STEAM LOCOMOTIVES

OF THE

NEW YORK CENTRAL LINES

PART 1

NEW YORK CENTRAL & HUDSON RIVER R.R.

"AMERICA'S GREATEST RAILROAD."

Compiled by William D. Edson

Assisted by Edward L. May
and H. L. Vail Jr.

March 1997

Published By
New York Central System Historical Society, Inc.
P. O. Box 81184
Cleveland, OH 44181-0184

Cover painting by Samuel B. McCausland.
Nearly new NYC & HR 2957, class I Atlantic with the westbound
Empire State Express along the Hudson River circa August 1902

NYC&HR 238, built at West Albany in 1888. Later class C-6a. See p. 112

ISBN 0-9659617-0-2

Library of Congress Catalog Number 97-68273

Contents

2

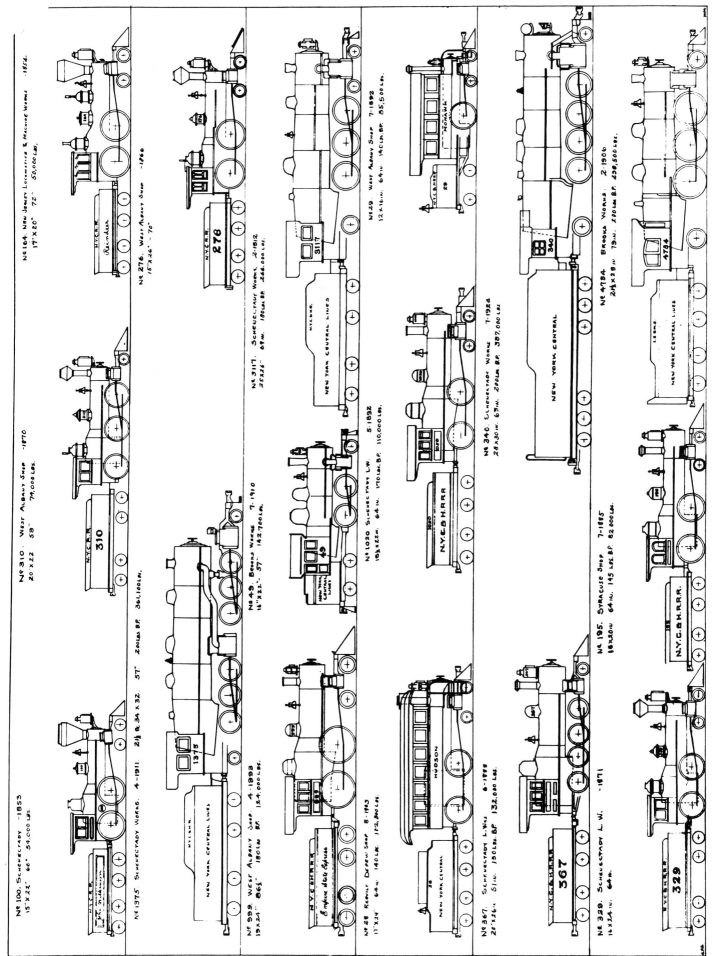

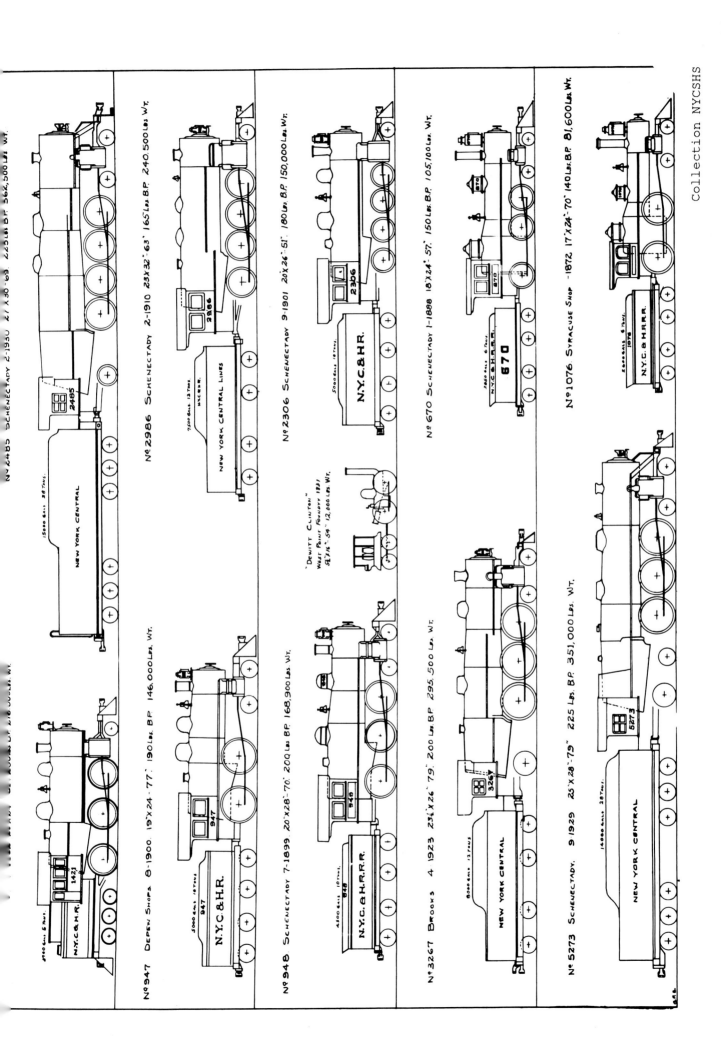

Nº 2485 Schenectady 2-1930 27"x30"-69" 225Lbs. B.P. 362,500 Lbs. Wt.

15000 Gals 28 Tons.

NEW YORK CENTRAL

2485

4700 Gals 6 Tons.

N.Y.C.&H.R.

1421

Nº 947 Depew Shops 8-1900 19"x24-77" 190Lbs. B.P. 146,000 Lbs. Wt.

5000 Gals 18 Tons.
947

N.Y.C.&H.R.

947

Nº 2986 Schenectady 2-1910 23"x32"-63" 165Lbs. B.P. 240,500 Lbs. Wt.

7500 Gals 12 Tons.
2986

NEW YORK CENTRAL LINES

Nº 948 Schenectady 7-1899 20"x28"-70" 200 Lbs. B.P. 168,900 Lbs. Wt.

4500 Gals 10 Tons.
948

N.Y.C.&H.R.R.

948

Nº 2306 Schenectady 9-1901 20"x26"-51" 180 Lbs. B.P. 150,000 Lbs. Wt.

2306

5000 Gals 18 Tons.

N.Y.C.&H.R.

"Dewitt Clinton"
West Point Foundry 1831
9¼"x16"-54" 12,000 Lbs. Wt.

Nº 3267 Brooks 4 1923 23½"x26" 79" 200 Lbs. B.P. 295,500 Lbs. Wt.

326

8000 Gals 13 Tons.

NEW YORK CENTRAL

Nº 670 Schenectady 1-1888 18"x24" 57" 150 Lbs. B.P. 105,100 Lbs. Wt.

670

7000 Gals 6 Tons.

N.Y.C.&H.R.R.

670

Nº 1076 Syracuse Shop -1872 17"x24"-70" 140Lbs. B.P. 81,600 Lbs. Wt.

1076

2600 Gals 6 Tons.

N.Y.C.&H.R.R.

Nº 5273 Schenectady. 9-1929 25"x28"-79" 225 Lbs. B.P. 351,000 Lbs. Wt.

527 3

15000 Gals 28 Tons.

NEW YORK CENTRAL

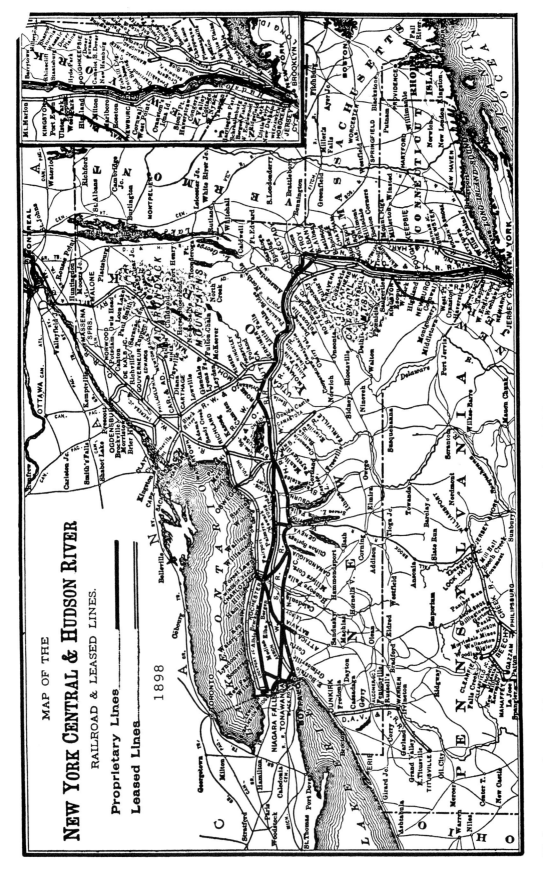

This map shows the extent of the NYC&HR in 1898, when total mileage of the leased lines far exceeded that of the parent company. Leased lines then included the N.Y.& Harlem; West Shore; Rome, Watertown & Ogdensburg; Beech Creek; and Dunkirk, Allegheny & Pitts.

INTRODUCTION

Over 6000 steam and electric locomotives are listed in this all-time roster of the
NYC&HR and its predecessors, starting in 1831. The listing continues through the
1914 merger with LS&MS, then lists subsequent New York Central power except former
B&A, Big Four, MC, OC and P&LE engines. These component lines are the subjects of
later parts.

Early locomotives are generally listed in chronological order; Later engines are
grouped under class headings which include wheel arrangement and specifications in
the following order: cylinder bore and stroke,* driver diameter over tires, boiler
pressure, engine weight, and tractive force. Each engine is listed only once, with
a complete record of renumbering, builders data, and disposition all on one line.
Renumberings were frequent, and some numbers were used by as many as nine different
engines. At the end of the roster is an index by road number, as well as a list of
rosters for all absorbed lines.   *The + with a cylinder dimension denotes 1/2 inch.

Many predecessor lines used their own systems of classifying locomotives. In 1901
the NYC&HR adopted the system which was later expanded to include the entire New
York Central Lines. All 0-4-0 switchers were assigned classes with prefix "A" such
as A-1, A-2, etc. Six wheel 0-6-0 switchers were assigned B-1, B-2, etc. A
complete list of classes by wheel arrangement appears on page 1 as part of the table
of contents.

As more and more engines were acquired along with subsidiary lines after 1900, the
class suffix numbers took on special meaning. Boston & Albany engines were assigned
classes with suffix numbers in the 30's such as A-30, B-32, C-35, etc. Class suffix
numbers in the 40's and 50's identified Lake Shore & Michigan Southern designs,
while 60's and 70's were used for Big Four power, 80's for Michigan Central, 90's
for Ohio Central Lines, and 100's for Pittsburgh & Lake Erie.

A common practice during the early days of railroads was to name locomotives, and
predecessors of the New York Central were no exception. Gradually numbers began to
appear, but with no particular pattern except to keep all engines within a solid
block starting with number 1. As engines were retired new ones were given the old
numbers, with the result that a group of identical engines bore random numbers.

In the nineties many roads indulged in elaborate renumbering to group engines in
orderly series. The NYC&HR went through three renumbering programs, in 1890, 1892,
and 1899. The last formed the basis for numbering applied to the entire New York
Central Lines, as follows.

1-3999	(original)	New York Central & Hudson River, and Boston & Albany.
4000-5999	(added 1905)	Lake Shore & Michigan Southern, incl. LE&W and CI&S.
6000-7499	(added 1905)	C.C.C.& St.L. (Big Four) incl. Peoria & Eastern.
7500-8999	(added 1905)	Michigan Central, incl. Canada Southern.
9000-9599	(added 1906)	Pittsburgh & Lake Erie, incl. PMcK&Y.
9500-9799	(added 1912)	Toledo & Ohio Central; Kanawha & Mich.(added 1924)

Sources for this roster material included numerous NYC locomotive diagram and
classification books, historical record cards, valuation records, locomotive
builders records, railroad annual reports, and many Bulletins of the Railway &
Locomotive Historical Society.

Photographs used in this volume came from several sources also. Many prints of the
oldest engines are from the New York Central negative collection now in the
possetion of the New York Central System Historical Society. C.M.Smith and H.L.Vail
arranged for prints from this collection as well as the Purinton and Tenniswood
collections of the society. Additional prints are from collections of George
Votava, Harold Vollrath,and others.

6

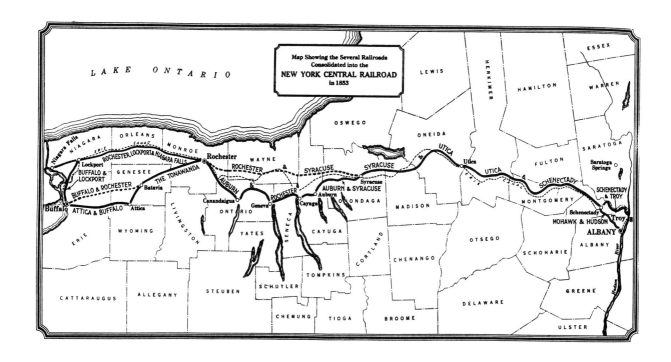

Map Showing the Several Railroads Consolidated into the NEW YORK CENTRAL RAILROAD in 1853

LOCOMOTIVES OF THE (FIRST) NEW YORK CENTRAL RAILROAD

In the long history of the "Water Level Route" there were actually two New York Central Railroads. The first was formed in May, 1853 as a consolidation of several lines between Buffalo and Albany. It lasted only until November, 1869 when it merged with the Hudson River Railroad to form the New York Central & Hudson River. The second New York Central was created in November, 1914 by the consolidation of the NYC&HR and the Lake Shore & Michigan Southern.

The roster which follows begins with the first New York Central and its predecessor roads. Prior to the 1853 consolidation, each of these lines named their locomotives, except the Utica & Schenectady which numbered theirs. Apparently the NYC did not develop its own numbering system until the year after it was formed.

New York Central Numbering System of 1854

1-34	Utica & Schenectady (Numbers unchanged)	See P. 8
40-44	Schenectady & Troy	P. 9
70-77	Albany & Schenectady (Was Mohawk & Hudson)	P. 9
78-97	Syracuse & Utica	P. 10
98-134	Rochester & Syracuse (Was Aub.& Syr. and Aub.& Roch.)	P. 12
135-150	Buffalo & Rochester (Was Tona.RR and Attica & Buflo.)	P. 13
151-179	Rochester, Lockport & Niagara Falls (Was Lock.& N.F.)	P. 14
180-183?	Buffalo & Niagara Falls	P. 14

After 1854, locomotives were moved around freely between divisions without any renumbering. New engines were assigned 35-39, 45-69, 184-219, and then vacant numbers as the oldest engines were retired. By 1869 the highest road number had reached 294. At that time all NYC engines simply became NYC&HR engines with no change in numbers. The roster which follows traces the history of each one, including ultimate disposition by the NYC&HR.

Experimental smokestack as applied to Utica & Schenectady's No.11, the NOAH VIBBARD, rebuilt in 1856 from a 4-2-0 type. (NYC photo 328)

The HENRY STEVENS was a Schenectady product of 1853. "No. 25" appeared in large letters on the tender. (NYC photo 4793)

8

UTICA & SCHENECTADY (1836-1854)

Orig.No. & Name	NYC	Re'67	Type	Bldr.,c/n,Date		Reblt.	Cyl. Drv. Wt.	Disposition
1	1?		4-2-0	BLW.	28 4/36		10+x16-56=27045	dr'53-56
2	–		"		29 "		12x16-56-36070	dr'53
3	–		"	"	32 6/36			dr by'52 (b)
4	–		"	"	33 "			dr by'45 (b)
5	5	(4-4-0)	"	"	35 "	'50	12x16-56-35515	dr by'62
6	–		"	"	36 "		12x16-56-36070	dr'53
7	–		"	"	37 7/36		10x18?54?	So'48 (b)
8	–		"	"	38 "		10+x16-56-27045	dr'52
9	–		"	"	83 6/37			dr by'46 (b)
10	–		"	"	85 7/37		12x20-56-34200	RB'53 4-4-0
11	11		"	"	86 "	'40,44	12x20-56-34200	RB'56 4-4-0
12	–		"		95 10/37			dr by'45 (b)
14	14		2-4-0?	"	186 11/43	'52	12x26-60-44340	?
"14	–		0-6-0	"	194 5/44			
15	–		"	"	195 6/44			dr by'51
" 4	4		-4-	Blackburn	/45?		15+x26-66-54900	dr by'53
"12	12		4-4-0	Norris	/45		13x22-66-41170	dr by'72
13	–		"	"	"		13x20-60-37150	dr'53
16	16	452	"	"	"		13x22-56-41170	Sc 8/79
17	17		"	"	"		13x22-56-41170	dr c.'68
18	18	454	"	"	"		13x20-60-41170	Sc 6/79
19	19		"	"	"		12x22-56-41170	dr c.'68
" 9	9		"	"	/46		11+x21-51-40150	dr c.'70
20	20	456	"	"	/48		14x24-60-51480	Sc 12/80
21	21		"	"	"		14x24-60-51480	dr c.'70
22 John Ellis	22		"	Schen.Shop	/49		14x24-60-51240	dr c.'70
23	23		"	" "	/50		14x24-72-54360	dr c.'65
24 L.Spraker	24		"	" "	/51		16x20-72-49700	Sc 2/76?
"15 Wm.C.Young	15		"	" "	/51		13+x18-60-43100	dr.c.'61
" 7	7	443	"	" "	/52	'56(c)	12x26-60-44550	dr c.'79
26 M.T.Reynolds	26	462	"	Schen.	8 3/52		16x20-72-53000	dr c.'78
27 Chauncey Vibbard	27	463	"	"	9 "	Ro'74	16x20-72-53240	Sc 8/84
" 8	8	444	"	"	19 11/52		16x22-60-50000	So 1/83 SLW
" 3 R.Higham	3	439	"	"	27 1/53		14x22-66-49050	So 5/82 Co&Ca
" 4 N.S.Benton	4	440	"	"	28 "		14x22-66-49050	" "
28 John V.L.Pruyn	28	464	"	"	29 2/53		15x22-72-56350	Sc 11/86
29 John Townsend	29	465	"	"	30 "		15x22-72-53850	So 5/82
25 Henry Stevens	25	461	"	"	38 4/53		16x22-72-55375	Sc 12/80
30 Erastus Corning	30	466	"	"	42 6/53	Ro'72	16x22-78-58400	Sc 10/89 (d)
31 Thomas Symonds	31	467	"	"	44 7/53	Sy'73	14x22-66-42000	Sc 12/89
32 Alonzo C.Paige	32	468	"	"	43 6/53		15x22-72-55100	Sc 12/80
33 David Wager (a)	33	469-723-1146	"	"	56 10/53	Ro'71	15x22-72-52800	dr by'02 (d)
34	34	470-234	"	"	57 "	Ro'72	16x22-60-48000	Sc 4/92 (e)
" 2	2	438	4-4-0	Hink.	476 9/53		15x24-60-42000	So 7/81
" 6	6		"	"	484 "		15x24-60-42000	RB'67 0-4-0
"10 Levi Worden	10		"	RB fr 4-2-0	'53		14x20-58-40000	dr by'66
"11 Noah Vibbard	11		"	" "	" '56		16x20-66-53000	dr by'76
"13	13		"	Lawrence	'53		17x20-60-52000	dr by'69

Note a: Original name "Edw.B.Johnson"   Note b: Six loco. sold to Central RR of Mich.
Note c: No.7 RB'56: 15x26-67-52000. Note d: RB to 16x22-66. Note e: RB to 17x22-60.

MOHAWK & HUDSON (1831-1847) and ALBANY & SCHENECTADY (1847-1853):

Name	NYC	Re'77	Type	Builder, c/n, Date	RB	Cyl. Dri. Wt.	Disposition
De Witt Clinton			0-4-0	W.Point Fndry. 6/31		5+x16-54-6758	Rt'33,Sc 4/35
John Bull (a)			4-2-0	Stephenson 24 6/31	'38	10x14-48-12742	RB'45 4-4-0
Brother Jonathan (b)			"	W.Point Fndry. 8/32	'33	9+x16-60-14000	RB'46 4-2-2?
Mohawk (c)			"	Stephenson 60 /34		10x14-48-	RB'47? 4-4-0
Hudson (c)			"	" 61 2/34		10x14-48-	RB'48? 4-4-0
Columbia			4-4-0	Rogers K&G 34 11/41		12x18-54-	RB'53
John T. Norton	70	506	"	Albany shop /42 (f)	'55	12x20-52-	Sc 10/86
Albany	75		"	Rogers K&G 50 12/43	'46	14x22-54-36000	dr c.'61
Rochester	71?		"	RB fr.4-2-0 McQ.'45			dr by'56
Brother Jonathan			4-2-2	RB fr.4-2-0 McQ.'46		12x18-54	dr by'56
Mohawk	73?		4-4-0	RB fr.4-2-0 McQ.'47		15x25-60-44000	dr by'56
Hudson	76?		"	RB fr.4-2-0 McQ.'48		15x25-60-44000	dr by'56
Mechanic	74	510	"	Albany shop 1849	'55	15x25-60-50000	dr c.'65
Superintendent	"73	509	"	Albbany shop	'55	17x24-60-64000	Sc 12/80
E.C.McIntosh	72	508	"	Schenectady 6 1/52	?	16x22-60-48000	Sc 12/89
George E. Gray	77		"	Albany shop '53		17x20-66-46000	So'76 (d)
Russell Sage	"71	507	"	New Jersey L&M '54		15x22-60-54000	So 2/81
G.B.Van Vorst	"76	512	"	Albany shop '55		15x22-60-48000	Sc 9/79

SCHENECTADY & TROY (1842-1853)

Name	NYC	Re'77	Type	Builder, c/n, Date	RB	Cyl. Dri. Wt.	Disposition
Samuel Tuell	1?		4-2-0	Wm.Norris '42		11x18-54-26000	dr c.'75
Ben Marshall (e)	53		"	Rogers K&G 39 8/42		11+x18-54-18000	dr c.'67
Syracuse	44		4-4-0?	Norris '50		14x26-60-44000	dr c.'69
Thomas Wallace	43	479	"	Schenectady 36 4/53		15x22-60-42000	So 5/82
(Note g)	41	(477	"	Amoskeag 160	11/53	15x24-60-53900	Sc 5/91
		(re 45-107					

Note a: RB 5/33 from 0-4-0; Perhaps originally named "Robert Fulton".
    b: Renamed 1834 from "Experiment".
    c: Perhaps originally named "Brother Jonathan" and "Robert Fulton".
    d: Perhaps originally U&S #40; Re'76 to to Hudson River RR #59.
    e: Renamed "General Chedell"?   Note f: Perhaps built as 0-6-0?
    g: Built Amos.c/n 6 in 1850 for unknown RR, named "Marmeluke".

Operating replica of the DE WITT CLINTON, built
in 1893 for display at the Chicago Exposition.

SYRACUSE & UTICA (1840-1853):

Name	NYC	Re'77	Type	Builder, c/n, Date			RB	Cyl. Dr. Wt.	Disposition
Oneida	?		4-2-0	Rogers K&G	22	6/40		11x18-54-	dr by'56
Onondaga	?		"	" "	25	10/40		11x18-54-	dr by'56
Schenedoah	?		4-2-2	" "	55	6/44		11x20-60-	dr by'56
Anteauga (a)	83		"	" "	57	7/44		11x20-60-32500	dr.c'77
Thayandanega	82		4-4-0	" "	110	10/47		14x20-60-42000	Expl.9/61
Garangula	?		"	" "	113	12/47		14x20-60-	dr by'56
Osceola	81		"	" "	116	1/48		14x20-60-42000	dr c'61
Logan	80		"	" "	138	8/48		14x20-60-42000	dr c'61
Goliah			"	Norris (Phila)		/48		13x24-56-44950	dr c'56
Hippomenes	84	519	"	" "		"		12x26-60-48000	dr c'83
Atalanta	85		"	" "		"		12x26-60-48000	dr c'67
Diomede	86		"	" "		/49		12x26-60-48000	dr c'59
Ajax	87		"	" "		"		12x26-60-48000	dr c'69
Achilles	88	523	"	" "		"	WA'63	12x26-60-48000	So 1/83 (b)
Lightning			6-2-0	Norris (Schen)		1/50		16x32-84-40000	Rt'51 (d)
Apollo	93		4-4-0	Lowell	97	/51		13x22-66-38000	dr c'69
Mercury	42		"	"	98	"		13x20-66-32000	dr c'69
Mars	95		"	"	103	"		14x20-66-40000	dr c'69
Bellona	94	527	"	"	104	"	Sch'68	14x20-66-40000	Sc 12/89 (e)
Perseus	92		"	Norris (Phila)		/52		15x22-60-50500	dr by'68
Theseus	91		"	" "		"		15x22-72-50500	dr by'70
Attila	90	525	"	" "		/53		15x22-66-54500	Sc 1/79
Alaric	89		"	" "		"		15x22-66-54500	dr c'61
Comet	96		"	Lawrence		"		17x20-66-50000	dr c'70
Aeolus	97	530	"	"		"		17x20-66-50000	Sc 7/81
	78			New Jersey L&M		"		13x22-60-52400	dr c'76

ROCHESTER & SYRACUSE: Engines built 1838-1850 for AUBURN & SYRACUSE:

Name		NYC	Re'77	Type	Builder, c/n, Date			RB	Cyl. Dr. Wt.	Disposition
Syracuse	1			4-2-0	Rogers K&G	7	10/38		10+x18-54-21000	dr by'56
Auburn	2			"	" "	8	11/38		10+x18-54-21000	dr by'56
Cayuga				(c) 4-4-0	" "	14	10/39	'51		dr by'56
Wyoming		181		" "	Dennis W&R		/40	AP'42	12x20-58-24000	dr by'70
Owasco				4-2-0	Dennis T&W		/40	AP'42		
Providence		180		"	Norris (Phila)		/42	AP	10x20-48-20000	dr c'68
E.P.Williams		182		4-4-0	Auburn Prison		/42		9x18-54-32000	dr c'60
Phoenix				"	Rogers K&G	67	6/45		12x18-54	dr by'56
Varnum				"	" "	103	7/47		12+x18 54	dr by'56
How		108		"	" "	139	8/48		13x20-72-45150	dr by'74
Conkling (f)		107		"	" "	183	8/49		14+x20-72-51900	dr by'76

Note a: Renamed "Ben Marshall".   Note b: RB to 15x26-57, Sold to Schen.L.W.
      c: Built as 4-2-0.   Note d: Returned to builder, boiler used on #195?
      e: RB to 16x24-66.   Note f: Originally named "Cayuga"?

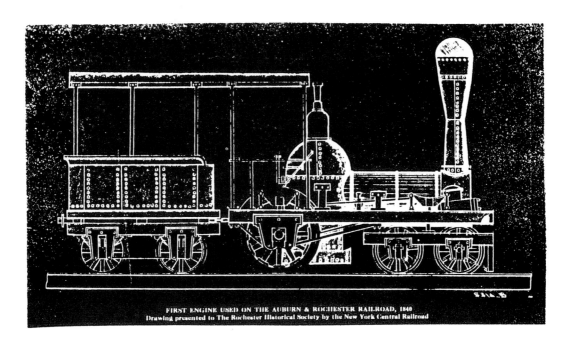

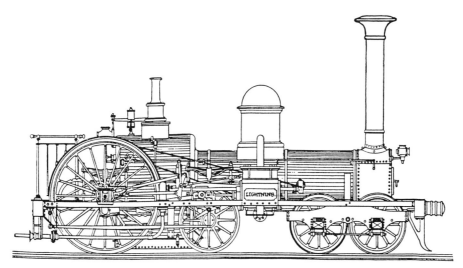

Norris built the LIGHTNING for Syracuse & Utica passenger service. It had a single pair of seven-foot drivers. It lasted less than a year.

More typical of power in the 1850's was the MERCURY, one of four built by Lowell for S&U.

ROCHESTER & SYRACUSE: Engines built 1840-1850 for AUBURN & ROCHESTER:

Name	NYC	Re'77	Type	Builder,	c/n.	Date	RB	Cyl.	Dr.	Wt.	Disposition
Young Lion	1		4-4-0?	Rogers K&G	23	9/40		12x18-54			So 6/52
Ontario	2		4-2-0	Wm.Norris		/40					
Columbus	3		"	"		"					
H.B.Gibson	4		"	"		"					
	5		"	"		"					
Maine (b)	115		4-4-0	Hinkley	114	8/47		15x20-60-47800			dr c'61
Oregon	119		"	"	119	9/47		" " "			dr c'76
Atlantic	118		"	"	167	5/48		15x20-54-47800			dr c'61
Pacific	122		"	"	173	5/48		" " "			dr c'61
President	121		"	"	182	6/48		" " "			dr c'70
Republic	116		"	"	184	7/48		" " "			dr c'72
Hercules (b)	117		"	"	216	12/48		" " "			dr c'61
Samson (b)	120		"	"	217	12/48		16x20-60-47800			dr c'77

ROCHESTER & SYRACUSE Engines built 1850-1854:

Name	NYC	Re'77	Type	Builder,	c/n.	Date	RB	Cyl.	Dr.	Wt.	Disposition
Canandaigua	105		4-4-0	Rogers K&G	260	4/51		15+x20-72-54700			dr c'70
Syracuse	106		"	" "	265	6/51		15+x20-72-54700			dr c'70
Rochester	123		"	Amoskeag	35	11/51		16x20-72-50570			dr c'64
Auburn	124		"	"	34	"		16x20-66-50570			dr c'65
Seymour	131		"	Norris (Schen.)		/51		16x22-60-45000			dr c.61
Sherwood	129		"	" "		"		16x20-60-44000			dr c'81
Palmyra	130		"	Norris (Phila.)		/52		16x20-60-52300			dr c'79
Lawrence	125		"	Lawrence		"		15x20-54-49700			Sc'64
Essex	126		"	"		"		15x20-60-49700			dr c'77
Geneva			"	Hinkley	363	4/52		15x24-60-			dr by'56
Vienna	114		"	"	372	5/52		16x20-66-50200			dr c'77
Clyde	113		"	"	382	7/52		16x20-66-50200			dr by'73
Pittsford	111		"	"	415	12/52	(d)	16x24-60-48100			So 7/80
Daniel Webster	112		"	"	416	1/53		16x20-66-50200			dr c'72
Victor	109	542?	"	"	422	12/52	(d)	16x24-60-48100			Sc 6/79
Clifton	110		"	"	428	3/53	(d)	16x24-60-48100			dr c'74
Nathaniel Thayer	104	537	"	Rogers K&G	370	2/53	'77	16x22-72-59400			Sc 3/89
Horace White	103	536?	"	" "	376	1/53		16x22-72-59400			Sc 9/80
Waterloo	99	532	"	Schen.	7	1/52		16x22-60-53000			dr c'83
John Wilkinson	100	533	"	"	25	12/52	'71	15x22-66-53500			dr c'83 (e)
Gen. Gould	101	534-239	"	"	26	"	'74	15x22-66-53500			Sc 7/91 (e)
J.W.Brooks	98	531	"	"	34	3/53		16x22-60-55000			Sc 7/79
J.H.Chedell (c)	102	235	"	"	84	5/54	'69	16x22-72-58700			Sc 5/87
G.Y.Lansing	132		"	"	72	2/54	Alb.	15x22-60-55600			Sc 2/82
E.Foster	133		"	"	73	3/54	Alb.	15x22-54-52000			Sc 8/81
Robt.H.Ives	127		"	Taunton	137	5/53		16x20-60-53200			dr c'77
Wm.F.Weld	128		"		131	3/53		16x20-60-53300			Sc 4/80

Note a: Re Watertown & Rome "Lion".   Note b: Re "Geneva","Tornado","Tempest".
Note c: NYC 102 re 235 by 1860.   Note d: Orig. 15x24 cyl.   Note e: RB to 16x22-66.
Note f: RB to 16x24-70.

See also NYC 48, 38, and 54 built for R&S, listed on page 16..

BUFFALO & ROCHESTER: Engines built for TONAWANDA RR (1836-1850):

Name		NYC	Type	Builder	c/n	Date	RB	Cyl.	Dr.	Wt.	Disposition
	1		4-2-0	Baldwin	50	9/36					dr by'56
	2		"	"	51	10/36					dr by'56
Batavia	3		"	Rogers	5	10/38					dr by'56
	4		?	Baldwin	184	6/43					dr by'56
Chili re Lewis Brooks		145	4-4-0	Rogers	137	8/48		14x20	60	40000	dr c'61
Byron re Joseph Field		146	"	"	158	1/49		"	"	"	Sc 6/80
Mumford		143	"	"	221	7/50		15x20	66	44000	So'63 (a)
Rochester		139	"	"	247	2/51		"	"	"	So'63 (a)
Buffalo		138	"	"	248	2/51		"	"	"	dr by'92

BUFFALO & ROCHESTER: Engines built for ATTICA & BUFFALO (1842-1850)

Name		NYC	Type	Builder	c/n	Date	RB	Cyl.	Dr.	Wt.	Disposition
	1		?	Rogers	38	8/42		11x18			dr c'56
Buffalo re Attica		183	-2-	Dennis W & R	/42			10x20	60	20000	dr c'59
Empire			?	Rogers	43	5/43					dr by'56
Winnebago		144	4-4-0	"	209	3/50	(b)	14+x20	66	44000	dr by'92

  Note: Eight additional 4-4-0 built 1849-1850 for A&B became Buff.Corn.& NY 16-23.

BUFFALO & ROCHESTER: Engines built 1851-1854:

Name	NYC	Type	Builder	c/n	Date	RB	Cyl.	Dr.	Wt.	Disposition
Batavia	141	4-4-0	Rogers	275	8/51		15x20	66	44000	Sc 6/81
Lancaster	142	"	"	312	4/52		"	"	"	dr by'74
Bergen	140	"	"	313	"		"	"	"	dr by'92
Pembroke	161	"	Hinkley	414	1/53		15x24	60	48000	dr by'92
Churchville	162	"	"	435	4/53		"	"	"	dr by'78
G.H.Burrows	150	"	Schen.	35	3/53	'68	15+x22	66	48000	dr c'82
Racer	148	"	"	37	4/53		16x22	72	50000	Sc 12/82
Dean Richmond	147	"	"	64	12/53		16x22	78	50000	So 5/81
David Upton	149	"	"	85	6/54		16x22	72	50000	Sc 12/86

Note a: 139 and 144 re RW&O 25 and 24.   Note b: 144 RB'63 to 16x22-57

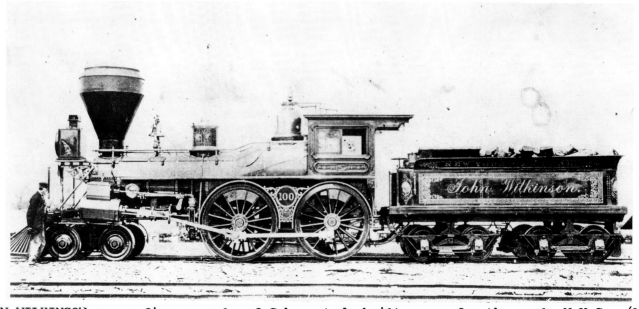

JOHN WILKINSON was a fine example of Schenectady-built power for the early N.Y.C. (WDE)

ROCHESTER, LOCKPORT & NIAGARA FALLS: Engines built for LOCK. & NIA. FALLS (1838-1850)

	NYC	Type	Builder,c/n,	Date	RB	cyl. dr. wt.	Disposition
Clinton		4-2-0	Rogers 3	4/38		10x18-	So 11/43 (a)
Downing		"	Dunham	/38			
Erie No. 2	179	4-4-0	Norris	/44		11x20-58-32000	dr c'72
Bird	172	"	"	/44	'68	11x22-54-36000	dr c'81
Cataract	171	"	"	/45		11x22-54-36000	dr c'74
Huron	173	"	"	/45		13x22-58-36000	So 4/81
Stranger	176	"	"	/45		13x22-58-36000	So 6/81
W.Hayden	177	"	"	/45		13x22-58-36000	So 8/81 (b)
Reliance	174	"	"	/46		13x26-58-36000	So 6/81
James Brisbane	175	"	"	/46		13x22-58-36000	So 6/81
Wende	178	"	"	/46		14x24-58-36000	So 8/81 (b)

ROCHESTER, LOCKPORT & NIAGARA FALLS: Engines built 1850-1854:

	NYC	Type	Builder,c/n,	Date	RB	cyl. dr. wt.	Disposition
W.W.Corcoran	136	4-4-0	Rogers 316	5/52		14x20-72-44000	dr by'92
John A. Willink	137	"	" 317	"		" " "	dr by'92
Iris (Note c)	170	"	Norris	/52		14+x22-58-44000	Sc 1/81
Ontario	159	"	Hinkley 365	4/52		15x24-60-48000	dr by'92
Erie	157	"	" 366	"		" " "	dr by'92
Niagara	153	"	" 369	5/52		15x20-66-46000	So 7/81
Michigan	158	"	" 373	"		15x24-60-48000	dr by'92
Genesee	154	"	" 378	6/52		15x20-66-46000	dr by'77
Superior	156	"	" 381	"		15x24-60-48000	So 5/82
St.Lawrence	160	"	" 423	1/53		" " "	dr by'92
Orleans	151	"	" 426	2/53		16x20-72-48000	dr c'80
Monroe	152	"	" 430	3/53		" " "	dr c'79
Rapid (B&NF)	155	"	" 436	5/53		15x20-66-46000	So 7/81
North Star	135	"	" 401	6/53		15+x22-78-50000	Sc 8/79
Henry Clay	169	"	Lawrence	/53		15+x20-66-44000	dr c'76
United States	168	"	"	/53		17x20-66-44000	dr c'81
Massachusetts	167	"	Springfield	/54	'69	16x22-60-48000	Sc 4/83
New York	166	"	"	/54		" " "	So'63 (d)
Albion	165	"	New Jer.L&M	/54		17x20-72-50000	dr c'78
Reindeer (e)	164	"	"	/54		" " "	dr c'79
Charlotte	163	"	Hinkley	?		12+x20-54-32000	dr by'69

ROCHESTER & LAKE ONTARIO. Leased 1855, perhaps including "Charlotte" above

BUFFALO & NIAGARA FALLS Leased 1855

		Type	Builder,c/n,	Date		cyl. dr. wt.	Disposition
Buffalo		2-2-0	Locks & Canals'35			11x16-60	dr by'56
Niagara		4-2-0	Dunham '36				dr by'56
Tonawanda		4-2-0	Baldwin 109	8/38			dr by'56
Niagara		4-2-2	Hinkley 41	5/45		11+x20-60	dr by'56

Note a - Re Erie & Kalamazoo "Tecumseh". Note b - Re N.Y.Texas & Mex. 1,2.
Note c - Re "J.D.Turrell". Note d - Re RW&O 23. Note e - Re "Brockport".

NYC 147, with the name DEAN RICHMOND all over the tender,
built by Schenectady in 1853. (NYC neg. 1166)

NYC 149, similar to the 147 except for smaller drivers. (Edson collection)

NEW YORK CENTRAL: Engines built 1853-1856:

Name	No.	Re'77	Type	Builder,c/n,Date			RB	Cyl. Dr. Wt.	Disposition
	35	471	4-4-0	Schen.	60	11/53		16x22-60-48000	Sc 8/80
Oneida	36	472	"	"	62	"		16x22-60-52500	Sc 12/82?
	37	473-235	"	"	63	12/53	'80	16x22-60-48000	So 8/92 (b)
G.C.Davidson (a)	38	474	"	("	45	7/53)		14x22-66-48000	So 11/82
Major Z.C.Priest	39	475	"	"	61	1/54	'63	16x22-72-55375	Sc 11/89
	40	476	"	"	68	2/54		16x22-66-50000	Sc 12/80
D.L.Fremyre	45	481	"	"	69	"		16x22-66-52600	Sc 8/79
	46	482	"	"	70	"		16x22-66-50000	Sc 12/86
E.Corning,Jr.	47	483	"	"	71	"		16x22-66-50000	Sc 10/81
(a)	48	484	"	("	47	8/53)		14x22-66-50950	Sc 9/79
J.F.Seymour	49		"	"	77	4/54		16x22-72-56090	dr c'76
	50	486				/77		15x26-60-	Sc 10/83
	51	487	4-4-0	Schen.	78	4/54	'73	16x22-60-55000	Sc 12/88 (g)
	52	488	"	"	79	"	'68	16x22-60-50000	So 12/86 (g)
Ben Marshall	53		4-2-0	(From S&T in '54)				11+x20-54-18000	dr c'67
Young America (a)	54		4-4-0	(Schen.	46	8/53)		14x22-66-53100	dr c'72
	55	491-100	"	"	88	7/54	'68	15x22-66-51749	So 7/90 (h)
	56	492	"	"	96	8/54		16x22-60-50000	Sc 8/79
W.R.Gifford	57	493	"	"	95	9/54		16x22-72-58000	dr c'82
Schuyler Livingston	58	494	"	"	98	"		16x22-66-54000	Sc 11/86
Russell Sage	59	495	"	"	102	11/54		16x22-66-42000	Sc 11/86
H.B.Gibson	60	496	"	"	103	"		16x22-66-56300	Sc 10/81
Isaac Townsend	61	497	"	"	106	12/54		15x22-66-52000	Sc 8/79
Henry W. Clark	62	498	"	"	110	4/55	'73	15x22-60-46000	Sc 6/88
	63	499	"	"	112	"		15x22-60-54000	So 5/82
Lyons	64	500	"	Norris				16x20-60-52300	dr c'83
	65	501	"	Schen.	108	3/55	'65	17x22-66-60550	Sc 5/82
	66	502	"	"	107	"		17x22-60-58500	So 11/82
President	67	503	4-6-0	"	113	"		17x20-48-60000	Sc 12/84
Edw.G.Faile	68	504	4-4-0	"	111	4/55		15x22-66-59500	Sc 12/80
H.W.Chittenden	69	505-55-162	"	"	118	6/55	'66	16x22-66-56450	So 5/95
	184		"	"	114	10/55		17x22-60-52000	Sc 6/79
	185		"	"	120	"		15x22-60-46000	So 3/81
Henry Martin	186	re'90 209	"	"	133	11/55	'71	16x22-66-50000	So 9/92 (d)
	187	" 75	"	"	126	10/55	'67	16x22-66-50000	So 10/90 (e)
S.Drullard	188		4-6-0	"	135	12/55	'75	17x22-54-64000	Sc 1/88
Thomas Hall	189		"	"	137	"		17x22-54-64000	dr by'77
	190		4-4-0	"	142	1/56		17x22-60-52000	Sc 12/88
	191		"	"	143	"		16x22-60-58400	Sc 6/85
	192		"	"	144	"		16x20-54-57600	Sc 12/80
Geo.H.Thatcher	193	(ex-?)	"	("	105	3/55)		15x22-66-50000	So 5/82
	194	(ex-?)	"	("	109	")		16x22-72-55375	So 5/81 T&F
Mohawk	195		"	Albany shop		5/56	'65	15x22-56-48000	Sc 7/85
Quickstep (Note c)	196		"	Rogers	340	9/52	(c)	15x20-66-55700	Sc 11/87

Note a - Built for R&S but assigned Eastern Div. nos. in 1854.   Note b - RB to 16x24-6-
Note c - Original owner L.G.B.Cannon for Rensselaer & Saratoga.   Note d - RB to 17x22.
Note e - Sold to George Vanderbilt.   Note g - RB to 15x22-60.   Note h - RB to 16x22.

West Albany erecting shop. (From W.H.Flynn stereoptican picture. NYC neg. 5218)

Shopmen at Albany relax after working on NYC 196, a Rogers engine of 1852.
(NYC neg 1264-1; H.L.Vail coll.)

NEW YORK CENTRAL Engines acquired 1856-1859:

Name	NYC	Type	Builder,c/n,Date	RB	Cyl. Dr. Wt.	Disposition
Medina	197	4-4-0	Detroit /56	'67	16x22-60-50000	Sc 8/87
Lockport	198	"	" "	'70	" " "	Sc 10/86
D.D.Williamson	199	"	Schen.152 9/56		16x22-56-48000	Sc 6/85
	200	"	" 155 "		16x22-60-59270	Sc 12/87
	201	"	" 162 "		16x22-66-60150	Sc 10/86
	202	"	" 153 "		16x22-66-59350	Sc 12/80
	203 ('90) 210	"	" 163 "	'71	16x22-66- (b)	Sc 1/92
	204	"	" 164 10/56		16x22-66	Sc 12/88
C.P.Nichols	205	"	" 165 "	'71	" " (b)	Sc 4/89
	206	"	" 170 11/56	'71	" " (b)	So 5/82
	207	"	" 169 "	'75	" " (b)	Sc 6/89
	208	"	" 173 12/56		16x22-56	Sc 6/89
Joseph Spraker	209	"	" 177 1/57		" "	Sc 6/89
	210	"	" 180 "		" "	Sc 12/86
	211	"	" 186 3/57		15x22-56	So 5/82
Col.Hamilton	212 ('90) 841	"	Schen. shop '67		16x24-70	So 2/92 (c)
H.Ledyard	213	"	Detroit /57?			dr by'64
	214	"	" /57?			dr by'64
Fred N.Collamer	215	"	" /57	'70	16x22-60	Sc 9/89
John Owen	216	"	" /57	'68	" "	Sc 8/88
	217	"	Schen.195 8/57		" "	Sc 11/82
	218	"	" 206 9/57		" "	Sc 6/89
Oxford	219	"	" 198 12/59		15x22-60	Sc 1/89
Alps	"183	"	" 199 "		16x22-54	Sc 11/89
	" 86 ('77) 521	"	" 192 6/59		16x22-60	Sc 12/86

CANANDAIGUA & NIAGARA FALLS (6'gage): Acquired 9/58 but NYC numbers unknown:

Name	NYC	Type	Builder,c/n,Date	Cyl. Dr. Wt.
Sam Rand		4-4-0	by'56	16x22-54
Joseph S.King		"	"	16x22-72
Sturncliff		"	"	" "
Benjamin Pringle		"	Rogers 357 12/52	16x22-60
Robert Bayard		"	" 361 "	16x22-72
Cataract		"	" 363 "	16x22-60
Wm.W.Gilbert		"	" 365 1/53	" "
Clifton		"	" 367 "	" "
Niagara	1	"	" 368 "	16x22-72
Rapids	2	"	" 374 2/53	" "
International	3	"	" 375 "	" "
The Hope		"	by'56	18x20-60
Sam Brown		"	"	" "
Irange		"	"	11x18-54

Note b : Specs. as rebuilt: 203= 17x22-66; 205= 16+x22-60; 206= 15x22-56; 207= 16x22-60.
Note c : 841 sold to Scott & McLain.

NYC&HR 499 had been renumbered in 1877 from 63, built by Schenectady in 1855. (NYC 5618)

Photographed at Grand Central, New York was NYC&HR 212, with extended smokebox. (Chaney)

NEW YORK CENTRAL Engines acquired 1860-1864. (All 4-4-0)

Orig.No.	Re'77	Re'90	Builder,c/n,Date			RB	Specs as RB	Disposition
"102	535		Schen.	212	2/60	Sy'71	16x22-66	Sc 11/87
220			"	214	1/60		15x22-60	So 1/83 Schen.L.W.
(a) "134			"	215	"		16x22-60	Sc 11/86
" 79	515	236	"	216	"	Ro'73	15x22-60	So 10/90 N.Y.Eq.Co.
"145			"	228	10/60			dr by 5/61
"182			"	229	"			So 3/81
"118		202	"	234	6/61	Ro'73	15x22-64	So 7/90 Amer.S.I.Co.
'"145		702	"	238	5/61	Ro'73	16x22-70	Wreck.8/90
" 75	511	726-1147	"	239	"	Ro'73	16x22-57	dr by'01
"115		81	"	240	"		16x24-64	Sc 1/91
" 15	451		"	241	"		16x24-60	Sc 11/86
"122			"	243	6/61		16x22-60	Sc 11/86
"117			"	244	"		16+x22-56	Sc 8/89
" 82	518		"	245	11/61	Sy'72	16x22-60	Sc 1/91?
"131			"	247	"		16x22-60	Sc 11/80
" 80	516	237	"	246	"	Ro'71	16x24-60	Sc 2/91
221			"	248	12/61	WA'72	16x24-56	Sc 10/89
222			Rochester		/62?	Ro'71	15x22-57	dr c'89
223			Schen.	249	1/62	Ro'67	16x24-60	Sc 10/87
" 5	441		"	253	3/62	(b)	" "	Sc 11/89
" 89	524		"	254	5/62		" "	Sc 7/87
224								
225			Schen.	256	5/62	Sy'72	16x24-60	Sc 11/87
226			"	260	7/62		" "	Sc 12/89
227		160	"	262	"	Ro'74	16x24-64	Sc 8/95
228		161	"	263	"	Ro'72	16x22-64	So 7/98
229								
230		82	Schen.	266	9/62		16x24-60	So 10/90 N.Y.Eq.Co.
231		212	"	268	10/62	Ro'76	16x24-64	Sc 8/95
232		86	"	273	12/62		" "	Sc 1/90
233		87	"	276	"		" "	Sc 5/90
234						Sy'69	16x22-60	Sc 12/89
235			(Reno. from 102; See p.12)					
" 81	517	238	Schen.	280	1/63	Sy'71	16x24-60	Sc 1/91
236		213	"	284	2/63	Ro'75	16x24-64	Sc 12/97
237			"	283	3/63		15x24-60	Sc 10/89
238			"	287	4/63		16x24-66	Sc 7/84
239			"	288	"	Ro'71	" "	Sc 11/87
"139		203	"	296	6/63	Ro'74	16x24-64	Sc 3/92 (b)
"143		732-1067	"	304	8/63	Sy'83	17x24-64	So 3/08 Ginsburg
(a) "213			"	357	11/64	Ro'69	16x22-60	Sc 5/86
"214		211	"	358	"	Ro'72	" "	So 10/90 N.Y.Eq.Co.
(a) "123			"	361	12/64	Sy'69	16x24-60	Sc 1/89 (b)
240			W.Albany?		/64		15x26-60	So 5/82
241			"			WA'73	" "	So 5/82
242			Rochester?		/64	Ro	16x24-60	Sc 12/89
243		214	"			Ro'73	" "	Sc 1/91

Note a - Names: 134 Com's L.Tracy; 145 Chili; 213 H.Ledyard; 123 J.M.Toucey.
Note b - Specs. as built 16x22-60.

NYC&HR 237 after front end changes. It never bore a name. (NYCSHS Purinton coll. 72)

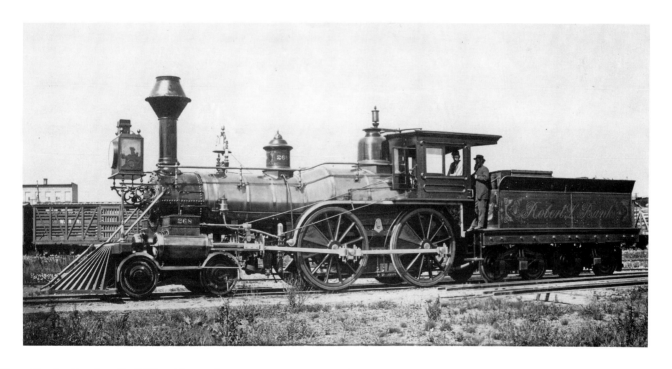

New York Central 268, the ROBERT L. BANKS, with his likeness painted on side of headlight. Built at West Albany 1865.   (NYC neg 4868)
                                                                    (H.L.Vail coll.)

NEW YORK CENTRAL Engines Acquired 1865-1867. All 4-4-0:

Name	Orig.	Re'77	Re'90	Re'92	Builder,c/n,Date		RB	Cyl. Dr.	Disposition
	244				Rochester	1/65	Sy'70	16x24-60	Sc 1/83
	245				W.Albany	"		15x26-60	Sc 12/89
	246		76		Rochester	6/65	Ro'67	16x24-60	Sc 6/91
H.H.M.	247				W.Albany	3/65		15x26-66	Sc 9/85
	248		215		Schen. 370	"	Ro'74	16x24-60	Sc 1/91
	249		88		" 372	"		" "	So 7/90 N.Y.Eq.Co.
	250		83		" 374	4/65			Sc 1/91
I.H.B.	251				W.Albany	5/65		15x26-60	Sc 1/89
	252		77	221	Rochester	9/65	Ro'67?	16x24-59	Sc 8/95
I.T.	253				"	12/65		16x24-66	Sc 1/89
	254		84		Schen. 375	6/65		16x24-60	Sc 6/90
	255				W.Albany	8/65		15x26-60	Sc 1/89
	256				"	"		" "	So 5/82
	"124				Schen. 378	6/65		16x24-60	Sc 6/88
	"125		701	1062 (a)	" 377	"	'76,'82	" "	So 2/08 Ginsburg
	257		89		" 391	8/65		" "	So 4/90 N.Y.Eq.Co.
	258		90		" 392	"		" "	So 7/90
Walter McQueen	259		91		" 393	9/65		16x24-66	Sc 3/91
Alonzo C. Paige	"23	459	476		" 394	"		" "	So 3/91
H.F.Chittenden	260	39	106		" 395	"		" "	Sc 3/91
Rosebloom	261		92		" 396	"		" "	So 4/90 N.Y.Eq.Co.
	262		93		" 397	10/65		16x24-60	So 4/90 N.Y.Eq.Co.
	263		94		" 398	"		" "	So 7/90 N.Y.Eq.Co.
	264				" 399	11/65		16x24-66	Sc 11/89
W.H.V.	265		95		" 400	"		" "	So 4/90 N.Y.Eq.Co.
Wm.G.Lapham	266		737	1070 (b)	" 401	"	'72,'84	16x24-70	So 7/03 Hy&Co.
E.D.W.	267				W.Albany	9/65			So 12/80
Robert L.Banks	268				"	10/65		15x26-66	Sc 4/89
E.F.S.	269				"	12/65		" "	Sc 11/89
L.I.L.	270				"	"		" "	Sc 11/86
John C.Ellis	271		96		Schen. 402	8/65		16x24-66	So 12/89
	272				" 403	12/65	Sy'71	" "	Sc 12/89
Wm.L.Doyle	273	62-113			" 408	"		" "	So 5/90 N.Y.Eq.Co.
Andrew D.White	274		97		" 409	1/66		" "	So 7/90 N.Y.Eq.Co.
Whitney	275		98		Rochester	5/66		" "	So 5/90 N.Y.Eq.Co.
H.E.C.	276				W.Albany	6/66		15x26-66	Sc 12/86
	277				"	9/66			Sc 1/79
	"10	446	294		Rochester	"	Ro'76	17x24-64	Sc 12/17
	278		163		Schen. 410	6/66	Sy'77	16x24-66	Sc 8/95
	279				W.Albany	11/66		15x26-66	Sc 11/86
Cephus Manning	280 (c)		842		"	1/67		16x24-60	So 11/90 N.Y.Eq.Co.
	281		78		Rochester	12/66	'68	" "	Sc 7/91
	282		99		Schen. 430	10/66		" "	Sc 6/93?
	283		300		Rochester	3/67	EB'77	" "	So 7/98
	"85	520			W.Albany	2/67		15x26-66	dr'85
	"53	489	744	1150	(Shops)	/67	Sy'82	16x24-70	Sc 9/92
Henry Keep	284		758	1084	W.Albany	4/67	WA'81	17x24-70	Sc 10/93

Note a - Re 1070, class Cx 17x24-70.   Note b - Class C-4 17x24-70
Note c - Re Wm.H.Vanderbilt.

NYC 271, named JOHN C. ELLIS, was a fine example of Schenectady's work in 1865. (NYC 5609)

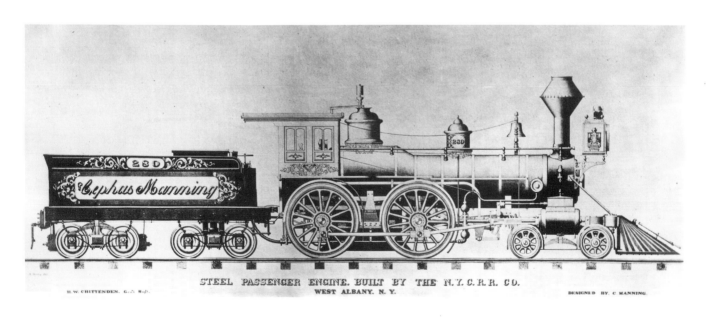

The CEPHUS MANNING, who claimed to be the designer, was built at West Albany in 1869.
(NYC neg 4938)

NEW YORK CENTRAL Engines Acquired 1867-1869:

Orig.	Re'77	Re'90	Re'92	Type	Builder,c/n,Date		RB	Cyl. Dr.	Disposition
" 6	442			0-4-0	W.Albany	/67		15x22-52	Sc 12/89
"229		756	1151	4-4-0	"	5/67	'73,'82		So 6/92 H.C.& B.
285		759	1085	"	"	6/67	WA'81	*17x24-70	Sc 11/93?
286		301	301	"	Rochester	8/67	EB'83	17x24-64	Sc 12/98
287		302	302	"	"	1/68	EB'83	" "	Sc 10/95
288		760	1086	"	W.Albany	7/67	WA'81	*17x24-70	Sc 12/94?
289		761	1087	"	"	8/67	'78,'81	*17x24-76	Sc 8/93?
290		762	1088	"	"	9/67	WA'79	* " "	Sc 9/92?
"224		755	1083	"	"	12/67	WA'81	*17x24-70	Sc 10/93
291		739		"	"	"	Sy'79	* " "	So 1/91
292		763	1089	"	"	3/68	WA'82	* " "	Sc 12/94
"166				"	Rochester	/68		16x22-57	Sc 12/89
"180		734	1068	"	"	"	Sy'83	*17x24-70	So 3/08 H.C.& B.
293		716	1142	"	"	6/68	EB'81		dr by'01
294		740	1072	"	W.Albany	7/68	'79,'87	*17x24-70	Sc 1/02
" 19	455	775	1096	"	"	8/68	WA'82	* " "	Sc 10/01
" 17	453	844	1125	"	"	11/68	WA'81	16x24-66	Sc 9/93
" 87	522			"	"	2/69		13x22-60	RB 12/89 Insp.

Note * - Specs as rebuilt.

LOCOMOTIVES OF THE NEW YORK CENTRAL & HUDSON RIVER RR

In November 1869 the first New York Central RR consolidated with the Hudson River RR to form the New York Central & Hudson River RR, forming a through line from New York to Buffalo via Albany. Surprisingly, there was no renumbering of power from either road until 1877. Meanwhile, additions to both rosters continued, and conflicting road numbers became more and more frequent.

Following are the locomotives added to the old NYC numbering system during this period. The complete Hudson River roster through 1877 starts on page 17.

Orig.	Reno.	Re'90	Re'92	Type	Builder,c/n,Date		Cyl. Dr.	Disposition
295		717		4-4-0	Rochester	12/69	16x24-60	Sc 6/91
296		718	1143	"	"	11/69	" "	dr'92-01
297		142		"	Schen. 612	1/70	16x24-56	So 7/90 N.Y.Eq.Co.
298		164		"	" 613	"	" "	Sc 4/92
299		165		"	" 614	"	" "	Sc 1/91
300		166		"	" 615	"	" "	So 5/95
301		167		"	" 619	3/70	" "	So 4/93 Ginsburg
302		168		"	" 623	4/70	" "	So 8/92 "
303		143		"	" 626	5/70	" "	So 4/90 N.Y.Eq.Co.
304		169		"	" 628	"	" "	Sc 1/91
305		170		"	" 630	"	" "	So 10/90 N.Y.Eq.Co.
306		171		"	" 631	"	" "	So 5/95
307		172		"	" 634	6/70	" "	So 5/95
308		79		"	" 635	"	" "	Sc 1/91
"121 (re'83)	244	162		"	Syracuse	4/70	16x24-60	So 8/92 Ginsburg
" 93 (re'77)	526	727	1148	"	Rochester	6/70	16x24-66	dr'92-01
" 21 "	457	158		"	W.Albany	/70?	16x24-60	So 11/90 N.Y.Eq.Co.
"181		709	1141	"	Rochester	12/70	16x24-63 (a)	dr'92-01

Note a - Later 70" drivers.

The 285's tender was still lettered N.Y.C.R.R., as built by West Albany in 1867.

Schenectady built dozens of engines just like NYC&HR 305 in 1870. (NYC neg 5703)

NYC&HR (NYC Division) Engines Acquired 1869-1872:

Orig.	Re'77	Re'90	Re'92	Type	Bldr.,c/n, Date		As Built	As Rebuilt		Disposition
" 13	449			2-6-0?	W.Albany	6/69	18x22-57	0-6-0? 18x22-52		Sc 10/85
" 44	480			"	"	9/69	" "	4-6-0? " "		Sc 12/89
" 42	478			"	"	11/69	15x22-57	0-6-0? 16x22-59		RB 10/84 (B-5)
"163				"	"	"	18x22-57	4-6-0? 18x22-52		Sc 9/89
" 95	528			"	"	12/69	" "	2-6-0? " "		Sc 12/89
" 9	445			"	"	1/70	15x22-57	0-6-0? 16x22-59		RB 8/86 (B-5)
" 22	458			"	"	5/70	" "	" " " "		RB 3/84 (B-5)
"105	538			"	"	"	18x22-57	2-6-0? 18x22-52		Re DAV&P 11
" 96	529			"	"	6/70	20x20-57	" 20x20-52		Sc 10/89
" 24	460			"	"	"	15x22-57	0-6-0? 15x22-52		RB (B-5)
309				"	"	8/70	" "	" "		RB 6/85 (B-5)
310				"	"		" "	" "		RB 7/88 (B-5)
311		144		4-4-0	"	10/70	16x24-60			So 4/90 NYEqCo
312		764	1090 (A)	"	"	"	" "	WA 2/84 17x24-70		Sc 12/01
313		765	1091	"	"	12/70	" "	WA 10/83 " "		Sc 10/93?
314		145		"	"	"	" "			So 7/90 NYEqCo
315		766	1092 (A)	"	"	2/71	" "	WA 2/83 17x24-70		dr'94-01
316		146		"	"	3/71	" "			So 7/90 NYEqCo
317	173			"	Schen.665	10/70	16x24-54			So 10/90 NYEqCo
318	80			"	" 666	"	" "			So 10/90 NYEqCo
319	174			"	" 667	11/70	" "			Sc 1/91
320	175			"	" 668	"	" "			So 5/93
321	176			"	" 669	"	" "			Sc 1/91
322	216			"	" 670	"	" "			Sc 10/95
323	177			"	" 674	"	" "			So 2/93
324	178			"	" 675	"	" "			Sc 6/90
325	147			"	" 676	12/70	" "			So 7/90 NYEqCo
326	179			"	" 677	"	" "			Sc 1/96
327	180			"	Grant	"	16x24-62	Sy'77		So 10/90 NYEqCo
" 14	450-774			"	W.Albany	7/71	16x24-66			Sc 6/91
328	148			"	Schen.712	"	16x24-60			So 7/90 NYEqCo
329	149			"	" 682	"	15x22-60			So 4/92 Gins.
330	181			"	" 697	"	16x24-64			Sc 1/91
331	217			"	" 698	"	" "			Sc 12/97
332	218			"	" 713	"	" "			Sc 12/97
333	150			"	" 730	10/71	" "			So 7/90 NYEqCo
334	182			"	" 731	"	" "			So 5/92 NYEqCo
335	219			"	" 732	"	" "			Sc 11/95
336	220			"	" 734	"	" "			So 6/96
337	255-482	482 (C)		"	" 744	12/71		c'93 17x24-64		dr'94-99 (a)
338	741	1073 (A)		"	" 745	"		Sy'83 17x24-70		So 3/02
339	221			"	" 748	1/72	16x24-64			So 8/92 Gins.
340	183			"	" 749	"				So 8/92 Gins.
341	742	1074 (C4)		"	" 750	"		EB'84 17x24-70		So 11/02
342	151	248		"	" 751	"	16x24-64			So 6/92 Gins.
343	184			"	" 752	"	" "			Sc 6/95
344	185			"	" 753	"	" "			So 7/98
345	186			"	" 754	"				Sc 4/92
" 12	448	722	1145	"	Rochester	4/72	16x24-64	16x24-70		dr by'01
"179		708	1140	"	"	10/72	" "	" "		dr by'01

Note a - No. 337 (re'89) 255 (re'90) 482, assigned 9/94 to RW&O.

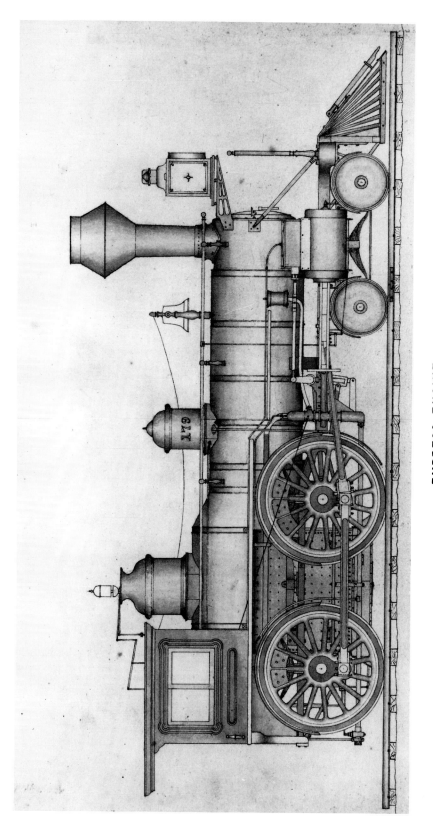

EXPRESS ENGINE

BUILT AT THE NEW YORK CENTRAL RAILROAD SHOPS ROCHESTER, N.Y. Oct. 1872.

The shop at Rochester turned out relatively few engines like this, NYC&HR 179. Drawing signed by D.Dorward.

NYC&HR (NYC Division) Engines Acquired 1872-1873. All 4-4-0.

Orig.	Re'77	Re'90	Re'92	Re'05	Builder,c/n,Date			RB	Cyl. DD	Disposition
346		767	1093		W.Albany		/72	WA'82	*17x24-70	Sc 12/94
347		719	1063	1069 Cx	Schen.	810	9/72	EB'83 * " "		So 11/07
348		743	1075		"	811	"	EB'82 * " "		Sc 10/95
"112		730	1066		"	812	"	'83 * " "		Sc 10/01
" 54	490	745	1076	Cx	"	813	"	Sy'83 * " "		So 7/02 Rut.RR
"116		201			"	816	"		16x24-60	So 7/95
349		222			"	815	"		" "	Sc 11/97
350		187			"	818	10/72		" "	Sc 6/95
351		480		(B)	"	817	"	WA'85 *17x24-64		Sc 8/93
352		481	"		"	819	"	WA'86 * " "		Sc 8/93
353		223			"	820	"		16x24-60	Sc 9/95
354		188			"	821	"		" "	Sc 1/91
355		189			"	822	"		" "	So 5/92 Ginsburg
356		720	1144		"	823	"		" "	dr'92-01
357		190			"	824	"		" "	Sc 10/95
358		843	1124	1086 Cx	"	825	"	(Note a)*17x24-64		So 3/08 CI&S Co.
359		191			"	826	"		16x24-60	So 5/92 Ginsburg
360		152			"	827	"		" "	Sc 5/91
361		224			"	828	"		" "	So'92 Adir.&StL 6
362		225			"	829	11/72		" "	Sc 9/95
363		192			"	830	"		" "	So 5/92 Ginsburg
364		193			"	831	"		" "	So 7/95
365		194			"	832	"		" "	So 7/95
366		226			"	833	"		" "	Sc 10/95
367 re'88		40-128			"	834	"		" "	Sc 5/91
368		195			"	835	"		" "	Sc 5/95
369		227			"	836	12/72		" "	Sc 9/95
370		153			"	837	"		" "	Sc 1/91
371		154			"	838	"		" "	So 7/90 (b)
372		196			"	840	"		" "	So 5/92 Ginsburg
373		228			"	839	"		" "	Sc 12/97
374					"	841	"		" "	Sc 9/85
375		155			"	842	"		" "	Sc 1/91
376		117			"	843	"		" "	So 5/92 Ginsburg
377		229			"	844	"		" "	Sc 1/96
378		156			"	845	"		" "	Sc 1/91
379		157			"	846	"		" "	So 7/90 (b)
380					"	847	"		" "	Re Hud.Riv. 44
381		230			"	848	"		" "	Sc 11/95
382		198			"	849	"		" "	Sc 4/92
383		231			"	850	2/73		" "	Sc 9/95
384		232			"	851	"		" "	Sc 10/95
385		768	1094		(Shops)		6/73	WA'83 *17x24-70		Sc 10/93?
386		769			"		"	*17x24-66		So 10/93? Ginsburg
387		770			"		"	*17x24-66		So 11/90 N.Y.Eq.Co
388		771			"		"	*17x24-70		So 7/90 N.Y.Eq.Co
389		772	1095		"		"	WA'80 *17x24-76		Sc 11/93?
390		773			"		"	*17x24-70		Sc 3/91
"113		700	1137		"		10/73		16x24-70	Sc 12/97

Note * - Specs as rebuilt.   Note a - #358 wrecked 6/84, replaced by Schen.c/n 1924
Note b - #154 and 157 re Florida Central & Peninsular 9 and 10.

This work train of the 1890's was headed by NYC&HR 479, built as 420 by Schenectady 1873.

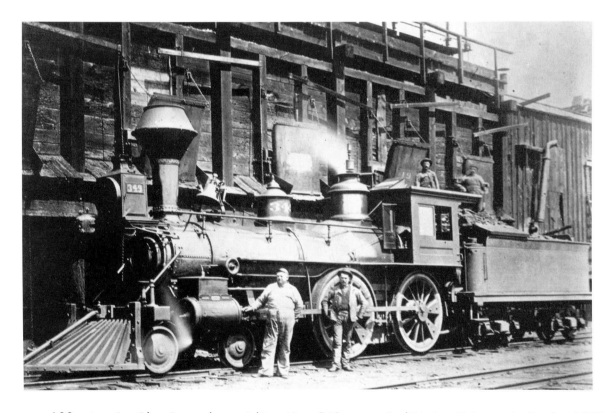

Well over 100 standardized engines like the 349 were built by Schenectady in 1870-1873.
(NYC neg. 5629)

NYC&HR (NYC Division) Engines Acquired 1873-1877. All 4-4-0. (@ 17x24-64).

Orig.	Re'90	Re'92	Re'99	Re'05	Class	Builder,c/n,Date	RB	Disposition
391	268					Schen. 906 7/73		@ So 5/92 Ginsburg
392	269	495				" 907 8/73		@ So 7/98
393	270	496				" 908 "		@ Sc 1/95
394	271	497				" 909 "		@ Sc 10/95
395	272					" 912 "		@ Sc 4/92
396	273	498				" 913 "		@ Sc 10/95
397	274	499-270	452			" 914 "		@ dr'99-01
398	275	500				" 915 9/73		@ Sc 8/95
399	276					" 916 "		@ So 11/90 N.Y.Eq.Co.
400	498	386	544	NY&O 2	B(C-9)	" 917 "	3/86	@ Sc'10 as NY&O 787
401	477					" 918 "		@ So 11/90 N.Y.Eq.Co.
402	277					" 919 "		@ Sc 11/93?
403	278					" 921 "		@ Sc 12/89?
404	279					" 923 "		@ Sc 10/95
405	280					" 924 "		@ Sc 9/95
406	281					" 925 10/73		@ Sc 10/95
407	478	478	478	813	B(C-9)	" 926 "	7/84	@ So 5/07 Jones & Galvin
408	282					" 927 "		@ So 5/90 N.Y.Eq.Co.
409	283					" 930 "		@ Sc 9/95
410	284					" 931 "		@ Sc 10/95
411	285					" 932 "		@ So 7/98
412	286					" 934 "		@ So 7/98
413	287					" 935 "		@ So 7/98
414	288					" 936 "		@ Sc 9/95
415	289					" 933 "		@ Sc 4/92
416	290					" 943 11/73		@ So 11/90 N.Y.Eq.Co.
417	475				B(C-9a)	" 944 12/73	12/83	@ So 8/08 Jones & Galvin
418	291					" 945 "		@ Sc 6/91
419	482	256	483	814	B(C-9)	" 946 "	7/85	@ So 10/05 Jones & Galvin
420	479				B(C-9)	" 947 "	3/84	@ So 1/05 Ginsburg
421	500	476	476	822	B(C-9)	" 948 "	10/89	@ So 10/05 Jones & Galvin
422	292					" 949 "		@ Sc 5/91

Orig.	Re'77	Re'90	Re'99	Class	Builder,c/n,Date	RB	Cyl,DD	Disposition
" 1	437	233			W.Albany /75		15x22-56	So 10/90 N.Y.Eq.Co.
"108	541	746	*1077	A(C-4)	Syracuse /74	Sy'85	16x24-64	Sc 5/09
"142	142	204			Rochester 2/74		16x22-64	Sc 7/92
"171	171	208			" /74		14x24-60	Sc 2/91
"106	539				Syracuse /75		16x24-64	Sc 11/87
"169	169	159			" /76		16x24-64	So 7/95
" 11	447				" "		" "	Sc 12/89
" 77	513	253		(4-2-4T)	W.Albany 6/76	(a)	12x16-64	Sc'96
"107	540	200			Schen. 999 12/76		16x24-64	So 7/98
" 49	485	295			" 1025 "		17x24-64	Sc 8/95
" 78	514	318			" 1026 "		" "	So 7/98
"119	293	293	497	B	" 1027 "		" "	Sc 12/98?
"120	296				" 1028 1/77		" "	So 7/98
"114	141				" 1029 "		16x24-64	Sc 6/91
"127	298				" 1030 "		17x24-64	Sc 3/96
"126	297				" 1031 "		" "	So 7/98
"189	735	735	*1069	Cx	" 1032 "	Sy'86	17x24-70	So 2/05
"380	303				" 1033 "		17x24-64	So 6/95
"154	299				" 1035 2/77		" "	So 7/98
423	304				" 1036 "		" "	Sc 10/99?
424	305				" 1037 "		" "	So 7/98
425	306				" 1038 3/77		" "	Sc 10/95
426	307				" 1039 "		" "	So 7/98
427	308	308	498	B(C-9)	" 1040 "		" "	So 8/03 Ginsburg
428	309	309	499	B(C-9)	" 1041 "		" "	dr'99-00
429	310				" 1042 "		" "	So 7/98
430	311				" 1043 "		" "	So 7/98
431	312	312	500	B(C-9)	" 1044 4/77		" "	So 2/05 H'y & Co.
432	313	3:3	501	B(C-9)	" 1045 "		" "	dr'99-01
433	314				" 1046 "		" "	So 7/98
434	315				" 1034 "		" "	So 6/95
435	316	316	502	B(C-9a)	" 1047 "		" "	So 11/04 Ginsburg
436	317				" 1048 "		" "	Sc 7/95

Note a - RB from Hud.Riv. 4-2-0 #59 as inspection loco."G.H.Burrows". See p.36.
    * - Renumbered 1892.

Many of the earlier diamond stack engines were rebuilt with extended smoke box including the 539, photographed here at the old Grand Central Station, New York. (Jos. Lavelle)

A freight train of the 1870's, in charge of a no-nonsense crew with NYC&HR 422. (NYC 2656)

In the roster which follows, locomotives are listed in approximate chronological order. Numbers were not assigned until after 1856, but the practice of naming engines continued until 1868. During the next year the Hudson River consolidated with the old NYC to form the New York Central & Hudson River, but separate rosters were maintained until 1877, when H.R. Nos. 1-109 became NYC&HR 1-109.

Name	Orig.	Re'90	Type	Builder,c/n,Date			Cyl. DD	RB	31st St.	Disposition
Ohio? re Erie	1		-2-	Springfield		9/49	14x20-66			Rt 12/73
Atlantic	2		4-4-0	Rogers	188	10/49	16x20-60			dr c'79
Pacific	3	125 (c)	"	"	190	"	16x20-72	7/75	17x22-70	Sc 5/91
Mohawk			4-2-2	Matteawan		12/49	15x20-72			dr by'79
Ontario	6	(c)	4-4-0	"		/49		/74	17x22-63	Sc 2/88
Champlain			"	Taunton	43	12/49	15x20-66			So 12/52 (e)
St.Lawrence	4		"	"	47	2/50	" "		15x20-54	So 10/81 (f)
Niagara	5		"	"	51	8/50	15x20-60		15x18-66	dr c'66?
Dana (note d)	8	(d)	4-2-2	Baldwin	381	5/50	15x20-72			Rt 12/73
Potomac			4-4-0	New Castle		6/50	15x20-66			dr by'77
Priam			"	" "		"	13x20-54			dr by'77
Croton	10		"	Lowell	91	7/51	12x20-66	2/77		(See p.37)
Spuyten Duyvil	11		"	"	92	9/51	" "	/67	16x24-60	So'81 (f)
West Point			"	"	93	"	" "			dr by'56
Albany			"	"	94	1/52	" "		14x18-66	dr by'64
S.W.Dana		(g)	4-2-2	(Rogers	99	5/47)	12x20-60			
Seneca	50?		4-4-0	Taunton	72	6/51	14x20-66			dr by'56
Oneida (i)	15		"	"	73	"	" "	/66	16x24-60	So 3/81
Canada	12		"	"	79	9/51	" "	6/78		(See p.38)
Chippewa	14		"	"	88	12/51	" "			So 10/81 (f)
Cayuga	7		"	S.Wilmarth		9/51	16x20-66	/76	16x22-63	Sc 4/86
New York	9	126	"	"		7/51	15x22-78	"	15x22-57	So 7/90 (h)
Dutchess	13	127	"	"		10/51	" "	2/73	15x22-63	Sc 4/93
Putnam	17		"	"		1/52	" "	/64		So 3/81
Westchester	18	105	"	"		2/52	" "	"	15x22-63	Sc 9/90
Richmond			"	"		7/52	" "			dr by'77
Boorman	29		"	"		9/52	15x20-66		15x29-56	Sc 3/87

Note b - to Ginsburg   Note c - Built as 4-2-2.   Note d - built as 6-2-0 "Susquehanna"
Note e - Rebuilt to N.Y.& Harlem "Mohawk".   Note f - re N.Y.Tex.& Mex.RR
Note g - Built for Troy & Greenbush RR, acquired 1851.   Note h - to N.Y.Equip.Co.
Note i - Re "Geo.B. McClellan" c.1862.

Additional locomotives listed at times, probably borrowed from nearby lines, named: Thomas Cornell, Clinton, C.H.Kendrick, Racer, Henry Clay, Livingston, Justice, Lenox.

Lithograph of Hudson River RR No.9, the NEW YORK. Title reads "Passenger Engine
Designed for the Hudson River Railroad by Walter McQueen. Built by Seth Wilmarth
Union Works, South Boston."

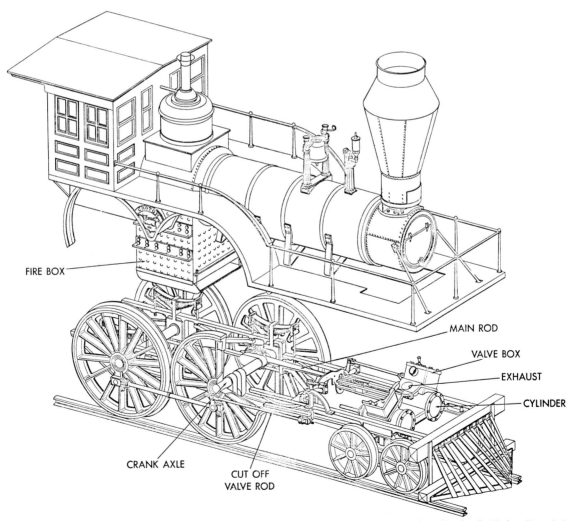

FIRE BOX

MAIN ROD

VALVE BOX

EXHAUST

CYLINDER

CRANK AXLE

CUT OFF
VALVE ROD

*Exploded view of the inside-connected 4–4–0 Croton of the 1850-51 period built by the Lowell Machine Shop for the Hudson River R.R.
Action of gab motion supplemented by a separate drive off the crankpin, giving a measure of expansive working. Eccentrics and hooks
of gab gear not shown. Cylinders 12 in. by 20 in.; wheels 5 ft. 6 in.*
(Courtesy: John H. White Jr.)

HUDSON RIVER RR Engines Acquired 1852-1861. All 4-4-0.

Name	Orig.	Re'90	Builder, c/n, Date	Cyl.	DD	RB	31st St.	Disposition
Mississippi			Essex	1/52	16x20-66				dr by'77
Merrimack	16	104	"	"	15x18-60		/63	15x22-63	Sc 7/93
Essex	28		"	9/52	15x20-54				Sc 2/76
Detroit			"	10/52	15x20-60				dr by'77
Montreal	21		"	11/52	15x18-60		/63	to 0-4-0?	Rt 12/73
Kinderhook	22		Lowell 95	3/52	13x20-66				RB'63 0-4-0T
Matteawan	24		" 96	5/52	" "				So 3/81?
Rensselaer	20 re 25		" 99	6/52	16+x22-72			16+x22-78	RB'72 (p.36)
Columbia	27		" 100	7/52	16+x22-84			16+x22-68	Sc 9/89
Hudson			" 101	8/52	16+x22-66			16+x22-72	dr by'77
Lowell			" 102	"	" "				dr by'77
Sing Sing	31		" 105	11/52	13x20-66			16x22-63	RB'60 (d)
Peekskill	30		" 106	10/52	" "		/63	16+x22-72	dr c'79
Rochester	22? re 20	256	" 109	2/53	16x22-66	9/71?		17x24-57	Sc 5/91?
Buffalo	19		" 110	"	" "			16x22-62	Sc 12/89
Schenectady(a)	23	250 401	Schen. 10	4/52	" "	11/89?		16x24-64	So 2/03
Saratoga	26		" 12	6/52	" "				Sc 8/89
Manchester			Amoskeag 74	12/52	" "		/74		dr by'90
Amoskeag	32		" 75	1/53	" "		/72		Sc 11/89
Young America	33		(Note c)				/65		RB 2/77 (p.37)
Utica	34		S.Wilmarth	2/53	16x22-66		/64		RB 3/77 (p.37)
Fulton	35		"	7/53	" "				Sc 11/74
Cumberland	36		Smith & Perk.	9/53	17x22-60		/64		RB 2/75 (p.37)
Huron	37		New Jer.L&M	1/54	15+x22-66		/65		So 7/74
Missouri	42		Schen. 65	12/53	16x22-72			16x22-57	Sc 11/89
St.Clair	38		" 66	1/54	" "			16x22-63	Sc 12/89
Fishkill	41		Lowell 129	2/54	16x22-66		/65		dr c'81
Rhinebeck	39		" 130	"	" "				Sc 4/88
Poughkeepsie	40		Danf.Cooke	"	" "		/65		Sc 5/88
Superior	43		Breese Knee.	3/54	16x22-78			16x22-63	Sc 11/89
Baltic	44		" "	4/54	" "			" "	Expl. 8/66
Arctic	45		" "	"	16x22-66			" "	Sc 5/88
Michigan	46		" "	6/54	" "			" "	Sc 5/85
Yonkers	47		" "	1/56	15x22-60			16x22-57	Sc 3/86
Tivoli	50		" "	2/57	16x22-78			" "	Sc 6/86
Edward Jones	48		Schen. 151	5/56	16x22-66			16x22-63	Sc 8/85
Stuyvesant	51	129	" 174	12/56	" "			17x20-64	So 5/90 NYEqCo
Irvington	49	108	Essex (Lawr.)	2/57				16x22-64	Sc 3/91
Seneca	52		N.Y.31st St.	/56	15x22-60	5/78		17x24-66	Sc 8/88
A.F.Smith	53		Schen. 209	10/57	16x22-60			16+x22-63	RB 5/78?(p.38)
West Point	54	109	" 224	7/60	16x22-66			16x22-70	So 5/90 NYEqCo
Storm King	55	110	" 225	8/60	16x24-60			16x22-64	So 2/92 (b)
Union	56		" 236	1/61	16x22-66				Sc 11/89
Constitution	57	111	" 237	"	" "				Sc 3/91

Note a – Renamed "Cornelius Oakley" #23 (re'90) 250 (re'99) 401?
b – to Scott & McLain.
c – Also listed as "Superior" built by Breese Kneeland 1853.
d – Rebuilt to 0-4-0T #31 "Jessie". Dr by'79

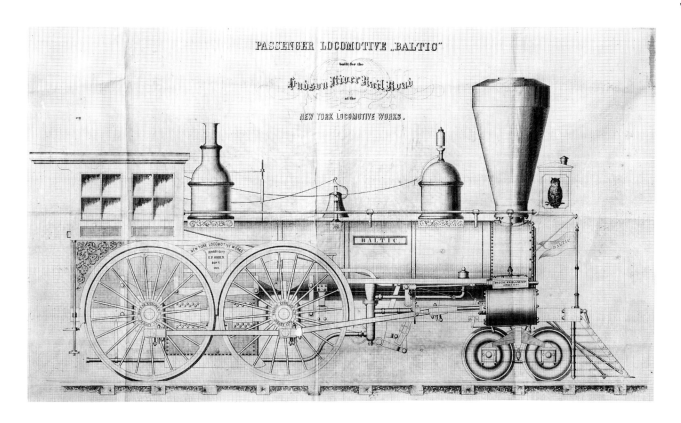

Lithograph of Hudson River 44, the BALTIC. Builder's plate reads "New York Locomotive Works, Jersey City. E.P.Gould, Supt. 1854"   (NYC neg 4062-6)

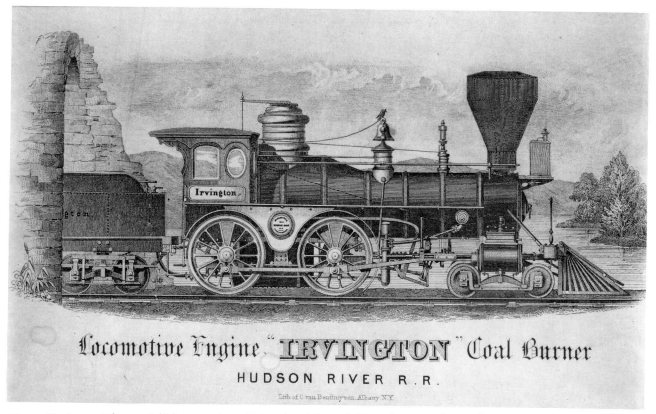

Another Hudson River lithograph, illustrating #49, the road's first coal burner.(NYC 4201)

HUDSON RIVER RR Engines Acquired 1861-1872:

Name & H.R.Orig.No.	Re'90	'92	Type	Builder,c/n,Date			Cyl. DD	RB	as RB	Disposition
Kinderhook ?	22	7	0-4-0T	NY 31st St.		/63		'75	Sc 8/95	
D.Thomas Vail	58	251	4-2-0	Danf.Cooke		8/61	11x15-56	WA'77	Inspec.	(See p.118)
Monitor	59		"	"	"	"	10x18-60	WA'76	"	Re NYC 77
John David Wolfe	60	112	"	"	"	11/62	" "			So 7/90 NYEq.
Moses H.Grinnell	61	830	"	"	"	12/62	" "			Sc 10/90
Winfield Scott	62		"	"	"	"	11x15-60			Sc 5/88
Wm.B.Kelly	63		"	"	"	1/63	" "			Sc 11/89
Minnesota	64	114	4-4-0	Schen.	282	2/63	16x24-60		16x22-64	Sc 9/90
Iowa	66		"	"	286	3/63	" "		" "	Sc 12/82
John Ericsson	65	115	"	Danf.Cooke		2/63	" "		" "	So 7/90 NYEq.
Erastus Corning	67	116	"	"	"	4/63	" "		" "	Sc 9/90
Brooklyn	68	117	"	"	"	2/64	" "		" "	So 7/90 NYEq.
Albany	69	118	"	"	"	"	" "		" "	So 2/93 Gins.
Sam Sloan	70	831	"	"	"	3/64	" "	NY'71	17x24-66	So 12/91 "
Troy	71	119	"	"	"	"	" "		16x22-70	So 7/90 NYE.
Augustus Schell	72	120	"	Schen.353?		11/64	" "			Sc 5/91
Cornelius Vander.	73	121	"	Danf.Cooke		"	" "		16x22-70	So 7/90 NYEq.
Leonard W.Jerome	74	130	"	"	"	"	" "		16x22-54	So 5/90 NYEq.
John M.Tobin	75	131	"	"	"	"	" "		" "	So 5/90 NYEq.
James H.Banker	76		"	"	"	"	" "		16x24-57	Sc 2/87
Horace F.Clark	77	132	"	NY31st St.		12/64	" "		16x22-70	Sc 9/90
John M.Toucey	78	122	"	"	"	"	" "			So 7/90 NYEq.
William Buchanan	79	832	"	"	"	7/65	17x24-70	WA'81	16x24-70	Re DAV&P (b)
Wm.H.Vanderbilt	80	833 1119	"	"	"	8/66	" "	WA'86	17x24-70	Re DAV&P (c)
Hudson River	81		"	"	"	/67	" "			dr c'81
Rueben E. Fenton	82	834 1120	"	"	"	12/67	" "	WA'83	17x24-	Sc'00
	83	389	"	"	"	8/68	17x24-64	WA'80		Sc 8/93?
	84	835 1121	"	"	"	/68	17x24-70	WA'82	17x24-66	Sc 10/93
	85	836 1122	"	"	"	12/69	" "	'83	" "	Sc 12/92
	86	837 1123	"	"	"	"	" "	WA'83	" "	Sc 10/93
	87	123	"	Schen.	605	12/69	16x24-54			So 7/90 NYEq.
	88	124	"	"	606	1/70	" "	" "		Sc 5/91
	89	133	"	"	608	"	" "	" "		Sc 5/91
	90	134 248	"	"	607	"	" "	" "	16x24-64	Re'94 DAV&P
	91	135	"	"	671	11/70	" "	" "		So 2/91 Gins.
	92	136	"	"	672	"	" "	" "		Sc 8/91
	93		"	"	673	"	" "	" "		Sc 3/90
	94	1	0-4-0	"	804	8/72			Class D	dr by'99
	95	2	"	"	805	"			"	Sc 5/96
	96	3 50	"	"	806	"			D (A-2)	So 4/03 Gins.
	97	257	4-4-0	"	807	9/72	17x24-66			So 5/90 NYEq.
	98	258	"	"	808	"	" "			Sc 3/91
	99	259	"	"	809	"	" "			Sc 3/91
	"25	821 1115	"	NY 31st St.		/72	17x24-63	/85		Re '94 DAV&P
(ex-NYC 380)	"44	825 1118	"	(Schen. 1872)			17x24-70	1/90		So 3/08 (d)

Note a - #59 re NYC 77 then 513 then 253. See p.30.
Note b - #832 re DAV&P 9, re 263, re 407 (class C-9).
Note c - #1119 re'05 1079, class C-4, old class A.
Note d - #1118 re'05 1065, class Cx to Ginsburg.

NYC&HR Hudson River Division Engines Acquired 1873-1877:

Orig.	Re'90	Re'92	Re'99	Re'05	Type	Builder,c/n,Date	RB	Cyl. DD	Disposition
100	260	487			4-4-0	Schen. 898 7/73		17x24-64	Sc 10/96
101	261	488			"	" 899 "		" "	Sc 12/98
102	262	489			"	" 900 "		" "	Sc 8/93
103	263				"	" 901 "		" "	Sc 5/91
104	264	491			"	" 902 "		" "	Sc 8/93
105	265				"	" 903 "		" "	So 5/90 N.Y.Eq.Co.
106	266	279	488	823	"	" 904 8/73	WA'89	" "	(Note a)
107	267				"	" 905 "		" "	Sc 3/91
108	4				0-4-0	" 938 11/73		Class D	So 2/98 StL&A 2
109	5	51			"	" 940 "		"	Re 5/91 DAV&P 51 (b)
"36	824	1117			4-4-0	NY 31st St. 2/75	/85	17x24-57	dr'92-01
"10	819	1113			"	" " 2/77		17x24-63	Sc 10/93
"33	822	1116			"	" " "		" "	Sc 11/99
"34	823				"	" " 3/77		" "	Sc 6/90

Note a - #266 re 5/91 to DAV&P 10, later 279-488-823, class C-9
Note b - DAV&P 51 sold 12/03 to Lowville & Beaver River RR.

HUDSON RIVER "Dummy" Engines:

For years the Hudson River RR operated service on the streets of lower Manhattan with a group of small locomotives with enclosed carbodies, called "Dummy" engines. Supposedly they frightened horses less easily than conventional steam locomotives. These engines were numbered in their own series, 1 to 8, as follows:

	No.	Type	Builder,c/n	Date	Cyl.	Disposition
	1	0-4-0T	NY 31st St.	6/61		RB'82 (2nd 1)
	2	"	" "	6/62		Sc 6/91
	3	"	" "	7/62		Sc 11/90
St.Lawrence	4	"	Schen. 438	2/67	11x15-42	Sc 2/88
Niagara	5	"	" 464	9/67	" "	Sc 11/90
Ontario	6	"	" 470	10/67	" "	Sc 2/90
Cayuga	7	"	" 474	12/67	" "	Sc 11/90
Dana	8	"	" 602	12/69	" "	Sc 2/88

For later Dummy engines, built 1882 to 1918, see P. 106.

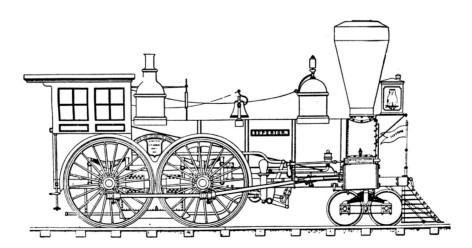

The Hudson River RR's SUPERIOR, later #43, built by Breese Kneeland.

NEW YORK CENTRAL & HUDSON RIVER Engines Acquired 1877-1879. All 4-4-0:

Note: In 1877, HR Division locomotives nos. 1-109 became NYC&HR 1-109, and NYC Division locomotives 1-109 (except three missing) became NYC&HR 437-542. Additions to the NYC&HR roster after April, 1877 are listed below in approximate chronological order.

Orig.	Re'90	Re'92	Re'99	Re'05	Class		Builder,c/n,Date		Cyl. DD	Disposition
543	333	271	457	(RW&O)	(B)C-9b	Schen.1049	4/77	17x24-60	So 2/03
544	334	334	514	"	" C-9a	"	1050	5/77	" "	So 1/05 Jones & Gal.
545	335				"	"	1051	"	" "	So 6/95
546	336		515	(RW&O)	" C-9a	"	1056	6/77	" "	So 4/04 Hy & Co.
547	337				"	"	1057	"	" "	Sc 1/98
548	338				"	"	1058	"	" "	Sc 1/98
549	319					"	1059	"	" "	dr'94-99
550	320		503		" C-9	"	1060	"	" "	So 7/98?
551	321		504		" "	"	1061	"	" "	So 11/04 Ginsburg
552	322		505		" "	"	1062	"	" "	So 9/03 Hy.& Co.
553	323					"	1063	"	" "	So 6/95
554	324					"	1064	"	" "	So 7/98
555	325		506			"	1067	9/77	" "	Sc 12/01
556	326		507	(RW&O)	C-9a	"	1068	"	" "	So 8/03 Jones & Gal.
557	327					"	1069	"	" "	Sc 3/96
558	328		508	(RW&O)		"	1070	"	" "	Sc 12/01
559						"	1073	10/77	" "	Re'78 CASO 559 re 54
560						"	1074	"	" "	" " 560 re 55
561						"	1075	"	" "	" " 561 re 56
562						"	1076	"	" "	" " 562 re 57
563						"	1077	"	" "	" " 563 re 58
564	728	1064				"	1052	5/77	17x24-66	So 7/98
565	747	1078				"	1053	"	" "	dr by'01
566	780	1099				"	1054	6/77	" "	Sc 12/98
567	781	1100				"	1055	"	" "	Sc 11/99
				(CS 600-603 re CS 50-53 blt. Schen.1079-1082 1/78)						
" 53	829					NY 31stSt.		5/78	17x24-66	Sc 10/90
" 12	820	1114				" "		6/78	17x24-57	RB 5/85, dr by'01
"165	207			(M&M)		E.Buffalo		/78	16x24-60	Sc 6/95
"462	199					Syracuse		/78	" "	So 10/91 Ginsburg
"162			(ex Cayuga Sou.)			(Hink.'72)acq.78			14x22-62	So 5/82
				(CS 564-591 re CS 59-86 blt. Schen.1083-1145 1-7/79)						
"443	331		511		C-9	Schen.1142	7/79	17x24-60	So 4/04 Hy.& Co.
592	339		516		(B)	"	1147	"	" "	Sc 12/01
"525	332		512			"	1152	9/79	" "	Sc 12/01
"277	738	1071			(A)C-4	"	1154	"	" "	RB'85, So 4/04 Hy.& C
"135	329		509			"	1156	"	" "	dr'99-01
"184	330					"	1157	"	" "	Wrk.8/90
"454	348		517		(B)	"	1158	"	" "	Sc 1/02
"492	350		519		" C-9	"	1159	"	" "	So 9/03 Ginsburg
"497	351		520		" "	"	1160	"	" "	So 11/04 Ginsburg
"531	353		521	800	" "	"	1161	"	" "	So 10/05 Ginsburg
"542	354		522		"	"	1162	"	" "	So 8/02
"559	355					"	1163	"	" "	Sc 1/98
"560	356		523	801	(B)C-9	"	1164	"	" "	So 10/05 Ginsburg
"561	357				"	"	1165	"	" "	dr'94-99
"562	358		524		" C-9	"	1166	"	" "	So 4/04 Hy.&Co.
"563	359				"	"	1167	"	" "	dr'94-99
"512	352				"	"	1168	"	" "	dr'94-99
568	360				"	"	1169	10/79	" "	dr'94-99
569	361		525		"	"	1170	"	" "	Sc 1/02
570	362		526		" C-9	"	1171	"	" "	So 5/04 Jones & Gal.
571	363				"	"	1172	"	" "	dr'94-99
572	364		527		"	"	1173	"	" "	dr'99-01

Schenectady builder's photo of NYC&HR 567, one of 25 identical machines delivered in 1877. Many survived to be grouped in class C-9 and C-9a. (NYC neg 5101)

NYC&HR 515, one of the C-9a engines in later years. (Joseph Lavelle)

Orig.	Re'90	Re'99	Re'05	Class	Type	Builder,c/n,Date			Cyl.	DD	Disposition
"130	731				4-4-0	Syracuse		/79	17x24-70		Sc 1/91
"164	206				"	E.Buffalo		5/79	17x22-64		Sc 10/95
"152	205				"	Rochester		9/79	16x24-64		Sc 10/95
" 2	38				0-6-0	N.Y.31st St.		7/79	16x24-50		So 5/90 N.Y.Eq.Co.
" 30	9	54		(D)	0-4-0	"	"	9/79	16x22-48		Sc 8/99
" 31	10	(55)		"	"	"	"	"	"	"	dr c'99
"481	349	518	824	(B)C-9a	4-4-0	Schen.	1174	10/79	17x24-64		So 5/07 Jones & Gal.
" 1	340			"	"	"	1175	"	17x24-60		dr'94-99
" 5	341			"	"	"	1176	"	"	"	Sc 10/95
" 8	342			"	"	"	1177	"	"	"	dr'94-99
" 21	343			"	"	"	1178	"	"	"	dr'94-99
" 28	344			"	"	"	1179	"	"	"	dr'94-99
" 35	345			"	"	"	1180	11/79	"	"	Sc 8/99
" 37	346			"	"	"	1181	"	"	"	Sc 10/93
" 59	347			"	"	"	1182	"	"	"	Sc 10/93
"484	381			"	"	"	1183	"	"	"	Sc 1/96
573	365	528		" C-9	"	"	1186	"	"	"	So 9/03 Ginsburg
574	366			"	"	"	1187	"	"	"	Re 12/93 DAV&P
575	367-278	487		"	"	"	1188	"	"	"	Sc 10/01 (Note a)
576	368	530	RW&O	" C-9	"	"	1189	"	"	"	So'04 Jones & Gal.
577	369	531		"	"	"	1190	"	"	"	dr'99-01
578	370	532		"	"	"	1191	"	"	"	dr'99-01
579	371	533	(802)	" C-9	"	"	1192	12/79	"	"	So 10/05 Ginsburg
580	372	534		" "	"	"	1193	"	"	"	So 8/03 Ginsburg
581	373	535		"	"	"	1194	"	"	"	dr'99-01
582	374	536		"	"	"	1195	"	"	"	dr'99-01
583	375	537		" C-9	"	"	1196	"	"	"	So 4/03 Ginsburg
584	376			"	"	"	1198	"	"	"	Sc 12/98
585	377	538	RW&O	" C-9	"	"	1199	"	"	"	So 8/03 Ginsburg
586	378			"	"	"	1200	"	"	"	Sc 8/97
587	379	539		" C-9	"	"	1201	"	"	"	So 1/04 Hy.& Co.
588	380			"	"	"	1202	1/80	"	"	dr'94-99
589	382	540		"	"	"	1203	"	"	"	dr by'02
590	383	541		" C-9	"	"	1204	"	"	"	So 8/02
591	384	542		" "	"	"	1205	"	"	"	So 4/04 Hy.& Co.
"151	703	1138		"	"	E.Buffalo		5/80	17x22-70		So 11/04 Ginsburg
593	847	1128		"	"	Schen.	1313	12/80	17x24-60		dr'92-01
594	385	546	803	C-9a	"	"	1292	10/80	"	"	Sc 8/08 (Note b)
595	386	547		C-9	"	"	1293	"	"	"	So 4/04 (Note c)
596	387	545	(B)		"	"	1294	"	"	"	Sc 3/02
597	388			"	"	"	1295	"	"	"	Sc 10/96
598				"	"	"	1296	"	"	"	Re 4/81 NY&H 18.
599				"	"	"	1312	12/80	"	"	" NY&H 23.
600	"Wm.H.Vanderbilt"				"	"	1290	10/80	18x24-72		RB 9/89 (See p.112
601					"	"	1291	"	"	"	RB 1/89 (See p.112
602			"		"	"	1320	1/81	17x24-60		Re 2/81 NY&H 12.
603			"		"	"	1318	"	"	"	" NY&H 17.
"267			"		"	"	1325	2/81	"	"	" NY&H 11.
"456			"		"	"	1327	"	"	"	" NY&H 15.
"131	402	402	RW&O	" C-9	"	"	1328	"	"	"	So 1/05 Jones & Gal.
"468	426	426	"	" "	"	"	1329	"	"	"	So 11/04 Ginsburg
"461	425	425		"	"	"	1330	"	"	"	Sc 8/02
"476	428	428		"	"	"	1331	"	"	"	dr'99-01
"509	431	431	804	" C-9	"	"	1333	"	"	"	So 10/05 Jones & Gal.

Note a - #575 (re'90) 367 (re) DAV&P 7 (re) 278 (re'99) 487.
Note b - #594 (re'90) 385 (re) DAV&P 11 (re) 388 (re'99) 546 (re'05) 803.
Note c - #595 (re'90) 386 (re) DAV&P 12 (re) 389 (re'99) 547. So 4/04 Jones & Gal.

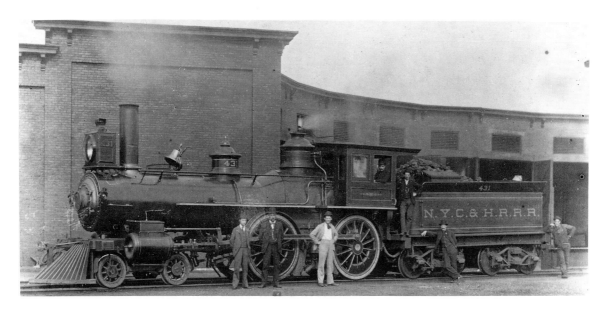

NYC&HR 431, as renumbered in 1890 from old #509.   (Purinton 90)

NYC&HR 151 as built at East Buffalo shop 1880 with clerestory cab roof. (NYC 2332)
                                                            (H.L.Vail coll.)

Somehow NYC&HR 600 was special, named WILLIAM H. VANDERBILT.   (NYC neg 327)
                                                            (H.L.Vail coll.)

NYC&HR Engines Acquired 1881:

Orig.	Re'90	Re'92	Re'99	Re'05	Class	Type	Builder,c/n,Date	Cyl. DD	Disposition
"172	704	1139				4-4-0	Syracuse 3/81	16x24-70	dr by'01
" 81	14	59		*	(D) A	0-4-0	N.Y.31st St.7/81	16x22-48	So 4/03
" 41	11	56			" "	"	" " 8/81	" "	So'06 Nwk.& Mar.2
" 11	6	52			" "	"	" " 9/81	" "	Sc 10/01
"507	430	Note d		* 808	(B)C-9	4-4-0	Schen.1400 7/81	17x24-60	So 10/05 J.& G.
604	437	"			"	"	1401	" " "	dr'99-01
605	438	"			" C-9	"	1404	" " "	So 8/02
"598	433				" "	"	1405	" " "	Sc 4/02
"599	434				" "	"	1406	" " "	So 11/04 Ginsburg
"602	435				" "	"	1407	" " "	So 11/02
"603	436				" "	"	1408	" " "	So 2/05 Hy.& Co.
"456	424				"	"	1409	" " "	Sc 8/02
"267	422				" C-9	"	1410	" " "	So 2/05 Hy.& Co.
"111	399		554		" "	"	1411	" " "	So 1/05 Ginsburg
"128	400				"	"	1412	" " "	So 8/02
"146	405			*	" C-9	"	1413	" " "	So 11/03 J.& G.
"170	410				" "	"	1414	" " "	So 11/04 Ginsburg
"192	419				" "	"	1415	" " "	So 9/03 Cont.I&SCo
"202	421				" "	"	1416	" " "	So 5/03 Cont.I&SCo
"471	427				" "	"	1417	" " "	So 11/02
"504	429				"	"	1418	" " "	dr'99-01
"536	432				" C-9	"	1419	" " "	So 2/05 Hy.& Co.
606	439				"	"	1420	" " "	dr'99-01
607	440				"	"	1421	" " "	dr'99-01
608	441				"	"	1422	" " "	So 8/02
" 4	394		550	*	"	"	1423	" " "	dr'94-01
" 15	396		552		"	"	1424	" " "	Sc 10/99
" 24	398				"	"	1425	" " "	Sc 8/95
"129	401				"	"	1426	" " "	Wrk. 8/90
"133	403			* 805	" C-9	"	1427	" " "	Sc'05
" 17	397		553		" "	"	1428	" " "	So 4/04 Hy.& Co.
"141	404			*	" "	"	1429	" " "	So 1/05 J.& G.
"147	406				" "	"	1430	" " "	dr.'03 (note a)
" 14	395		551	*	"	"	1431	" " "	dr'94-01 (note b)
"153	407				"	"	1436 10/81	" "	Sc 8/99
"155	408				"	"	1437 "	" "	dr'94-99
"168	409				"	"	1438	" "	So 11/01 J.& G.
"173	411				"	"	1445	" "	So 8/02 Ginsburg?
"174	412				"	"	1446	" "	dr'99-01
"175	413				"	"	1449	" "	So 8/02
"176	414				"	"	1450	" "	Sc 10/99
"177	415			* 806	" C-9	"	1453	" "	So 10/05 J.& G.
"178	416			*	" "	"	1465 11/81	" "	So 11/04 Ginsburg
"182	417			807	" C-9a	"	1469 12/81	" "	So 7/08 Cont.I&SCo?
"185	418				"	"	1470	" "	Sc 8/95
"194	420				" C-9	"	1471	" "	So 11/04 Ginsburg
"438	423				" "	"	1472	" "	Sc 5/03 R.L.G.& Son

Note a - #406 perhaps re NY&O 787.   Note b - #551 (re) No.Adir.2, then NY&O 2 (Cx)
Note d - Earlier 507,604,605 built Schen.c/n 1332,1334,1335 2/81 as Michigan Central,
         re MC 220-222. See MC Roster.   * Assigned to RW&O.

NYC&HR 472, built as #533 in 1883 along with 35 others.   (George M. Sittig)

A branch line crew enjoying a pleasant layover beside the 456 in 1880's. (NYC neg 8160)

NYC&HR Engines Acquired 1882-1883:

Orig.	Re'90	Re'92	Re'99	Re'05	Class	Type	Builder,c/n,Date	Cyl. / DD	Disposition
"136	17			62	(D) A	0-4-0	E.Buffalo 3/82	16x22-48	So 7/06 Butter Bros.
"157	21			66	" "	"	" 6/82	" "	Sc 5/02
"159	23			68	" "	"	" 10/82	" "	So 7/06 Skaneateles
"150	733		1149			4-4-0	Syracuse 9/82	16x24-70	Sc /94
"110	729		1065		Cx	"	"	17x24-76	So 11/04 Ginsburg
"132	444				(B)	"	Schen.1647 9/82	17x24-63 " "	Sc 11/99
"156	445	NY&O 1		786	" Cx	"	" 1648	"	dr.by'09
"162	446				"	"	" 1649	17x24-64	Sc 10/99
"193	447				"	"	" 1650	" " "	Sc 11/99
"206	448				"	"	" 1651	" " "	Sc 8/95
"211	449	RW&O			" C-9	"	" 1652	" " "	So 1/05 Jones & Gal.
"240	450				" C-	"	" 1653	" " "	So 4/04 Hy. & Co.
"241	451				"	"	" 1654	" " "	dr'99-02
"256	452				"	"	" 1655	" " "	Re 11/98 StL&Adir.11
"439	453				"	"	" 1656	" " "	Sc 1/02
"440	454	DAV&P 4		809	" C-9a	"	" 1657	" " "	Wrk. 5/08
"452	455				" C-9	"	" 1658	" " "	So 11/04 Ginsburg
"465	456				"	"	" 1659	" " "	Sc 8/02
"479	457				"	"	" 1660	" " "	Sc 8/95
"483	458				" C-9	"	" 1661	" " "	So 9/03 Hy. & Co.
"493	459				" "	"	" 1662	" " "	So 1/05 Ginsburg
"496	460				"	"	" 1663	" " "	So 11/04 Ginsburg
" 66	461				"	"	" 1702 1/83	" " "	Sc 11/99
"121	462				"	"	" 1703	" " "	Sc 12/98
"148	463				" C-9	"	" 1704	" " "	Sc 11/04 Ginsburg
"217	464				" "	"	" 1705	" " "	So 12/02
"474	845	1126		810	" C-9a	"	" 1706	" " "	Sc 7/11
"499	465				" C-9	"	" 1707	" " "	So 4/03 Ginsburg
"500	466				" "	"	" 1708	" " "	So 9/03 Ginsburg
"501	467	DAV&P		811	" C-9a	"	" 1709	" " "	Sc 12/10
"502	468				" C-9	"	" 1710	" " "	Sc 5/02
"519	469			(812)	" "	"	" 1711	" " "	So 10/05 Ginsburg
"530	470				"	"	" 1712	" " "	dr'99-02
"532	471				"	"	" 1713	" " "	Re 7/02 Rut.176
"533	472				" C-9	"	" 1714	" " "	So 11/02
609	473				" "	"	" 1715	" " "	So 1/04 Jones & Gal.
610	474				" "	"	" 1716 2/83	" " "	So 9/03 Pough.& Eas.7
611	748		1079		(A)	"	" 1767 6/83	17x24-70	Sc 11/01
612	749		1080		" C-4	"	" 1768	" " "	So 10/05 Ginsburg
613	750		1081		" "	"	" 1769	" " "	So 4/03 Ginsburg
614	751		1082		" "	"	" 1770	" " "	So 11/05 Ginsburg
"161	25			70	(D) A	0-4-0	E.Buffalo 2/83	16x22-48	Sc 5/01
"160	24			69	" "	"	" 3/83	" "	So 4/08 Ginsburg
"138	19			64	" "	"	" 5/83	" "	So 8/03 DeGrassePaper
"167	26			71	" "	"	" 7/83	" "	So 6/05 Kilby & Co.
"486	33			77	" "	"	" 10/83	" "	So 10/05 Ginsburg

45

Class C-9

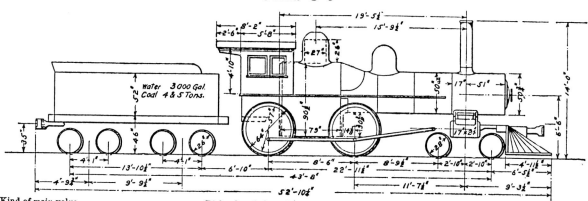

Kind of main valve .... Richardson balanced	Weight of tender, empty .... 29.800 pounds
Firebox length inside .... 72 inches	Steam pressure .... 140 p unds
Firebox width inside .... 35½ inches	Rating .... 13.0 per cent.
Grate area .... 17.5 square feet	
Tubes number 160	**EXCEPTIONS.**
Tubes, length over sheets .... 11 feet 5 inches	Engine No. 407: Boiler, 48 inches;. firebox. 60 x 35 inches; 169 tubes.
Tubes, diameter outside .... 2 inches	11 feet 2 inches; cylinders, 16 x 24 inches; driving wheel centers. 63
Heating surface, tubes .... 956.44 square feet	inches.
Heating surface, firebox .... 117.82 square feet	Engines Nos. 476, 478, 479, 483. 488: 50 inch boiler; 180 tubes, 11 feet
H ating surface total .... 1,074 26 square feet	inches long; total weight, 85 800 pounds
Weight on drivers, working order .... 52,200 pounds	Engines, Nos. 482 484 to 486 inclusive: 4 9, 491 to 496 inclusive, 529, 543:
Weight on truck, working order .... 27,600 pounds	50 inch boiler; 198 tubes, 11 feet 8 inches long; total weight, 85 800
Weight total of engine, working order .... 79 800 pounds	pounds
Weight of tender, loaded .... 64,000 pounds	Engines Nos. 498 500, 5"4. 505: Firebox. 62 x 35½ inches; 138 tubes, 11
	feet 4 inches long, 2¼ inches diameter; total weight, 76,000 pounds.

Class C-4

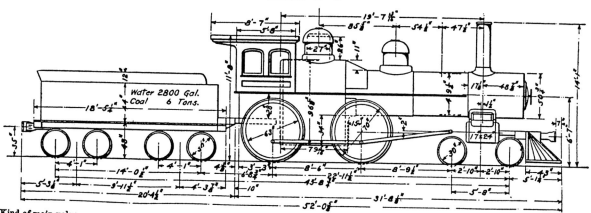

Kind of main valve .... Richardson balanced	Heating surface, total .... 1,353 square feet
Firebox, length inside .... 72¾ inches	Weight on drivers, working order .... 55,000 pounds
Firebox, width inside .... 36 inches	Weight on truck, " " .... 33,000 pounds
Grate area .... 18 square feet	Weight, total of engine " " .... 88,000 pounds
Tubes, number 198	Weight of tender. loaded .... 62,200 pounds
Tubes, length over sheets .... 11 feet 8½ inches	Weight of tender, empty .... 27,000 pounds
Tubes diameter outside .... 2 inches	Steam pressure .... 145 pounds
Heating surface, tubes .... 1,200 square feet	Rating .... 12.6 per cent.
Heating surface, firebox .... 153 square feet	

Class B-5

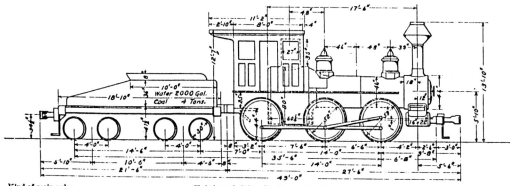

Kind of main valve .... Unbalanced slide	Heating surface, firebox .... 76 square feet
Firebox, length inside .... 53 inches	Heating surface, total .... 1,006 square feet
Firebox, width inside .... 35½ inches	Weight on drivers, working order .... 74,000 pounds
Grate area .... 13.0 square feet	Weight, total of engine " " .... 74,000 pounds
Tubes, number 140	Weight of tender, loaded .... 50,000 pounds
Tubes, length over sheets .... 11 feet	Weight of tender, empty .... 25,300 pounds
Tubes, diameter outside .... 2 inches	Steam pressure .... 145 pounds
Heating surface, tubes .... 930 square feet	Rating .... 12.2 per cent.

NYC&HR Engines Acquired 1884-1886:

Orig.	Re'90	Re'92	Re'99	Re'05	Class	Type	Builder,c/n,Date	Cyl.	DD	Disposition
"137	18		63		(D)A	0-4-0	E.Buffalo 1/84	16x22-48		So 7/06 Butter Bros.
"155	22	67			" "	"	" 5/84	"	"	So 1/05 Mar.& Otis.L
"463	32	76			" "	"	" 8/84	"	"	So 6/05 Kilby & Co.
"140	20	65			" "	"	" 1/85	"	"	So 3/08 Cont.I&S Co.
" 46	12	57			" "	"	" 5/85	"	"	So 11/04 Ginsburg
" 48	13	58			" "	"	" 8/85	"	"	So 1/05 Jones & Gal.
"213	31	75			" "	"	" 5/86	"	"	So 8/08 Cont.I&S Co.
" 29	8	53			" "	"	" 8/86	"	"	So 10/05 Holcomb Stl
"198	29	73			" "	"	" 10/86	"	"	So 10/05 Ginsburg
"458	42	204			(E2)B-5	0-6-0	W.Albany(a) 3/84	16x22-59		So 12/03 Kilby & Co.
"460	43				"	"	" (a) ?	"	"	So 10/90 N.Y.Eq.Co.
"478	44	205			" B-5	"	" (a)10/84	"	"	So 12/03 Kilby & Co.
"309	39	201			" "	"	" (a) 6/85	"	"	So 1/05 Hy.&Co.
"445	41	203	194-424		" "	"	" 8/86	"	"	So 4/08 Ginsburg
"310	40	202			" "	"	" (a) 7/88	"	"	So 8/03 Ginsburg
"503	846	1127			(A)C-4	4-4-0	W.Albany 12/84	17x24-70		So 8/02
"520	778	1098		1076	" "	" "	" 9/85	"	"	So 12/06 Jones & Gal
"510	777	1097			" "	" "	" 3/86	"	"	Sc 11/99
"199	840	1134	1134	1133	(A2)C-7	4-4-0	W.Albany 6/85	17x20-64		So 3/08 Cont.I&S Co.
"191	838	1132			" "	" "	E.Buffalo 6/85	"	"	So 8/08 " "
"195	839	1133			" "	" "	Syracuse 7/85	"	"	Sc 5/03
"374	721	1135			" "	" "	E.Buffalo 12/85	"	"	So 4/05 Hy.& Co.
" 47	826	1130			" "	" "	" 3/86	"	"	So 3/08 Cont.I&S Co.
" 50	827	1131			" "	" "	" 6/86	"	"	Sc 10/99
" 7	818	1129			" "	" "	Syracuse 7/86	"	"	So 3/08 Cont.I&S Co.
"488	725	1136	1131		" "	" "	E.Buffalo 12/86	"	"	So 3/08 " "
"122	483	257	484	816	(B)C-9	4-4-0	Schen.2210 12/86	17x24-64		So 10/05 Hy.& Co.
"134	484	258	485		" "	" "	" 2211	"	"	So 2/05 Hy.& Co.
"210	486	263	490		"	"	" 2212	"	"	dr'99-01
"270	488	266	493	819	" C-9	"	" 2213	"	"	So 3/08 (Note c)
"279	490	276	482	815	" "	"	" 2214	"	"	So 12/06 Kilby
"451	491	282	489	817	" "	"	" 2215	"	"	So 1/06 Hy.& Co.
"464	492	290	491	818	" "	"	" 2216	"	"	So 2/05 Jones & Gal
"196#	495	330	510		" "	"	" 2217	"	"	Sc 12/01
"225#	496	367	529	(b)	" C-9	"	" 2218	"	"	So'02-05 Ginsburg
"149	485	259	486		" "	"	" 2219	"	"	So 10/03 Jones & Gal
"220	487	265	492		"	"	" 2220	"	"	So 8/02
"276	489	267	494		"	"	" 2221	"	"	Re 4/00 StL&Adir.12
" 76#	493	291	495	820	" C-9	"	" 2222	"	". "	So 2/06 Jones & Gal.
"144#	494	292	496	RW&O	" "	"	" 2223	"	"	So 5/04 " "
"239#	497	385	543	821	" "	"	" 2224	"	"	Sc'05

Note # - Delivered as 494,495,472,482,521, renumbered 1887
Note a - Class E-2 rebuilt from 2-6-0 or 4-6-0. See P.26.
Note b - 367 re DAV&P 6.   Note c - to Hazard,Coates & Bennett.

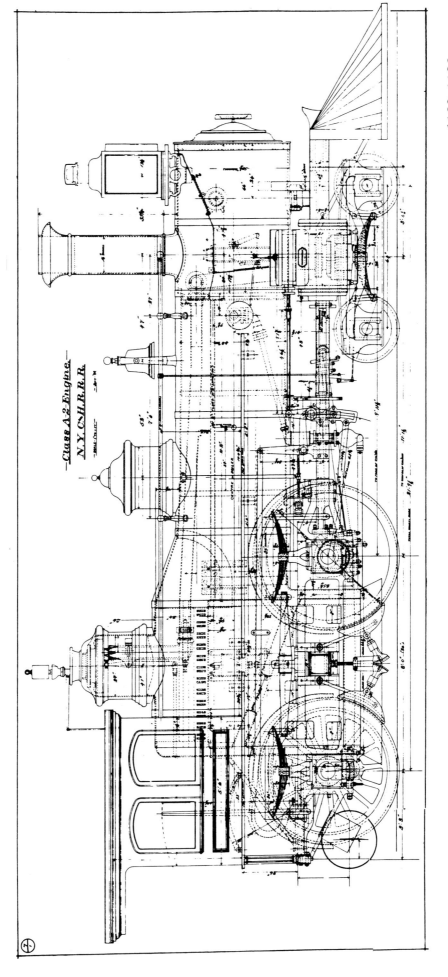

Class A-2 Engine
N.Y.C.H.R.R.

Side Elevation drawing for the eight engines in class A-2, later C-7. In 1892 they were renumbered 1129-1136.

47

NEW YORK & HARLEM RR 1836-1886:

The New York & Harlem was leased to the New York Central & Hudson River in April, 1873, but the Harlem retained its own locomotive roster until 1886. During that year NY&H nos. 1-44 were renumbered NYC&HR 616-659, but not in sequence. In the roster which follows NY&H engines are listed in approximate chronological order. The road did not assign numbers until about 1863.

NY&H Name & No.	Re'86	Re'90	Type	Builder,c/n,Date	RB	Cyl. DD Wt.	Disposition
Dykers			0-4-0?	W.Point Fndy.'36		9x16-60-22000	Rt by'56
New York			4-2-0	Dunham '37		11x16-45	" "
Harlaem			"	" "		" "	" "
Manhattanville			"	" "		" "	" "
Yorkville			"	" "		" "	" "
Westchester			"	Wm.Norris '40		" "	" "
White Plains			2-4-2	Rogers 46 8/43			" "
Jacob Little			4-4-0	" 62 12/44		11x18-54	" "
Putnam			"	Norris /45		13x22-60-40000	dr by'63
Rensselaer			"	" "		13x22-66-40000	" "
Columbia			"	" "		13x22-60-40000	" "
Dutchess			"	" "		" " "	Rt 9/56
Mahopic			"	" /49		12x20-60-36000	dr by'63
Dover			"	Rogers 163 3/49		13x20-72-40000	" "
Albany 27			"	" 166 "		14x22-66-42000	So LIRR
Thomas Rogers			"	" 194 11/49		13x20-72-40000	dr by'63
Chatham 9	636		"	" 214 5/50		14x20-66-42000	dr by'90
Pocahontas 12			"	" 234 10/50	(b)	13x20-60-42000	Sc 1/81
Amenia 22			"	" 242 12/50		14x20-66-42000	So'81 Sara.Lake
Gouver.Morris 8	635	799	"	" 293 12/51	'85	16x18-66-48000	Sc 10/92 (d)
Philo Hurd (c) 6	633	797	"	" 297 1/52	'85	15+x22-78-56000	So 2/92 (d)
Atlantic 14	639	803	"	" 300 2/52	'82	" " "	So 2/92 (d)
Pacific 17			"	" 301 "		" " "	So 6/81 (1)
Troy (f) 10			"	" 303 3/52		14x20-72-48000	So 10/80 Leb.Spr
New York (f) 13	638?		"	" 304 "		" " "	So 81 Col.& Can.
Sharon 1			"	Hink. 353 2/52		16x20-60-44000	So'62 USMR 1
Hillsdale 24			"	" 355 "		" " "	dr by'76
Croton 5			"	" 356 "		16x20-66-44000	Sc'83
E.J.Crosby 2			"	" 358 3/52		16x20-54-44000	So'62 USMR 2
Governor Jay 18	(Note h)		"	Rogers 321 5/52		16x18-66-48000	So 2/81 Savage
Fordham (h) 7	634		"	" 332 8/52	(b)	13x20-60-42000	dr c'89
Morrisania 25	644	807	"	" 334 "	(b)	" " "	Sc 3/91 (g)
Cayuga (i) 16			"	Hink. 393 /52		15x18-60-40000	dr by'86
Mohawk (k) 3	630		"	Taun. 124 12/52		16x20-60-52000	dr c'89
Tuscarora (j) 4	631		"	" 128 2/53		" " "	RB'88 See p.112.

Note b - RB as 0-4-0. Note c - 6,14,17 orig. names "Tempest. Tornado, Terror".
Note d - RB as 16x22-70.   Note f - Diverted from New Haven & New London.
Note g - RB as 17x24-70.   Note h - 7,18 renamed "Old Danger" and "Isaac C.Buckhout"
Note i - formerly Wes.Vermont "Danby". Note j - RB Taun.320 '64, re C.Godfrey Gunther
Note k - RB from Hud.Riv. "Champlain", re "Seneca". Note 1 - to Milw.Lake Shore & Wes.

New York & Harlem 17, formerly NYC&HR 603 when delivered by Schenectady. (NYC 7036)

NYC&HR 623 after renumbering from New York & Harlem 23. (NYC neg 2551; C.W.Page coll.)

NEW YORK & HARLEM - Continued. Additions 1853-1886:

NH&H Name & No.		Re '86	Re '90	Re '92	Re '99	Type	Builder,c/n,date		RB	Cyl.	DD	Disposition
Uncas	26					4-4-0	Rogers 364	1/53		15x20-54		dr by'71
Onondaga	21	642	806			"	" 366	"	'81	Note a		So'90 NYEqCo.
Red Rover	19	640	804			"	" 535	10/54		16x20-60		Sc 8/91
Water Witch (b)	28					"	" 536	"		" "		So'81 Sara.L.
Pilot	15					"	" 545	11/54		15x20-60		So'81 SeaBeach
Young America	**20**	**641**	**805**			"	" 546	"	'85	" "		**So'90 NYEqCo.**
Geo.L.Schuyler	11					"	D.Cooke /54			" "		So'80 Leb.Spr.
United States	"3					"	Jer.City LW /59			" "		So'81 Leb.Spr.
Island Belle	23					"	" " "					So'81 Leb.Spr.
?		33	650	810		"	Schen. 235	12/60		16x22-60		So'92 Ginsburg
?		32				"	Rogers 1046	11/62		17x22-54		Sc 9/83
?		31	649			"	New Jer.LW	6/63		16x24-60		Sc 5/87
?		30	652			"	" " "			" "		Sc 5/87
?		29	647	808	101?	"	Taun. 308	11/63		16x22-60		So'90 NYEqCo.
?		34				"	" 309	12/63		16x24-60		Sc 6/88
Corn.Vanderbilt	35	648	102			"	BLW. 1193	12/63		" "		So'90 NYEqCo.
Horace F.Clark	36	616	788	1101		"	" 1205	1/64	'86	(old B)		So'04 Ginsburg
J.H.Banker	37	653	103			"	" 1206	"		16x24-60		Sc 9/90
Augustus Schell	"1	628				"	Mason 179	11/64		16x24-66		Sc 3/88
John M.Tobin	"2					"	" 181	12/64		" "		Sc'85
Abram B.Baylies	38	654	140			"	" 182	"		" "		So'90 NYEqCo.
Wm.C.Wetmore	43	617	499	401		"	" 184	"	'86	(old A)		Sc'92-99
Commodore	44	659				"	" 185	"		16x24-66		Sc 4/88
John B.Dutcher	39	655				"	Taun. 337	/64		" "		Sc 3/87
Wm.H.Vanderbilt	40	656	814	1112		"	" 339	"	'81	(old A)		Sc 11/93
President	41	657	815			"	" 344	/65		16x24-66		So'90 NYEqCo.
Governor	42	658	816			"	" 345	/65	'84	" "		So'91 Ginsburg
	"26					0-4-0	Hinkley 9/71			15x22-48		Re'73 GCDepot1
	"27					"	" "			" "		" " " 2
	"24	643	137			0-4-4T	Schen.1005	6/76		15x20-50		Sc 8/90
	"26	645	138	249		"	" 1006	"		" "		RB'99 0-4-0 82
	"27	646	139			"	" 1007	"		" "		So'91 Ginsburg
Ex-NYC&HR 267	"11	618	442			4-4-0	(Schen.1325	2/81)		(old B)		So'03 Hy.&Co.
" 602	"12	619	390			"	(" 1320	10/80)		"		Sc'94-99
" 456	"15	620	443			"	(" 1327	2/81)		"		Sc 8/95
" 603	"17	621	391			"	(" 1318	10/80)		"		Sc'94-99
" 598	"18	622	392		548	"	(" 1296	")		"		So'04 Ginsburg
" 599	"23	623	393		549	"	(" 1312	")		"		So'05 Hy.&Co.
Ex- ?	"10?	637?				"	Acq'81					dr by'90
	" 5	632	16		61	0-4-0	E.Buffalo	6/83		(old D)		So'05 Hy.&Co.
	" 2	629	15		60	"	N.Y.43rd St.	9/85		"		So'04 Ginsburg
Ex-NYC&HR 238	"34?	651	811		1111	4-4-0	(W.Albany	7/84)		(old A)		Sc 10/01
	"16	624	790	(c)	1102	"	Schen.2140	6/86		"		So'08 Cont.I&S
	"22	625	791		1103	"	" 2141	"		"		Sc'99-02
	"28	626	792		1104	"	" 2142	"		"		Sc 10/01
	"32	627	793		1105	"	" 2143	"		"		Sc'99-02

Note a - RB to 17x24-66   Note b - Renamed Isaac D.Barton
Note c - 1102 re'05 1078.

New York & Harlem 41, named PRESIDENT, as built by Taunton in 1865,   (NYC neg 5611)

For a while, Rogers was a favorite of the New York & Harlem. No. 20 was delivered in
1854 with the name YOUNG AMERICA.   (NYC neg 7039)

NYC&HR Locomotives Acquired 1886-1890:

Type	NYC&HR Numbers	Old Class	Builder	Date	Cyl. DD	1902 Class
0-4-0	188,197,205,498	D	E.Bflo.	1887-89	16x22-48	A p.94
"	37,124,207	D-1	Syracuse	1888-89	17x24-52	A-1 p.94
0-4-0T	11,12	Dummy	Schen.	1888	15x22-46	- p.106
0-6-0	223,237,247,449	E	W.A.,E.B.	1886-87	17x24-51	B-3 p.98
"	26,27,93,163,183,190,204	E-1	W.Albany	1888-90	17x24-52	B-3a p98
	208,209,215,218,226,255,262	E-1	W.Albany	1888-90	17x24-52	B-3a p98
2-6-0	221,235,466,537,715-720	J	Brooks	1889	19x26-64	E p122
"	166,234,242,272,447,467,508,698,708,726-736	J	Rome	1889-90	" "	Ea p122
"	123,200,219,251,253,264,269,441,475	J-1	Schen.	1889	" "	Ed p126
"	245,442,480,527-529,721-725	J-1	Schen.	1889	" "	Ed p126
2-8-0	260,273,367,477	D-2	Schen.	1888	20x26-51	G p146
4-2-4T	117		W.Albany	1889	Inspection Pony	p118
4-4-0	522		W.Albany	1889	Inspection Pony	p118
"	52,201,506,615,660	A-1	Syra,WA	1886-89	18x24-70	C-5 p112
"	238,538,600,601,661,677-689	A-1x	WA,Rome,Schen.	'87-89	18x24-70	C-6 p112
"	216,222,481,628,631,649,652,655,659	A-3	WA,Syr,EB	'87-90	18x20-64	C-8 p112
"	123,200,219,251,253,690-704	B-1	Schen,Rome	'88-89	18x24-64	C-10 112
"	705-714	F	Schen,Rome	'89	18x24-70	C-11 116
"	630,634,636-638	H	Schen,Rome	'90	17x24-64	C-13 116
4-6-0	444,523,524,535,539,662-676	C	Schen.	'87-88	18x24-57	F 136
"	472,482,494,495,521	C	Rome	'87	" "	Fa 136

NYC&HR First Classification System:

During the late 1880's a great variety of locomotive designs began to appear on the NYC&HR. No longer was a single class of dual-service 4-4-0's sufficient. As shown above, the six-wheel switcher, Mogul, Ten Wheeler, and Consolidation types made their debuts, and several designs of passenger and freight 4-4-0's were introduced. At this time the railroad developed a classification system to group the more recent power, as follows:

Class	Type	Cyl. DD	Intro.	1902 Class	Class	Type	Cyl. DD	Intro.	1902 Class
A	4-4-0	17x24-70	1881	C-4	I-3	4-4-0	19x24-77	1900	C-3
A-1	"	18x24-70	1886	C-5	I-4	4-4-2	20+x26-79	1901	I,Ia,Ib
A-1x	"	18x24-70	1887	C-6	J	2-6-0	19x26-64	1889	E,Ea,Eb
A-2	"	17x20-64	1887	C-7	J-1	"	19x26-57	1889	Ec,Ed/Ee
A-3	"	18x20-60	1887	C-8	J-2	"	" "	1898	Ef
B	"	17x24-64	1873	C-9,a	K	0-6-0	18x24-51	1890	B
B-1	"	18x24-64	1888	C-10	K-1	"	19,29x26-51	1896	B-1,B-4
C	4-6-0	18x24-57	1887	F, Fa	K-2	"	19x26-51	1900	B-2
D	0-4-0	16x22-52	1882	A, A-2	L	"	19x24-51	1890	B-6
D-1	"	17x24-52	1887	A-1	M	2-6-6T	18x22-64	1891	E-4
D-2	2-8-0	20x26-51	1888	G	N	4-4-0	19x24-86	1893	C-14a
E	0-6-0	17x24-51	1885	B-3	P	2-6-0	20x28-57	1898	E-1,a
E-1	"	" "	1888	B-3a	P-1	"	" "	1899	E-1b
E-2	"	16x22-59	1884	B-5	P-2	"	" "	1900	E-1c
F	4-4-0	18x24-70	1889	C-11	P-3	"	" "	1900	E-1d
G	"	18+x22-64	1891	C-12,a	P-4	"	22+,35x28-57	1900	E-2
H	"	17x24-64	1890	C-13	P-5	"	20x28-63	1900	E-1e
I	"	19x24-70	1889	C,Ca	Q	4-6-0	20x28-70	1899	F-3a
I-1	"	19x24-78	1896	Cb	Q-1	"	20x28-75	1899	F-3
I-2	"	19x24-70	1896	Cc,Cd					

New York & Harlem 26, one of three tank engines supplied by Schenectady in 1886.

NYC&HR 32, the last engine built specifically for the New York & Harlem. (NYC neg 5648)

NYC&HR RENUMBERING OF 1890

In May, 1890 the NYC&HR began its first general renumbering of locomotives. Apparently
the scheme was to group all switchers together, then freight engines, and then passenger
power. Within these groups, number blocks were assigned to the major classes, and further
sub-groups were established by operating division.

1-34	class D	0-4-0	Switcher	(2 groups)
35-37	" D-1	"	"	
38		0-6-0	"	
39-44	class E-2	"	"	
45-62	" E, E-1	"	"	(3 groups)
75-136		4-4-0	"	(5 groups)
137-139		0-4-4T	"	
140-250		4-4-0		(4 groups)
251-254		Inspection		
255-500	class B	4-4-0	Freight	(10 groups)
501-504	" D-2	2-8-0	"	
505-554	" J	2-6-0	"	(3 groups)
655-679	class C	4-6-0	Passenger	
680-699	" B-1	4-4-0	"	(2 groups)
700-859	Miscellaneous	4-4-0	"	(5 groups)

NYC&HR Engines Acquired 1890-1892:

0-4-0T	3,5,6,7......Dummy	Schen.	1890		See p.106	
0-6-0	38,63-65.......E-1	(Shops)	1890	B-3a	p.98	
"	75-142 ....K	Schen.	1890-91	B	p.96	
"	146-153.........L	"	1890	B-6	p.98	
2-6-0	482-500.........J	"	1891	Ed	p.126	
"	555-654.........J	Brks,Rog,Sch.1890	E,Eb,Ed	p.122,124	
2-6-6T	829,830,832.....M	Schen.	1891	J	p.182	
4-4-0	805,806........A-1x	W.Albany	1890,91	C-6	p.112	
"	823.............G	Schen.	1891	C-12	p.116	
	860-912.........I	"	1890-92	C	p.108	

NYC&HR RENUMBERING OF 1892

Just two years after the general renumbering of 1890, the jumble of 700 and 800 series
passenger engines were reassigned new numbers in the 900-1000-1100 series, grouped by
class. The lower numbers vacated were then filled by new 2-6-0 and other types in
following years.

913-922	Class I	4-4-0	
953-987	" F,A-1x	"	
1008-1018	" G	"	
1050-1052	" M	2-6-6T	
1053-1061	" A-3	4-4-0	
1062-1105	" A	"	
1106-1110	" H	"	
1111-1128	" A	"	
1129-1136	" A-2	"	
1137-1152	(16x24)	"	
700-718	Class J	2-6-0 (ex-482-500)	
483-500	" B	4-4-0 (ex-256-275)	

RW&O 5, the ORVILLE HUNGERFORD, photographed in 1854 at Ogdensburg.   (Vollrath coll.)

Another early Taunton engine was RW&O No. 17 the ANTWERP.   (NYCSHS Purinton coll.335)

RW&O 38, the GARDNER COLBY, home-built in 1868.   (NYCSHS Purinton coll.339)

(NYC&HR): ROME, WATERTOWN & OGDENSBURG   All-Time Roster:

The RW&O began service in 1849 as the Watertown & Rome, and became the Rome, Watertown & Ogdensburg in July, 1861. It was leased by the NYC&HR in March, 1891, and its engines were renumbered into the NYC&HR series the following year.

RW&O Name & Number		Re'92	Type	Builder,c/n,Date	Acq.	Cyl.	DD	Wt.	Disp'n.
Pierrepont re Watertown	1		4-4-0	Taunton 56 9/50		14x20	-60	-45000	dr by'83
Rome	2		"	" 61 11/50		"	"	"	dr by'83
Adams	3		"	" 65 2/51		"	"	"	Expl.'69
Com.Perry (ex-Prov.& Worc.)	35		"	(Rogers 108 10/47)'51		14x18	-66	-27500	dr by'66
Kinston	4		"	Hink. 330 9/51		15x24	-60	-45000	dr by'83
Orville Hungerford	5		"	Taunton 80 "		14x20	-60	-43000	dr by'83
E.Kirby			"	" 86 11/51		"	"		(note a)
Col.Edmund Kirby	6		"	" 89 12/51		"	"	"	dr by'83
N.M.Woodruff	7		"	" 94 2/52		"	"	"	dr by'85
Camden	8		"	" 96 3/52		"	"	"	dr by'81
Cape Vincent re J.L.Grant	9		"	" 98 "		"	"	"	dr by'81
Lion (ex-Aub.& Roch.)			4-2-0	(Rogers 23 9/40)'52		11x18	-54	-	Expl.'58
North Star (ex-Conn.Riv.11)	14		4-4-0	(Taunton 17 7/48) 52		15x18	-60	-38000	dr by'75
Toronto re Job Callamor	10		"	" 111 8/52		14x20	-60	-44000	dr by'85
Jefferson	11		"	" 117 10/52		"	"	"	dr by'85
R.B.Doxtater	12		"	" 134 5/53		15x20	-57	-47000	dr by'84
O.V.Brainard	13		"	" 145 9/53		"	"	"	dr by'83
St.Lawrence	19		"	" 168 6/54 (b)		"	"	"	dr by'88
W.C.Pierrepont	18		"	" 177 10/54		"	"	"	dr by'88
Roxbury (ex-Bos.& Prov.15)	34		2-2-2?	(B&PRR 11/50) by'56		9x16	-54		So by'74

POTSDAM & WATERTOWN: Acquired by RW&O in July, 1860.

Silas Wright	16		4-4-0	Taun. 192 6/55		14x20	-66		dr by'87
Antwerp (ex-Platts.& Mont.)	17 (c)		"	(" 106 6/52)'53		"	"		dr by'88
Potsdam (ex-C.R."Chicopee")	20		"	(Springfield /53)'56		14x	-60		dr by'88
Ontario (ex- ?)	21								dr by'88
Montreal (ex-C.R. "Mont.")	22		4-4-0	(New Castle /48)'53					dr by'88

RW&O Additions 1860-1868:

T.J.Camp (ex-AB&P; note e)	15		4-4-0	(Taun. 93 2/52)'63		16x24	-54		dr by'67
New York (ex-NYC 166)	23		"	(Springfield /53)'63		16x22	-60		dr by'73
Ogdensburg (ex-NYC 143)	24		"	(Rogers 221 7/50)'63		15x20	-66		dr by'73
Oswego (ex-NYC 139)	25		"	(" 247 2/51)'63		"	"		dr by'92
Delos De Wolf	26		"	RW&O Shops /64					dr by'92
D.Utley	27		"	" " /66					dr by'92
M.Massey	28		"	" " "					dr by'92
H.Moore	29		"	" " "					dr by'92
Calvert Comstock	30	235	"	Schen. 413 3/66		15x22	-60		So 6/93
S.F.Phelps	31		"	" 414 "		"	"		dr by'92
Col.William Lord	32	236	"	" 417 5/66		"	"		So 6/93
H.Alexander,Jr.	33	237	"	" 421 "		"	"		Sc 6/94
Com.Perry	"35		"	RW&O Shops /66					dr by'93
C.E.Hill re Lewiston 36 re"14			"	" " "					dr by'86
Gen.S.D.Hungerford	37		"	" " /67					dr by'90
Gardner Colby	38		"	" " /68					Expl.c.93

Note a - Wrecked during delivery, sold by'56 to Rut.& Wash. "Bates".
Note b - RB Taunton 180 11/54.   Note c - Orig. Platts.& Mont."Platts.",re P&W "Saranac"
Note d - to NY Loco Wks for sta.boiler.   Note e - ex-Am.Belch.& Palmer "Palmer". RB'74

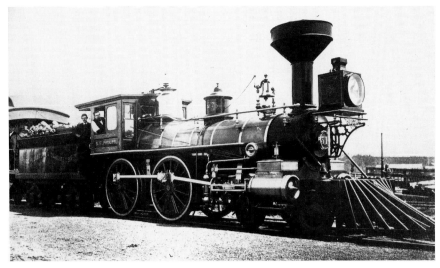

Schenectady built only a few engines for the RW&O. One of them was #31. (Purinton 337)

RW&O 33, the H.ALEXANDER,JR. lasted until 1894.   (NYCSHS Purinton coll. 338)

RW&O 40 was home-built in 1872. Photographed at Watertown,N.Y.   (Vollrath collection)

(NYC&HR) ROME, WATERTOWN & OGDENSBURG Engines Acquired 1870-1873:

RW&O Name & No.	Re'92	Re'99	Classes		Type	Builder,c/n,Date			Cyl. DD	Disposition
C.Zabriskie	39				4-4-0	Schen.	656	9/70	15x20-60	dr by'93
Theodore Irwin	40				"	RW&O Shops		/72		dr by'93
John Denny	41				"	"	"	"		dr by'93
W.M.White	42				"	"	"	"		dr by'93
J.S.Farlow	"23	234			"	"	"	/73	15+x20-64	So 9/94
J.W.Moak	"24				"	"	"	"		dr by'92

LAKE ONTARIO RR. Consolidated 1/75 in RW&O. Formerly LAKE ONTARIO SHORE 1873 to 1874.

RW&O Name & No.	Re'92	Re'99	Classes		Type	Builder,c/n,Date			Cyl. DD	Disposition
Oswego 43 re "34		238			4-4-0	Hinkley		5/72	15x22-54	Sc 9/94
Hannibal	44				"	"		6/72	*16x24-64	dr by'92
Wolcott	45				"	"		/72	* " "	dr by'92
Sodus	46				"	"		11/72	* " "	dr by'92
Williamson	47				"	"		2/73	* " "	dr by'92
Ontario	48	239			"	"		4/73	* " "	So 6/93

SYRACUSE & NORTHERN. Consolidated 12/75 in RW&O.

RW&O Name & No.	Re'92	Re'99	Classes		Type	Builder,c/n,Date			Cyl. DD	Disposition
1 Pulaski	49				4-4-0	Manch.	272	8/70	15x24-60	dr by'92
2 Brewerton	50				"	"	273	"	" "	dr by'92
3 Sandy Creek	51				"	"	360	7/71	16x24-60	dr by'92
4 Parish	52	240			"	"	361	11/71	" "	So 6/93
5 Syracuse	53				"	Rogers 2302		7/73	15x20-66	dr by'92

RW&O Engines acquired 1875-1886:

RW&O Name & No.	Re'92	Re'99	Classes		Type	Builder,c/n,Date			Cyl. DD	Disposition
Moses Taylor 14"35					4-4-0	RW&O Shops		/75		dr by'92
	54				"	" " "		"		dr by'90
Cataract 55 re"37					"	" " "		/76		dr by'93
Samson 56 re "8	852	1803			2-6-0	BLW.	3933	7/76	18x24-50	Sc 11/01
Goliath 57 re "9	853	1804			"	"	3934	"	" " "	Sc 3/02
(ex-M&E 25) a	"56				4-4-0	(D.Cooke'64)		7/81	15x22-66	dr by'89
(ex-M&E 39) a	"57				"	(" '66)		"	" " "	dr by'89
Genesee	58	267			"	Dickson 343		4/83	17x24-64	So 8/95
	59	268			"	RW&O Shops		/83	17x24-57	Sc 12/98
	60	269			"	" " "		"	" " "	So 6/93
	"1	845	1796	J-2 E-5	2-6-0	R.I.	1406	8/83	18x24-56	Sc 7/09
	"2	846	1797	" "	"	"	1407	"	" " "	So 1/08 J&G
	"3	847	1798	" "	"	"	1408	"	" " "	Sc 3/09
	"4	848	1799	" "	"	"	1410	"	" " "	So'06 Kilby
	"5	849	1800	J-3 E-5a	"	Rome	50	10/83	" "	So'06 Kilby
	"6	850	1801	" "	"	"	51	"	" " "	Sc 10/01
"12 (re'86)	61				4-4-0	RW&O Shops		/84		dr by'92
"13 "	62	270			"	" " "		/83	17x24-57	Sc 9/94
(ex-L.& P.212) "7	851	1802	J-3 E-5a		2-6-0	(Rome 58 '83) (b)			18x24-57	Sc 9/05
(" 211) "10	854				4-6-0	(" 52 ")		"	" " "	So 9/94
(" 204) "11	855				"	(" 57 ")		"	" " "	Sc 8/96
(Note c) "12					2-6-0	Rome	123	9/86	" " "	(note e)
"13	856	1805	J-3 E-5a		"	"	122	2/86	" " "	So 10/05 J&G
"14	857	1806	J-2 E-5		"	R.I.	1642	3/86	" " "	So'05 Hy.&Co

Note a - Acq.7/81 from Morris & Essex RR   Note b - Acq.2/85 from Lack. & Pitts. RR
Note c - Possibly ex-Lack.& Pitts. 203, re RW&O 12, NYC&HR 841,500,1795.
    * - Orig. 15x22-54.   Note e - re Carthage & Adirondack #2.

RW&O 46, originally named SODUS, was a Hinkley engine. (NYCSHS Purinton coll. 340)

RW&O Mogul 2nd 6 was built at Rome in 1883. Later in NYC&HR class E-5a. (Purin.334-2)

Class E-5

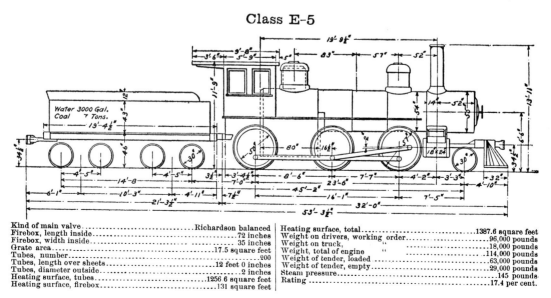

Kind of main valve...........................Richardson balanced	Heating surface, total............................1387.6 square feet
Firebox, length inside................................72 inches	Weight on drivers, working order......................96,000 pounds
Firebox, width inside................................35 inches	Weight on truck, ...18,000 pounds
Grate area......................................17.5 square feet	Weight, total of engine............................114,000 pounds
Tubes, number.......................................200	Weight of tender, loaded............................63,000 pounds
Tubes, length over sheets........................12 feet 0 inches	Weight of tender, empty............................29,000 pounds
Tubes, diameter outside.............................2 inches	Steam pressure...................................145 pounds
Heating surface, tubes...........................1256 6 square feet	Rating...17.4 per cent.
Heating surface, firebox............................131 square feet	

60

(NYC&HR) UTICA & BLACK RIVER. Acq.4/1886 by RW&O. Formerly Black River & Utica until 5/61

U&BR Name & Number	Re '86	Re '92	Re '99	Builder,c/n,Date	Specs.(All 4-4-0)	Disp'n.
T.S.Faxton 1				Breese Knee.12/53	14x22-60-44000	dr by'74
Boonville 2				" " 8/54	14x20-60-38000	dr by'78
J.Butterfield 3				" " 3/55	14x22-60-44000	dr by'84
D.C.Jenne (Note a) 4	71			Schen. 134 11/55	16x22-56-50000	dr by'92
John Thorn 5	81	248		" 469 1/68	15x22-60	dr by'98
Isaac Maynard 6	82			". 472 "	" " "	Sc'92
James Sayre 7	83			" 620 4/70	15x24-60	dr by'92
E.A.Graham 8	84			" 726 10/71	" "	dr by'92
Russell Wheeler 9	73			" 727 "	16x24-60	dr by'92
David Jones (Note c) 10	88			(R.I. 366 ")	14x22-60	dr by'86
W.E.Hopkins " 11	89			(" 367 ")	" "	dr by'86
De Witt C.West 12	85			Schen. 765 3/72	15x24-60	dr by'92
Thos.Foster 13	74	242		" 781 5/72	16x24-60	So 6/93
Robt.Lennox Kennedy 14	75	243		" 882 5/73	" "	So 6/95
A.J.Williams 15	76	244		" 960 4/74	" "	So 9/94
Wm.J.Bacon "1	72	241		" 961 7/74	" "	So 9/94
Ludlow Patton 16	77			" 963 11/74	" "	dr by'93
A.G.Brower 17	86			" 977 2/75	" "	dr by'93
J.Fred Maynard 18	87			" 978 6/75	" "	dr by'93
D.B.Goodwin "2	80	247		" 1000 3/78	15x24-60	So 8/95
Lewis Lawrence 19	78	245		" 1285 9/80	16x24-60	So 9/94
Theo.Butterfield 20	79	246-267	448	" 1289 10/80	" " (C-9c)	So 11/03 J&G
John S.Sayre 21	64	272	462	" 1382 6/81	17x24-60	Sc 3/02
Fred S.Easton 22	65	273	477	" 1384 "	" " (C-9)	So 4/04 Hy&Co
H.W.Hammond 23	66	274	480	" 1718 2/83	" " "	So 11/04 Gins
George W.Egart 24	97	275	481	" 1719 "	" " "	So 11/04 Gins
John Butterfield "3	63	271-333	513-678	" 1851 1/84		Rt'05
E.A.Van Horne 25	68	264	408	" 1852 "	(C-20)	So 11/04 Gins
David Crouse 26	69	265	418	" 1902 12/85	"	So 11/04 Gins
John J.Crouse 27	70	266	443	" 1912 "	"	So 1/05 J&G

RW&O Engines Acquired 1886-1888:

	Re '86			Builder,c/n,Date	Specs.	Disp'n.
	"88			RW&O Shops 1886		dr by'92
	"89			" " "		"
	90			" " "		"
	91			" " "		"
Ex-L.E.& StL. 13 (b)	92			Rome RB 1887	17x24-62	"
" " 17 "	93			" " "	" "	"
	94			RW&O Shops 1888		"
	95			" " "		"
	96			" " "		"
	97			" " "		"
	98			" " "		"
	99			" " "		"

Note a - Renamed Charles Millar, RB'72.   Note b - ex Louisville, Evansville & StLouis.
Note c - Built for Carthage, Watertown & Sacketts Harbor, named Norris Winslow
     L.D.Doolittle. #89 later 15x22-69.

Utica & Black River's first engine was the T.S.FAXTON, built in 1853.   (NYC neg 8103)

U&BR 11, the W.E.HOPKINS, was acquired with the Carthage,Watertown & Sacketts Harbor RR.
(NYC neg 8102)

Almost the entire U&BR roster came from Schenectady, including #27.   (NYC neg 8104)

(NYC&HR) ROME. WATERTOWN & OGDENSBURG Engines Acquired 1887-1890:

RW&O	Re'92	Re'99	Classes		Type	Bldr.,c/n,Date			Cyl. DD	Disposition
"15	858	1807	J-3	E-5a	2-6-0	Rome	265	6/87	18x24-57	So 10/05 Ginsburg
"16	859	1808	"	"	"	"	266	"	" "	So 3/07 Jones & Galvin
"17	860	1809	"	"	"	"	355	5/88	" "	Sc 3/05
"18	861	1810	"	"	"	"	353	4/88	" "	So 1/06 Kilby L&M Co.(a)
"19	862	1811	"	"	"	"	354	"	" "	So 12/06 SI&E Co.
"20	863	1812	"	"	"	"	356	5/88	" "	So 3/06 Kilby L&M Co.(a)
"56	1006	1006	A-1x	C-6	4-4-0	"	473	3/89	18x24-70	Sc 4/09
"57	1007	1007	"	"	"	"	474	"	" "	So 5/08 Cont.I&S Co.
100	864	2204	D-3	G-8	2-8-0	"	485	7/89	21x26-51	Sc 2/11
101	865	2205	"	"	"	"	486	"	" "	Sc 5/10
102	866	2206	"	"	"	"	487	"	" "	Sc 5/11
103	867	2207	"	"	"	"	616	6/90	" "	So 7/10 Birm.R&L Co.(b)
104	868	2208	"	"	"	"	617	"	" "	Sc 5/10
105	869	2209	"	"	"	"	618	"	" "	Sc 12/10
"54	1004	1004	A-1x	C-6	4-4-0	"	621	"	18x24-70	Sc 4/09
"55	1005	1005	"	"	"	"	622	"	" "	Sc 1/07 Marc.& Otisco L.

NYC&HR Engines Acquired 1892-1893:

1019-1028	4-4-0	class G,	later C-12	Schen.	5,6/92	See p.116
719-748	2-6-0	" J	" Ed	"	6,9/92	p.126
749-783	"	" J-1	" Ec	"	9-11/92	p.124
66	0-6-0	" E-1	" B-3a	W.Albany	10/92	p. 98
143	"	" K	" B	Schen.	4/93	p. 96
999	4-4-0	" N	" C-14	W.Albany	4/93	p.116
255	4-2-4T	Inspection Pony		"	7/92	p.118

CARTHAGE & ADIRONDACK Leased 5/1893 to NYC&HR:

	1	988	988	1083	C-21	4-4-0	Rome	198	12/86	18x24-64	Sc 8/08
(Ex-RW&O 12)	2	841	500	1795	E-5b	2-6-0	(Rome	123	9/86)	18x24-57	Sc 9/08
(Ex-NYO&W 4)	?	(Acquired '87)				4-4-0	(R.I.	109	/69)	17x22-60	

NEW YORK & OTTAWA leased 2/05 to NYC&HR. Formerly NORTHERN ADIRONDACK 12/83-5/95,
                then NORTHERN NEW YORK till 10/97.

NY&O		Re'05	Re'13		Type	Bldr.,c/n,Date		Cyl. DD	Disposition
1	(ex-NYC&HR 445)	786		Cx	4-4-0	(Schen.1882)		17x24-63	dr by'09
2	(" 551)			Cx	"	(Schen.1881)		" "	
"2	(" 544)	787		Cx	"	(Schen.'73,RB'86)		" "	Sc /10
3	"Santa Clara"	788	1076	Cx	"	Rh.Is.	1373 1/84	17x24-63-107000	Sc 12/14
4	"Buck Mountain"	785		Cx	"	Rh.Is.	1308 4/85	16x24-62-95000	dr'10
5	"Tupper Lake"	789	1077	Cx	"	Rh.Is.	1578 /85	17x24-63-109000	Sc 12/14
6	"Bay Pond"	790		Cx	"	Rh.Is.	1378 7/87	17x24-63-107000	dr'10
7	"Mountaineer"	2199		Fx	4-6-0	Rh.Is.	2780 8/92	19x26-63-134000	RT'14 (c)
?	(ex- ?)	423		Bx	0-6-0	(Porter '80)		9+x14-26-24000	dr by'09

Also assigned after 1905: C-11 #1082-1084, and Eb 1537,1544,1568,1570, and Ed 1585.

Note a - 1810 or 1812 resold to Mobile, Jackson & Kansas City RR
Note b - 2207 resold 5/13 to Allen Gravel Co., Miss.
Note c - NY&O 7 built as compound with 19&28x26 cylinders.

Class G—8

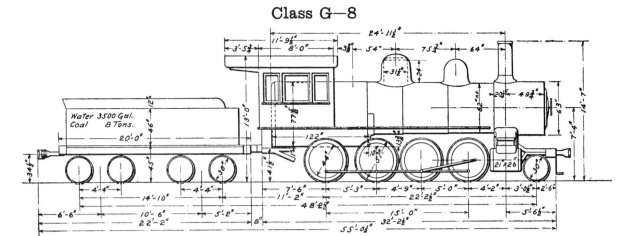

Kind of main valve.....................Allen-Richardson balanced	Heating surface, total....................1818.8 square feet
Firebox, length inside.................................113¼ inches	Weight on drivers, working order........116,000 pounds
Firebox, width inside...................................42⅜ inches	Weight on truck....................................11,000 pounds
Grate area......................................32.9 square feet	Weight, total of engine, " ....127,000 pounds
Tubes, number..219	Weight of tender, loaded.....................73,000 pounds
Tubes, length over sheets...............13 feet 0¼ inches	Weight of tender, empty.....................28,000 pounds
Tubes, diameter outside....................................2¼ inches	Steam pressure....................................140 pounds
Heating surface, tubes..................1676.8 square feet	Rating...27.3 per cent.
Heating surface, firebox.................142.0 square feet	

Class C-6

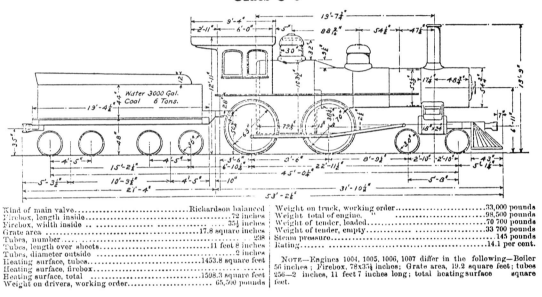

Kind of main valve.....................Richardson balanced	Weight on truck, working order............33,000 pounds
Firebox, length inside..................................72 inches	Weight total of engine, " ....98,500 pounds
Firebox, width inside ....35½ inches	Weight of tender, loaded.....................70 700 pounds
Grate area ....17.8 square inches	Weight of tender, empty......................33 700 pounds
Tubes, number..238	Steam pressure....................................145 pounds
Tubes, length over sheets...............11 feet 8 inches	Rating...14.1 per cent.
Tubes, diameter outside....................................2 inches	
Heating surface, tubes..................1453.8 square feet	NOTE—Engines 1004, 1005, 1006, 1007 differ in the following—Boiler
Heating surface, firebox	56 inches ; Firebox, 78x35½ inches; Grate area, 19.2 square feet; tubes
Heating surface, total ....1598.3 square feet	256—2 inches, 11 feet 7 inches long; total heating surface square
Weight on drivers, working order............... 65,500 pounds	feet.

N. Y. & O.

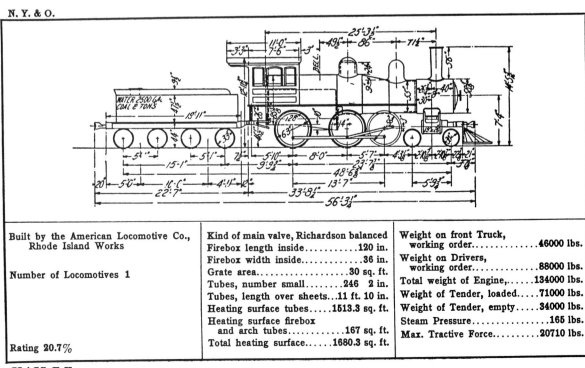

Built by the American Locomotive Co., Rhode Island Works	Kind of main valve, Richardson balanced	Weight on front Truck, working order..............46000 lbs.
	Firebox length inside...........120 in.	Weight on Drivers, working order..............88000 lbs.
Number of Locomotives 1	Firebox width inside.............36 in.	
	Grate area..........................30 sq. ft.	Total weight of Engine,......134000 lbs.
	Tubes, number small.......246 2 in.	Weight of Tender, loaded....71000 lbs.
	Tubes, length over sheets..11 ft. 10 in.	Weight of Tender, empty.....34000 lbs.
	Heating surface tubes.....1513.3 sq. ft.	Steam Pressure.................165 lbs.
	Heating surface firebox and arch tubes...........167 sq. ft.	Max. Tractive Force.........20710 lbs.
Rating 20.7%	Total heating surface......1680.3 sq. ft.	

CLASS F-X

HERKIMER, NEWPORT & POLAND   (3'6" gauge) Acquired 6/92 by Mohawk & Malone.

```
              1 Edward W.Burns   4-4-0  BLW.5627 5/81 Acq. 9/83 10x16-42  Re Cen.Vt. 9
(Ex-N.Bruns.) 2 Henry W.Dexter   2-4-4T (Mason 1874)   Acq. 9/83 12x16-36
(Ex-Ga.L&L.)  3 J.C.Anderson     2-6-0  (BLW.4286 2/78)          14x18-42  Re Cen.Vt. 12
```

(NYC&HR) MOHAWK & MALONE leased 5/93 to NYC&HR. Formerly ADIRONDACK & ST.LAWRENCE and
          HERKIMER, NEWPORT & POLAND until merged in 6/92 to form M&M.

First group of A&StL engines transferred almost immediately to RUTLAND RR:

```
     1     0-4-0  Schen. 3510     6/91  16x24-51  Re Rut. 211        See class A-5 #80,50,97
   11,12   4-4-0    "    3511,12  5/91  18x24-69    "   232,233.  See class C-1 #862,863
   31,32   4-6-0    "    3505,06  6/91  18x24-57    "   235,234.  See class F-14 2156,2155
```

Second group of A&StL engines transferred almost immediately to CENTRAL VERMONT RR:

```
     2     0-4-0  Schen. 3515     7/91  16x24-51  Re CV  20
     6     4-4-0  (ex-NYC&HR 224 1/92) 16x24-64    "    13
   11,12    "     Schen. 3593,94 11/91 17x24-63    "    31,30
   13,14    "       "    3513,14  7/91 18x24-69    "    107,108
   30,31   4-6-0    "    3707,06  3/92 19x24-63    "    118,119 re Leh.Val. 706,707.
   32,33    "       "    3722,23  5/92  "    "      "    116,117
   34-37    "     R.I.2730,60-62  "    19x24-56     "    113,110,111,115.
   38,39    "       "    2726,27  "     "    "      "    112,114
     99    Insp.  Schen. 3639     2/92 16x22-61     "    109 "St.Lawrence"
    101    4-4-0    "    3878     7/92 19x24-78     "    129
  116-120  2-6-0    "    4114-18  6/93 19x26-58     "    130-134
```

A&StL Engines Acquired by NYC&HR:

Re'94	Re'99	Re'05	Class	Type	Builder,c/n,Date			Cyl.	DD	Disposition
15	993	2025	F-7	4-6-0	Schen.	3754	5/92	20,30x26-70		Rt'14-15
16	994	2026	"	"	"	3755	"	"	"	So 12/09
17	995	2027	"	"	"	3825	6/92	"	"	Sc 5/11
50	842	1813	E-10	2-6-0	Schen.	3686	4/92	20,30x26-50		Sc 9/13
51	843	1814	"	"	"	3687	"	"	"	Sc 12/13
52	844	1815	"	"	"	3826	6/92	"	"	Sc 6/12
60	996	2210	G-13	2-8-0	Schen.	4055	4/93	22,32x26-51		So 10/07 Kilby L&M Co
61	997	2211	"	"	"	4056	"	"	"	So 10/07 Kilby L&M Co
80	998	2089	2186	F-8	4-6-0	Schen.	3879	7/92	19,28x24-69	Sc 12/21
81	1000	2090	2187	"	"	"	3880	"	"	"	So 8/19 E.Caro. 6
82	1001	2091	2188	"	"	"	3883	"	"	"	Sc 4/20
83	1002	2092	2189	F-8a	"	"	3884	"	"	"	Sc 10/19
84	1003	2093	2190	"	"	"	3885	"	"	"	Sc 8/22

```
  4  99 (ex-N.Y.Elev.45) Insp. 2-4-4T (R.I. 710 8/78)   11x16-42        ? See p.118.
```

Adirondack & St.Lawrence 15, 50, and 61, all Schenectady compounds built in 1892-93.
The NYC&HR assigned classes F-7, E-10, and G-13. (Schenectady History Center)
(H.L.Vail collection)

A&StL Inspection Pony #99, rebuilt from a New York Elevated Forney.   (NYC neg. 4957)

NYC&HR 1815, ex-A&StL 52. At West Albany 1901. Later class E-10.   (Vollrath coll.)

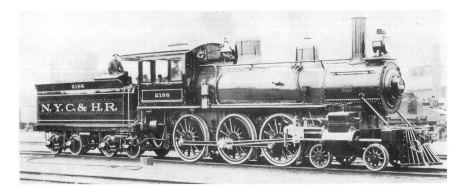

NYC&HR 2188, originally A&StL 82. Later class F-8.   (Joseph Lavelle.)

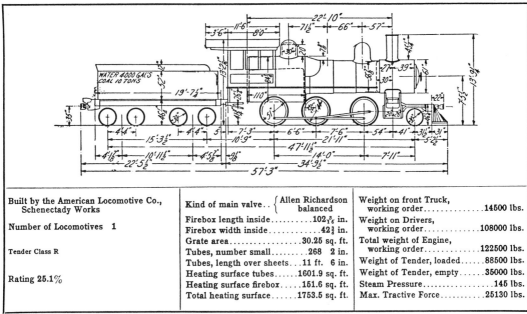

Built by the American Locomotive Co.,
Schenectady Works

Number of Locomotives   1

Tender Class R

Rating 25.1%

Kind of main valve . . { Allen Richardson balanced
Firebox length inside..........102 7/16 in.
Firebox width inside...........42 3/4 in.
Grate area.................30.25 sq. ft.
Tubes, number small........268   2 in.
Tubes, length over sheets...11 ft. 6 in.
Heating surface tubes......1601.9 sq. ft.
Heating surface firebox.....151.6 sq. ft.
Total heating surface......1753.5 sq. ft.

Weight on front Truck,
  working order.............14500 lbs.
Weight on Drivers,
  working order............108000 lbs.
Total weight of Engine,
  working order............122500 lbs.
Weight of Tender, loaded......88500 lbs.
Weight of Tender, empty......35000 lbs.
Steam Pressure.................145 lbs.
Max. Tractive Force..........25130 lbs.

CLASS E-10

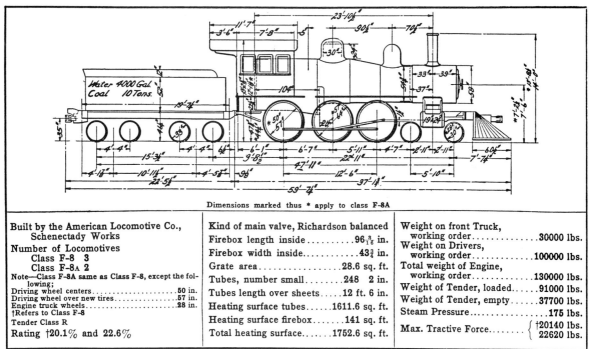

Dimensions marked thus * apply to class F-8A

Built by the American Locomotive Co.,
  Schenectady Works
Number of Locomotives
    Class F-8   3
    Class F-8A 2
Note—Class F-8A same as Class F-8, except the following;
Driving wheel centers.....................50 in.
Driving wheel over new tires...............57 in.
Engine truck wheels......................28 in.
†Refers to Class F-8
Tender Class R
Rating †20.1% and 22.6%

Kind of main valve, Richardson balanced
Firebox length inside..........96 3/16 in.
Firebox width inside............43 3/4 in.
Grate area.................28.6 sq. ft.
Tubes, number small........248   2 in.
Tubes length over sheets.....12 ft. 6 in.
Heating surface tubes......1611.6 sq. ft.
Heating surface firebox......141 sq. ft.
Total heating surface......1752.6 sq. ft.

Weight on front Truck,
  working order.............30000 lbs.
Weight on Drivers,
  working order............100000 lbs.
Total weight of Engine,
  working order............130000 lbs.
Weight of Tender, loaded......91000 lbs.
Weight of Tender, empty......37700 lbs.
Steam Pressure.................175 lbs.
Max. Tractive Force........ { †20140 lbs.
                              22620 lbs.

CLASS F-8 and F-8A

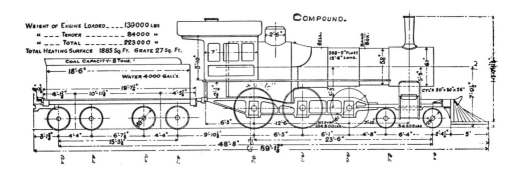

(NYC&HR) NEW YORK & NORTHERN. Leased 1/94 to NYC&HR.
           Formerly NEW YORK CITY & NORTHERN 1879 to 1887.

No.	Re'94	Re'99	Re'05	Class	Type	Builder, c/n, Date			Cyl. DD	Disposition
1					4-4-0	Brooks	359	6/79	17x24-56	dr by'94
2	1112				"	"	361	7/79	" "	Sc 8/99
3	1113				"	"	362	10/79	" "	Sc 8/99
4					"	"	363	"	" "	dr by'94
5	1121				"	"	452	9/80	" "	Sc 8/99
6	1122				"	"	453	"	" "	Sc 8/99
7	1123				"	"	454	"	" "	Sc 8/99
8	43				0-4-0T	"	466	10/80	15X22-55	Sc 8/99
?	(Note a)				2-4-2T	(Grant		10/78)	10x20-44	dr by'92
?										dr by'92
11	836?				4-4-0	Portland	411	12/81	17x24-61	dr c94 Pough.& Eas. 3?
12					2-6-0	"	408	10/81	18x24-54	dr by'89
13					"	"	409	"	" "	dr by'89
14					"	"	410	12/81	" "	dr by'89
?										
?										
?										
18	1151	1400	40	D	2-4-4T	Rogers	3891	1/88	14x22-55	Sc 7/11
19	1152	1401	41	"	"	"	3892	2/88	" "	Sc 12/10
20	1153	1402	42	"	"	"	3913	3/88	" "	So 6/10 SI&E 760 (b)
21	1154	1403	43	"	"	"	3926	4/88	" "	Sc 2/13
22	1155	1404	44	"	"	"	3927	"	" "	So 6/10 SI&E 761 (c)
23	1156	1405	45	"	"	"	4502	5/91	" "	So 6/15 C.W.Lane 27
24	1157	1406	46	"	"	"	4719	6/92	" "	Sc 2/13 or 2/11
12	837	496	1791	E-9	2-6-0	Rogers	4209	11/89	18x24-50	So 3/08 Cont.I&S Co.
13	838	497	1792	"	"	"	4210	"	" "	So 3/06 Hicks
14	839	498	1793	"	"	"	4216	"	" "	So 6/07 SI&ECo.
15	840	499	1794	"	"	"	4217	"	" "	So 10/07 Kilby L&M Co.
9	991	1084	1084	C-27	4-4-0	Rogers	4503	5/91	18x24-64	Sc 4/11
10	992	1085	1085	"	"	"	4721	6/92	" "	Sc 12/10

        Note a - Ex-Manhattan Ry. 232, acquired 3/81.
        Note b - re 5/11 to Cia.Cpe.Phos.de la Floride, Pembroke,Fla.
        Note c - re 3/13 to Mitchell Mountain Coal & Iron Co.

NYC&HR Engines Acquired 1896-1900:

0-6-0	243-248	Class K-1	Schen.	1898-99	See class B-1, p.96	
2-6-0	786,788-814	" P	"	1898-99	" " E-1,a p.130	
"	787	" J-2	W.Albany	1898	" " Ef, p.126	
"	815-817	" P-1	Depew,WA	1899-00	" " E-1b P.130	
4-2-4T	251,253	(Inspec.)	" "	1897,96	" " Pony p.118	
4-4-0	1029-1038	Class G	Schen.	1897	" " C-12 p116	
"	923	" I	W.Albany	1896	" " C, p108	
"	924-928,934-938	" I-1	Schen.	1896,98	" " Cb p106	
"	870	" "	W.Albany	1898	" " " "	
"	929-933,939-943	" I-2	Schen.	1898	" " Cc "	
"	945,946	" "	WA,Depew	1898,99	" " Cb,Cc p.108	

New York City & Northern #2 as built by Brooks 1879.　　　　(NYC neg 4986)
(H.L.Vail coll.)

Builder's photo of New York City & Northern #8, as delivered by Brooks in 1880.(NYC 2658)
(H.L.Vail coll.)

NYC&N #11, one of four built by Portland in 1881.   Photo at Mahopac Mines in 1888.
(NYC neg 1766; H.L.Vail coll.)

NYC&HR 1793, class E-9, ex-NY&Nor. 14, Rogers 1889.   (NYC neg 5654)

Class D

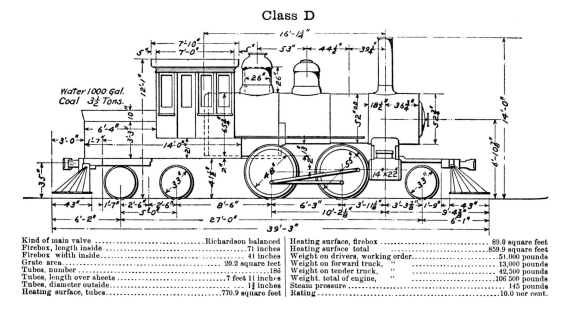

Kind of main valve	Richardson balanced
Firebox, length inside	71 inches
Firebox width inside	41 inches
Grate area	20.2 square feet
Tubes, number	186
Tubes, length over sheets	7 feet 11 inches
Tubes, diameter outside	1¾ inches
Heating surface, tubes	770.9 square feet

Heating surface, firebox	89.0 square feet
Heating surface total	859.9 square feet
Weight on drivers, working order	51,000 pounds
Weight on forward truck, "	13,000 pounds
Weight on tender truck, "	42,500 pounds
Weight, total of engine, "	106,500 pounds
Steam pressure	145 pounds
Rating	10.0 per cent.

The Putnam Division had a fleet of seven tank engines for the Getty Square service. One of these double enders was NYC&HR 45, built 1891 as NY&N 23. (Arthur Curran)

Another Putnam Forney, No. 40, built by Rogers in 1888. (W.D.E.collection)

NYC&HR Renumbering and Classification System of 1899:

During the 1880's and 1890's the NYC&HR had acquired several lines in New York and Pennsylvania, including the West Shore, the Beech Creek, and the Fall Brook. However, their locomotives had not been renumbered, and no doubt the duplication of road numbers gradually became a problem. In 1899 it was decided to establish a new numbering scheme for all the NYC&HR and its component lines, and this scheme was to last almost 40 years. The assigned number groups are listed below, together with a new classification system adopted about the same time.

```
    1-10     0-4-0T Dummy
   25-30     Inspection Pony
   50-81     0-4-0  Classes A-2, A, A-1  Old classes D, D-1.
  200-310    0-6-0    "      B-3, B-5, B, B-6  Old classes E, E-2, K, L.
  351-374      "      "      B-7, B-8, B-9  ex-West Shore, Beech Creek.
* 400-554    4-4-0    "      C-9  Old class B
  555-679      "      "      C-15 to C-19  ex-West Shore.
* 680-699      "      "      C-10  Old class B-1
  700-714      "      "      C-19, C-22 to C-26  ex-Wallkill Valley, Beech Creek, Fall Brook
* 870-948      "      "      C, Ca, Cb, Cc, C-3  Old classes I, I-1, I-2, I-3.
* 960-1049     "      "      C-5, C-6, C-11, C-12, C-14  Old classes A-1, A-1x, F, G, N.
*1053-1136     "      "      C-8, C-4, C-13, C-7  Old classes A-3, A, H, A-2.
 1400-1406   2-4-4T   "      D
 1407-1422   2-6-6T   "      J
 1450-1720   2-6-0    "      E-4, E, Ea, Eb, Ec, Ed, Ef, E-1  Old M, J, J-1, J-2, P, P-1.
 1791-1815     "      "      E-9, E-5, E-10  ex-N.Y. & N., R.W.& O. and A.& StL.
 1816-1858     "      "      Ef, E-8, E-7  ex-West Shore, Beech Creek, Fall Brook.
 2000-2027   4-6-0    "      F, F-7  Old class C.
 2089-2102     "      "      F-8, F-5, F-6, F-9  ex-West Shore, Beech Creek, Fall Brook.
 2200-2211   2-8-0    "      G, G-8, G-13  Old class D-2.
 2212-2301     "      "      G-7, G-11, G-9, G-10, G-12  ex-W.Shore, Beech Creek, Fall Brook
 2600-2631   4-8-0    "      H, H-1, H-3  ex-Beech Creek.
```

        * Indicates old numbers retained.

WALLKILL VALLEY. Leased May, 1899 to NYC&HR. Operated by the Erie 1871-1877.

```
WV 1  (ex-Erie 99)              4-4-0 (Hinkley    12/50)  15x22-66  dr by'77
WV 2  re "1                       "    Danf.  1039  /77   17x24     dr by'99
WV 3  re  4                       "     "     1040   "      "       dr by'99
WV 2         re'99  700  C-19     "    Schen. 2307 3/87   16x24-64  So 11/01 S.C.& Ga.Ext.
WV "3          "    701   "       "     "     2308  "      "   "    So 11/04 Ginsburg
```

SYRACUSE, ONTARIO & NEW YORK. Acquired 6/91 by NYC&HR. Formerly SYRACUSE & CHENANGO VALLEY until 5/73, then SYRACUSE & CHENANGO until 4/77, then SYRACUSE, CHENANGO & NEW YORK until 1/83, then SO&NY.

```
  1  "Syracuse"                4-4-0  Schen.  684  6/71   15x24-60
  2  "Manlius"                   "      "     741 11/71    "    "
  3  "Cazenovia"                 "      "     814  9/72   16x24-60
  4  re WS 221 re 126 re 1842?  2-6-0  Pitts. 753  1/85   17x24-62
```

Wallkill Valley's first engine was this Hinkley inherited from the Erie. (NYC neg 5602)

WV second #2, built Schenectady 1887. It became NYC&HR class C-19.   (NYC neg 902)

Rosendale bridge on the Wallkill Valley. Engine is first #2.   (NYC neg 1150)

(NYC&HR) WEST SHORE. Leased 1/86 to NYC&HR. Formerly NEW YORK, WEST SHORE & BUFFALO until 12/85. Locomotives renumbered 1899 into NYC&HR series.

WS No.	WS Class	Re'99	Re'05	Re'13	Class	Type	Builder, c/n,	Date	RB	Disposition
1	A2	555	778		C-16	4-4-0	Rogers 3021	6/82	1/90	So 3/08 Cont.I&S Co.
2	Ab	556	776		C-16b,c	"	" 3024	"	8/88	So 12/07 Ginsburg
3	Ab	557	767	1087	C-16c	"	" 3028	7/82	4/92	Sc 12/13 (b)
4	A	558			C-15a	"	" 3032	"		So 1/05 Ginsburg
5	A2	559	775		C-16a	"	" 3035	"	4/96	Sc 6/11
6	Ab	560	777		C-16b,c	"	" 3037	"	2/93	Sc 5/12
7	A2	561	761		C-16a	"	" 3257	5/83	10/93	Sc 5/11
8	A2	562	762		"	"	" 3258	"	4/91	Sc 7/12
9	Ab	563	763		C-16c	"	" 3261	"	4/89	Sc 11/11
10	"	564	764		C-16b,c	"	" 3265	"	8/89	Sc 8/11
11	"	565	765		C-16b	"	" 3266	"	"	So 10/05 Ginsburg
12	"	566	766		C-16c	"	" 3267	6/83	2/88	Sc 11/09
13		567				"	" 3272	"	5/88	Sc 4/02 (b)
14	Ab	568	768		C-16c	"	" 3274	"	8/87	Sc 11/09
15	"	569	769		"	"	" 3278	"	8/90	Sc 8/11
16	A	570	700		C-15	"	" 3285	"		So 11/05 Hy.&Co.
17	"	571			"	"	" 3286	"		So 4/03
18	A2	572	772		C-16	"	" 3288	"	3/94	Sc 7/08
19	Ab	573	773		C-16b	"	" 3300	7/83	4/93	Sc 9/07
20	A2	574	774		C-16a	"	" 3297	6/83	8/94	Sc 5/10
21		575				"	" 3303	7/83		Sc 9/02
22		576				"	" 3305	"		Sc 9/02
23	A	577			C-15a	"	" 3307	"	2/91	So 11/04 Ginsburg
24	"	578	701		"	"	" 3308	"	4/93	So 11/05 Hy.&Co.
25	A2	579	779		C-16,a	"	" 3316	8/83	3/95	Sc 12/10
26	Ab	580	780		C-16c	"	" 3317	"	1/90	So 3/08 Hicks L&C
27	"	581	781		C-16b,c	"	" 3326	"	2/89	Sc 10/11
28	"	582	782		C-16b	"	" 3328	"	6/90	So 3/08 Cont.I&S Co.
29	A2	583	783		C-16a	"	" 3338	"	9/92	Sc 12/10
30	Ab	584	784		C-16c	"	" 3341	10/83	4/92	Sc 10/10
31	B	585				4-4-0	Rogers 3362	9/83		dr by'02
32	"	586	625		C-17a	"	" 3363	"		So 11/05 Ginsburg
33	"	587	626		"	"	" 3365	"		So 11/05 Hy.&Co.
34	"	588	627		"	"	" 3366	10/83		So 12/05 Hy.&Co.
35	"	589	628		"	"	" 3367	"		So'05 Ginsburg
36	"	590	630		"	"	" 3368	"		So'05 Jones & Gal.
37	"	591			C-17	"	" 3391	"		So'05 Ginsburg
38	"	592	635		C-17a	"	" 3392	"	4/89	Sc'05
39	"	593	636		"	"	" 3393	"		So 10/06 Hy.&Co.
40	"	594	641		C-17	"	" 3422	"		So 7/07 Ginsburg
41	"	595	643		C-17a	"	" 3419	11/83		So 11/07 Cont.I&S Co
42	"	596			C-17	"	" 3420	"		So 1/05 Ginsburg
43	"	597	652		C-17a	"	" 3435	12/83		So 7/07 Ginsburg
44	"	598	654		C-17	"	" 3436	"		So 2/07 Haz.Co.& Ben
45	"	599	655		C-17a	"	" 3437	11/83		Sc 10/09
46	"	600			C-17	"	" 3438	12/83		So 3/08 Ginsburg
47	"	601			"	"	" 3450	4/84		So 6/05 Kilby & Co.
48	"	602			C-17a	"	" 3451	"		So 4/06 H'y.& Co.
49	"	603			"	"	" 3453	"		So 7/07 Ginsburg
50	"	604			C-17	"	" 3454	"		So 4/07 Kilby (a)

Note a - re Carolina & Northwestern 121.   Note b - Boiler 3272 to #557 in 1902.

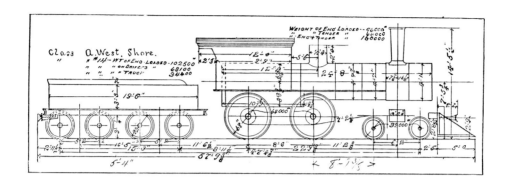

Class C-16

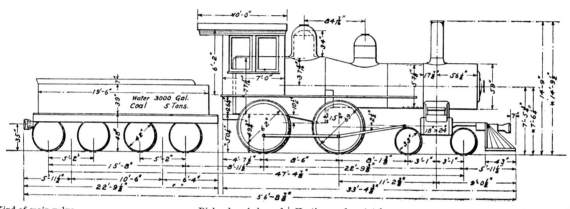

Kind of main valve	Richardson balanced	Heating surface, total	1,504 square feet
Firebox, length inside	120½ inches	Weight on drivers, working order	73 800 pounds
Firebox, width inside	38½ inches	Weight on truck, "	34,500 pounds
Grate area	32 square feet	Weight, total of engine, "	108,300 pounds
Tubes, number	236	Weight of tender loaded	64,000 pounds
Tubes, length over sheets	10 feet 11 15/16 inches	Weight of tender, empty	29,000 pounds
Tubes diameter outside	2 inches	Steam pressure	150 pounds
Heating surface, tubes	1,349 square feet	Rating	14.8 per cent.
Heating surface, firebox	155 square feet	NOTE.—Dimensions marked thus * apply to Class C-16A.	

Rogers builder's photo of NYWS&B #1, first of a large fleet of 4-4-0's.　　(NYC neg 5649)
(H.L.Vail coll.)

(NYC&HR) WEST SHORE   Engines 51-100:

WS No.	WS Class	Re'99	Class	Type	Builder,	c/n,	Date	Disposition
51	B	605	C-17	4-4-0	Rogers	3053	8/82	So 3/08 Haz,Coates & Benn.
52	"	606	C-17,a	"	"	3054	"	So 12/06 Kilby & Co.
53	"	607	C-17	"	"	3057	"	So 2/05 H'y & Co.
54	"	608	"	"	"	3059	"	So 3/06 Jones & Galvin
55	"	609	C-17a	"	"	3061	"	So 11/04 Ginsburg
56	"	610	C-17	"	"	3062	"	Sc 5/10 (on DAV&P)
57	"	611	C-17a	"	"	3083	9/82	So 10/04 F.M.Hicks
58	"	612	"	"	"	3084	"	So 10/05 Ginsburg
59	"	613	C-17	"	"	3086	"	So 3/08 Ginsburg
60	"	614	"	"	"	3116	10/82	So 10/05 Jones & Galvin
61	"	615		"	"	3117	"	Sc 8/02
62	"	616	C-17a	"	"	3118	"	So 7/07 Ginsburg
63	"	617	"	"	"	3139	11/82	So 3/08 Ginsburg
64	"	618	C-17	"	"	3140	"	So 4/04 Hy.& Co.
65	"	619	C-17a	"	"	3141	"	Sc 5/09 (on DAV&P)
66	"	620	"	"	"	3142	"	So 3/08 Ginsburg
67	"	621	C-17	"	"	3143	12/82	So 2/04 Norfolk Sou. 18
68	"	622	"	"	"	3144	"	So 9/03 H'y.& Co.
69	"	623	"	"	"	3150	"	So 5/08 Cont.I&S Co.
70	"	624	C-17a	"	"	3151	"	So 4/06 H'y.& Co.
71	"	625	C-17	"	"	3152	"	So 11/04 Ginsburg
72	"	626	"	"	"	3153	"	So 12/02
73	"	627	C-17a	"	"	3154	"	So 2/04 Norfolk Sou. 19
74	"	628	C-17	"	"	3155	"	So 2/04 Norfolk Sou. 20
75	"	629	"	"	"	3156	"	So 2/05 H'y.& Co.
76	"	630	"	"	"	3157	"	So 10/04 F.M.Hicks
77	"	631	C-17a	"	"	3158	"	So 8/07 Ginsburg
78	"	632	C-17	"	"	3162	"	So 2/06 Jones & Galvin
79	"	633	C-17a	"	"	3163	"	So 5/06 Ginsburg
80	"	634	C-17,a	"	"	3187	2/83	Sc 8/08
81	"	635	C-17a	"	"	3190	"	So 11/04 Ginsburg
82	"	636	C-17	"	"	3192	"	So 11/04 Ginsburg
83	"	637	C-17a	"	"	3195	"	So 11/07 Jones & Galvin
84	"	638	"	"	"	3213	3/83	So 9/07 Haz.Coates & Benn.
85	"	639	"	"	"	3214	"	So 10/05 Ginsburg
86	"	640	"	"	"	3215	"	So 2/05 H'y.& Co.
87	"	641	C-17	"	"	3216	"	So 9/03 H'y.& Co.
88	"	642	"	"	"	3229	"	So 12/07 Ginsburg
89	"	643		"	"	3230	"	Sc 10/01
90	"	644	C-17a	"	"	3231	"	So 3/05 H'y.& Co.
91	"	645	"	"	"	3232	4/83	So 10/05 Ginsburg
92	"	646	"	"	"	3241	"	So 4/06 H'y.& Co.
93	"	647	"	"	"	3242	"	So 8/07 Ginsburg
94	"	648	C-17	"	"	3243	3/83	So 3/08 Ginsburg
95	"	649	"	"	"	3244	7/83	So 10/05 Ginsburg
96	"	650	"	"	"	3247	4/83	So 1/07
97	"	651	C-17a	"	"	3249	"	So 11/06 Jones & Galvin
98	"	652	"	"	"	3254	5/83	So 11/04 Ginsburg
99	"	653	"	"	"	3255	"	So 1/08 Ginsburg
100	"	654	"	"	"	3256	"	Sc 2/04

NYWS&B 51, built Rogers 1882, in West Shore class B, later NYC&HR class C-17.(NYC 5650)

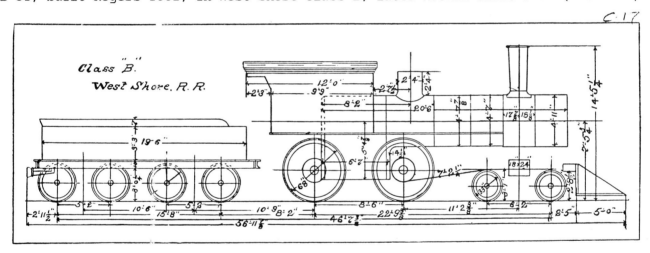

NYC&HR 593 with oversizwe cab, built as West Shore 39; Renumbered 1899. (NYC neg 5653)

(NYC&HR) WEST SHORE Engines 101-150:

WS No.	WS Class	Re '99	Re '05	Class	Type	Builder	c/n	Date	RB	Disposition
101	D	351			0-6-0	Baldwin	6908	9/83		So 8/02
102	"	352	195	B-7	"	"	6916	"		So 4/06 Hy.&Co.
103	"	353	196	B-7b	"	"	6919	"		So 10/06 "
104	"	354		B-7a	"	"	6922	"		So 9/02 Woodstock I&S Co. 2
105	"	355	200	"	"	"	6931	"	6/14	Sc 7/34 (Note a)
106	"	356		"	"	"	6929	"		So 8/02
107	"	357			"	"	6943	"		dr by'01
108	"	358			"	"	6945	"	Cooke	So Fleischmann Yeast Co.
109	"	359		B-7b	"	"	6951	10/83		So 1/05 Hy.&Co.
110	"	360			"	"	6954	"		dr by'02
111	"	361		B-7b	"	"	6958	"		So 1/05 Hy.&Co.
112	"	362		B-7a	"	"	6960	"	11/12	Re Dummy 2
113	"	363	197	B-7b	"	"	6962	"		So 4/06 Hy.&Co.
114	"	364	198-201	"	"	"	6970	"	2/07	Re Dummy 10
115	"	365		B-7a	"	"	6971	"		So 9/02
116	"	366			"	"	6973	"		dr by'02
117	"	367			"	"	6977	"		Sc 10/01
118	"	368			"	"	6986	"		So c'02 McDonald & Onderdonk
119	"	369	199-202	B-7b	"	"	6992	"		So 5/08 Hicks L&C Co.
120	"	370		"	"	"	6996	11/83		So 5/04 Kilby & Co.
121	C	2212		G-7a	2-8-0	Baldwin	7019	11/83		So 10/07 Kilby & Co.
122	"	2213		"	"	"	7024	"		So 12/06 Sou.I&E Co.
123	"	2214		"	"	"	7030	"		So 4/07 Woodstock I&S Co.(b)
124	"				"	"	7031	"		So 5/86 N.Y.Ont.& Wes. 88
125	"				"	"	7036	"		" " " 87
126	"				"	"	7044	"		" " " 80
127	"	2215		G-7a	"	"	7046	12/83		So 1/08 Hicks L&C Co.
128	"	2216		"	"	"	7049	"		So 1/06 Kilby & Co.
129	"	2217		G-7	"	"	7063	"	6/97	Sc 11/11
130	"				"	"	7068	"		So 5/86 N.Y.Ont.& Wes. 84
131	"				"	"	7072	"		So 10/87 " " 81
132	"				"	"	7074	"		" " " 82
133	"	2218		G-7a	"	"	7077	"		So 7/07 SI&E re E.Coast L.Co.
134	"	2219		"	"	"	7085	"		So 10/07 (b) re Alger Sull.5
135	"				"	"	7091	"		So 5/86 N.Y.Ont.& Wes. 83
136	"	2220		G-7a	"	"	7097	1/84		So 1/08 Ginsburg
137	"	2221		"	"	"	7099	"		So 5/09 Empire Coal & Coke Co
138	"	2222		"	"	"	7103	"		So 9/02 Caro.& No.Wes.267 (b)
139	"	2223		G-7	"	"	7114	"	4/98	Rt 4/22, Sc
140	"				"	"	7115	"		So'87 N.Y.Ont.& Wes. 86
141	"	2224		G-7a	"	"	7124	2/84		So 07 Kilby re'11 Escambia 7
142	"	2225		G-7	"	"	7126	"	7/95	Sc 3/12
143	"				"	"	7131	"		So'87 N.Y.Ont.& Wes. 85
144	"				"	"	7155	"		" " " 89
145	"				"	"	7157	"		So 12/86 Buff.Roch.& Pitts.67
146	"	2226		G-7a	"	"	7159	"		So 3/08 Cont.I&S Co.
147	"	2227		"	"	"	7170	"		So 10/07 Kilby, re A.C.I.2227
148	"	2228		"	"	"	7172	"		So 10/06 Kilby
149	"				"	"	7212	3/84		So 12/86 Buff.Roch.& Pitts.68
150	"	2229		"	"	"	7216	"		Sc 8/02

Note a: #200 re 76 re 1924, converted 9/31 to Work Equip.   Note b - Sold through Kilby.

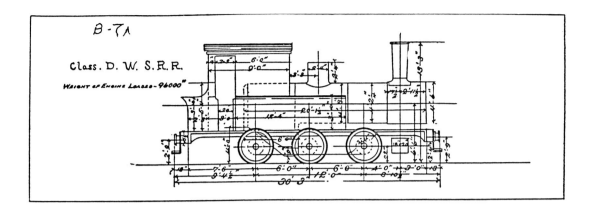

Class B-7

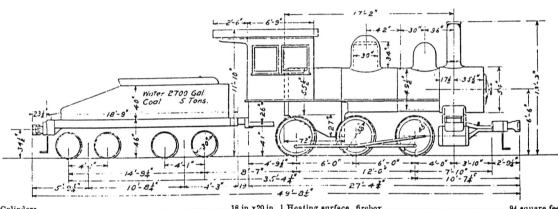

Cylinders..18 in x20 in.
Kind of main valve....................Richardson balanced
Firebox, length inside ....62¼ inches
Firebox, width inside ....34½ inches
Grate area...16 square feet
Tubes, number.......................................169
Tubes, length over sheets...............9 feet 10½ inches
Tubes, diameter outside ....2 inches
Heating surface, tubes.....................868 square feet

Heating surface, firebox........................94 square feet
Heating surface, total.........................952 square feet
Weight on drivers, working order ....79,200 pounds
Weight, total of engine, working order.....79,200 pounds
Weight of tender, loaded....................57,400 pounds
Weight of tender, empty.....................25,400 pounds
Steam pressure.....................................140 pounds
Rating...17.9 per cent.

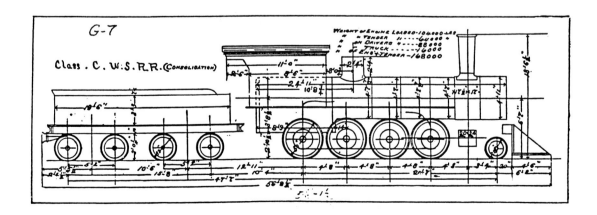

(NYC&HR) WEST SHORE Engines 151-200:

WS No.	WS Class	Re '99	Class	Type	Builder, c/n, Date		RB	Disposition
151	C	2230	G-7	2-8-0	Dickson	361 9/83	8/98	Sc 11/09
152	"	2231	"	"	"	362 "	2/97	Sc 10/11
153	"	2232	G-7A	"	"	363 "		So 4/08 Haz.Coa.& Benn.
154	"	2233		"	"	364 "		So 9/02 Carolina & NW 268
155	"	2234	G-7a	"	"	365 10/83	6/97	Sc 8/07
156	"	2235	G-7	"	"	366 "	12/96	So 5/07 Ginsburg
157	"	2236	G-7a	"	"	367 "		So 10/07 Ginsburg
158	"	2237	"	"	"	368 "		So 8/07 HC&B
159	"	2238	"	"	"	369 "		So 10/07 Kilby
160	"	2239	G-7	"	"	370 11/83	8/98	Sc 1/12
161	"	2240	G-7a	"	"	371 12/83		So 11/07 Hicks L&C Co.
162	"	2241	G-7	"	"	372 "	2/01	Sc 1/12
163	"	2242	G-7a	"	"	373 "		Sc 12/06
164	"	2243	"	"	"	374 5/84		So 10/07 Jones & Galvin
165	"	2244	"	"	"	375 "		So 3/06 Kilby
166	"	2245	"	"	"	376 "		So 8/07 Ginsburg
167	"	2246	G-7	"	"	377 "	6/97	So 4/11 BR&L re Ball & Peters
168	"	2247	G-7a	"	"	378 4/84		So 12/07 Ginsburg
169	"	2248	"	"	"	379 5/84		Sc 7/09
170	"	2249	G-7	"	"	380 "	10/96	Sc 1/12
171	"	2250	G-7a	"	"	381 7/84		Sc 12/05
172	"	2251	G-7	"	"	382 "	7/96	Sc 4/12
173	"	2252	G-7a	"	"	383 "		So 10/07 HC&B
174	"	2253	G-7	"	"	384 "	12/96	Sc 12/10
175	"	2254	"	"	"	385 "	2/97	So 3/08 Cont.I&S Co.
176	H	1816	Ee	2-6-0	Schen.	3673 1/92	8/06	Sc 8/23
177	"	1817	"	"	"	3674 "	10/07	Rt 12/16, Sc
178	"	1818	"	"	"	3675 "	3/08	Rt 12/16, Sc
179	"	1819	"	"	"	3676 "		Sc 9/11
180	"	1820	"	"	"	3677 "		Sc 5/10
181	"	1821	"	"	"	3678 2/92	5/06	Sc 7/23
182	"	1822	"	"	"	3679 "	12/08	Sc 11/23
183	"	1823	"	"	"	3680 "		Sc 9/11
184	"	1824	"	"	"	3681 "		Sc 5/10
185	"	1825	"	"	"	3682 "		Sc 2/11
186	"	1826	"	"	"	3688 "	1/05	Rt 10/15
187	"	1827	"	"	"	3689 "	10/07	Sc 3/19
188	"	1828	"	"	"	3690 "	2/08	Rt 12/21
189	"	1829	"	"	"	3691 "	8/05	Rt 12/16, Sc
190	"	1830	"	"	"	3692 "	1/05	Rt 1/17, Sc
191	"	1831	"	"	"	3693 "	8/06	Sc 9/29
192	"	1832	"	"	"	3694 "		Sc 5/10
193	"	1833	"	"	"	3695 "		Sc 11/11
194	"	1834	"	"	"	3696 "		Sc 10/11
195	"	1835	"	"	"	3697 "	8/08	Rt 2/17, Sc
196	"	1836	"	"	"	3698 "	5/06	Rt 12/21, Sc
197	"	1837	"	"	"	3699 "	9/08	Sc 11/25
198	"	1838	"	"	"	3700 "	3/06	Rt 12/21, Sc
199	"	1839	"	"	"	3701 "		Sc 11/10
200	"	1840	"	"	"	3702 "	3/06	Sc 3/15

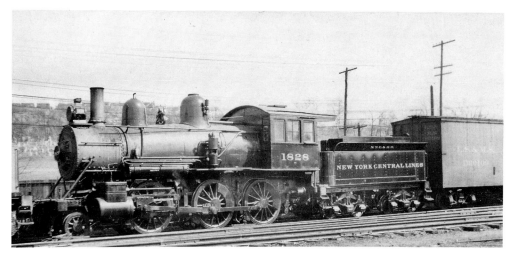

NYC&HR 1828 was one of the 25 Moguls delivered to the West Shore by Schenectady in 1892.

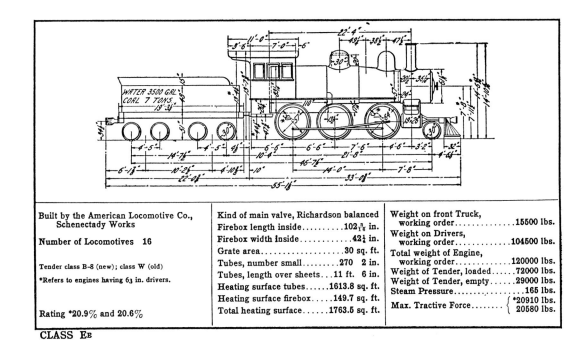

Built by the American Locomotive Co., Schenectady Works

Number of Locomotives 16

Tender class B-8 (new); class W (old)

*Refers to engines having 63 in. drivers.

Rating *20.9% and 20.6%

Kind of main valve, Richardson balanced
Firebox length inside..........102$\frac{3}{16}$ in.
Firebox width inside...........42$\frac{1}{4}$ in.
Grate area...................30 sq. ft.
Tubes, number small........270 2 in.
Tubes, length over sheets...11 ft. 6 in.
Heating surface tubes......1613.8 sq. ft.
Heating surface firebox.....149.7 sq. ft.
Total heating surface......1763.5 sq. ft.

Weight on front Truck,
   working order..............15500 lbs.
Weight on Drivers,
   working order............104500 lbs.
Total weight of Engine,
   working order............120000 lbs.
Weight of Tender, loaded......72000 lbs.
Weight of Tender, empty......29000 lbs.
Steam Pressure................165 lbs.
Max. Tractive Force........{ *20910 lbs.
                            20580 lbs.

CLASS E_B

The West Shore bought 25 Consolidations like this one from Dickson in 1883. (NYC neg 5049)
(H.L.Vail coll.)

(NYC&HR) WEST SHORE   Additions 1885-1888:

WS No.	WS Class	Re '99	Re '02	Class	Type	Builder, c/n, Date			Disposition
201	E	660		C-18	4-4-0	Rogers	3567	8/85	So 1/05 Ginsburg
202	"	661		"	"	"	3568	"	So 2/06 Jones & Galvin
203	"	662			"	"	3570	"	Sc 8/02
204	"	663		C-18	"	"	3571	"	So 1/05 H'y & Co.
205	"	664		C-18a	"	"	3573	"	So 4/04 H'y & Co.
206	"	665		C-18	"	"	3583	10/85	So 9/03 Ginsburg
207	"	666		"	"	"	3584	"	So 11/02
208	"	667		"	"	"	3585	"	So 9/03 Pough. & Eas. 6
209	"	668		"	"	"	3586	"	So 11/04 Ginsburg
210	"	669		"	"	"	3587	"	Sc 8/08
211	"	670		"	"	"	3588	"	So 7/07 Ginsburg
212	"	671		"	"	"	3589	"	So 9/03 Ginsburg
213	"	672		"	"	"	3590	"	So 1/05 Ginsburg
214	"	673		"	"	"	3591	"	So 1/04 Kilby Mach. Co.
215	"	674		"	"	"	3592	11/85	Sc 3/07
216	"	675		C-18a	"	"	3593	"	So 4/03
217	"	676		"	"	"	3594	"	Sc 5/03
218	"	677		"	"	"	3595	"	Sc 4/09
219	"	678			"	"	3596	"	dr by'02
220	"	679		C-18	"	"	3597	"	So 1/05 Ginsburg
221		126	1842?		2-6-0	(Pitts.	753	1/85)	Ex Syr.Ont.& NY 4
"124	F	655		C-19	4-4-0	Schen.	2148	8/86	So 1/05 Ginsburg
"125	"	656		"	"	"	2149	"	So 10/05 Ginsburg
"130	"	657		"	"	"	2150	"	So 11/04 Ginsburg
"135	"	658		"	"	"	2151	9/86	So 4/04 H'y & Co.
"140	"	659		"	"	"	2152	"	So 11/04 Ginsburg
"143	G	2096	2193	F-5	4-6-0	Rogers	3761	6/87	So 3/08 Cont.I&S Co.
"145	"	2098	2195	"	"	"	3762	"	Sc 8/02
"131	"	2094	2191	"	"	"	3922	4/88	So 11/06 Jones & Galvin
"132	"	2095	2192	"	"	"	3923	"	So 3/08 Cont.I&S Co.
"144	"	2097	2194	"	"	"	3924	"	So 4/07 Kilby re BFB&C 4
"149	"	2099	2196	"	"	"	3925	"	Sc 9/05

BEECH CREEK. Leased 10/90 to NYC&HR. Formerly BEECH CREEK, CLEARFIELD & SOUTHWESTERN until 6/86. Locomotives renumbered 1899 into NYC&HR series.

No.		Re '99	Re '02	Class	Type	Builder, c/n, Date			Disposition
1		2255		G-9a	2-8-0	Schen.	1775	1/84	So 8/07 Ginsburg
2	(a)	2256		G-11	"	"	1868	"	So 3/08 Kilby L&M Wks.
3	(a)	2257		"	"	"	1869	"	Sc 4/11
4	(a)			"	"	"	1870	"	dr by'87
5		2259		G-11	"	"	1871	"	So 7/87 Sou.I&E.Co.
6		2260		G-11b,a	"	"	2203	12/86	Rt '14-15
7		2261		"	"	"	2204	"	So 1/08 Hicks L&C Co.
" 4		2258		"	"	"	2331	3/87	Sc 10/10
8		2262		"	"	"	2332	4/87	Sc 7/09
9		2263		"	"	"	2333	5/87	So 3/08 Kilby L&M
10		2264		"	"	"	2334	"	So 4/08 Haz.Coa.& Benn.
21		1841		E-8	2-6-0	Schen.	1877	6/84	So 3/07 Kilby L&M
22	P&E 1	1998	1842	"	"	"	1878	"	Sc 4/09
23		1843		"	"	"	1879	"	Sc 2/04
24	(b)	2100	2197	F-6	4-6-0	Schen.	1947	1/85	Wrk. 8/00
25		2101	2198	"	"	"	1948	"	So 6/07 Sou.I&E Co.

Note a: 2-4 named Clinton, Centre, Snowshoe.   Note b: 24 named Woodland.

In 1885 the West Shore got 20 more eight-wheelers from Rogers. Later C-18. (Alco H.P.)

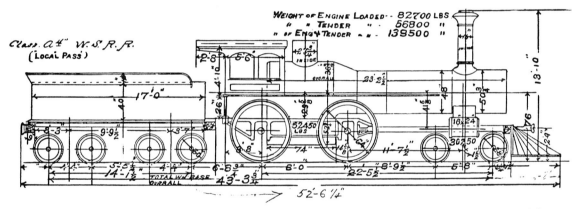

Diagram for the five W.S. class F local passenger engines. Later A-4, then C-19.

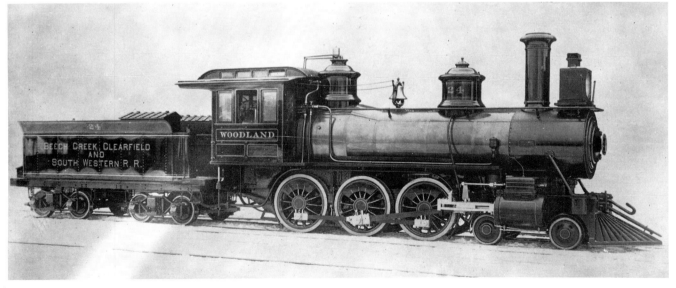

Early Beech Creek power included two ten-wheelers #24 named WOODLAND.   (NYC neg 8177)
(H.L.V. coll.)

(NYC&HR)   BEECH CREEK - Continued

BC	Re'99	Re'05	Re'12	Re'13	Class	Type	Builder,c/n,Date		Disposition
30	371				B-9	0-6-0	Schen.1931	8/84	So 11/04 F.M.Hicks
31	372	201			B-8	"	" 2674	4/88	So 6/07 Sou.I&E Co.
32	373	202			"	"	" 3605	11/91	So 12/06 SI&E 554 (note a)
33	374	203			"	"	" 4030	3/93	RB 2/11 Dummy 9
41	702				C-26	4-4-0	Schen.1865	1/84	So 5/07 Ginsburg
42	703				"	"	" 1866	"	So 3/06 Jones & Galvin
43	704				"	"	" 1867	"	Sc 5/10
44	705				C-26a	"	" 2858	4/89	Sc 11/11
11	2600	3600			H	4-8-0	Schen.2422	3/88	So 4/06 Hicks (note b)
12	2601	3601			"	"	" 2423	"	So 1/08 Cont.I&S Co.
13	2602	3602			"	"	" 2424	"	Sc 9/11
14	2603	3603			Ha	"	" 2859	4/89	Sc 11/09
15	2604	3604			H	"	" 3216	10/90	Sc 5/10
16	2605	3605			"	"	" 3217	"	Sc 10/09
17	2606	3606			"	"	" 3218	11/90	Sc 11/09
18	2607	3607			"	"	" 3219	"	So 6/08 Hicks (note b)
19	2608	3608			"	"	" 3220	"	Sc 5/11
20	2609	3609	621	79	H,X	"	" 3606	1/92	Sc 7/15
50	2610	3610			H	"	" 3607	2/92	Sc 11/11
51	2611	3611			"	"	" 3608	1/92	Sc 5/10
52	2612	3612			"	"	" 3609	2/92	Sc 8/11
53	2613	3613			H-1	"	" 3999	2/93	Sc 3/12
54	2614	3614			"	"	" 4000	"	Sc 5/11
55	2615	3615	615	75	H-1,X-1	"	" 4001	"	Sc 11/14
56	2616	3616	616	76	" "	"	" 4002	"	Sc 10/13
57	2617	3617			H-1	"	" 4029	3/93	Sc 2/12
58	2618	3618	618	77	H-1,X-1	"	" 4186	12/93	Sc 7/15
59	2619	3619	619	78	" "	"	" 4187	"	Sc 11/14
60	2620	3620			H-1	"	" 4188	"	Sc 3/12
61	2621	3621			"	"	" 4189	"	Sc 2/12
62	2622	3622			"	"	" 4190	"	Sc 3/12
63	2623	3623	623		"	"	" 4191	"	Sc 2/13
64	2624	3624			H-3,X-3	"	" 4532	2/97	Re Raq.Lake 2, Sc 1/15
65	2625	3625			H-3	"	" 4533	"	Sc 5/12
66	2626	3626	626		"	"	" 4534	3/97	Sc 2/13
67	2627	3627			"	"	" 4698	2/98	Sc 3/12
68	2628	3628	628	80	H-3,X-3	"	" 4699	"	Sc 11/14
69	2629	3629	629	81	" "	"	" 4700	"	Re Raq.Lake 1, Sc 2/16
70	2630	3630	630		H-3	"	" 4701	"	Sc 2/13
71	2631	3631			"	"	" 4702	"	Sc 3/12

Note a: Re 4/07 Tecumseh Iron Co. 202.   Note b: Re Denver,Laramie & N.W. 5,6

PITTSBURGH & EASTERN Acquired 1899 by NYC&HR:

1						2-8-0	Schen.4395	6/96	Re Fall Brook 81
2 (ex-Mont Alto RR 1)	1999		16x24-44			4-6-0	(BLW. 2945 9/72)		Acq'96, Sc 11/01

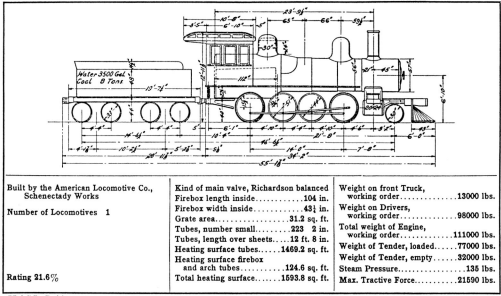

Built by the American Locomotive Co., Schenectady Works	Kind of main valve, Richardson balanced	Weight on front Truck,

Built by the American Locomotive Co., Schenectady Works

Number of Locomotives   1

Rating 21.6%

Kind of main valve, Richardson balanced
Firebox length inside............104 in.
Firebox width inside............43¼ in.
Grate area.................31.2 sq. ft.
Tubes, number small........223   2 in.
Tubes, length over sheets.....12 ft. 8 in.
Heating surface tubes......1469.2 sq. ft.
Heating surface firebox
  and arch tubes..........124.6 sq. ft.
Total heating surface......1593.8 sq. ft.

Weight on front Truck,
  working order.............13000 lbs.
Weight on Drivers,
  working order.............98000 lbs.
Total weight of Engine,
  working order...........111000 lbs.
Weight of Tender, loaded.....77000 lbs.
Weight of Tender, empty......32000 lbs.
Steam Pressure................135 lbs.
Max. Tractive Force.........21590 lbs.

CLASS G-11A

Class B-8

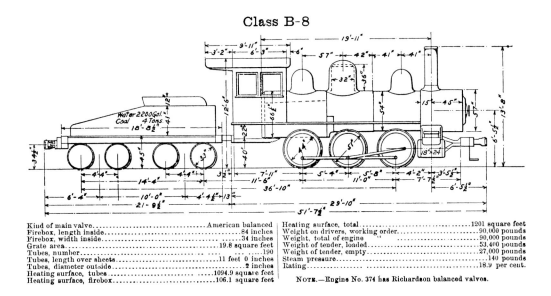

Kind of main valve...................................American balanced
Firebox, length inside................................84 inches
Firebox, width inside................................34 inches
Grate area...19.8 square feet
Tubes, number...190
Tubes, length over sheets.............................11 feet 0 inches
Tubes, diameter outside...............................2 inches
Heating surface, tubes ....1094.9 square feet
Heating surface, firebox..............................106.1 square feet

Heating surface, total.................................1201 square feet
Weight on drivers, working order.......................90,000 pounds
Weight, total of engine   '' ....90,000 pounds
Weight of tender, loaded...............................53,400 pounds
Weight of tender, empty................................27,000 pounds
Steam pressure...140 pounds
Rating...18.9 per cent.

NOTE.—Engine No. 374 has Richardson balanced valves.

Class H—3

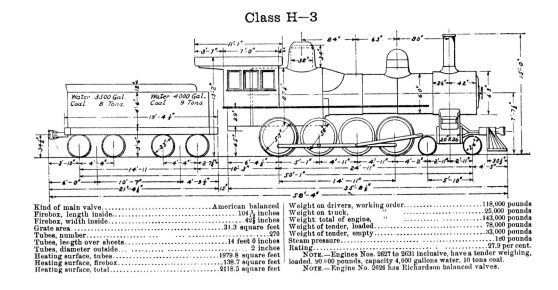

Kind of main valve...................................American balanced
Firebox, length inside................................104 3/8 inches
Firebox, width inside................................42¾ inches
Grate area...31.3 square feet
Tubes, number...270
Tubes, length over sheets.............................14 feet 0 inches
Tubes, diameter outside...............................2 inches
Heating surface, tubes ....1979.8 square feet
Heating surface, firebox..............................138.7 square feet
Heating surface, total.................................2118.5 square feet

Weight on drivers, working order......................118,000 pounds
Weight on truck,
Weight, total of engine,   '' ....25,000 pounds
Weight of tender, loaded..............................143,000 pounds
Weight of tender, empty...............................78,000 pounds
Steam pressure...33,000 pounds
Rating...180 pounds
                                                      27.9 per cent.

NOTE.—Engines Nos. 2627 to 2631 inclusive, have a tender weighing, loaded, 90,000 pounds, capacity 4,000 gallons water, 10 tons coal.
NOTE.—Engine No. 2626 has Richardson balanced valves.

The Beech Creek believed in big power from the start. No.2 was one of 10 2-8-0's. (NYC 817

Builder's photo of BC 11, first of 32 4-8-0's.   (Alco Historic Photos)

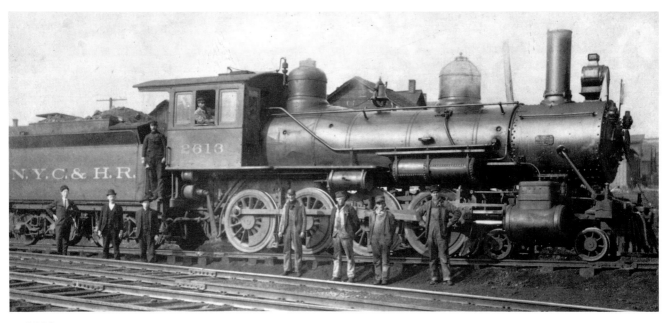

NYC&HR 2613, class H-1. The BC 4-8-0's were the only ones on the NYC&HR. (NYC neg 8174)

Fall Brook Coal Co. switcher #11 with the name WARD on sand box. (Vollrath collection)

The Fall Brook owned a few passenger engines like the JAMES H. RUTTER #20. (R.C.Schmid)

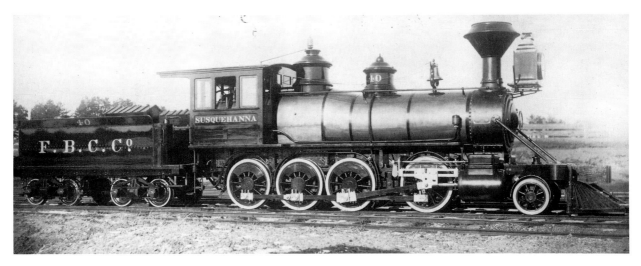

The Fall Brook had a variety of power, all of them named. #40 was SUSQUEHANA. (SHS)
(H.L.Vail coll.)

(NYC&HR) FALL BROOK. Leased 5/1899 to NYC&HR. Formerly TIOGA COAL,IRON,MINING & MFG.CO.
1839 to 4/1851, then CORNING & BLOSSBURG till 5/54, then BLOSSBURG
& CORNING till 1859, then FALL BROOK COAL CO. till 7/92, then FBRR.

F.B. Name & Number		Re'99	Class	Type	Builder,c/n,Date	Cyl.	DD	Disposition
Chemung	1				Alby.Iron Wks.'39			dr by'60
Tioga re Benjamin	4			4-2-0	Baldwin 131 10/39			
Canisteo re Jonathon	5			"	" 159 8/40			
Conhocton	3?			"	" 150 5/41	12x16-54		RB 4-4-0 #7?
Tuscarora	2			4-4-0	Rogers 29 /41	12x18-48		dr by'63
Susquehanna	6			0-6-0	Baldwin 287 4/47	13x18-42		RB'60 4-4-0
Fall Brook	"1			4-4-0	N.J.Loco. /60			
Seymour	"2			"	" /63			
Schuyler	8			2-6-0	" /63			
Seneca re Wedgewood	9			4-4-0	Schen. 302 8/63	16x24-54		
Deacon Lovejoy	"3			"	N.J.Loco. /64			So'66 (a)
Lark	7			"	RB fr."Conhocton"?			
Chemung	10			"	Schen. 419 5/66	17+x24-64		
Ward re Linden	11			2-6-0T	NJLoco. 465 /66			
Paul (ex- ?)	"6				(Swinburne) Acq/69	RB'80		dr by'93
Steuben	12			4-6-0	Schen. 880 5/73	18x24-54		dr by'99
Salt Point re Sam Hatch	13			"	" 883 "	" "	"	"
Antrim	14			"	" 964 6/74	" "	"	"
Lawrenceville (Note b)	15				(Acq.1/76)			"
Haskin " "	16			2-6-0	" "	"	"	"
Nearing " "	17				" "	"	"	"
Beaver(ex-McKean & Bflo)	18			4-4-0	(Brooks 226 ' 73)	15x22-61		"
Dundee	19			"	Schen. 1078 12/77	17x24-60		"
Jas.H.Rutter	20	714	Cx	"	" 1086 4/78	" "	"	So 8/02
Yates	21			"	" 1118 4/79	" "	"	dr by'99
Ontario (Note c)	22			2-6-0	(Rogers 2271 '73)	17x24-50		"
Tioga	"3			4-6-0	Schen. 1265 /80	18x24-54		"
Wayne	23	2102	F-9	"	" 1271 "	" "	"	So 1/04 (d)
New York	24	713	C-25	4-4-0	" 1341 1/81	17x24-63		So 1/05 Gins.
Pennsylvania	25			4-6-0	" 1372 5/81	18x24-54		dr by'99
Reading (ex- ?)	26	1844	Ex	2-6-0	(Schen.'69? RB'85)	18x24-56		So 11/05 Gins
Corning	27	1845	"	"	Schen. 1578 6/82	" "	"	So 3/08 HC&B.
Geneva	28			"	" 1579	" "	"	dr by'05
Morris Run	29	2265	G-9	2-8-0	" 1677 /83	20x24-51		So 11/04 Hicks
Blossburg	30	2266	"	"	" 1678 "	" "	"	So 10/07 Kilby
Wellsboro	31	2267	"	"	" 1679 "	" "	"	So 11/05 Gins.
Stokesdale	32	2268	"	"	" 1680 "	" "	"	So 1/06 H'y&Co
Middlebury	33	2269	"	"	" 1681 "	" "	"	So 3/06 Kilby
Lathrop re Elkland	34			"	" 1682 "	" "	"	dr by'99
Osceola	35	2270	G-9	"	" 1683 "	" "	"	Sc 7/10
Westfield	36	2271	"	"	" 1684 "	" "	"	dr by'09
Knoxville	37	2272	"	"	" 1685 "	" "	"	So 4/07 Kilby
Lindley	38	2273	"	"	" 1686 "	" "	"	So 10/06 Kilby
Pine Creek re Morrisbury	39	2274	"	"	" 1687 "	" "	"	So 3/06 (e)
Susquehanna	40	2275	"	"	" 1688 "	" "	"	Sc 9/11
Lycoming	41	2276	"	"	" 1689 "	" "	"	So 3/06 Kilby
Williamsport	42	2277	"	"	" 1690 "	" "	"	dr by'09
Jersey Shore	43	2278	"	"	" 1691 "	" "	"	So 2/08 Kilby

Note a: to Blossburg Coal Mining & RR Co.   Note b: ex-Morris Run Coal Mining Co.
Note c: ex-Ind.Bloom.& Wes. 60, acq.'79. Note d: 2102 re 2199, re H.Weston Lbr.Co. 7
Note e: 2274 re H.Weston Lbr.Co. 10.

Class G—9

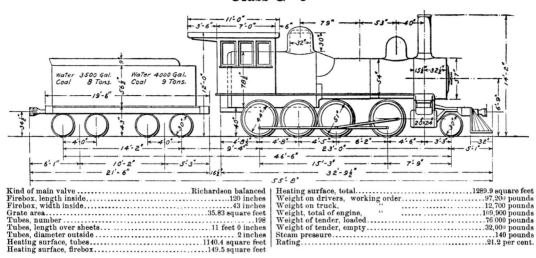

Kind of main valve...................................Richardson balanced	Heating surface, total.........................1289.9 square feet
Firebox, length inside...120 inches	Weight on drivers, working order.......................97,200 pounds
Firebox, width inside..43 inches	Weight on truck, " ....12,700 pounds
Grate area..35.83 square feet	Weight, total of engine, " ....109,900 pounds
Tubes, number...198	Weight of tender, loaded...........................76,000 pounds
Tubes, length over sheets...........................11 feet 0 inches	Weight of tender, empty............................32,000 pounds
Tubes, diameter outside..................................2 inches	Steam pressure...........................140 pounds
Heating surface, tubes.........................1140.4 square feet	Rating.....................................21.2 per cent.
Heating surface, firebox........................149.5 square feet	

Fall Brook Coal Co. #50, the MERCHANTS DESPATCH, later class E-7 on NYC&HR. (NYC 4958)
(H.L.Vail coll.)

Class E-7

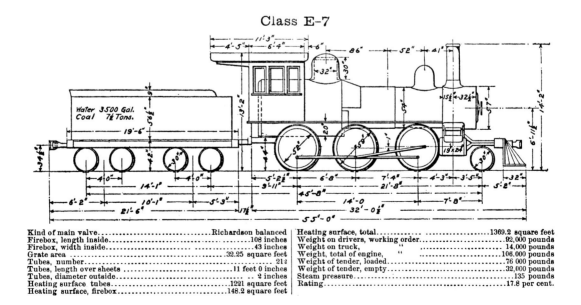

Kind of main valve..................................Richardson balanced	Heating surface, total.........................1369.2 square feet
Firebox, length inside...108 inches	Weight on drivers, working order.......................92,000 pounds
Firebox, width inside..43 inches	Weight on truck, " ....14,000 pounds
Grate area..32.25 square feet	Weight, total of engine, " ....106,000 pounds
Tubes, number...212	Weight of tender, loaded...........................76,000 pounds
Tubes, length over sheets...........................11 feet 0 inches	Weight of tender, empty............................32,000 pounds
Tubes, diameter outside..................................2 inches	Steam pressure...........................135 pounds
Heating surface, tubes.........................1221 square feet	Rating.....................................17.8 per cent.
Heating surface, firebox........................148.2 square feet	

(NYC&HR) FALL BROOK - Continued.

F.B. Name and Number		Re'99	Re'13	Class	Type	Builder,c/n,Date		Disposition
Potter (Note a)	44			(14x16-60)	0-4-0	(BLW'64)	Acq.'83	dr by'99
Mulhollon (Note b)	45			(13x24-60)	4-4-0	(BLW'57)	Acq.'83	dr by'99
Blue Line	46	1846	(d)	E-7	2-6-0	Schen.1872	5/84	Sc 11/11
White Line	47	1847		"	"	" 1873	"	So 4/06 H'y & Co
Red Line	48	1848		"	"	" 1874	"	Sc 1/09
Nickel Plate	49	1849		"	"	" 1875	"	Sc 6/09
Merchants Despatch	50	1850		"	"	" 1876	"	So 11/05 Ginsburg
Watkins	51	1851		"	"	" 1942	1/85	So 5/08 Cont.I&S Co.
Himrods	52	1852	(d)	"	"	" 1943	"	Sc 7/10
Dresden	53	1853	(d)	"	"	" 1944	"	Sc 7/09
Lyons	54	1854	(d)	"	"	" 1945	"	Sc 10/09
Penn Yan	55	1855	(d)	"	"	" 1946	"	Sc 12/09
J.P.Haskin	"16			(18x24-56)	"	" 2001	5/85	dr by'99
W.S.Nearing	"17			" "	"	" 2002	"	dr by'99
Cowanesque	56	1856		E-7	"	" 2004	6/85	Sc 4/09
Post Creek	57	1857	(d)	"	"	" 2132	10/86	Sc 3/15
Rock Stream	58	1858	(d)	"	"	" 2133	"	Sc 12/13
Interstate	"7	1085		Cx	4-4-0	" 2238	5/88?	Sc 12/10 (18x24-69)
Nelson	"34 re 77	2297		G-10	2-8-0	" 2546	3/88	Sc 10/09
Slate Run	59	2279		"	"	" 2547	"	So 5/08 Atlan.Equip
Newberry	60	2280		"	"	" 2548	"	So 2/09 Atlan.Equip.
Keuka	61	2281		"	"	" 2725	2/89	So 8/08 Hicks L&C Co.
Cedar	62	2282		"	"	" 2805	"	Sc 2/12
Lathrop	63	2283		"	"	" 2992	1/90	Sc 5/10
Gammal	64	2284		"	"	" 2993	"	Rt '14-15
Ansonia	65	2285		"	"	" 2994	"	Sc 4/08 Hicks L&C Co.
John			Insp.	4-2-2		Corning Shop /90?		
Duncan S. Ellsworth	66	2286		G-10	2-8-0	Schen.3051	2/90	Sc 12/09
John Magee Ellsworth	67	2287		"	"	" 3052	"	So 9/08 Cinti.Equip.
John Magee, Jr.	68	2288		"	"	" 3053	"	So 5/08 (Note c)
Southern Tier	69	2289		"	"	" 3534	8/91	Sc 5/10
Northern Tier	70	2290		"	"	" 3535	"	Sc 2/13
Tiadaghion	71	2291		"	"	" 3683	2/92	Sc 6/11
Blackwells	72	2292		"	"	" 3684	"	So 10/12 Central C&L
Harrison	73	2293		"	"	" 3685	"	Rt'13
Cascade	74	2294		"	"	" 3757	4/92	Sc 9/11
Moreland	75	2295		"	"	" 3758	"	So 3/10 Atlan.Equip.
Roundtop	76	2296		"	"	" 3759	"	So 7/10 (Note e)
Ulysses	"4	706	1092	C-24	4-4-0	" 4125	6/93	Sc 5/15
Columbus	"5	707	1093	"	"	" 4126	"	Sc 4/16
Paul (ex-CRRofPa)	"6	708		"	"	" 4144	"	dr by'02
Holiday	78	2298		G-10	2-8-0	" 4233	10/94	Sc 11/11
Earle	79	2299		"	"	" 4234	"	Rt'14-15
Waterville	80	2300		"	"	" 4235	"	Rt'14-15
Pritchard	"8	709	1088	C-22	4-4-0	" 4236	11/94	Sc 12/25
Presho	"10	711	1089	"	"	" 4237	"	Sc 8/23
(ex-Pitts.& Eas. 1)	81	2301		G-12	2-8-0	" 4395	6/96	Sc 11/13
	"9	710	1090	C-23	4-4-0	" 4540	3/97	Sc 11/16
	"11	712	1091	"	"	" 4541	"	Sc 4/15

Note a: #44 RB from Phila.& Rdg. 0-6-0 299 BLW.1730 6/68?
Note b: #45 from Riverside Iron Works, ex-P&R 312. Other sources list #45 ex-PRR 81,
         2-6-0 Norris 1854, from E.H.Wilson. Note c: to Atlan.Equip.Co., re Coal Fields
Note d: Assigned to DAV&P.   Note e: To Birm.R&L Co., re 7/12 to Liberty-White RR.

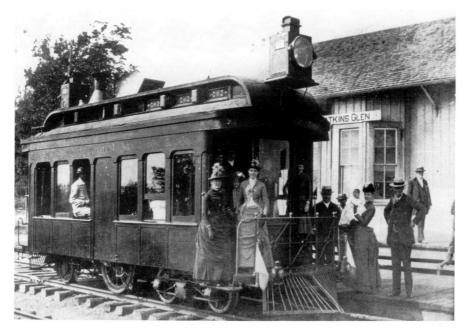

Fall Brook inspection engine JOHN, home-built at Corning Shops.

Class G—10

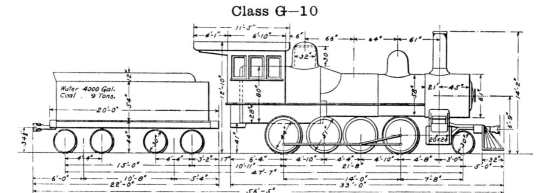

Kind of main valve	Richardson balanced	
Firebox, length inside	104 inches	
Firebox, width inside	43 inches	
Grate area	31.3 square feet	
Tubes, number	233	
Tubes, length over sheets	12 feet 10 inches	
Tubes, diameter outside	2 inches	
Heating surface, tubes	1586 square feet	
Heating surface, firebox	145.8 square feet	

Heating surface, total	1731.8 square feet
Weight on drivers, working order	109,300 pounds
Weight on truck, "	13,500 pounds
Weight, total of engine, "	122,800 pounds
Weight of tender, loaded	86,000 pounds
Weight of tender, empty	35,000 pounds
Steam pressure	160 pounds
Rating	25.8 per cent.

Fall Brook second # 9, one of a pair delivered by Schenectady in 1897. (Schen.Hist.Ctr.)
(H.L.Vail coll.)

(NYC&HR) BOSTON & ALBANY. Leased 7/1900 to the NYC&HR. All B&A power was promptly
renumbered into the new NYC&HR series, as follows:

84-101	0-4-0	Class A-30		2030-2031	4-6-0	Class F-31
386-400	0-6-0	"	B-30,31,32	2158-2159	4-6-0	"	F-30
715-760	4-4-0	"	C-30,31	2506-2569	2-8-0	"	G-30,31
1139-1225	4-4-0	"	C-32 to 39	2632-2642	4-8-0	"	H-30

In 1912, all B&A locomotives were renumbered again into a new system entirely separate
from the NYC&HR. Details are shown in the all-time B&A roster beginning on page 249.

GRAND CENTRAL STATION. Locomotives lettered GRAND CENTRAL DEPOT until c. 1887.

```
 1 (ex-N.Y.& Har.26)   15x22-48      0-4-0 (Hinkley       9/71) So 6/87 Ft.Orange Paper Co.
 2 (    "    "  27)     "    "         "    "              "     So 7/87 Colwell & Canning
 3 ('87) 7              "    "         "    "              /73   So 6/92 Empire Cement Co.
 4                      "    "         "    "              "     So 5/93 Manhattan Equip.Co.
 5                     15x22-50        "    Schen. 1597  7/82   So 7/93 S.A.Rorke
 6                     16x22-50        "      "     1921  6/84   So 11/93 Empire Cement Co.
"1 ('96) 83 ('05) 51        A-3        "    Rome    246  3/87   So 1/95 DAV&P. Sc 12/08
"2                          "          "      "     247   "     So'94 Fort Orange Paper Co.
"3                          "          "      "     248         So 5/95 S.A.Rorke
 8 ('05) 425           Bx   0-6-0 Schen. 2708  8/88   RB 6/09 Dummy 14
 9  "    426           "     "    Rome    482  5/89   Sc 11/09
10  "    427           B-11  "    Schen. 2991 12/89   RB 12/08 Dummy 13
11  "    428           "     "      "    3460  3/91   RB 3/13 Dummy 11
12  "    429           "     "      "    3572 10/91   SS 4/08 J.Joseph & Sons
13     (430)           "     "      "    3804  4/92   RB 12/07 Dummy 12
"7                     Ba    "      "    3972 11/92   Re 10/07 B&A 423-439-97.
14 ('95) 3 ('07) 430 ('08) 224 "   "    3973   "     Sc 6/12
"5 ('08) 225           "     "      "    4162  5/93   Sc 10/13
"2                     "     "      "    4201  1/94   Re 10/07 B&A 422-438-98.
"4 ('08) 226           "     "      "    4202   "     Sc 8/12
"6  "    227           "     "      "    4203  2/94   So 12/13 Fitzhugh-Luther
"1 ('02) 266 ('05) 204 B-4a  "      "    4440  4/96   Sc 12/15
14 ('08) 371           B-2   "      "    5570  5/00   So 12/22 Gen.Equip.Co.
15  "    372           "     "      "    6069  5/01   So 5/23 Adir.Lt.& Power Co.
16  "    373           "     "    Alco-S 28407 4/03   So 12/23 Gen.Equip.Co.
17  "    374           "     "      "    28408   "    So 12/22  "    "    "
18  "    375           "     "      "    28409   "    So 12/22 G.E.Co., Jeff.SW
"1       (ex-NYC&HR 266) B   "    (Schen.3145 '90)'02 So 10/07 B&A 421-437-99
19 ('08) 197           B-10  "    Alco-S 29600 4/04   Sc 12/26
20  "    198           "     "      "    29601   "    Sc 11/26
21 ('15) 442  (Note a)  "    "      "    29602   "    Sc 5/33  (Super. 7/16)
22 ('08) 199           "     "      "    29603   "    Sc 9/28
23  "    596 ('12) 440  "    "      "    29604   "    So 8/26 P&E 440, Sc 6/34
24 ('07) 195           "     "      "    30989  6/05   Sc 9/29  (Super. 11/13)
25  "    196           "     "      "    30990   "    So'34 Corrigan McKinney Stl
26 ('15) 443  (Note a)  "    "      "    30991   "    Sc 6/36  (Super. 12/15)
27  "    444     "      "    "      "    30992   "    Sc 8/34  (Super. 7/16)
28 ('08) 599 ('12) 441  "    "      "    30993   "    Sc 5/33  (Super. 2/19)
```

    Note a: GCS 21,26,27 owned one-third by NYNH&H, purchased 9/15 by NYC.

LITTLE FALLS & DOLGEVILLE. Consolidated 1913 in NYC&HR.

```
1                     Fx  4-6-0 Schen. 3807  6/92 17x24-55-140-90000-15280  Sc 10/14
2                     Cx  4-4-0  "     4336  7/95 17x24-61-145-89000-14070  Sc 10/14
3 (ex-NYC&HR 1658)    Ec  2-6-0 (Sch.'92) Acq.9/10 19x26-57-160-120000-22400 So'16 P&S 101
4 (     "    1668)    "    "     "        Acq.3/12   "    "    "    "      "   Re'16 NYC 1668
```

Grand Central Depot heavy 0-4-0 #6, built Schenectady 1884.   (Alco Historic Photos)

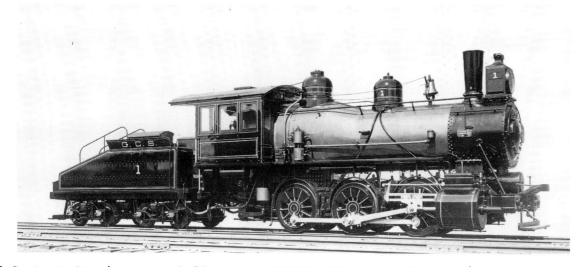

Grand Central Station second #1 became NYC&HR 266, class B-4a.   (H.L.Vail collection)

GCS 23 as built at Schenectady 1904. Class B-10.   (Alco Historic Photos)

NYC&HR CLASSIFICATION SYSTEM OF 1902:

A new system of classifying locomotives was adopted by the NYC&HR in February, 1902.
Prefix letters were assigned by wheel arrangement, with numerals and small letters
indicating mechanical differences. This system was followed for the entire N.Y.C. Lines
until the end of steam. Listed below are the prefix letters, with dates introduced:

A	0-4-0	1902		"J	2-6-2	1905 (LS&MS)		U	0-8-0	1913	
B	0-6-0	1902		"L	2-6-6T	1906 (Later D)		"L	4-8-2	1916	
C	4-4-0	1902		T	1-D-1	1906 (Electric)		Z	2-10-2	1919 (B&A)
D	2-4-4T	1902		S	2-D-2	1907 (Electric)		"A	2-8-4	1924 (B&A)
E	2-6-0	1902		R	B-B	1910 (Electric)		Q	B-B	1926 (Electric)
F	4-6-0	1902		N	2-6-6-2	1910 (Later NE)		"J	4-6-4	1927	
G	2-8-0	1902		"H	2-8-2	1912		"D	4-6-6T	1928 (B&A)
H	4-8-0	1902 (Later R,X)		P	0-8-8-0	1913 (Later NU)		"P	2-C-C-2	1929 (CUT Elec.)
I	4-4-2	1902		"R	4-8-0	1913 (Old H)		HS	4-8-4	1931 (Exper.)
J	2-6-6T	1902		X	4-8-0	1913 (Old R)		"D	2-6-6T	1940 (Old L)
K	4-6-2	1903		NB	0-6-6-0	1913		"S	4-8-4	1945	
L	1-D-1	1904 (Electric)		NE	2-6-6-2	1913 (Old N)		Dummy		1900 (Encl.Body)
M	0-10-0	1905		NU	0-8-8-0	1913 (Old P)		Pony		1900 (Inspec.)
				"T	B-B-B-B	1913 (Electric)		Shay		1923 (Geared)

The remainder of this NYC&HR roster lists locomotives by class designation.

CLASS A : 0-4-0 SWITCHER

NYC&HR CLASS A 0-4-0:   16x22-52-135-54900-12900. Old Class D.

52,56,59		N.Y.31st St. 1881	- See p.42	
60		N.Y.43rd St. 1885	- See p.50	
53,57,58,61-71,73,75-77		E.Buffalo 1882-86	- See pp.44,46.	
188 ('90) 27		E.Buffalo 1/88	So 7/99	
197 " 28 ('99) 72		" 8/87	So 1/06 H'y&Co.	
205 " 30 " 74		" 4/89	So 7/06 Hyman Const. Co., re Newark & Mar.3
498 " 34 " 78		" 6/88	So 11/04 Ginsburg	

NYC&HR CLASS A-1 0-4-0:   17x24-52-135-63600-15000. Old Class D-1.

124 ('90) 35 ('99) 79	Syracuse	6/88	So 3/08 Cont.I&S Co.
207 " 36 " 80	"	6/89	Sc 10/09
37 " 81	"	/92	Sc 7/11 (RB 5/98)

NYC&HR CLASS A-2 0-4-0:   15x22-52-135-52700-11400. Old Class D.

50, 51	Schen. '72,73	- See pp.36,37

GCS CLASS A-3 0-4-0:   16x24-52-135-60000-14100.

GCD 1-3 re 83, 51	Rome '87	- See p.92

NYC&HR CLASS A-4 0-4-0:   15x20-50-135-66700-10800. RB From 0-4-4T 249.

82 ('05) 52	Rebuilt 6/99	So 3/08 Cont.I&S Co.

RUTLAND CLASS A-5 0-4-0:   16x24-51-130-64800-13900. Built for A&StL.

ex-Rut.211-80 ('04) 50	Schen.'91	Re '15 Rutland 97. See P.64

LATER B&A CLASS A 2-8-4 berkshire: See B&A roster p. 304

Adirondack & St.Lawrence #1 became Rutland 211, class A-5. (Schen. History Center)

(H.L.Vail coll.)

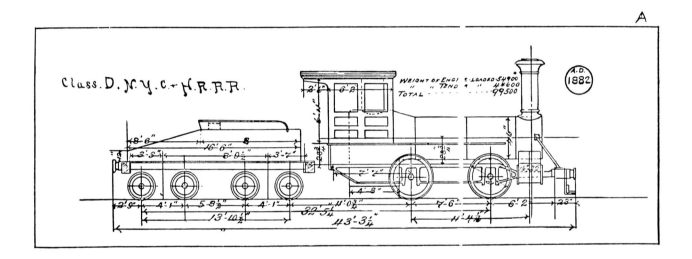

Class A-1

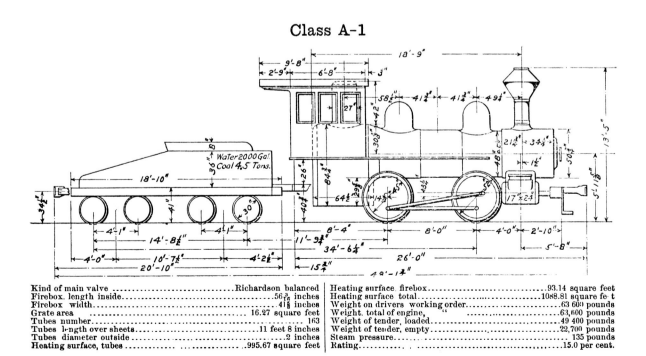

Kind of main valve ....Richardson balanced	Heating surface, firebox..............................93.14 square feet
Firebox. length inside...............................56¾ inches	Heating surface total..........................1088.81 square fe t
Firebox width..........................41⅝ inches	Weight on drivers working order................63 600 pounds
Grate area ....16.27 square feet	Weight, total of engine, " ....63,600 pounds
Tubes number............................163	Weight of tender, loaded..............................49 400 pounds
Tubes l-ngth over sheets......................11 feet 8 inches	Weight of tender, empty.............................22,700 pounds
Tubes diameter outside ....2 inches	Steam pressure................................... 135 pounds
Heating surface, tubes ....995.67 square feet	Rating..15.0 per cent.

CLASS B. 0-6-0 SWITCHER

NYC&HR CLASS B 0-6-0: 18x24-51-145-97000-19600. Old Class K. Some later 160 bp.

	Re'99	(Note a)						Re'99	(Note a)		
75	228	Schen.3124	5/90	Sc 11/11		110	269	Schen.3148	7/90	So 7/10 GaC&LCo.127
76	229	" 3125	"	Sc 5/10		111	270	" 3149	"	RB 10/05,12/18 Dummy 16
77	230	" 3126	"	Sc 10/11		112	271(f)	" 3150	6/90	So 9/21 M.D.T.
78	231	" 3127	"	So 7/10 BR&LCo.(b)		113	272	" 3151	"	Sc 8/11
79	232	" 3128	"	So 2/12 Warner Eq.Co.		114	273	" 3152	"	Sc 10/13
80	233	" 3129	"	Sc 5/12		115	274	" 3153	"	Sc 10/13
81	234	" 3155	7/90	So 3/13 Gen.Eq.Co.		116	275	" 3154	"	Sc 10/11
82	235	" 3156	"	Sc 7/11		117	276	" 3268	11/90	Sc 12/10
83	236	" 3157	"	Sc 5/10		118	277	" 3269	"	Sc 5/12
84	237	" 3158	"	Sc 8/11		119	278	" 3270	"	Sc 7/11
85	238	" 3159	"	Sc 10/11		120	279	" 3271	"	So 5/08 Hicks L&C Wks.
86	239	" 3160	"	Sc 10/11		121	280	" 3272	"	Sc 3/13
87	240	" 3161	8/90	Sc 12/10		122	281	" 3273	"	Sc 10/13
88	241	" 3162	"	RB 9/14 Dummy 10		123	282	" 3274	12/90	Sc 7/17
89	242	" 3163	"	So 9/10 M.D.T.		124	283	" 3275	"	So 4/14 Fitz.Luther (d)
90	249	" 3164	"	Sc 4/16		125	284(g)	" 3276	"	RB 11/07, Sc 11/23
91	250	" 3165	"	Sc 5/10		126	285	" 3277	"	Rt 9/15
92	251	" 3130	6/90	Sc 9/11		127	286	" 3278	"	Rt 9/15
93	252	" 3131	"	So 3/13 Gen.Eq.Co.		128	287	" 3279	"	Sc 4/12
94	253	" 3132	"	RB 12/07,Sc 2/11		129	288	" 3280	"	Sc 10/13
95	254	" 3133	"	Sc 8/14		130	289	" 3281	"	RB 10/13 Dummy 6
96	255	" 3134	"	RB 5/13 Dummy 5		131	290	" 3282	"	Sc 3/13
97	256	" 3135	"	So 6/13 Gen.Eq.Co.		132	291	" 3283	"	Sc 12/13
98	257	" 3136	"	Sc 11/10		133	292	" 3284	"	Sc 3/12
99	258	" 3137	"	Sc 7/13		134	293	" 3285	"	Sc 12/13
100	259(c)	" 3138	"	RB 8/05,Sc 7/32		135	294	" 3286	"	Sc 11/10
101	260	" 3139	"	Sc 10/13		136	295	" 3287	"	Sc 12/13
102	261	" 3140	"	Sc 12/10		137	296	" 3288	1/91	Sc 10/11
103	262	" 3141	"	Sc 8/12		138	297	" 3289	"	So 12/13 Fitz.Luther
104	263	" 3142	7/90	Sc 7/11		139	298	" 3290	"	Sc 5/10
105	264	" 3143	"	So 12/08 Atlan.Eq.Co.		140	299	" 3291	"	Sc 12/13
106	265	" 3144	"	So 12/13 Fitz.Luther		141	300	" 3292	"	Sc 11/11
107	266(e)	" 3145	"	Sc 1/15		142	301	" 3293	"	So 3/12 J.T.Gardner
108	267	" 3146	"	Sc 10/11		143	302	" 4127	4/93	So 12/08 Atlan.Eq.Co (h)
109	268	" 3147	"	RB 10/07,9/18 Dummy 15						

GCS CLASS Ba 0-6-0: 18x24-51-140-97000-18900. See p. 92.

NY&O CLASS Bx 0-6-0: 9+x14-26-120-24000-5400.

423	Porter	1880	Dr by'09

NYC&HR CLASS B-1 0-6-0: Compound 19&29x26-51-180-125000-29400. Old Class K-1.
NYC&HR CLASS B-1a 0-6-0: Converted to 19x26-51-175-126000-27380.

243 ('19)	70 ('22)	1921	Schen. 4973	1/99	Sc 10/24	
244			" 4974	"	So 8/16 Gen.Eq.Co. re Amer.Manganese Co.	
245			" 4889	9/98	So 7/14 Central Loco. & Car CO.	
246			" 4890	"	Sc 9/15	
247			" 4891	10/98	Sc 9/15	
248			" 4892	"	Sc 9/15	

Note a: NYC&HR diagram books list Schen.c/n 3130-3165 in order for #81 - 116
Note b: 231 sold to Birm.R&L Co., re Blytheville, Leachville & Ark. Sou. 9.
Note c: 259 (re'19) 71 (re'22) 1922 as 0-6-0T, wt.112000.   Note d: 283 re F.T.Ley 7
Note e: 266 (re'02) GCS 1 ('07) B&A 421 ('10) 437 ('12) 99.   Note f: 271 (re 9/20) 72.
Note g: 284 RB 11/07 (re'19) 73 (re'22) 1923.   Note h: 302 re Gouver.& Osweg.1.

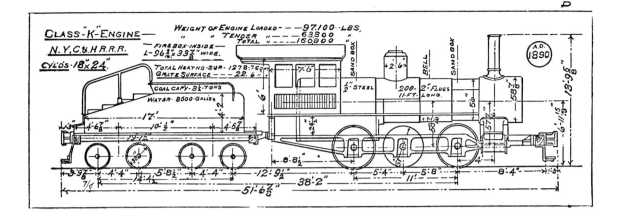

Classes B-1 and B-4

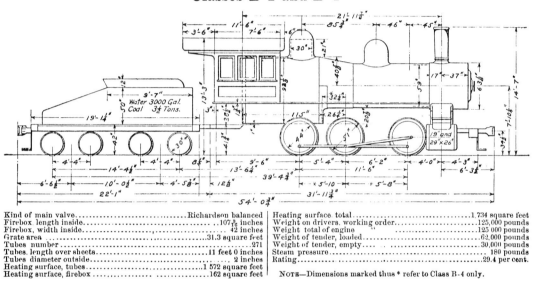

Kind of main valve...............................Richardson balanced	Heating surface, total..................................1,734 square feet
Firebox, length inside.................................107⅞ inches	Weight on drivers, working order..................125,000 pounds
Firebox, width inside...................................42 inches	Weight total of engine ....125,000 pounds
Grate area......................................31.3 square feet	Weight of tender, loaded............................62,000 pounds
Tubes number 271	Weight of tender, empty.... ....30,000 pounds
Tubes, length over sheets.......................11 feet 0 inches	Steam pressure......................................180 pounds
Tubes diameter outside................................2 inches	Rating...29.4 per cent.
Heating surface, tubes.........................1,572 square feet	
Heating surface, firebox ....162 square feet	NOTE—Dimensions marked thus * refer to Class B-4 only.

NYC&HR 228, first of the class B switchers, built by Schenectady in 1890, (NYC neg   )

CLASS B-2: 19x26-51-180-133000-29300. Old class K-2.

Orig.	Re'22	Re'23	Builder,c/n,Date	Disposition
311	78	1926	Schen.5508 3/00	RB 9/18, So 12/23*
312	79	1927	" 5509 "	So 12/23*
313	(80)		" 5510 "	So 9/22* GrBay&W 80
314			" 5511 "	So 10/19* NEMfgCo 5
315	81	1928	" 5512 "	So 12/23*
316	82	1929	" 5513 4/00	So 12/23*
317	83	1930	" 5514 "	So 12/23*
318	84	1931	" 5515 "	Sc 11/23
319	85	1932	" 5516 "	So 12/23*
320	(1954)		" 5517 "	So 6/23 M.D.T.
321	1955-6799		" 5518 "	Sc 7/37
322			" 5519 "	So 12/23*
323			" 5520 "	So 6/23 M.D.T.
324			" 5521 "	So'23 Asb.& Dan.19
325			" 5522 5/00	So 1/21* AB&A 18
326			" 5523 "	Sc 10/15
327			" 5524 "	So 12/22*
328			" 5525 "	So'23 Asb.& Dan.23
329			" 5526 "	So 12/23*
330			" 5527 "	So 12/23*
331			" 5528 "	So'22* Asb.& Dan.24
332			" 5529 "	So 12/22*
333			" 5530 "	So 1/19*
334			" 5531 "	So 12/22*
335			" 5532 "	So 9/16* MoOk&Gulf 3
336			" 5586 10/00	So 12/22*
337			" 5587 "	So 12/23*
338			" 5588 "	So 7/23 Asb.& Dan.21
339			" 5589 "	So 8/16*
340			" 5590 "	So 12/23*
357	(re'05)	376	Alco-S 25000 8/01	Sc 11/23
377			" 25001 "	So 4/20*
378			" 25002 9/01	So 12/22*
379			" 25003 "	So 12/22*
380			" 25004 "	So 11/23 PaWood&Iron
381			" 25005 "	Sc 4/33
382			" 25006 "	So 12/22*
383			" 25007 10/01	So 12/22*
384			" 25008 "	So 1/24 Asb.& Dan.22
385			" 25009 "	Sc 12/26
341	(B.C.Ext.)		Alco-C 25231 3/02	Sc 7/19
342	1956		" 25232 "	RB 10/18, Sc 6/33
343	(B.C.Ext.)		" 25233 "	So 12/22*
344	"		" 25234 "	So 11/20* AB&A 17
345	"		" 25235 "	So 1/21* AB&A 19
346	1957		" 25236 "	Sc 7/28
347	(B.C.Ext.)		" 25237 "	So 12/23*
348	1958		" 25238 "	RB 10/14, Sc 7/29
349			" 25239 "	So 12/23*
350	1959		" 25240 "	Sc 11/26
360	(re'05)	351	" 25241 "	Sc 12/15
366	"	352	" 25242 "	So 12/22*
368	"	353	" 25243 "	So 12/22*
375	"	354	" 25244 "	So 12/23*
376	"	355	" 25245 "	Sc 11/23
190	"	356	" 27139 2/03	So 12/23*
191	"	357	" 27140 3/03	So 12/22*
192	"	358	" 27141 "	So 12/22*
193	"	359	" 27142 2/03	So 12/23*
194	"	360	" 27143 "	So 12/23*
195	"	361	" 27144 "	Sc 10/23
196	"	362	" 27145 "	So 12/22*
197	"	363	" 27146 "	So 3/23 M.D.T.
198	"	364	" 27147 "	So 12/23*
351	"	365	" 27148 3/03	So 9/23 Asb.& Dan.20
354	"	366	" 27149 "	So 12/23*
356	"	367	" 27150 "	So 12/22*
358	"	368	" 27151 "	So 12/22*
365	"	369	" 27152 "	So 11/23 PaWood&Iron
367	"	370	" 27153 "	So 12/23* Lima-Def.

GCS 14-18 re 371-375 See page 92.

RUTLAND CLASS B-2a: 19x26-51-180-136000-28160.

Rut	Builder, c/n, Date	Disposition
445	Alco-C 43035 6/07	Re'14 Rutland 100
446	" 43036 "	" " " 101

RUTLAND CLASS B-2b: 19x26-51-180-136000-28160.

450	Alco-M 53286 /13	Re'14 Rutland 105

RUTLAND CLASS B-2c: 20x26-51-180-136000-31200,

451	Alco-S 54887 /14	Re'14 Rutland 106

CLASS B-3: 17x24-51-140-75000-16800. Old Class E.

NYC&HR	Re'90	Re'99		Disposition
247	56	217	W.Albany 9/85	So 8/07 Ginsburg
449	59	220	" 7/86	So 11/06 Ginsburg
237	55	216	" 5/87	So 3/08 Cont.I&S.
223	46	207	E.Buffalo 10/87	Sc 5/09

CLASS B-3a: 17x24-51-145-82300-17500. Old Class E-1.

215	45	206	E.Buffalo 9/89	So 3/08 Ginsburg
163	47	208	W.Albany 9/89	So'07 Moose Riv.L.
183	48	209	" 11/89	So 3/08 Cont.I&S.
190	49	210	" 12/88	Sc 11/08
204	50	211	" "	So 4/08 J.Joseph
208	51	212	" 6/89	So 5/07 Kilby
209	52	213	" 5/89	So 3/08 Cont.I&S.
218	53	214	" 6/89	So 3/08 Ginsburg
226	54	215	" 12/89	So'07 Fleisch.Yst.
255	57	218	" 1/89	Sc 3/07
262	58	219	" 4/89	So 3/08 Ginsburg
26	60	221	" 8/89	So 3/08 Cont.I&S.
27	61	222	" 9/89	So 11/06 Jones & G
93	62	223	" 3/90	So 3/08 Cont.I&S.
	63	224	" 5/90	So 3/08 Cont.I&S.
	64	225	" 6/90	So 3/08 Cont.I&S.
	65	226	" 9/90	So 5/07 Kilby L&M
	66	227	" 10/92	So 3/08 Cont.I&S.
	38	200-205	E.Buffalo 10/90	So 3/08 Ginsburg

CLASS B-4: Comp.19&29x24-51-180-125000-29400. Old K-1
Converted to B-4a: 19x24-51-180-122200-26000.
GCS 1 re 266 re 204 See page 92.

CLASS B-5: 16x22-59-145-74000-12200. Old Class E-2.
NYC&HR 201-205. Converted from 2-6-0? See page 46

CLASS B-6: 19x24-51-145-102000-21800. Old Class L.

146	303	Schen.3102 5/90	So 8/11*
147	304	" 3103 "	Sc 10/11
148	305	" 3104 "	So 8/11*
149	306	" 3105 "	Sc 6/11
150	307	" 3106 "	Sc 3/12
151	308	" 3107 "	So 6/13*
152	309 (b)	" 3108 "	Sc 12/23
153	310	" 3109 "	Sc 9/15

CLASS B-7: 18x20-45-140-79200-17900. Old WS Class D.
CLASS B-7a: 18x20-45-140-96000-17900. RB to 0-6-0T.
CLASS B-7b: 18x20-46-140-79200-17500.
351-370 re 195-202,76,1924 See Page 78

CLASS B-8: 18x24-51-140-90000-18900. Old Beech Creek
372-374 re 201-203. See page 84

CLASS B-9: 18x24-51-125-85000-16900. Old Beech Creek
371 See page 84

RUTLAND CLASS B-9: 18x24-51-180-101700-23900.

81	(re'04)	447	Alco-M 26419 6/02	Re'14 Rut.102
82	"	448	" 26420 "	" " 103
83	"	449	" 26421 "	" " 104

Note * Sold to General Equipment Co.

NYC&HR 326, class B-2, built at Alco Schenectady works in 1900. (Alco builders photo,HLV)

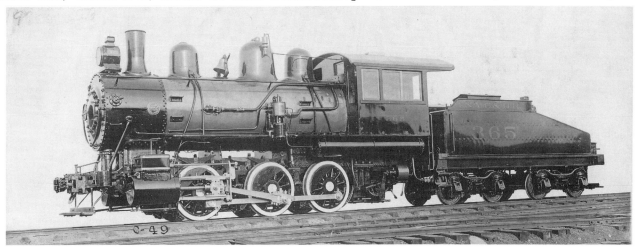

NYC&HR 365, class B-2, built at Alco Cooke works in 1903. (Alco builders photo; H.L.Vail)

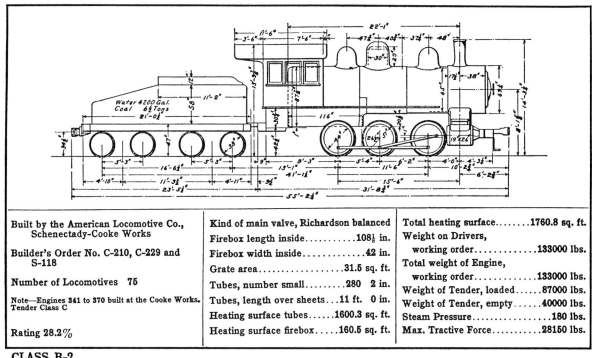

Built by the American Locomotive Co., Schenectady-Cooke Works	Kind of main valve, Richardson balanced	Total heating surface........1760.8 sq. ft.
Builder's Order No. C-210, C-229 and S-118	Firebox length inside..........108⅛ in.	Weight on Drivers, working order............133000 lbs.
	Firebox width inside............42 in.	Total weight of Engine, working order............133000 lbs.
Number of Locomotives 75	Grate area................31.5 sq. ft.	Weight of Tender, loaded......87000 lbs.
Note—Engines 341 to 370 built at the Cooke Works. Tender Class C	Tubes, number small........280 2 in.	Weight of Tender, empty......40000 lbs.
	Tubes, length over sheets...11 ft. 0 in.	Steam Pressure.................180 lbs.
Rating 28.2%	Heating surface tubes.....1600.3 sq. ft.	Max. Tractive Force..........28150 lbs.
	Heating surface firebox.....160.5 sq. ft.	

CLASS B-2

NYC&HR 382, class B-2, built at Alco Schenectady works in 1901.   (Chaney collection)

Class B-3

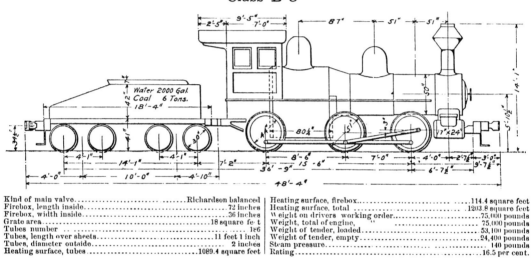

Kind of main valve..........................Richardson balanced	Heating surface, firebox............................114.4 square feet
Firebox, length inside..................................72 inches	Heating surface, total............................1203.8 square feet
Firebox, width inside..................................36 inches	Weight on drivers working order....................75,000 pounds
Grate area..18 square feet	Weight, total of engine, " ....75,000 pounds
Tubes number 186	Weight of tender, loaded...........................53,100 pounds
Tubes, length over sheets.......................11 feet 1 inch	Weight of tender, empty............................24,400 pounds
Tubes, diameter outside..................................2 inches	Steam pressure...140 pounds
Heating surface, tubes..........................1089.4 square feet	Rating...16.5 per cent.

NYC&HR 225, class B-3a, one of 17 built at West Albany in the late 1880's.(Vollrath col.)

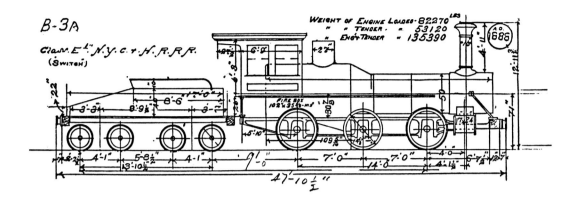

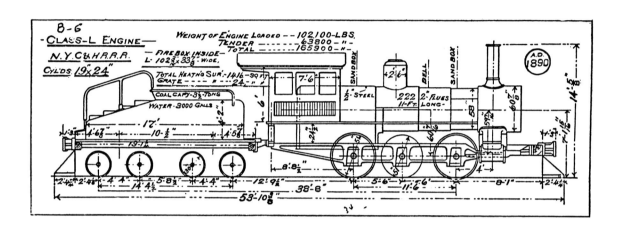

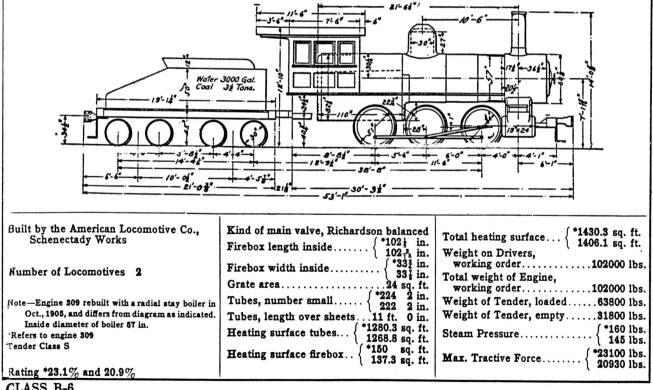

Built by the American Locomotive Co., Schenectady Works	Kind of main valve, Richardson balanced	Total heating surface...	*1430.3 sq. ft. / 1406.1 sq. ft.

Built by the American Locomotive Co., Schenectady Works

Number of Locomotives 2

Note—Engine 309 rebuilt with a radial stay boiler in Oct., 1905, and differs from diagram as indicated. Inside diameter of boiler 57 in.
*Refers to engine 309
†Tender Class S

Rating *23.1% and 20.9%

Kind of main valve, Richardson balanced
Firebox length inside....... { *102½ in. / 102¾ in.
Firebox width inside......... { *33¾ in. / 33⅞ in.
Grate area................... 24 sq. ft.
Tubes, number small...... { *224 2 in. / 222 2 in.
Tubes, length over sheets...11 ft. 0 in.
Heating surface tubes... { *1280.3 sq. ft. / 1268.8 sq. ft.
Heating surface firebox.. { *150 sq. ft. / 137.3 sq. ft.

Total heating surface... { *1430.3 sq. ft. / 1406.1 sq. ft.
Weight on Drivers, working order.............102000 lbs.
Total weight of Engine, working order.............102000 lbs.
Weight of Tender, loaded......63800 lbs.
Weight of Tender, empty......31800 lbs.
Steam Pressure.............. { *160 lbs. / 145 lbs.
Max. Tractive Force........ { *23100 lbs. / 20930 lbs.

CLASS B-6

NYC LINES CLASSES B-10 and B-11 0-6-0: 21x28-57-180-152000 to 171000-33140. Later 58"DD, 32570TF.

These were standard switchers for most of the NYC Lines for many years. Listed below are classes assigned to component lines. As classes B-10 thru B-10u were superheated they were reclassed B-9's, then B-10's again.

B-10	(B-9a)	NYC&HR and GCS	B-10m		B&A	B-11c	MC
B-10a		MC (Ind.Har.)	B-10n		MC and CS	B-11d	CCC&StL
B-10b		CCC&StL (re B-10y,z)	B-10o	(B-9o)	NYC&HR	B-11e	MC
B-10b	(B-9b)	NYC&HR	B-10p		IHB	B-11f	Det.Term.
B-10c		LS&MS (CI&S)	B-10q		CCC&StL	B-11g	MC
B-10d	(B-9d)	NYC&HR	B-10r		MC	B-11h	CCC&StL
B-10e		LS&MS	B-10s		B&A	B-11j	IHB
B-10f		MC	B-10t		CCC&StL	B-11k	NYC&HR
B-10g		CCC&StL	B-10u	(B-9u)	NYC&HR	B-11l	B&A
B-10h	(B-9h)	NYC&HR	B-10v		NYC&HR	B-11m	Det.Term.
B-10i		LS&MS and B&A	B-10w,x		MC and CS	B-11n	CCC&StL
B-10j	(B-9j)	NYC&HR	B-10y,z		CCC&StL (ex B-10b)	B-11o	B&A
B-10k		LS&MS	B-11a		MC	B-11p	CCC&StL
B-10l	(B-9l)	NYC&HR	B-11b		CS	B-11q	L&JB&RR

NYC&HR CLASS B-10: 21x28-57-180-152500-33140 (B-9a)

Orig.	Builder,	c/n,	Date	Super.	Scrap.
150	Alco-S	27830	11/03	6/14	11/32
151	"	27831	"	7/16	4/32
152	"	27832	"	7/23	4/33
153	"	27833	"	5/14	12/32
154	"	27834	"	9/13	8/27
155	"	27835	"	no	7/27
156	"	27836	"	no	12/25
157	"	27837	"	7/23	6/35
158	"	27838	"	no	8/26
159	"	27839	"	no	11/26
160	"	27840	"	7/17	6/33
161	"	27841	"	8/23	6/33
162	"	27842	"	4/15	6/29
163	"	27843	"	4/14	6/29
164	"	27844	"	no	6/27
165	"	27845	"	8/13	5/33
166	"	27846	"	8/13	6/33
167	"	27847	"	11/14	11/26
168	"	27848	"	6/17	9/28
169	"	27849	"	6/16	11/32
125	"	29605	10/04	9/17	7/33
126	"	29606	"	6/17	8/29
127	"	29607	"	no	9/26
128	"	29608	"	no	8/26
129	"	29609	"	4/15	10/32
130	"	29610	"	/17	9/28
131	"	29611	"	9/22	9/29
132	"	29612	"	5/14	4/32
133	"	29613	"	no	12/26
134	"	29614	"	7/16	11/32
135	"	29615	"	no	8/27
136	"	29616	"	12/17	12/32
137	"	29617	"	9/13	6/33
138	"	29618	"	9/14	12/26
139	"	29619	"	6/19	4/32
140	"	29620	"	8/13	6/32
141	"	29621	"	1/13	8/29
142	"	29622	"	4/14	4/32
143	"	29623	"	4/15	4/32
144	"	29624	"	4/14	12/32
145	"	29625	"	3/16	8/29
146	"	29626	"	7/15	8/29
147	"	29627	"	10/16	6/33
148	"	29628	"	8/13	5/33
149	"	29629	"	10/16	4/32

GCS 19-28 re 195-199,440-444,596,599 - See p.92

Note a: 446 re 8/26 P&E.   Note b: to Asb.& Dan.26
Note c: 633 RB 9/31 0-6-0T, re'36 6766, re'40 X6766.

NYC&HR CLASS B-10b: 21x28-57-180-154000-33140 (B-9b)

Orig.	Re'22		Builder,	c/n,	Date	Super.	Scrap.
100	1933		Alco-S	37944	10/05	'18	5/33
101	1934		"	37945	"	'19	6/33
102	1935		"	37946	"	'20	10/32
103	1936		"	37947	"	no	9/28
104	1937		"	37948	"	9/14	6/32
105	1938		"	37949	"	'18	6/33
106	1939		"	37950	"	no	3/32
107	1940		"	37951	"	'19	8/36
108	1941		"	37952	"	by'14	11/34
109	('19)	445	"	37953	"	9/16	7/32
110	"	446 (a)	"	37954	"	no	4/34
111	1942		"	37955	"	'24	4/34
112	1943		"	37956	"	no	4/32
113	1944		"	37957	"	'18	6/33
114	1945		"	37958	"	no	9/28
115	1946		"	37959	"	no	9/28
116	1947		"	37960	"	no	11/32
117	1948		"	37961	"	7/14	6/33
118	1949		"	37962	"	'18	6/33
119	1950		"	37963	"	by'14	4/32
120	1951		"	37964	"	'17	6/32
121	1952		"	37965	"	8/13	5/32
122	1953		"	37966	"	11/14	5/32
123			"	37967	"	11/18	5/33
124			"	37968	"	8/18	9/28
170			Alco-C	30159	12/05	5/15	4/33
171			"	30160	"	8/17	11/32
172			"	30161	"	7/14	11/30
173			"	30162	"	9/15	5/33
174			"	30163	"	2/18	7/33
175			"	30164	"	no	12/16
176			"	30165	"	12/20	11/30
177	('36)	6753	"	30166	"	3/14	3/39
178			"	30167	"	1/15	9/28
179			"	30168	1/06	11/13	5/33
180			"	30169	"	8/13	3/32
181			"	30170	"	8/13	6/35
182			"	30171	"	2/14	6/33
183	('26)	447	"	30172	"	5/15	1/36 Rt
184	"	448	"	30173	"	10/14	12/34 Rt
185	"	449	"	30174	2/06	2/14	8/29
186	"	630	"	30175	"	4/15	4/34
187	"	631	"	30176	"	10/17	7/35
188	"	632	"	30177	"	8/17	6/32
189	"	633	"	30178	"	4/16	4/52 (c)
190	"	634	"	30179	"	5/17	7/32
191	('36)	6754	"	30180	"	8/13	6/37 (b)
192			"	30181	"	8/18	8/34
193			"	30182	"	1/18	6/33
194			"	30183	"	5/16	5/33

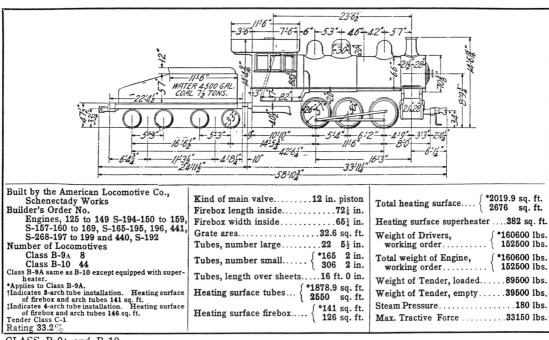

Built by the American Locomotive Co.,
Schenectady Works
Builder's Order No.
Engines, 125 to 149 S-194-150 to 159,
S-157-160 to 169, S-165-195, 196, 441,
S-268-197 to 199 and 440, S-192
Number of Locomotives
Class B-9A   8
Class B-10   44
Class B-9A same as B-10 except equipped with super-
heater.
*Applies to Class B-9A.
†Indicates 3-arch tube installation.   Heating surface
of firebox and arch tubes **141** sq. ft.
‡Indicates 4-arch tube installation.   Heating surface
of firebox and arch tubes **146** sq. ft.
Tender Class C-1
Rating 33.2%

Kind of main valve	12 in. piston
Firebox length inside	72⅛ in.
Firebox width inside	65¼ in.
Grate area	32.6 sq. ft.
Tubes, number large	22 5½ in.
Tubes, number small	{ *165 2 in. 306 2 in.
Tubes, length over sheets	16 ft. 0 in.
Heating surface tubes	{ *1878.9 sq. ft. 2550 sq. ft.
Heating surface firebox	{ *141 sq. ft. 126 sq. ft.

Total heating surface	{ *2019.9 sq. ft. 2676 sq. ft.
Heating surface superheater	382 sq. ft.
Weight of Drivers, working order	{ *160600 lbs. 152500 lbs.
Total weight of Engine, working order	{ *160600 lbs. 152500 lbs.
Weight of Tender, loaded	89500 lbs.
Weight of Tender, empty	39500 lbs.
Steam Pressure	180 lbs.
Max. Tractive Force	33150 lbs.

CLASS B-9A and B-10

NYC&HR 121, class B-10, the switcher that served the entire system.   (C.B.Chaney)

NYC&HR CLASS B-10d: 21x28-57-180-158000-33140 (B-9d)

Orig.	Re'36	Builder,	c/n,	Date	Super.	Scrap.	
450		Alco-H	41033	12/06		4/29	
451		"	41034	"		12/25	
452	6757	"	41035	"	/25	6/37	Note a
453		"	41036	"	12/23	6/33	
454		"	41037	"	9/18	4/32	
455		"	41038	"	1/25	4/34	
456	(6758)	"	41039	"	2/23	6/36	
457		"	41040	"		11/27	
458		"	41041	"	10/25	9/35	
459		"	41042	1/07		8/26	
460		"	41043		8/23	7/32	
461		"	41044		5/22	6/33	
462		"	41045			8/27	
463		"	41046		8/14	6/33	
464		"	41047		10/13	5/33	
465	(6759)	"	41048		2/20	7/36	
466	(6760)	"	41049		5/22	1/36	
467		"	41050		12/13	11/32	
468		"	41051			8/26	
469		"	41052		3/17	10/30	
470		"	41053		4/19	5/27	M.D.T.
471		"	41054		12/18	11/32	
472		"	41055	2/07	9/19	6/35	
473	(6761)	"	41056	"	4/20	6/36	
474		"	41057	"	10/17	4/34	

NYC&HR CLASS B-10h: 21x28-57-180-158000-33140 (B-9h)

Orig.	Re'36	Builder,	c/n,	Date	Super.	Scrap.
475		Alco-J	42572	3/07	6/15	6/32
476		"	42573	"	5/18	10/34
477		"	42574	"	8/15	9/32
478		"	42575	"	11/17	4/34
479		"	42576	"	6/23	9/35

NYC&HR CLASS B-10j: 21x28-57-180-158000-33140 (B-9j)

Orig.	Re'36	Builder,	c/n,	Date	Super.	Scrap.
480		Alco-H	43776	9/07	6/15	8/28
481		"	43777	"	5/15	12/30
482		"	43778	"	3/15	6/33
483		"	43779	"	5/16	11/32
484		"	43780	"	7/14	8/35
485		"	43781	"	3/18	8/27
486		"	43782	"		8/26
487		"	43783	"	5/17	8/35
488	6762	"	43784	"	/24	1/39
489		"	43785	"	5/22	9/35
490		"	43786	10/07	7/16	12/30
491		"	43787	"	7/19	6/35
492		"	43788	"	2/18	9/35
493		"	43789	"	11/16	9/35
494		"	43790	"	6/23	6/35
495	6763	"	43791	"	11/24	12/47
496	6764	"	43792	"	5/15	11/40
497		"	43793	"	6/15	7/35
498	(6765)	"	43794	"	9/13	5/36
499		"	43795	"	7/15	11/32

Note a: 6757 re Asbestos & Danville 26 or 27.
Note b: 6610 So 1/37 Despatch Shops 6.
Note c: 516 So 8/35 Despatch Shops, Inc.
Note d: 532 So 11/27 Procter & Gamble.
Note e: Second 538,539 delivered as 542,543.
Note f: 6640 So 3/45 Despatch Shops 6.
Note g: 6642 So 5/49 Despatch Corp.
Note h: 6644 So 4/52 Delray Connecting RR
Note i: 6650 So 5/48 M.D.T.

NYC&HR CLASS B-10L: 21x28-57-180-163000-33140 (B-9L)

Orig.	Re'36	Builder,	c/n,	Date	Super.	Scrap.	
500	6600	Alco-B	45477	9/08	/21	11/40	
501	6601	"	45478	"	3/23	11/47	
502	6602	"	45479	"	5/18	12/47	
503	6603	"	45480	"	7/16	11/47	
504		"	45481	"	4/19	8/28	
505	6605	"	45482	"	3/23	12/47	
506		"	45483	"	12/17	9/35	
507	6607	"	45484	"	4/16	12/47	
508		"	45485	"	10/16	3/32	
509	6609	"	45486	"	5/17	10/47	
510	6610	"	45487	"	/18	1/37	Note b
511	6611	"	45488	"	12/16	10/47	
512		"	45489	"	7/19	8/35	
513	6613	"	45490	"	8/19	10/47	
514		"	45491	"	10/14	8/28	
515	6615	"	45492	"	9/15	11/47	
516		"	45493	"	6/15	8/35	Note c
517	6617	"	45494	"	4/17	11/47	
518	6618	"	45495	"	5/17	11/47	
519	6619	"	45496	"	6/16	11/47	
520	6620	"	45497	"	6/18	11/47	

NYC&HR CLASS B-10o: 21x28-57-180-163000-33140 (B-9o)

Orig.	Re'36	Builder,	c/n,	Date	Super.	Scrap.	
521		Alco-S	46979	3/10		7/27	
522	6622	"	46980	"	6/24	11/47	
523		"	46981	"		8/28	
524	6624	"	46982	"	9/24	11/47	
525	6625	"	46983	"	1/18	11/47	
526		"	46984	"		7/27	
527	6627	"	46985	"	1/18	1/48	
528	6628	"	46986	"	2/25	11/47	
529		"	46987	"		11/26	
530		"	46988	"		8/28	
531	6631	"	46989	"	/17	7/40	
532		"	46990	"		11/27	note d
533	6633	"	46991	"	6/18	11/47	
534	6634	"	46992	"	9/23	11/47	
535	6635	"	46993	"	12/21	11/47	
536		"	46994	"		8/26	
537	6637	"	46995	"	6/19	11/47	
538		"	46996	"		Re'10 B&A 418	
539		"	46997	"		Re'10 B&A 419	
540		"	46998	"		Re'10 B&A 420	
541		"	46999	"		Re'10 B&A 421	
538(e)6638		"	47000	"	/21	11/47	
539(e)6639		"	47001	"		9/28	

NYC&HR CLASS B-10u: 21x28-57-180-167000-33140 (B-10u)

Orig.	Re'36	Builder,	c/n,	Date	Super.	Scrap.	
540	6640	Alco-B	49429	3/11	/23	3/45	Note f
541	6641	"	49430	"	1/26	11/52	
542	6642	"	49431	"	6/20	5/49	Note g
543	6643	"	49432	"		7/48	
544	6644	"	49433	"	4/16	4/52	Note h
545	6645	"	49434	"	10/27	3/50	
546		"	49435	"		11/26	
547	6647	"	49436	"	4/23	2/49	
548		"	49437	"		11/26	
549	6649	"	49438	"		7/50	
550	6650	"	49439	"	5/23	5/48	Note i
551	6651	"	49440	"		5/50	
552	6652	"	49441	"	6/18	3/49	
553	6653	"	49442	"		9/50	
554	6654	"	49443	"	1/23	3/49	
555	6655	"	49444				
556	6656	"	49445	"		2/50	
557	6657	"	49446	"	2/28	2/49	
558	6658	"	49447	"		7/50	
559	6659	"	49448	"	/26	8/51	

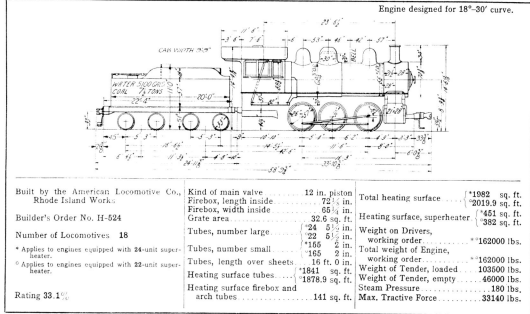

Engine designed for 18°–30' curve.

Built by the American Locomotive Co., Rhode Island Works	Kind of main valve .... 12 in. piston	Total heating surface .... { *1982 sq. ft. / °2019.9 sq. ft.
	Firebox, length inside........72½ in.	
Builder's Order No. H-524	Firebox, width inside .... 65¼ in.	Heating surface, superheater. { *451 sq. ft. / °382 sq. ft.
	Grate area................32.6 sq. ft.	
Number of Locomotives 18	Tubes, number large { *24 5½ in. / °22 5½ in.	Weight on Drivers, working order...........*°162000 lbs.
* Applies to engines equipped with 24-unit super-heater.	Tubes, number small { *155 2 in. / °165 2 in.	Total weight of Engine, working order...........*°162000 lbs.
° Applies to engines equipped with 22-unit super-heater.	Tubes, length over sheets .. 16 ft. 0 in.	Weight of Tender, loaded ... 103500 lbs.
	Heating surface tubes..... { *1841 sq. ft. / °1878.9 sq. ft.	Weight of Tender, empty...... 46000 lbs.
Rating 33.1%	Heating surface firebox and arch tubes................ 141 sq. ft.	Steam Pressure................180 lbs.
		Max. Tractive Force..........33140 lbs.

CLASS B-10ᴅ

(Printed Jan. 1, 1930)

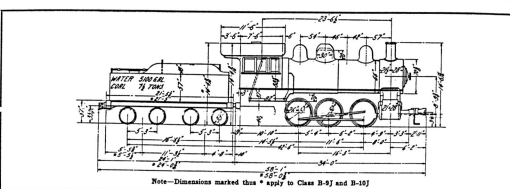

Note—Dimensions marked thus * apply to Class B-9J and B-10J

Built by the American Locomotive Co., Rhode Island Works	Kind of main valve..........12 in. piston	Total heating surface..... { *2019.9 sq. ft / 2692.7 sq. ft.
Builder's Order No. H-531	Firebox length inside............72½ in.	
Number of Locomotives	Firebox width inside...........65¼ in.	Heating surface superheater....382 sq. ft.
Class B-10J 19	Grate area..................32.6 sq. ft.	Weight on Drivers, working order........... { *...... lbs. / 158000 lbs.
Class B-9J 1	Tubes, number large........22 5½ in.	
Class B-9J same as B-10J except equipped with superheater.	Tubes, number small { *165 2 in. / 308 2 in.	Total weight of Engine, working order........... { *...... lbs. / 158000 lbs.
*Applies to Class B-9J.	Tubes, length over sheets....16 ft. 0 in.	Weight of Tender, loaded.....102400 lbs.
†Indicates 3-arch tube installation. Heating surface of firebox and arch tubes 141 sq. ft.	Heating surface tubes .. { *1878.9 sq. ft. / 2566.7 sq. ft.	Weight of Tender, empty......46000 lbs
‡Indicates 4-arch tube installation. Heating surface of firebox and arch tubes 146 sq. ft.		Steam Pressure.................180 lbs
Tender Class C-3A	Heating surface firebox.... { *141 sq. ft. / 126 sq. ft.	Max. Tractive Force..........33150 lbs.
Rating 33.2%		

CLASS B-9ᴊ and B-10ᴊ

Engine designed for 18°–30' curve.

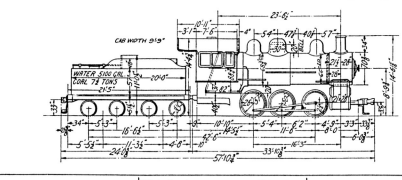

Built by the American Locomotive Co., Brooks Works	Kind of main valve.........12 in. piston	Total heating surface..... { *1982 sq. ft. / 2674.4 sq. ft.
	Firebox length inside............72½ in.	
Builder's Order No. B-1271	Firebox width inside...........65¼ in.	Heating surface, superheater...451 sq. ft.
	Grate area.................32.6 sq. ft.	Weight on Drivers, working order........... { *171000 lbs. / 167000 lbs.
Number of Locomotives 18	Tubes, number large....... *24 5½ in.	
	Tubes, number small...... { *155 2 in. / 304 2 in.	Total weight of Engine, working order........... { *171000 lbs. / 167000 lbs.
* Applies to engines equipped with 24-unit super-heater.	Tubes, length over sheets.....16 ft. 0 in.	Weight of Tender, loaded.....105000 lbs.
	Heating surface tubes.... { *1841 sq. ft. / 2533.4 sq. ft.	Weight of Tender, empty......47500 lbs.
	Heating surface firebox and arch tubes............141 sq. ft.	Steam Pressure.................180 lbs.
Rating 33.1%		Max. Tractive Force.........33140 lbs.

CLASS B-10ᴜ

(Printed July 1, 1927)

NYC&HR CLASS B-10v: 21x28-57-180-170000-33140

Orig.	Re'36	Builder, c/n, Date		Rt	Sc/SS
560	6660	Alco-P	51970 10/12	1/49	3/49
561	6661	"	51971 "	3/53	5/53
562	6662	"	51972 "	1/50	2/50
563	6663	"	51973 "	2/49	4/49
564	6664	"	51974 "	4/51	7/51
565	6665	"	51975 "	3/50	6/50
566	6666	"	51976 "	3/52	4/52
567	6667	"	51977 "	1/49	2/49
568	6668	"	51978 "	6/51	7/51
569	6669	"	51979 "	7/52	9/52
570	6670	"	51980 "	3/52	4/52
571	6671	"	51981 "	5/50	7/50
572	6672	"	51982 "	8/51	10/51
573	6673	"	51983 "	10/50	11/50
574	6674	"	51984 "	10/50	12/50
575	6675	"	51985 "	1/49	4/49
576	6676	"	51986 "	1/49	2/49
577	6677	"	51987 "	3/50	6/50
578	6678	"	51988 "	2/49	3/49
579	6679	"	51989 "	1/49	2/49
580	6680	"	51990 11/12	3/52	5/52
581	6681	"	51991 "	12/52	2/53
582	6682	"	51992 "	6/49	10/49
583	6683	"	51993 "	3/50	5/50
584	6684	"	51994 "	1/53	2/53
585	6685	"	51995 "	3/50	5/50
586	6686	"	51996 "	3/53	6/53
587	6687	"	51997 "	12/43	So M.D.T.
588	6688	"	51998 "	10/49	12/49
589	6689	"	51999 "	1/49	3/49
590	6690	"	52079 "	2/52	3/52
591	6691	"	52080 "	2/49	4/49
592	6692	"	52081 "	1/49	2/49
593	6693	"	52082 "	4/49	7/49
594	6694	"	52083 "	2/53	5/53
595	6695	"	52084 "	6/51	6/51

NYC&HR CLASS B-10v - Continued

Orig.	Re'36	Builder, c/n, Date		Rt	Sc/SS
596	6696	Alco-P	52085 11/12	4/50	8/50
597	6697	"	52086 "	10/49	12/49
598	6698	"	52087 "	3/49	10/49
599	6699	"	52088 "	10/49	11/49
600	6700	"	52089 "	1/50	5/50
601	6701	"	52090 "	3/52	4/52
602	6702	"	52091 "	3/50	6/50
603	6703	"	52092 "	12/51	3/52
604	6704	"	52093 12/12	3/51	4/51
605	6705	"	52094 "	3/50	4/50
606	6706	"	52095 "	6/51	7/51
607	6707	"	52096 "	3/52	5/52
608	6708	"	52097 "	1/50	4/50
609	6709	"	52098 "	6/51	6/51

NYC&HR CLASS B-11k: 21x28-57-180-171000-33140

Orig.	Re'36	Builder, c/n, Date		Rt	Sc/SS
610		Alco-S	54064 12/13	10/18	So LE&W 4275
611	6711	"	54065 "	6/51	6/51
612		"	54066 "	5/19	So LE&W 4276
613	6713	"	54067 "	6/51	6/51
614	6714	"	54068 "	10/50	12/50
615	6715	"	54069 "	6/51	6/51
616	6716	"	54070 "	6/51	7/51
617	6717	"	54071 "	4/57	
618	6718	"	54072 "	1/53	2/53
619	6719	"	54073 "	6/51	6/51
620	6720	"	54074 "	11/52	1/53
621	6721	"	54075 "	9/53	So (Note a)
622	6722	"	54076 "	10/50	11/50
623	6723	"	54077 "	11/51	11/51
624	6724	"	54078 "	3/52	4/52
625	6725	"	54079 "	11/51	11/51
626	6726	"	54080 "	6/51	6/51
627	6727	"	54081 "	10/50	11/50
628		"	54082 "	10/18	So LE&W 4277
629	6729	"	54083 "	7/53	/54

GCS CLASS B-11: 17x24-52-140-86700-16500. Coke Burners.
   GCS 8-13 re 425-430. (425 & 426 Class Bx. Weight 84200, 78400) See P.92.

NYC&HR "DUMMY" O-4-OT: 15x22-46-135-74000-12900. Enclosed Carbody. Numbered in Separate Series.
   Hudson River 1-8. See p.37.

1		NY 31st St.	RB 1882	Sc 10/07	
9		Schen.	1482 1/82	So 4/08	Ginsburg
10		"	1485 "	So 4/08	Ginsburg
11 re 4		"	2480 2/88	Sc 11/08	
12 re 8		"	2481 "	Sc 7/09	
6		"	2954 2/90	Sc 9/13	
5		"	3265 11/90	Sc 9/13	
7		"	3266 "	Sc 10/10	
3		"	3267 "	Sc 10/07	

NYC&HR "DUMMY" O-6-OT: Various Specs. Enclosed Carbody. Separate Number Series Until 1923.

10		RB W.Alby.	2/07	from B-7b 201	17x20-46-160-108500-17100	Sc /14	
12	1906	" "	12/07	" B-11 GCS 13	18x24-51-145-138200-18750	Rt 4/32	
13	1907	" "	12/08	" B-11a 427	17x24-51-150-118500-17340	Rt 7/24	
14	1908	" "	6/09	" Bx 425	17x24-51-150-115000-17340	Rt 7/24	
9	1903	" "	2/11	" B-8 203	18x24-51-140-127300-18150	Rt 2/24	
2		" "	11/12	" B-7a 362 (b)	17x20-45-140-118000-16000	So 12/22	Note b
11	1905	" "	3/13	" B-11 428 (c)	17x24-51-150-122400-17340	Rt 7/24	
5	1901	" "	5/13	" B 255	17x24-51-160-135000-18500	Rt 7/24	
6	1902	" "	10/13	" B 289	17x24-51-160-135000-18500	Rt 4/32	
10	1904	" "	9/14	" B 241	18x24-51-160-133000-20750	Rt 12/32	
15	1909	" "	9/18	" B 268	18x24-51-160-136800-20750	Rt 5/32	
16	1910	" "	12/18	" B 270	18x24-51-160-129740-20750	Rt 5/32	

   Note a: 6721 to Central Illinois Public Service Co. 7, Huttonville, Ill.
   Note b: 2 reno. 1/05 from 362. Sold to Penn. Wood & Iron Co.   Note c: 11 reno. 10/07 fr.428.

NYC 6674, class B-10v, in storage at Wesleyville, Pa.　　(P.W.Prescott collection)

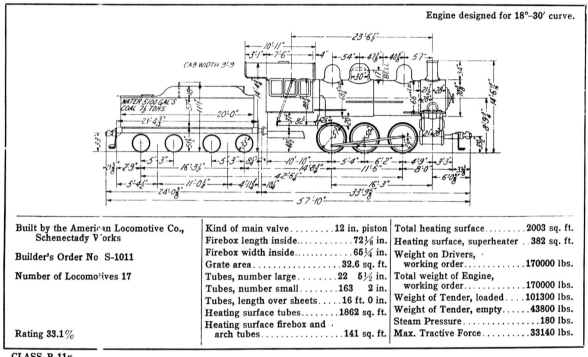

Engine designed for 18°–30' curve.

Built by the American Locomotive Co., Schenectady Works	Kind of main valve........12 in. piston	Total heating surface........2003 sq. ft.
Builder's Order No S-1011	Firebox length inside............72⅛ in.	Heating surface, superheater ..382 sq. ft.
Number of Locomotives 17	Firebox width inside............65¼ in.	Weight on Drivers, working order............170000 lbs.
	Grate area.................32.6 sq. ft.	
	Tubes, number large........22　5½ in.	Total weight of Engine, working order............170000 lbs.
	Tubes, number small.......163　2 in.	
	Tubes, length over sheets.....16 ft. 0 in.	Weight of Tender, loaded....101300 lbs.
	Heating surface tubes........1862 sq. ft.	Weight of Tender, empty......43800 lbs.
	Heating surface firebox and arch tubes.................141 sq. ft.	Steam Pressure................180 lbs.
Rating 33.1%		Max. Tractive Force.........33140 lbs.

CLASS B-11ᴋ

NYC&HR 9, four wheel Dummy used on New York City's west side streets.　(H.L.Vail coll.)

CLASS C. 4-4-0 EIGHT WHEEL

NYC&HR CLASS C 4-4-0: 19x24-78-180-120000-20980. Some RB to 125000 weight. Old Class I.

Orig.	Re'92	Re'13	Builder	c/n	Date	Rebuilt	Scr.	Orig.	Re'13	Builder	c/n	Date	Rebuilt	Scr.
860	913	1027	Schen.	3055	3/90	'01,'18	8/35	882	1008	Schen.	3238	11/90	7/01	10/15
861	914	1028	"	3056	"	12/03	4/16	883	1009	"	3239	"	8/05	12/20
862	915	1029	"	3057	"	12/01	4/16	884	1010	"	3240	"	12/06	8/34
863	916	1030	"	3058	"	1/01	2/17	885	1011	"	3241	"	6/05	12/25
864	917	1031	"	3059	"	10/06	4/16	886	1012	"	3242	12/90	5/05	7/33
865	918	1032	"	3060	"	3/05	12/24	887	1013(d)	"	3243	"	4/07	9/37
866	919	1033	"	3061	4/90	8/05	12/16	888	1014	"	3244	"	6/03	9/23
867	920	1034	"	3062	"	6/07	8/34	889	1015	"	3245	"	11/05	8/35
868	921	1035	"	3063	"	7/04	10/26	890	1016	"	3246	"	6/06	6/23
869	922	1036	"	3064	"	8/05	8/34	891	1017	"	3247	"	5/05	10/34
870	944	1038(b)	"	3065	"	'98,'05	6/37	892	1018	"	3248	"	6/07	12/25
873		1000	Schen.	3229	10/90	12/05	12/25	899	1019	Schen.	3589	11/91	10/03	6/33
874			"	3230	"	4/05	Expl.1/12	900	1020	"	3590	"	5/01	4/32
875		1001	"	3231	"	5/05	12/24	901	1021	"	3591	"	'04,'17	3/32
876		1002	"	3232	"	2/05	7/23	902	1022	"	3592	"	11/07	12/25
877		1003(c)	"	3233	"	6/05	11/36	909	1023	Schen.	3647	3/92	6/06	6/34
878		1004(c)	"	3234	11/90	8/04	10/36	910	1024	"	3648	"	'06,'18	7/35
879		1005	"	3235	"	2/05	8/34	911	1025	"	3649	"	4/07	10/15
880		1006	"	3236	"	9/04	10/16	912	1026	"	3650	"	8/04	12/25
881		1007	"	3237	"	9/01	10/23	923	1037(d)	W.Albany		8/96	6/18	9/37

NYC&HR CLASS Ca 4-4-0: 19x24-78-180-120000-17400. Old class I.

Orig.	Re'13	Builder	c/n	Date	Rebuilt	Scr.	Orig.	Re'13	Builder	c/n	Date	Rebuilt	Scr.
871	1039	Schen.	3066	4/90	7/04	12/24	898	1046	Schen.	3588	11/91	6/04	12/20
872	1040	"	3228	10/90	9/94	9/17	903	1047	"	3641	2/92	1/02	8/23
893	1041	"	3583	11/91	5/05	7/23	904	1048	"	3642	"	11/01	3/16
894	1042	"	3584	"	6/03	8/23	905	1049	"	3643	"	6/05	4/15
895	1043	"	3585	"	5/05	8/23	906	1050	"	3644	"	'04,'17	12/25
896	1044	"	3586	"	4/01	11/15	907	1051	"	3645	"	3/06	6/16
897	1045	"	3587	"	7/05	8/23	908	1052	"	3646	"	2/07	11/24

NYC&HR CLASS Cb 4-4-0: 19x24-78-180-134500-17400. Old class I-1, re C-1. Later 144,500 wt.

Orig.	Re'13	Builder	c/n	Date	Rebuilt	Scr.	Orig.	Re'13	Builder	c/n	Date	Rebuilt	Scr.
924	1054	Schen.	4486	8/96	5/13	10/23	935	1060	Schen.	4650	1/98	1/15	So 10/23 (e)
925	1055	"	4487	"		10/15	936	1061	"	4651	"	5/13	12/25
926	1056	"	4488	"	5/14	8/35	937	1062	"	4652	"	12/14	So 10/23 (e)
927	1057	"	4489	"		5/16	938	1063	"	4653	"	1/14	11/23
928	1058	"	4490	"	9/12	12/24	870	1053	W.Albany		11/98		6/16
934	1059	"	4649	1/98		4/16	945	1064	(f) "		12/98	1/14	So 10/23 (e)

NYC&HR CLASS Cc 4-4-0: 19x24-70-180-131000-14500. Old class I-2, re C-2. Later 133,500 wt.

Orig.	Re'13	Builder	c/n	Date	Rebuilt	Scr.	Orig.	Re'13	Builder	c/n	Date	Rebuilt	Scr.
929	1065	Schen.	4491	8/96		12/16	939	1070	Schen.	4654	1/98	2/14	7/25
930	1066	"	4492	"	6/13	9/35	940	1071	"	4655	"		8/15
931	1067	"	4493	"		10/19	941	1072	"	4656	"		10/20
932	1068	"	4494	"		4/15	942	1073	"	4657	"		8/23
933	1069	"	4495	"		8/15	943	1074	"	4658	"		6/16
							946	1075	(f) Depew		1/99	9/13	3/29

RUTLAND CLASS C-1 and C-1a 4-4-0: 18x24-69-160-106000-15800. Acq.1905 with Rut.RR. Old class C-5,C-4
862-865 (Ex-Rut.182,183,180,181) Schen. 1891, 1894.

RUTLAND CLASS C-1b 4-4-0: 18x24-69-190-110600-16500. Acquired 1905 with Rutland RR. Old class C-6.
866-869 (Ex-Rut.184-187) Schen. 1897, 1899.

RUTLAND CLASS C-2 4-4-0: 18x26-68-200-126500-19900. Acquired 1905 with Rutland RR. Old class C-ℊ.
1000,1001 (Ex-Rut.190,191) Brooks 1897.

RUTLAND CLASS C-2a 4-4-0: 18x26-64-180-126500-____
1002 re 1078 (Ex-StL&A 6) Brooks 1897.

          Note b: 870 (re'98) 944 (re'13) 1038 (re'36) 4304. Later 19x24-78.
          Note c: 1003, 1004 scheduled to be (re'36) 4300, 4301.   Note d: 1013,1037 (re'36) 4302,4303.
          Note e: to Penn. Wood & Iron Co.   Note f: Formerly class Cd.

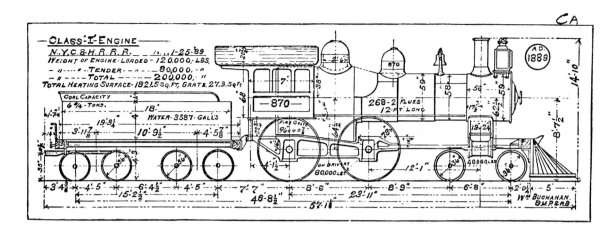

92

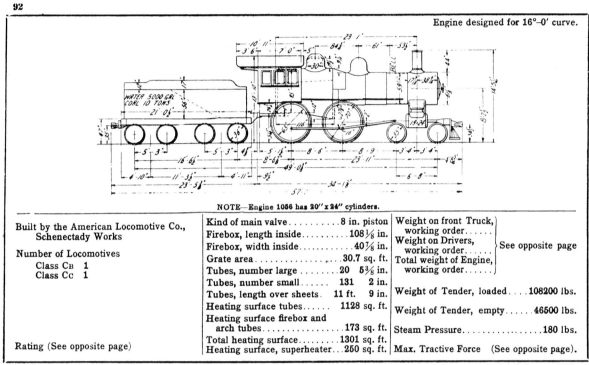

Engine designed for 16°–0' curve.

NOTE—Engine 1056 has 20" x 24" cylinders.

Built by the American Locomotive Co.,
Schenectady Works

Number of Locomotives
Class Cв 1
Class Cc 1

Rating (See opposite page)

Kind of main valve . . . . 8 in. piston	Weight on front Truck, working order . . . . . .
Firebox, length inside . . . . 108⅛ in.	Weight on Drivers, working order . . . . . .
Firebox, width inside . . . . 40⅞ in.	Total weight of Engine, working order . . . . . .
Grate area . . . . 30.7 sq. ft.	
Tubes, number large . . . . 20 5⅜ in.	
Tubes, number small . . . . . . 131 2 in.	
Tubes, length over sheets . 11 ft. 9 in.	Weight of Tender, loaded . . . . 108200 lbs.
Heating surface tubes . . . . . . 1128 sq. ft.	Weight of Tender, empty . . . . . . 46500 lbs.
Heating surface firebox and arch tubes . . . . 173 sq. ft.	Steam Pressure . . . . 180 lbs.
Total heating surface . . . . 1301 sq. ft.	
Heating surface, superheater . . . 250 sq. ft.	Max. Tractive Force (See opposite page).

See opposite page

CLASS Cв and Cc   (Printed Jan. 1, 1930)

NYC class C #1003 lasted until 1936, when it was scheduled to be renumbered 4300. (WDE)

NYC&HR 932, Class Cc, photographed in 1906 in N.Y. Third Rail Territory. (Vollrath coll.)

NYC&HR 897, another of the Buchanan eight-wheelers. Class Ca. (Adrian Buyse collection)

NYC&HR 921, class C, later #1035. Photo at Harmon before 1913.   (NYC neg 5673)

NYC 1013, class C, at Yorktown Heights, NY on the Putnam Division in 1926. (H.Ameling)

NYC 1038, another Putnam Division 4-4-0, at Briarcliff Manor, NY, in November, 1929.

NYC&HR 870, later 1053, class Cb. One of a pair built at West Albany in 1898.

NYC&HR CLASS C-3 4-4-0: 19x24-77-190-146400-18700. Old Class I-3.
```
                947 (re 10/13)  1079   Depew Shops 8/00  Sc 12/25
                948     "       1080     "    "    1/01  Sc  7/26
```

NYC&HR CLASS C-4 4-4-0: 17x24-70-145-88000-12600. Old Class A. Some Class Cx with 64" and 76" Drivers.
(Ex 700, 800 Series)   1062-1127   Rebuilt 1881-1887: See PP.44,46

NYC&HR CLASS C-5 4-4-0: 18x24-70-145-90300-14100. Old Class A-1.
```
Orig.  Re'90  Re'92  Re'99  Re'05
201    736    960    960    960       Syracuse   10/86  Sc  8/07
506    776    965    965    965       W.Albany   10/86  So  3/08  Paul Smiths 1
 52    828    975    975    975 (b)     "         3/88  So  3/08  Cont. Iron & Stl. Co.
615    848    976    976    976         "         2/89  So  3/08    "     "    "
660    849    977    977    977         "         7/87  Sc  7/09
```

NYC&HR CLASS C-6 4-4-0: 18x24-70-125-98500-14100. Old Class A-1x.
```
678    752    961    961    961       Rome  344   5/88  Sc  5/12
679    851    979    979    979        "    345    "    Sc 12/10
680    753    962    962    962        "    346   6/88  Sc 10/11
681    785    970                      "    347    "    Wrecked 9/92
682    852    980    980    980        "    348    "    Sc  8/12
683    786    971    971    971        "    349    "    Sc 12/10
684    853    981    981    981     Schen. 2569  6/88  Sc  4/11
685    754    963    963    963        "   2570    "    Sc  5/10
686    854    982    982    982        "   2571    "    Sc 12/10
687    787    972    972    972        "   2572    "    Sc 12/10
688    855    983   1086    959        "   2573    "    So  4/08  J.Joseph
689    856    984   1087    970        "   2574    "    Sc  7/11
661    784    969    969    969     West Albany 12/87  Sc 12/10
677    850    978    978    978        "    "    2/88  Sc 11/10
238    757    964 (re'13) 1081 (c)     "    "    5/88  RB 11/07  So 12/22 Penn.Wood & Iron Co.
538    779    966    966    966         "    "    9/88  So  3/08  Cont.Iron & Stl. Co.
600    782    967    967    967 (a)     "    "    8/88  Sc  6/11
601    783    968    968    968 (a)     "    "    1/89  So  5/08  Cont.Iron & Stl. Co.
       805    973    973    973         "    "    9/90  Sc  6/11
       806    974    974    974         "    "    5/91  Sc  5/10
```

NYC&HR CLASS C-7 4-4-0: 17x20-64-145-78100-11500. Old Class A-2.
(Ex-700,800 series)   1129-1136   WA,Syra.,E.Buf. 1885-86. See P.46

NYC&HR CLASS C-8 4-4-0: 18x20-64-145-82000-12100. Old Class A-3.
```
Orig.  Re'90  Re'92                      Orig. Re'90 Re'92
216    710   1053  E.Buf. 8/88 Sc 12/02 | 649   809  1058  E.Buf.  5/87 So 11/01
222    715   1054(d) "    4/90 So  3/08 | 652   812  1059  Syra.   5/87 Wrecked 8/93
487    724   1055    " 12/88 Sc 10/02   | 655   813  1060  W.Alby. 3/87 Wrecked 8/93
628    794   1056    "  3/88 Sc by'02   | 659   817  1061   "      7/88 Sc  8/02
631    796   1057    "  6/88 Sc 10/11   |
```

NYC&HR CLASS C-9 4-4-0: 17x24-64-140-85800-12300. Old Class B. (Class C-9a wt. 79800)
400-554 (re'05) 800-824   Schen. 1873-86. See pp.38-46

NYC&HR CLASS C-10 4-4-0: 18x24-64-145-96000-14900. Old Class B-1.
```
Orig. Re ? Re'90                          Orig. Re ? Re'90
123    32   680  Rome   450  2/89 Sc  8/12 | 690              Schen. 2757 12/88 So 11/07 (e)
200    42   681   "     451   "   Sc 10/95 | 691                  "    2758  "   So by'01 Rutland 68
219    43   682   "     452   "   So 11/08 (e)| 692               "    2759  "   Sc 11/09
251    56   683   "     453   "   So  3/08 (f)| 693               "    2760  "   Sc  7/09
253    63   684   "     454   "   Sc  4/11 | 694                  "    2761  "   Sc  4/09
700         685  Schen.2767 1/89  Sc 10/09 | 695                  "    2762  "   Sc 11/09
701    38   686   "    2768  "    So  3/08 (e)| 696   789  696    "    2763  "   Sc  8/02
702         687   "    2769  "    So  3/08 (e)| 697               "    2764 1/89 So  5/08 (e)
703         688   "    2770  "    So  3/08 (f)| 698    19  698    "    2765  "   So by'01 Rutland 69
704 (g)     689   "    2771  "    Sc  7/13  | 699                 "    2766  "   Sc  2/12
```

```
Note a:  600,601 RB from old class B.    Note b:  975 class C-5a with 73" drivers)
Note c:  1081 class C-6a 17x24-64-160)   Note d:  1054 (re'05) 1056.
Note e:  to Hicks Loco. & Car Co.        Note f:  to Cont.Iron & Stl. Co.
Note g:  689 (re 5/90) 808 (re 3/92) 774 (re  ) 689.
```

Class C-3

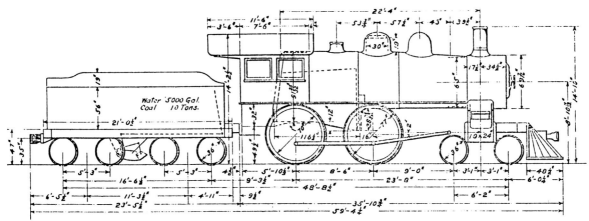

Kind of main valve....................Richardson balanced
Firebox, length inside ....108½ inches
Firebox width inside............................40⅞ inches
Grate area........................30.7 square feet
Tubes, number..................................354
Tubes, length over sheets....................12 feet 1 inch
Tubes, diameter outside........................2 inches
Heating surface, tubes ....2,224 square feet
Heating surface, firebox.................180.1 square feet

Heating surface, total...................2404.1 square feet
Weight on drivers, working order,............90 400 pounds
Weight on truck,   "   ....56 000 pounds
Weight, total of engine,   "   ....146,400 pounds
Weight of tender, loaded..................108,000 pounds
Weight of tender empty...................46,500 pounds
Steam pressure............................190 pounds
Rating..................................18.7 per cent.

Class C-5

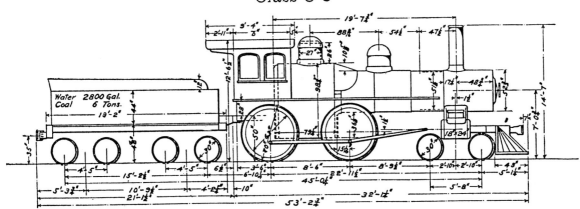

Kind of main valve....................Richardson balance
Firebox, length inside.........................72½ inches
Firebox width inside ....35½ inches
Grate area ....17.5 square feet
Tubes, number ... .238
Tubes, length over sheets.................11 feet 8 inches
Tubes, diameter outside........................2 inches
Heating surface, tubes ....1,454.5 square feet
Heating surface, firebox...................160 square feet
Heating surface, total................1,614.5 square feet

Weight on drivers, in working order..........57,300 pounds
Weight on truck, ...33 000 pounds
Weight, total of engine.   "   ....90,300 pounds
Weight of tender, loaded...............70 000 pounds
Weight of tender, empty...............35 000 pounds
Steam pressure.......................145 pounds
Rating.............................13.5 per cent.

NOTE—Engine No. 960 has firebox 40½ inches wide, with grate area of 20 square feet.

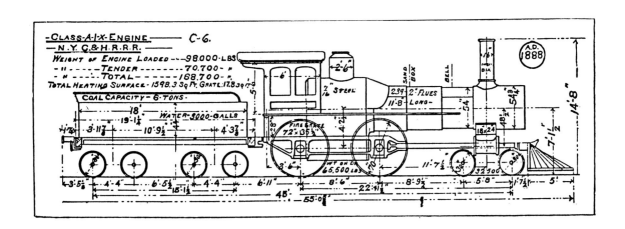

114

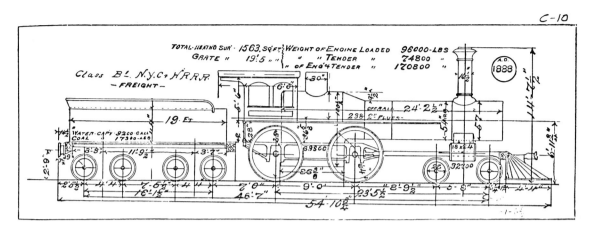

Diagram for NYC&HR class B-1, later C-10. Total of 20 built by Rome and Schenectady.

Rome-built 680, as it looked after renumbering in 1890. Class B-1, later C-10.(NYC 4309)

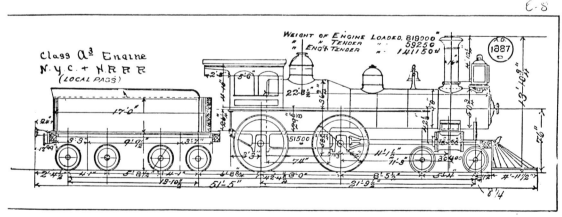

Diagram for the 9 engines in class A-3, later C-8. They were built in company shops in 1887-1890 for local passenger service.

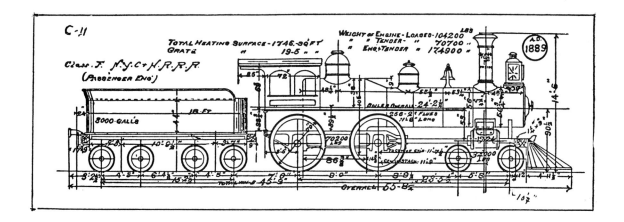

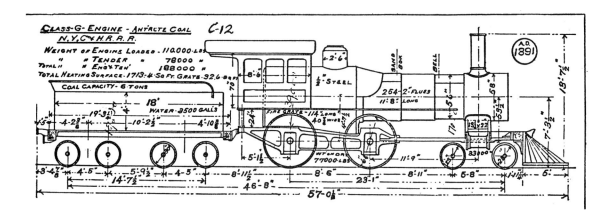

NYC 1405, class C-12 at Highbridge, N.Y. in August, 1920.   (Paul Prescott collection)

NYC&HR CLASS C-11 4-4-0: 18x24-70-155-104200-15100. Old Class F.

Orig.	Re'92	Re'99	Re'13						Orig.	Re'92	Re'99	Re'13				
705	953	988		Schen.	2850	3/89	Sc	8/08	710	859	987	1084	Rome	468	3/89	Sc 12/13 (g)
706	954	989	1085	"	2851	"	So	11/23(d)	711	956	991		"	469	"	Sc 6/11
707	955	990		"	2852	"	Sc	1/12	712	957	992		"	470	"	Sc 4/11
708	857	985		"	2853	"	Sc	12/09	713	958	983		"	471	"	Sc 10/10
709	858	986	1083	"	2854	"	Sc	12/13(g)	714	959	984	1082	"	472	"	Sc 12/13 (g)

Also: 1004-1007 (Ex class C-6) Rome 1889-90 as RW&O 54-57. 18x24-64. See p.62.

NYC&HR CLASS C-12 4-4-0: 18+x22-64-170-110000-17500. Old Class G

Orig.	Re'92	Re'13		Reblt.						Orig.	Re'13		Reblt.				
823	1049		Schen.	3427	2/91		Sc	2/13		1023	1410	Schen.	3831	5/92	6/14	So 1/22 (a)
802	1008	1400	"	3670	1/92		Sc	4/16		1024	1411	"	3832	"	12/14	So 1/22 (a)
803	1009		"	3661	"		Sc	6/12		1025	1412	"	3833	"	4/14	So 12/20
804	1010	1401(e)	"	3662	"		Sc	8/23		1026	1413	"	3834	"	2/11	So 11/24 (b)
807	1011		"	3663	"		Sc	7/12		1027		"	3835	6/92		Sc 12/09
808	1012	1402	"	3671	"		Sc	11/14		1028	1414	"	3836	"	7/12	So 11/22 (a)
810	1013	1403	"	3664	"	7/14	So	12/22 (a)		1029	1415	"	4634	12/97		So 10/15
815	1014		"	3665	"		Sc	5/10		1030	1416	"	4635	"	12/13	So 11/23 (b)
816	1015	1404	"	3666	"	3/12	Sc	9/23		1031	1417	"	4636	"	8/13	Sc 12/20
831	1016	1405	"	3667	"	3/14	So	11/22 (a)		1032	1418	"	4637	"	6/15	So 11/22 (a)
841	1017	1406	"	3668	"	4/13	So	11/22 (a)		1033	1419	"	4638	"		Sc 12/16
842	1018		"	3669	"		Sc	7/12		1034	1420	"	4639	"	8/14	Sc 12/20
	1019	1407	"	3827	5/92	8/15	Sc	12/25		1035	1421	"	4640	"	2/15	So 11/22 (c)
	1020	1408	"	3828	"	5/08	Sc	3/17		1036	1422	"	4641	"	9/13	Sc 11/20
	1021	1409	"	3829	"		Sc	11/14		1037	1423	"	4642	"	12/13	Sc 12/20
	1022		"	3830	"		Sc	6/11		1038	1424	"	4643	"	5/14	So 11/22 (a)

NYC&HR CLASS C-13 4-4-0: 17x24-64-140-85000-12900. Old Class H.

	Re'90		Re'92						
630	795		1106	Rome	572	2/90	So	6/15	Kilby Mach. Co.
634	798		1107	"	573	"	So	1/05	Ginsburg
636	800		1108	Schen.	2951	1/90	So	4/06	Jones & Galvin
637	801		1109	"	2952	"	RB	8/03	Insp. Pony 28. See p118
638	802	re 773	1110	"	2953	"	So	1/05	Ginsburg

NYC&HR CLASS C-14a 4-4-0: 19x24-70-180-124000-18940. Old Class N.
(As Built: 19x24-86-190-129000-   ). Rebuilt 6/99 with 70" drivers.
999 (re'13) 1086 (re'21) 999 W.Albany 4/1893. RB 5/06 Oswego. RT 7/23. To Chicago Museum S.& I. 9/62

NYC&HR CLASS C-15 4-4-0: 18x24-69-140-96000-13800. Old WS Class A.
NYC&HR CLASS C-15a 4-4-0: 18x24-70-140-96000-13600. Old WS Class A.
NYC&HR CLASS C-16 4-4-0: 18x24-69-150-108300-14800. Old WS Class A2.
NYC&HR CLASS C-16a 4-4-0: 18x24-70-150-108300-14600. Old WS Class A2.
NYC&HR CLASS C-16b 4-4-0: 18x24-69-150-109100-14800. Old WS Class Ab.
NYC&HR CLASS C-16c 4-4-0: 18x24-70-150-109100-14800. Old WS Class Ab.
 (ex-WS 1-30)   555-584 (re'05) 700,761-784 Rogers 1882-83. See p.74.

NYC&HR CLASS C-17 4-4-0: 18x24-69-140-94500-13800. Old WS Class B. (C-17a had 70" drivers)
 (ex-WS 31-100)   585-654 (some re'05) Rogers 1882-84. See pp.74,76

NYC&HR CLASS C-18 4-4-0: 17x24-63-140-92000-13500. Old WS Class E. (C-18a had 64" drivers)
 (ex-WS 201-220)   660-679   Rogers 1885. See p.82

NYC&HR CLASS C-19 4-4-0: 16x24-64-140-82700-11800. Old WS Class F.
 (ex-WS 124,125,130,135,140) 655-659   Schen. 1886. See p.82.
 (ex-Walkill Valley 2,3)   700,701   Schen. 1887. See p.72.

NYC&HR CLASS C-20 4-4-0: 17x24-64-140-87900-13300. Built for Utica & Black River.
 (ex-264-266,333)   408,418,443,513   Schen. 1884,85 See P.60

NYC&HR CLASS C-21 4-4-0: 18x24-64-140-90000-13700. Built for Carthage & Adirondack.
 (ex- C&A 1)   988 (re'13) 1083 Rome 1886. See P.62.

Note a: to Penn. Wood & Iron Co.   Note b: to StLouis & Hannibal.
Note c: to Rochester Iron & Metal Co. Note d: RB 2/06; So 11/23 to StL&H.
Note e: 1401 RB 4/15.   Note g: to N.Y.& Ottawa in 1910.

The famed 999 as she looked when new in 1893. The 86" drivers didn't last long.(Vollrath)

Class C-14

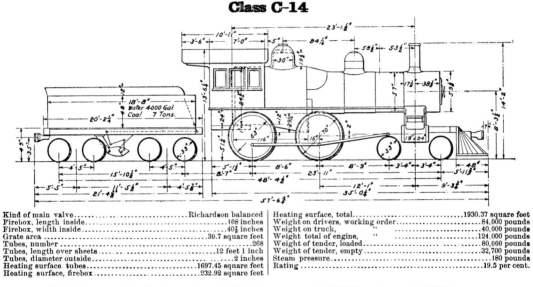

Kind of main valve............................Richardson balanced	Heating surface, total.......................1930.37 square feet
Firebox, length inside...................................108 inches	Weight on drivers, working order.....................84,000 pounds
Firebox, width inside....................................40⅝ inches	Weight on truck, " ....40,000 pounds
Grate area ....30.7 square feet	Weight total of engine, " ....124,000 pounds
Tubes, number 268	Weight of tender, loaded................................80,000 pounds
Tubes, length over sheets.... ....12 feet 1 inch	Weight of tender, empty.............................32,700 pounds
Tubes, diameter outside..................................2 inches	Steam pressure...180 pounds
Heating surface, tubes......................1697.45 square feet	Rating ....19.5 per cent.
Heating surface, firebox ....232.92 square feet	

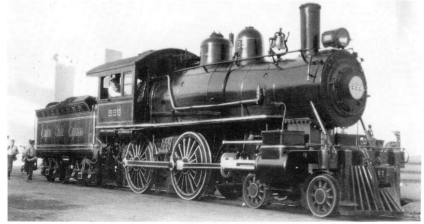

The 999 in later days, as an exhibition engine at the Chicago 1933 Fair.   (C.T.Andrews)

NYC&HR CLASS C-22 4-4-0: 19x24-69-155-119000-17000. Old Fall Brook Class G.
(ex-FB 8,10)   709,711 (re'13) 1088, 1089   Schen. 1894 See p. 90

NYC&HR CLASS C-23 4-4-0: 20x24-69-155-124000-18900. Old Fall Brook.
(ex-FB 9,11)   710,712 (re'13) 1090, 1091   Schen. 1897 See p. 90

NYC&HR CLASS C-24 4-4-0: 18x24-69-155-104800-15300. Old Fall Brook Class G.
(ex-FB 4-6)   706-708 (re'13) 1092, 1093   Schen. 1893 See p. 90

NYC&HR CLASS C-25 4-4-0: 17x24-63-135-70900-10800. Old Fall Brook Class H. (714 class Cx)
(ex-FB 24,20)   713,714   Schen. 1881,78 See p.88.

RUTLAND CLASS C-25 4-4-0: 17x24-64-140-84500-13300. Old Rutland Class C-1.
(ex-Rut.170,171) 793,794   Schen. 1886.

NYC&HR CLASS C-26 4-4-0: 17x24-64-125-80000-11900. Old Beech Creek. (705 class C-26a)
(ex-BC 41-44)   702-705   Schen. 1884,89. See p 84.

NYC&HR CLASS C-27 4-4-0: 18x24-64-145-100000-15500. Built as N.Y.& Nor. 9,10.
(ex-991,992)   1084,1085   Rogers 1891,92. See p.68

RUTLAND CLASS C-28 4-4-0: 17x24-64-145-87900-12700. Old Rutland Class C-2.
(ex-Rut.172,173) 795,796   BLW 1890.

RUTLAND CLASS C-29 4-4-0: 17x24-63-130-80000-11800. Old Rutland Class C-3.
(ex-Rut.174,175) 797,798   BLW 1890.

RUTLAND CLASS Cx 4-4-0:

(ex-Rut.77)	791	15x20-60	D.Cooke
" 78	792	14x22-56	Brooks 1883
" 65	1058	16x24-69-72500	St.Albans 1873
" 76	1059	16x24-64-66200	Malone 1872
" 60	1060	16x24-69-77000	Schen. 1869
" 61	1061	16x24-70-77000	" "
" 177	1062	17x24-70-81300	Syracuse RB'83
" 193	1063	18x24-64-96000	Schen. 1889
" 64	1064	16x24-64-68100	Taunton 1868

PONY INSPECTION ENGINES

NYC&HR "PONY" CLASS 4-2-4T INSPECTION ENGINES: 12x16-64-140-85500-4400. *As Rebuilt: 160-102000-4900

		Re'99	Names	(See Note a)				
	(2nd)	251	25 "Monitor" (re) "Catskill"	W.Alby. 10/97	(RB WA 6/14) *	Sc 12/25		
117	(re 5/90)	252	28 "Mohawk" (re'92) "Ontario"	W.Alby. 8/89	(RB Oswego 11/10)*	Sc 9/20		
513	(re /90)	253		W.Alby. 6/76	(See pp.16,19)	Sc /96		
	(2nd)	253	27 "Niagara"	Depew 8/96	(RB Depew 4/14) *	Sc 2/28		
		255	29 "Mohawk" (re'23) 26 "Ontario"	W.Alby. 7/92	(RB WA 5/14) *	Sc 12/25		
251	(re /97)	256	30 "Monitor" (re) "Chemung"	W.Alby. 3/90	(11x15-56-140)	So 12/03	Kilby	

NYC&HR "PONY" CLASS 4-4-0 INSPECTION ENGINE: 13x22-64-140-66400-6915. As Rebuilt: 160-75720-7900
522 (re 7/90) 254 28 "Hudson" re 30 "Steuben" re 32 "Corning" WA 12/89 (RB Avis 4/15) Sc 10/29

NYC&HR "PONY" CLASS 4-4-0 INSPECTION ENGINE: 17x24-64-140-102300-13300. As Rebuilt: 160-108500-14740
(2nd) 28 "Hudson" (ex C-13 #1109) Depew 8/03 (RB WA 11/14) Sc 9/29

RUTLAND "PONY" CLASS 4-4-0 INSPECTION ENGINE: 14X22-63-80900. Built as StL&A 10.
Rut.49 re 100 re 33 "Ne-Ha-Sa-Ne" Schen.4401 3/96 Re'14 RUT 99

NYC&HR "PONY" CLASS 0-4-4T INSPECTION ENGINES:
Ex-Utica & MV   23 "Oneida" (Built as N.Y.Elev.278 by Man.Ry.'89) Dr by'09
Ex-A&StL 4   99 (p.64) (Built as N.Y.Elev. 45 by R.I. 710 8/78) RB to 2-4-4T 10x14-39.

Note a - Numbers discontinued in 1922. Names only used thereafter.

Inspection Engines 25-26-27-29.

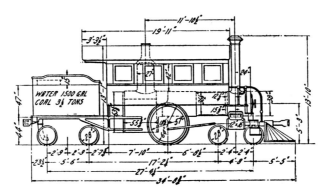

Kind of main valve...............................	Heating surface, firebox.........................77 square feet
Firebox, length inside........................48¾ inches	Heating surface, total.......................562.9 square feet
Firebox, width inside.........................35¼ inches	Weight on drivers, working order............24,000 pounds
Grate area...............................12 square feet	Weight on forward truck, working order........22,500 pounds
Tubes, number...................................100	Weight on rear truck, working order..........39,000 pounds
Tubes, length over sheets...................9 feet 3 inches	Weight, total of engine, working order.......85,500 pounds
Tubes, diameter outside........................2 inches	Steam pressure..............................140 pounds
Heating surface, tubes.....................485.9 square feet	Rating....................................4.4 per cent.

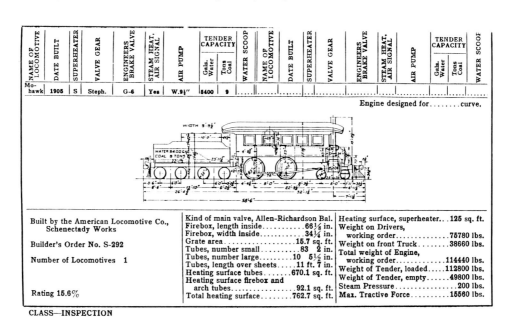

NAME OF LOCOMOTIVE	DATE BUILT	SUPERHEATER	VALVE GEAR	ENGINEERS BRAKE VALVE	STEAM HEAT, AIR SIGNAL	AIR PUMP	TENDER CAPACITY		WATER SCOOP	NAME OF LOCOMOTIVE	DATE BUILT	SUPERHEATER	VALVE GEAR	ENGINEERS BRAKE VALVE	STEAM HEAT, AIR SIGNAL	AIR PUMP	TENDER CAPACITY		WATER SCOOP
							Gals. Water	Tons Coal									Gals. Water	Tons Coal	
Mo-hawk	1905	S	Steph.	G-6	Yes	W.9½"	5400	9											

Engine designed for........curve.

Built by the American Locomotive Co., Schenectady Works	Kind of main valve, Allen-Richardson Bal.	Heating surface, superheater..125 sq. ft.
	Firebox, length inside...........66⅛ in.	Weight on Drivers,
Builder's Order No. S-292	Firebox, width inside............34¼ in.	working order............75780 lbs.
	Grate area..................15.7 sq. ft.	Weight on front Truck.......38660 lbs.
Number of Locomotives 1	Tubes, number small..........83 2 in.	Total weight of Engine,
	Tubes, number large.........10 5½ in.	working order............114440 lbs.
	Tubes, length over sheets.....11 ft. 7 in.	Weight of Tender, loaded.....112800 lbs.
	Heating surface tubes.......670.1 sq. ft.	Weight of Tender, empty......49800 lbs.
	Heating surface firebox and	Steam Pressure................200 lbs.
Rating 15.6%	arch tubes.................92.1 sq. ft.	Max. Tractive Force..........15560 lbs.
	Total heating surface.......762.7 sq. ft.	

CLASS—INSPECTION

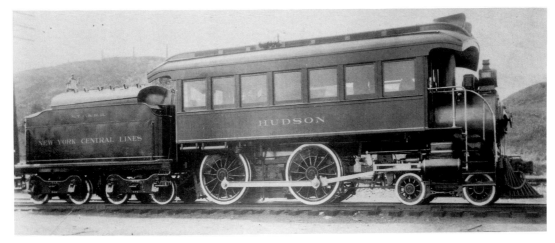

NYC&HR second HUDSON, assembled at Depew shop in 1903 from C-13 #1109.   (H.W.Ameling)

NYC&HR 251, the MONITOR, as built at West Albany in 1897.   (NYC negative 5608)

NYC&HR 25, named CATSKILL; the MONITOR as rebuilt in 1914.   (Vollrath collection)

NYC&HR #26, the ONTARIO, as rebuilt 1914 at West Albany.   (C.B.Chaney collection)

NYC #27, the NIAGARA, as rebuilt 1914 at Depew. It lasted until 1928. (NYC neg 3916)

CLASS D. 2-4-4T TANK

NYC&HR CLASS D 2-4-4T: 14x22-55-145-106500-10000. Built as New York & Northern #18-24.
   (Ex-1151-1157) 1400-1406 (re'05) 40-46 Rogers 1888-92 See p.68

NYC&HR CLASS D-1a and D-2a 2-4-4T: 16x22-57-160-142700-13440. (37-41 class D-2a wt. 140300.

	Re'22								Re'22					
37	1911	Alco-B	51790	9/12	RT	12/26		"42	1916	Alco-B	48420	7/10	RT	12/26.
38	1912	"	51791	"	RT	12/26		"44	1917	"	48421	"	RT	12/26.
39	1913	"	51792	"	So	12/26 (a)		47	1918	"	48422	"	So	12/26 (b)
"40	1914	"	51793	"	Rt	12/26		48	1919	"	48423	"	So	12/26 (b)
"41	1915	"	51794	"	So	12/26 (a)		49	1920	"	48424	"	So	7/26 (c)

CLASS E, 2-6-0 MOGUL

NYC&HR CLASS E 2-6-0: 19x26-64-160-120000-20600. Old Class J. Orig. 63"dd-19950tf

	Re'90	Re'99				Reblt.				Re'99				Reblt.			
221	505	1453	Brooks	1567	10/89	3/06	Sc	6/27	562	1510	Brooks	1731	9/90		Sc	9/11	
235	506	1454	"	1568	"	9/06	Sc	11/16	563	1511	"	1732	"	8/06	Sc	12/16	
466	507	1455	"	1569	"	6/07	Sc	6/27	564	1512	"	1733	"	8/07	Sc	5/17	
537	508	1456	"	1570	"	6/07	Sc	12/16	565	1513	"	1734	"	9/07	Sc	12/20	
715	509	1457	"	1571	"	1/08	So	12/22 (d)	566	1514	"	1735	"	11/07	Sc	4/19	
716	510	1458	"	1572	"	7/07	Sc	10/16	567	1515	"	1736	"	5/07	Sc	12/20	
717	511	1459	"	1573	"	2/06	Sc	12/20	568	1516	"	1737	"	8/07	Sc	12/16	
718	512	1460	"	1574	"	5/07	Sc	8/23	569	1517	"	1738	"	7/07	So	10/23 (d)	
719	513	1461	"	1575	"		Sc	12/10	570	1518	"	1739	"	5/06	Sc	12/20	
720	514	1462	"	1576	"	10/07	Sc	7/23	571	1519	"	1740	"		Sc	5/10	
									572	1520	"	1741	"		Sc	10/10	
	555	1503	Brooks	1724	9/90	10/08	RT	10/15	573	1521	"	1742	10/90	5/01	Sc	12/18	
	556	1504	"	1725	"	7/07	Sc	12/20	574	1522	"	1743	"	7/07	So	10/23 (d)	
	557	1505	"	1726	"	8/05	Sc	12/21	575	1523	"	1744	"	3/06	Sc	12/20	
	558	1506	"	1727	"	11/05	Sc	11/29	576	1524	"	1745	"	3/01	Sc	8/15	
	559	1507	"	1728	"	10/07	So	11/23 (d)	577	1525	"	1746	"	8/07	So	10/23 (d)	
	560	1508	"	1729	"		Sc	4/10	578	1526	"	1747	"	8/07	Sc	11/16	
	561	1509	"	1730	"	8/03	Sc	12/20	579	1527	"	1748	"	7/05	Sc	3/15	

NYC&HR CLASS Ea 2-6-0: 19x26-64-160-120000-20600. Old Class J, then E.

	Re'90	Re'99								Re'90	Re'99							
166	535	1483	Rome	542	12/89		Sc	10/11	727	545	1493	Rome	552	1/90	10/08	Sc	8/23	
234	536	1484	"	543	"		Sc	10/10	728	546	1494	"	553	"	4/04	Sc	12/20	
242	537	1485	"	544	"	12/04	Sc	8/23	729	547	1495	"	554	"	5/08	Sc	12/20	
272	538	1486	"	545	"	1/08	So	10/23 (d)	730	548	1496	"	555	"	6/07	Sc	1/22	
447	539	1487	"	546	"	7/07	Sc	9/16	731	549	1497	"	556	"		Sc	5/10	
467	540	1488	"	547	"		Sc	7/10	732	550	1498	"	557	"	7/05	So	3/18 (f)	
508	541	1489	"	548	"	6/07	Sc	3/17	733	551	1499	"	558	"		Sc	5/10	
698	542	1490	"	549	"	8/08	So	11/22 (d)	734	552	1500	"	559	"	4/04	Sc	8/23	
701	543	1491	"	550	"		Sc	6/10	735	553	1501	"	560	"	2/06	Sc	7/23	
726	544	1492	"	551	"	10/05	So	12/22 (d)	736	554	1502	"	561	"		Sc	12/10	

Note a: To General Equip. Co.; 1913 re Lima-Defiance RR #1.
Note b: To F.C.Rio Mayo 10, 9 (Mexico).   Note c: To Carroll Bros., Buffalo.
Note d: To Penn.Wood & Iron Co.   Note e: To Rochester Iron & Metal Co.
Note f: To General Equip. Co.; Re Arrow Coal & Mining Co.

NYC&HR 37, one of ten late model tank engines for the Getty Square line.(Alco Hist.Photo)

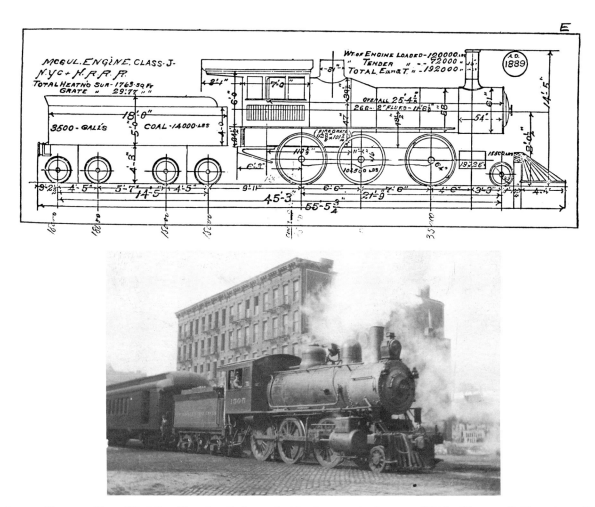

C 1505, class E, on the "Dolly Varden" local that ran between 30th St. and Spuyten Duyvil.

124

NYC&HR CLASS Eb 2-6-0: 19x26-64-160-120000-20600. Old Class J, then E.

No.	Re'99	Bldr	Bldr#		Reblt.	Disp		Note
580	1528	Rogers	4323	6/90	8/05	Sc	11/19	
581	1529	"	4324	"	6/08	So	12/22	(b)
582	1530	"	4325	"	6/06	Sc	8/23	
583	1531	"	4326	"		Sc	9/11	
584	1532	"	4332	7/90	9/05	Sc	8/23	
585	1533	"	4333	"	10/05	Sc	12/21	(r)
586	1534	"	4334	"	4/06	So	10/23	(b)
587	1535	"	4335	"		Sc	12/10	
588	1536	"	4338	"	10/04	RT	4/17	
589	1537(p)	"	4339	"	9/05	Rt	10/15	
590	1538	"	4346	8/90	3/06	Sc	12/23	
591	1539	"	4347	"	3/07	So	12/22	(b)
592	1540(a)	"	4348	"	8/08	Sc	4/32	
593	1541	"	4349	"	12/07	Sc	12/20	
594	1542	"	4351	"		Sc	7/09	
595	1543	"	4352	"	4/08	Sc	10/16	
596	1544(p)	"	4353	9/90	12/07	Sc	3/15	
597	1545	"	4354	"	3/06	Sc	9/22	
598	1546	"	4355	"	9/05	RT	10/15	
599	1547	"	4356	"	6/03	RT	11/16	
600	1548	"	4357	"	9/05	Sc	5/20	
601	1549	"	4358	"	11/05	Sc	12/20	
602	1550	"	4359	"	10/07	Sc	12/20	
603	1551	"	4360	"	5/07	Sc	4/19	
604	1552	"	4361	"		Sc	11/11	
605	1553	Rogers	4362	9/90	2/06	Sc	11/23	
606	1554	"	4363	"		Sc	12/10	
607	1555	"	4364	"	9/08	RT	7/16	
608	1556	"	4365	"	11/03	RT	11/16	
609	1557	"	4366	"	12/07	Sc	6/27	
610	1558	"	4369	"		Sc	9/11	
611	1559	"	4370	"	8/06	Sc	7/23	
612	1560	"	4371	"		Sc	5/10	
613	1561	"	4372	"	11/07	RT	10/16	
614	1562	"	4373	"	9/07	Sc	12/24	
615	1563	"	4375	"	3/06	RT	10/16	
616	1564	"	4376	"	11/05	So	11/22	(b)
617	1565	"	4377	"	5/08	Sc	12/20	
618	1566	"	4378	"	1/08	Sc	12/24	
619	1567	"	4379	"	8/08	Sc	1/22	
620	1568(p)	"	4380	"	5/07	RT	2/17	
621	1569	"	4381	"	10/06	RT	12/21	
622	1570(p)	"	4382	"	11/05	Sc	12/14	
623	1571	"	4383	"	11/05	Sc	6/15	
624	1572	"	4384	"		Sc	10/09	
625	1573	"	4385	"	3/06	So	11/22	(c)
626	1574	"	4386	"	3/06	Sc	12/20	
627	1575	"	4387	"	8/05	Sc	12/20	
628	1576	"	4388	"		Sc	10/09	
629	1577	"	4389	"	10/07	Sc	11/23	

NYC&HR CLASS Ec 2-6-0: 19x26-57-160-120000-22390. Old Class J-1, then E-1.

No.	Re'99	Bldr	Bldr#		Reblt.	Disp		Note
749	1652	Schen.	3894	9/92	12/04	Sc	9/48	(d)
750	1653	"	3895	"	3/01	So	5/19	(e)
751	1654	"	3896	"	12/04	Sc	3/32	
752	1655	"	3897	"	10/07	So	11/22	(g)
753	1656	"	3898	"		So	8/11	(f)
754	1657	"	3899	"	11/07	So	12/16	(h)
755	1658(i)	"	3900	"	6/05	So	8/16	(j)
756	1659	"	3901	"	9/07	So	12/22	(b)
757	1660	"	3902	10/92	8/07	So	1/19	(g)
758	1661	"	3903	"	9/07	Sc	12/25	
759	1662	"	3904	"		So	8/11	(f)
760	1663	"	3905	"	2/04	So	12/16	(f,k)
761	1664	"	3906	"		So	8/13	(f)
762	1665	"	3907	"	10/05	Sc	12/23	
763	1666	"	3908	"		Sc	4/04	
764	1667	"	3909	"		So	7/10	(1)
765	1668(i)	"	3910	"	9/08	So	12/22	(b)
766	1669	"	3911	"	12/06	So	8/16	(e)
767	1670	Schen.	3912	10/92	5/08	Sc	8/22	
768	1671	"	3913	"	8/05	So	12/22	(b)
769	1672	"	3914	"	9/07	So	11/22	(c)
770	1673	"	3915	"	5/07	So	12/17	(f,n)
771	1674	"	3916	"	10/02	So	11/22	(c)
772	1675	"	3917	"		Sc	10/11	
773	1676	"	3918	"		Sc	11/11	
774	1677	"	3919	"	9/06	So	4/17	(f,o)
775	1678	"	3920	"	4/07	So	12/22	(g)
776	1679(d)	"	3921	"	12/07	Sc	8/48	
777	1680	"	3922	"	1/05	Sc	11/25	
778	1681	"	3923	"	12/06	So	10/18	(f)
779	1682	"	3924	11/92		Sc	7/13	
780	1683	"	3925	"	10/02	So	11/22	(c)
781	1684	"	3926	"		Sc	7/12	
782	1685	"	3927	"		So	5/10	(1)
783	1686	"	3928	"	11/05	So	1/17	(q)
784	1687(m)	"	4130	12/93	3/08	So	8/16	(e)

Note a: 1540 (re'30) 1640.   Note b: To Penn.Wood & Iron Co.   Note c: To Rochester Iron & Metal Co.
Note d: 1652,1679 (re'36) 1900,1901.   Note e: 1653,1669,1687 to Pitts.& Shawmut 101-103.
Note f: to General Equip. Co.   Note g: 1655,1660,1678 to Grasse River 61,60,68.   Note h: to N.Y.& Penn.
Note i: to Little Falls & Dolge. 3,4 until 1913.   Note j: to Arcade & Attica 2.
Note k: to Consol.Rol.Mills & Furn.Co.(Mex.).   Note 1: to Hicks Loco, & Car Co.   Note m: 784 ex-StL&A 1
Note n: to E&A Noriego   Note o: to Clin.& Okla.Wes. 104.   Note p: to NY&Ott. 4/12,7/09,1/12,12/05.
Note q: to Wis.& Nor. 6.   Note r: to Salina Northern 1.

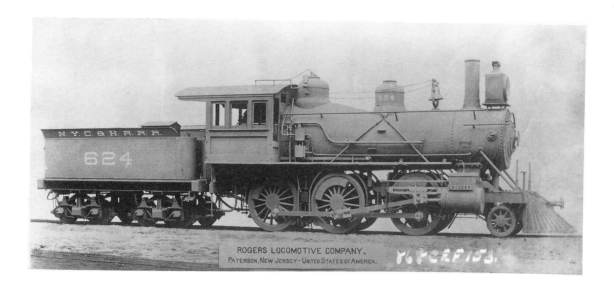

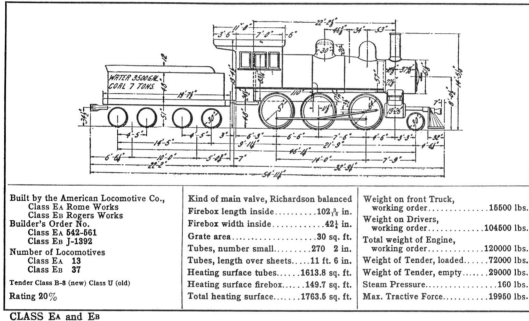

Built by the American Locomotive Co.,
   Class Eᴀ Rome Works
   Class Eʙ Rogers Works
Builder's Order No.
   Class Eᴀ 542-561
   Class Eʙ J-1392
Number of Locomotives
   Class Eᴀ 13
   Class Eʙ 37
Tender Class B-8 (new) Class U (old)

Rating 20%

Kind of main valve, Richardson balanced	
Firebox length inside	102⅜ in.
Firebox width inside	42¼ in.
Grate area	30 sq. ft.
Tubes, number small	270 2 in.
Tubes, length over sheets	11 ft. 6 in.
Heating surface tubes	1613.8 sq. ft.
Heating surface firebox	149.7 sq. ft.
Total heating surface	1763.5 sq. ft.

Weight on front Truck, working order	15500 lbs.
Weight on Drivers, working order	104500 lbs.
Total weight of Engine, working order	120000 lbs.
Weight of Tender, loaded	72000 lbs.
Weight of Tender, empty	29000 lbs.
Steam Pressure	160 lbs.
Max. Tractive Force	19950 lbs.

CLASS Eᴀ and Eʙ

NYC&HR 1482, one of 95 Moguls in class Ed.　　　　　(C.B.Chaney collection)

NYC&HR CLASS Ed 2-6-0: 19x26-64-160-120000-20600. Old Class J-1. then E-1.

No.	Re'90	Re'99	Bldr	S#	Date	Reblt.	Disp.
123	515	1463	Schen.	2932	11/89	6/06	Sc 9/16
200	516	1464	"	2933	"	4/05	So 11/22(a)
219	517	1465	"	2934	"		Sc 10/09
245	518	1466	"	2942	12/89		Sc 8/11
251	519	1467	"	2935	11/89	4/07	So 3/27(b)
253	520	1468	"	2936	"	4/06	Sc 10/19
264	521	1469	"	2937	"	7/07	Sc 11/23
269	522	1470	"	2938	"		Sc 7/12
441	523	1471	"	2939	"	4/07	Sc 12/19
442	524	1472	"	2943	12/89		Sc 4/11
475	525	1473	"	2940	11/89	6/05	Sc 10/16
480	526	1474	"	2944	12/89	5/06	So 7/14(c)
527	527	1475	"	2941	11/89	8/06	So 10/23(d)
528	528	1476	"	2945	12/89	10/06	Sc 1/17
529	529	1477	"	2862	10/89	10/08	Sc 12/16
721	530	1478	"	2946	12/89	8/05	Sc 12/16
722	531	1479	"	2947	"		Sc 5/10
723	532	1480	"	2948	"	6/07	Sc 11/23
724	533	1481	"	2949	"	9/07	So 12/22(e)
725	534	1482	"	2950	"		Sc 4/11
	630	1578(f)	"	3183	8/90	11/05	To B&A 12/03
	631	1579(g)	"	3184	"	10/05	Sc 10/47
	632	1580	"	3185	"		Sc 2/13
	633	1581	"	3186	"		Sc 5/10
	634	1582	"	3187	"	6/01	Rt 3/17
	635	1583	"	3188	9/90		Sc 10/09
	636	1584	"	3189	"	3/06	Sc 2/17
	637	1585(1)	"	3190	"		Sc 12/13
	638	1586	"	3191	"		Sc 10/10
	639	1587	"	3192	"	4/06	Sc 12/20
	640	1588	"	3193	"		Sc 3/11
	641	1589	"	3194	"	3/09	Sc 9/23
	642	1590	"	3195	"	6/05	RT 12/16
	643	1591	"	3196	"	4/07	Sc 3/14
	644	1592	"	3197	"	10/05	Sc 8/23
	645	1593	"	3198	"	6/08	Sc 1/22
	646	1594	"	3199	"	8/07	Sc 3/15
	647	1595	"	3200	"		Sc 10/11
	648	1596	"	3201	"	3/08	So 11/23(d)
	649	1597	"	3202	"		Sc 4/12
	650	1598	"	3203	10/90	5/08	So 11/22(a)
	651	1599	"	3204	"	8/06	Rt 11/15
	652	1600	"	3205	11/90	11/07	Sc 5/33
	653	1601	"	3206	"	7/08	Sc 12/20
	654	1602	"	3207	"		Sc 12/10
482	700	1603(h)	"	3595	12/91		Sc 10/10
483	701	1604(h)	"	3596	"	10/07	Sc 12/21
484	702	1605(h)	"	3597	"		Sc 10/12
485	703	1606	Schen.	3598	12/91	2/02	Sc 12/20
486	704	1607	"	3599	"		Sc 7/12
487	705	1608	"	3600	"	2/99	Sc 11/11
488	706	1609	"	3601	"	12/07	RT 11/16
489	707	1610	"	3602	"	6/08	Sc 12/25
490	708	1611	"	3603	"	4/07	RT 1/17
491	709	1612(g)	"	3604	"	1/06	Sc 7/37
492	710	1613	"	3620	"	10/07	RT 7/16
493	711	1614	"	3621	"		Sc 9/11
494	712	1615	"	3622	"	3/08	Rt 11/16
495	713	1616(g)	"	3623	"	7/05	Sc 6/39
496	714	1617	"	3624	"	9/00	Sc 7/23
497	715	1618	"	3625	"	8/07	Sc 11/23
498	716	1619	"	3626	"	9/05	Sc 1/22
499	717	1620	"	3627	"	10/00	Sc 8/23
500	718	1621	"	3628	"	9/08	So 12/16(i)
	719	1622	"	3848	6/92		Sc 6/11
	720	1623	"	3849	"		Sc 5/10
	721	1624	"	3850	"	8/07	Sc 4/19
	722	1625(g)	"	3851	"	4/06	Sc 12/47
	723	1626	"	3852	"		Sc 5/10
	724	1627	"	3853	7/92		Sc 12/10
	725	1628	"	3854	"		Sc 9/11
	726	1629	"	3855	"		Sc 5/10
	727	1630(g)	"	3856	"	6/07	SS 12/50
	728	1631	"	3857	"	9/05	Rt 1/17
	729	1632	"	3858	"		Sc 6/11
	730	1633	"	3859	"	7/06	Rt 7/16
	731	1634	"	3860	"	3/08	Sc 12/20
	732	1635	"	3861	"		Sc 11/05
	733	1636	"	3862	"	2/05	Rt 10/16
	734	1637	"	3863	8/92	8/07	Sc 12/25
	735	1638(f)	"	3864	"	12/06	To B&A 12/03
	736	1639	"	3865	"	9/08	So 4/14(j)
	737	1640	"	3866	"		Sc 10/10
	738	1641	"	3867	"		Sc 12/09
	739	1642	"	3868	"		Sc 5/10
	740	1643	"	3869	"		Sc 5/10
	741	1644	"	3870	"	5/08	So 11/22(a)
	742	1645	"	3871	"		Sc 9/11
	743	1646	"	3872	"	5/06	Sc 9/24
	744	1647	"	3873	"	7/05	Sc 11/19
	745	1648	"	3874	8/92		Sc 10/11
	746	1649	"	3875	"		Sc 6/11
	747	1650	"	3876	"	12/04	So 11/22(a)
	748	1651	"	3877	"	11/04	Rt 11/16
(k)785		1688	"	4393	10/95		Sc 6/12

NYC&HR CLASS Ee 2-6-0: 19x26-64-165-120000-21200. Old Class J-1. Built for West Shore.

(Ex WS 176-200) 1816-1840 Schen. 1892. See pp.80

NYC&HR CLASS Ef 2-6-0: 19x26-57-160-144700-23200. Old Class J-2.

787 (re'99) 1690 West Albany 10/98 So 10/12 Fitz.Luther, re Ashley, Drew & Nor. 102

Note a: to Rochester Iron & Metal Co.   Note b: to Virginia Cen.RR   Note c: to Cen.Loco.& Car Wks.
Note d: to Penn.Wood & Iron Co.   Note e: to L.Katz.   Note f: 1578,1638 (re'13) B&A 600,601.
Note g: 1579,1612,1616,1625,1630 (re'36) 1902-1906.   Note h: 482-484 (re'92) 700-702.
Note i: 1621 to Wis.& Nor. 7.   Note j: to Gen.Equip.Co.   Note k: StL&A 2 (re'96) 785. Note 1: NY&Ott

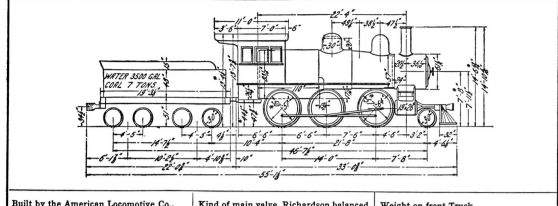

Built by the American Locomotive Co., Schenectady Works

Number of Locomotives
- Class Ec   24
- Class Ed   57

Note—Diagram of Class Ec same as class Ed except the following:
- Driving wheel centers.....................50 ins.
- Driving wheel over new tires.............57 ins.
- *Refers to Class Ec as well as all dimensions marked *
- Tender Class B-8 (new) Class W (old)

Rating 22.4% and 20%

Kind of main valve, Richardson balanced
Firebox length inside..........$102\frac{3}{16}$ in.
Firebox width inside............$42\frac{1}{4}$ in.
Grate area....................30 sq. ft.
Tubes, number small........270 2 in.
Tubes, length over sheets...11 ft. 6 in.
Heating surface tubes......1613.8 sq. ft.
Heating surface firebox.....149.7 sq. ft.
Total heating surface.......1763.5 sq. ft.

Weight on front Truck,
    working order.............15500 lbs.
Weight on Drivers,
    working order............104500 lbs.
Total weight of Engine,
    working order............120000 lbs.
Weight of Tender, loaded......72000 lbs.
Weight of Tender, empty......29000 lbs.
Steam Pressure.................160 lbs.
Max. Tractive Force........{ *22400 lbs.
                              19950 lbs.

CLASS Ec and Ed

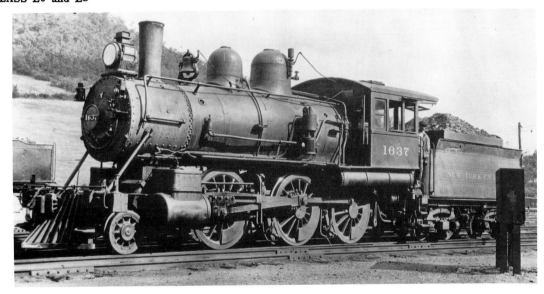

NYC 1637, class Ed, photographed at Corning, N.Y. in August, 1916. (Vollrath collection)

NYC&HR 1688, one-of-a-kind class Ed, acquired with the St.Lawrence & Adirondack.(Winters)

NYC&HR 1541, class Eb, heading what appears to be a solid mail and express train. (NYC 5683)

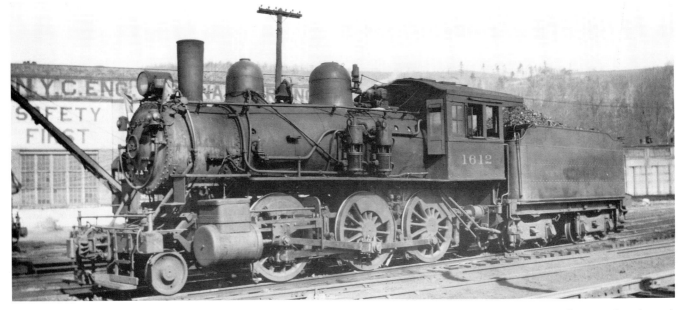

NYC 1612, class Ed, at Corning, N.Y. in the 1920's. Reno. 1936 to 1903. (Jay Williams)

NYC&HR 786 became Pittsburgh & Eastern 12, then 1689, class E-1. (Schen.History Ctr.)
(H.L.Vail coll.)

NYC&HR 1762, a Schenectady compound, soon converted to class E-2a. (Schen.History Ctr.)
(H.L.Vail coll.)

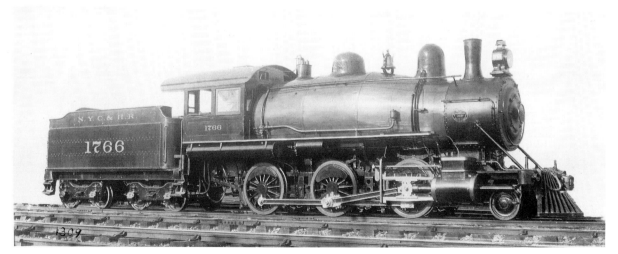

NYC&HR 1766, class E-1f, one of a pair built by Baldwin,   (R.Street collection)
both built with a Vanderbilt Firebox.

NYC&HR CLASS E-1 2-6-0: 20x28-57-180-146000-30060. Old Class P.

786 re Pitts.& Eas.12 re 1689 Schen.4909 9/98 RT 12/15

NYC&HR CLASS E-1a 2-6-0: 20x28-57-180-152000-30060. Old Class P.

No.	Re'99	Re'36	Builder	Bldr#	Date	Reblt.	Disp.		No.	Re'99	Re'36	Builder	Bldr#	Date	Reblt.	Disp.	
788	1691		Schen.	4975	1/99		Sc 3/15		812	1715		Schen.	4999	3/99		So 8/23	
789	1692	1907	"	4976	"	8/15	Sc 3/49		813	1716		"	5000	"		Sc 5/15	
790	1693		"	4977	"		Sc 11/24		814	1717		"	5001	"	7/18	Sc 9/26	
791	1694		"	4978	"		Sc 12/22										
792	1695	1908	"	4979	"	3/19	Sc 8/50			1721	1911	Schen.	5189	9/99	10/18	Sc 3/49	
793	1696		"	4980	"		Sc 12/24			1722		"	5190	"		Rt 12/22	
794	1697		"	4981	2/99		Sc 7/19			1723		"	5191	"		Sc 12/22 (a)	
795	1698		"	4982	"	8/16	Sc 8/26			1724		"	5192	"		Sc 12/25	
796	1699		"	4983	"	9/17	Sc 7/32			1725		"	5193	"		Sc 12/24	
797	1700		"	4984	"	3/19	Sc 3/29			1726		"	5194	10/99	1/19	So 11/23 (a)	
798	1701	1909	"	4985	"	4/18	Sc 12/47			1727		"	5195	"	5/19	Sc 4/33	
799	1702		"	4986	"		Rt 12/15			1728		"	5196	"	5/18	Sc 3/32	
800	1703		"	4987	"	11/15	Sc 11/23			1729		"	5197	"		Sc 11/23	
801	1704	1910	"	4988	"	8/18	Sc 12/39			1730		"	5198	"	8/16	Sc 9/28	
802	1705		"	4989	"	/18?	Sc 8/23			1731		"	5199	"	10/18	Sc 9/28	
803	1706		"	4990	"		Sc 12/24			1732		"	5200	"		Sc 7/27	
804	1707		"	4991	"		Sc 3/14			1733		"	5201	11/99		Sc 12/24	
805	1708		"	4992	"	12/15	Sc 12/25			1734		"	5202	"		So 11/23 (a)	
806	1709		"	4993	3/99	6/18	Sc 5/33			1735		"	5203	"		Sc 8/23	
807	1710		"	4994	"		Rt 12/15			1736	1912	"	5204	"	9/14	Sc 10/49	
808	1711		"	4995	"		Sc 12/24			1737		"	5205	"		Rt 12/15	
809	1712		"	4996	"		Sc 12/24			1738		"	5206	"		Sc 11/05	
810	1713		"	4997	"		Sc 12/24			1739		"	5207	"	5/17	So 12/23 (a)	
811	1714		"	4998	"		Sc 7/32			1740		"	5208	"		Rt 12/15	

NYC&HR CLASS E-1b 2-6-0: 20x28-57-180-160600-30060. Old Class P-1 (J-4)

No.	Re'99	Re'36	Builder	Date	Reblt.	Disp.		No.	Builder	Date	Reblt.	Disp.
815	1718	1913	Depew Shops	7/99	8/18	Sc 9/48		1878	W.Albany	6/00		Sc 12/24
816	1719		W.Albany	6/99	4/18	Sc 6/33		1874	Depew Shops	7/01		Sc 10/26
817	1720		Depew Shops	4/00		Sc 12/14		1875	Depew Shops	10/01	10/14	Sc 12/25

NYC&HR CLASS E-1c 2-6-0: 20x28-57-190-156800-31730. Old Class P-2. * Some 63"DD- 28710 tf.

No.	Re'36	Builder	Bldr#	Date	Reblt.	Disp.		No.	Builder	Bldr#	Date	Reblt.	Disp.
1768		BLW.	17774	5/00		Sc 12/25		1780	BLW.	17840	6/00		Sc 11/23
1769*	1914	"	17775	"	1/18	SS 12/50		1781*	"	17841	"		Sc 10/24
1770*		"	17776	6/00	8/14	Sc 12/25		1782*	"	17864	7/00		Sc 12/24
1771	1915	"	17777	"	8/17	Sc 11/48		1783*	"	17865	"	12/18	Sc 6/33
1772*		"	17778	"		Sc 10/24		1784*	"	17866	"		Rt 11/15
1773		"	17779	"	1/15	Sc 11/26		1785	"	17888	"	7/17	Sc 8/27
1774*		"	17809	"		Rt 11/15		1786*	"	17889	"		So 12/22 (a)
1775*		"	17810	"		Sc 11/24		1787*	"	17902	"	12/18	Sc 9/26
1776*		"	17825	"		Rt 12/24		1788*	"	17903	"		Sc 8/23
1777*	1916	"	17826	"	9/18	Sc 3/49		1789*	"	17924	"		Sc 3/15
1778*		"	17827	"		Sc 11/24		1790*	"	17951	"	6/15	Sc 12/30
1779*	1917	"	17839	"		Sc 4/42							

NYC&HR CLASS E-1d 2-6-0: 20x28-57-190-155200-31730. Old Class P-3. *Some later 63"DD-28710tf.

No.	Re'36	Builder	Bldr#	Date	Reblt.	Disp.		No.	Re'36	Builder	Bldr#	Date	Reblt.	Disp.	
1741*	1918	Schen.	5483	2/00	5/18	Sc 5/49		1754*	1921	Schen.	5496	6/00		SS 11/50	
1742*		"	5484	"	5/17	Sc 6/33		1755	1922	"	5497	"	5/18	Sc 12/47	
1743*	1919	"	5485	"	6/17	Sc 12/50		1756		"	5498	"		Sc 12/24	
1744*		"	5486	"		Sc 8/23		1757*		"	5499	"		Sc 8/23	
1745*		"	5487	"		Sc 8/23		1758*		"	5500	"		Sc 12/23	
1746*		"	5488	3/00	5/18	Sc 7/28		1759*		"	5501	7/00	11/17	Sc 8/27	
1747*		"	5489	"		Sc 12/25		1760*		"	5502	"		Sc 8/23	
1748		"	5490	"	7/17	So 9/26 (b)		1761		"	5503	8/00	12/17	Sc 10/26	
1749*		"	5491	"		Sc 12/24									
1750		"	5492	"		Sc 3/14		1884	(c)	Schen.	5591	10/00		Re'14 RUT.	
1751*		"	5493	6/00		Sc 12/25		1885	(c)	"	5592	"		" " "	
1752*		"	5494	"	1/15	Sc 5/33		1876		Depew Shops	10/02	1/19	Sc 3/32	
1753*	1920	"	5495	"		Sc 7/50		1877		" "	1/03		Sc 12/14	

Note a: to Penn. Wood & Iron Co.   Note b: 1748 re Susq.& N.Y. 117.
Note c: StL&A 3,4 (re 2/02) Rutland 320,321 (re'04) 1884,1885 (re'14) 144,145.

Most of the E-1 Moguls had smaller drivers than the E's. NYC&HR 1701 was an E-1a.

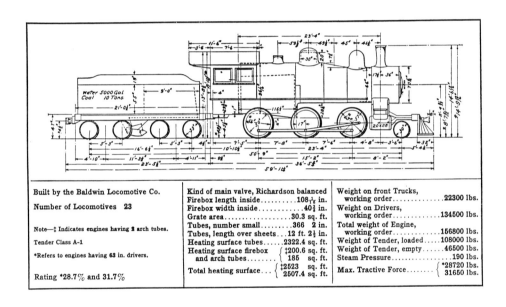

Built by the Baldwin Locomotive Co.	Kind of main valve, Richardson balanced	Weight on front Trucks,
	Firebox length inside..........108 1/16 in.	working order..............22300 lbs.
Number of Locomotives 23	Firebox width inside............40 3/4 in.	Weight on Drivers,
	Grate area.................30.3 sq. ft.	working order.............134500 lbs.
Note—‡ Indicates engines having 2 arch tubes.	Tubes, number small........366 2 in.	Total weight of Engine,
	Tubes, length over sheets...12 ft. 2½ in.	working order.............156800 lbs.
Tender Class A-1	Heating surface tubes......2322.4 sq. ft.	Weight of Tender, loaded.....108000 lbs.
	Heating surface firebox { ‡200.6 sq. ft.	Weight of Tender, empty......46500 lbs.
*Refers to engines having 63 in. drivers.	and arch tubes........ { 185 sq. ft.	Steam Pressure.................190 lbs.
		Max. Tractive Force........ { *28720 lbs.
Rating *28.7% and 31.7%	Total heating surface... { ‡2523 sq. ft. 2507.4 sq. ft.	31650 lbs.

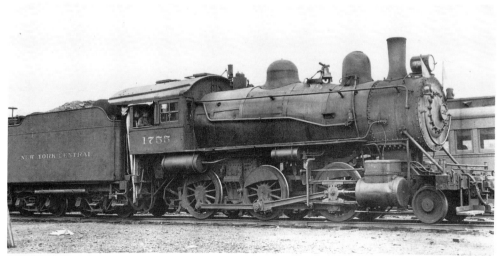

NYC 1755, class E-1d, at Brewster,N.Y. in December, 1931. Became #1922 (Vollrath coll.)

NYC&HR CLASS E-1e 2-6-0: 20x28-63-200-157100-31200. Old Class P-5.

```
                            RB                                         RB
  1859  1923  Schen. 5571  8/00  6/17  Sc  3/49   |   1867        Schen. 5579  9/00         Sc 11/26
  1860         "     5572   "          Sc 11/23   |   1868  1925    "    5580   "    11/18  Sc  9/48
  1861  1924   "     5573   "    4/19  Sc  9/48   |   1869          "    5581   "           Sc  1/22
  1862         "     5574   "          Sc 11/23   |   1870  1926    "    5582   "     8/18  SS 11/50
  1863         "     5575   "          Sc 12/23   |   1871          "    5583   "           Sc 11/24
  1864         "     5576  9/00        Sc 12/24   |   1872          "    5584   "           Sc  8/23
  1865         "     5577   "    9/19  Sc  5/33   |   1873          "    5585   "    12/14  Sc  7/32
  1866         "     5578   "          Sc 12/25   |
```

NYC&HR CLASS E-1f 2-6-0: 20x28-63-190-159200-28710. Formerly Class E-3.

```
  1766        BLW.  17637  4/00  9/04  Sc 10/24   |   1767 (b) 1927  BLW. 17638 4/00  4/04  Sc 11/41
```

NYC&HR CLASS E-1g 2-6-0: 20x28-63-190-160000-28710. Formerly Class E-3a.

```
  1763        Schen. 5505  8/00  9/05  Rt 11/15   |   1764 (a) 1928  Schen.5506 8/00 10/05  Sc 12/47
                                                  |   1765      1929    "   5507  "    8/05  Sc  9/48
```

NYC&HR CLASS E-2 2-6-0: 22+& 35x28-57-190-165000-33000. Old Class P-4.
          Converted to E-2a: 20x28-63-190-165000-28710.
  1762   Schen. 5504 8/00   Sc 11/24

NYC&HR CLASS E-3 2-6-0: 20x28-57-190-167500-32900. Old Class V-1. Later Class E-1f, above.

NYC&HR CLASS E-3a 2-6-0: 20x28-57-190-171000-32900. Old Class V-2. Later Class E-1g, above.

NYC&HR CLASS E-4 2-6-0: 18x22-64-160-120700-15600. Rebuilt from 2-6-6T Old Class M.

  (ex 829,830,832) 1050-1052 re 1450-1452. Schen. 1891. See p.182

NYC&HR CLASS E-5 2-6-0: 18x24-57-145-114000-17400. Old RW&O Class J-2. Built as RW&O 1-4.

  (ex 845-848)   1796-1799   Rhode Island 1883. See p.58

NYC&HR CLASS E-5a 2-6-0: 18x24-57-145-116000-17400., Old RW&O Class J-3. Built as RW&O 5-9,13-20.

  (ex 849-853)   1800-1804   Rome, BLW. 1883,76. See p.58
  (ex 856-863)   1805-1812   Rome, R.I. 1886-88. See p.58,62

NYC&HR CLASS E-5b 2-6-0: 18x24-57-145-100000-17400. Old RW&O Class J-5. Built as RW&O 12.

  (ex 841 re 500)   1795   Rome 1886   See p.58

NYC&HR CLASS Ex 2-6-0: 18x24-56-   Built for Fall Brook Coal Co.

  (ex FB 26,27)   1844,1845   Schen. 1885,82. See p.88

NYC&HR CLASS E-7 2-6-0: 19x24-59-135-106000-17800. Old Fall Brook Class C.

  (ex FB 46-58)   1846-1858   Schen. 1884,86. See p.90.

NYC&HR CLASS E-8 2-6-0: 19x24-59-125-98000-16200. Built for Beech Creek, Clear. & S.W.

  (ex BC 21-23)   1841-1843   Schen. 1884. See P.82

NYC&HR CLASS E-9 2-6-0: 18x24-51-145-101300-19600. Built as NY&Nor. 12-15. (1794 E-9a with 55"DD)

  (ex 496-499)   1791-1794   Rogers 1889. See P.68

NYC&HR CLASS E-10 2-6-0: 20x26-51-145-122500-25400. Built as Adiron. & St.Law. 50-52.

  (ex 842-844)   1813-1815   Schen. 1892. See p.64.

        Note a: 1764 (re'16) Raq.Lake 1.   Note b: 1767 (re'14) Raq.Lake 2..

NYC 1867, class E-1e, at Sedgwick Avenue, Bronx, in Putnam Division service. (A.Curran)

Class E—3

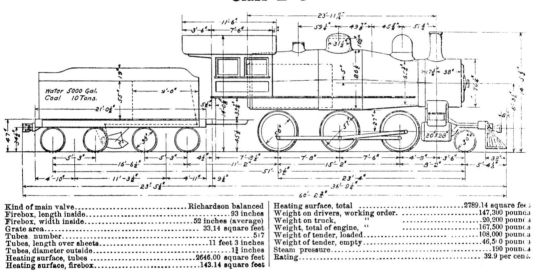

Kind of main valve..............................Richardson balanced	Heating surface, total....................2789.14 square feet
Firebox, length inside................................93 inches	Weight on drivers, working order. ....147,300 pounds
Firebox, width inside....................52 inches (average)	Weight on truck, " ....20,200 pounds
Grate area.....................................33.14 square feet	Weight, total of engine, " ....167,500 pounds
Tubes, number..517	Weight of tender, loaded......................108,000 pounds
Tubes, length over sheets........................11 feet 3 inches	Weight of tender, empty.......................46,500 pounds
Tubes, diameter outside.............................1¾ inches	Steam pressure....................................190 pounds
Heating surface, tubes ....2646.00 square feet	Rating...32.9 per cent.
Heating surface, firebox.....................143.14 square feet	

Class E-4

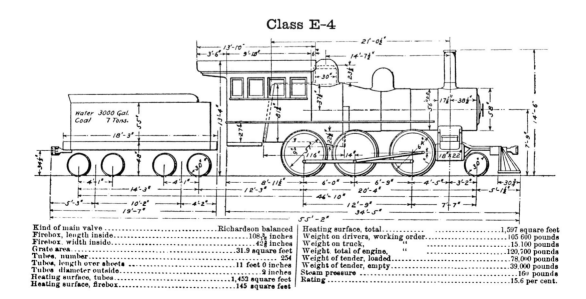

Kind of main valve..............................Richardson balanced	Heating surface, total...........................1,597 square feet
Firebox, length inside................................108⅜ inches	Weight on drivers, working order. ....105,600 pounds
Firebox, width inside....................42⅜ inches	Weight on truck, " ....15,100 pounds
Grate area.....................................31.9 square feet	Weight, total of engine, " ....120,700 pounds
Tubes, number..254	Weight of tender, loaded......................78,000 pounds
Tubes, length over sheets........................11 feet 0 inches	Weight of tender, empty.......................39,000 pounds
Tubes, diameter outside.............................2 inches	Steam pressure....................................160 pounds
Heating surface, tubes ....1,452 square feet	Rating...15.6 per cent.
Heating surface, firebox.....................145 square feet	

NYC&HR CLASS E-11,a 2-6-0: 20x24-63-200-160000-26800. Rebuilt from 2-6-6T Class J and Ja.

1407	E-11		Rebuilt c.1905	Sc	2/13		1415	E-11a		Rebuilt c.1905	Sc	3/13	
1408	"	(a)	"	"	Sc	2/13		1416	"	(a,b)	"	"	Sc	3/13	
1409	"		"	"	Sc	3/13		1417	"	(b)	"	"	Sc	3/13	
1410	"	(b)	"	"	Sc	3/13		1418	"		"	"	Sc	3/13	
1411	"		"	"	Sc	3/13		1419	"	(a,b)	"	"	Sc	3/13	
1412	"	(b)	"	"	Sc	3/13		1420	"	(b)	"	"	Sc	2/13	
1413	"	(b)	"	"	Sc	3/13		1421	"	(b)	"	"	So	1/12	(c)
1414	"	(b)	"	"	Sc	3/13		1422	"		"	"	Sc	9/11	

RUTLAND CLASS Ex 2-6-0: 17x24-57-125-74300-13400. Old Rut. Class E-1. Built as CV 81, re 38, re 228

	Re'04						
(ex Rut. 370)	1879	BLW.	2454	5/71	Sc	6/09

RUTLAND CLASS E-12 2-6-0: 18x24-55-160-104000-19600. Old Rut. Class E-2. Built as Benn.& Rut. 5,6.

(ex Rut. 380)	1880	Schen.	3351	2/91	Sc	7/18
(" 381)	1881	"	3352	"	Sc	12/20

RUTLAND CLASS E-13 2-6-0: 18x24-58-135-82300-15500. Old Rut. Class E-3. Built as Ogden.& L.C. 317,319

(ex Rut. 382)	1882	Port.	456	6/82	Sc	7/11
(" 383)	1883	"	457	"	Sc	11/09

RUTLAND CLASS E-14 2-6-0: 19x26-57-180-121000-24200. Old Rut. Class E-4,a. Built as CV 239,240,245-248.

(ex Rut. 386)	1886	Schen.	5009	3/99	Re'14 Rut.	146
(" 387)	1887	"	5010	"	" "	147
(" 388)	1888	"	5405	/00	" "	148
(" 389)	1889	"	5404	"	" "	149
(" 390)	1890	"	5406	"	" "	150
(" 391)	1891	"	5407	"	" "	151

RUTLAND CLASS E-15 2-6-0: 19x24-58-140-98600-18400. Old Rut. Class E-5. Built as O&LC 314,321.

(ex Rut. 392)	1892	BLW.	8309	12/86	So	11/15
(" 395)	1893	"	8310	"	Sc	5/13

RUTLAND CLASS E-16 2-6-0: 19x24-58-140-100700-18400. Old Rut. Class E-6. Built as O&LC 329,330.

(ex Rut. 398)	1898	Rh.Is.	1584	11/85	Sc	9/13
(" 399)	1899	"	1585	"	Sc	12/14

RUTLAND CLASS E-17 2-6-0: 19x26-58-160-110000-21600. Old Rut. Class E-7. Built as O&LC 320,318,322,323.

(ex Rut. 394)	1894	BLW.	10914	/90	Re'14 Rut.	152
(" 393)	1895	"	10638	"	" "	153
(" 396)	1896	"	10916	"	" "	154
(" 397)	1897	"	10917	"	" "	155

Note a: 19x24 cyl.-24800tf. Note b: to B&A 6/08. Note c: to Susq.& NY 109.

NYC&HR 1419, class E-11a with wide firebox. Converted from 2-6-6T class J. (Vollrath)

Class E-11.

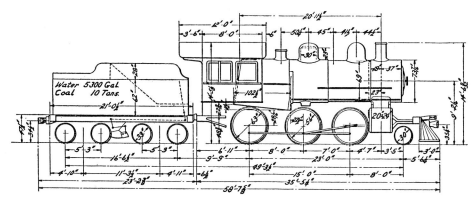

Kind of main valve..................................10 inch Piston	Heating surface, total.............................2437 square feet
Firebox, length inside................................92¾ inches	Weight on drivers, working order...................135,200 pounds
Firebox, width inside.................................97⅞ inches	Weight on truck, working order.....................24,800 pounds
Grate area...63.2 square feet	Weight, total of engine, working order..............160,000 pounds
Tubes, number...365	Weight of tender, loaded...........................114,000 pounds
Tubes, length over sheets................................12 feet	Weight of tender, empty.............................46,700 pounds
Tubes, diameter outside...................................2 inches	Steam pressure..200 pounds
Heating surface, tubes............................2275 square feet	Rating...26.8 per cent.
Heating surface, firebox...........................162 square feet	

NYC&HR 1410, class E-11. Towing an electric motor.   (H.L.Goldsmith)

CLASS F: 4-6-0 TEN WHEEL

NYC&HR CLASS F and Fa 4-6-0: 18x24-57-150-105100-18000. Old Class C. (2160-2164 later class Fa)

Re'90	Re'99	Re'00								Re'90	Re'99	Re'00					
472	655	2000	2160	Rome	311	12/87	So	5/08	(b)		667	2012	2172	Schen. 2449	1/88	So 10/06	(e)
482	656	2001	2161	"	312	"	So	3/08	(c)		668	2013	2173	" 2450	"	So 7/07	(h)
494	657	2002	2162	"	313	"	So	10/07	(f)		669	2014	2174	" 2451	"	Sc 1/06	
495	658	2003	2163(a)	"	314	"	Sc	2/14			670	2015	2175	" 2452	"	So 10/07	(g)
521	659	2004	2164	"	315	"	So	3/08	(c)		671	2016	2176	" 2453	"	So 10/07	(i)
											672	2017	2177	" 2454	"	So 8/08	(c)
444	660	2005	2165	Schen.	2439	11/87	So	3/06	(d)		673	2018	2178	" 2455	"	So 10/06	(e)
523	661	2006	2166	"	2440	"	So	10/06	(e)		674	2019	2179	" 2456	"	So 3/07	(i)
	662	2007	2167	"	2444	1/88	So	1/06	(d)		675	2020	2180	" 2457	"	So 3/07	(i)
	663	2008	2168	"	2445	"	So	2/09			676	2021	2181	" 2458	"	So 10/06	(e)
	664	2009	2169	"	2446	"	dr	by'09		524	677	2022	2182	" 2441	11/87	dr by'02	
	665	2010	2170	"	2447	"	Sc	5/09		535	678	2023	2183(a)	" 2442	"	Sc 4/12	
	666	2011	2171	"	2448	"	So	10/06	(e)	539	679	2024	2184	" 2443	"	So 1/07	(i)

NYC&HR CLASS F-1 4-6-0: 20x28-61-180-160000-26700. Old Class V. 19+x26 cyl.
Converted to F-1a: 20x28-61-190-170000-30700.
947 re 2025 re 2185 W.Albany 8/99 Reblt. 2/05 to StL&A. 11/10. Sc 10/16.

NYC&HR CLASS F-2 4-6-0: 22x26-69-200-194500-31900. Reclassified F-12 when superheated, wt. 199500.

	Re'36	Re'48				Super.					Re'36	Re'48				Super.		
2085			Alco-S	37969	10/05	by'17	Rt	8/29		2093			Alco-S	37977	10/05	(no)	Rt	8/26
2086			"	37970	"	'19	Rt	5/32		2094			"	37978	"	(no)	Rt	8/26
2087			"	37971	"	by'17	Rt	7/32		2095			"	37979	"	by'17	Rt	8/29
2088			"	37972	"	"	Rt	3/32		2096			"	37980	"	"	Rt	10/26
2089			"	37973	"	"	Rt	11/26		2097			"	37981	"	"	Rt	10/28
2090			"	37974	"	'19	Rt	7/29		2098	819	1232	"	37982	"	"	Rt	7/52
2091			"	37975	"	'18	Rt	5/32		2099			"	37983	11/05	'17	Rt	3/29
2092			"	37976	"	by'17	Rt	7/29										

NYC&HR CLASS F-2a 4-6-0: 22x26-69-200-194500-31900. Reclassified F-12a when superheated. 199500 wt.

2065			Alco-S	41058	11/06	'17	Rt	11/29		2075			Alco-S	41068	11/06	'23	Rt	3/32
2066	820	1233	"	41059	"	'19	Rt	10/51		2076			"	41069	"	'24	Rt	11/26
2067			"	41060	"	4/15	Rt	4/32		2077			"	41070	"	by'17	Rt	3/29
2068			"	41061	"	'16	Rt	5/32		2078			"	41071	"	'23	Rt	10/32
2069			"	41062	"	by'17	Rt	8/29		2079			"	41072	"	'17	Rt	5/29
2070	821	1234	"	41063	"	"	Rt	12/51		2080	823	1236	"	41073	"	by'17	Sc	2/49
2071	822	1235	"	41064	"	'17	Rt	7/52		2081			"	41074	"	(no)	Rt	8/26
2072			"	41065	"	'18	Rt	3/29		2082			"	41075	"	4/14	Rt	10/26
2073			"	41066	"	'18	Rt	5/32		2083			"	41076	"	by'17	Rt	7/29
2074			"	41067	"	'20	Rt	10/32		2084	824	1237	"	41077	"	'20	Rt	12/51

NYC&HR CLASS F-2b 4-6-0: 22x26-69-200-198500-31900. Reclassified F-12b when superheated. 203500 wt.

2100	Alco-S	41530	11/06	(no)	Rt	12/25		2106	Alco-S	41536	11/06 by'17 Rt 6/29
2101	"	41531	"	(no)	Rt	8/26		2107	"	41537	" '18 Rt 10/32
2102	"	41532	"	'23	Rt	8/28		2108	"	41538	" '20 Rt 5/32
2103	"	41533	"	by'17	Rt	7/28		2109	"	41539	" '23 Rt 10/32
2104	"	41534	"	11/15	Rt	5/29		2110	"	41540	" '18 Rt 8/28
2105	"	41535	"	by'17	Rt	8/28		2111	"	41541	" by'17 Rt 10/26

B&A CLASS F-2c 4-6-0: See B&A 704-713, ex 1900-1909.

Note a: 2163,2183 re'02 Raq.Lake 1,2.   Note b: to Hicks Loco.& Car Co.   Note c: to Cont.Iron & Stl.Co.
Note d: to Kilby Loco. & Mach. Co.   Note e: to "H'y & Co."   Note f: to SI&E 644, re Apal.Nor. 121.
Note g: to SI&E 643 re Sou.States Lbr.Co.10.   Note h: to SI&E 627 re Asherton & Gulf 1.
Note i: to Jones & Galvin.

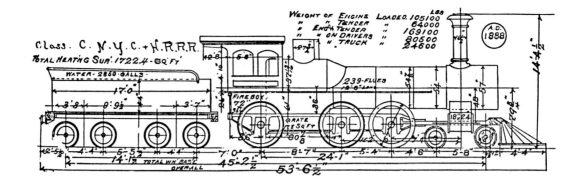

Class F-1

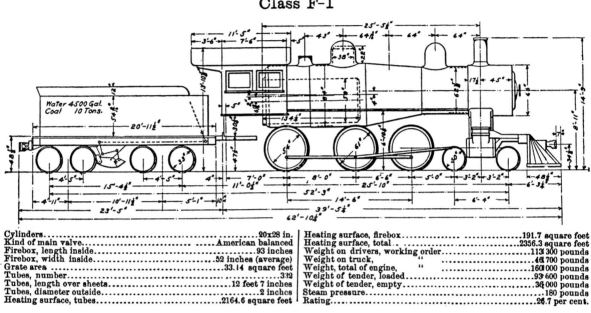

Cylinders....................20x28 in.	Heating surface, firebox...............191.7 square feet
Kind of main valve...............American balanced	Heating surface, total...............2356.3 square feet
Firebox, length inside................93 inches	Weight on drivers, working order...........113300 pounds
Firebox, width inside............52 inches (average)	Weight on truck, " ....46700 pounds
Grate area ....33.14 square feet	Weight, total of engine, " ....160000 pounds
Tubes, number...................332	Weight of tender, loaded............93600 pounds
Tubes, length over sheets............12 feet 7 inches	Weight of tender, empty............36000 pounds
Tubes, diameter outside................2 inches	Steam pressure....................180 pounds
Heating surface, tubes............2164.6 square feet	Rating....................26.7 per cent.

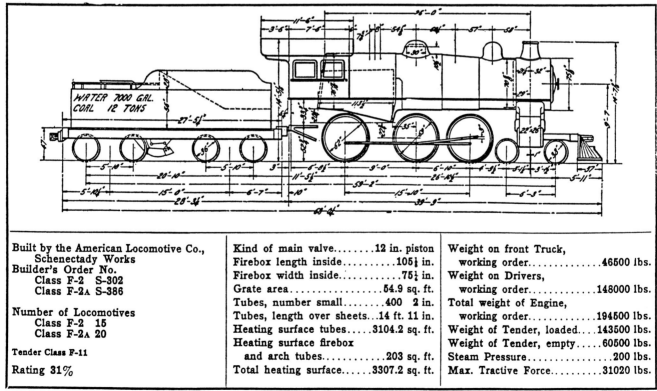

Built by the American Locomotive Co., Schenectady Works	Kind of main valve........12 in. piston	Weight on front Truck, working order..............46500 lbs.

Builder's Order No.
    Class F-2   S-302
    Class F-2A S-386
	Firebox length inside..........105¼ in.
	Firebox width inside...........75¼ in.
		Weight on Drivers, working order............148000 lbs.

Number of Locomotives
    Class F-2   15
    Class F-2A 20
	Grate area.................54.9 sq. ft.
	Tubes, number small........400 2 in.
	Tubes, length over sheets...14 ft. 11 in.
		Total weight of Engine, working order............194500 lbs.
		Weight of Tender, loaded....143500 lbs.

Tender Class F-11	Heating surface tubes.....3104.2 sq. ft. Heating surface firebox	Weight of Tender, empty.....60500 lbs.
Rating 31%	and arch tubes...........203 sq. ft. Total heating surface.....3307.2 sq. ft.	Steam Pressure................200 lbs. Max. Tractive Force.........31020 lbs.

CLASS F-2 and F-2A

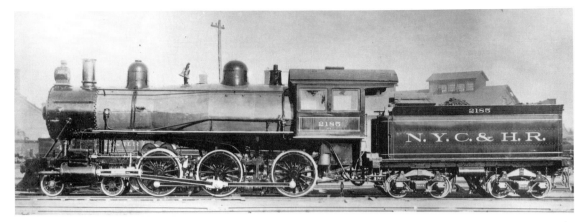

NYC&HR 2185 class F-1,with Vanderbilt firebox   (Vollrath collection)

NYC 2098, one of many F-12's assigned to Putnam Division.   June 1936. (Prescott coll.)

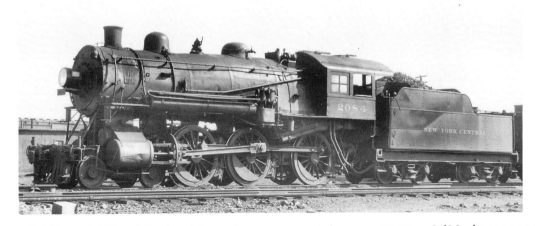

NYC 2084 class F-12a, still with inside valve gear. Niagara Falls 9/23.(Prescott coll.)

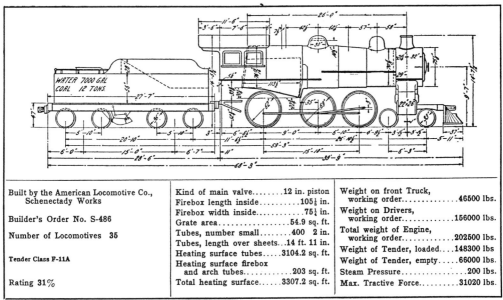

Built by the American Locomotive Co., Schenectady Works	Kind of main valve........12 in. piston	Weight on front Truck, working order.............46500 lbs.
Builder's Order No. S-486	Firebox length inside..........105⅛ in.	Weight on Drivers, working order............156000 lbs.
	Firebox width inside...........75¼ in.	
Number of Locomotives 35	Grate area.................54.9 sq. ft.	Total weight of Engine, working order.............202500 lbs.
	Tubes, number small........400 2 in.	
	Tubes, length over sheets...14 ft. 11 in.	Weight of Tender, loaded....148300 lbs
Tender Class F-11A	Heating surface tubes.....3104.2 sq. ft.	Weight of Tender, empty.....66000 lbs.
	Heating surface firebox and arch tubes...........203 sq. ft.	Steam Pressure...............200 lbs.
Rating 31%	Total heating surface......3307.2 sq. ft.	Max. Tractive Force.........31020 lbs.

CLASS F-2D

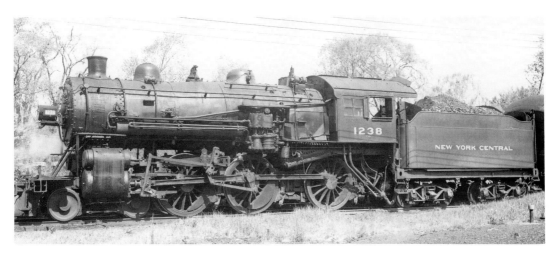

NYC 1238, class F-12e, converted from F-2e when superheated in 1913.

NYC 2114, another F-12e, at Yorktown Heights, N.Y. in June, 1936. (Prescott Collection)

NYC&HR CLASS F-2d 4-6-0: 22x26-69-200-202500-31900. Reclassified F-12d when superheated. 207500 wt.

	Re'36	Re'48				Super.		
1965			Alco-S	43614	7/07	/23	Rt	10/26
1966			"	43615	"	/17	Rt	10/32
1967			"	43616	"	by'17	Rt	9/32
1968			"	43617	"	/17	Rt	11/26
1969			"	43618	"	4/16	Sc	6/32
1970			"	43619	"	11/15	Rt	3/29
1971			"	43620	"	/24	Rt	4/32
1972			"	43621	"	by'17	Rt	4/29
1973			"	43622	"	3/15	Rt	4/29
1974			"	43623	"	by'17	Rt	3/29
1975			"	43624	"	7/15	Rt	3/32
1976			"	43625	"	/21	Rt	6/32
1977			"	43626	8/07	/17	Rt	10/26
1978			"	43627	"	/20	Rt	10/32
1979			"	43628	"	by'17	Rt	5/29
1980			"	43629	"	by'17	Rt	3/32
1981			"	43630	"	1/16	Rt	10/26
1982			"	43631	"	1/16	Rt	10/26

	Re'36	Re'48				Super.		
1983			Alco-S	43632	8/07	/17	Rt	6/29
1984			"	43633	"	11/17	Sc	5/29
1985			"	43634	"	7/15	Rt	3/32
1986			"	43635	"	4/15	Rt	7/29
1987			"	43636	"	/24	Rt	6/29
1988			"	43637	"	4/15	Rt	3/29
1989			"	43638	"	8/15	Sc	10/34
1990			"	43639	"	by'17	Rt	6/32
1991			"	43640	"	/17	Rt	7/28
1992			"	43641	"	/24	Rt	4/32
1993			"	43642	"	9/15	Rt	4/29
1994			"	43643	"	by'17	Rt	4/32
1995			"	43644	"	by'17	Rt	3/32
1996			"	43645	"	12/22	Sc	4/33
1997			"	43646	"	by'17	Rt	5/29
1998			"	43647	"	8/19	Sc	5/29
1999			"	43648	"	by'17	Sc	7/28

NYC&HR CLASS F-2e 4-6-0: 22x26-69-200-208000-31900. Reclassified F-12e when superheated.

2112	825	1238	Alco-S	43649	11/07	1/13	Rt	12/51
2113	826	1239	"	43650	"	1/14	Rt	12/51
2114	827	1240	"	43651	"	3/15	Rt	3/50
2115	828	1241	"	43652	"	7/13	Rt	12/51
2116	829	1242	"	43653	"	3/15	Rt	9/49
2117	830	1243	"	43654	"	10/12	Rt	12/51
2118	831	1244	"	43655	"	2/16	Rt	2/52
2119	832	1245	"	43656	"	8/13	Rt	2/49
2120	833	1246	"	43657	"	1/13	Rt	2/49
2121	834	1247	"	43658	"	1/13	Rt	11/48

2122	835	1248	Alco-S	43659	11/07	1/15	Rt	8/51
2123	836	1249	"	43660	"	12/12	Rt	10/51
2124	837	1250	"	43661	"	by'17	Rt	7/52
2125	838	1251	"	43662	"	3/14	Rt	5/5
2126	839	1252	"	43663	"	1/13	Rt	12/51
2127	840	1253	"	43664	"	/18	Rt	12/51
2128	841	1254	"	43665	"	1/15	Rt	8/51
2129	842	1255	"	43666	"	7/14	Rt	6/49
2130	843	1256	"	43667	"	7/14	Rt	10/51
2131	844	1257	"	43668	"	5/15	Rt	5/52

B&A CLASS F-2f. See B&A 714-723, ex 1910-1919.

NYC&HR CLASS F-2g 4-6-0: 22x26-69-200-208000-31900. Reclassified F-12g when superheated.

2132	845	1258	Alco-S	45348	9/08	12/15	Rt	12/51
2133			"	45349	"	11/14	Rt	10/26
2134	846	1259	"	45350	"	1/16	Rt	8/51
2135	847	1260	"	45351	"	by'17	Rt	12/51
2136	848	1261	"	45352	"	9/14	Rt	4/49
2137	849	1262	"	45353	"	3/14	Rt	12/51
2138	850	1263	"	45354	"	1/15	Rt	12/51
2139	851	1264	"	45355	"	by'17	Rt	8/51
2140			"	45356	"	3/13	Rt	10/26
2141	852	1265	"	45357	"	2/15	Rt	6/51
2142	853	1266	"	45358	"	4/14	Rt	1/49
2143	854	1267	"	45359	"	5/15	Rt	12/51
2144	855	1268	"	45360	"	1/16	Rt	12/51
2145	856	1269	"	45361	"	8/13	Rt	4/51
2146	857	1270	"	45362	"	1/16	Rt	12/51
2147	858	1271	"	45363	10/08	1/14	Rt	1/49
2148	859	1272	"	45364	"	/18	Rt	5/52
2149	860	1273	"	45365	"	/18	Rt	12/51

2150	861	1274	Alco-S	45366	10/08	12/12	Rt	12/51
2151	862	1275	"	45367	"	11/13	Rt	6/49
2152	863	1276	"	45368	"	/25	Rt	5/52
2153	864	1277	"	45369	"	12/12	Rt	8/51
2154	865	1278	"	45370	"	by'17	Rt	12/51
2155	866	1279	"	45371	"	/17	Rt	11/51
2156	867	1280	"	45372	"	11/13	Rt	5/52
2157	868	1281	"	45373	"	/17	Rt	12/51
2158	869	1282	"	45374	"	12/12	Rt	10/51
2159	870	1283	"	45375	"	12/13	Rt	1/49
2160	871	1284	"	45376	"	/17	Rt	4/49
2161			"	45377	"		Rt	12/25
2162	872	1285	"	45378	"	/19	Rt	12/51
2163	873	1286	"	45379	"	9/13	Rt	12/51
2164	874	1287	"	45380	"	/23	Rt	12/51
2165	875	1288	"	45381	"	by'17	Rt	5/52
2166	876	1289	"	45382	"	11/13	Rt	1/49

RUTLAND CLASS F-2h 4-6-0: 22x26-69-200-204000-31900. Later F-2k with 22+x26 cylinders, 32430 tf.

2036-2039 re 2070-2073 Alco-S 47308-47311 2/10 Re'14 Rut. 70-73.

RUTLAND CLASS F-2j 4-6-0: 22+x26-69-200-211000-32430.

2074-2079 Alco-S 51564-51569 6/12 Re'14 Rut. 74-79.

NYC 861 class F-12g at White Plains North Station in May, 1938.   (Prescott collection)

NYC 1267 class F-12g at Yorktown Heights N.Y. in 1949.   (Bob Lorenz collection)

Alco builders photo of NYC&HR 2146, class F-2g, in 1908.

NYC&HR CLASS F-3 4-6-0: 20x28-75-200-175000-26100. Old Class Q-1.

Re'99	Re'00						Re'99	Re'00				
2036	2010	BLW.	17626	4/00	Rt	7/16	2044	2018	BLW.	17669	5/00	Rt '14-17
2037	2011	"	17627	"	Rt	11/16	2045	2019	"	17670	"	" "
2038	2012	"	17628	"	Rt	7/16	2046	2020	"	17698	"	" "
2039	2013	"	17647	"	Rt	12/16	2047	2021	"	17702	"	" "
2040	2014	"	17648	"	Rt	12/16	2048	2022	"	17714	"	" "
2041	2015	"	17649	"	Sc	6/15	2049	2023	"	17715	"	" "
2042	2016	"	17667	5/00	Rt	/16	2050	2024	"	17716	"	" "
2043	2017	"	17668	"	Rt'14-17							

NYC&HR CLASS F-3a 4-6-0: 20x28-70-200-168900-28000. Old Class Q. 165500 wt.

948	2026	2000	Schen.5179	7/99	Sc	8/34	953	2031	2005(a)	Schen.	5184	7/99	Sc	4/15
949	2027	2001	" 5180	"	Sc	8/34	954	2032	2006	"	5185	"	Rt	4/17
950	2028	2002(a)	" 5181	"	Sc	5/34	955	2033	2007	"	5186	"	Rt	8/16
951	2029	2003(a)	" 5182	"	Rt	9/16	956	2034	2008	"	5187	"	Sc	10/34
952	2030	2004	" 5183	"	Sc	11/34	957	2035	2009	"	5188	"	Rt	4/17

NYC&HR CLASS F-4 4-6-0: 20x26-57-180-150600-28900. Acquired 1902 from St.Lawrence & Adirondack.
(ex SL&A 2 re 4 "Kushaqua") 2029 Brooks 2677 7/96 So 6/11 Fitzhugh Luther Co.
("   3 "Cascapedia") 2028   "   2678   "   "   "   "

NYC&HR CLASS F-5 4-6-0: 18x24-57-140-108600-16800. Old West Shore Class G.
(ex WS 131,132,143-145,149) 2094-2099 re 2191-2196   Rogers 1887,88.   See p. 82.

NYC&HR CLASS F-6 4-6-0: 19x24-56-125-102000-17100. Built for Beech Creek.
(ex BC 24,25)   2100-2101 re 2197-2198   Schen. 1885. See p.82.

NYC&HR CLASS F-7 4-6-0: 19x26-64-175-138400-22500. Built as Adir.& St.Lawr. (20&30x26 compound)
(ex A&SL 15-17)   993-995   re 2025-2027   Schen. 1892. See p.64.

NYC&HR CLASS F-8 4-6-0: 19x24-64-175-125000-20800. Built as A.& St.L. (19&28x24 compound)
(ex A&SL 80-82) 998,1000,1001 re 2089-2091 re 2186-2188 Schen. 1892. See p.64.

NYC&HR CLASS F-8a 4-6-0: 19x24-57-175-130300-23400. Built as A.& St.L. (19&28x24 compound)
(ex A&SL 83-84)   1002-1003 re 2092-2093 re 2189-2190 Schen. 1892 See p.64.

NYC&HR CLASS F-9 4-6-0: 18x23-56-175-78300-13600. Built for Fall Brook Coal Co.
(ex FB 23)   2102   re   2199   Schen. 1880. See p.88.

NYC&HR CLASS Fx 4-6-0: 19x26-63-165-134000-20710. Built as Nor.Adir. "Mountaineer".
(ex NY&O 7)   2199   Rhode Is. 1892. See p62

RUTLAND CLASS F-11a 4-6-0: 21x26-63-200-165000-30600. Old Rutland Class F-1.
(ex Rut. 212,213,422,423,482-485) 2050-2057   Alco-S 1902 re'14 Rut. 50-57

RUTLAND CLASS F-12 4-6-0: 20x26-69-200-154000-26400. Old Rutland Class F.
(ex Rut. 200-207,210,211)   2040-2049   Alco-S,M 1902 re'14 Rut. 40-49

RUTLAND CLASS F-13 4-6-0: 20x28-61-200-161000-28900. Built as St.Law.& Adir. 8,9. Old Rut. Class F-2.
(ex Rut. 251,252 re 420,421) 2153-2154 re 2063-2064   Schen. 1898 re'14 Rut. 63,64

RUTLAND CLASS F-14 4-6-0: 18x24-57-160-116000-19200. Built as Adir.& St.Law. 32,31. Old Rut. Class F-3.
(ex Rut. 234,235 re 480,481) 2155-2156 re 2061-2062   Schen. 1891 re'14 Rut. 61,62

RUTLAND CLASS F-15 4-6-0: 19x24-57-140-112000-18700. Built as Ogdens.& L.C. 336-338. Old Class F-4.
(ex Rut. 491-493)   2157-2159 re 2058-2060   Rhode.Is. 1894 re'14 Rut. 58-60

NYC&HR CLASS F-46c,d 4-6-0: 17x24-69-180-115000-15800. Acquired 1910-11 from Lake Shore & Mich. Sou.
(ex LS&MS 5032,5030,5033,5043)   2192-2195   Brooks 1891 See LS&MS roster.

Note a - 2002,2003,2005 re'02 StLaw.& Adir. 10-12, re'13 2002,2003,2005.

Class F-3

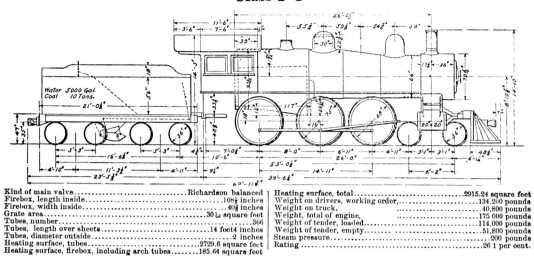

Kind of main valve............................Richardson balanced	Heating surface, total.........................2915.24 square feet
Firebox, length inside.........................108¾ inches	Weight on drivers, working order,............134,200 pounds
Firebox, width inside..........................40⅝ inches	Weight on truck, `` ....40,800 pounds
Grate area.....................................30⅘ square feet	Weight, total of engine, `` ....175,000 pounds
Tubes, number.................................366	Weight of tender, loaded.......................114,000 pounds
Tubes, length over sheets..................14 feet 4 inches	Weight of tender, empty.......................51,800 pounds
Tubes, diameter outside........................2 inches	Steam pressure................................200 pounds
Heating surface, tubes.........................2729.6 square feet	Rating..26 1 per cent.
Heating surface, firebox, including arch tubes........185.64 square feet	

Class F-4.

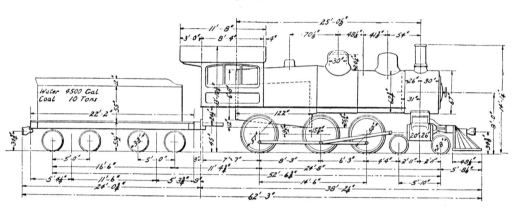

Kind of main valve............................Richardson balanced	Heating surface, total..........................2009 square feet
Firebox, length inside.........................113 inches	Weight on drivers, working order.............125,600 pounds
Firebox, width inside..........................39¼ inches	Weight on truck, working order...............25,000 pounds
Grate area.....................................31.29 square feet	Weight, total of engine, working order...........150,600 pounds
Tubes, number.................................278	Weight of tender, loaded.......................92,500 pounds
Tubes, length over sheets..................12 feet 7½ inches	Weight of tender, empty.......................39,000 pounds
Tubes, diameter outside........................2 inches	Steam pressure................................180 pounds
Heating surface, tubes.........................1834.5 square feet	Rating..28.9 per cent.
Heating surface, firebox.......................174.5 square feet	

Class F-5

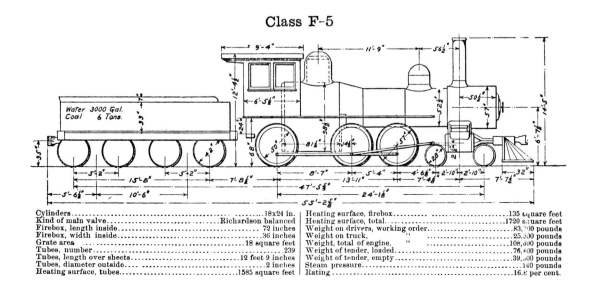

Cylinders.....................................18x24 in.	Heating surface, firebox........................135 square feet
Kind of main valve............................Richardson balanced	Heating surface, total..........................1720 square feet
Firebox, length inside.........................72 inches	Weight on drivers, working order..............83,700 pounds
Firebox, width inside..........................36 inches	Weight on truck,..............................25,300 pounds
Grate area.....................................18 square feet	Weight, total of engine, `` ....108,600 pounds
Tubes, number.................................239	Weight of tender, loaded.......................76,400 pounds
Tubes, length over sheets..................12 feet 9 inches	Weight of tender, empty.......................39,000 pounds
Tubes, diameter outside........................2 inches	Steam pressure................................140 pounds
Heating surface, tubes.........................1585 square feet	Rating..16.8 per cent.

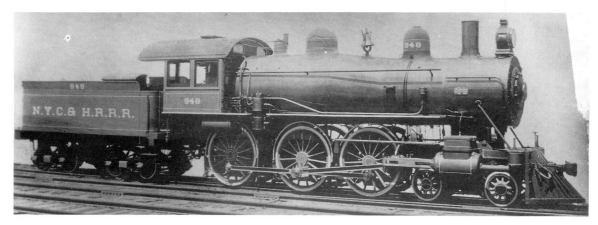

NYC&HR 949, one of ten in old class Q, built by Schenectady in 1899. Later class F-3a.
(W.D.Edson coll.)

NYC&HR class F-3 was built by Baldwin in 1900 with 75 inch drivers for passenger service.
(W.D.Edson coll.)

NYC F-3a #2004 at Sedgwick Avenue, Bronx, in February 1934.   (George Votava collection)

The NYC&HR acquired only four 2-8-0 types before 1901, One was the 367, class D-2, later G.

(Edson coll.)

NYC&HR 2399, class G-2a, built as a tandem compound.   (Chaney collection)

NYC&HR class G-2c #2402, at Utica in September 1914.   (Vollrath collection)

CLASS G: 2-8-0 CONSOLIDATION

NYC&HR CLASS G 2-8-0: 20x26-51-150-132000-27100. Old Class D-2. Later 160 bp.

260	(re'90)	501	(re'99)	2200	Schen.	2601	6/88	RB	8/07	So 6/25	Roux Crate Co.
273	"	502	"	2201	"	2602	"	"	"	" "	" "
367	"	503	"	2202	"	2603	"	RB	10/07	Rt 11/22	
477	"	504	"	2203	"	2604	"	RB	5/09	Rt 11/23	

NYC&HR CLASS G-1 2-8-0: Compound 23&35x32-63-210-190000-38500.

2332 Schen. 5709 1/01   Rt 2/24

NYC&HR CLASS G-2 2-8-0: Compound 23&35x34-63-210-192000-39100. Reclassified G-2d when superheated.

			Super.						Super.		
2333	Schen.	5779	11/01	7/14	Rt 5/27	2366	Schen.	6084	12/01	Re 7/06	MC 7758
2334	"	5781	7/01	4/13	Rt 5/27	2367	"	6085	"	9/13 Rt 9/25	
2335	"	5782	8/01	12/13	Rt 12/24	2368	"	6086	1/02	Re 7/06	MC 7759
2336	"	5783	"	1/13	Rt 9/25	2369	"	6087	"	11/13 Rt 10/26	
2337	"	5784	11/01	4/13	Rt 5/27	2370	"	6088	"	8/14 Rt 12/24	
2338	"	5785	"	10/12	Rt 12/25	2371	"	6089	2/02	10/14 Rt 12/24	
2339	"	5786	"	12/12	Rt 11/24	2372	"	6090	3/02	7/13 Rt 12/24	
2340	"	5787	"	2/13	Rt 5/27	2373	"	6091	"	8/12 Rt 12/25	
2341	"	5788	"	2/13	Rt 5/27	2374	"	6092	"	Re 7/06	MC 7760
2342	"	5780	5/01		Re 7/06 MC 7747	2375	"	6093	"	12/12 Rt 5/27	
2343	"	6043	10/01	5/12	Rt 11/24	2376	"	6094	"	Re 9/07	MC 7755
2344	"	6044	"	11/12	Rt 11/24	2377	"	6095	"	Re 9/07	MC 7756
" 2345	"	6045	"		Re 8/07 CS 7604	2378	"	6096	7/02	1/13 Rt 8/25	
2346	"	6046	"	6/13	Rt 10/26	2379	"	6097	"	Re 6/07	CS 7601
2347	"	6047	11/01		Re 6/07 MC 7749	2380	"	6098	8/02	9/12 Rt 12/24	
2348	"	6048	"		Re 7/06 MC 7750	2381	"	6099	"	• 3/13 Rt 5/27	
2349	"	6049	"		Re 7/06 MC 7751	2382	"	6100	"	2/13 Rt 10/26	
2350	"	6050	12/01		Re 6/07 MC 7752	2383	"	6101	"	Re 8/07	CS 7602
2351	"	6051	"		Re 7/06 MC 7753	2384	"	6102	"	10/13 Rt 5/27	
2352	"	6052	"	6/13	Rt 12/24	2385	"	6103	"	Re 8/07	CS 7603
2353	"	6071	"		Re 7/06 MC 7754	2386	"	6104	"	12/13 Rt 12/23	
2354	"	6072	"	9/13	Rt 12/25	2387	"	6105	"	7/13 Rt 12/24	
2355	"	6073	"	5/14	Rt 10/25	2388	Alco-S	25010	9/01	Re 9/07	MC 7757
2356	"	6074	"	3/14	Rt 12/25	2389	"	25011	"	Re 8/07	CS 7607
2357	"	6075	"		Re 8/07 CS 7605	2390	"	25012	10/01	3/13 Rt 11/24	
2358	"	6076	"	8/12	Rt 11/25	2391	"	25013	"	Re 7/06	MC 7748
2359	"	6077	"		Re 6/07 MC 7501	2392	"	25014	"	9/12 Rt 12/24	
2360	"	6078	"	5/12	Rt 5/27	2393	"	25015	"	1/13 Rt 10/24	
2361	"	6079	"	6/12	Rt 12/24	2394	"	25016	4/02	3/12 Rt 5/27	
2362	"	6080	"		Re 8/07 CS 7606	2395	"	25017	"	9/12 Rt 11/24	
2363	"	6081	"	3/13	Rt 12/24	2396	"	25018	"	3/13 Rt 12/24	
2364	"	6082	"	12/12	Rt 11/25	2397	"	25019	"	Re 8/07	CS 7608
2365	"	6083	"	5/13	Rt 11/25	2398	"	25020	"	Re 7/06	CS 7600

NYC&HR CLASS G-2a 2-8-0: Tandem Compound 15&28x34-63-210-200000-39100.
Converted to G-2c: 21x30-63-210-200000-37490. Reclassified G-2e when superheated. Wt. 206900.

2399	Alco-S	25021	4/02	/23	Rt 5/27	2407	Alco-S	27161	2/03	/19	Rt 12/25
2400	"	27154	2/03	/23	Rt 7/28	2408	"	27162	"	by'17	Rt 9/28
2401	"	27155	"		Rt 8/26	2409	"	27163	"	/18	Rt 12/25
2402	"	27156	"	by'17	Rt 7/28	2410	"	27164	"	/23	Rt 5/27
2403	"	27157	"	1/18	Sc 8/34	2411	"	27165	"	/19	Rt 5/33
2404	"	27158	"	/23	Rt 9/28	2412	"	27166	3/03	9/15	Rt 7/34
2405	"	27159	"	/23	Rt 4/33	2413	"	27167	"	10/17	Rt 6/27
2406	"	27160	"	by'17	Rt 6/27	2414re2398	"	27168	"	/17	Rt 10/26

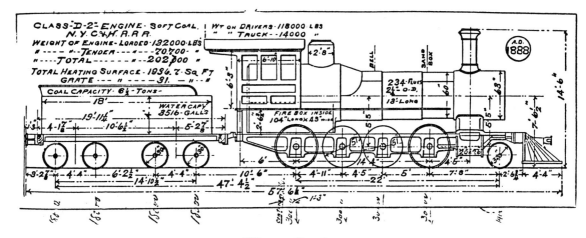

Class G—2

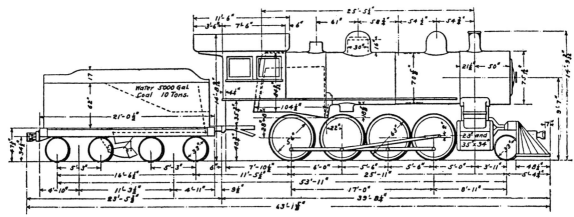

Kind of main valve.......... {14-inch piston, H. P. / Allen-Richardson balanced, L. P.}
Firebox, length inside......................96⅛ inches
Firebox, width inside......................75⅜ inches
Grate area.............................50.32 square feet
Tubes, number...............................396
Tubes, length over sheets.............15 feet 6 inches
Tubes diameter outside........................2 inches
Heating surface, tubes.............3194.48 square feet
Heating surface, firebox, including arch tubes.....189.39 square feet

Heating surface, total...................3383.87 square feet
Weight on drivers, working order............166,000 pounds
Weight on truck, "...........26,000 pounds
Weight, total of engine, "...........192,000 pounds
Weight of tender, loaded................114,000 pounds
Weight of tender, empty................46,700 pounds
Steam pressure...............................210 pounds
Rating.......................................39.1 per cent.

NOTE.—For exceptions see page 180.

160

Engine designed for........curve.

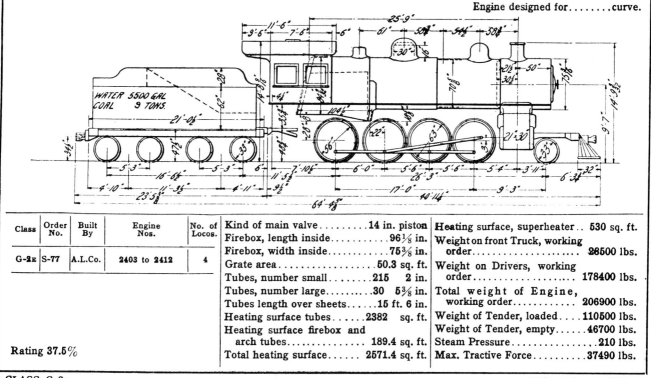

Class	Order No.	Built By	Engine Nos.	No. of Locos.
G-2ᴇ	S-77	A.L.Co.	2403 to 2412	4

Rating 37.5%

Kind of main valve.........14 in. piston
Firebox, length inside...........96⅛ in.
Firebox, width inside...........75⅜ in.
Grate area.................50.3 sq. ft.
Tubes, number small.......215   2 in.
Tubes, number large.........30 5⅜ in.
Tubes length over sheets......15 ft. 6 in.
Heating surface tubes......2382 sq. ft.
Heating surface firebox and arch tubes............189.4 sq. ft.
Total heating surface......2571.4 sq. ft.

Heating surface, superheater.. 530 sq. ft.
Weight on front Truck, working order.................. 28500 lbs.
Weight on Drivers, working order.................. 178400 lbs.
Total weight of Engine, working order.......... 206900 lbs.
Weight of Tender, loaded....110500 lbs.
Weight of Tender, empty......46700 lbs.
Steam Pressure...............210 lbs.
Max. Tractive Force..........37490 lbs.

CLASS G-2ᴇ

(Printed Jan. 1, 1929)

NYC&HR CLASS G-3 2-8-0: 20x26-51-180-150000-32500. Converted to G-3b, wt. 152000.

2302		Schen.	6003	8/01	Rt 10/26		2317 re'36 904	Schen.	6018	2/02	Sc 6/37
2303		"	6004	"	Rt 7/27		2318	"	6019	"	Rt 6/27
2304		"	6005	"	Rt 6/27		2319	"	6020	"	Rt 6/27
2305		"	6006	9/01	Rt 10/26		2320	"	6021	"	Rt 10/26
2306		"	6007	"	Rt 6/27		2321	"	6022	"	Rt 6/27
2307		"	6008	12/01	Rt 7/27		2322	"	6023	4/02	Rt 8/28
2308		"	6009	"	Rt 6/27		2323	"	6024	"	So 10/31 (a)
2309 (G-3a)		"	6010	"	Rt 6/27		2324	"	6025	"	Rt 10/26
2310		"	6011	"	Sc 10/35		2325	"	6026	"	Rt 10/26
2311		"	6012	"	Sc 8/35		2326	"	6027	"	Rt 8/26
2312		"	6013	2/02	Sc 9/35		2327	"	6028	"	Rt 10/26
2313		"	6014	"	Rt 10/28		2328	"	6029	"	Rt 10/26
2314		"	6015	"	Rt 10/26		2329	"	6030	"	Rt 11/32
2315		"	6016	"	Rt 8/26		2330	"	6031	"	Rt 7/27
2316		"	6017	"	Rt 10/28		2331	"	6032	"	Rt 8/26

NYC&HR CLASS G-4 2-8-0: Tandem Compound 16&30x30-51-210-225000-46600. Converted to G-4a 23x30-180.

	re'05							re'05				
2415	2685	Alco-S	27124	3/03	Rt 7/27		2423	2693	Alco-S	27132	3/03	Rt 7/27
2416	2686	"	27125	"	Rt 10/26		2424	2694	"	27133	"	So 8/27 (b)
2417	2687	"	27126	"	Rt 7/27		2425	2695	"	27134	"	Rt 12/25
2418	2688	"	27127	"	So 5/27 (b)		2426	2696	"	27135	"	Rt 12/25
2419	2689	"	27128	"	Rt 10/27		2427	2697	"	27136	"	Rt 10/27
2420	2690	"	27129	"	So 8/27 (b)		2428	2698	"	27137	4/03	Rt 10/27
2421	2691	"	27130	"	Rt 12/25		2429	2699	"	27138	"	So 4/27 (c)
2422	2692	"	27131	"	Rt 12/25							

Note a: to St.Regis Paper Co.   Note b: to Kan.City,Mex.& Orient 21-23.   Note c: to Susq.& NY 118.

NYC LINES CLASSES G-5, G-6, and G-16 2-8-0: 23x32-63-200-220200 to 246000-45680.

These were standard freight engines for many of the New York Central Lines for several years. Listed below are classes assigned to component lines. For a time, some engines were reclassified to G-16 as they were superheated. Starting in 1912 many were rebuilt to 2-8-2 types and assigned class H-5.

G-5 and G-5a	NYC&HR	G-5y re G-6ya	LS&MS
G-5a	LS&MS	G-5z re G-16za	LS&MS
G-5b and G-5c	NYC&HR	G-6a re G-16a	NYC&HR
G-5c,G-5d,G-5e	LS&MS	G-6b	LS&MS
G-5f	NYC&HR	G-6c and G-6d	CCC&StL
G-5g	B&A	G-6e	B&A
G-5h	CI&S (IH)	G-6f re G-16f	NYC&HR
G-5ha re G-6ha	CCC&StL	G-6g re G-16g	NYC&HR
G-5i re G-6ia,b	CCC&StL	G-6h	B&A
G-5j	NYC&HR	G-6j	MC
G-5k re G-6ka	LS&MS	G-6k re G-16k	NYC&HR
G-5l	CI&S (IH)	G-6l	NYC&HR
G-5m re G-6ma	LS&MS	G-6m	CI&S, LS&MS
G-5n	NYC&HR	G-6n	CCC&StL
G-5o (ex G-5h)	CCC&StL	G-6o	MC
G-5p and G-5q	NYC&HR	G-6p	CS
G-5r and G-6ra	LS&MS	G-6q re G-16q	B&A
G-5s	MC	G-6s	CCC&StL
G-5t	CCC&StL	G-6t	MC
G-5u and G-16ua	CCC&StL	G-6u	CS
G-5v	NYC&HR	G-6v	LS&MS
G-5w	B&A	G-16v	LE&W
G-5x	CI&S (IH)	G-16w	LE&W

Class G—3

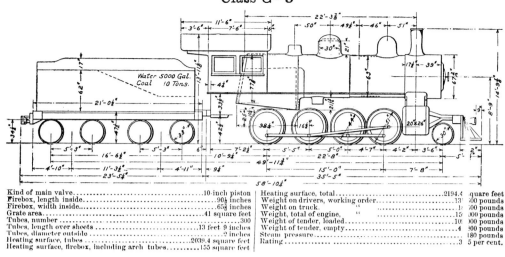

Kind of main valve.................10-inch piston
Firebox, length inside.....................90⅛ inches
Firebox, width inside......................65⅜ inches
Grate area...............................41 square feet
Tubes, number............................300
Tubes, length over sheets.............13 feet 9 inches
Tubes, diameter outside..................2 inches
Heating surface, tubes..................2039.4 square feet
Heating surface, firebox, including arch tubes..........155 square feet

Heating surface, total....................2194.4 square feet
Weight on drivers, working order.....................13?500 pounds
Weight on truck, " ....1?500 pounds
Weight, total of engine, " ....15?000 pounds
Weight of tender, loaded............10?000 pounds
Weight of tender, empty..................4?00 pounds
Steam pressure.........................180 pounds
Rating.............................3?5 per cent.

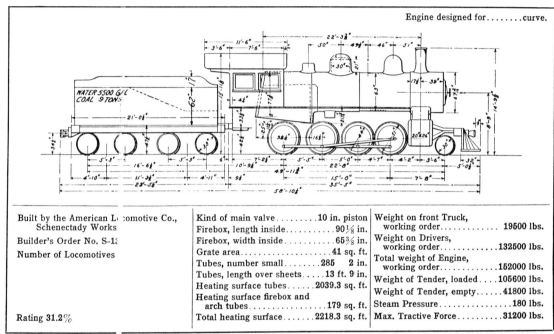

Engine designed for........curve.

Built by the American Locomotive Co., Schenectady Works

Builder's Order No. S-13?

Number of Locomotives

Rating 31.2%

Kind of main valve.........10 in. piston
Firebox, length inside...........90⅛ in.
Firebox, width inside...........65⅜ in.
Grate area....................41 sq. ft.
Tubes, number small.......285   2 in.
Tubes, length over sheets.....13 ft. 9 in.
Heating surface tubes.....2039.3 sq. ft.
Heating surface firebox and arch tubes.................179 sq. ft.
Total heating surface......2218.3 sq. ft.

Weight on front Truck, working order...... 19500 lbs.
Weight on Drivers, working order............132500 lbs.
Total weight of Engine, working order............152000 lbs.
Weight of Tender, loaded....105600 lbs.
Weight of Tender, empty......41800 lbs.
Steam Pressure................180 lbs.
Max. Tractive Force.........31200 lbs.

CLASS G-3ʀ

(Printed Jan. 1, 1929)

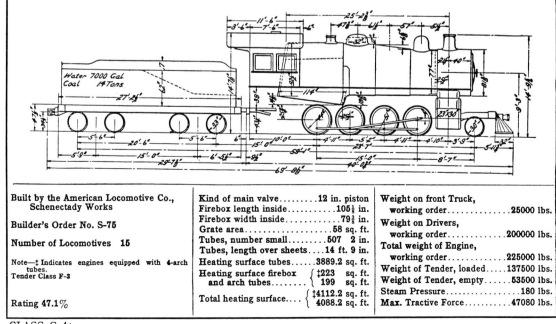

Built by the American Locomotive Co., Schenectady Works

Builder's Order No. S-75

Number of Locomotives 15

Note—‡ Indicates engines equipped with 4-arch tubes.
Tender Class F-3

Rating 47.1%

Kind of main valve........12 in. piston
Firebox, length inside...........105⅛ in.
Firebox width inside............79⅜ in.
Grate area....................58 sq. ft.
Tubes, number small........507   2 in.
Tubes, length over sheets....14 ft. 9 in.
Heating surface tubes.....3889.2 sq. ft.
Heating surface firebox and arch tubes........ ‡223 sq. ft. / 199 sq. ft.
Total heating surface.... ‡4112.2 sq. ft. / 4088.2 sq. ft.

Weight on front Truck, working order..............25000 lbs.
Weight on Drivers, working order............200000 lbs.
Total weight of Engine, working order............225000 lbs.
Weight of Tender, loaded.....137500 lbs.
Weight of Tender, empty......53500 lbs.
Steam Pressure................180 lbs.
Max. Tractive Force..........47080 lbs.

CLASS G-4ᴀ

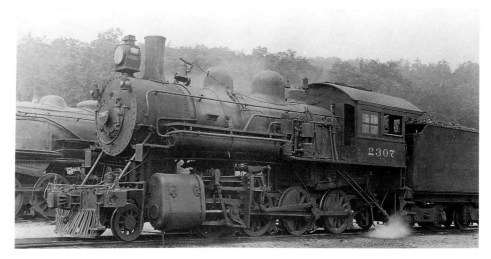

NYC&HR 2307, G-3b. Corning, N.Y. August, 1916.   (K.Schlachter)

NYC&HR 2306, class G-3; Schenectady delivered 30 of these engines in 1901-02. Later G-3b
(Edson Coll.)

NYC 2685 , built as tandem compound and later simpled as class G-4a.   (W. Landon)

(Railway Age 1903)

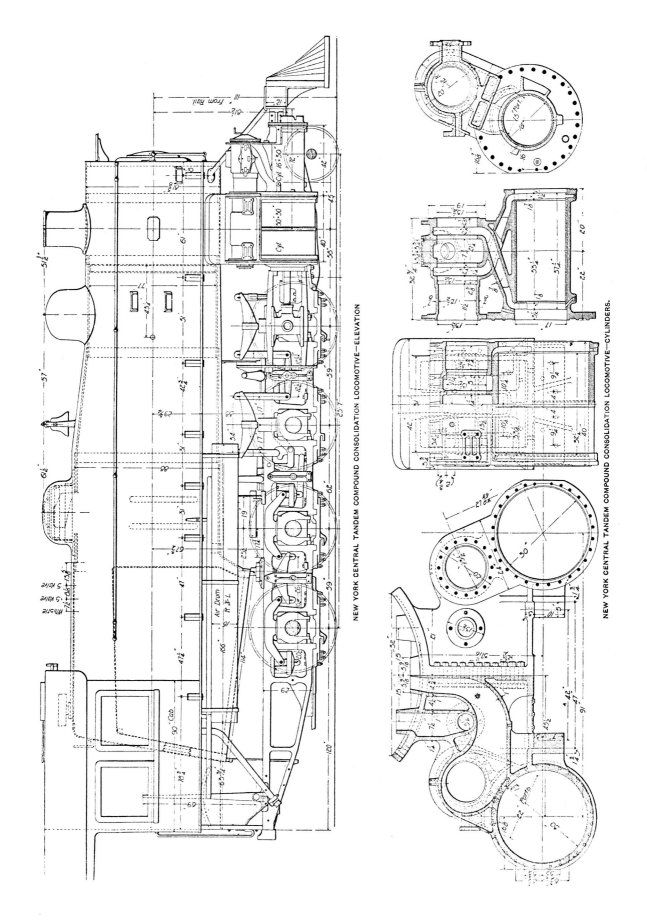

NEW YORK CENTRAL TANDEM COMPOUND CONSOLIDATION LOCOMOTIVE—ELEVATION

NEW YORK CENTRAL TANDEM COMPOUND CONSOLIDATION LOCOMOTIVE—CYLINDERS.

NYC&HR Class G-5 2-8-0: 23x32-63-200-220200-45680

No.	Builder	C/N	Date	RB	Date	Class	No.	Note
2477	Alco-S	27850	10/03	RB	7/12	H-5e	3664	
2478	"	27851	"	"	9/12	"	3629	
2479	"	27852	"	"	7/12	"	3654	
2480	"	27853	"	"	6/12	H-5d	3683	
2481	"	27854	"	"	12/12	H-5e	3712	(a)
2482	"	27855	"	"	11/12	"	3705	
2483	"	27856	"	"	7/12	"	3674	
2484	"	27857	"	"	4/12	H-5c	3687	
2485	"	27858	"	"	10/12	H-5e	3611	
2486	"	27859	11/03	"	9/12	"	3646	
2487	"	27860	"	"	3/12	H-5c	3692	
2488	"	27861	"	"	9/12	H-5e	3670	
2489	Alco-S	27862	11/03	RB	9/12	H-5e	3624	
2490	"	27863	"	"	8/12	"	3644	(a)
2491	"	27864	"	"	12/12	"	3719	
2492	"	27865	"	"	11/12	"	3601	
2493	"	27866	"	"	9/12	"	3625	
2494	"	27867	"	"	8/12	"	3651	(a)
2495	"	27868	"	"	6/12	H-5d	3680	
2496	"	27869	"	"	4/12	H-5c	3686	
2497	"	27870	"	"	7/12	H-5e	3659	
2498	"	27871	"	"	8/12	"	3632	
2499	"	27872	12/03	"	7/12	"	3658	

Note a: Boiler replaced 1909.

NYC&HR Class G-5a 2-8-0: 23x32-63-200-220200-45680

No.	Builder	C/N	Date	RB	Date	Class	No.
2452	Alco-B	29635	7/04	RB	8/12	H-5e	3650
2453	"	29636	"	"	10/12	"	3616
2454	"	29637	"	"	6/12	H-5d	3681
2455	"	29638	"	"	9/12	H-5e	3645
2456	"	29639	8/04	"	9/12	"	3662
2457	"	29640	"	"	12/12	"	3713
2458	"	29641	"	"	9/12	"	3643
2459	"	29642	"	"	10/12	"	3623
2460	"	29643	"	"	11/12	"	3706
2461	"	29644	"	"	7/12	"	3673
2462	"	29645	"	"	7/12	"	3672
2463	"	29646	"	"	7/12	"	3661
2464	"	29647	"	"	9/12	"	3647
2465	Alco-S	29648	10/04	RB	8/12	H-5e	3649
2466	"	29649	"	"	7/12	"	3668
2467	"	29650	"	"	10/12	"	3607
2468	"	29651	"	"	12/12	"	3711
2469	"	29652	"	"	12/12	"	3718
2470	"	29653	"	"	10/12	"	3621
2471	"	29654	"	"	10/12	"	3606
2472	"	29655	"	"	7/12	"	3660
2473	"	29656	"	"	3/12	H-5c	3693
2474	"	29657	"	"	11/12	H-5e	3710
2475	"	29658	"	"	12/12	"	3714
2476	"	29659	"	"	10/12	"	3614

NYC&HR CLASS G-5b 2-8-0: 23x32-63-200-220200-45680

No.	Builder	C/N	Date	RB	Date	Class	No.	Note
2427	Alco-S	30348	12/04	RB	7/12	H-5e	3671	
2428	"	30349	"	"	7/12	H-5d	3679	
2429	"	30350	"	"	8/12	H-5e	3648	
2430	"	30351	"	"	8/12	"	3655	
2431	"	30352	"	"	3/12	H-5a	3699	
2432	"	30353	"	"	9/12	H-5e	3636	
2433	"	30354	"	"	7/12	"	3667	(b)
2434	"	30355	"	"	11/12	"	3701	
2435	"	30356	"	"	11/12	"	3703	
2436	"	30357	"	"	10/12	"	3612	
2437	"	30358	"	"	9/12	"	3641	
2438	"	30359	"	"	3/12	H-5c	3694	
2439	"	30360	"	"	10/12	H-5e	3617	
2440	Alco-S	30361	12/04	RB	10/12	H-5e	3620	
2441	"	30362	"	"	12/12	"	3717	
2442	"	30363	"	"	12/12	"	3715	
2443	"	30364	"	"	8/12	"	3663	
2444	"	30365	"	"	11/12	"	3707	
2445	"	30366	"	"	9/12	"	3628	
2446	"	30367	"	"	12/12	"	3720	
2447	"	30368	"	"	6/12	H-5d	3678	
2448	"	30369	"	"	6/12	"	3684	
2449	"	30370	1/05	"	11/12	H-5e	3702	
2450	"	30371	"	"	6/12	H-5d	3682	
2451	"	30372	"	"	9/12	H-5e	3635	

Note b: Boiler replaced 4/07.

NYC&HR CLASS G-5c 2-8-0: 23x32-63-200-220200-45680.

No.	Builder	C/N	Date	RB	Date	Class	No.
2700	Alco-S	30795	2/05	RB	3/12	H-5b	3695
2701	"	30796	"	"	11/12	H-5e	3709
2702	"	30797	"	"	12/12	"	3721
2703	"	30798	"	"	3/12	H-5b	3696
2704	"	30799	"	"	11/12	H-5e	3600
2705	"	30800	"	"	9/12	"	3657
2706	"	30801	"	"	9/12	"	3642
2707	"	30802	"	"	12/12	"	3716
2708	"	30803	"	"	7/12	"	3653
2709	"	30804	"	"	8/12	"	3637
2710	"	30805	"	"	10/12	"	3604
2711	"	30806	"	"	3/12	H-5b	3697
2712	"	30807	"	"	10/12	H-5e	3615
2713	"	30808	"	"	6/12	H-5d	3677
2714	"	30809	"	"	9/12	H-5e	3626
2715	"	30810	"	"	11/12	"	3602
2716	"	30811	"	"	11/12	"	3603
2717	"	30812	"	"	7/12	"	3666
2718	"	30813	3/05	"	9/12	"	3639
2719	"	30814	"	"	8/12	"	3631
2720	"	30815	"	"	4/12	H-5c	3685
2721	"	30816	"	"	3/12	"	3691
2722	"	30817	"	"	3/12	"	3690
2723	"	30818	"	"	9/12	H-5e	3640
2724	"	30819	"	"	8/12	"	3633
2725	Alco-S	30820	3/05	RB	10/12	H-5e	3608
2726	"	30821	"	"	10/12	"	3619
2727	"	30822	"	"	8/12	"	3627
2728	"	30823	"	"	8/12	"	3634
2729	"	30824	"	"	7/12	H-5d	3676
2730	"	30825	"	"	8/12	H-5e	3638
2731	"	30826	"	"	7/12	"	3656
2732	"	30827	"	"	8/12	"	3669
2733	"	30828	"	"	3/12	H-5b	3698
2734	"	30829	"	"	11/12	H-5e	3700
2735	"	30830	"	"	11/12	"	3708
2736	"	30831	"	"	10/12	"	3605
2737	"	30832	"	"	10/12	"	3609
2738	"	30833	"	"	3/12	H-5c	3689
2739	"	30834	"	"	10/12	H-5e	3610
2740	"	30835	"	"	8/12	"	3665
2741	"	30836	"	"	8/12	"	3652
2742	"	30837	"	"	9/12	"	3630
2743	"	30838	"	"	10/12	"	3622
2744	"	30839	"	"	11/12	"	3704
2745	"	30840	"	"	7/12	H-5d	3675
2746	"	30841	"	"	10/12	H-5e	3618
2747	"	30842	"	"	10/12	"	3613
2748	"	30843	"	"	4/12	H-5c	3688
2749 (G-5f)		30970	5/05	"	/12	G-10f	699

NYC&HR 2482, among the first group of G-5's, many of which were converted to H-5 2-8-2's.

Class **G-5.**

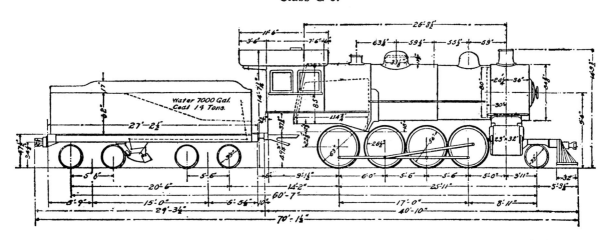

Kind of main valve	14-inch piston
Firebox, length inside	105¹⁄₈ inches
Firebox, width inside	75¼ inches
Grate area	54.9 square feet
Tubes, number	458
Tubes, length over sheets	15 feet 6 inches
Tubes, diameter outside	2 inches
Heating surface, tubes	3717 square feet
Heating surface, firebox, including arch tubes	220 square feet

Heating surface, total	3937 square feet
Weight on drivers, working order	200,000 pounds
Weight on truck, working order	20,200 pounds
Weight, total of engine, working order	220,200 pounds
Weight of tender, loaded	137,500 pounds
Weight of tender, empty	53,500 pounds
Steam pressure	200 pounds
Rating	47.1 per cent.

NYC&HR 2737, G-5c built 1905, rebuilt just 7 years later to class H-5e #3609.(Edson Coll.)

2750	Alco-S	38731	12/05	RB	6/16	H-5p	3877	2778	Alco-S	38759	1/06	RB	2/17	H-5p	3879
2751	"	38732	"	"	8/13	H-5f	2601	2779	"	38760	"	"	9/16	"	3880
2752	"	38733	"	"	8/13	"	2611	2780	"	38761	"	"	1/14	H-5k	3829
2753	"	38734	"	"	1/14	H-5k	3828	2781	"	38762	"	"	8/13	H-5f	2615
2754	"	38735	"	"	1/16	H-5p	3866	2782	"	38763	"	"	12/15	H-5q	3862
2755	"	38736	"	"	8/13	H-5f	2609	2783	"	38764	"	"	8/13	H-5f	2607
2756	"	38737	"	"	2/17	H-5p	3872	2784	"	38765	"	"	1/14	H-5k	3823
2757	"	38738	"	"	2/16	"	3865	2785	"	38766	"	"	3/18	H-5q	3881
2758	"	38739	"	"	9/16	"	3873	2786	"	38767	"	"	1/14	H-5k	3826
2759	"	38740	"	"	1/17	"	3874	2787	"	38768	"	"	8/13	H-5f	2610
2760	"	38741	"	"	7/16	H-5q	3875	2788	"	38769	"	"	8/13	"	2603
2761	"	38742	"	"	8/13	H-5f	2617	2789	"	38770	"	"	8/13	"	2612
2762	"	38743	"	"	7/15	H-5p	3853	2790	"	38771	"	"	1/17	H-5p	3882
2763	"	38744	"	"	8/13	H-5f	2620	2791	"	38772	"	"	8/13	H-5f	2608
2764	"	38745	"	"	8/13	"	2616	2792	"	38773	"	"	12/17	H-5q	3883
2765	"	38746	"	"	9/16	H-5p	3876	2793	"	38774	"	"	1/14	H-5k	3825
2766	"	38747	"	"	6/16	"	3871	2794	"	38775	"	"	9/16	H-5p	3884
2767	"	38748	"	"	1/14	H-5k	3827	2795	"	38776	"	"	1/16	"	3863
2768	"	38749	"	"	8/13	H-5f	2613	2796	"	38777	"	"	5/16	"	3870
2769	"	38750	"	"	8/13	"	2614	2797	"	38778	"	"	1/14	H-5k	3824
2770	"	38751	1/06	"	8/13	"	2600	2798	"	38779	"	"	9/16	H-5p	3885
2771	"	38752	"	"	8/13	"	2605	2799	"	38780	"	"	8/13	H-5f	2619
2772	"	38753	"	"	8/13	"	2602	2800	"	38781	"	"	1/17	H-5p	3886
2773	"	38754	"	"	8/13	"	2606	2801	"	38782	"	"	8/13	H-5f	2618
2774	"	38755	"	"	7/15	H-5p	3857	2802	"	38783	"	"	2/16	H-5p	3867
2775	"	38756	"	"	9/16	"	3878	2803	"	38784	"	"	1/14	H-5k	3822
2776	"	38757	"	"	11/15	"	3860	2804	"	38785	"	"	3/14	"	3830
2777	"	38758	"	"	8/13	H-5f	2604								

NYC&HR CLASS G-5n 2-8-0: 23x32-63-200-229000-45680

2805	Alco-S	40968	10/06	RB	8/13	H-5g	2623	2828	Alco-S	40991	1/07	RB	9/13	H-5g	2639
2806	"	40969	"	"	1/14	H-5m	3848	2829	"	40992	"	"	7/15	H-5p	3858
2807	"	40970	"	"	12/18	H-5q	3887	2830	"	40993	"	"	9/13	H-5g	2632
2808	"	40971	"	"	9/16	H-5p	3888	2831	"	40994	2/07	"	11/15	H-5p	3861
2809	"	40972	"	"	3/14	H-5m	3843	2832	"	40995	"	"	2/17	"	3893
2810	"	40973	"	"	1/14	"	3851	2833	"	40996	"	"	8/13	H-5g	2624
2811	"	40974	"	"	9/13	H-5g	2633	2834	"	40997	"	"	8/13	"	2621
2812	"	40975	"	"	9/13	"	2638	2835	"	40998	"	"	1/16	H-5p	3864
2813	"	40976	"	"	7/18	H-5q	3889	2836	"	40999	"	"	7/15	"	3859
2814	"	40977	"	"	9/13	H-5g	2630	2837	"	41000	"	"	7/15	"	3854
2815	"	40978	"	"	9/13	"	2634	2838	"	41001	"	"	9/16	"	3894
2816	"	40979	"	"	12/16	H-5p	3890	2839	"	41002	"	"	1/17	"	3895
2817	"	40980	"	"	8/13	H-5g	2625	2840	"	41003	"	"	1/14	H-5m	3847
2818	"	40981	"	"	2/17	H-5p	3891	2841	"	41004	"	"	1/17	H-5p	3896
2819	"	40982	"	"	1/14	H-5m	3850	2842	"	41005	"	"	9/13	H-5g	2631
2820	"	40983	"	"	1/17	H-5p	3892	2843	"	41006	"	"	9/13	"	2636
2821	"	40984	"	"	9/13	H-5g	2635	2844	"	41007	"	"	9/13	"	2640
2822	"	40985	"	"	9/13	"	2629	2845	"	41008	"	"	9/13	"	2627
2823	"	40986	"	"	8/13	"	2626	2846	"	41009	"	"	1/14	H-5m	3645
2824	"	40987	"	"	2/16	H-5p	3868	2847	"	41010	"	"	6/16	H-5p	3897
2825	"	40988	1/07	"	1/14	H-5m	3846	2848	"	41011	"	"	9/13	H-5g	2628
2826	"	40989	"	"	8/13	H-5g	2622	2849	"	41012	"	"	1/14	H-5m	3849
2827	"	40990	"	"	9/13	"	2637								

NYC&HR CLASS G-5p 2-8-0: 23x32-63-200-229000-45680

2850	Alco-S	41542	1/07	RB	5/15	H-5p	3869	2856	Alco-S	41548	1/07	RB	7/15	H-5p	3856
2851	"	41543	"	"	2/17	"	3898	2857	"	41549	"	"	9/13	H-5g	2642
2852	"	41544	"	"	1/14	H-5m	3844	2858	"	41550	"	"	1/17	H-5p	3901
2853	"	41545	"	"	7/17	H-5q	3899	2859	"	41551	"	"	3/15	H-5m	3852
2854	"	41546	"	"	1/17	H-5p	3900	2860	"	41552	"	"	11/17	H-5q	3723
2855	"	41547	"	"	7/15	"	3855	2861	"	41553	"	"	9/13	H-5g	2641

NYC&HR 2806, G-5n   (W.D.Edson coll.)

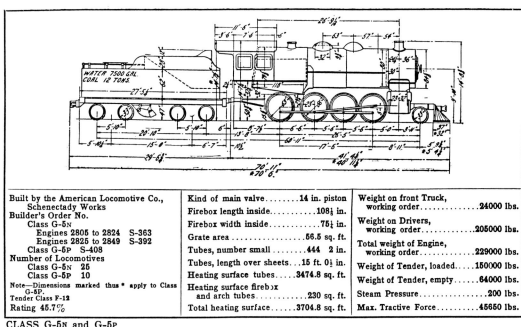

Built by the American Locomotive Co., Schenectady Works	Kind of main valve........14 in. piston	Weight on front Truck, working order.............24000 lbs.
Builder's Order No.	Firebox length inside..........108⅛ in.	Weight on Drivers, working order.............205000 lbs.
Class G-5N	Firebox width inside...........75¼ in.	
Engines 2805 to 2824 S-363	Grate area ....56.5 sq. ft.	Total weight of Engine, working order.............229000 lbs.
Engines 2825 to 2849 S-392	Tubes, number small ....444 2 in.	
Class G-5P S-408	Tubes, length over sheets...15 ft. 0½ in.	Weight of Tender, loaded.....150000 lbs.
Number of Locomotives	Heating surface tubes.....3474.8 sq. ft.	Weight of Tender, empty......64000 lbs.
Class G-5N 25	Heating surface firebox	Steam Pressure................200 lbs.
Class G-5P 10	and arch tubes...........230 sq. ft.	
Note—Dimensions marked thus * apply to Class G-5P.	Total heating surface......3704.8 sq. ft.	Max. Tractive Force.........45650 lbs.
Tender Class F-12		
Rating 45.7%		

CLASS G-5N and G-5P

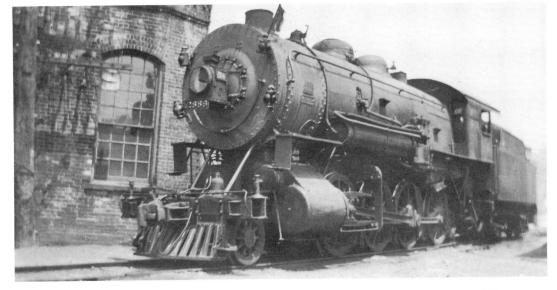

NYC&HR 2886, G-5q. Note centered headlight and steel pilot.   (Chaney collection)

NYC&HR CLASS G-5q 2-8-0: 23x32-63-200-230000-45680.

2862	Alco-S	41849	2/07	RB	2/17	H-5p	3902
2863	"	41850	"	"	2/18	H-5q	3903
2864	"	41851	"	"	8/15	H-5p	3904
2865	"	41852	"	"	9/16	"	3905
2866	"	41853	"	"	9/16	"	3906
2867	"	41854	"	"	12/15	"	3907
2868	"	41855	"	"	1/17	"	3908
2869	"	41856	"	"	8/16	H-5q	3909
2870	"	41857	"	"	7/15	H-5p	3910
2871	"	41858	"	"	2/14	H-5n	3831
2872	"	41859	"	"	12/15	H-5p	3911
2873	"	41860	"	"	2/14	H-5n	3832
2874	"	41861	"	"	5/16	H-5p	3912
2875	Alco-S	41862	2/07	RB	9/16	H-5p	3913
2876	"	41863	"	"	3/14	H-5n	3833
2877	"	41864	"	"	7/16	H-5q	3914
2878	"	41865	3/07	"	3/16	H-5p	3915
2879	"	41866	"	"	9/16	"	3916
2880	"	41867	"	"	3/14	H-5n	3834
2881	"	41868	"	"	2/14	"	3835
2882	"	41869	"	"	1/16	H-5p	3917
2883	"	41870	"	"	12/16	H-5q	3918
2884	"	41871	"	"	1/17	H-5p	3919
2885	"	41872	"	"	11/15	"	3920
2886	"	41873	"	"	5/18	H-5q	3921

NYC&HR CLASS G-5v 2-8-0: 23x32-63-200-230000-45680.

2887	Alco-S	42577	3/07	RB	3/14	H-5n	3836
2888	"	42578	"	"	2/14	"	3837
2889	"	42579	"	"	3/14	"	3838
2890	"	42580	"	"	8/15	H-5p	3922
2891	"	42581	"	"	1/16	"	3923
2892	"	42582	"	"	12/15	H-5q	3924
2893	"	42583	"	"	1/16	"	3925
2894	"	42584	"	"	1/16	"	3926
2895	"	42585	"	"	8/16	"	3927
2896	"	42586	"	"	7/17	"	3928
2897	Alco-S	42587	3/07	RB	1/16	H-5q	3929
2898	"	42588	"	"	5/16	H-5p	3930
2899	"	42589	"	"	1/16	"	3931
2900	"	42590	"	"	3/14	H-5n	3839
2901	"	42591	"	"	6/16	H-5p	3932
2902	"	42592	"	"	1/17	"	3933
2903	"	42593	"	"	2/14	H-5n	3840
2904	"	42594	"	"	3/14	"	3841
2905	"	42595	"	"	2/14	"	3842
2906	"	42596	"	"	5/16	H-5p	3934

NYC&HR CLASS G-6a 2-8-0: 23x32-63-200-236000-45680. Reclassified G-16a when superheated. Wt. 239000.

2907	Alco-S	44053	10/07	SH	by'17	Rt	7/29	
2908	"	44054	"	"	2/15	Sc	10/32	
2909	"	44055	"	"	1/16	So	8/27	(a)69
2910	"	44056	"		by'17	Rt	11/26	
2911	"	44057	"	"	12/15	Rt	8/29	
2912	"	44058	"		by'17	Sc	3/32	
2913	"	44059	"	"	12/15	Rt	10/30	
2914	"	44060	"	"	1/16	Rt	8/29	
2915	"	44061	"	"	7/15	So	5/27	(a)51
2916	"	44062	"	"	5/15	Rt	10/30	
2917	Alco-S	44063	10/07	SH	3/14	Rt	9/29	
2918	"	44064	11/07	"	12/15	Rt	10/30	
2919	"	44065	"	"	10/13	Rt	11/26	
2920	"	44066	"	"	by'17	Sc	10/32	
2921	"	44067	"	"	11/13	Rt	6/27	
2922	"	44068	"	"	1/14	So	8/27	(a)63
2923	"	44069	"	"	by'17	Rt	7/29	
2924	"	44070	"	"	1/16	Rt	10/30	
2925	"	44071	"	"	3/15	So	5/27	(a)52
2926	"	44072	"	"	by'17	Sc	10/32	

NYC&HR CLASS G-6f 2-8-0: 23x32-63-200-236000-45680. Reclassified G-16f when superheated. Wt. 239000.

2927	Alco-S	45185	1/08	SH	6/13	Rt	10/30	
2928	"	45186	"	"	by'17	Rt	7/27	
2929	"	45187	"	"	12/13	so	5/27	(a)53
2930	"	45188	"	"	12/15	Rt	10/29	
2931	"	45189	"	"	2/13	Rt	10/26	
2932	"	45190	"	"	10/15	Rt	10/26	
2933	"	45191	"		by'17	Rt	8/27	
2934	"	45192	"	"	12/13	So	8/27	(a)62
2935	"	45193	"	"	/23	Rt	5/32	
2936	"	45194	"		by'17	So	5/27	(a)54
2937	Alco-S	45195	1/08	SH	12/13	Rt	7/29	
2938	"	45196	"	"	by'17	Sc	10/32	
2939	"	45197	"	"	6/14	Rt	10/31	
2940	"	45198	"	"	by'17	So	5/27	(a)55
2941	"	45199	"	"	by'17	Rt	3/32	
2942	"	45200	"	"	9/13	Rt	4/29	
2943	"	45201	2/08	"	by'17	Rt	8/29	
2944	"	45202	"	"	11/13	Rt	4/29	
2945	"	45203	"	"	11/15	Rt	7/27	
2946	"	45204	"	"	4/14	Rt	11/31	

NYC&HR CLASS G-6g 2-8-0: 23x32-63-200-236000-45680. Reclassified G-16g when superheated. Wt. 239000.

2947	Alco-S	45383	11/08	SH	5/15	Rt	9/29	
2948	"	45384	"	"	1/14	So	8/27	(a)65
2949	"	45385	"	"	10/14	Rt	6/27	
2950	"	45386	"	"	/17	Rt	4/29	
2951	"	45387	"		by'17	Rt	7/27	
2952	"	45388	"	"	10/13	Rt	10/30	
2953	"	45389	"	"	2/15	So	8/27	(a)67
2954	"	45390	"	"	7/15	Rt	3/32	
2955	Alco-S	45391	11/08	SH	by'17	Rt	7/27	
2956	"	45392	"	"	by'17	Rt	4/29	
2957	"	45393	"	"	by'17	Rt	7/28	
2958	"	45394	"	"	9/13	Rt	4/29	
2959	"	45395	"	"	4/15	Rt	4/29	
2960	"	45396	12/08	"	by'17	Sc	11/32	
2961	"	45397	"	"	1/14	Rt	5/29	

Note a: to Kan.City, Mex. & Orient

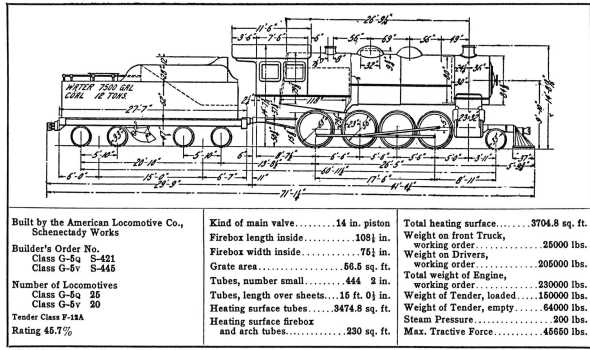

Built by the American Locomotive Co.,
Schenectady Works

Builder's Order No.
Class G-5q S-421
Class G-5v S-445

Number of Locomotives
Class G-5q 25
Class G-5v 20

Tender Class F-12A

Rating 45.7%

Kind of main valve.........14 in. piston
Firebox length inside..........108⅛ in.
Firebox width inside...........75¼ in.
Grate area.................56.5 sq. ft.
Tubes, number small........444 2 in.
Tubes, length over sheets....15 ft. 0½ in.
Heating surface tubes......3474.8 sq. ft.
Heating surface firebox
  and arch tubes.............230 sq. ft.

Total heating surface........3704.8 sq. ft.
Weight on front Truck,
  working order..............25000 lbs.
Weight on Drivers,
  working order..............205000 lbs.
Total weight of Engine,
  working order.............230000 lbs.
Weight of Tender, loaded.....150000 lbs.
Weight of Tender, empty......64000 lbs.
Steam Pressure.................200 lbs.
Max. Tractive Force..........45650 lbs.

CLASS G-5q and G-5v

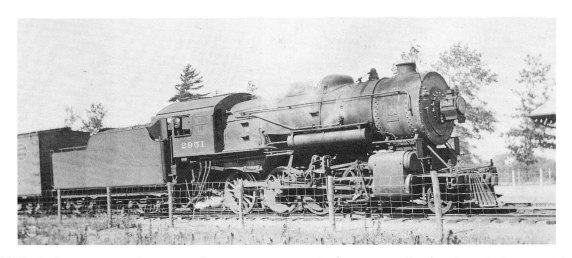

NYC 2951 G-6g, among the few that were not rebuilt to H-5 Mikados.(Edson coll.)

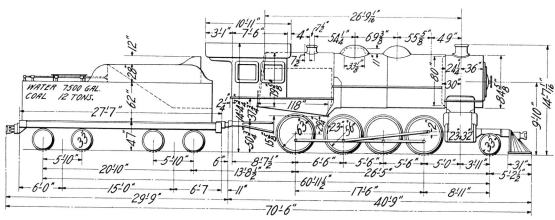

CONSOLIDATION LOCOMOTIVE No. 2947
CLASS G-6-G.

158

NYC&HR CLASS G-6k 2-8-0: 23x32-63-200-244500-45680. Briefly reclassified G-16k when superheated.

```
2962  Alco-B 47002  1/10  SH  1/15   Rt   4/29        2974  Alco-B 47014  1/10  SH  12/14  Rt   7/29
2963    "    47003   "    "   by'17  Rt  11/26        2975    "    47015   "    "    /23   So   5/27  KCMO 59
2964    "    47004   "    "   3/14   Sc   6/32        2976    "    47016   "    "   6/14   So   8/27  KCMO 66
2965    "    47005   "    "    /23   So   5/27 KCMO 56 2977   "    47017   "    "   by'17  Rt   8/29
2966    "    47006   "    "   9/12   So   8/27 KCMO 68 2978   "    47018   "    "   11/14  So   5/27  KCMO 60
2967    "    47007   "    "    /23   Rt   7/29        2979    "    47019   "    "    /23   Rt   5/32
2968    "    47008   "    "   5/14   So   8/27 KCMO 64 2980   "    47020  2/10  "    5/14  Rt   5/29
2969    "    47009   "    "          Rt  10/26        2981    "    47021   "    "    /22   Rt   3/32
2970    "    47010   "    "   by'17  Rt   4/29        2982    "    47022   "    "   11/44  So   5/27  KCMO 61
2971    "    47011   "    "   by'17  So   5/27 KCMO 57 2983   "    47023   "    "   by'17  Rt  11/26
2972    "    47012   "    "   1/15   So   5/27 KCMO 58 2984   "    47024   "    "   6/14   Sc  10/32
2973    "    47013   "    "    /23   Rt   5/32        2985    "    47025   "    "   1/16   Rt   6/29
```

NYC&HR CLASS G-6L 2-8-0: 26x32-63-165-240500-48150. Formerly 23x32-63-200-45680. Built with superheater

```
2986   Alco-B 47026 2/10  Rt 8/27
```

NYC&HR CLASS G-7 2-8-0: 20x24-51-165-104000-24950. Old West Shore class C. (G-7a: 135bp-20700tf)

   (ex WS 121-175 series)   2212-2254   BLW,Dickson 1883,84. See pp.78,80.

NYC&HR CLASS G-8 2-8-0: 21x26-51-140-127000-27300. Built as RW&O Class D-3 #100-105.

   (ex 864-869)   2204-2209   Rome 1889,90. See p.62.

NYC&HR CLASS G-9 2-8-0: 20x24-51-140-109900-22900. Old Fall Brook Class B. (G-9a 2255 ex G-11a)

   (ex FB 29-33,35-43)   2265-2278   Schen. 1883. See p.88.

NYC&HR CLASS G-10 2-8-0: 20x24-51-160-122800-25800. Old Fall Brook Class A.

   (ex FB 59-80)   2279-2300   Schen. 1888-94. See p 90

NYC&HR CLASS G-10f 2-8-0: 23x32-63-200-220200-45700. Rebuilt from class G-5f for switching service.

   (ex 2749)   699 Alco-S '05; RB '12.   RB 1/17 to 2-8-2 class H-5f 3722.

NYC&HR CLASS G-11 2-8-0: 20x24-51-125-108000-20800. Built for Beech Creek. (G-11a: 135bp-225000wt.)

   (ex BC 1-10)   2255-2264   Schen. 1884-87. See p.82

NYC&HR CLASS G-12 2-8-0: 20x26-51-180-142000-29700. Built as Pittsburgh & Eastern 1

   (ex Fall Brook 81)   2301   Schen. 1896. See p.90.

NYC&HR CLASS G-12a 2-8-0: 20x26-51-170-145500-29400. Built as Hoover. & S.W. 10, acquired 1913.

   (ex H&SW 10)   2nd 2298   Alco-S 38878 11/05 So 12/15 Okla.N.M. & Pac. 101.

NYC&HR CLASS G-13 2-8-0: Compound 22&32x26-51-140-149400-31300. Built as Adiron. & StLaw. 60,61.

   (ex 996,997)   2210,2211   Schen. 1893. See p.64.

RUTLAND CLASS G-14a 2-8-0: Compound 22&34x28-54-200-153000-31200. Built as Ogdens.& L.C. 339-341.

   (ex Rut.550-552) 2424-2426 re 2401-2403. Schen. 4645-4647 12/97. Conv. to 19x28 G-14. Re'14 RUT. 10-12

RUTLAND CLASS Gx 2-8-0: 19x24-51-140-108200-21000. Acquired from WNY&P by O&LC.

   (ex Rutland 519)   (2nd) 2265   BLW 4392 7/78. Sc 12/11

RUTLAND CLASS G-34's 2-8-0: 22+x30-63-195-209000 to 214000-39960.

```
G-34a  2418-2423  Alco-S  43037-43042  4/07  Re'14 Rutland 18-23
G-34b  2414-2417    "     48011-48014  4/10   "     "   14-17
G-34c  2424-2425    "     50150-50151  6/11   "     "   24-25
G-34d  2426-2431    "     53280-53285  6/13   "     "   26-31
```

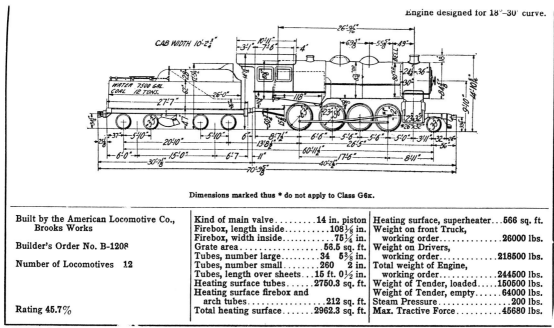

Engine designed for 18°–30° curve.

Dimensions marked thus * do not apply to Class G6κ.

Built by the American Locomotive Co., Brooks Works	Kind of main valve.........14 in. piston	Heating surface, superheater...566 sq. ft.
	Firebox, length inside..........108⅛ in.	Weight on front Truck,
Builder's Order No. B-1208	Firebox, width inside............75¼ in.	working order..............26000 lbs.
	Grate area..................56.5 sq. ft.	Weight on Drivers,
Number of Locomotives 12	Tubes, number large........34 5⅜ in.	working order............218500 lbs.
	Tubes, number small.......260 2 in.	Total weight of Engine,
	Tubes, length over sheets..15 ft. 0½ in.	working order............244500 lbs.
	Heating surface tubes.....2750.3 sq. ft.	Weight of Tender, loaded.....150500 lbs.
	Heating surface firebox and	Weight of Tender, empty......64000 lbs.
	arch tubes.................212 sq. ft.	Steam Pressure.................200 lbs.
Rating 45.7%	Total heating surface......2962.3 sq. ft.	Max. Tractive Force.........45680 lbs.

CLASS G-6κ   (Printed Jan. 1, 1929)

NYC&HR 2986, class G-6L, the first 2-8-0 built with superheater.   (Chaney collection)

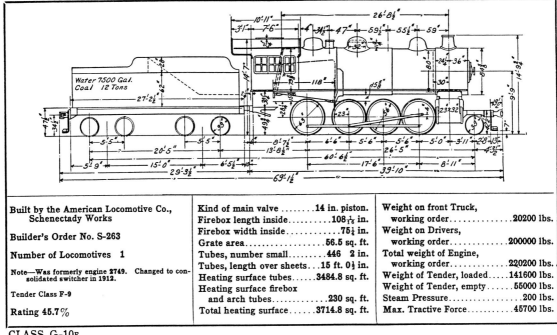

Built by the American Locomotive Co., Schenectady Works	Kind of main valve ....14 in. piston.	Weight on front Truck,
	Firebox length inside..........108 1/16 in.	working order..............20200 lbs.
Builder's Order No. S-263	Firebox width inside............75¼ in.	Weight on Drivers,
	Grate area..................56.5 sq. ft.	working order............200000 lbs.
Number of Locomotives 1	Tubes, number small........446 2 in.	Total weight of Engine,
Note—Was formerly engine 2749. Changed to consolidated switcher in 1912.	Tubes, length over sheets..15 ft. 0¾ in.	working order............220200 lbs.
	Heating surface tubes.....3484.8 sq. ft.	Weight of Tender, loaded.....141600 lbs.
Tender Class F-9	Heating surface firebox and arch tubes............230 sq. ft.	Weight of Tender, empty......55000 lbs.
		Steam Pressure.................200 lbs.
Rating 45.7%	Total heating surface.....3714.8 sq. ft.	Max. Tractive Force.........45700 lbs.

CLASS G-10F

CLASS H. 2-8-2 MIKADO

NYC LINES CLASS H-5 2-8-2: 25x32-63-180-274000 to 308700-48570.

Starting in 1912 hundreds of G-5 and G-6 Consolidations were rebuilt to Mikados in this class, followed by many more built new to this design. Listed below are H-5 subclasses assigned to component lines:

H-5a to H-5f	NYC&HR	
H-5g	NYC&HR and B&A	
H-5h	NYC&HR	
H-5j	B&A	
H-5k	NYC&HR	
H-5L	NYC&HR, LS&MS, CCC&StL	
H-5La	CCC&StL (ex LS&MS H-5L)	

H-5m, H-5n	NYC&HR	
H-5o	CCC&StL	
H-5p, H-5q	NYC	
H-5r	IHB	
H-5s	CCC&StL	
H-5t	NYC and CCC&StL	
H-5u, H-5v	IHB	

NYC&HR CLASS H-5a 2-8-2: 25x32-63-180-274000-48570

	re'36	re'48							
3699			RB from G-5b 2431	Baldwin 3/12				Sc	8/34

NYC&HR CLASS H-5b 2-8-2: 25x32-63-180-274000-48570

3695	(1235)	RB from G-5c 2700	Baldwin 3/12	Sc	7/36
3696		" " " 2703	" "	Sc	7/34
3697		" " " 2711	" "	Rt	7/33, Sc
3698		" " " 2733	" "	Rt	9/33, Sc

NYC&HR CLASS H-5c 2-8-2: 25x32-63-180-274000-48570

3685	1230	1300	RB from G-5c 2720	Alco-B	4/12	(GO-24576-10)	Rt	2/52, SS 2/52
3686			" " G-5 2496	" "		" -9	Sc	6/34
3687			" " " 2484	" "		" -8	Rt	8/33, Sc
3688	(1231)		" " G-5c 2748	" "		" -7	Sc	7/36
3689	1232		" " " 2738	" "	3/12	" -6	So	7/37 DSS&A 1050
3690	1253	1301	" " " 2722	" "		" -4	Rt	3/52, SS 8/52
3691			" " " 2721	" "		" -5	Rt	9/33, Sc
3692			" " G-5 2487	" "		" -2	Rt	8/33, Sc
3693	1234		" " G-5a 2473	" "		" -3	So	3/41 AB&C 235
3694			" " G-5b 2438	" "		" -1	Rt	8/33, Sc

NYC&HR CLASS H-5d 2-8-2: 25x32-63-180-274000-48570

3675		RB from G-5c 2745	Alco-B	7/12	(GO-24576-18)	Sc	9/34
3676	1226	" " " 2729	" "		" -20	So	5/37 TA&G 304
3677		" " " 2713	" "	6/12	" -16	Sc	7/34
3678		" " G-5b 2447	" "		" -17	Rt	8/33, Sc
3679	1227	" " " 2428	" "	7/12	" -19	Sc	10/47
3680	(1228)	" " G-5 2495	" "	6/12	" -11	Sc	1/36
3681		" " G-5a 2454	" "		" -12	Rt	8/33, Sc
3682		" " G-5b 2450	" "		" -13	Rt	7/33, Sc
3683		" " G-5 2480	" "		" -14	Sc	6/34
3684	1229	" " G-5b 2448	" "		" -15	Sc	11/37

NYC&HR CLASS H-5e 2-8-2: 25x32-63-180-274000-48570

3600	P&E 20 (a)	RB from G-5c 2704	Alco-B	11/12	(GO-24576-95)	Rt	1/51 (NB 4/14)
3601		" " G-5 2492	" "		" -94	Sc	7/34
3602		" " G-5c 2715	" "		" -93	Rt	8/33, Sc
3603		" " " 2716	" "		" -92	Rt	9/33, Sc
3604		" " " 2710	" "	10/12	" -91	Sc	9/34
3605		" " " 2736	" "		" -90	Sc	7/35
3606		" " G-5a 2471	" "		" -89	Sc	9/34
3607	P&E 21 (a)	" " " 2467	" "		" -88	Rt	12/50, SS 2/51
3608		" " G-5c 2725	" "		" -87	Rt	8/33, Sc

Note a: 3600 and 3607 assigned 10/27 to P&E, were scheduled to be renumbered in 1936 to 1200 and 1201, but were renumbered P&E 20 and 21 in 3/37.

NYC&HR 3699, class H-5a, the first conversion from 2-8-0. Baldwin did the work.(E.L.May)

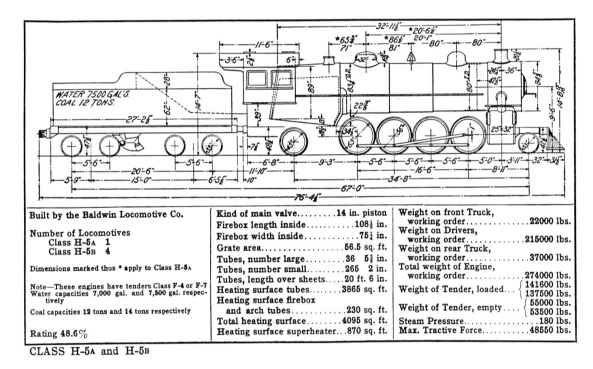

Built by the Baldwin Locomotive Co.

Number of Locomotives
    Class H-5ᴀ 1
    Class H-5ʙ 4

Dimensions marked thus * apply to Class H-5ᴀ

Note—These engines have tenders Class F-4 or F-7
Water capacities 7,000 gal. and 7,500 gal. respectively

Coal capacities 12 tons and 14 tons respectively

Rating 48.6%

Kind of main valve	14 in. piston
Firebox length inside	108⅛ in.
Firebox width inside	75¼ in.
Grate area	56.5 sq. ft.
Tubes, number large	36 5¾ in.
Tubes, number small	265 2 in.
Tubes, length over sheets	20 ft. 6 in.
Heating surface tubes	3865 sq. ft.
Heating surface firebox and arch tubes	230 sq. ft.
Total heating surface	4095 sq. ft.
Heating surface superheater	870 sq. ft.

Weight on front Truck, working order	22000 lbs.
Weight on Drivers, working order	215000 lbs.
Weight on rear Truck, working order	37000 lbs.
Total weight of Engine, working order	274000 lbs.
Weight of Tender, loaded	141600 lbs. 137500 lbs.
Weight of Tender, empty	55000 lbs. 53500 lbs.
Steam Pressure	180 lbs.
Max. Tractive Force	48550 lbs.

CLASS H-5ᴀ and H-5ʙ

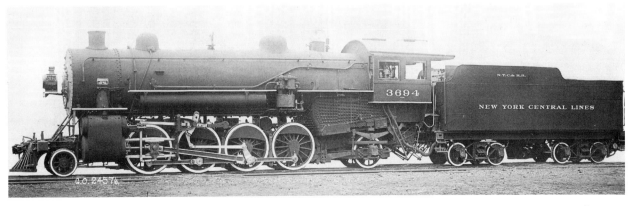

Alco builder's photo for NYC&HR 3694, Alco's first H-5 conversion (from G-5b 2438).(Edson)

NYC&HR CLASS H-5e 2-8-2: Continued.

No.	re'36	re'48	RB from	class	bldr	Alco-B	date	GO	suffix	disposition
3609			RB from	G-5c	2737	Alco-B	10/12	(GO-24576-86)		Sc 8/34
3610	1202	1400	" "	"	2739	"	"	"	-85	Rt 7/50, Sc
3611	1203		" "	G-5	2485	"	"	"	-84	So 10/39 AB&C 232
3612	1204		" "	G-5b	2436	"	"	"	-83	So 12/38 TA&G 306
3613	1205		" "	G-5c	2747	"	"	"	-82	Rt 1/39, Sc 8/39
3614			" "	G-5a	2476	"	"	"	-81	Sc 8/34
3615			" "	G-5c	2712	"	"	"	-80	Sc 9/34
3616	1206		" "	G-5a	2453	"	"	"	-79	Rt 12/39, Sc 7/40
3617			" "	G-5b	2439	"	"	"	-78	Sc 8/34
3618			" "	G-5c	2746	"	"	"	-77	Sc 10/34
3619	1207	1401	" "	G-5c	2726	"	"	"	-76	Rt 5/51, SS
3620	1208		" "	G-5b	2440	"	"	"	-75	Rt 12/39, Sc 8/40
3621			" "	G-5a	2470	"	"	"	-74	Rt 8/33, Sc
3622			" "	G-5c	2743	"	"	"	-73	Rt 12/34, Sc 4/35
3623	1209	1402	" "	G-5a	2459	"	10/12	"	-72	Rt 10/49, Sc
3624	1210	1403	" "	G-5	2489	"	9/12	"	-71	Rt 12/49, Sc
3625			" "	"	2493	"	"	"	-70	Rt 9/33, Sc
3626			" "	G-5c	2714	"	"	"	-69	Rt 12/34, Sc
3627			" "	"	2727	"	8/12	"	-49	Rt 8/33, Sc
3628			" "	G-5b	2445	"	9/12	"	-68	Sc 5/35
3629			" "	G-5	2478	"	"	"	-67	Sc 7/34
3630			" "	G-5c	2742	"	"	"	-66	Sc 11/34
3631			" "	"	2719	"	8/12	"	-46	Sc 10/34
3632			" "	G-5	2498	"	"	"	-48	Rt 9/33, Sc
3633			" "	G-5c	2724	"	"	"	-45	Sc 7/34
3634	1211		" "	"	2728	"	"	"	-44	Sc 7/39
3635			" "	G-5b	2451	"	9/12	"	-60	Sc 6/34
3636	(1212)		" "	"	2432	"	"	"	-53	Sc 3/36
3637	(1213)		" "	G-5c	2709	"	8/12	"	-52	Sc 3/36
3638			" "	"	2730	"	"	"	-51	Sc 10/34
3639			" "	"	2718	"	9/12	"	-58	Rt 8/33, Sc
3640			" "	"	2723	"	"	"	-57	Sc 7/35
3641			" "	G-5b	2437	"	"	"	-56	Rt 9/33, Sc
3642			" "	G-5c	2706	"	"	"	-55	Rt 9/33, Sc
3643			" "	G-5a	2458	"	"	"	-54	Sc 7/34
3644			" "	G-5	2490	"	8/12	"	-50	Rt 8/33, Sc
3645			" "	G-5a	2455	"	9/12	"	-59	Sc 9/34
3646	1214	1404	" "	G-5	2486	"	"	"	-62	Rt 9/55
3647			" "	G-5a	2464	"	"	"	-61	Sc 5/34
3648	(1215)		" "	G-5b	2429	"	8/12	"	-43	Sc 5/36
3649			" "	G-5a	2465	"	"	"	-42	Sc 7/35
3650	(1216)		" "	"	2452	"	"	"	-41	Sc 6/36
3651			" "	G-5	2494	"	"	"	-40	Sc 8/34
3652			RB from	G-5c	2741	"	"	"	-47	Sc 10/34
3653	(1217)		" "	"	2708	"	7/12	"	-34	Sc 3/36
3654			" "	G-5	2479	"	"	"	-35	Rt 9/33, Sc
3655	1218		" "	G-5b	2430	"	8/12	"	-36	Sc 7/39
3656	(1219)		" "	G-5c	2731	"	7/12	"	-25	Sc 7/36
3657			" "	"	2705	"	9/12	"	-63	Sc 7/35
3658			" "	G-5	2499	"	7/12	"	-32	Sc 6/35
3659			" "	"	2497	"	"	"	-26	Sc 8/34
3660	(1220)		" "	G-5a	2472	"	"	"	-30	Sc 1/36
3661	1221	1405	" "	"	2463	"	"	"	-27	Rt 9/55
3662			" "	"	2456	"	9/12	"	-64	Sc 10/34
3663	1222	1406	" "	G-5b	2443	"	8/12	"	-37	SS 6/51
3664			" "	G-5	2477	"	7/12	"	-31	Sc 8/34
3665			" "	G-5c	2740	"	8/12	"	-39	Rt 8/33, Sc
3666	1223	1407	" "	"	2717	"	7/12	"	-29	Rt 2/53, SS 6/53
3667			" "	G-5b	2433	"	"	"	-28	Rt 8/33, Sc
3668	(1224)		" "	G-5a	2466	"	"	"	-33	Sc 7/36
3669	(1225)		" "	G-5c	2732	"	8/12	"	-38	Sc 6/36
3670			" "	G-5	2488	"	9/12	"	-65	Rt 8/33, Sc
3671			" "	G-5b	2427	"	7/12	"	-24	Rt 8/33, Sc
3672			" "	G-5a	2462	"	"	"	-23	Rt 8/33, Sc
3673			" "	"	2461	"	"	"	-22	Sc 8/34
3674			" "	G-5	2483	"	"	"	-21	Sc 6/34

NYC 3615, class H-5e at Collinwood in 1920. Note large electric headlight.   (Prescott)

NYC 1209 class H-5e (ex-3623), at Fremont, Ohio.   (H.W.Ameling collection)

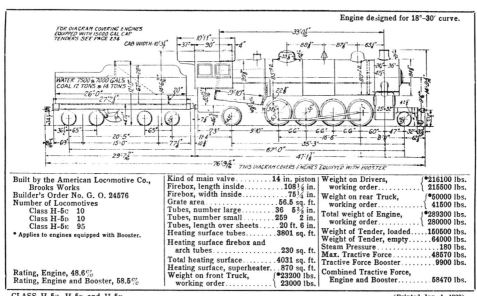

Built by the American Locomotive Co.,
  Brooks Works
Builder's Order No. G. O. 24576
Number of Locomotives
  Class H-5c   10
  Class H-5d   10
  Class H-5e   95
* Applies to engines equipped with Booster.

Rating, Engine, 48.6%
Rating, Engine and Booster, 58.5%

Kind of main valve	14 in. piston
Firebox, length inside	108⅛ in.
Firebox, width inside	75¼ in.
Grate area	56.5 sq. ft.
Tubes, number large	36 5⅜ in.
Tubes, number small	259 2 in.
Tubes, length over sheets	20 ft. 6 in.
Heating surface tubes	3801 sq. ft.
Heating surface firebox and arch tubes	230 sq. ft.
Total heating surface	4031 sq. ft.
Heating surface, superheater	870 sq. ft.
Weight on front Truck, working order	*23200 lbs. / 23000 lbs.

Weight on Drivers, working order	*216100 lbs. / 215500 lbs.
Weight on rear Truck, working order	*50000 lbs. / 41500 lbs.
Total weight of Engine, working order	*289300 lbs. / 280000 lbs.
Weight of Tender, loaded	150500 lbs.
Weight of Tender, empty	64000 lbs.
Steam Pressure	180 lbs.
Max. Tractive Force	48570 lbs.
Tractive Force Booster	9900 lbs.
Combined Tractive Force, Engine and Booster	58470 lbs.

CLASS H-5c, H-5d and H-5e   (Printed Jan. 1, 1929)

NYC&HR CLASS H-5e 2-8-2: Continued.

	re'13	re'36	re'48		from						
3700		1236		RB from	G-5c	2734	Alco-B	11/12	(GO-24576-96)	Rt 1/39, Sc 8/39
3701		1237		"	G-5b	2434	"	"	-97	Rt 1/39, Sc 7/39
3702				"	"	2449	"	"	" -98	Sc 7/34
3703		1238		"	"	2435	"	"	" -99	Rt 1/39, Sc 8/39
3704		1239	1408	"	G-5c	2744	"	"	" -200	Rt 8/51, SS 10/51
3705				"	G-5	2482	"	"	" -201	Sc 8/34
3706				"	G-5a	2460	"	"	" -202	Sc 8/34
3707				"	G-5b	2444	"	"	" -203	Sc 9/34
3708		1240	1409	"	G-5c	2735	"	"	" -204	Rt 1/50, Sc
3709		1241		"	"	2701	"	"	" -205	Rt 7/39, Sc
3710				"	G-5a	2474	"	"	" -206	Sc 7/34
3711				"	"	2468	"	12/12	" -207	Sc 6/34
3712				"	G-5	2481	"	"	" -208	Sc 7/34
3713				"	G-5a	2457	"	"	" -209	Rt 12/34, Sc 9/35
3714		1242	1410	"	"	2475	"	"	" -210	Rt 6/51, SS
3715				"	G-5b	2442	"	"	" -211	Sc 6/34
3716				"	G-5c	2707	"	"	" -212	Rt 12/34, Sc 7/35
3717		1243		"	G-5b	2441	"	"	" -213	So 5/37 TA&G 305
3718		1244		"	G-5a	2469	"	"	" -215	So 10/39 AB&C 233
3719		(1245)		"	G-5	2491	"	"	" -214	Rt 1/36, Sc 6/36
3720		(1246)		"	G-5b	2446	"	"	" -217	Rt 1/36, Sc 3/36
3721		1247		"	G-5c	2702	"	"	" -216	So 1/38 (GC&L) A&StAB 404

NYC&HR CLASS H-5f 2-8-2: 25x32-63-180-277000-48570.   Note a: 3781 scheduled to be reno.1279.

	re'13	re'36	re'48		from					
2600	3775	1276	1520	RB from	G-5j	2770	Alco-B	8/13	(GO-30835-225)	Rt 3/52, SS
2601	3776			"	"	2751	"	"	" -226	Sc 8/34
2602	3777	1277		"	"	2772	"	"	" -227	So 10/37 (GC&L) TC 727
2603	3778			"	"	2788	"	"	" -228	Sc 6/34
2604	3779			"	"	2777	"	"	" -231	Rt 12/34, Sc 8/35
2605	3780	1278	1522	"	"	2771	"	"	" -232	Rt 2/52, SS
2606	3781	P&E 22 (a)		"	"	2773	"	"	" -233	Rt 1/51, SS
2607	3782	1280		"	"	2783	"	"	" -235	Rt 12/36, Sc 11/37
2608	3783			"	"	2791	"	"	" -236	Rt 12/34, Sc 10/35
2609	3784			"	"	2755	"	"	" -237	Rt 12/34, Sc 5/35
2610	3785	1281	1523	"	"	2787	"	"	" -238	Rt 5/52, SS 11/52
2611	3786			"	"	2752	"	"	" -239	Rt 12/34, Sc 5/35
2612	3787	1282	1524	"	"	2789	"	"	" -240	Rt 5/57
2613	3788	1283		"	"	2768	"	"	" -241	So 10/40 (GC&L) TA&G 307
2614	3789	1284	1525	"	"	2769	"	"	" -242	Sc 7/50
2615	3790			"	"	2781	"	"	" -243	Sc 9/34
2616	3791			"	"	2764	"	"	" -244	Rt 12/34, Sc 5/35
2617	3792	1285		"	"	2761	"	"	" -245	Sc 3/36
2618	3793			"	"	2801	"	"	" -246	Sc 9/34
2619	3794			"	"	2799	"	"	" -247	Rt 12/34, Sc 8/35
2620	3795	1286		"	"	2763	"	"	" -248	Rt 12/39, Sc 10/40

NYC&HR CLASS H-5g 2-8-2: 25x32-63-180-277000-48570.   See also B&A Class H-5g.

	re'13	re'36	re'48		from					
2621	3796	1287		RB from	G-5n	2834	Alco-B	8/13	(GO-30835-229)	Rt 12/39, Sc 8/40
2622	3797			"	"	2826	"	"	" -230	Sc 9/34
2623	3798			"	"	2805	"	"	" -234	Rt 12/34, Sc 5/35
2624	3799	1288		"	"	2833	"	"	" -249	Rt 12/39, Sc 8/40
2625	3800			"	"	2817	"	"	" -250	Rt 12/34, Sc 8/35
2626	3801			"	"	2823	"	"	" -251	Rt 12/34, Sc 9/35
2627	3802	1289	1512	"	"	2845	"	9/13	" -252	SS 4/52
2628	3803			"	"	2848	"	"	" -253	Sc 9/34
2629	3804	(1290)		"	"	2822	"	"	" -254	Rt 1/36, Sc
2630	3805	1291	1513	"	"	2814	"	"	" -255	Rt 11/51, SS
2631	3806			"	"	2842	"	"	" -256	Rt 12/34, Sc 8/35
2632	3807			"	"	2830	"	"	" -257	Rt 12/34, Sc 6/35
2633	3808			"	"	2811	"	"	" -258	Rt 12/34, Sc 9/35
2634	3809			"	"	2815	"	"	" -259	Rt 12/34, Sc 5/35
2635	3810			"	"	2821	"	"	" -260	Rt 12/34, Sc 9/35
2636	3811			"	"	2843	"	"	" -261	Rt 12/34, Sc 6/35
2637	3812	1292		"	"	2827	"	"	" -262	Rt 1/39, Sc 7/39
2638	3813			"	"	2812	"	"	" -263	Rt 12/34, Sc 5/35
2639	3814			"	"	2828	"	"	" -264	Rt 12/34, Sc 7/35
2640	3815	1293	1514	"	"	2844	"	"	" -265	Rt 6/56
2641	3816	1294	1515	"	G-5p	2861	"	"	" -266	Rt 7/51, SS
2642	3817			"	"	2857	"	"	" -267	Sc 5/35

NYC 1524 H-5f spent her last days on the Big Four. Lafayette,IN. 2/56.   (M.D.McCarter).

NYC&HR 2603 H-5f, on exhibit in 1913, just before renumbering to 3778. Former G-5j 2788.

(H.W.Ameling coll.)

NYC&HR CLASS H-5h 2-8-2:   25x32-63-180-284000-48570

	re'36	re'48					
3725			Alco-S	52397	1/13	Sc	5/35
3726			"	52398	"	Sc	9/35
3727	(1250)		"	52399	"	Sc	4/36
3728	(1251)		"	52400	"	Sc	3/36
3729	(1252)		"	52401	"	Sc	7/36
3730			"	52402	"	Sc	9/35
3731			"	52403	"	Sc	10/35
3732			"	52404	"	Sc	8/35
3733	1253	1411	"	52405	"	Rt	11/55,SS
3734	1254	1412	"	52406	"	Rt	6/51,SS
3735	1255	1413	"	52407	"	Rt	12/49,Sc
3736	(1256)		"	52408	"	Sc	6/36
3737			"	53409	"	Sc	4/35
3738	1257		"	53410	"	Sc	2/48
3739	1258	1414	"	53411	"	Rt	8/55,SS
3740	(1259)		"	53412	"	Sc	6/36
3741			"	53413	"	Sc	7/35
3742			"	53414	"	Sc	6/35
3743			"	53415	"	Sc	7/35
3744			"	53416	"	Sc	9/35
3745	1260	1415	"	53417	"	Rt	6/57
3746			"	53418	"	Sc	6/35
3747	1261		"	53419	"	Sc	11/37
3748	1262		"	53420	"	Sc	11/37
3749			"	53421	"	Sc	4/35

	re'36	re'48					
3750			Alco-S	52422	1/13	Sc	7/35
3751			"	52423	"	Sc	7/35
3752			"	52424	"	Sc	8/35
3753	1263		"	52425	"	Sc	3/36
3754			"	52426	"	Sc	5/35
3755			"	52427	"	Sc	6/35
3756			"	52428	"	Sc	7/35
3757			"	52438	"	Sc	8/35
3758	(1264)		"	52430	"	Sc	3/36
3759	1265	1416	"	52439	"	Rt	4/52,SS
3760			"	52432	"	Sc	7/35
3761	1266	1417	"	52440	"	Rt	10/51,SS
3762	1267	1418	"	52434	"	Rt	11/51,SS
3763	1268	1419	"	52441	"	Rt	4/50,Sc
3764			"	52436	"	Sc	10/35
3765	1269	1420	"	52442	"	Rt	4/56
3766			"	52429	"	Sc	7/35
3767	1270	1421	"	52443	2/13	Rt	3/50,Sc
3768			"	52431	1/13	Sc	7/35
3769	(1271)		"	52444	2/13	Sc	6/36
3770	1272	1422	"	52433	1/13	Rt	9/53,Sc
3771	1273	1423	"	52445	2/13	Rt	12/51,Sc
3772			"	52435	1/13	Sc	5/35
3773	1274	1424	"	52446	2/13	Rt	5/52,SS
3774	1275		"	52437	1/13	So	3/41
						AB&C 234	

NYC&HR CLASS H-5k 2-8-2:   25x32-63-180-277000-48570.   Note a: 3829 to P&E 10/27, was to be 1301 in 1936.

3822	1297	1516	RB from G-5j	2803	Alco-B	1/14	(GO-34567-L114)	Rt	10/51, SS 1/52
3823			"	"	2784	"	"	"	L115	Sc	5/34
3824	(1298)		"	"	2797	"	"	"	L116	Sc	5/36
3825	(1299)		"	"	2793	"	"	"	L117	Sc	6/36
3826	(1300)		"	"	2786	"	"	"	L118	Sc	6/36
3827			"	"	2767	"	"	"	L119	Sc	10/35
3828			"	"	2753	"	"	"	L120	Sc	5/35
3829	P&E 23 (a)		"	"	2780	"	"	"	L121	Rt	7/50,SS
3830			"	"	2804	"	3/14	"	L129	Sc	5/35

NYC&HR CLASS H-5L 2-8-2:   25x32-63-180-277000-48570

	re'14	re'36								
2643	3818		RB from G-5a	5900	Alco-B	10/13	(GO-32200-278)	Sc	6/35
2644	3819	1295	" "	5901	"	"	" -274	Sc	10/38
2645	3820		" "	5902	"	"	" -272	Sc	8/35
2646	3821	(1296)	" "	5903	"	"	" -281	Sc	6/36

NYC&HR CLASS H-5m 2-8-2:   25x32-63-180-277000-48570

	3843		RB from G-5n	2809	Alco-B	3/14	(GO-34567-L135)	Rt	9/33,
	3844	1309	" G-5p	2852	"	1/14	"	L136	Rt	8/51,SS
	3845	1310	" G-5n	2846	"	"	"	L137	Sc	9/40
	3846		" "	2825	"	"	"	L138	Sc	5/35
	3847		" "	2840	"	"	"	L139	Sc	8/35
	3848	1311	" "	2806	"	"	"	L140	Rt	11/51,SS
	3849		" "	2849	"	"	"	L141	Sc	6/34
	3850	1312	" "	2819	"	"	"	L142	So	1/37 TC 725
	3851	1313	" "	2810	"	"	"	L143	Rt	10/54,SS
	3852	1314	" G-5p	2859	W.Alby.	3/15		L164	Sc	8/40

NYC&HR CLASS H-5n 2-8-2:   25x32-63-180-277000-48570

	re'16									
2871	3831		RB from G-5q	2871	Alco-B	2/14	(GO-34567-L122)	Sc	5/35
2873	3832	1302	" "	2873	"	"	"	L123	Rt	11/51,SS
2876	3833	1303	" "	2876	"	3/14	"	L130	Rt	6/51,SS
2880	3834	1304	" "	2880	"	"	"	L134	So	7/37 DSS&A 1051
2881	3835	1305	" "	2881	"	2/14	"	L124	Rt	6/57
2887	3836		" G-5v	2887	"	3/14	"	L131	Sc	9/35
2888	3837		" "	2888	"	2/14	"	L125	Sc	5/35
2889	3838		" "	2889	"	3/14	"	L127	Sc	9/35
2900	3839	1306	" "	2900	"	"	"	L132	Sc	6/49
2903	3840	1307	" "	2903	"	2/14	"	L128	Sc	4/49
2904	3841		" "	2904	"	3/14	"	L133	Sc	5/35
2905	3842	1308	" "	2905	"	2/14	"	L126	Rt	2/52,SS

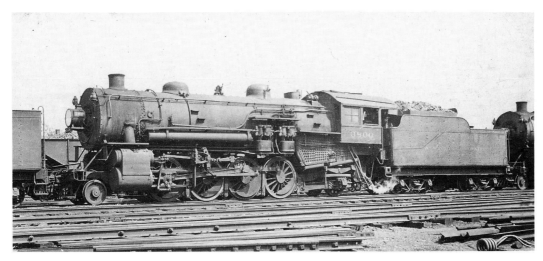

NYC 3800, class H-5g rebuilt 1913 from class G-5n Consolidation.   (C.B.Chaney collection)

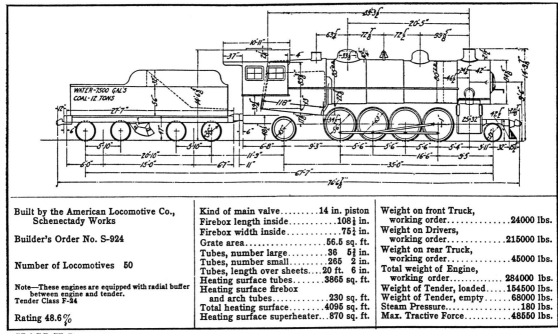

Built by the American Locomotive Co.,
Schenectady Works

Builder's Order No. S-924

Number of Locomotives 50

Note—These engines are equipped with radial buffer
between engine and tender.
Tender Class F-24

Rating 48.6%

Kind of main valve	14 in. piston
Firebox length inside	108¼ in.
Firebox width inside	75¼ in.
Grate area	56.5 sq. ft.
Tubes, number large	36 5¾ in.
Tubes, number small	265 2 in.
Tubes, length over sheets	20 ft. 6 in.
Heating surface tubes	3865 sq. ft.
Heating surface firebox and arch tubes	230 sq. ft.
Total heating surface	4095 sq. ft.
Heating surface superheater	870 sq. ft.

Weight on front Truck, working order ... 24000 lbs.
Weight on Drivers, working order ... 215000 lbs.
Weight on rear Truck, working order ... 45000 lbs.
Total weight of Engine, working order ... 284000 lbs.
Weight of Tender, loaded ... 154500 lbs.
Weight of Tender, empty ... 68000 lbs.
Steam Pressure ... 180 lbs.
Max. Tractive Force ... 48550 lbs.

CLASS H-5H

NYC 1260, later 1415, class H-5h with booster.   At Three Rivers, Mich. 6/48. (W.Whittaker)

NYC CLASS H-5p 2-8-2:   25x32-63-180-274000 to 295300-48570. Some had booster, 9900 tf.

	re'36							
3853	1315	RB from	G-5j	2762	Alco-B	7/15	(GO-39781-3)	Rt 11/51, SS 1/52
3854	1316	"	G-5n	2837	"	"	" -4	Rt 3/49, Sc 4/49
3855		"	G-5p	2855	"	"	" -6	Rt 12/34, Sc 6/35
3856	1317	"	"	2856	"	"	" -5	So 11/38 AB&C 227
3857	1318	"	G-5j	2774	"	"	" -13	Rt 12/39 Sc 11/40
3858		"	G-5n	2829	"	"	" -17	Rt 12/34 Sc 7/35
3859		"	"	2836	"	"	" -19	Rt 12/34 Sc 5/35
3860	1319	"	G-5j	2776	"	11/15	(GO-40774-13)	Rt 6/51, SS 8/51
3861		"	G-5n	2831	"	"	" -14	Sc 7/34
3863	1321	"	G-5j	2795	"	1/16	" -32	Rt 12/39, Sc 8/40
3864		"	G-5n	2835	"	"	" -35	Rt 12/34 Sc 8/35
3865		"	G-5j	2757	"	2/16	" -36	Rt 9/33, Sc
3866	1322	"	"	2754	"	1/16	" -38	Rt 1/50, Sc 2/50
3867	1323	"	"	2802	"	2/16	" -43	So 1/41 DSS&A 1052
3868	1324	"	G-5n	2824	"	"	" -37	So 3/37 (GC&L) A&StAB 403
3869	1325	"	G-5p	2850	"	5/16	" -52	Rt 12/39 Sc 9/40
3870	1326	"	G-5j	2796	"	"	" -53	Rt 6/51, SS 8/51
3871	1327	"	"	2766	"	6/16	" -56	So 1/41 DSS&A 1053
3872		"	"	2756	"	2/17	" -88	Rt 12/34 Sc 9/35
3873	1328	"	"	2758	"	9/16	" -67	Rt 2/52, SS 3/52
3874		"	"	2759	"	1/17	" -77	Rt 12/34, Sc 10/35
3876	1330	"	"	2765	"	9/16	" -66	Rt 2/52, SS 4/52
3877	1331	"	"	2750	"	6/16	" -57	Rt 6/51, SS 6/51
3878	1332	"	"	2775	"	9/16	" -68	Rt 5/52, SS 10/52
3879	1333	"	"	2778	"	2/17	" -90	Rt 7/55, SS 8/55
3880		"	"	2779	"	9/16	" -60	Rt 12/34 Sc 7/35
3882	1334	"	"	2790	"	1/17	" -76	Rt 6/57
3884	1336	"	"	2794	"	9/16	" -70	Rt 5/51, SS 11/51
3885	1337	"	"	2798	"	"	" -61	Rt 12/36, Sc 11/37
3886	1338	"	"	2800	"	1/17	" -74	Rt 2/52, SS 3/52
3888		"	G-5n	2808	"	9/16	" -69	Rt 12/34, Sc 8/35
3890	1340	"	"	2816	"	12/16	" -72	Rt 10/49 Sc 2/50
3891		"	"	2818	"	2/17	" -85	Sc 7/34
3892	1341	"	"	2820	"	1/17	" -79	Rt 7/52, SS 10/52
3893	1342	"	"	2832	"	2/17	" -86	So 3/37 (GC&L) A&StAB 401
3894	1343	"	"	2838	"	9/16	" -71	Rt 2/49, Sc 6/49
3895	1344	"	"	2839	"	1/17	" -78	Rt 3/52, SS 4/52
3896	1345	"	"	2841	"	"	" -84	Rt 3/50, Sc 4/50
3897	1346	"	"	2847	"	6/16	" -58	Rt 12/39 Sc 8/40
3898	1347	"	G-5p	2851	"	2/17	" -89	Rt 7/53, SS 8/53
3900	1349	"	"	2854	"	1/17	" -83	Rt 11/51, SS 11/51
3901		"	"	2858	"	"	" -75	Rt 12/34, Sc 6/35
3902	1350	"	G-5q	2862	"	2/17	" -87	So 3/37 (GC&L) A&StAB 402
*3904	1351	"	"	2864	"	8/15	(GO-39781-20)	Rt 4/50 Sc 7/50
3905	1352	"	"	2865	"	9/16	(GO-40774-62)	Rt 12/39, Sc 10/40
3906	1353	"	"	2866	"	9/16	" -65	Rt 7/55, SS 8/55
*3907	1354	"	"	2867	"	11/15	" -20	Rt 7/54, SS 12/54
3908	1355	"	"	2868	"	1/17	" -73	Rt 12/36, Sc 10/37
*3910	1357	"	"	2870	"	7/15	(GO-39781-16)	Rt 5/53, SS 8/53
*3911	1358	"	"	2872	"	12/15	(GO-40774-21)	Rt 12/36, Sc 11/37
3912	1359	"	"	2874	"	5/16	" -51	Rt 10/54, SS
3913	1360	"	"	2875	"	9/16	" -63	Rt 6/52, SS 10/52
*3915	1362	"	"	2878	"	3/16	" -44	Rt 7/52, SS 10/52
3916		"	"	2879	"	9/16	" -64	Rt 12/34, Sc 6/35
*3917	1363	"	"	2882	"	1/16	" -33	Rt 2/53, SS 7/53
3919	1364	"	"	2884	"	1/17	" -82	Rt 11/55, SS 12/55
*3920	1365	"	"	2885	"	11/15	" -12	Rt 7/56
3922	1367	"	G-5v	2890	"	8/15	(GO-39781-14)	Rt 2/52, SS 3/52
*3923	1368	"	"	2891	"	1/16	(GO-40774-34)	Rt 3/57
3930	P&E 24(a)	"	"	2898	"	5/16	" -54	SS 2/51
*3931	1374	"	"	2899	"	1/16	" -31	Rt 12/36, Sc 5/38
3932		"	"	2901	"	6/16	" -59	Rt 12/34, Sc 9/35
3933	1375	"	"	2902	"	1/17	" -80	Rt 3/52, SS 4/52
3934	1376	"	"	2906	"	5/16	" -55	Rt 1/50, Sc 2/50
3722	1248 (b)	"	G-5f	699	"	1/17	" -81	SS 6/55, Rt 3/55

Note * : Old number used until 4/16.   Note a: 3930 to P&E 10/27, was to be 1373 in 1936.
Note b: 1248 reno. 8/48 to second 1380.

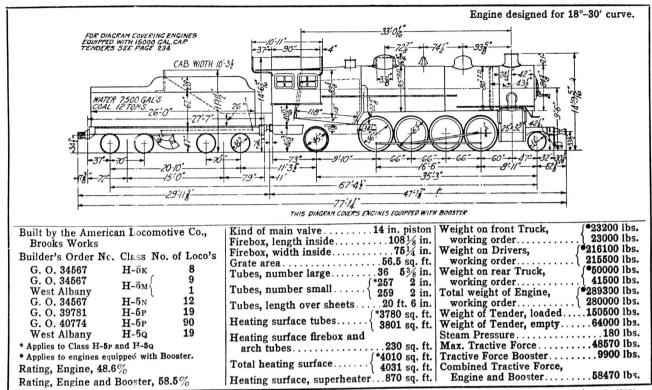

Engine designed for 18°–30' curve.

FOR DIAGRAM COVERING ENGINES
EQUIPPED WITH 15000 GAL. CAP.
TENDERS SEE PAGE 234

CAB WIDTH 10'-3½

WATER 7500 GAL'S
COAL 12 TONS

THIS DIAGRAM COVERS ENGINES EQUIPPED WITH BOOSTER

Built by the American Locomotive Co., Brooks Works			
Builder's Order No.	Class	No. of Loco's	
G. O. 34567	H-5K	8	
G. O. 34567	H-5M {	9	
West Albany		1	
G. O. 34567	H-5N	12	
G. O. 39781	H-5P	19	
G. O. 40774	H-5P	90	
West Albany	H-5Q	19	

* Applies to Class H-5p and H-5q
● Applies to engines equipped with Booster.
Rating, Engine, 48.6%
Rating, Engine and Booster, 58.5%

Kind of main valve	14 in. piston
Firebox, length inside	108⅛ in.
Firebox, width inside	75¼ in.
Grate area	56.5 sq. ft.
Tubes, number large	36 5⅜ in.
Tubes, number small	*257 2 in.
	259 2 in.
Tubes, length over sheets	20 ft. 6 in.
Heating surface tubes	*3780 sq. ft.
	3801 sq. ft.
Heating surface firebox and arch tubes	230 sq. ft.
Total heating surface	*4010 sq. ft.
	4031 sq. ft.
Heating surface, superheater	870 sq. ft.

Weight on front Truck, working order	●23200 lbs. / 23000 lbs.
Weight on Drivers, working order	●216100 lbs. / 215500 lbs.
Weight on rear Truck, working order	●50000 lbs. / 41500 lbs.
Total weight of Engine, working order	●289300 lbs. / 280000 lbs.
Weight of Tender, loaded	150500 lbs.
Weight of Tender, empty	64000 lbs.
Steam Pressure	180 lbs.
Max. Tractive Force	48570 lbs.
Tractive Force Booster	9900 lbs.
Combined Tractive Force, Engine and Booster	58470 lbs.

CLASS H-5K, H-5M, H-5N, H-5P and H-5Q

(Printed Jan. 1, 1929)

NYC 1368 H-5p, helping on the B&A before retirement in 1957.   (Rail Photo Service).

NYC CLASS H-5p 2-8-2: Continued.

4071	1377	RB from	G-5x	5456	Alco-B	3/16	(GO-40774-45)	Rt 10/52, Sc 2/53
4072	1378	"	"	5458	"	"	"	-47	Rt 5/52, SS 10/52
4073	1379	"	"	5459	"	2/16	"	-39	Rt 11/49 Sc 1/50
4074	1380	"	"	5462	"	3/16	"	-50	Rt 12/36, Sc 5/38
4075	1381	"	"	5464	"	"	"	-41	Rt 12/51 SS 1/52
4076	1382	"	G-5L	5474	"	"	"	-40	Rt 1/50, SS 2/50
4077	1383	"	G-5h	5480	"	"	"	-46	Rt 8/49, Sc 9/49
4078	1384	"	"	5481	"	"	"	-49	Rt 1/50 SS 1/50
4079	1385	"	"	5487	"	2/16	"	-42	Rt 10/54, SS 3/55
4080	1386	"	"	5489	"	"	"	-48	Rt 7/55, SS 8/55
4081	1387	"	G-5k	5463	"	1/16	"	-24	Rt 12/39, Sc 10/40
4082	1388	"	"	5465	"	"	"	-30	Rt 3/55, SS 4/55
4083	1389	"	"	5468	"	12/15	"	-23	Rt 2/49, Sc 6/49
4084	1390	"	G-5L	5476	"	1/16	"	-29	Rt 11/51, SS 12/51
4085	1391	"	"	5478	"	"	"	-25	Rt 5/52, SS 10/52
4086	1392	"	"	5479	"	"	"	-26	Rt 2/49, Sc 8/49
4087		"	G-5h	5491	"	12/15	"	-22	Sc 7/34
4088	1393	"	"	5494	"	1/16	"	-27	Rt 3/52, SS 5/52
4089		"	"	5496	"	"	"	-28	Rt 12/34, Sc 7/35
4090	1394	"	G-5L	5471	"	11/15	"	-17	Rt 5/57
4091	1395	"	"	5472	"	12/15	"	-18	Rt 10/55, SS 11/55
4092		"	"	5475	"	11/15	"	-15	Rt 12/34, Sc 7/35
4093		"	G-5h	5482	"	12/15	"	-16	Rt 12/34, Sc 9/35
4094	1396	"	"	5488	"	11/15	"	-19	Rt 7/53, Sc 12/53
4095		"	G-5x	5469	"	10/15	"	-2	Sc 8/34
4096	1397	"	G-5h	5497	"	"	"	-1	Rt 6/52, SS 10/52
4097	1398	"	G-5L	5473	"	"	"	-6	Rt 12/39, Sc 10/40
4098		"	G-5h	5495	"	"	"	-7	Sc 7/34
4099	1399	"	"	5485	"	11/15	"	-10	Rt 4/50, Sc 7/50
4100	1589	"	"	5493	"	10/15	"	-3	Rt 9/54, SS 12/54
4101	1590	"	G-5x	5457	"	"	"	-4	Rt 12/39, Sc 10/40
4102		"	"	5461	"	11/15	"	-8	Sc 8/33
4103	1591	"	G-5h	5486	"	"	"	-11	Rt 7/55, SS 8/55
4104	1592	"	G-5L	5470	"	10/15	"	-5	Rt 4/49, SS 8/49
4105	1593	"	G-5h	5484	"	11/15	"	-9	Rt 11/51, SS 2/52
4106	1594	"	"	5490	"	8/15	(GO-39781-18)	Rt 6/57
4107	1595	"	G-5x	5455	"	7/15	"	-15	Rt 2/52, SS 3/52
4108	1596	"	"	5460	"	"	"	-12	Rt 2/49, Sc 7/49
4109	1597	"	"	5466	"	"	"	-7	Rt 12/39 Sc 10/40
4110	1598	"	"	5467	"	"	"	-8	Rt 12/39 Sc 10/40
4111	1599	"	G-5h	5483	"	"	"	-9	Sc 4/47
4112	1527	"	"	5492	"	"	"	-11	Rt 12/39, Sc 7/40
4113	1528	"	"	5499	"	"	"	-10	Rt 5/52, SS 9/52
4114	1529	"	G-5L	5477	"	"	"	-2	Rt 10/51, SS 11/51
4115	1530	"	G-5h	5498	"	"	"	-1	Rt 12/36, Sc 11/37

NYC CLASS H-5q 2-8-2: 25x32-63-180-274000 to 295300-48570.   Some had booster, 9900 tf.

3723a	1249	RB from	G-5p	2860	West Albany	11/17	L206	Rt 9/53, SS '54
3862	1320	"	G-5j	2782	" "	12/15	L174	Rt 4/57
3875	1329	"	"	2760	" "	7/16	L182	Rt 4/50, Sc 8/50
3881		"	"	2785	" "	3/18	L207	Rt 12/34, Sc 10/35
3883	1335	"	"	2792	" "	12/17	L208	Rt 2/52, SS 2/52
3887	1339	"	G-5n	2807	" "	12/18	L209	Rt 12/52, SS 1/53
3889		"	"	2813	" "	7/18	L210	Sc 5/34
3899	1348	"	G-5p	2853	" "	7/17	L211	Rt 3/50, Sc 4/50
3903		"	G-5q	2863	" "	2/18	L212	Sc 8/34
3909	1356	"	"	2869	" "	8/16	L184	Rt 6/50, Sc 6/50
3914	1361	"	"	2877	" "	7/16	L185	Rt 10/54, SS 12/54
3918		"	"	2883	" "	12/16	L183	Rt 12/34, Sc 7/35
3921	1366	"	"	2886	" "	5/18	L213	Rt 8/55, SS 9/55
*3924	1369	"	G-5v	2892	" "	12/15	L175	Rt 3/53, SS 6/53
*3925	1370	"	"	2893	" "	1/16	L176	Rt 6/57
*3926	1371	"	"	2894	" "	"	L177	Rt 12/39, Sc 8/40
3927	1372	"	"	2895	" "	8/16	L186	Rt 2/52, SS 3/52
3928		"	"	2896	" "	7/17	L214	Rt 12/34, Sc 6/35
*3929		"	"	2897	" "	1/16	L178	Sc 8/34

Note * : Old number retained until 3/16.   Note a: 1249 reno. 8/48 to 1371.

NYC 3925, class H-5q. There were 19 in this class, all converted at West Albany. (Votava)

NYC 1348, another H-5q, at Fremont, Ohio in July 1948.   (Prescott collection)

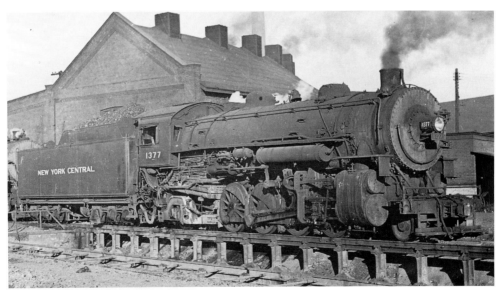

NYC 1377 H-5p, on the ash pit at Ashtabula in August, 1951.   (Prescott collection.)

NYC CLASS H-5t 2-8-2:   25x32-63-180-283000 to 297700-48570. Some had booster, 9900 tf. See also CCC&StL.

	re'36	re'51							re'36	re'51			
3935	1435		Lima	5226	9/16	Rt	7/54, SS	9/54	3960	1460		Lima 5251 10/16	So 3/37 HPT&D 1460
3936	1436		"	5227	"	Rt	12/36, Sc	5/37	3961	1461		" 5252 "	Rt 9/54, SS 12/54
3937	1437		"	5228	"	Rt	7/55, SS	8/55	3962	1462		" 5253 "	Re 2/41 B&A 1227
3938	1438		"	5229	"	Rt	7/54, SS	1/55	3963	1463		" 5254 "	Re 3/39 B&A 1224
3939	1439		"	5230	"	Rt	6/54 SS	10/54	3964	1464		" 5255 "	Re 9/41 B&A 1228
3940	1440		"	5231	"	Rt	4/57		3965	1465		" 5256 "	Rt 3/56
3941	1441		"	5232	"	Re	12/41 B&A 1229		3966	1466		" 5257 "	Rt 7/55, SS 8/56
3942	1442		"	5233	"	Rt	11/54, SS		3967	1467		" 5258 "	Rt 1/53, SS 2/53
3943	1443		"	5234	"	Rt	10/52, Sc	12/52	3968			" 5259 "	Rt 8/33, Sc
3944	1444		"	5235	"	Rt	10/55, SS	11/55	3969	1469		" 5260 "	Rt 3/57
3945	1445		"	5236	10/16	Rt	12/55, SS	12/55	3970	1470		" 5261 11/16	Rt 9/53, SS 9/54
3946	1446		"	5237	"	Rt	5/49, Sc	7/49	3971	1471		" 5262 "	Rt 10/53, SS /54
3947	1447		"	5238	"	Rt	3/55, SS	6/55	3972	1472		" 5263 "	Rt 11/51, SS 2/52
3948	1448		"	5239	"	Rt	6/57		3973	1473		" 5264 "	Rt 4/57
3949	1449		"	5240	"	Rt	8/49, Sc	10/49	3974	1474		" 5265 "	Rt 5/52, SS 10/52
3950	1450		"	5241	"	Rt	4/57		3975	1475		" 5266 "	Rt 6/54, SS
3951	1451		"	5242	"	Rt	6/57		3976	1476		" 5267 "	Rt 12/36, Sc 5/37
3952	1452		"	5243	"	Rt	10/54, SS	12/54	3977	1477		" 5268 "	Rt 8/55, SS 9/55
3953	1453		"	5244	"	Re	2/41 B&A 1226		3978	1478		" 5269 "	Rt 4/55, SS 6/55
3954	1454		"	5245	"	Rt	3/55, SS	4/55	3979	1479		" 5270 "	So 3/37 HPT&D 1479
3955	1455		"	5246	"	Rt	5/52, SS	10/52	3980	1480		" 5271 "	Re 10/40 B&A 1225
3956	1456		"	5247	"	Rt	2/56		3981	1481		" 5272 "	Rt 7/54, SS 11/54
3957	1457		"	5248	"	Rt	2/52, SS	10/52	3982	1482		" 5273 "	Rt 2/53, SS 4/53
3958	1458		"	5249	"	Rt	7/55, SS	12/55	3983	1483		" 5274 "	Rt 9/54, SS 12/54
3959	1459		"	5250	"	Rt	11/55, SS	12/55	3984	1484		" 5275 "	Rt 5/52, SS 9/52

NYC H-6a 2-8-2:   26x30-63-200-300500-54720. USRA. Orig. Wt. 292000. See also LE&W, CCC&StL, MC, T&OC, IHB.

	re'36	re'51								re'36	re'51				
5100	1800	6359	Alco-S	59695	11/18	Rt 10/54, SS		5152	1852	6394	Lima 5752 11/18	Rt	5/56
5101	1801	6360	"	59696	"	Rt 9/53, SS		5153	1853	6395	" 5753 "	(Boos.) Rt 8/55
5102	1802	6361	"	59697	"	Rt 7/54, SS		5154	1854	6396	" 5754 "	Rt	5/56
5103	1803	6362	"	59698	"	Rt 7/53, SS		5155	1855	6397	" 5755 "	Rt 10/54, SS
5104	1804		"	59699	"	Rt 3/46, Sc		5156	1856	6398	" 5756 "	Rt	2/56
5105	1805	6363	"	59700	"	Rt 3/53, SS		5157	1857	6399	" 5757 "	Rt	4/56
5106	1806		"	59701	"	Rt 12/47, Sc		5158	1858	(6400)	" 5758 "	Rt 5/52, SS
5107	1807	6364	"	59702	"	Rt 7/53, Sc		5159	1859	6401	" 5759 "	Rt 10/54, SS
5108	1808	6365	"	59703	"	Rt 10/53, SS		5160	1860	6402	" 5760 "	Rt 10/54, SS
5109	1809	6366	"	59704	"	Rt 7/53, Sc		5161	1861	6403	" 5761 "	Rt 2/54, SS
(5110-5116 assigned'20 to Pere Marquette 1034-1040)								5162	1862	6404	" 5762 "	Rt 3/55, SS
5117	1817	6367	Alco-S	59712	12/18	Rt 11/55, SS		5163	1863	6405	" 5763 12/18	Rt 10/54, SS
5118	1818	6368	"	59713	"	Rt 3/54, SS		5164	1864	6406	" 5764 "	Rt 10/54, SS
5119	1819	6369	"	59714	"	Rt 9/54, SS		5165	1865	6407	" 5765 "	Rt 11/54
5120	1820	6370	"	59715	"	Rt 11/54, SS		5166	1866	6408	" 5766 "	Rt 3/55, SS
5121	1821		"	59716	"	Rt 10/46, Sc		5167	1867	(6409)	" 5767 "	Rt 12/51, SS
5122	1822	6371	"	59717	"	Rt 4/56		5168	1868	6410	" 5768 "	Rt 10/54, SS
5123	1823	6372	"	59718	"	Rt 3/52		5169	1869	6411	" 5769 "	NB'23,Rt 7/53
5124	1824	6373	"	59719	"	Rt 10/54, SS		5170	1870	6412	" 5770 "	Rt 5/56, SS
5125	1825	6374	"	60275	"	Rt 3/52, SS		5171	1871	6413	" 5771 "	Rt 3/56, SS
5126	1826	6375	"	60276	"	Rt 5/52, SS		5172	1872	6414	" 5772 "	Rt 10/53, SS
5127	1827	6376	"	60277	"	Rt 4/52, SS		5173	1873	6415	" 5773 "	Rt 10/54, SS
5128	1828	6377	"	60278	"	Rt 3/55, SS		5174	1874	6416	" 5774 "	Rt 2/52, SS
5129	1829	6378	"	60279	"	NB'24,Rt 7/53		5175	1875		" 5775 "	Rt 9/37, Sc
(5130-5133 assigned'20 to Pere Marquette 1030-1033)								5176	1876		" 5776 "	Rt 7/53, Sc
5134	1834	6379	Alco-S	60284	12/18	Rt 3/52, SS		5177	1877		" 5777 "	Rt 4/56
5135	1835	6380	"	60285	"	Rt 7/53, SS		5178	1878		" 5778 "	Rt 9/54, SS
5136	1836	6381	"	60286	"	Rt 9/54, SS		5179	1879		" 5779 "	Rt 7/54, SS
5137	1837	6382	"	60287	"	Rt 10/51, SS		5180	1880		" 5780 "	Rt 7/52, SS
5138	1838	6383	"	60288	"	Rt 7/53, SS		5181	1881		" 5781 "	Rt 2/56
5139	1839	6384	"	60289	"	Rt 9/54, SS		5182	1882		" 5782 "	Rt 11/54, SS
5140	1840	6385	"	60290	"	Rt 3/56		5183	1883		" 5783 "	Rt 6/54, SS
5141	1841	6386	"	60291	"	Rt 6/54, SS		5184	1884		" 5784 "	Rt 10/54, SS
5142	1842	6387	"	60292	"	Rt 7/54, SS		5185	1885		" 5785 "	Rt 10/53, Sc
5143	1843		"	60293	"	Rt 10/46, Sc		5186	1886		" 5786 "	Rt 7/48, Sc
5144	1844	6388	"	60294	"	Rt 2/53, SS		5187	1887		" 5787 "	Rt 3/52, SS
5145	1845	(6389)	"	60295	"	Rt 3/52, SS		5188	1888		" 5788 "	Rt 10/46, Sc
5146	1846		"	60296	"	Rt 3/50, Sc		5189	1889		" 5789 1/19	Rt 8/55, SS
5147	1847	6390	"	60297	"	Rt 11/54, SS		5190	1890		" 5790 "	Rt 3/56
5148	1848	6391	"	60298	"	Rt 4/56		5191	1891		" 5791 "	Rt 8/54, SS
5149	1849		"	60299	"	Rt 10/46, Sc		5192	1892		" 5792 "	Rt 3/56
5150	1850	6392	Lima	5750	11/18	Rt 10/54, SS		5193	1893		" 5793 "	Rt 8/55, SS
5151	1851	6393	"	5751	"	Rt 10/54, SS		5194	1894		" 5794 "	Rt 10/54, SS

(Prescott)

NYC 1473, class H-5t, one of 50 built by Lima in 1916. Front air pumps, booster, small tank.

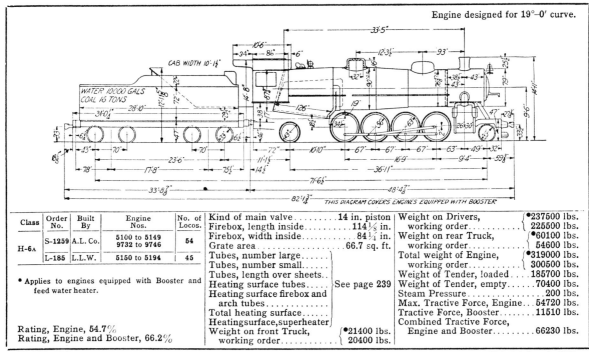

Engine designed for 19°–0′ curve.

Class	Order No.	Built By	Engine Nos.	No. of Locos.
H-6A	S-1259	A.L. Co.	5100 to 5149 9732 to 9746	54
	L-185	L.L.W.	5150 to 5194	45

• Applies to engines equipped with Booster and feed water heater.

Rating, Engine, 54.7%
Rating, Engine and Booster, 66.2%

Kind of main valve	14 in. piston
Firebox, length inside	114⅛ in.
Firebox, width inside	84¼ in.
Grate area	66.7 sq. ft.
Tubes, number large	
Tubes, number small	
Tubes, length over sheets	See page 239
Heating surface tubes	
Heating surface firebox and arch tubes	
Total heating surface	
Heating surface, superheater	
Weight on front Truck, working order	•21400 lbs. / 20400 lbs.

Weight on Drivers, working order	•237500 lbs. / 225500 lbs.
Weight on rear Truck, working order	•60100 lbs. / 54600 lbs.
Total weight of Engine, working order	•319000 lbs. / 300500 lbs.
Weight of Tender, loaded	185700 lbs.
Weight of Tender, empty	70400 lbs.
Steam Pressure	200 lbs.
Max. Tractive Force, Engine	54720 lbs.
Tractive Force, Booster	11510 lbs.
Combined Tractive Force, Engine and Booster	66230 lbs.

CLASS H-6A   (Printed Jan. 1, 1930)

NYC 6410, H-6a, ex-1868, USRA Lima 1918. At Bellefontain 1953.   (McCarter collection)

NYC CLASS H-10a 2-8-2: 28x30-63-200-342500-63470+11000 booster.

				re'36		
1	*	2101	Lima	6357	9/22	Rt 10/51, SS 2/52
2		2102	"	6358	11/22	Rt 5/52, SS 10/52
3		2103	"	6359	"	Rt 10/51, SS 2/52
4	*	2104	"	6360	"	Rt 8/52, SS 9/52
5	*	2105	"	6361	"	Rt 10/51, SS 2/52
6	*	2106	"	6362	"	Rt 6/50, SS
7		2107	"	6363	12/22	Rt 10/51, SS 1/52
8		2108	"	6364	"	Rt 11/51, SS 2/52
9	*	2109	"	6365	"	Rt 6/50, SS
10		2110	"	6366	"	Rt 10/51, SS 2/52
11	*	2111	"	6367	"	Rt 12/51, SS 2/52
12		2112	"	6368	"	NB 1/31, Rt 6/50
13	*	2113	"	6369	"	Rt 6/50, SS
14	*	2114	"	6370	"	Rt 10/51, SS 2/52
15	*	2115	"	6371	"	Rt 4/52, SS 11/52
16		2116	"	6372	"	Rt 3/53, SS 5/53
17		2117	"	6373	"	Rt 10/51, SS 2/52
18		2118	"	6374	"	Rt 10/51, SS 10/51
19		2119	"	6375	"	Rt 10/51, SS 11/51
20	*	2120	"	6376	"	Rt 6/50, SS
21		2121	"	6377	1/23	Rt 10/51, SS 11/51
22		2122	"	6378	2/23	Rt 12/52, SS 2/53
23		2123	"	6379	"	Rt 3/53, SS 5/53
24	*	2124	"	6380	"	Rt 10/51, SS 2/52
25	*	2125	"	6381	"	Rt 6/50, SS
26		2126	"	6382	"	Rt 5/52, SS 10/52
27		2127	"	6383	"	Rt 3/53, SS 4/53
28	*	2128	"	6384	"	Rt 6/50, SS
29	*	2129	"	6385	"	Rt 10/51, SS 2/52
30		2130	"	6386	"	Rt 3/52, SS 4/52
31	*	2131	"	6397	"	Rt 10/51, SS 2/52
32	*	2132	"	6398	"	Rt 10/51, SS 11/51
33		2133	"	6399	3/23	Rt 12/51, SS 2/52
34	*	2134	"	6400	"	Rt 10/51, SS 2/52
35		2135	"	6401	"	Rt 10/51, SS 11/51
36		2136	"	6402	"	Rt 7/50, SS
37		2137	"	6403	"	Rt 3/52, SS 4/52
38		2138	"	6404	"	Rt 5/52, SS 10/52
39		2139	"	6405	"	Rt 6/53, SS 8/53
40		2140	"	6406	"	Rt 3/53, SS 5/53
41		2141	"	6407	"	Rt 6/50, SS
42	*	2142	"	6408	"	Rt 6/50, SS
43		2143	"	6409	"	Rt 5/52, SS 10/52
44		2144	"	6410	"	Rt 10/51, SS 11/51
45		2145	"	6411	"	Rt 6/53, SS 7/53
46		2146	"	6412	"	Rt 10/51, SS 12/51
47		2147	"	6413	"	Rt 10/51, SS 10/51
48	*	2148	"	6414	"	Re 4/50 P&LE 213
49		2149	"	6415	"	Rt 6/52, SS 10/52
50	*	2150	"	6416	"	Rt 10/51, SS 2/52
51		2151	"	6417	"	Rt 12/51, SS 2/52
52		2152	"	6418	"	Rt 6/50, SS
53		2153	"	6419	"	Rt 7/52, SS 10/52
54		2154	"	6420	"	Rt 3/53, SS 5/53
55		2155	"	6421	"	Rt 6/50, SS
56		2156	"	6422	5/23	Rt 10/51, SS 1/52
57		2157	"	6423	3/23	Rt 6/50, SS
58		2158	"	6424	"	Rt 10/51, SS 12/51
59		2159	"	6425	"	NB 4/27, Rt 10/51
60		2160	"	6426	5/23	Rt 6/50, SS
61		2161	"	6427	3/23	Rt 12/51, SS 1/52
62		2162	"	6428	5/23	Rt 10/51, SS 12/51
63		2163	"	6429	4/23	Rt 2/53, SS 6/53
64		2164	"	6430	"	Rt 10/51, SS 10/51
65		2165	"	6431	"	Rt 6/50, SS

				re'36		
66	2166	Alco-S	63667	1/23	Rt 6/50, SS
67	2167	"	63668	"	Rt 5/52, SS 10/52
68	2168	"	63669	"	Rt 12/51, SS 2/52
69	2169	"	63670	"	Rt 10/51, SS 12/51
70	2170	"	63671	"	Rt 10/51, SS 12/51
71	2171	"	63672	"	Rt 5/52, SS 10/52
72	2172	"	63673	"	Rt 10/51, SS 11/51
73	2173	"	63674	"	Rt 6/52, SS 11/52
74	2174	"	63675	"	Rt 6/50, SS
75	2175	"	63676	"	Rt 6/53, SS 9/53
76	2176	"	63677	"	Rt 2/53, SS 6/53
77	2177	"	63678	"	Rt 7/50, SS
78	2178	"	63679	"	Rt 12/51, SS 2/52
79	2179	"	63680	"	Rt 5/52, SS 10/52
80	2180	"	63681	"	Rt 3/52, SS 4/52
81	2181	"	63682	"	Rt 1/52, SS 2/52
82	2182	"	63683	"	Rt 7/50, SS
83	2183	"	63697	2/23	Rt 10/51, SS 2/52
84	2184	"	63698	"	Rt 3/53, SS 4/53
85	2185	"	63699	"	Rt 1/53, SS 5/53
86	2186	"	63700	"	Rt 5/52, SS 10/52
87	2187	"	63701	"	Rt 10/51, SS 11/51
88	2188	"	63702	"	Rt 10/51, SS 12/51
89	2189	"	63703	"	Rt 7/52, SS 10/52
90	2190	"	63704	"	Rt 6/52, SS 11/52
91	2191	"	63705	"	Rt 6/50, SS
92	2192	"	63706	"	Rt 12/52, SS 2/53
93	2193	"	63707	"	Rt 6/52, SS 11/52
94	2194	"	63708	"	NB 1/30, Rt 6/50
95	2195	"	63709	"	Rt 10/51, SS 2/52
96	2196	"	63710	3/23	Rt 5/52, SS 10/52
97	2197	"	63999	"	Rt 4/52, SS 11/52
98	2198	"	64000	"	Rt 2/52, SS 3/52
99	2199	"	64001	"	Rt 6/53, SS 7/53
100	2200	"	64002	"	Rt 10/51, SS 11/51
101	2201	"	64003	"	Rt 10/51, SS 11/51
102	2202	"	64004	"	Rt 5/52, SS 9/52
103	2203	"	64005	"	Rt 7/50, SS
104	2204	"	64006	"	Rt 6/52, SS 11/52
105	2205	"	64007	"	Rt 6/50, SS
106	2206	"	64008	"	Rt 6/50, SS
107	2207	"	64009	"	Rt 2/53, SS 5/53
108	2208	"	64010	"	Rt 10/51, SS 11/51
109	2209	"	64011	"	Rt 5/52, SS 11/52
110	2210	"	64012	"	Rt 10/51, SS 11/51
111	2211	"	64013	"	Rt 10/51, SS 2/52
112	2212	"	64014	"	Rt 7/52, SS 9/52
113	2213	"	64015	"	Rt 5/52, SS 10/52
114	2214	"	64016	"	Rt 1/53, SS 2/53
115	2215	"	64017	"	Rt 10/51, SS 10/51
116	2216	"	64018	"	Re 4/50 P&LE 214
117	2217	"	64019	"	Rt 10/51, SS 2/52
118	2218	"	64020	"	Rt 2/53, SS 5/53
119	2219	"	64021	"	Rt 5/52, SS /54
120	2220	"	64022	"	Rt 10/51, SS 11/51
121	2221	"	64023	"	Rt 6/50, SS
122	2222	"	64024	"	Rt 6/53, SS /54

Other Class H-10a:

123-132 re 2223-2232 MC.
133-182 re 2233-2282 CCC&StL.
183-190 re 2283-2290 B&A.
191-200 (not reno.) P&LE.

* Note: Leased to CCC&StL in 1926 without change of number.

NYC 2101 H-10a, ex-#1, the first H-10a. Ashtabula, Ohio in March 1947. (Paul Prescott)

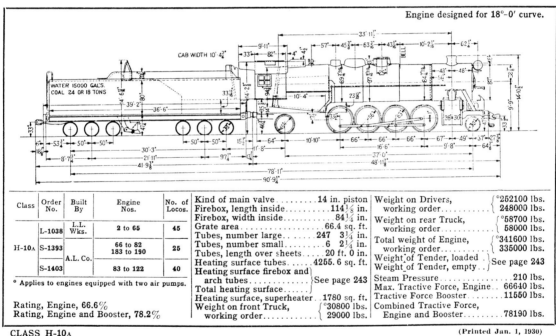

Engine designed for 18°-0′ curve.

CAB WIDTH 10′-4¾″

WATER 15000 GALS.
COAL 24 OR 18 TONS

Class	Order No.	Built By	Engine Nos.	No. of Locos.
H-10ᴀ	L-1038	L.L. Wks.	2 to 65	45
	S-1393	A.L. Co.	66 to 82 183 to 190	25
	S-1403		83 to 122	40

° Applies to engines equipped with two air pumps.

Rating, Engine, 66.6%
Rating, Engine and Booster, 78.2%

Kind of main valve . . . . .14 in. piston
Firebox, length inside . . . . .114⅛ in.
Firebox, width inside . . . . 84¼ in.
Grate area . . . . .66.4 sq. ft.
Tubes, number large 247   3¼ in.
Tubes, number small 6   2¼ in.
Tubes, length over sheets . . . . 20 ft. 0 in.
Heating surface tubes . . . . . 4255.6 sq. ft.
Heating surface firebox and⎫
  arch tubes . . . . ⎬See page 243
Total heating surface . . . . . .⎭
Heating surface, superheater . .1780 sq. ft.
Weight on front Truck, ⎧°30800 lbs.
  working order . . . .⎨ 29000 lbs.

Weight on Drivers, ⎧°252100 lbs.
  working order . . . . ⎨ 248000 lbs.
Weight on rear Truck, ⎧°58700 lbs.
  working order . . . .⎨ 58000 lbs.
Total weight of Engine, ⎧°341600 lbs.
  working order . . . .⎨ 335000 lbs.
Weight of Tender, loaded . ⎫See page 243
Weight of Tender, empty . .⎭
Steam Pressure . . . . .210 lbs.
Max. Tractive Force, Engine . . 66640 lbs.
Tractive Force Booster . . . . . . .11550 lbs.
Combined Tractive Force,
  Engine and Booster . . . . .78190 lbs.

CLASS H-10ᴀ

(Printed Jan. 1, 1930)

NYC 19, another H-10a, at Youngstown in 1927.   (G.A.Doeright)

	re'36								re'36					
320	d	2360	Alco-S	65562	6/24	Rt 12/51, SS 1/52	345	a	2385	Alco-S	65587	7/24	Rt 5/52, Sc 8/52
321	a	2361	"	65563	"	Rt 5/52, SS 1/53	346	a	2386	"	65588	"	Rt 5/52, Sc 11/53
322	a	2362	"	65564	"	Rt 3/52, SS 4/52	347	d	2387	"	65589	"	Rt 7/52, SS 12/52
323	d	2363	"	65565	"	Rt 4/52, SS 11/52	348	c	2388	"	65590	"	Rt 1/53, SS 6/53
324	a	2364	"	65566	"	Rt 7/52, SS 10/52	349	a	2389	"	65591	"	Rt 5/52, Sc 2/53
325	a	2365	"	65567	"	Rt 1/52, SS 2/52	350	c	2390	"	65592	"	Rt 4/52, SS 11/52
326	a	2366	"	65568	"	Rt 6/52, Sc 1/53	351	c	2391	"	65593	"	Rt 2/53, SS 5/53
327	d	2367	"	65569	"	Rt 3/52, SS 4/52	352	c	2392	"	65594	"	Rt 11/52, SS 2/53
328	c	2368	"	65570	"	Rt 11/51, SS 11/51	353	d	2393	"	65595	"	Rt 7/50, SS 11/50
329	a	2369	"	65571	"	Rt 6/52, SS 11/53	354	c	2394	"	65596	"	Rt 12/52, SS 2/53
330	a	2370	"	65572	"	Rt 6/50, SS	355	b	2395	"	65597	"	Rt 7/52, SS 12/52
331	a	2371	"	65573	"	Rt 5/52, SS 2/53	356	d	2396	"	65598	"	Rt 8/52, SS 10/52
332	d	2372	"	65574	"	Rt 11/51, SS 1/52	357	a	2397	"	65599	"	Rt 6/52, SS /54
333	b	2373	"	65575	"	Rt 1/52, SS 2/52	358	b	2398	"	65600	"	Rt 4/52, SS 10/52
334	d	2374	"	65576	"	Rt 7/52, SS 10/52	359	b	2399	"	65601	"	Rt 11/51, SS 11/51
335	c	2375	"	65577	"	Rt 7/52, SS 11/52	360	a	2080	"	65602	8/24	Rt 5/52, Sc 3/53
336	c	2376	"	65578	"	Rt 6/50, SS	361	d	2081	"	65603	"	Rt 7/52, SS 11/52
337	b	2377	"	65579	"	Rt 6/52, SS 10/52	362	a	2082	"	65604	"	Rt 5/52, Sc 2/53
338	a	2378	"	65580	"	Rt 6/52, Sc 2/53	363	c	2083	"	65605	"	Rt 7/50, SS
339	d	2379	"	65581	"	Rt 7/52, SS 12/52	364	d	2084	"	65606	"	Rt 6/53, SS 9/53
340	b	2380	"	65582	7/24	Rt 3/52, SS 4/52	365	b	2085	"	65607	"	Rt 4/52, SS 12/52
341	c	2381	"	65583	"	Rt 1/52, SS 2/52	366	d	2086	"	65608	"	Rt 4/53, SS 6/53
342	a	2382	"	65584	"	Rt 5/52, Sc 8/52	367	b	2087	"	65609	"	Rt 4/52, SS 11/52
343	d	2383	"	65585	"	Rt 7/52, SS 11/52	368	b	2088	"	65610	"	Rt 11/52, SS 1/53
344	d	2384	"	65586	"	Rt 9/52, SS 11/52	369	b	2089	"	65611	"	Rt 1/53, SS 6/53

```
Other Class H-10b:  P&LE     201-211 (Not reno.)    .
                    CCC&StL  212-236 re 2312-2336. .
                    MC  .    237-251 re 2337-2351.
```

Note a: Leased to CCC&StL in 1926 without change of numbers.
Note b: Leased to Michigan Central in 1928 without change of numbers.
Note c: "   "   "   "   " 1929 "   "   "   "
Note d: "   "   "   "   " 1930 "   "   "   "

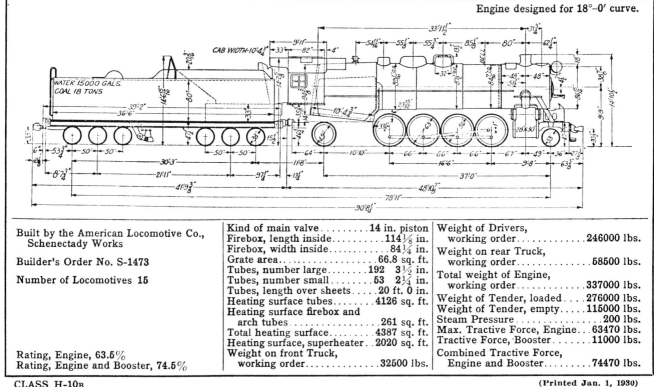

Engine designed for 18°-0' curve.

Built by the American Locomotive Co., Schenectady Works	Kind of main valve........14 in. piston	Weight of Drivers, working order..........246000 lbs.
Builder's Order No. S-1473	Firebox, length inside.........114⅛ in.	Weight on rear Truck, working order.............58500 lbs.
	Firebox, width inside...........84¼ in.	
	Grate area....................66.8 sq. ft.	
Number of Locomotives 15	Tubes, number large.......192 3½ in.	Total weight of Engine, working order............337000 lbs.
	Tubes, number small.....53 2¼ in.	
	Tubes, length over sheets.....20 ft. 0 in.	Weight of Tender, loaded....276000 lbs.
	Heating surface tubes.......4126 sq. ft.	Weight of Tender, empty.....115000 lbs.
	Heating surface firebox and arch tubes................261 sq. ft.	Steam Pressure............200 lbs.
		Max. Tractive Force, Engine..63470 lbs.
	Total heating surface........4387 sq. ft.	Tractive Force, Booster......11000 lbs.
	Heating surface, superheater .2020 sq. ft.	
Rating, Engine, 63.5%	Weight on front Truck, working order.............32500 lbs.	Combined Tractive Force, Engine and Booster........74470 lbs.
Rating, Engine and Booster, 74.5%		

CLASS HS : 4-8-4 EXPERIMENTAL

NYC CLASS HS-1a 4-8-4 Three Cylinder, High Pressure, Experimental Locomotive.

23x30 (2) and 13+x30 (1) - 69- 250, 850, 1300, 1700 - 435000 - 66000 + 13750 Booster.

800 (re'36) 80 Alco-S 68055 9/31. Sc 8/39.

Niagara Type Freight Locomotive, Class HS-1A.
Built by American Locomotive Co.,Schenectady, N.Y., October, 1931.
N.Y.C. No. 800   Order No. S-1663

Cylinder, diameter & stroke - outside	23" x 30"	Heating surface,sq.ft.-Superheater,L.P.steam	1021
Cylinder, diameter & stroke - middle	13¼" x 30"	Wheel base, driving	19'-2"
Steam pressure, high pressure, lbs.	850	Wheel base, total engine	44'-5"
Steam pressure, low pressure, lbs.	250	Wheel base, total engine and tender	67'-2"
Steam pressure, closed circuit, lbs.	1350	Length over couplers, eng. & tender	99'5-1/4"
Drivers, diameter	69"	Weight, working order,lbs.on front truck	66,500
Firebox, length, inside	129 - 3/8"	Weight, working order,lbs., on drivers	252,000
Firebox, width, inside	78"	Weight,working order,lbs.rear truck,fr.axle	55,000
Grate area, Sq.Ft. - (118-3/8" x 79")	65.0	Weight,working order,lbs.rear truck,rear axle	61,500
Boiler, diameter, inside 1st course	80"	Weight,working order,lbs.total engine	435,000
L.P. Boiler Tubes, large, number and size	174- 3-1/2"	Weight, tender, empty	132,500
L.P. Boiler Tubes, small, number and size	-	Weight, tender, loaded	312,700
L.P. Boiler Tubes, length over sheets	18'2-1/8"	Weight, engine and tender, total	747,700
Heating surface, sq.ft. - tubes	3215	Maximum tractive force, engine	66,000
Heating surface, sq.ft. - firebox and arch tubes	-	Tractive force, booster	13,750
Heating surface, sq.ft. - L.P. Boiler Tube Sheet	15	Combined tractive force,engine and booster	79,750
Heating surface, sq.ft. -P.B.Tubes, closed circuit	430	Factor of adhesion, engine	3.82
Heating surface, sq.ft. -H.P. Boiler Transfer Coils	660	Factor of adhesion, booster	4.47
Heating surface, sq.ft. - Total	4320	Tender capacity, coal tons	28
Heating surface, sq.ft. - Superheater, H.P.exhaust	777	Tender capacity, water gallons	15,000

CLASS I: 4-4-2 ATLANTIC

NYC&HR CLASS I 4-4-2: 20+x26-79-200-178000-22400. Old Class I-4. Reclassified I-10 when superheated.

```
      re'05 re'13              Super.                      re'05 re'13              Super.
2999  3999  999  Schen. 5708 1/01      So 11/22 (a)    2969  3969  969  Schen. 6106 5/01      So 11/23 (b)
                                                       2970  3970  970    "    6107  "        Sc 10/24
2979  3979  979    "    5728 1/01 8/17 Sc 12/25        2971  3971  971    "    6108 7/01      Sc  8/25
2980  3980  980    "    5729  "   1/24 SS  6/28        2972  3972  972    "    6109  "   /18  Sc  6/28
2981  3981  981    "    5730  "        So 11/22 (a)    2973  3973  973    "    6110  "        Sc  9/24
2982  3982  982    "    5731  "        So 11/22 (a)    2974  3974  974    "    6111 1/02      Sc 12/25
2983  3983  983    "    5732  "        So 11/22 (a)    2975  3975  975    "    6112  "        So 11/22 (b)
2984  3984  984    "    5733  "        So 12/22 (b)    2976  3976  976    "    6113 2/02      Sc 12/25
2985  3985  985    "    5734 2/01      Sc  7/23        2977  3977  977    "    6114  "        So 11/23 (b)
2986  3986  986    "    5735  "        So 12/23 (b)    2978  3978  978    "    6115  "   /23  SS  6/28
2987  3987  987    "    5736  "        Sc  8/25
2988  3988  988    "    5737  "        Sc  7/23        2954  3954  954  Alco-S 25022 5/02     Sc  7/25
2989  3989  989    "    5738  "        Sc 11/25        2955  3955  955    "    25023  "       Sc 11/23
2990  3990  990    "    5739  "   3/19 Sc  6/33        2956  3956  956    "    25024  "       Sc 10/25
2991  3991  991    "    5740 3/01      So 11/23 (b)    2957  3957  957    "    25025  "       So 11/22 (a)
2992  3992  992    "    5741  "        Sc 11/23        2958  3958  958    "    25026  "       So 11/23 (b)
2993  3993  993    "    5742  "        Sc  8/23        2959  3959  959    "    25027  "       Sc  6/26
2994  3994  994    "    5743  "        So 12/22 (b)    2960  3960  960    "    25028  "       So 11/22 (a)
2995  3995  995    "    5744 4/01      So 11/22 (a)    2961  3961  961    "    25029  "  7/17 Sc  7/25
2996  3996  996    "    5745  "        Sc 10/22        2962  3962  962    "    25030  "       Sc  9/24
2997  3997  997    "    5746  "        Sc 12/25        2963  3963  963    "    25031  "       Sc  8/23
2998  3998  998    "    5747 3/01      So 12/22 (b)    2964  3964  964    "    25032  "  4/19 Sc  7/26
                                                       2965  3965  965    "    25033  "       Sc  8/23
                                                       2966  3966  966    "    25034  "  /24  Sc  6/29
                                                       2967  3967  967    "    25035  "  1/24 SS  6/28
                                                       2968  3968  968    "    25036  "  1/24 Sc  9/32
```

NYC&HR CLASS Ia 4-4-2: 20+x26-79-200-176000-22400. Reclassified I-10a when superheated. Wt. 181000.

```
2923  3923  923  Alco-S 26637  9/02  So 11/22 (a)     2935  3935  935  Alco-S 26649 10/02      Sc  7/23
2924  3924  924    "    26638   "    So 11/22 (a)     2936  3936  936    "    26650  "          Sc  7/23
2925  3925  925    "    26639   "    Sc  7/23         2937  3937  937    "    26651  "          Sc  6/26
2926  3926  926    "    26640   "    Sc  8/23         2938  3938  938    "    26652 11/02       Sc  9/23
2927  3927  927    "    26641   "    So 11/22 (b)     2939  3939  939    "    26653 12/02 '24   Sc  5/29
2928  3928  928    "    26642   "    So 11/22 (a)     2940  3940  940    "    26654  "          So 11/22 (b)
2929  3929  929    "    26643   "    Sc 12/25         2941  3941  941    "    26655  "          So 11/22 (a)
2930  3930  930    "    26644   "    Sc  8/25         2942  3942  942    "    26656  "          Sc 12/25
2931  3931  931    "    26645 10/02  So 11/22 (a)     2943  3943  943    "    26657  "          So 11/23 (b)
2932  3932  932    "    26646   "    So  8/22 (b)     2944  3944  944    "    26658  "          So 11/22 (a)
2933  3933  933    "    26647   "    So  8/22 (b)     2945  3945  945    "    26659  "          So 11/23 (b)
2934  3934  934    "    26648   "  '18 Sc  7/28       2946  3946  946    "    26660  "          So 11/22 (a)
                                                      2947  3947  947    "    26661  "          Sc  7/25
```

B&A CLASS Ib 4-4-2: See B&A 2948-2953, on p. 290

NYC&HR CLASS Ib (later Ic): 20+x26-79-200-183000-22400

```
2916  3916  916  Alco-S 27873 11/03  So 12/22 (b)
2917  3917  917    "    27874   "    Sc  8/23
2918  3918  918    "    27875   "    Sc  6/25
2919  3919  919    "    27876 12/03  Sc  8/23
2920  3920  920    "    27877   "    Sc  9/25
2921  3921  921    "    27878   "    So 11/22 (b)
2922  3922  922    "    27879   "    Sc  8/23
```

Note a; to Rochester Iron & Metal Co.

Note b: to Penn. Wood & Iron Co.

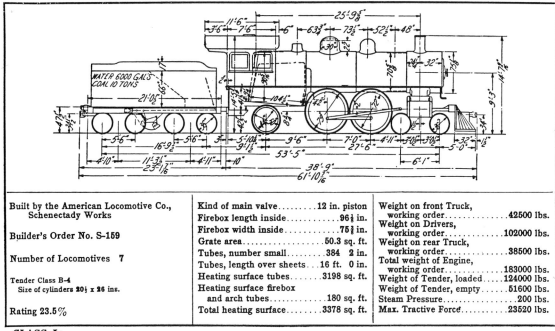

Built by the American Locomotive Co.,
Schenectady Works

Builder's Order No. S-159

Number of Locomotives 7

Tender Class B-4
  Size of cylinders 20½ x 26 ins.

Rating 23.5%

Kind of main valve	12 in. piston
Firebox length inside	96¼ in.
Firebox width inside	75¾ in.
Grate area	50.3 sq. ft.
Tubes, number small	384 2 in.
Tubes, length over sheets	16 ft. 0 in.
Heating surface tubes	3198 sq. ft.
Heating surface firebox and arch tubes	180 sq. ft.
Total heating surface	3378 sq. ft.

Weight on front Truck, working order	42500 lbs.
Weight on Drivers, working order	102000 lbs.
Weight on rear Truck, working order	38500 lbs.
Total weight of Engine, working order	183000 lbs.
Weight of Tender, loaded	124000 lbs.
Weight of Tender, empty	51600 lbs.
Steam Pressure	200 lbs.
Max. Tractive Force	23520 lbs.

CLASS Ic

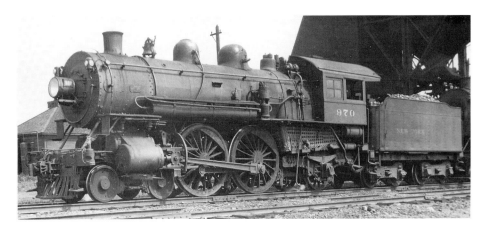

NYC 970, class I,   at Niagara Falls in 1923.   It was scrapped a year later.   (Edson)

NYC&HR 2990, class I, with oil headlight, wood pilot.   (Bob Lorenz collection)

NYC&HR CLASS Ib (later Id) 4-4-2: 20+x26-79-200-186000-22400. | Reclassified I-10d when superheated. Wt. 191000

	re'05	re'13								re'05	re'13						
2896	3896	896	Alco-S	29580	4/04	11/17	Sc	8/25	2906	3906	906	Alco-S	29590	5/04		So	11/22 (a)
2897	3897	897	"	29581	"	9/18	Sc	5/28	2907	3907	907	"	29591	"	6/24	So	5/29
2898	3898	898	"	29582	"	/23	Sc	6/29	2908	3908	908	"	29592	"		Sc	10/25
2899	3899	899	"	29583	5/04		Sc	6/26	2909	3909	909	"	29593	"	11/18	SS	6/28
2900	3900	900	"	29584	"		Sc	9/25	2910	3910	910	"	29594	"		Sc	7/25
2901	3901	901	"	29585	"		So	12/22 (a)	2911	3911	911	"	29595	"		Sc	9/25
2902	3902	902	"	29586	"		Sc	8/23	2912	3912	912	"	29596	"		Sc	6/26
2903	3903	903	"	29587	"		So	12/22 (a)	2913	3913	913	"	29597	"	1/24	Sc	6/32
2904	3904	904	"	29588	"		Sc	8/23	2914	3914	914	"	29598	"	1/24	Sc	7/29
2905	3905	905	"	29589	"		Sc	7/26									

NYC&HR CLASS Ic (later Ie) 4-4-2: 20+x26-79-200-186000-22400. | Orig. Cole Superhtr. removed 1/09, not replaced.

2915	3915	915	Alco-S	29599	6/04	Sc	7/23

NYC&HR CLASS If 4-4-2: 21+x26-79-185-190000-24500. | Reclassified I-10f when superheated. Wt. 195000.

B.C.E.	3876	876	Alco-S	37838	7/05	11/12	Sc	6/27	3856	856	Alco-S	38711	2/06	8/14	Sc	5/29
"	3877	877	"	37839	"	8/17	Sc	6/26	3857	857	"	38712	"	11/12	Sc	7/32
"	3878	878	"	37840	"	7/15	Sc	5/27	3858	858	"	38713	"	11/16	Sc	4/29
"	3879	879	"	37841	"	6/16	Sc	5/28	3859	859	"	38714	"	8/12	Sc	10/29
"	3880	880	"	37842	"	10/15	Sc	6/26	3860	860	"	38715	"	8/13	Sc	5/32
"	3881	881	"	37843	"	2/14	Sc	5/28	3861	861	"	38716	"	8/23	Sc	9/32
"	3882	882	"	37844	"	7/14	SS	5/28	3862	862	"	38717	"	2/15	Sc	7/26
"	3883	883	"	37845	"	7/18	Sc	5/28	3863	863	"	38718	"	7/13	Sc	7/26
"	3884	884	"	37846	"	12/16	Sc	6/28	3864	864	"	38719	"	6/12	Sc	6/26
"	3885	885	"	37847	"	8/16	Sc	5/33	3865	865	"	38720	"	5/13	Sc	10/27
"	3886	886	"	37848	"	12/13	Sc	6/28	3866	866	"	38721	"	10/16	Sc	6/27
"	3887	887	"	37849	"	11/23	Sc	6/26	3867	867	"	38722	"	12/13	Sc	7/26
"	3888	888	"	37850	"	10/13	Sc	12/25	3868	868	"	38723	"	1/24	Sc	6/28
"	3889	889	"	37851	"	11/13	SS	5/28	3869	869	"	38724	"	11/13	Sc	5/34
"	3890	890	"	37852	"	8/16	Sc	4/33	3870	870	"	38725	"	5/14	Sc	6/32
"	3891	891	"	37853	"	7/16	Sc	7/26	3871	871	"	38726	"	4/18	Sc	4/32
"	3892	892	"	37854	"	12/12	Sc	5/27	3872	872	"	38727	"	9/14	Sc	7/26
"	3893	893	"	37855	"	5/24	Sc	5/33	3873	873	"	38728	"	10/13	Sc	8/26
"	3894	894	"	37856	"	6/12	Sc	5/33	3874	874	"	38729	"	10/13	Sc	5/32
"	3895	895	"	37857	"	5/14	Sc	9/24	3875	875	"	38730	"	8/13	Sc	6/28

NYC&HR CLASS Ig 4-4-2: 21+x26-79-185-191000-24500. | Reclassified I-10g when superheated. Wt. 195000

	re'06	re'07	re'13	Alco c/n						re'13						
3836	3851		851	40187	6/06	11/12	Sc	6/26	3831	831	Alco-S	41013	10/06	9/12	Sc	6/27
3837	4803	3785	785	40188	"	9/17	Sc	7/26	3832	832	"	41014	"	1/14	Sc	12/25
3838	4804	3786	786	40189	"	8/15	Sc	7/26	3833	833	"	41015	"	9/13	Sc	6/28
3839	4805	3787	787	40190	"	11/15	Sc	7/26	3834	834	"	41016	"	12/13	Sc	9/29
3840	4806	3788	788	40191	"	2/18	Sc	7/26	3835	835	"	41017	"	6/13	Sc	6/33
3841	4800	3789	789	40192	"	10/15	Sc	6/28	3836	836	"	41018	"	5/12	Sc	5/33
3842	3852		852	40193	"	12/19	Sc	3/29	3837	837	"	41019	"	4/14	Sc	5/32
3843	4807	3790	790	40194	"	11/12	Sc	7/29	3838	838	"	41020	"	7/17	Sc	7/26
3844	4808	3791	791	40195	"	11/12	Sc	7/26	3839	839	"	41021	"	10/16	Sc	7/26
3845	4809	3792	792	40196	"	3/12	Sc	7/26	3840	840	"	41022	"	6/14	Sc	8/26
3846	3853		853	40197	"	8/13	Sc	6/27	3841	841	"	41023	"	4/14	Sc	5/28
3847	4801	3793	793	40198	"	1/13	Sc	5/33	3842	842	"	41024	"	9/13	Sc	6/29
3848	3854		854	40199	"	1/15	Sc	6/32	3843	843	"	41025	"	3/17	Sc	5/32
3849	4810	3794	794	40200	"	1/14	Sc	5/33	3844	844	"	41026	"	5/14	Sc	12/25
3850	3855		855	40201	"	8/13	Sc	5/28	3845	845	"	41027	"	9/13	Sc	8/25
3851	4802	3795	795	40202	"	7/15	Sc	7/26	3846	846	"	41028	"	12/16	Sc	6/27
3852	4811	3796	796	40203	"	10/15	Sc	10/32	3847	847	"	41029	"	1/21	Sc	6/32
3853	4812	3797	797	40204	"	4/15	Sc	5/29	3848	848	"	41030	"	5/12	Sc	10/32
3854	4813	3798	798	40205	"	2/17	Sc	11/26	3849	849	"	41031	"	10/13	Sc	7/26
3855	4814	3799	799	40206	"	3/14	SS	6/28	3850	850	"	41032	"	2/16	Sc	6/26

Note: 4800 series operated on LS&MS.

Note a : to Penn. Wood & Iron Co.

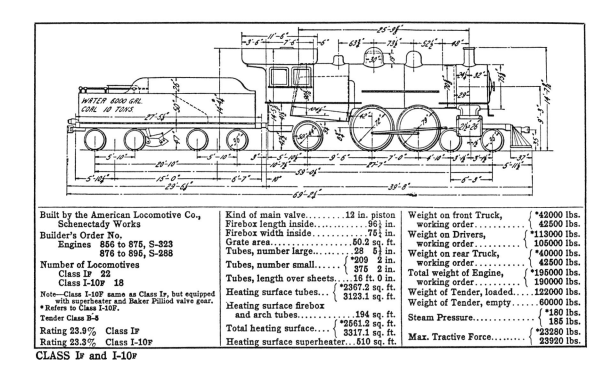

Built by the American Locomotive Co.,
  Schenectady Works

Builder's Order No.
  Engines   856 to 875, S-323
            876 to 895, S-288

Number of Locomotives
  Class IF   22
  Class I-10F 18

Note—Class I-10F same as Class IF, but equipped
  with superheater and Baker Pilliod valve gear.
* Refers to Class I-10F.

Tender Class B-5

Rating 23.9%   Class IF
Rating 23.3%   Class I-10F

Kind of main valve	12 in. piston
Firebox length inside	96⅜ in.
Firebox width inside	75¼ in.
Grate area	50.2 sq. ft.
Tubes, number large	28 5⅜ in.
Tubes, number small	*209 2 in. 375 2 in.
Tubes, length over sheets	16 ft. 0 in.
Heating surface tubes	*2367.2 sq. ft. 3123.1 sq. ft.
Heating surface firebox and arch tubes	194 sq. ft.
Total heating surface	*2561.2 sq. ft. 3317.1 sq. ft.
Heating surface superheater	510 sq. ft.

Weight on front Truck, working order	*42000 lbs. 42500 lbs.
Weight on Drivers, working order	*113000 lbs. 105000 lbs.
Weight on rear Truck, working order	*40000 lbs. 42500 lbs.
Total weight of Engine, working order	*195000 lbs. 190000 lbs.
Weight of Tender, loaded	122000 lbs.
Weight of Tender, empty	60000 lbs.
Steam Pressure	*180 lbs. 185 lbs.
Max. Tractive Force	*23280 lbs. 23920 lbs.

CLASS IF and I-10F

NYC 790, class I-10g with superheater and Baker-Piliod valve gear.   (W.G.Landon)

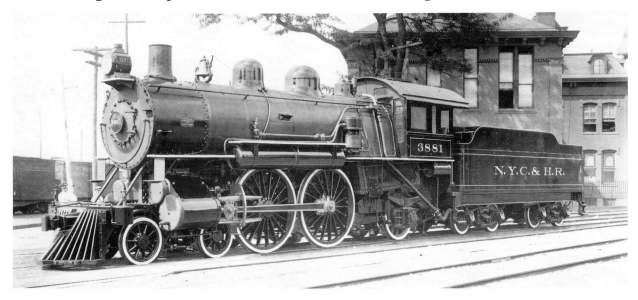

NYC&HR 3881 class If, as built by Alco at Schenectady Works in 1905.(Alco Historic Photos)

NYC&HR CLASS Ih 4-4-2: 21+x26-79-185-191000-24500.   Reclassified I-10h when superheated.   Wt. 195000.

	re'13				Super.					re'13				Super.	
3816	816	Alco-S	41756	11/06	5/12	Sc	5/33	3824	824	Alco-S	41764	11/06	11/12	So	5/34
3817	817	"	41757	"	2/15	Sc	8/26	3825	825	"	41765	"	7/13	Sc	8/34
3818	818	"	41758	"	4/16	Sc	9/34	3826	826	"	41766	"	4/14	Sc	10/32
3819	819	"	41759	"	1/17	Sc	6/28	3827	827	"	41767	"	3/14	Sc	7/26
3820	820	"	41760	"	5/15	Sc	12/30	3828	828	"	41768	"	12/16	Sc	10/32
3821	821	"	41761	"	7/14	Sc	8/26	3829	829	"	41769	"	8/20	Sc	9/32
3822	822	"	41762	"	4/13	Sc	5/33	3830	830	"	41770	"	1/24	Sc	9/34
3823	823	"	41763	"	7/12	Sc	7/26								

CCC&StL CLASS Ij 4-4-2:   See CCC&StL 6940-6959

NYC&HR CLASS Ik 4-4-2: 21+x26-79-185-193000-24500.   Reclassified I-10k when superheated.   Wr.198000.

3806	806	Alco-S	43604	6/07	1/13	Sc	6/32	3811	811	Alco-S	43609	6/07	/21	Sc	5/32
3807	807	"	43605	"	2/14	Sc	7/26	3812	812	"	43610	"	2/24	Sc	10/32
3808	808	"	43606	"	7/13	Sc	6/27	3813	813	"	43611	"	5/17	Sc	7/26
3809	809	"	43607	"	6/13	Sc	6/28	3814	814	"	43612	"	3/24	Sc	10/32
3810	810	"	43608	"	7/12	Sc	7/26	3815	815	"	43613	"	8/13	Sc	5/27

NYC&HR CLASS IL 4-4-2: 21+x26-79-185-193000-24500.   Reclassified I-10L when superheated.   Wt.198000.

3775	775	Alco-S	44039	9/07	2/15	Sc	8/26	3780	780	Alco-S	44044	9/07	/23	Sc	6/32
3776	776	"	44040	"	11/17	Sc	6/26	3781	781	"	44045	"	4/14	Sc	4/29
3777	777	"	44041	"		Sc	10/24	3782	782	"	44046	"	10/16	Sc	7/26
3778	778	"	44042	"	1/24	Sc	6/28	3783	783	"	44047	"	3/15	Sc	7/26
3779	779	"	44043	"	9/23	Sc	5/27	3784	784	"	44048	"	9/16	Sc	9/34

NYC&HR CLASS I-1 4-4-2: Four Cylinder Compound 15+&26x26-79-220-200000-25900.

3000 (re'05) 3803 (re'13) 803   Alco-S 29418 12/04   Sc   11/13

NYC&HR CLASS I-2 4-4-2: 19x26-69-200-168000-22420.   Built for StLawrence & Adirondack.

SL&A	10	(re'01)	2900	(re'04)	2800	(re'05)	3800	(re'13)	800	Schen.	6128	6/01	So 12/22	Roch.Iron & Metal Co
"	11	"	2901	"	2801	"	3801	"	801	"	6136	"	So 11/22	" " " "
"	12	"	2902	"	2802	"	3802	"	802	"	6137	"	So 12/22	" " " "

NYC&HR CLASS I-3 4-4-2: Four Cylinder Compound 15+&26x26-79-220-204500-25900.

3804 (re'13) 804   BLW. 25000 3/05 Sc 11/13

EARLY CLASS J.   2-6-6T TANK

NYC&HR Old Class M 2-6-6T : 18x22-64   Rebuilt to Class E-4 2-6-0. See P132

829	re 1050	Schen.	3528	7/81	Rebuilt to 2-6-0	1450	Sc 9/11
830	re 1051	"	3529	"	" " " "	1451	Sc 10/11
832	re 1052	"	3530	"	" " " "	1452	Sc 5/10

NYC&HR CLASSES J and Ja 2-6-6T: 20x24-63-200-216000-26800.   Rebuilt to Class E-11, E-11a 2-6-0.

1407		Schen.	6144	8/01	RB by'05	1415	(Ja)	Alco-S	25044	6/02	RB by'05
1408		Alco-S	25037	2/02	" "	1416	"	"	25045	"	" "
1409		"	25038	"	" "	1417	"	"	25046	"	" "
1410		"	25039	"	" "	1418	"	"	25047	"	" "
1411		"	25040	"	" "	1419	"	"	25048	7/02	" "
1412		"	25041	3/02	" "	1420	"	"	25049	"	" "
1413		"	25042	5/02	" "	1421	"	"	25050	"	" "
1414	(Ja)	"	25043	6/02	" "	1422	"	"	25051	"	" "

NYC&HR 3804 was truly something special. It was a four cylinder balanced compound, and Baldwin assigned it their construction number 25000.   (BLW)

NYC 820, class I-10h at Buffalo in October, 1917.   (Vollrath collection)

184

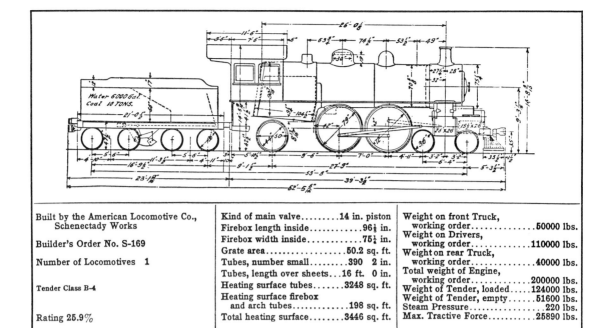

Built by the American Locomotive Co., Schenectady Works

Builder's Order No. S-169

Number of Locomotives   1

Tender Class B-4

Rating 25.9%

Kind of main valve........14 in. piston
Firebox length inside...........96⅛ in.
Firebox width inside...........75¼ in.
Grate area.................50.2 sq. ft.
Tubes, number small........390   2 in.
Tubes, length over sheets...16 ft.   0 in.
Heating surface tubes......3248 sq. ft.
Heating surface firebox
  and arch tubes............198 sq. ft.
Total heating surface.......3446 sq. ft.

Weight on front Truck,
  working order.............50000 lbs.
Weight on Drivers,
  working order............110000 lbs.
Weight on rear Truck,
  working order.............40000 lbs.
Total weight of Engine,
  working order............200000 lbs.
Weight of Tender, loaded....124000 lbs.
Weight of Tender, empty......51600 lbs.
Steam Pressure...............220 lbs.
Max. Tractive Force..........25890 lbs.

CLASS I-1

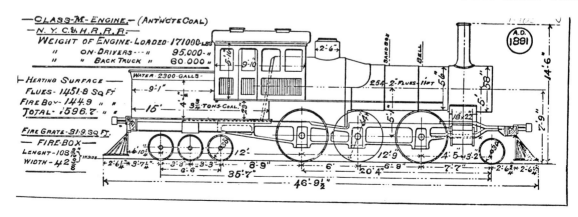

(Alco Hist. Photos)

185

NYC&HR 3000, class I-1 four-cylinder compound. (Alco builders photo; H.L.Vail coll.)

Class J

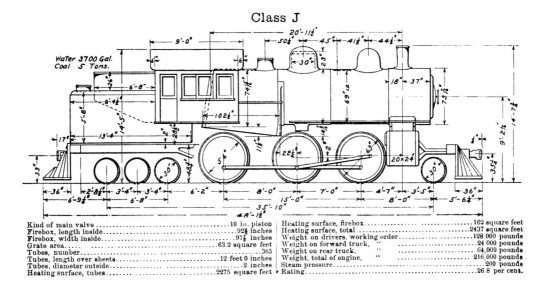

Kind of main valve ....10 in. piston	Heating surface, firebox........................162 square feet
Firebox, length inside...........................92⅝ inches	Heating surface, total ....2437 square feet
Firebox, width inside...........................97⅞ inches	Weight on drivers, working order..............128,000 pounds
Grate area....................................63.2 square feet	Weight on forward truck, " ....24,000 pounds
Tubes, number.....................................365	Weight on rear truck, " ....64,000 pounds
Tubes, length over sheets....................12 feet 0 inches	Weight, total of engine, " ....216,000 pounds
Tubes, diameter outside............................2 inches	Steam pressure...................................200 pounds
Heating surface, tubes.......................2275 square feet	Rating...26.8 per cent.

NYC&HR 1407, class J, built 1901 for N.Y.Suburban runs, but rebuilt to 2-6-0 class E-11.

(Votava)

CLASS J :4-6-4 HUDSON

NYC CLASS J-1a 4-6-4: 25x28-79-225-359800-42360 (b)

5200 Alco-S 67165 2/27 Rt 4/53, Sc 7/53

NYC CLASS J-1b 4-6-4: 25x28-79-225-359800-42360 (b)

5201	Alco-S	67432	9/27	Rt	7/53	
5202	"	67433	"	Rt	7/53, SS	/54
5203	"	67434	"	Rt	7/53, SS	/54
5204	"	67435	"	Rt	3/55, SS	5/55
5205	"	67436	"	Rt	7/53, SS	/54
5206	"	67437	"	Rt	7/53, SS	/54
5207	"	67438	"	Rt	7/53, SS	/54
5208	"	67439	"	Rt	4/53, Sc	6/53
5209	"	67440	"	Rt	4/53, Sc	5/53
5210	"	67441	"	Rt	5/54, SS	
5211	"	67442	"	Rt	8/55, SS	9/55
5212	"	67443	"	Rt	7/53, Sc	11/53
5213	"	67444	"	Rt	7/53, SS	/54
5214	"	67445	"	Rt	7/53, SS	/54
5215	"	67446	"	Rt	7/53, SS	/54
5216	"	67447	"	Rt	9/53, SS	10/53
5217	"	67448	"	Rt	7/53, SS	/54
5218	"	67449	"	Rt	4/53, Sc	6/53
5219	"	67450	"	Rt	7/53, SS	/54
5220	"	67451	"	Rt	11/54, SS	
5221	"	67452	"	Rt	5/54, SS	
5222	"	67453	"	Rt	8/55, SS	9/55
5223	"	67454	10/27	Rt	1/55, SS	4/55
5224	"	67455	"	Rt	5/54, SS	
5225	"	67456	"	Rt	2/54, SS	
5226	"	67457	"	Rt	7/53, SS	/54
5227	"	67458	"	Rt	9/53, SS	/54
5228	"	67459	"	Rt	7/53, SS	/54
5229	"	67460	"	Rt	7/53, SS	/54
5230	"	67461	"	Rt	9/53, SS	
5231	"	67462	"	Rt	12/54, SS	
5232	"	67463	"	Rt	9/54, SS	
5233	"	67464	"	Rt	4/54, SS	
5234	"	67465	"	Rt	4/53, Sc	12/53
5235	"	67466	"	Rt	10/53, SS	/54
5236	"	67467	"	Rt	5/53, SS	12/53
5237	"	67468	"	Rt	8/53, SS	/54
5238	"	67469	"	Rt	9/55, SS	9/55
5239	"	67470	"	Rt	2/54, SS	

Note a - 5265-5274 weight 361000.

NYC CLASS J-1b 4-6-4: Continued

5240	Alco-S	67471	10/27	Rt	4/53, SS	6/53
5241	"	67472	"	Rt	5/54, SS	
5242	"	67473	"	Rt	9/53, SS	/54
5243	"	67474	"	Rt	7/53, SS	/54
5244	"	67475	"	Rt	4/53, Sc	12/53
5245	"	67476	11/27	Rt	4/53, SS	6/53
5246	"	67477	"	Rt	7/53, SS	/54
5247	"	67478	"	Rt	3/56	
5248	"	67479	"	Rt	11/53, Sc	12/53
5249	"	67480	"	Rt	4/53, SS	7/53

MC CLASS J-1b: See MC 8200-8209 re 5345-5354

NYC CLASS J-1c 4-6-4: 25x28-79-225-358900-42360 (b)

5250	Alco-S	67712	12/28	Rt	7/53, SS	/54	
5251	"	67713	"	Rt	7/53, SS	/54	
5252	"	67714	"	Rt	10/53, Sc	11/53	
5253	"	67715	"	Rt	5/54, SS		
5254	"	67716	"	Rt	5/54, SS		
5255	"	67717	"	Rt	4/53, Sc	9/53	
5256	"	67718	"	Rt	10/53, SS	/54	
5257	"	67719	"	Rt	4/53, Sc	12/53	
5258	"	67720	"	Rt	11/53, Sc	2/54	
5259	"	67721	1/29	Rt	4/53, Sc	11/53	
5260	"	67722	12/28	Rt	3/56		
5261	"	67723	"	Rt	9/55, SS	9/55	
5262	"	67724	"	Rt	4/53, SS	6/53	
5263	"	67725	"	Rt	8/55, SS	9/55	
5264	"	67726	"	Rt	4/53, SS	6/53	
5265	"	67727	"	Rt	4/53, SS	6/53	(a)
5266	"	67728	"	Rt	3/55, SS	5/55	(a)
5267	"	67729	"	Rt	5/55, SS	6/55	(a)
5268	"	67730	1/29	Rt	3/53, SS	6/53	(a)
5269	"	67731	"	Rt	3/56		(a)
5270	"	67732	"	Rt	11/54, SS		(a)
5271	"	67733	"	Rt	3/55, SS	5/55	(a)
5272	"	67734	"	Rt	4/53, SS	/54	(a)
5273	"	67735	"	Rt	3/56		(a)
5274	"	67736	"	Rt	5/54, SS		(a)

MC CLASS J-1c: See MC 8210-8214 re 5355-5359.

Note b - Booster adds 10900 tf.

NYC 5200 class J-1a, the Central's first Hudson, as she looked in later years. (Lorenz)

NYC 5205, class J-ib at the 1927 "Fair of the Iron Horse" near Baltimore.

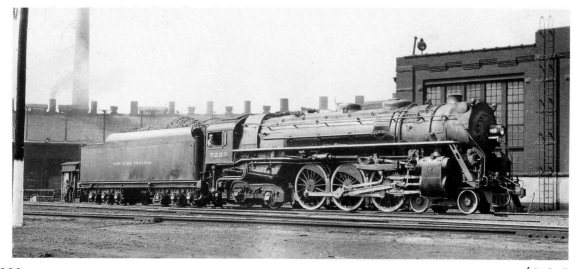

NYC 5229, another J-1b, at Youngstown, 1929. (G.A.Doeright)

188

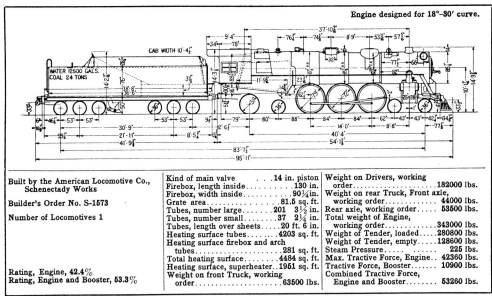

Engine designed for 18°–30' curve.

Built by the American Locomotive Co., Schenectady Works	Kind of main valve . . . .14 in. piston Firebox, length inside. . . . . .130 in. Firebox, width inside. . . . . .90½ in. Grate area. . . . . .81.5 sq. ft. Tubes, number large. . . . . .201 3½ in.	Weight on Drivers, working order. . . . . .182000 lbs. Weight on rear Truck, Front axle, working order. . . . . 44000 lbs.
Builder's Order No. S-1573	Tubes, number small. . . . . . .37 2¼ in. Tubes, length over sheets. . . .20 ft. 6 in. Heating surface tubes. . . . . . .4203 sq. ft.	Rear axle, working order. . . . . 53500 lbs. Total weight of Engine, working order. . . . . .343000 lbs.
Number of Locomotives 1	Heating surface firebox and arch tubes. . . . . .281 sq. ft. Total heating surface. . . . . . .4484 sq. ft.	Weight of Tender, loaded. . . . .280800 lbs. Weight of Tender, empty. . . . .128600 lbs. Steam Pressure. . . . . 225 lbs.
	Heating surface, superheater. .1951 sq. ft. Weight on front Truck, working	Max. Tractive Force, Engine. . 42360 lbs. Tractive Force, Booster. . . . . . .10900 lbs.
Rating, Engine, 42.4% Rating, Engine and Booster, 53.3%	order. . . . . .63500 lbs.	Combined Tractive Force, Engine and Booster. . . . . . . .53260 lbs.

CLASS J-1A

(Printed Jan. 1, 1929)

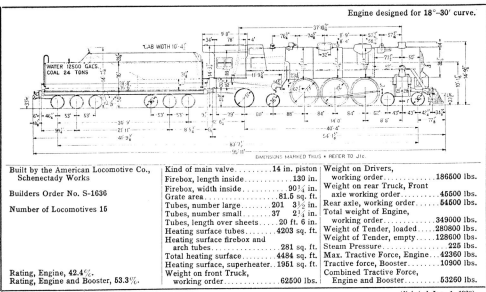

Engine designed for 18°–30' curve.

DIMENSIONS MARKED THUS • REFER TO J1c.

Built by the American Locomotive Co., Schenectady Works	Kind of main valve. . . . . . . .14 in. piston Firebox, length inside. . . . . .130 in. Firebox, width inside. . . . . .90¼ in. Grate area. . . . . .81.5 sq. ft.	Weight on Drivers, working order. . . . . .186500 lbs. Weight on rear Truck, Front axle working order. . . . . 45500 lbs.
Builders Order No. S-1636	Tubes, number large. . . . . .201 3½ in. Tubes, number small. . . . . . .37 2¼ in. Tubes, length over sheets. . . . .20 ft. 6 in.	Rear axle, working order. . . . . 54500 lbs. Total weight of Engine, working order. . . . . .349000 lbs.
Number of Locomotives 15	Heating surface tubes. . . . . . .4203 sq. ft. Heating surface firebox and arch tubes. . . . . .281 sq. ft.	Weight of Tender, loaded. . . . .280800 lbs. Weight of Tender, empty. . . . .128600 lbs. Steam Pressure. . . . . .225 lbs.
	Total heating surface. . . . . . . .4484 sq. ft. Heating surface, superheater. .1951 sq. ft. Weight on front Truck,	Max. Tractive Force, Engine. .42360 lbs. Tractive force, Booster. . . . . . .10900 lbs. Combined Tractive Force,
Rating, Engine, 42.4%. Rating, Engine and Booster, 53.3%.	working order. . . . . .62500 lbs.	Engine and Booster. . . . . . . .53260 lbs.

CLASS J-1C (Eng's #5250-5264)

(Printed Jan. 1, 1930)

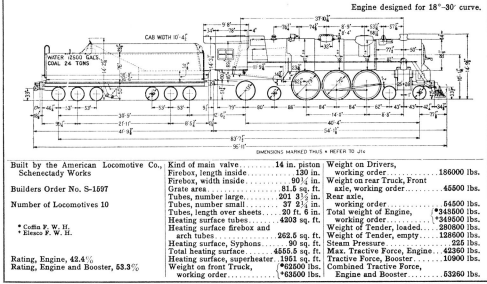

Engine designed for 18°–30' curve.

DIMENSIONS MARKED THUS • REFER TO J1c

Built by the American Locomotive Co., Schenectady Works	Kind of main valve. . . . . . . .14 in. piston Firebox, length inside. . . . . .130 in. Firebox, width inside. . . . . .90¼ in. Grate area. . . . . .81.5 sq. ft.	Weight on Drivers, working order. . . . . .186000 lbs. Weight on rear Truck, Front axle, working order. . . . . 45500 lbs.
Builders Order No. S-1597	Tubes, number large. . . . . .201 3½ in. Tubes, number small. . . . . . .37 2¼ in. Tubes, length over sheets. . . . .20 ft. 6 in.	Rear axle, working order. . . . . 54500 lbs. Total weight of Engine, { •348500 lbs.
Number of Locomotives 10	Heating surface tubes. . . . . . .4203 sq. ft. Heating surface firebox and arch tubes. . . . . .262.5 sq. ft.	working order. . . . . . { +349500 lbs. Weight of Tender, loaded. . . . .280800 lbs. Weight of Tender, empty. . . . .128600 lbs.
• Coffin F. W. H. + Elesco F. W. H.	Heating surface, Syphons. . . . .90 sq. ft. Total heating surface. . . . . . .4555.5 sq. ft. Heating surface, superheater. .1951 sq. ft.	Steam Pressure. . . . . .225 lbs. Max. Tractive Force, Engine. . .42360 lbs. Tractive Force, Booster. . . . . . .10900 lbs.
Rating, Engine, 42.4% Rating, Engine and Booster, 53.3%	Weight on front Truck, { •62500 lbs. working order. . . . . . { +63500 lbs.	Combined Tractive Force, Engine and Booster. . . . . . . .53260 lbs.

CLASS J-1B (Eng's. #5240-5249).

(Printed Jan. 1, 1929)

NYC 5246 J-1b at Chicago in November 1946. (A.F.Staufer collection)

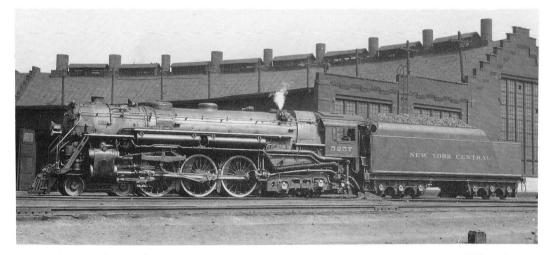

NYC 5257 class J-1c, still with Walschaert valve gear. Youngstown, 1929. (G.A.Doeright)

NYC 5274 class J-1c, with "centipede" PT tank. Lima built 50 of these tenders in 1944-45

NYC CLASS J-1d 4-6-4: 25x28-79-225-362500-42360 (a)

5275	Alco-S	68153	11/29	Rt	1/56, SS	2/56
5276	"	68154	"	Rt	9/53, SS	/54
5277	"	68155	"	Rt	12/54, SS	
5278	"	68156	"	Rt	6/53, SS	8/53
5279	"	68157	"	Rt	10/53, SS	/54
5280	"	68158	"	Rt	6/53, SS	8/53
5281	"	68159	"	Rt	10/53, SS	/54
5282	"	68160	12/29	Rt	5/53, SS	9/53
5283	"	68161	"	Rt	10/53, SS	/54
5284	"	68162	"	Rt	3/54, SS	
5285	"	68163	"	Rt	12/54, SS	
5286	"	68164	"	Rt	9/53, SS	/54
5287	"	68165	"	Rt	2/55, SS	3/55
5288	"	68166	"	Rt	8/55, SS	9/55
5289	"	68167	"	Rt	10/53, SS	/54
5290	"	68168	"	Rt	11/53, SS	/54
5291	"	68169	"	Rt	8/54, SS	
5292	"	68170	"	Rt	11/54, SS	
5293	"	68171	"	Rt	9/53, SS	/54
5294	"	68172	"	Rt	10/53, SS	11/53
5295	"	68173	1/30	Rt	11/54, SS	
5296	"	68174	"	Rt	9/55, SS	9/55
5297	"	68175	"	Rt	9/54, SS	
5298	"	68176	"	Rt	4/53, Sc	7/53
5299	"	68177	"	Rt	4/53, Sc	12/53
5300	"	68178	"	Rt	4/55, SS	6/55
5301	"	68179	"	Rt	9/53, SS	/54
5302	"	68180	"	Rt	9/53, SS	/54
5303	"	68181	"	Rt	10/54, SS	
5304	"	68182	"	Rt	4/53, Sc	7/53
5305	"	68183	"	Rt	11/53, SS	/54
5306	"	68184	"	Rt	6/53, SS	9/53
5307	"	68185	"	Rt	3/54, SS	
5308	"	68186	"	Rt	6/54, SS	
5309	"	68187	"	Rt	5/54, SS	
5310	"	68188	"	Rt	3/56	
5311	"	68189	"	So	1/48	TH&B 501
5312	"	68190	2/30	Rt	2/56	
5313	"	68191	"	So	2/48	TH&B 502
5314	"	68192	"	Rt	4/56	

MC CLASS J-1d: See MC 8215-8229 re 5360-5374.

CCC&StL J-1d: See CCC&StL 6600-6609 re 5375-5384

NYC CLASS J-1e 4-6-4: 25x28-79-225-361700-42360 (a).

5315	Alco-S	68551	4/31	Wrk.	4/40, Sc	6/40
5316	"	68552	5/31	Rt	11/53, SS	/54
5317	"	68553	4/31	Rt	4/53, SS	/54
5318	"	68554	5/31	Rt	9/55, SS	12/55
5319	"	68555	"	Rt	5/53, SS	6/53
5320	"	68556	"	Rt	4/53, SS	/54
5321	"	68557	"	Rt	4/53, SS	/54
5322	"	68558	"	Rt	9/53, SS	9/53
5323	"	68559	"	Rt	1/53, Sc	5/53
5324	"	68560	"	Rt	9/53, SS	/54
5325	"	68561	"	Rt	7/53, SS	/54
5326	"	68562	"	Rt	5/53, SS	/54
5327	"	68563	"	Rt	10/53, SS	/54
5328	"	68564	"	Rt	6/54, SS	
5329	"	68565	"	Rt	5/53, SS	7/53
5330	"	68566	"	Rt	7/53, SS	/54
5331	"	68567	6/31	Rt	5/53, SS	9/53
5332	"	68568	"	Rt	11/53, SS	/54
5333	"	68569	"	Rt	10/53, SS	/54
5334	"	68570	"	Rt	11/53, Sc	12/53

NYC CLASS J-1e 4-6-4: Continued.

5335	Alco-S	68571	6/31	Rt	10/53, SS	/54
5336	"	68572	"	Rt	6/53, SS	6/53
5337	"	68573	"	Rt	8/53, SS	/54
5338	"	68574	"	Rt	3/55, SS	5/55
5339	"	68575	"	Rt	4/53, Sc	6/53
5340	"	68576	"	Rt	3/56	
5341	"	68577	7/31	Rt	8/53, SS	/54
5342	"	68578	9/31	Rt	4/53, SS	7/53
5343	"	68579	10/31	Rt	11/54, SS	
5344(c)	"	68580	11/31	Rt	7/53, SS	/54

CCC&StL J-1e: See CCC&StL 6610-6629 re 5385-5404

NYC CLASS J-3a 4-6-4: 22+x29-79-265-365500-41860 (b)

5405	Alco-S	68839	9/37	Rt	3/56	
5406	"	68840	"	Rt	2/56	
5407	"	68841	"	Rt	5/54, SS	
5408	"	68842	"	Rt	3/56	
5409	"	68843	"	Rt	2/56	
5410	"	68844	"	Rt	11/53, Sc	2/54
5411	"	68845	"	Rt	3/56	
5412	"	68846	"	Rt	9/55, SS	11/55
5413	"	68847	"	Rt	3/56	
5414	"	68848	"	Rt	4/56	
5415	"	68849	10/37	Rt	3/56	
5416	"	68850	"	Rt	4/54, SS	
5417	"	68851	"	Rt	10/54, SS	
5418	"	68852	"	Rt	3/55, SS	6/55
5419	"	68853	"	Rt	4/53, Sc	7/53
5420	"	68854	"	Rt	11/54, Sc	
5421	"	68855	"	Rt	11/54, SS	
5422	"	68856	"	Rt	3/56	
5423	"	68857	"	Rt	2/56	
5424	"	68858	"	Rt	11/55, SS	12/55
5425	"	68859	"	Rt	1/56	
5426(d)	"	68860	"	Rt	2/56	
5427	"	68861	"	Rt	7/53, Sc	9/53
5428	"	68862	"	Rt	4/53, Sc	9/53
5429(e)	"	68863	"	Rt	12/55, SS	2/56
5430	"	68864	"	Rt	1/55, SS	6/55
5431	"	68865	"	Rt	10/54, SS	
5432	"	68866	"	Rt	4/53, Sc	10/53
5433	"	68867	"	Rt	3/56, SS	4/56
5434	"	68868	"	Rt	1/56	
5435	"	68869	"	Rt	4/56	
5436	"	68870	"	Rt	10/55, SS	11/55
5437	"	68871	11/37	Rt	4/56	
5438	"	68872	"	Rt	4/53, Sc	5/53
5439	"	68873	"	Rt	3/56	
5440	"	68874	"	Rt	2/56	
5441	"	68875	"	Rt	4/56	
5442	"	68876	"	Rt	4/56	
5443	"	68877	12/37	Rt	3/56	
5444	"	68878	"	Rt	10/54, SS	
5445	"	68879	3/38	De-Str.	12/47. Rt	11/55
5446	"	68880	"	"	3/47. Rt	3/56
5447	"	68881	"	"	11/47. Rt	2/56
5448	"	68882	"	"	12/46. Rt	4/53
5449	"	68883	"	"	3/47. Rt	4/56
5450	"	68884	4/38 (f)	"	3/45. Rt	8/55
5451	"	68885	"	"	3/47. Rt	2/56
5452	"	68886	"	"	3/47 Rt	4/56
5453	"	68887	"	"	3/47. Rt	8/55
5454	"	68888	"	"	4/46. Rt	10/54

Note a: Booster adds 10900 tf.
Note b: Booster adds 12100 tf.

Note c: Streamlined 12/34 to 7/39, and 7/39 to 10/45.
  Specs as RB: 23 3/4 x 28-79-250-370000-42480 (b)
Note d: Stream. 12/41 to 11/50. Note e: 12/41 to 6/49
Note f: Boiler exploded 9/43. Rebuilt 9/44.

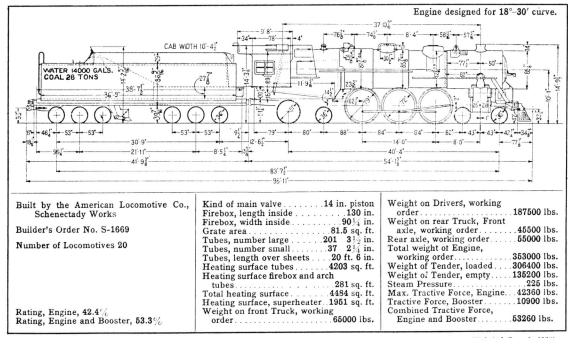

Engine designed for 18°-30' curve.

CAB WIDTH 10'-4½"

WATER 14000 GAL'S.
COAL 28 TONS

Built by the American Locomotive Co., Schenectady Works	Kind of main valve . . . . . . 14 in. piston	Weight on Drivers, working
	Firebox, length inside . . . . 130 in.	order . . . . 187500 lbs.
Builder's Order No. S-1669	Firebox, width inside . . . . 90¼ in.	Weight on rear Truck, Front
	Grate area . . . . 81.5 sq. ft.	axle, working order . . . . 45500 lbs.
Number of Locomotives 20	Tubes, number large . . . . . 201 3½ in.	Rear axle, working order . . . . . 55000 lbs.
	Tubes, number small . . . . . . 37 2¼ in.	Total weight of Engine,
	Tubes, length over sheets . . . 20 ft. 6 in.	working order . . . . 353000 lbs.
	Heating surface tubes . . . . . . 4203 sq. ft.	Weight of Tender, loaded . . . 306400 lbs.
	Heating surface firebox and arch	Weight of Tender, empty . . . . 135200 lbs.
	tubes . . . . 281 sq. ft.	Steam Pressure . . . . 225 lbs.
	Total heating surface . . . . . . 4484 sq. ft.	Max. Tractive Force, Engine . . 42360 lbs.
	Heating surface, superheater . 1951 sq. ft.	Tractive Force, Booster . . . . . . 10900 lbs.
Rating, Engine, 42.4%	Weight on front Truck, working	Combined Tractive Force,
Rating, Engine and Booster, 53.3%	order . . . . 65000 lbs.	Engine and Booster . . . . 53260 lbs.

CLASS J-1ᴅ   (Printed Jan. 1, 1930)

J-1d   Alco Builders photo.   (H.L.Vail coll.)

NYC 5313 class J-1d, before sale in 1948 to Toronto, Hamilton & Buffalo RR. (Hirsimaki)

NYC 5297, class J-1d with Castleton Cut-off Bridge in background.   (Edson collection)

J-1e   Alco Builders photo. (Edson coll.)

NYC 5332, class J-1e.   (Roy Carlson collection)

The 5344 in disguise as the "Commodore Vanderbilt". Elkhart, 1930's.   (R.C.Schell)

The 5344 in her second streamlining. Light weight rods had been applied earlier.

J-3a #5430 was typical of the 40 non-streamlined J-3's with PT tank. Chicago, Aug. 1948.

194

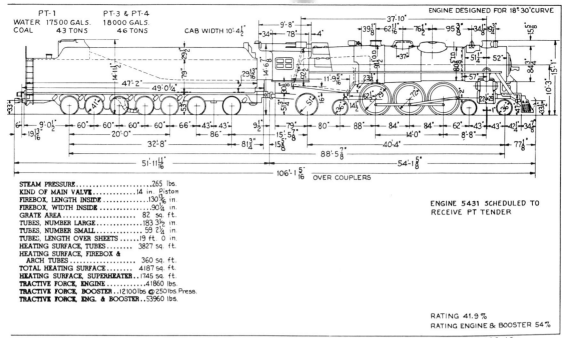

STEAM PRESSURE.................265 lbs.
KIND OF MAIN VALVE............14 in. Piston
FIREBOX, LENGTH INSIDE..........130¹³⁄₁₆ in.
FIREBOX, WIDTH INSIDE...........90¼ in.
GRATE AREA.................... 82 sq. ft.
TUBES, NUMBER LARGE......183 3½ in.
TUBES, NUMBER SMALL.........59 2¼ in.
TUBES, LENGTH OVER SHEETS......19 ft. 0 in.
HEATING SURFACE, TUBES....... 3827 sq. ft.
HEATING SURFACE, FIREBOX &
   ARCH TUBES.............. 360 sq. ft.
TOTAL HEATING SURFACE....... 4187 sq. ft.
HEATING SURFACE, SUPERHEATER..1745 sq. ft.
TRACTIVE FORCE, ENGINE....41860 lbs.
TRACTIVE FORCE, BOOSTER..12100 lbs @ 250 lbs. Press.
TRACTIVE FORCE, ENG. & BOOSTER..53960 lbs.

ENGINE 5431 SCHEDULED TO
RECEIVE PT TENDER

RATING 41.9 %
RATING ENGINE & BOOSTER 54%

CLASS J3A

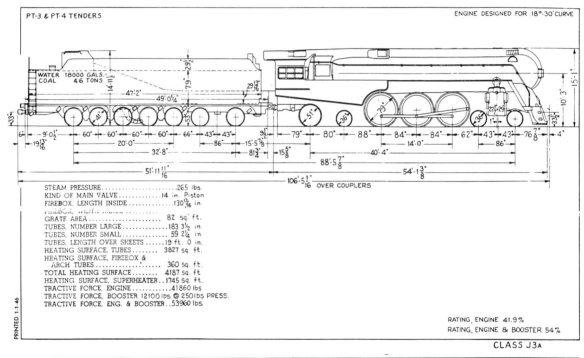

WATER 18000 GALS.
COAL 46 TONS

STEAM PRESSURE.....................265 lbs.
KIND OF MAIN VALVE............14 in. Piston
FIREBOX, LENGTH INSIDE.............130¹³⁄₁₆ in.
FIREBOX, WIDTH INSIDE.................90¼ in.
GRATE AREA.................. 82 sq. ft.
TUBES, NUMBER LARGE............183 3½ in.
TUBES, NUMBER SMALL.............59 2¼ in.
TUBES, LENGTH OVER SHEETS......19 ft. 0 in.
HEATING SURFACE, TUBES........ 3827 sq. ft.
HEATING SURFACE, FIREOX &
   ARCH TUBES................... 360 sq. ft.
TOTAL HEATING SURFACE....... 4187 sq. ft.
HEATING SURFACE, SUPERHEATER...1745 sq. ft.
TRACTIVE FORCE, ENGINE...........41860 lbs
TRACTIVE FORCE, BOOSTER 12100 lbs.@ 250 lbs. PRESS.
TRACTIVE FORCE, ENG. & BOOSTER...53960 lbs.

PRINTED 1-1-46

RATING, ENGINE 41.9%
RATING, ENGINE & BOOSTER 54%

CLASS J3A

WATER 18000 GALS
COAL 46 TONS

STEAM PRESSURE....................265 lbs.
KIND OF MAIN VALVE.............14 in. Piston
FIREBOX, LENGTH INSIDE.............130¹³⁄₁₆ in.
FIREBOX, WIDTH INSIDE ....90¼ in.
GRATE AREA.................... 82 sq. ft.
TUBES, NUMBER LARGE............183 3½ in.
TUBES, NUMBER SMALL.............59 2¼ in.
TUBES, LENGTH OVER SHEETS .....19 ft. 0 in.
HEATING SURFACE, TUBES....... 3827.0 sq. ft.
HEATING SURFACE, FIREBOX &
   ARCH TUBES.................. 360 sq. ft.
TOTAL HEATING SURFACE....... 4187 sq. ft.
HEATING SURFACE, SUPERHEATER.. 1745 sq. ft.
TRACTIVE FORCE, ENGINE ....41860 lbs.
TRACTIVE FORCE, BOOSTER 12100 lbs @ 250 lbs. Press.
TRACTIVE FORCE, ENG. & BOOSTER..53960 lbs.

PRINTED 1-1-46

CYL. SIZE 22½" x 29"

ENGINE 5426 EQUIPPED WITH PT
TENDER. ENGINE 5429 SCHEDULED
TO BE EQUIPPED.

RATING, ENGINE 41.9 %
RATING, ENGINE & BOOSTER 54%

CLASS J3A

Streamlined J-3a #5452. Five of these engines were built with disc drivers.(Votava)

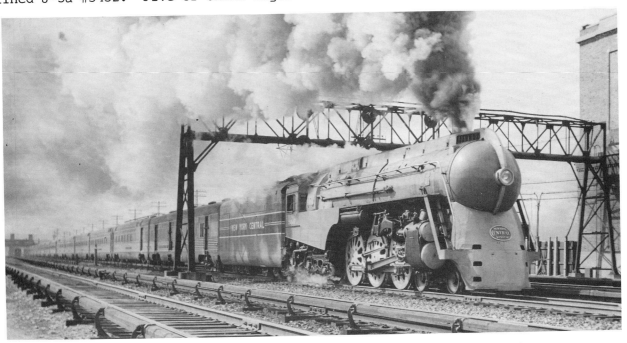

The "Empire" leaving Harmon with the 5447 in charge.   (Robert E. Huke)

The 5426 was usually assigned to the "Empire", later handled the "Mercury" on the M.C.

CLASS K : 4-6-2 PACIFIC

B&A CLASS K 4-6-2 2795-2799 re 3595-3599: See B&A
B&A CLASS Ka,Kc,Kd,Ke,Kj 4-6-2 3510-3549: See B&A
CCC&StL CLASS Kb,Kf,etc. 4-6-2 6400-6454: See CCC&SL
B&A CLASS K-1 4-6-2 2700-2709 re 3500-3509: See B&A
LS&MS CLASS K-2a,b,c,d 4-6-2 4800-4844: See LS&MS.

NYC&HR CLASS K-2e 4-6-2: 22x28-79-200-262000-29160
    re'36

3555		Alco-S	45244	2/08	Rt 11/32
3556		"	45245	"	Rt 3/32
3557		"	45246	"	Rt 11/32
3558		"	45247	"	Rt 6/33
3559		"	45248	"	Rt 11/32
3560		"	45249	"	Rt 9/29
3561		"	45250	"	Rt 9/29
3562		"	45251	"	Rt 5/33
3563		"	45252	3/08	Rt 11/29
3564	4652	"	45253	"	Rt 11/38
3565		"	45254	"	Rt 10/29
3566		"	45255	"	Rt 12/32
3567		"	45256	"	Rt 9/29
3568		"	45257	"	Rt 5/33
3569		"	45258	"	Rt 6/32
3570		"	45259	"	Rt 6/32
3571		"	45260	"	Rt 5/33
3572		"	45261	"	Rt 5/29
3573		"	45262	"	Rt 6/33
3574		"	45263	"	Rt 11/29
3575		"	45264	"	Rt 11/29
3576		"	45265	"	Rt 5/33
3577		"	45266	"	Rt 9/29
3578	4653	"	45267	4/08	Rt 11/38
3579		"	45268	"	Rt 11/29
3580		"	45269	"	Rt 5/33
3581		"	45270	"	Rt 5/33
3582		"	45271	"	Rt 6/28
3583		"	45272	5/08	Rt 4/32
3584		"	45273	"	Rt 10/30
3585		"	45274	"	Rt 11/32
3586		"	45275	"	Rt 5/32
3587		"	45276	"	Rt 11/33
3588		"	45277	"	Rt 5/33
3589		"	45278	"	Rt 10/30
3590		"	45279	"	Rt 11/32
3591		"	45280	"	Rt 11/32
3592		"	45281	"	Rt 6/33
3593		"	45282	"	Rt 11/29
3594		"	45283	"	Rt 10/32

NYC&HR CLASS K-2f 4-6-2: 22x28-79-200-262000-29160

3450	Alco-S	45303	8/08	Rt 4/32
3451	"	45304	"	Rt 11/32
3452	"	45305	"	Rt 8/28
3453	"	45306	"	Rt 4/33
3454	"	45307	"	Rt 5/33
3455	"	45308	"	Rt 10/29
3456	"	45309	"	Rt 8/28
3457	"	45310	"	Rt 11/32
3458	"	45311	9/08	Rt 5/32
3459	"	45312	"	Rt 7/32

NYC&HR CLASS K-2g 4-6-2: 22x28-79-200-262000-29160.

3460	Alco-S	45313	9/08	Rt 10/29
3461	"	45314	"	Rt 12/32
3462	"	45315	"	Rt 6/27
3463	"	45316	"	Rt 4/33
3464	"	45317	"	Rt 3/32

NYC&HR CLASS K-2h 4-6-2: 22x28-79-200-262000-29160.

3465	Alco-S	45318	9/08	Rt 11/32
3466	"	45319	"	Rt 11/29
3467	"	45320	"	Rt 6/32
3468	"	45321	"	Rt 5/33
3469	"	45322	"	Rt 10/32

NYC&HR CLASS K-2i 4-6-2: 22x28-79-200-262000-29160.

3470	Alco-S	46954	2/10	Rt 11/32
3471	"	46955	"	Rt 11/32
3472	"	46956	"	Rt 11/29
3473	"	46957	"	Rt 4/32
3474	"	46958	"	Rt 6/32
3475	"	46959	"	Rt 11/32
3476	"	46960	"	Rt 5/33
3477	"	46961	"	Rt 6/33
3478	"	46962	"	Rt 5/32
3479	"	46963	"	Rt 5/33
3480	"	46964	"	Rt 6/32
3481	"	46965	"	Rt 5/33
3482	"	46966	"	Rt 5/33
3483	"	46967	"	Rt 5/33
3484	"	46968	"	Rt 6/32
3485	"	46969	"	Rt 4/32
3486	"	46970	"	Rt 4/32
3487	"	46971	"	Rt 11/32 (NB 1/12)
3488	"	46972	"	Rt 5/33
3489	"	46973	"	Rt 4/33
3490	"	46974	3/10	Rt 11/32
3491	"	46975	"	Rt 4/32
3492	"	46976	"	Rt 7/32
3493	"	46977	"	Rt 11/32

NYC&HR CLASS K-2j 4-6-2: 22x28-79-200-262000-29160.

3494	Alco-S	46978	3/10	Rt 5/32

NYC&HR CLASS K-2k 4-6-2: 22x28-79-200-262000-29160.

3438	Alco-S	47577	5/10	Rt 10/30
3439	"	47578	"	Rt 7/32
3440	"	47579	"	Rt 3/32
3441	"	47580	"	Rt 7/33
3442	"	47581	"	Rt 4/32
3443	"	47582	"	Rt 6/33
3444	"	47583	"	Rt 10/29
3445	"	47584	"	Rt 4/32
3446	"	47585	"	Rt 10/29
3447	"	47586	"	Rt 7/32
3448	"	47587	"	Rt 6/27
3449	"	47588	"	Rt 11/32

LS&MS CLASS K-2L 4845-4894: See LS&MS

Note: All K-2 superheated 1911-13. Wt. 271500.

NYC 3585, one of 40 in class K-2e, first Pacifics on the NYC&HR.   (Chaney collection)

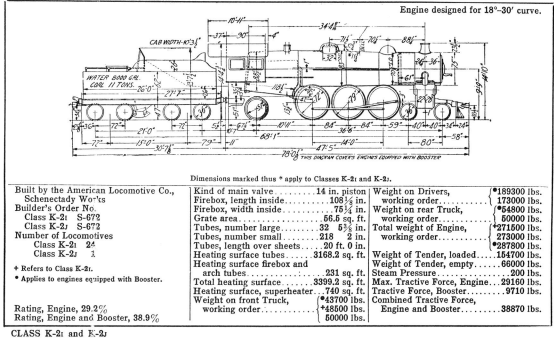

Engine designed for 18°–30' curve.

Dimensions marked thus * apply to Classes K-2ɪ and K-2ᴊ.

Built by the American Locomotive Co., Schenectady Works	Kind of main valve.........14 in. piston	Weight on Drivers, working order.......... { •189300 lbs. / 173000 lbs. }
Builder's Order No.	Firebox, length inside..........108⅛ in.	
Class K-2ɪ S-672	Firebox, width inside..........75¼ in.	Weight on rear Truck, working order.......... { •54800 lbs. / 50000 lbs. }
Class K-2ᴊ S-672	Grate area.................56.5 sq. ft.	
Number of Locomotives	Tubes, number large........32 5⅜ in.	Total weight of Engine, working order.......... { +271500 lbs. / 273000 lbs. / •287800 lbs. }
Class K-2ɪ 24	Tubes, number small........218 2 in.	
Class K-2ᴊ 1	Tubes, length over sheets.....20 ft. 0 in.	
+ Refers to Class K-2ɪ.	Heating surface tubes.....3168.2 sq. ft.	Weight of Tender, loaded.....154700 lbs.
• Applies to engines equipped with Booster.	Heating surface firebox and arch tubes..............231 sq. ft.	Weight of Tender, empty......66000 lbs.
	Total heating surface......3399.2 sq. ft.	Steam Pressure................200 lbs.
	Heating surface, superheater...740 sq. ft.	Max. Tractive Force, Engine...29160 lbs.
Rating, Engine, 29.2%	Weight on front Truck, working order.......... { •43700 lbs. / +48500 lbs. / 50000 lbs. }	Tractive Force, Booster........9710 lbs.
Rating, Engine and Booster, 38.9%		Combined Tractive Force, Engine and Booster........38870 lbs.

CLASS K-2ɪ and K-2ᴊ

NYC&HR 3441, class K-2k, fresh from the shops.   (Gene Baxter)

NYC LINES CLASS K-3 4-6-2: Subclasses built for component lines:

K-3a	NYC&HR	K-3f	MC	K-3m	MC
K-3b	LS&MS	K-3g	NYC&HR	K-3n	NYC
K-3c,d	NYC&HR	K-3h,i	MC	K-3p,q	NYC,CCC&StL,MC
K-3e	LS&MS	K-3j,k,l	CCC&StL	K-3r	CCC&StL

NYC&HR CLASS K-3a 4-6-2: 23+x26-79-200-269000-30900.

re'36

3418		Alco-S	49449	2/11	Rt 11/32
3419	(4805)	"	49450	"	Rt 1/36
3420		"	49451	"	Rt 6/32
3421		"	49452	"	Rt 11/32
3422	4806	"	49453	"	Sc 10/38
3423		"	49454	"	Rt 7/32
3424		"	49455	"	Rt 11/32
3425		"	49456	"	Rt 5/29
3426		"	49457	"	Rt 11/32
3427		"	49458	"	Rt 3/32
3428	4807	"	49459	"	Sc 12/39
3429		"	49460	"	Rt 11/32
3430	4808	"	49461	"	Rt 1/39
3431		"	49462	"	Rt 5/32 (NB 8/12)
3432		"	49463	"	Rt 5/32
3433	4809	"	49464	"	Sc 5/38
3434	4810	"	49465	"	Sc 9/38
3435	(4811)	"	49466	"	Sc 6/36
3436	4812	"	49467	"	Sc 5/39
3437	(4813)	"	49468	3/11	Sc 6/36

NYC&HR CLASS K-3c 4-6-2: 23+x26-79-200-269000-30900.

3398	4821	Baldwin	37423	1/12	Sc 11/38
3399		"	37424	"	Rt 7/33
3400	4822	"	37425	"	Sc 5/39
3401		"	37426	"	Rt 3/32
3402	4823	"	37427	"	Sc 6/39
3403	4824	"	37428	"	Sc 11/48
3404	4825	"	37429	"	Rt 5/50
3405		"	37430	"	Rt 7/33
3406		"	37431	2/12	Rt 6/32
3407	4826(a)	"	37432	1/12	Sc 7/46
3408	4827	"	37468	"	Sc 9/47
3409		"	37469	"	Rt 6/33
3410		"	37470	"	Rt 11/32
3411		"	37471	"	Rt 7/32
3412		"	37472	"	Rt 4/32
3413		"	37491	2/12	Rt 11/32
3414		"	37492	"	Rt 7/33
3415	4828	"	37493	"	Sc 9/38
3416	4829	"	37494	"	Sc 10/38
3417	4830	"	37495	"	Sc 10/38

NYC&HR CLASS K-3d 4-6-2: 23+x26-79-200-272000-30900

3378		Alco-S	51740	8/12	Rt 7/33
3379		"	51741	"	Rt 4/32
3380		"	51742	"	Rt 3/32
3381		"	51743	"	Rt 4/32
3382	4831	"	51744	"	Rt 1/38
3383		"	51745	"	Rt 11/32
3384		"	51746	"	Rt 3/32
3385		"	51747	"	Rt 11/32
3386		"	51748	"	Rt 11/32
3387	4832	"	51749	"	Rt 1/39
3388		"	51750	"	Rt 11/32
3389	4833	"	51751	"	Sc 5/39
3390	4834	"	51752	"	Sc 5/48
3391	4835	"	51753	"	Rt 3/49
3392		"	51754	"	Rt 7/32
3393		"	51755	"	Rt 7/33
3394	4836	"	51756	"	Sc 9/38
3395		"	51757	9/12	Rt 10/32
3396		"	51758	"	Rt 7/32
3397		"	51759	"	Rt 7/32

NYC&HR CLASS K-3g 4-6-2: 23+x26-79-200-271000-30900.

re'36

3358		Alco-S	54044	9/13	Rt 6/33
3359	4848(a)	"	54045	"	Rt 1/51
3360		"	54046	"	Rt 8/33
3361		"	54047	"	Rt 10/28
3362		"	54048	"	Rt 5/29
3363		"	54049	"	Rt 11/32
3364	4849	"	54050	"	Rt 1/38
3365		"	54051	"	Rt 6/33
3366		"	54052	"	Rt 7/33
3367		"	54053	"	Rt 9/33
3368		"	54054	"	Rt 7/33
3369		"	54055	"	Rt 10/32
3370	4850	"	54056	"	Rt 9/48
3371		"	54057	"	Rt 7/32
3372	4851	"	54058	"	Rt 1/49
3373	4852	"	54059	"	Sc 8/38
3374	4853	"	54060	"	Sc 6/39
3375		"	54061	"	Rt 10/32
3376	4854	"	54062	"	Sc 7/48
3377		"	54063	"	Rt 9/32

NYC CLASS K-3n 4-6-2: 23+x26-79-200-269000-30900 (b)

3323	4723	Alco-B	58098	2/18	Rt 12/51, SS 1/52
3324	4724	"	58099	"	Rt 3/49, Sc 10/49
3325	4725	"	58100	"	Rt 3/49, Sc 10/49
3326	4726	"	58101	"	Rt 8/49, Sc 10/49
3327	4727	"	58102	"	Re 3/38 B&A 504
3328	4728	"	58103	"	Rt 8/50, Sc 8/50
3329	4729	"	58104	"	Rt 3/50, Sc 5/50
3330	4730	"	58105	"	Rt 1/49, Sc 4/49
3331	4731	"	58106	"	Rt 1/50, Sc 3/50
3332	4732	"	58107	"	Rt 4/53, SS 7/53
3333	4733	"	58108	" (c)	Rt 3/49, Sc 11/49
3334	4734	"	58109	"	Rt 1/50, Sc 1/50
3335	4735	"	58110	"	Rt 1/49, Sc 3/49
3336	4736	"	58111	"	Rt 6/51, SS 8/51
3337	4737	"	58112	"	Re 10/37 B&A 500
3338	4738	"	58113	"	Re 10/37 B&A 501
3339	4739	"	58114	"	Rt 3/52, SS 9/52
3340	4740	"	58115	"	Rt 2/49, Sc 7/49
3341	4741	"	58116	"	Re 3/38 B&A 505
3342	4742	"	58117	"	Rt 6/51, SS 8/51
3343	4743	"	58118	"	Rt 6/51, SS 6/51
3344	4744	"	58119	"	Rt 2/49, Sc 3/49
3345	4745	"	58120	"	Re 10/37 B&A 502
3346	4746	"	58121	"	Rt 6/51, SS 7/51
3347	4747	"	58122	"	Re 10/37 B&A 503
3348	4748	"	58123	"	Rt 12/51, SS 1/52
3349	4749	"	58124	"	Rt 6/53, Sc 10/53
3350	4750	"	58125	"	Rt 11/51, SS 1/52
3351	4751	"	58126	"	Rt 6/51, SS 7/51
3352	4752	"	58127	"	Rt 12/51, SS 3/52
3353	4753	"	58128	"	Rt 6/51, SS 6/51
3354	4754	"	58129	"	Rt 6/51, SS 6/51
3355	4755	"	58130	"	Rt 6/51, SS 7/51
3356	4756	"	58131	"	Rt 3/52, SS 4/52
3357	4757	"	58132	"	Re 2/39 B&A 506

Note a: 4826 and 4848 re 4/38 to P&E 60 and 61.

Note b: Wt. 290200 with booster, 40610 tf.

Note c: 3333 NB 3/19, boiler L-241.

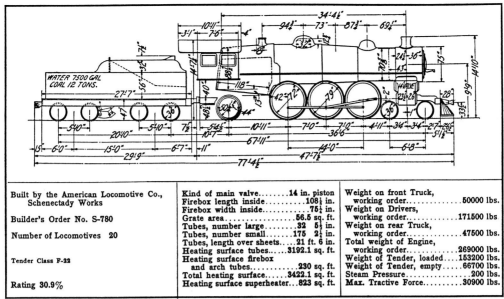

Built by the American Locomotive Co., Schenectady Works	Kind of main valve........14 in. piston	Weight on front Truck,

Built by the American Locomotive Co., Schenectady Works

Builder's Order No. S-780

Number of Locomotives 20

Tender Class F-22

Rating 30.9%

Kind of main valve........14 in. piston
Firebox length inside..........108¼ in.
Firebox width inside............75½ in.
Grate area.................56.5 sq. ft.
Tubes, number large.......32   5½ in.
Tubes, number small......175   2¼ in.
Tubes, length over sheets....21 ft. 6 in.
Heating surface tubes.....3192.1 sq. ft.
Heating surface firebox
   and arch tubes.........230 sq. ft.
Total heating surface.....3422.1 sq. ft.
Heating surface superheater...823 sq. ft.

Weight on front Truck,
   working order.............50000 lbs.
Weight on Drivers,
   working order..........171500 lbs.
Weight on rear Truck,
   working order............47500 lbs.
Total weight of Engine,
   working order..........269000 lbs.
Weight of Tender, loaded....153200 lbs.
Weight of Tender, empty.....66700 lbs.
Steam Pressure...............200 lbs.
Max. Tractive Force.........30900 lbs.

CLASS K-3A

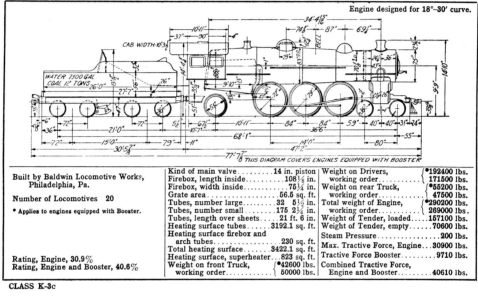

Engine designed for 18°–30′ curve.

Built by Baldwin Locomotive Works, Philadelphia, Pa.

Number of Locomotives 20

* Applies to engines equipped with Booster.

Rating, Engine, 30.9%
Rating, Engine and Booster, 40.6%

Kind of main valve........14 in. piston
Firebox, length inside..........108⅛ in.
Firebox, width inside............75¼ in.
Grate area.................56.5 sq. ft.
Tubes, number large........32   5½ in.
Tubes, number small........175 2¼ in.
Tubes, length over sheets....21 ft. 6 in.
Heating surface tubes......3192.1 sq. ft.
Heating surface firebox and
   arch tubes.............230 sq. ft.
Total heating surface.......3422.1 sq. ft.
Heating surface, superheater...823 sq. ft.
Weight on front Truck,
   working order...........*42600 lbs. / 50000 lbs.

Weight on Drivers,
   working order..........*192400 lbs. / 171500 lbs.
Weight on rear Truck,
   working order...........*55200 lbs. / 47500 lbs.
Total weight of Engine,
   working order..........*290200 lbs. / 269000 lbs.
Weight of Tender, loaded.....157100 lbs.
Weight of Tender, empty......70600 lbs.
Steam Pressure.................200 lbs.
Max. Tractive Force, Engine...30900 lbs.
Tractive Force Booster.........9710 lbs.
Combined Tractive Force,
   Engine and Booster.......40610 lbs.

CLASS K-3C

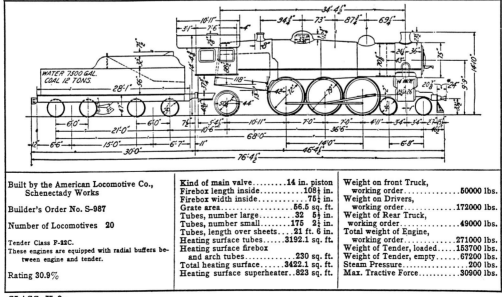

Built by the American Locomotive Co., Schenectady Works

Builder's Order No. S-987

Number of Locomotives 20

Tender Class F-22C.
These engines are equipped with radial buffers between engine and tender.

Rating 30.9%

Kind of main valve.........14 in. piston
Firebox length inside...........108¼ in.
Firebox width inside............75½ in.
Grate area.................56.5 sq. ft.
Tubes, number large........32   5½ in.
Tubes, number small.......175 2¼ in.
Tubes, length over sheets....21 ft. 6 in.
Heating surface tubes.....3192.1 sq. ft.
Heating surface firebox
   and arch tubes............230 sq. ft.
Total heating surface......3422.1 sq. ft.
Heating surface superheater..823 sq. ft.

Weight on front Truck,
   working order..............50000 lbs.
Weight on Drivers,
   working order............172000 lbs.
Weight of Rear Truck,
   working order.............49000 lbs.
Total weight of Engine,
   working order............271000 lbs.
Weight of Tender, loaded....153700 lbs.
Weight of Tender, empty......67200 lbs.
Steam Pressure.................200 lbs.
Max. Tractive Force..........30900 lbs.

CLASS K-3G

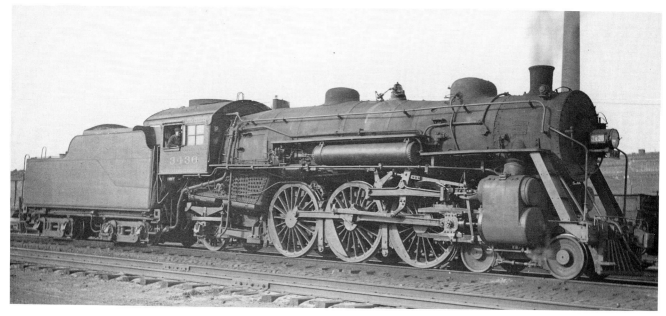

NYC 3436, class K-3a, at Harmon April 1936.   K-3 appearance was similar to the K-2.
(E.L.May)

NYC 3416, class K-3c, still in as-built condition.   (Chaney collection)

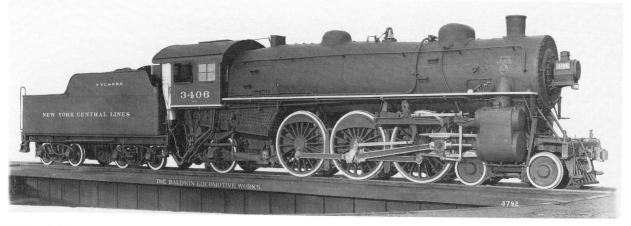

NYC&HR 3406, class K-3c.   One of the few engines built by Baldwin for NYC Lines.
(BLW builder's photo. R.B.Street coll.)

NYC 3380, class K-3q, still unadorned with booster, electric headlight, etc.   (Chaney)

NYC 3359, K-3g. North Adams, Mass. 7/33.   Renumbered 4848, then Peoria & Eastern 61.
(Chaney)

MYC 3342, class K-3n, with booster, running board ladders. At Albany, April 1936. (Votava)

NYC CLASS K-3p 4-6-2: 23+x26-79-200-283500-30900 (a)

	re'36							
3297	4697	Alco-S	62312	11/20	Rt	6/52,	SS	8/52
3298	4698	"	62313	"	Rt	6/51,	SS	6/51
3299	4699	"	62314	"	Rt	5/47,	Sc	8/47
3300	4700	"	62315	"	Rt	7/40,	Sc	10/40
3301	4701	"	62316	"	Rt	6/51,	SS	8/51
3302	4702	"	62317	"	Rt	6/51,	SS	6/51
3303	4703	"	62318	"	Rt	6/51,	SS	8/51
3304	4704	"	62319	"	Rt	10/52,	SS	10/52
3305	4705	"	62320	12/20	Rt	6/51,	SS	10/51
3306	4706	"	62321	"	Rt	6/51,	SS	7/51
3307	4707	"	62322	"	Rt	3/52,	SS	4/52
3308	4708	"	62323	"	Rt	6/51,	SS	8/51
3309	4709	"	62324	"	Rt	9/52,	SS	10/52
3310	4710	"	62325	"	Rt	3/52,	SS	5/52
3311	4711	"	62326	"	Rt	7/52,	SS	11/52
3312	4712	"	62327	"	Rt	10/51,	SS	11/51
3313	4713	"	62328	"	Rt	9/52,	SS	11/52
3314	4714	"	62329	"	Rt	3/52,	SS	4/52
3315	4715	"	62330	"	Rt	6/51,	SS	6/51
3316	4716	"	62331	"	Rt	7/52,	SS	9/52
3317	4717	"	62352	"	Rt	1/50,	Sc	1/50
3318	4718	"	62353	"	Rt	12/51,	SS	2/52
3319	4719	"	62354	"	Rt	4/52,	SS	9/52
3320	4720	"	62355	"	Rt	6/52,	SS	9/52
3321	4721	"	62356	"	Rt	2/52,	SS	3/52
3322	4722	"	62357	"	Rt	5/52,	SS	11/52

NYC CLASS K-3q 4-6-2: 23+x26-79-200-298800-30900 (b)

	re'36							
3267	4667	Alco-B	63949	2/23	Rt	10/52,	SS	10/52
3268	4668	"	63950	3/23	Rt	4/50,	Sc	7/50
3269	4669	"	63951	"	Rt	4/52,	SS	8/52
3270	4670	"	63952	"	Rt	7/52,	SS	9/52
3271	4671	"	63953	"	Rt	6/51,	SS	7/51
3272	4672	"	63954	"	Rt	6/51,	SS	7/51
3273	4673	"	63955	"	Rt	10/52,	SS	10/52
3274	4674	"	63956	"	Rt	6/51,	SS	8/51
3275	4675	"	63957	"	Rt	9/52,	SS	11/52
3276	4676	"	63958	"	Rt	6/51,	SS	6/51
3277	4677	"	63959	"	Rt	4/50,	Sc	7/50
3278	4678	"	63960	"	Rt	7/52,	SS	12/52
3279	4679	"	63961	2/23	Rt	10/51,	SS	1/52
3280	4680	"	63962	3/23	Rt	6/51,	SS	8/51
3281	4681	"	63963	"	Rt	3/52,	SS	4/52
3282	4682	"	63964	"	Rt	6/51,	SS	6/51
3283	4683	"	63965	"	Rt	7/52,	SS	9/52
3284	4684(c)	"	63966	"	Rt	10/52,	SS	2/53
3285	4685	"	63967	"	Rt	6/51,	SS	8/51
3286	4686	"	63968	"	Rt	4/52,	SS	10/52
3287	4687	"	63969	4/23	Rt	6/51,	SS	6/51
3288	4688	"	63970	"	Rt	6/51,	SS	6/51
3289	4689	"	63971	"	Rt	6/51,	SS	8/51
3290	4690	"	63972	"	Rt	4/52,	SS	9/52
3291	4691	"	63973	"	Rt	6/51,	SS	6/51
3292	4692	"	63989	"	Rt	8/50,	Sc	9/50
3293	4693	"	63990	"	Rt	7/52,	SS	8/52
3294	4694	"	63991	"	Rt	6/51,	SS	6/51
3295	4695	"	63992	"	Rt	12/51,	SS	2/52
3296	4696	"	63993	"	Rt	3/52,	SS	4/52

Note a: Wt. 291300 with booster, 40610 tf.
Note b: Built with booster, 40610 tf.
Note c: 3284 converted to 4-6-4 11/26 until 10/27.

NYC CLASS K-5 4-6-2: 26x28-79-200-303000-40700 +9800 booster. Later 25x28-205-38600 +9950.

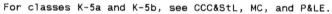

5000 Alco-S 65000 2/24. Re 11/27 to CCC&StL 6525 re 4925.

For classes K-5a and K-5b, see CCC&StL, MC, and P&LE.

NYC 3271, class K-3q, later 4671. Photographed at Albany June 1935. (Chaney collection)

NYC 4704, class K-3p, at Harmon, February 1937, in Poughkeepsie local service. (E.L.May)

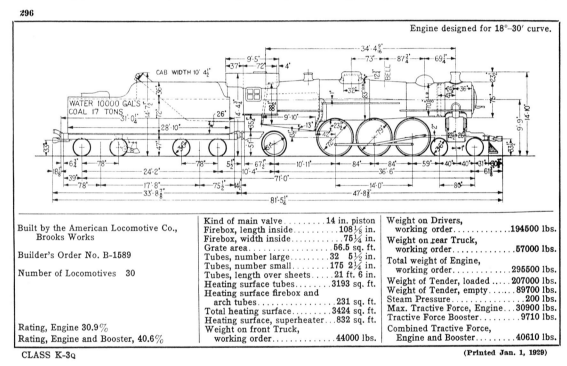

296

Engine designed for 18°–30' curve.

CAB WIDTH 10' 4½"

WATER 10000 GAL'S
COAL 17 TONS

Built by the American Locomotive Co.,
Brooks Works

Builder's Order No. B-1589

Number of Locomotives 30

Rating, Engine 30.9%
Rating, Engine and Booster, 40.6%

Kind of main valve........14 in. piston
Firebox, length inside.........108⅛ in.
Firebox, width inside..........75¼ in.
Grate area.................56.5 sq. ft.
Tubes, number large........32 5½ in.
Tubes, number small.......175 2¼ in.
Tubes, length over sheets....21 ft. 6 in.
Heating surface tubes.......3193 sq. ft.
Heating surface firebox and
  arch tubes...............231 sq. ft.
Total heating surface........3424 sq. ft.
Heating surface, superheater...832 sq. ft.
Weight on front Truck,
  working order.............44000 lbs.

Weight on Drivers,
  working order............194500 lbs.
Weight on rear Truck,
  working order.............57000 lbs.
Total weight of Engine,
  working order............295500 lbs.
Weight of Tender, loaded ....207000 lbs.
Weight of Tender, empty......89700 lbs.
Steam Pressure................200 lbs.
Max. Tractive Force, Engine...30900 lbs.
Tractive Force Booster........9710 lbs.
Combined Tractive Force,
  Engine and Booster........40610 lbs.

CLASS K-3Q

(Printed Jan. 1, 1929)

NYC 4719, another K-3p, one of many equipped with booster in 1920's.   (Chaney collection)

```
NYC&HR CLASS K-10a 4-6-2: 24x26-69-200-266000-36900
(Re K-11a when superheated 1912: 26x26-180-38970)
          re'36
3000           Alco-S 49255 12/10  RB 10/25 K-14a
3001  4401(a)    "     49256   "    Rt  9/52
3002             "     49257   "    Rt  6/32
3003             "     49258   "    Rt  8/33
3004             "     49259  1/11  Sc  5/34
3005  4405       "     49260   "    Sc  8/47
3006             "     49261   "    Rt  9/33
3007             "     49262   "    Rt  7/33
3008             "     49263   "    Rt  8/33
3009             "     49264   "    RB  9/25 K-14a
3010             "     49265   "    Rt  8/33
3011             "     49266   "    RB  9/25 K-14a
3012  4412       "     49267   "    Rt  5/47
3013  4413       "     49268   "    Rt  1/53
3014  4414       "     49269   "    Rt  5/47
3015             "     49270   "    Rt  4/32
3016             "     49271   "    Rt  9/32
3017             "     49272   "    NB 6/11; Sc 6/34
3018             "     49273   "    Sc  8/34
3019             "     49274   "    Rt  7/32
3020             "     49275   "    Rt  7/33
3021             "     49276   "    Rt  7/33
3022  4422       "     49277   "    Rt  5/47
3023             "     49278   "    Rt  7/53
3024             "     49279   "    Rt  7/33
3025             "     49280   "    Rt  9/33
3026             "     49281 12/10  Rt  8/33
3027  4427       "     49282   "    Rt  5/47
3028             "     49283   "    Rt  7/33
3029             "     49284   "    Rt  7/33
3030             "     49285  1/11  Rt  1/36
3031  4431       "     49286   "    Rt  5/47
3032             "     49287   "    Rt  7/33
3033             "     49288   "    Rt  8/33
3034             "     49289   "    Rt  7/33
3035             "     49290   "    Rt  9/33
3036             "     49291   "    Rt  7/33
3037             "     49292   "    Rt  1/36
3038             "     49293   "    Rt  7/33
3039  4439       "     49294   "    Rt 10/52
3040             "     49295   "    Sc  2/36
3041  4441       "     49296   "    Rt 12/51
3042             "     49297   "    Rt  9/33
3043             "     49298   "    Rt  1/36
3044  4444       "     49299   "    Rt  3/50
3045             "     49300   "    Rt  8/33
3046             "     49301   "    Rt  7/33
3047  4447       "     49302   "    Rt  7/52
3048             "     49303   "    Rt  6/32
3049             "     49304   "    Rt  8/33


NYC&HR CLASS K-11a 4-6-2: 26x26-69-180-266000-38970
3090  4490  Alco-B 49245  2/11  Rt  7/52
3091  4491    "    49246   "    NB 5/24; Rt 4/52
3092          "    49247   "    Rt  1/36
3093          "    49248   "    Rt  7/33
3094          "    49249   "    Rt  1/36
3095          "    49250   "    Rt  1/36
3096          "    49251   "    Rt  7/33
3097          "    49252   "    Rt  7/33
3098  4498    "    49253   "    Rt  7/52
3099          "    49254   "    Rt  1/36
```

```
NYC&HR CLASS K-11b 4-6-2: 26x26-69-180-266000-38970
          re'36
3080           Alco-S 50672 12/11  Rt  7/33
3081  (d)        "     50673   "    RB  1/30 K-14b
3082             "     50674   "    Rt  7/33
3083  4483       "     50675   "    Rt  3/52
3084  (d)        "     50676   "    RB  7/29 K-14b
3085             "     50677   "    Rt  1/36
3086  4486       "     50678   "    Sc  9/47
3087             "     50679   "    Rt  8/33
3088             "     50680   "    Rt  1/36
3089             "     50681   "    Rt  8/33
3100  4500       "     50682  1/12  Sc 10/40
3101  4501       "     50683   "    Sc  2/40
3102  4502       "     50684   "    Sc  4/39
3103  4503       "     50685   "    Rt  1/50
3104  4504(b)    "     50686   "    Rt  2/52
3105  4505       "     50687   "    Sc  2/48
3106  4506       "     50688   "    Rt  5/47
3107  4507(c)    "     50689   "    Rt  7/52
3108  (d)        "     50690   "    RB  9/29 K-14b
3109  4509       "     50691   "    Rt  6/52
3110  4510       "     50692   "    Rt  5/47
3111  4511       "     50693   "    Rt  9/50
3112  4512       "     50694   "    Rt  3/49
3113  4513       "     50695   "    Rt 10/50
3114  4514       "     50696  2/12  Rt  1/50
3115  4515       "     50697   "    Rt  7/52
3116  4516       "     50698   "    Sc  5/48
3117  4517       "     50699   "    Sc  6/40
3118  4518       "     50700   "    Rt  2/52
3119  4519       "     50701   "    Rt 12/51


NYC&HR CLASS K-11c 4-6-2: 26x26-69-180-266000-38970
3050  4450  Baldwin 37260 12/11  Rt  4/52
3051          "     37261   "    Sc  8/34
3052          "     37262   "    RB 10/25 K-14c
3053  4453    "     37263   "    Rt  3/52
3054          "     37264   "    Sc  6/34
3055  4455    "     37265   "    Rt  8/51
3056          "     37266   "    Sc  8/34
3057  4457    "     37267   "    Rt  2/54
3058          "     37354   "    Sc  8/34
3059  4459    "     37355   "    Rt 10/50
3060  4460    "     37356   "    Sc 10/47
3061  4461    "     37357   "    Rt 10/52
3062          "     37358   "    Sc  7/34
3063          "     37359   "    Sc  8/34
3064  (e)     "     37360   "    RB  9/25 K-14c
3065          "     37361   "    Sc  6/34
3066          "     37362   "    Sc  7/34
3067  4467    "     37363   "    Sc  6/40
3068  4468    "     37364   "    Sc  6/48
3069  4469    "     37365   "    Rt  4/52
3070          "     37366   "    Sc  6/34
3071  4471    "     37367   "    Rt 10/51
3072          "     37368  1/12  Rt  1/36
3073  4473    "     37369 12/11  Rt  8/52
3074  4474    "     37370   "    Rt  3/50
3075  4475    "     37371   "    Sc  5/48
3076  4476    "     37372   "    Rt  3/49
3077  4477    "     37373  1/12  Rt 10/49
3078  4478    "     37374   "    Rt  1/53
3079  4479    "     37375   "    Rt  2/48
```

Note a: 4401 re 2/48 to 4492.   Note b: 4504 re'51 4574.   Note c: 4507 re'51 4577.
Note c: 3081,3084,3108 sold 10/27 to P&E; later RB to K-14b and re 3/37 to P&E 17, 18, 19.
Note e: 3064 re'24 to B&A 589, later class K-14h.

NYC&HR 3068, class K-11c, Baldwin builder's print.   (Richard Street collection)

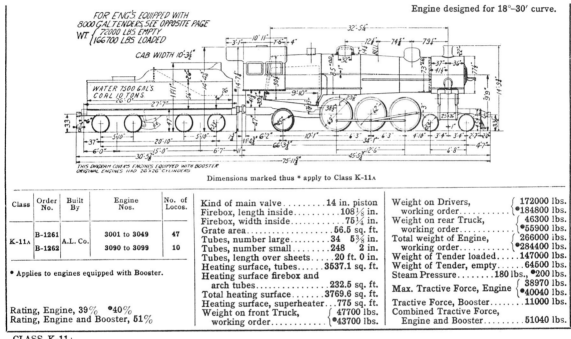

Engine designed for 18°–30′ curve.

Dimensions marked thus * apply to Class K-11A

Class	Order No.	Built By	Engine Nos.	No. of Locos.
K-11A	B-1261	A.L. Co.	3001 to 3049	47
	B-1262		3090 to 3099	10

• Applies to engines equipped with Booster.

Rating, Engine, 39% •40%
Rating, Engine and Booster, 51%

Kind of main valve.........14 in. piston
Firebox, length inside...........108⅛ in.
Firebox, width inside............75¼ in.
Grate area...................56.5 sq. ft.
Tubes, number large........34   5⅜ in.
Tubes, number small.......248   2 in.
Tubes, length over sheets.....20 ft. 0 in.
Heating surface, tubes......3537.1 sq. ft.
Heating surface firebox and
    arch tubes.................232.5 sq. ft.
Total heating surface.......3769.6 sq. ft.
Heating surface, superheater...775 sq. ft.
Weight on front Truck,   { 47700 lbs.
    working order........... •43700 lbs.

Weight on Drivers,   { 172000 lbs.
    working order........... •184800 lbs.
Weight on rear Truck,   { 46300 lbs.
    working order........... •55900 lbs.
Total weight of Engine,   { 266000 lbs.
    working order........... •284400 lbs.
Weight of Tender loaded.....147000 lbs.
Weight of Tender, empty......64500 lbs.
Steam Pressure........180 lbs., •200 lbs.
Max. Tractive Force, Engine { 38970 lbs.
                            { •40040 lbs.
Tractive Force, Booster........11000 lbs.
Combined Tractive Force,
    Engine and Booster.........51040 lbs.

CLASS K-11A

NYC 4498, class K-11a, built for freight service, at Weehawken, May 1939.   (J. Quinn)

```
NYC&HR CLASS K-11d 4-6-2: 26x26-69-180-266000-38970
      re'36
3120  4520  Alco-S 51184  4/12  Rt  1/50
3121  4521    "    51185   "    Rt  9/52
3122  4522    "    51186   "    Rt  1/50
3123  4523    "    51187   "    Rt  6/51
3124  4524    "    51188   "    Rt  4/50
3125  4525    "    51189   "    Rt 10/52
3126          "    51190   "    Rt 12/34
3127  4527    "    51191   "    Rt  2/52
3128  4528    "    51192   "    Rt  3/53
3129  4529    "    51193   "    Rt  5/52
3130  4530    "    51194   "    Rt 11/49
3131  4531    "    51195   "    Rt  2/52
3132  4532    "    51196   "    Rt 10/49
3133  4533    "    51197   "    Rt  2/50
3134          "    51198   "    Rt  8/28
3135  4535    "    51199   "    Rt  5/47
3136  4536    "    51200   "    Rt 11/51
3137  4537    "    51201   "    Rt  7/51
3138  4538    "    51202   "    Sc  7/40
3139  4539    "    51203   "    Rt  3/52


NYC&HR CLASS K-11e 4-6-2: 26x26-69-160-266000-38970
3140  4540  Alco-S 51760  8/12  Rt  3/52
3141  4541    "    51761   "    Rt  6/51
3142  4542    "    51762   "    Rt 10/50
3143  4543    "    51763   "    Rt  7/52
3144          "    51764   "    Rt 12/34
3145  4545    "    51765   "    Rt  6/51
3146  4546    "    51766   "    Rt  1/38
3147  4547    "    51767   "    Rt  4/50
3148          "    51768  9/12  Rt 12/34
3149  4549    "    51769   "    Rt  5/53
3150  4550    "    51770   "    Rt  4/52
3151  4551    "    51771   "    Rt 12/51
3152  4552    "    51772   "    Rt  6/51
3153  4553    "    51773   "    Rt  6/51
3154  4554    "    51774   "    Rt  2/52
3155  4555    "    51775   "    Rt  2/49
3156  4556    "    51776   "    Rt 10/51
3157  4557    "    51777   "    Rt  7/51
3158  4558    "    51778   "    Rt  3/52
3159          "    51779   "    RB  6/25 K-14e
3160  4560    "    51780   "    Rt  2/52
3161  4561    "    51781   "    Rt  3/52
3162  4562    "    51782   "    Rt  1/50
3163  4563    "    51783   "    Rt  2/52
3164  4564    "    51784   "    Rt  6/51
3165          "    51785   "    RB  7/25 K-14e
3166  4566    "    51786   "    Rt  9/52
3167  4567    "    51787   "    Rt 12/39
3168  4568    "    51788   "    Rt  6/52
3169  4569    "    51789   "    Rt  8/52


NYC&HR CLASS K-11f 4-6-2: 26x26-69-180-272000-38970 (c)
3170  4570  Alco-S 54167  9/13  Rt 10/49
3171          "    54168   "    RB  1/21 K-14f (a)
3172          "    54169   "    RB  5/23   "   (a)
3173          "    54170   "    RB  6/23   "   (a)
3174          "    54171   "    RB  8/24   "
3175          "    54172   "    RB 12/20   "   (a)
3176          "    54173 10/13  RB  1/21   "   (a)
3177          "    54174   "    RB 11/22   "   (a)
3178  4578    "    54175   "    Rt  3/52
3179          "    54176   "    RB  5/23 K-14f (a)
3180  4580    "    54177   "    Rt 10/51
3181          "    54178   "    RB  9/21 K-14f (a)
3182          "    54179   "    RB 12/20   "   (a)
3183          "    54180   "    RB  7/25   "
3184          "    54181   "    RB  6/23   "   (a)
```

```
NYC&HR CLASS K-11f 4-6-2:  Continued.
      re'36
3185          Alco-S 54182 10/13  RB  6/23 K-14f (a)
3186  4586    "      54183   "    Rt  3/52
3187  4587    "      54184   "    Rt  3/52
3188          "      54185   "    RB  7/23 K-14f (a)
3189  4589    "      54186   "    Rt 10/49
3190          "      54187   "    RB  8/20 K-14f (a)
3191          "      54188   "    RB  9/25   "
3192          "      54189   "    RB  1/21   "   (a)
3193          "      54190   "    RB 10/25   "
3194  4594    "      54191   "    Rt  7/49
3195  4595    "      54192   "    Rt  5/47
3196  4596    "      54193   "    Rt  8/50
3197  4597    "      54194   "    Rt  5/53
3198  4598    "      54195   "    Rt  3/52
3199  4599    "      54196   "    Rt  2/52


NYC CLASS K-14a 4-6-2: 25x26-72-200-281500-38370 (b)
3000  4390  RB B.Grove 10/25 fr.K-11a  Rt  9/52
3009  4391   "    "     9/25    "      Rt  5/52
3011  4392   "    "     9/25    "      Rt  7/52


P&E CLASS K-14b 4-6-2: 25x26-72-180-278900-34530
3081  P&E 17  RB Urbana  1/30 fr.K-11b  Rt  1/51
3084   "  18   "         7/29    "      Rt  1/51
3108   "  19   "         9/29    "      Rt 12/50


NYC CLASS K-14c 4-6-2: 25x26-72-200-287700-38370 (b)
3052  4393  RB B.Grove 10/25 fr.K-11c  Rt  3/52
3064        RB W.Spring.9/25    "      re'24 B&A 589


NYC CLASS K-14e 4-6-2: 25x26-72-200-287700-38370 (b)
3159  4394  RB W.Albany 6/25 fr.K-11e  Rt  3/52
3165  4395   "      "   7/25    "      Rt  3/52


NYC CLASS K-14f 4-6-2: 25x26-72-200-290400-38370 (b)
3171        RB W.Albany 1/21 fr.K-11f  re'21 B&A 575
3172         "      "   5/23    "      re'23  "  583
3173         "      "   6/23    "      re'23  "  584
3174  4396   "      "   8/24    "      Rt  8/52
3175         "      "  12/20    "      re'21 B&A 576
3176         "      "   1/21    "      re'21  "  577
3177         "      "  11/22    "      re'23  "  582
3179         "      "   5/23    "      re'23  "  585
3181         "      "   9/21    "      re'21  "  581
3182         "      "  12/20    "      re'21  "  578
3183  4397   "      "   7/25    "      Rt  5/52
3184         "      "   6/23    "      re'23 B&A 586
3185         "      "   6/23    "      re'23  "  587
3188         "      "   7/23    "      re'23  "  588
3190         "      "   8/20    "      re'21  "  579
3191  4398   "      "   9/25    "      SS  4/52
3192         "      "   1/21    "      re'21 B&A 580
3193  4399   "      "  10/25    "      Rt  3/52


B&A CLASS K-14g 4-6-2: 26x26-72-190-275500-39420
  See B&A 575-588  RB from K-14f.

B&A CLASS K-14h 4-6-2: 26x26-72-190-269500-39420
  See B&A 589  RB from K-14c.


        Note a:  Later B&A 575-588, conv.'24-25 to K-14g.
        Note b:  Booster adds 11000 tf.
        Note c:  Some K-11f later 25x26-287700-40040 tf
                 with booster.
```

NYC 4414, class K-11a, in Lakefront shuttle service at Linndale, OH 1937. (Jay Williams)

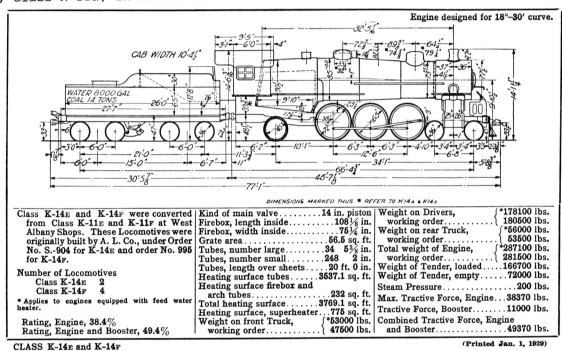

Engine designed for 18°–30' curve.

CAB WIDTH 10'-4½"

WATER 8000 GAL
COAL 14 TONS

DIMENSIONS MARKED THUS ■ REFER TO K14A & K14c

Class K-14E and K-14F were converted from Class K-11E and K-11F at West Albany Shops. These Locomotives were originally built by A. L. Co., under Order No. S.-904 for K-14E and order No. 995 for K-14F.

Number of Locomotives
Class K-14E   2
Class K-14F   4
* Applies to engines equipped with feed water heater.

Rating, Engine, 38.4%
Rating, Engine and Booster, 49.4%

Kind of main valve	14 in. piston
Firebox, length inside	108⅛ in.
Firebox, width inside	75¼ in.
Grate area	56.5 sq. ft.
Tubes, number large	34 5⅜ in.
Tubes, number small	248 2 in.
Tubes, length over sheets	20 ft. 0 in.
Heating surface tubes	3537.1 sq. ft.
Heating surface firebox and arch tubes	232 sq. ft.
Total heating surface	3769.1 sq. ft.
Heating surface, superheater	775 sq. ft.
Weight on front Truck, working order	*53000 lbs. / 47500 lbs.

Weight on Drivers, working order	*178100 lbs. / 180500 lbs.
Weight on rear Truck, working order	*56000 lbs. / 53500 lbs.
Total weight of Engine, working order	*287100 lbs. / 281500 lbs.
Weight of Tender, loaded	166700 lbs.
Weight of Tender, empty	72000 lbs.
Steam Pressure	200 lbs.
Max. Tractive Force, Engine	38370 lbs.
Tractive Force, Booster	11000 lbs.
Combined Tractive Force, Engine and Booster	49370 lbs.

CLASS K-14E and K-14F

(Printed Jan. 1, 1929)

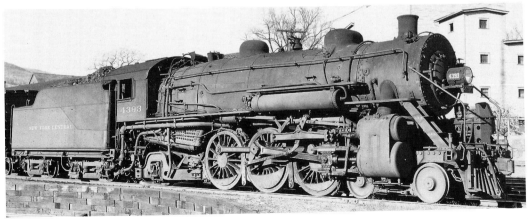

NYC 4393, class K-14c as rebuilt from K-11c #3052. N,Adams,Mass.   (P.H.Bonnet)

NYC&HR CLASS L: 1-D-1 Electric. Later class T-1, then S-1. See p. 234.

CLASS L : 4-8-2 MOHAWK

NYC CLASS L-1a 4-8-2: 28x28-69-200-364500-54080(a,b)

2500	Alco-S 56000	7/16	Rt 6/51, SS 7/51 (c)
2501	" 56027	11/16	Rt 6/51, SS 8/51
2502	" 56028	"	Rt 3/49, Sc 10/49
2503	" 56029	"	Rt 1/52, Sc 3/52
2504	" 56030	"	Rt 1/39, Sc 3/39
2505	" 56031	"	Rt 12/34, Sc 8/35
2506	" 56032	"	So 5/31 re 3/37 P&E 40
2507	" 56033	"	Rt 5/50, SS 6/50
2508	" 56034	"	Rt 3/50, Sc 5/50
2509	" 56035	"	Rt 5/50, SS 7/50
2510	" 56036	"	Rt 1/36, Sc 4/36
2511	" 56037	"	Rt 5/50, SS 7/50
2512	" 56038	"	Rt 6/53, SS 7/53
2513	" 56039	"	Rt 5/49, Sc 8/49
2514	" 56040	"	Rt 1/50, Sc 3/50
2515	" 56041	"	Rt 6/51, SS 7/51
2516	" 56042	"	Rt 2/53, SS 7/53
2517	" 56043	"	Rt 7/49, Sc 10/49
2518	" 56044	"	NB 4/25, Sc 11/47
2519	" 56045	"	So 5/31, Re 3/37 P&E 41
2520	" 56046	"	Rt 1/36, Sc 8/36
2521	" 56047	"	Rt 1/36, Sc 4/36
2522	" 56048	"	Rt 1/36, Sc 4/36
2523	" 56049	"	Rt 7/49, Sc 10/49
2524	" 56050	"	Rt 1/36, Sc 4/36
2525	" 56051	12/16	Rt 6/50, SS 7/50
2526	" 56052	"	Rt 5/47, Sc 9/47
2527	" 56053	"	Rt 12/51, SS 1/52
2528	" 56054	"	Rt 1/36, Sc 4/36
2529	" 56055	"	Rt 3/49, Sc 10/49

NYC CLASS L-1b 4-8-2: 28x28-69-200-343000-54080.(a,b)

2530	Alco-S 56910	12/17	Rt 4/49, Sc 6/49
2531	" 56911	"	Rt 1/39, Sc 3/39
2532	" 56912	"	Rt 2/52, SS 3/52
2533	" 56913	"	Rt 1/52, SS 2/52
2534	" 56914	"	Rt 1/36, Sc 5/36
2535	" 56915	"	Rt 12/52, SS 1/53
2536	" 56916	"	Rt 1/36, Sc 4/36
2537	" 56917	1/18	Rt 5/49, So 9/49
2538	" 56918	12/17	Rt 12/34, Sc 9/35
2539	" 56919	1/18	Rt 12/52, SS 1/53
2540	" 56920	"	Rt 1/36, Sc 7/36
2541	" 56921	12/17	Rt 1/38, Sc 11/38
2542	" 56922	"	Rt 6/49, SS 9/49
2543	" 56923	"	Rt 12/49, Sc 1/50
2544	" 56924	1/18	Rt 12/49, Sc 1/50
2545	" 56925	"	Rt 12/52, SS 1/53
2546	" 56926	12/17	Rt 7/50, Sc 7/50
2547	" 56927	"	Rt 5/49, Sc 8/49
2548	" 56928	"	Rt 5/52, SS 10/52
2549	" 56929	"	Rt 6/52, SS 11/52
2550	" 56930	1/18	So 12/32 re 3/37 P&E 42
2551	" 56931	12/17	Rt 2/53, SS 7/53
2552	" 56932	1/18	Rt 1/36, Sc 4/36
2553	" 56933	"	Rt 12/34, Sc 10/35
2554	" 56934	"	Rt 1/36, Sc 7/36
2555	" 56935	"	Rt 7/49, Sc 10/49
2556	" 56936	"	Rt 1/36, Sc 4/36
2557	" 56937	"	Rt 12/34, Sc 10/35
2558	" 56938	"	Rt 7/49, Sc 10/49
2559	" 56939	"	Rt 2/52, SS 3/52

NYC CLASS L-1b 4-8-2: Continued.

2560	Alco-S 56940	1/18	So 6/40 re 3/37 P&E 39
2561	" 56941	"	Rt 3/50, Sc 4/50
2562	" 56942	"	Rt 2/53, SS 7/53
2563	" 56943	"	Rt 1/39, Sc 3/39
2564	" 56944	"	Rt 1/50, Sc 2/50
2565	" 56945	"	Rt 3/50, Sc 5/50
2566	" 56946	"	Rt 1/36, Sc 7/36
2567	" 56947	"	Rt 10/49, Sc 11/49
2568	" 56948	" (d)Rt 1/36, Sc 4/36 (c)
2569	" 56949	"	Rt 1/36, Sc 7/36 (c)
2570	" 56950	"	So 7/36 re 3/37 P&E 43
2571	" 56951	"	Rt 12/51, SS 1/52
2572	" 56952	"	Rt 8/49, Sc 9/49
2573	" 56953	"	Rt 2/53, SS 7/53
2574	" 56954	"	Rt 1/36, Sc 4/36
2575	" 56955	"	Rt 2/53, SS 7/53
2576	" 56956	"	Rt 2/47, Sc 2/47
2577	" 56957	"	Rt 2/52, SS 3/52
2578	" 56958	2/18	Rt 12/34, Sc 8/35
2579	" 56959	"	Rt 7/52, SS 10/52
2580	" 56960	"	Rt 10/49, Sc 11/49
2581	" 56961	"	Rt 2/53, SS 7/53
2582	" 56962	"	Rt 12/51, SS 2/52
2583	" 56963	"	Rt 12/51, SS 1/52
2584	" 56964	"	Rt 1/36, Sc 2/36

NYC CLASS L-1c 4-8-2: 28x28-69-200-343000-54080

2585	Lima 5499	1/18	Rt 1/50, Sc 2/50
2586	" 5500	"	Rt 5/49, Sc 11/49
2587	" 5501	"	Rt 5/52, SS 10/52
2588	" 5502	"	Rt 5/47, Sc 9/47
2589	" 5503	2/18	Rt 5/50, SS 7/50
2590	" 5504	"	Rt 12/49, Sc 1/50
2591	" 5505	"	Rt 5/49, Sc 8/49
2592	" 5506	"	Rt 5/49, Sc 6/49
2593	" 5507	"	Rt 12/52, SS 2/53
2594	" 5508	"	Rt 4/49, Sc 6/49
2595	" 5509	"	Rt 12/34, Sc 8/35
2596	" 5510	"	Re 6/40 P&E 49
2597	" 5511	"	Rt 10/34, Sc 8/35
2598	" 5512	"	Rt 6/50, Sc 6/50
2599	" 5513	"	Rt 12/34, Sc 8/35
2600	" 5514	"	Rt 5/47, Sc 10/47
2601	" 5515	3/18	Rt 1/36, Sc 2/36
2602	" 5516	"	Rt 10/49, Sc 11/49
2603	" 5517	"	Rt 1/39, Sc 4/39
2604	" 5518	"	Rt 1/36, Sc 4/36
2605	" 5519	"	Rt 12/34, Sc 5/35
2606	" 5520	"	Rt 2/52, SS 3/52
2607	" 5521	"	Rt 8/51, Sc 12/51
2608	" 5522	"	Rt 3/50, SS 5/50
2609	" 5523	"	Rt 10/49, Sc 11/49
2610	" 5524	"	Rt 1/52, SS 2/52
2611	" 5525	"	Rt 10/49, Sc 11/49
2612	" 5526	"	Rt 12/34, Sc 7/35
2613	" 5527	4/18	Rt 12/34, Sc 6/35
2614	" 5528	"	So 5/36 re 3/37 P&E 44
2615	" 5529	"	Re 2/41 P&E 50
2616	" 5530	"	Rt 6/51, SS 8/51
2617	" 5531	"	Rt 1/36, Sc 5/36
2618	" 5532	"	Rt 12/52, SS 1/53
2619	" 5533	"	Rt 12/34, Sc 6/35

Note a: L-1a,b orig.190-348000-51400.   Note b: Booster adds 11000 tf.   Note c: 2500 orig. 185-343000-50000.
Note c: 2568 and 2569 RB 9/22 and 1/24 to 3-cylinder: 25x28-69-200-368000 and 372500-64670. Note d: NB 9/22

NYC 2500, class L-1a, the Central's first 4-8-2, Alco builder's photo. (R.Lorenz)

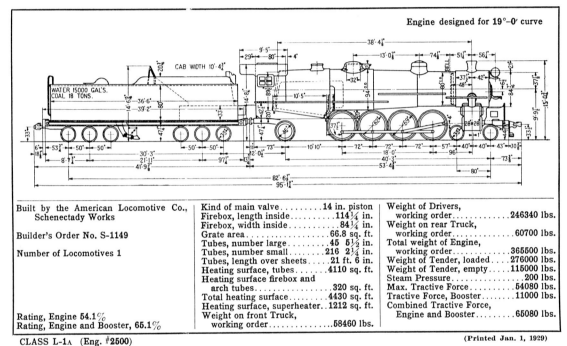

Engine designed for 19°-0' curve

Built by the American Locomotive Co., Schenectady Works

Builder's Order No. S-1149

Number of Locomotives 1

Rating, Engine 54.1%
Rating, Engine and Booster, 65.1%

Kind of main valve.........14 in. piston
Firebox, length inside..........114¼ in.
Firebox, width inside...........84¼ in.
Grate area....................66.8 sq. ft.
Tubes, number large........45 5½ in.
Tubes, number small.......216 2¼ in.
Tubes, length over sheets.....21 ft. 6 in.
Heating surface, tubes......4110 sq. ft.
Heating surface firebox and
 arch tubes.................320 sq. ft.
Total heating surface........4430 sq. ft.
Heating surface, superheater..1212 sq. ft.
Weight on front Truck,
 working order..............58460 lbs.

Weight of Drivers,
 working order.............246340 lbs.
Weight on rear Truck,
 working order..............60700 lbs.
Total weight of Engine,
 working order.............365500 lbs.
Weight of Tender, loaded....276000 lbs.
Weight of Tender, empty.....115000 lbs.
Steam Pressure................200 lbs.
Max. Tractive Force..........54080 lbs.
Tractive Force, Booster........11000 lbs.
Combined Tractive Force,
 Engine and Booster........65080 lbs.

CLASS L-1A (Eng. #2500)

(Printed Jan. 1, 1929)

NYC 2511 class L-1a, one of many assigned to the Pennsylvania Division. At Avis, Pa, 6/50
(E.L.May)

NYC CLASS L-1c 4-8-2: Continued

2620	Lima	5534	4/18	Rt	12/52,	SS	1/53
2621	"	5535	"	Rt	1/36,	Sc	2/36
2622	"	5536	"	Rt	2/52,	SS	3/52
2623	"	5537	"	Rt	3/50,	SS	5/50
2624	"	5538	"	Rt	5/49,	Sc	8/49
2625	"	5539	"	Rt	10/49,	Sc	11/49
2626	"	5540	"	Rt	12/34,	Sc	5/35
2627	"	5541	"	Rt	1/50,	Sc	2/50
2628	"	5542	"	Rt	5/47,	Sc	9/47
2629	"	5543	"	Rt	8/49,	Sc	9/49
2630	"	5544	"	Rt	5/49,	Sc	9/49
2631	"	5545	"	Rt	8/49,	Sc	9/49
2632	"	5546	"	So	12/32 re 3/37 P&E 45		
2633	"	5547	"(a)	So	12/41 re P&E 52		
2634	"	5548	"	Rt	3/53,	SS	7/53
2635	"	5549	"	Rt	5/50,	SS	6/50
2636	"	5550	"	Rt	5/49,	Sc	9/49
2637	"	5551	"	Rt	12/34,	Sc	9/35
2638	"	5552	5/18	Rt	12/34,	Sc	9/35
2639	"	5553	6/18	Rt	12/34,	Sc	6/35

NYC CLASS L-1d 4-8-2: 28x28-69-200-343000-54080.

2640	Lima	5585	7/18	Rt	,	Sc	12/44
2641	"	5586	"	Rt	1/36,	Sc	4/36
2642	"	5587	8/18	Rt	12/52,	SS	1/53
2643	"	5588	"	Rt	1/36,	Sc	8/36
2644	"	5589	"	Rt	12/52,	SS	1/53
2645	"	5590	"	Rt	6/51,	SS	7/51
2646	"	5591	"	Rt	1/52,	SS	2/52
2647	"	5592	"	Rt	12/51,	SS	1/52
2648	"	5593	"	Rt	5/49,	Sc	8/49
2649	"	5594	"	.Rt	1/26,	Sc	4/36
2650	"	5595	"	Rt	12/34,	Sc	6/55
2651	"	5596	"	Rt	3/49,	SS	10/49

NYC CLASS L-1d 4-8-2: Continued

2652	Lima	5597	7/18	Rt	6/49,	Sc	7/49
2653	"	5598	"	Rt	2/52,	SS	3/52
2654	"	5599	"	Rt	3/50,	Sc	5/50
2655	"	5600	"	Rt	10/49,	Sc	11/49
2656	"	5601	"	Rt	11/52,	SS	1/53
2657	"	5602	"	Rt	12/51,	SS	2/52
2658	"	5603	"	Rt	8/41,	Sc	9/41
2659	"	5604	"	Rt	3/52,	SS	4/52
2660	"	5605	"	Rt	1/36,	Sc	3/36
2661	"	5606	"	Rt	5/47,	Sc	9/47
2662	"	5607	"	Rt	6/52,	SS	10/52
2663	"	5608	"	Rt	10/49,	Sc	11/49
2664	"	5609	"	Rt	5/49,	Sc	9/49
2665	"	5610	"	Rt	1/39,	Sc	3/39
2666	"	5611	"	So	3/36 re 3/37 P&E 46		
2667	"	5612	9/18	Rt	8/49,	Sc	9/49
2668	"	5613	"	Rt	5/47,	Sc	10/47
2669	"	5614	"	Rt	1/39,	Sc	4/39
2670	"	5615	"	So	5/36 re 3/37 P&E 47		
2671	"	5616	"	So	2/41 P&E 51		
2672	"	5617	"	Rt	12/34,	Sc	9/35
2673	"	5618	"	Rt	1/36,	Sc	8/36
2674	"	5619	"	Rt	12/51,	SS	2/52
2675	"	5620	"	Rt	2/52,	SS	3/52
2676	"	5621	"	Rt	1/36,	Sc	5/36
2677	"	5622	"	Rt	1/50,	Sc	3/50
2678	"	5623	"	Rt	6/51,	SS	8/51
2679	"	5624	"	Rt	3/50,	Sc	6/50
2680	"	5625	11/18	So	5/32 re 3/37 P&E 48		
2681	"	5626	"	Rt	10/49,	Sc	11/49
2682	"	5627	"	Rt	12/34,	Sc	8/35
2683	"	5628	"	Rt	2/52,	SS	3/52
2684	"	5629	"	Rt	12/34,	Sc	9/35

Note a :   2633 new boiler 2/23

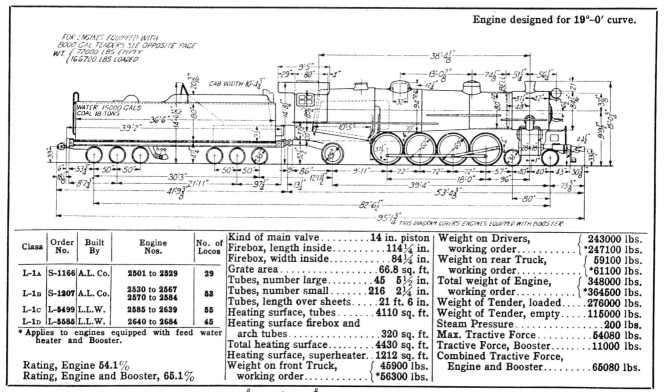

Engine designed for 19°–0' curve.

FOR ENGINES EQUIPPED WITH 8000 GAL TENDERS SEE OPPOSITE PAGE
WT. { 72000 LBS EMPTY / 166700 LBS LOADED

WATER 15000 GALS COAL 18 TONS

THIS DIAGRAM COVERS ENGINES EQUIPPED WITH BOOSTER

Class	Order No.	Built By	Engine Nos.	No. of Locos
L-1A	S-1166	A.L. Co.	2501 to 2529	29
L-1B	S-1207	A.L. Co.	2530 to 2567 / 2570 to 2584	53
L-1C	L-5499	L.L.W.	2585 to 2639	55
L-1D	L-5585	L.L.W.	2640 to 2684	45

* Applies to engines equipped with feed water heater and Booster.

Rating, Engine 54.1%
Rating, Engine and Booster, 65.1%

Kind of main valve.........14 in. piston
Firebox, length inside..........114¼ in.
Firebox, width inside...........84¼ in.
Grate area...................66.8 sq. ft.
Tubes, number large........45 5½ in.
Tubes, number small......216 2¼ in.
Tubes, length over sheets....21 ft. 6 in.
Heating surface, tubes......4110 sq. ft.
Heating surface firebox and arch tubes.................320 sq. ft.
Total heating surface.......4430 sq. ft.
Heating surface, superheater..1212 sq. ft.
Weight on front Truck, { 45900 lbs. / working order...........*56300 lbs.

Weight on Drivers, { 243000 lbs. / working order..........*247100 lbs.
Weight on rear Truck, { 59100 lbs. / working order...........*61100 lbs.
Total weight of Engine, { 348000 lbs. / working order.........*364500 lbs.
Weight of Tender, loaded....276000 lbs.
Weight of Tender, empty.....115000 lbs.
Steam Pressure................200 lbs.
Max. Tractive Force..........54080 lbs.
Tractive Force, Booster......11000 lbs.
Combined Tractive Force, Engine and Booster........65080 lbs.

CLASS L-1A, L-1B, L-1C, L-1D (Except Engs #2500, #2568, #2569)

(Printed Jan. 1, 1929)

NYC 2568, class L-1b, converted to 3 cylinder. Alco Builders photo. (H.L.Vail coll.)

NYC 2569, class L-1b, converted to 3 cylilnder with original boiler.
Alco Builders photo. (H.L.Vail coll.)

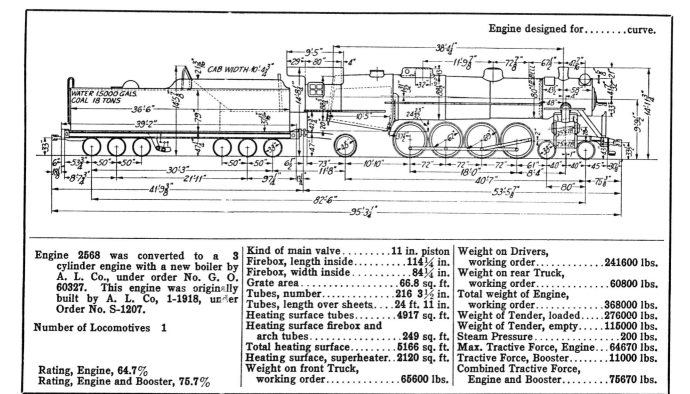

Engine designed for........curve.

Engine 2568 was converted to a 3 cylinder engine with a new boiler by A. L. Co., under order No. G. O. 60327. This engine was originally built by A. L. Co, 1-1918, under Order No. S-1207.

Number of Locomotives 1

Rating, Engine, 64.7%
Rating, Engine and Booster, 75.7%

Kind of main valve	11 in. piston
Firebox, length inside	114¼ in.
Firebox, width inside	84¼ in.
Grate area	66.8 sq. ft.
Tubes, number	216 3½ in.
Tubes, length over sheets	24 ft. 11 in.
Heating surface tubes	4917 sq. ft.
Heating surface firebox and arch tubes	249 sq. ft.
Total heating surface	5166 sq. ft.
Heating surface, superheater	2120 sq. ft.
Weight on front Truck, working order	65600 lbs.
Weight on Drivers, working order	241600 lbs.
Weight on rear Truck, working order	60800 lbs.
Total weight of Engine, working order	368000 lbs.
Weight of Tender, loaded	276000 lbs.
Weight of Tender, empty	115000 lbs.
Steam Pressure	200 lbs.
Max. Tractive Force, Engine	64670 lbs.
Tractive Force, Booster	11000 lbs.
Combined Tractive Force, Engine and Booster	75670 lbs.

CLASS L-1ʙ (Eng. #2568)　　　　　　　　　　　　　　　　(Printed Jan. 1, 1929)

NYC CLASS L-2a 4-8-2: 27x30-69-225-363400-60620 (b)

2700	Alco-S	66281	3/25	Rt	5/52, SS 11/52
2701	"	66578	2/26	Rt	9/52, SS 11/52
2702	"	66579	"	Rt	5/52, SS 9/52
2703	"	66580	"	Rt	6/52, SS 8/52
2704	"	66581	"	Rt	6/52, Sc 8/52
2705	"	66582	"	Rt	7/53, SS /54
2706	"	66583	"	Rt	6/52, SS 11/52
2707	"	66584	"	Rt	5/52, SS 11/52
2708	"	66585	"	Rt	6/52, Sc 8/52
2709	"	66586	"	Rt	5/52, SS 11/52
2710	"	66587	"	Rt	6/52, Sc 8/52
2711	"	66588	"	Rt	6/52, Sc 12/52
2712	"	66589	"	Rt	2/53, SS 7/53
2713	"	66590	"	Rt	5/52, SS 9/52
2714	"	66591	"	Rt	7/52, SS 12/52
2715	"	66592	"	Rt	7/52, SS 12/52
2716	"	66593	"	Rt	2/53, SS 7/53
2717	"	66594	"	Rt	6/52, Sc 9/52
2718	"	66595	"	Rt	7/52, SS 11/52
2719	"	66596	"	Rt	7/52, SS 12/52
2720	"	66597	"	Rt	2/53, SS 7/53
2721	"	66598	"	Rt	10/52, SS /54
2722	"	66599	"	Rt	6/53, SS 7/53
2723	"	66600	"	Rt	5/52, SS 9/52
2724	"	66601	"	Rt	7/52, SS 12/52
2725	"	66602	"	Rt	6/52, Sc 9/52
2726	"	66603	"	Rt	2/53, SS 7/53 (c)
2727	"	66604	"	Rt	8/53, SS /54
2728	"	66605	"	Rt	5/52, SS 11/52
2729	"	66606	"	Rt	5/52, SS 11/52
2730	"	66607	"	Rt	5/52, SS 1/53
2731	"	66608	"	Rt	7/52, SS 12/52
2732	"	66609	"	Rt	5/52, SS 10/52
2733	"	66610	3/26	Rt	5/52, SS 9/52
2734	"	66611	"	Rt	6/52, SS 8/52
2735	"	66612	"	Rt	5/52, SS 9/52
2736	"	66613	"	Rt	9/52, Sc 8/53
2737	"	66614	"	Rt	6/52, Sc 11/52
2738	"	66615	"	Rt	5/52, SS 9/52
2739	"	66616	"	Rt	9/53, SS /54
2740	"	66617	"	Rt	5/52, SS 7/52
2741	"	66618	"	Rt	5/52, SS 10/52
2742	"	66619	"	Rt	7/53, SS 8/53
2743	"	66620	"	Rt	5/52, SS 10/52
2744	"	66621	"	Rt	6/52, SS 8/52
2745	"	66622	"	Rt	5/52, SS 8/52
2746	"	66623	"	Rt	5/52, Sc 8/53
2747	"	66624	"	Rt	5/52, SS 11/52
2748	"	66625	"	Rt	5/52, SS 12/52
2749	"	66626	"	Rt	7/52, SS 11/52
2750	"	66627	"	Rt	9/52, SS 3/53
2751	"	66628	"	Rt	5/52, SS 9/52
2752	"	66629	"	Rt	6/52, SS 9/52
2753	"	66630	"	Rt	5/52, SS 12/52
2754	"	66631	"	Rt	5/52, SS 10/52
2755	"	66632	"	Rt	6/53, SS 8/53
2756	"	66633	"	Rt	7/52, Sc 9/52
2757	"	66634	"	Rt	9/53, SS /54
2758	"	66635	"	Rt	1/53, SS 3/53 (a)
2759	"	66636	"	Rt	5/52, SS 9/52
2760	"	66637	"	Rt	5/52, SS 9/52
2761	"	66638	"	Rt	6/52, SS 10/52
2762	"	66639	"	Rt	7/53, SS 8/53
2763	"	66640	"	Rt	5/52, SS 11/52
2764	"	66641	"	Rt	5/52, SS 10/52
2765	"	66642	"	Rt	8/51, Sc 3/52
2766	"	66643	"	Rt	7/52, SS 9/52
2767	"	66644	"	Rt	5/52, SS 10/52

NYC CLASS L-2a: Continued

2768	Alco-S	66645	3/26	Rt	5/52, SS 10/52
2769	"	66646	"	Rt	7/52, SS 10/52
2770	"	66647	"	Rt	7/52, SS 11/52
2771	"	66648	"	Rt	5/52, SS 10/52
2772	"	66649	4/26	Rt	5/52, SS 9/52
2773	"	66650	"	Rt	5/52, SS 8/52
2774	"	66651	"	Rt	9/52, Sc 2/53
2775	"	66652	"	Rt	5/53, SS 7/53
2776	"	66653	"	Rt	8/53, SS /54
2777	"	66654	"	Rt	5/52, SS 9/52
2778	"	66655	"	Rt	1/53, SS 4/53
2779	"	66656	"	Rt	6/52, Sc 12/52
2780	"	66657	"	Rt	7/52, SS 9/52
2781	"	66658	"	Rt	3/53, SS 4/53
2782	"	66659	"	Rt	5/52, SS 11/52
2783	"	66660	"	Rt	5/52, SS 11/52
2784	"	66661	"	Rt	11/52, SS 2/53
2785	"	66662	"	Rt	5/52, SS 9/52
2786	"	66663	"	Rt	9/52, Sc 8/53
2787	"	66664	"	Rt	7/52, SS 11/52
2788	"	66665	"	Rt	7/52, SS 12/52
2789	"	66666	"	Rt	5/52, SS 9/52
2790	"	66667	"	Rt	7/52, SS 10/52
2791	"	66668	"	Rt	5/52, SS 10/52
2792	"	66669	"	Rt	5/52, SS 10/52
2793	"	66670	"	Rt	11/52, Sc 3/53
2794	"	66671	"	Rt	2/53, SS 6/53
2795	"	66672	"	Rt	5/52, SS 9/52
2796	"	66673	"	Rt	5/52, SS 9/52
2797	"	66674	"	Rt	6/52, Sc 9/52
2798	"	66675	"	Rt	5/52, SS 8/52
2799	"	66676	"	Rt	5/52, SS 10/52

CCC&StL CLASS L-2b 6200-6224, re 2900-2924. See CCC&SL

NYC CLASS L-2c 4-8-2: 27x30-225-69-366550-60620 (b)

2800	Alco-S	67821	4/29	Rt	4/57
2801	"	67822	"	Rt	9/53, SS /54
2802	"	67823	"	Rt	4/57
2803	"	67824	"	Rt	4/57
2804	"	67825	"	Rt	3/55, SS 5/55
2805	"	67826	"	Rt	10/53, SS /54
2806	"	67827	"	Rt	6/53, SS 7/53
2807	"	67828	"	Rt	11/53, SS /54
2808	"	67829	"	Rt	7/55, SS 8/55
2809	"	67830	"	Rt	6/53, SS 9/53
2810	"	67831	"	Rt	11/53, SS /54
2811	"	67832	"	Rt	10/55, SS 11/55
2812	"	67833	"	Rt	10/53, Sc 12/53
2813	"	67834	"	Rt	11/53, SS /54
2814	"	67835	"	Rt	8/53, Sc 10/53
2815	"	67836	5/29	Rt	4/57
2816	"	67837	"	Rt	6/53, SS 9/53
2817	"	67838	"	Rt	5/53, SS 7/53
2818	"	67839	"	Rt	11/54, SS
2819	"	67840	"	Rt	7/55, SS 8/55
2820	"	67841	"	Rt	8/55, SS 9/55
2821	"	67842	"	Rt	6/56
2822	"	67843	"	Rt	3/52, Sc 5/52
2823	"	67844	"	Rt	8/53, Sc 10/53
2824	"	67845	"	Rt	12/54, SS
2825	"	67846	"	Rt	3/55, SS 5/55
2826	"	67847	"	Rt	7/56
2827	"	67848	"	Rt	4/53, SS 8/53
2828	"	67849	"	Rt	4/53, SS 7/53
2829	"	67850	"	Rt	6/56

Note a: 2758 NB 1/28.   Note b: 73020 tf w/booster

Note c: L-2a 2726 equipped with Scullin Disc driving wheels by NYC.

NYC 2795, class L-2a, one of the few classes never renumbered. Weehawken, June 1950.
(E.L.May)

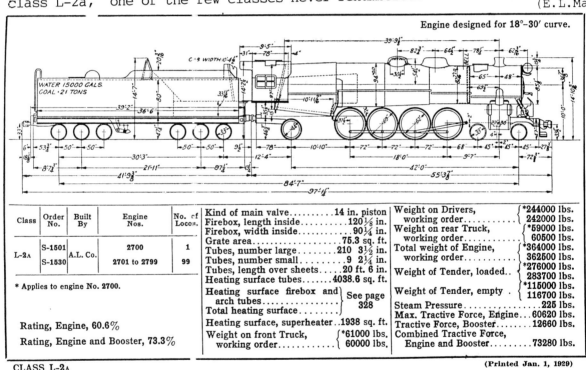

Engine designed for 18°-30' curve.

CLASS L-2ᴀ

Class	Order No.	Built By	Engine Nos.	No. of Locos.
L-2ᴀ	S-1501	A.L. Co.	2700	1
	S-1530		2701 to 2799	99

* Applies to engine No. 2700.

Rating, Engine, 60.6%

Rating, Engine and Booster, 73.3%

Kind of main valve.........14 in. piston
Firebox, length inside.........120⅛ in.
Firebox, width inside...........90¼ in.
Grate area...................75.3 sq. ft.
Tubes, number large.......210 3½ in.
Tubes, number small........9 2¼ in.
Tubes, length over sheets.....20 ft. 6 in.
Heating surface tubes.......4038.6 sq. ft.
Heating surface firebox and arch tubes................} See page 328
Total heating surface........}
Heating surface, superheater..1938 sq. ft.
Weight on front Truck, working order...........{ *61000 lbs. / 60000 lbs.

Weight on Drivers, working order..........{ *244000 lbs. / 242000 lbs.
Weight on rear Truck, working order..........{ *59000 lbs. / 60500 lbs.
Total weight of Engine, working order..........{ *364000 lbs. / 362500 lbs.
Weight of Tender, loaded..{ *276000 lbs. / 283700 lbs.
Weight of Tender, empty .{ *115000 lbs. / 116700 lbs.
Steam Pressure.................225 lbs.
Max. Tractive Force, Engine...60620 lbs.
Tractive Force, Booster.......12660 lbs.
Combined Tractive Force, Engine and Booster.........73280 lbs.

(Printed Jan. 1, 1929)

NYC 2800   class L-2c

Alco Builders photo. (H.L.V. coll.)

214

NYC CLASS L-2c 4-8-2: Continued

2830	Alco-S	67851	4/29	Rt	1/55,	SS	4/55
2831	"	67852	"	Rt	7/56		
2832	"	67853	"	Rt	6/52,	Sc	8/52
2833	"	67854	"	Rt	10/55,	SS	11/55
2834	"	67855	"	Rt	4/53,	SS	7/53
2835	"	67856	"	Rt	6/53,	SS	9/53
2836	"	67857	"	Rt	4/53,	SS	7/53
2837	"	67858	"	Rt	9/54,	SS	
2838	"	67859	"	Rt	12/55,	SS	12/55
2839	"	67860	"	Rt	3/55,	SS	5/55
2840	"	67861	"	Rt	6/53,	SS	9/53
2841	"	67862	"	Rt	6/54,	SS	
2842	"	67863	"	Rt	10/54,	SS	
2843	"	67864	"	Rt	11/53,	Sc	2/54
2844	"	67865	"	Rt	7/55,	SS	9/55
2845	"	67866	"	Rt	3/54,	SS	
2846	"	67867	"	Rt	2/56		
2847	"	67868	"	Rt	8/55,	SS	9/55
2848	"	67869	"	Rt	4/55,	SS	6/55
2849	"	67870	"	Rt	5/29,	SS	2/59
2850	"	67871	"	Rt	11/53,	Sc	2/54
2851	"	67872	"	Rt	6/52,	SS	5/53
2852	"	67873	"	Rt	10/54,	SS	
2853	"	67874	"	Rt	6/53,	SS	7/53
2854	"	67875	"	Rt	6/54,	SS	
2855	"	67876	6/29	Rt	10/54,	SS	
2856	"	67877	"	Rt	6/53,	SS	9/53
2857	"	67878	"	Rt	6/53,	SS	/54
2858	"	67879	"	Rt	3/57		
2859	"	67880	"	Rt	9/54,	SS	
2860	"	67881	"	Rt	11/53,	SS	/54
2861	"	67882	"	Rt	8/55,	SS	9/55
2862	"	67883	"	Rt	10/54,	SS	
2863	"	67884	"	Rt	1/55,	SS	4/55
2864	"	67885	"	Rt	4/53,	SS	7/53
2865	"	67886	"	Rt	11/53,	Sc	12/53
2866	"	67887	"	Rt	11/53,	SS	/54
2867	"	67888	"	Rt	3/53,	SS	6/53
2868	"	67889	"	Rt	11/53,	Sc	1/54
2869	"	67890	"	Rt	12/55,	Sc	2/56
2870	"	67891	"	Rt	4/53,	SS	6/53
2871	"	67892	"	Rt	6/54,	SS	
2872	"	67893	"	Rt	11/53,	SS	/54
2873	"	67894	4/29	Rt	5/53,	SS'54	(a)
2874	"	67895	"	Rt	6/54,	SS	
2875	"	67896	"	Rt	6/53,	SS	7/53
2876	"	67897	"	Rt	3/57		
2877	"	67898	"	Rt	1/55,	SS	3/55
2878	"	67899	"	Rt	2/56		
2879	"	67900	7/29	Rt	6/53,	SS	7/53
2880	"	67901	"	Rt	4/53,	SS	7/53
2881	"	67902	"	Rt	4/53,	SS	9/53
2882	"	67903	"	Rt	9/55,	SS	11/55
2883	"	67904	"	Rt	6/54,	SS	
2884	"	67905	"	Rt	3/55,	SS	5/55
2885	"	67906	8/29	Rt	9/53,	SS	/54
2886	"	67907	"	Rt	2/59,	SS	
2887	"	67908	"	Rt	2/59,	SS	
2888	"	67909	"	Rt	6/53,	SS	/54
2889	"	67910	"	Rt	5/55,	SS	6/55
2890	"	67911	"	Rt	8/55,	SS	9/55
2891	"	67912	"	Rt	6/53,	SS	/54
2892	"	67913	"	Rt	9/54,	SS	
2893	"	67914	"	Rt	3/55,	SS	5/55
2894	"	67915	9/29	Rt	3/55,	SS	5/55
2895	"	67916	"	Rt	3/55,	SS	5/55
2896	"	67917	"	Rt	11/53,	SS	/54
2897	"	67918	"	Rt	6/53,	SS	/54
2898	"	67919	"	Rt	1/55,	SS	4/55
2899	"	67920	"	Rt	6/53,	SS	9/53

NYC CLASS L-2d 4-8-2: 27x30-69-225-370150-60620 (b) re'36

2450	2950	Alco-S	68068	11/29	Rt	1/53,	Sc	6/53
2451	2951	"	68069	"	Rt	4/55,	SS	6/55
2452	2952	"	68070	"	Rt	11/53,	SS	/54
2453	2953	"	68071	"	Rt	1/54,	SS	
2454	2954	"	68072	"	Rt	2/59,	SS	4/59
2455	2955	"	68073	"	Rt	4/55,	SS	6/55
2456	2956	"	68074	"	Rt	11/53,	Sc	3/54
2457	2957	"	68075	"	Rt	10/53,	SS	/54
2458	2958	"	68076	"	Rt	10/54,	SS	
2459	2959	"	68077	"	Rt	12/54,	SS	
2460	2960	"	68078	"	Rt	3/55,	SS	5/55
2461	2961	"	68079	"	Rt	11/53,	SS	/54
2462	2962	"	68080	"	Rt	6/53,	SS	7/53
2463	2963	"	68081	"	Rt	6/53,	SS	6/53
2464	2964	"	68082	"	Rt	7/53,	SS	/54
2465	2965	"	68083	"	Rt	3/53,	SS	5/53
2466	2966	"	68084	"	Rt	1/54,	SS	
2467	2967	"	68085	"	Rt	3/55,	SS	6/55
2468	2968	"	68086	"	Rt	12/53,	SS	/54
2469	2969	"	68087	"	Rt	12/54,	SS	
2470	2970	"	68088	"	Rt	10/54,	SS	
2471	2971	"	68089	"	Rt	6/53,	SS	/54
2472	2972	"	68090	"	Rt	10/54,	SS	
2473	2973	"	68091	"	Rt	5/55,	SS	6/55
2474	2974	"	68092	"	Rt	8/53,	Sc	11/53
2475	2975	"	68093	2/30	Rt	12/55,	SS	12/55
2476	2976	"	68094	"	Rt	12/55,	SS	12/55
2477	2977	"	68095	"	Rt	8/53,	SS	/54
2478	2978	"	68096	"	Rt	10/55,	SS	11/55
2479	2979	"	68097	"	Rt	6/53,	SS	9/53
2480	2980	"	68098	"	Rt	10/54,	SS	
2481	2981	"	68099	"	Rt	11/53,	Sc	12/53
2482	2982	"	68100	"	Rt	7/55,	SS	8/55
2483	2983	"	68101	"	Rt	10/55,	SS	11/55
2484	2984	"	68102	"	Rt	9/53,	SS	/54
2485	2985	"	68103	"	Rt	4/55,	SS	6/55
2486	2986	"	68104	3/30	Rt	7/53,	SS	8/53
2487	2987	"	68105	"	Rt	7/54,	SS	
2488	2988	"	68106	"	Rt	5/55,	SS	6/55
2489	2989	"	68107	"	Rt	6/53,	SS	9/53
2490	2990	"	68108	"	Rt	12/53,	SS	/54
2491	2991	"	68109	"	Rt	9/54,	SS	
2492	2992	"	68110	"	Rt	10/53,	SS	11/53
2493	2993	"	68111	"	Rt	9/53,	SS	/54
2494	2994	"	68112	"	Rt	11/53,	Sc	12/53
2495	2995	"	68113	"	Rt	10/53,	SS	/54 (c)
2496	2996	"	68114	"	Rt	3/55,	SS	5/55
2497	2997	"	68115	"	Rt	6/55,	SS	8/55
2498	2998	"	68116	"	Rt	3/53,	SS	5/53 (c)
2499	2999	"	68117	"	Rt	4/53,	SS	7/53

CCC&StL CLASS L-2d 6225-6249 re 2925-2949. See CCC&StL

Note a: 2873 streamlined 2/36 to 12/36
         for nation-wide tour of Rexall Train.

Note b: 73030 tf with booster.

Note c: 2995 and 2998 RB 8/39 for dual service.
         Specs 25+x30-69-250-385100-60100.
         73850 t.f. with booster.

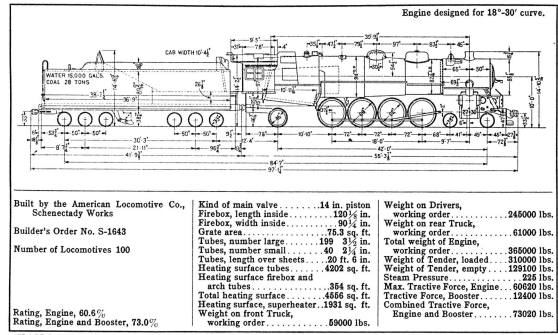

Engine designed for 18°-30' curve.

Built by the American Locomotive Co., Schenectady Works	Kind of main valve........14 in. piston	Weight on Drivers,
	Firebox, length inside.........120⅛ in.	working order...........245000 lbs.
Builder's Order No. S-1643	Firebox, width inside..........90¼ in.	Weight on rear Truck,
	Grate area..................75.3 sq. ft.	working order............61000 lbs.
Number of Locomotives 100	Tubes, number large.......199 3½ in.	Total weight of Engine,
	Tubes, number small......40 2¼ in.	working order..........365000 lbs.
	Tubes, length over sheets....20 ft. 6 in.	Weight of Tender, loaded....310000 lbs.
	Heating surface tubes.......4202 sq. ft.	Weight of Tender, empty....129100 lbs.
	Heating surface firebox and	Steam Pressure...............225 lbs.
	arch tubes.................354 sq. ft.	Max. Tractive Force, Engine..60620 lbs.
	Total heating surface.......4556 sq. ft.	Tractive Force, Booster......12400 lbs.
	Heating surface, superheater..1931 sq. ft.	Combined Tractive Force,
Rating, Engine, 60.6%	Weight on front Truck,	Engine and Booster........73020 lbs.
Rating, Engine and Booster, 73.0%	working order...........59000 lbs.	

CLASS L-2c   (Printed Jan. 1; 1930)

NYC 2889, another of the 100 class L-2c engines. At Harmon in 1936.   (D.A.Somerville)

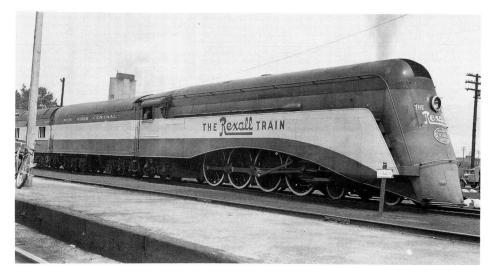

NYC 2873, streamlined for the Rexall exhibition train. At Green Bay, Wis.7/36 (Prescott)

NYC 2990, class L-2d at Niles, Mich. in June 1953. Wood pilot on M.C.   (A.F.Staufer)

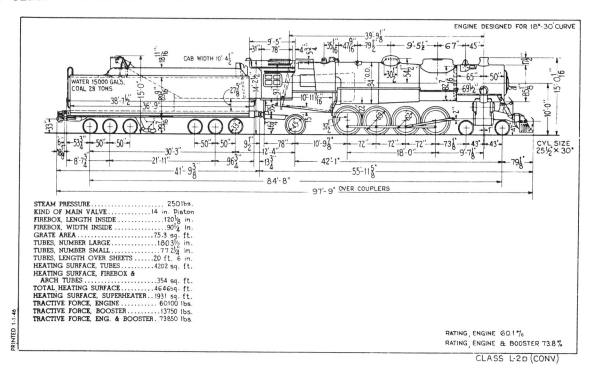

```
ENGINE DESIGNED FOR 18°-30' CURVE
CAB WIDTH 10' 4½
WATER 15000 GALS.
COAL 28 TONS
CYL. SIZE
25½ x 30"

STEAM PRESSURE.....................250 lbs.
KIND OF MAIN VALVE..............14 in. Piston
FIREBOX, LENGTH INSIDE.............120⅛ in.
FIREBOX, WIDTH INSIDE..............90¼ in.
GRATE AREA.......................75.3 sq. ft.
TUBES, NUMBER LARGE.............180 3½ in.
TUBES, NUMBER SMALL.............77 2¼ in.
TUBES, LENGTH OVER SHEETS......20 ft. 6 in.
HEATING SURFACE, TUBES.........4202 sq. ft.
HEATING SURFACE, FIREBOX &
    ARCH TUBES ...................354 sq. ft.
TOTAL HEATING SURFACE.........4646 sq. ft.
HEATING SURFACE, SUPERHEATER..1931 sq. ft.
TRACTIVE FORCE, ENGINE..........60100 lbs.
TRACTIVE FORCE, BOOSTER.........13750 lbs.
TRACTIVE FORCE, ENG. & BOOSTER.73850 lbs.

PRINTED 1-1-46

RATING, ENGINE 60.1%
RATING, ENGINE & BOOSTER 73.8%

CLASS L-2D (CONV.)
```

L-2d 2995 and 2998 were converted for passenger service, Here is 2995 near Chicago, 7/194
(A.F.Staufer coll.

NYC 3013 class L-3a at Collinwood, April 1953. This class never had boosters. (Prescott)

NYC 3004 L-3a with last steam run 4/16/51, from Boston, B&A used 12 L-3a's. (NYC 9429)

CAB WIDTH 10'-1½" (FRONT)
9'-10" (REAR)

WATER 15500 GALS.
COAL 43 TONS

STEAM PRESSURE.....................250 lbs.(SEE NOTE)
KIND OF MAIN VALVE.............14 in. Piston
FIREBOX, LENGTH INSIDE.............120⅛ in.
FIREBOX, WIDTH INSIDE.............90¼ in.
GRATE AREA.....................75.3 sq. ft.
TUBES, NUMBER LARGE.............198 3½ in.
TUBES, NUMBER SMALL.............50 2¼ in.
TUBES, LENGTH OVER SHEETS......20 ft. 6 in.
HEATING SURFACE, TUBES........4303.0 sq. ft.
HEATING SURFACE, FIREBOX &
ARCH TUBES ....373.0 sq. ft.
TOTAL HEATING SURFACE.......4676.0 sq. ft.
HEATING SURFACE, SUPERHEATER..2082 sq. ft.
TRACTIVE FORCE, ENGINE...........60100 lbs.
TRACTIVE FORCE, BOOSTER.........
TRACTIVE FORCE, ENG. & BOOSTER..

NOTE :
ENG 3000 HAS 260 LBS BOILER PRESSURE, 72"DRIVING
AND 36" ENG.TRUCK WHEELS. ENG. HEIGHT ABOVE
RAIL 1½" GREATER THAN SHOWN.

RATING 60.1%

NYC CLASS L-3a 4-8-2: 25+x30-69-250-388500-60100

3000	Alco-S	69337	10/40	Rt	4/57	(a)
3001	"	69338	"	So	2/57	(b)
3002	"	69339	"	Rt	11/54, SS	
3003	"	69340	"	Rt	1/55, SS	6/55
3004	"	69341	"	Rt	1/55, SS	3/55
3005	"	69342	"	Rt	5/56	
3006	"	69343	"	Rt	10/54, SS	
3007	"	69344	"	Rt	10/54, SS	
3008	"	69345	11/40	Rt	11/54, SS	
3009	"	69346	"	Rt	12/54, SS	
3010	"	69347	"	Rt	4/57	
3011	"	69348	"	Rt	10/54, SS	
3012	"	69349	"	Rt	8/56	
3013	"	69350	"	Rt	3/55, SS	6/55
3014	"	69351	"	Rt	4/57	
3015	"	69352	"	Rt	10/54, SS	
3016	"	69353	"	Rt	10/54, SS	
3017	"	69354	12/40	Rt	4/55, SS	6/55
3018	"	69355	"	Rt	10/54, SS	
3019	"	69356	"	Rt	10/54, SS	
3020	"	69357	"	Rt	6/54, SS	11/54
3021	"	69358	"	Rt	11/54, SS	
3022	"	69359	"	Rt	1/55, SS	6/55
3023	"	69360	"	Rt	5/55, SS	6/55
3024	"	69361	"	Rt	10/54, SS	

NYC CLASS L-3b 4-8-2: 25+x30-69-250-393500-60100 (c)

3025	Alco-S	69362	12/40	Rt	6/53, SS	9/53
3026	"	69363	1/41	Rt	12/53, Sc	3/54
3027	"	69364	"	Rt	11/53, Sc	1/54
3028	"	69365	"	Rt	10/53, SS	/54
3029	"	69366	"	Rt	6/54, SS	
3030	"	69367	"	Rt	6/53, SS	9/53
3031	"	69368	"	Rt	11/54, SS	
3032	"	69369	"	Rt	6/56	
3033	"	69370	"	Rt	4/55, SS	6/55
3034	"	69371	"	Rt	11/54, SS	
3035	Lima	7779	11/40	Rt	11/53, Sc	1/54
3036	"	7780	"	Rt	11/53, Sc	1/54
3037	"	7781	"	Rt	6/56	
3038	"	7782	"	Rt	12/55, SS	12/55
3039	"	7783	"	Rt	10/53, SS	/54
3040	"	7784	"	Rt	6/53, SS	7/53
3041	"	7785	12/40	Rt	6/53, SS	9/53
3042	"	7786	"	Rt	9/53, Sc	10/53
3043	"	7787	"	Rt	8/53, Sc	10/53
3044	"	7788	"	Rt	7/53, Sc	10/53
3045	"	7789	"	Rt	5/55, SS	6/55
3046	"	7790	"	Rt	11/53, Sc	6/54
3047	"	7791	"	Rt	4/57	
3048	"	7792	"	Rt	5/55, SS	6/55
3049	"	7793	1/41	Rt	3/57	

NYC CLASS L-3c 4-8-2: 25+x30-69-250-398000-60100 (c)

3050	Alco-S	69745	3/42	Rt	7/53, Sc	10/53
3051	"	69746	"	Rt	9/53, SS	/54
3052	"	69747	"	Rt	6/53, SS	9/53
3053	"	69748	"	Rt	12/55, SS	12/55
3054	"	69749	"	Rt	11/53, Sc	7/54
3055	"	69750	"	Rt	10/53, SS	/54
3056	"	69751	"	Rt	6/53, SS	8/53
3057	"	69752	"	Rt	5/52, Sc	12/52
3058	"	69753	"	Rt	4/55, SS	6/55
3059	"	69754	"	Rt	10/52, SS	/54
3060	"	69755	"	Rt	10/53, SS	/54
3061	"	69756	"	Rt	10/53, SS	/54
3062	"	69757	"	Rt	3/54, SS	
3063	"	69758	"	Rt	2/54, SS	
3064	"	69759	4/42	Rt	12/55, SS	12/55

NYC CLASS L-4a 4-8-2: 26x30-72-250-397300-59000

3100	Lima	7978	12/42	Rt	3/55, SS	6/55
3101	"	7979	"	Rt	12/54, SS	
3102	"	7980	"	Rt	3/56	
3103	"	7981	"	Rt	3/55, SS	6/55
3104	"	7982	"	Rt	12/55, SS	12/55
3105	"	7983	"	Rt	10/55, SS	11/55
3106	"	7984	"	Rt	3/57	
3107	"	7985	"	Rt	11/54, SS	
3108	"	7986	"	Rt	11/55, SS	12/55
3109	"	7987	"	Rt	3/55, SS	6/55
3110	"	7988	"	Rt	9/55, SS	11/55
3111	"	7989	"	Rt	3/55, SS	6/55
3112	"	7990	1/43	Rt	3/55, SS	6/55
3113	"	7991	"	Rt	4/55, SS	6/55
3114	"	7992	"	Rt	11/54, SS	
3115	"	7993	"	Rt	7/56	
3116	"	7994	"	Rt	10/55, SS	11/55
3117	"	7995	"	Rt	12/55, SS	2/56
3118	"	7996	"	Rt	4/57	
3119	"	7997	"	Rt	10/55, SS	11/55
3120	"	7998	"	Rt	3/57	
3121	"	7999	2/43	Rt	6/56	
3122	"	8000	"	Rt	11/54, SS	
3123	"	8001	"	Rt	8/55, SS	11/55
3124	"	8002	3/43	Rt	2/56	

NYC CLASS L-4b 4-8-2: 26x30-72-250-401100-59900

3125	Lima	8292	10/43	Rt	6/56	
3126	"	8293	"	Rt	3/56	
3127	"	8294	"	Rt	3/57	
3128	"	8295	"	Rt	4/57	
3129	"	8296	11/43	Rt	2/56, SS	4/56
3130	"	8297	"	Rt	10/54, SS	
3131	"	8298	"	Rt	2/56	
3132	"	8299	"	Rt	1/57	
3133	"	8300	"	Rt	3/55, Rt	6/55
3134	"	8301	"	Rt	12/55, SS	12/55
3135	"	8302	12/43	Rt	12/56	
3136	"	8303	"	Rt	10/54, SS	
3137	"	8304	"	Rt	3/56	
3138	"	8305	"	Rt	10/54, SS	
3139	"	8306	"	Rt	9/55, SS	11/55
3140	"	8307	"	Rt	10/54, SS	
3141	"	8308	"	Rt	10/55, SS	9/55
3142	"	8309	"	Rt	10/54, SS	
3143	"	8310	"	Rt	8/55, SS	9/55
3144	"	8311	"	Rt	11/55, SS	12/55 (d)
3145	"	8312	"	Rt	4/55, SS	6/55
3146	"	8313	1/44	Rt	4/55, SS	6/55
3147	"	8314	"	Rt	10/54, Sc	11/54
3148	"	8315	"	Rt	6/56 (d)	
3149	"	8316	"	Rt	11/54, SS	

Note a: 3000 had 72" drivers and 260 bp for a while.

Note b: 3001 taken to Dallas, Tex. Fair grounds, then returned to Elkhart for restoration.

Note c: Booster added 14000 tf.

Note d: 3144 and 3148 equiped with Timken roller bearing rods by NYC.

NYC 3035 class L-3b, ready for freight service at Lima in 1941.   (P.E.Buchert)

NYC 3049 Class L-3b, in later days at Bellefontaine, Ohio.   (M.D.McCarter)

NYC 3051 class L-3c. It grew elephant ears later. Elkhart, Ind.   (Staufer collection)

220

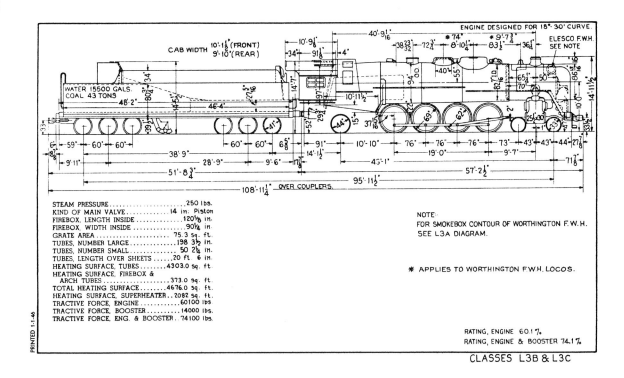

STEAM PRESSURE.....................250 lbs.
KIND OF MAIN VALVE.............14 in. Piston
FIREBOX, LENGTH INSIDE.............120⅛ in.
FIREBOX, WIDTH INSIDE ....90¼ in.
GRATE AREA .... 75.3 sq. ft.
TUBES, NUMBER LARGE............198 3½ in.
TUBES, NUMBER SMALL............ 50 2¼ in.
TUBES, LENGTH OVER SHEETS .....20 ft. 6 in.
HEATING SURFACE, TUBES........4303.0 sq. ft.
HEATING SURFACE, FIREBOX &
    ARCH TUBES .... 373.0 sq. ft.
TOTAL HEATING SURFACE ....4676.0 sq. ft.
HEATING SURFACE, SUPERHEATER..2082 sq. ft.
TRACTIVE FORCE, ENGINE ....60100 lbs.
TRACTIVE FORCE, BOOSTER..........14000 lbs.
TRACTIVE FORCE, ENG. & BOOSTER. 74100 lbs.

NOTE:
FOR SMOKEBOX CONTOUR OF WORTHINGTON F.W.H.
    SEE L3A DIAGRAM.

✳ APPLIES TO WORTHINGTON F.W.H. LOCOS.

RATING, ENGINE 60.1 %
RATING, ENGINE & BOOSTER 74.1 %

CLASSES L3B & L3C

NYC 3100, first L-4a, at Ypsilanti, Mich. in 1955.   (Ron Morgan)

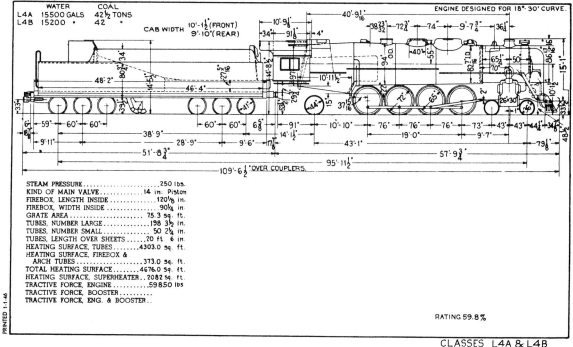

STEAM PRESSURE.....................250 lbs.
KIND OF MAIN VALVE.............14 in. Piston
FIREBOX, LENGTH INSIDE.............120⅛ in.
FIREBOX, WIDTH INSIDE ....90¼ in.
GRATE AREA .... 75.3 sq. ft.
TUBES, NUMBER LARGE............198 3½ in.
TUBES, NUMBER SMALL............ 50 2¼ in.
TUBES, LENGTH OVER SHEETS .....20 ft. 6 in.
HEATING SURFACE, TUBES........4303.0 sq. ft.
HEATING SURFACE, FIREBOX &
    ARCH TUBES .... 373.0 sq. ft.
TOTAL HEATING SURFACE ....4676.0 sq. ft.
HEATING SURFACE, SUPERHEATER..2082 sq. ft.
TRACTIVE FORCE, ENGINE ....59850 lbs.
TRACTIVE FORCE, BOOSTER.........
TRACTIVE FORCE, ENG. & BOOSTER..

RATING 59.8 %

CLASSES L4A & L4B

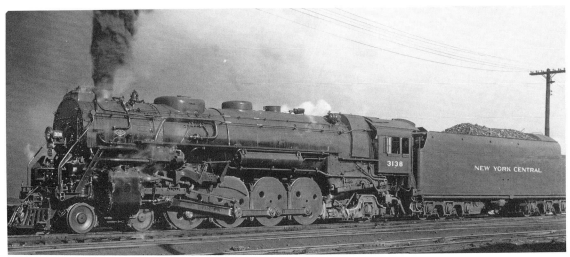

NYC 3138, L-4b, at Elkhart. Highly successful dual service engine. (Staufer collection)

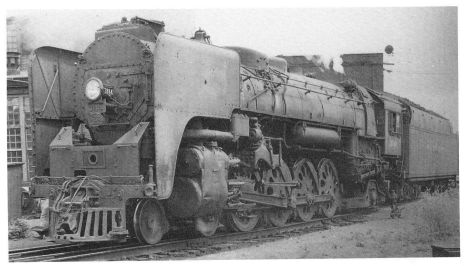

NYC 3114, class L-4a. At Buffalo in August, 1953.   (Paul Prescott collection)

NYC&HR 1300 class NB-1a(orig. class N)   Alco Builder's photo. (H.L.Vail coll.)

CLASS M : 0-10-0 SWITCHER

```
NYC&HR CLASS M 0-10-0: 24x28-51-210-270000-56450
      re'12 re'17
   3650  97  4601  Alco-B 37751  7/05  Rt  5/33
   3651  98  4602    "    37752   "    Rt  6/33
   3652  99  4603    "    37753   "    Sc  9/34

NYC&HR CLASS M-1f 0-10-0: 24x28-52-210-269000-55360
          95  4600  Alco-B 48646  9/10  Sc  6/34
          96          "    48647   "    Re'13 MC 8998
```

LS&MS CLASS M-1 and M-1a: See LS&MS 4592-4599.

LS&MS CLASS M-1b: See CI&S 4590, 4591.

CCC&StL CLASS M-1c: See CCC&StL 7498, 7499.

MC CLASS M-1d: See MC 8790 re 8990 re 7190.

MC CLASS M-1e: See MC 8991 re 7191.

CLASS N : MALLET COMPOUND

```
NYC&HR NB-1a 0-6-6-0: 21+&34x30-51-220-361000-72650C
(Originally Class N.  Weight 348000)
   1300    Alco-S 54238 12/13  Rt  3/32

NYC&HR NE-1a 2-6-6-2: 20+&33x32-57-210-342000-60770C
(Orig. B&A Class N-1a. Acquired from B&A c.1912)
   1374  Ex-B&A 1249   Alco-S 46714 1/10 Rt 4/32

NYC&HR NE-2a 2-6-6-2: 21+&34x32-57-200-354000-63030C
(Originally Class N-2)
   1375  Alco-S 49556  4/11  Rt  9/32
   1376    "    49557   "    Rt 10/32
   1377    "    49558   "    Rt  3/32
   1378    "    49559   "    Rt  9/32
   1379    "    49560   "    Rt  9/32
   1380    "    49561   "    Rt  3/32
   1381    "    49562   "    Sc  9/34
   1382    "    49563   "    Sc  6/34
   1383    "    49564   "    Rt 10/32
   1384    "    49565   "    Rt  9/32
   1385    "    49566   "    Sc  5/34
   1386    "    49567   "    Sc  9/32
   1387    "    49568   "    Sc  9/32
   1388    "    49569   "    Rt  9/32
   1389    "    49570   "    Rt  5/33
   1390    "    49571   "    Rt  9/32
   1391    "    49572   "    Rt  3/32
   1392    "    49573   "    Rt  5/33
   1393    "    49574   "    Rt  7/33
   1394    "    49575   "    Sc  9/34
   1395    "    49576   "    Sc  9/34
   1396    "    49577   "    Sc  9/34
   1397    "    49578   "    Rt  9/32
   1398    "    49579   "    Sc  9/34
   1399    "    49580  5/11  Rt  9/32

B&A CLASS NE-2b 2-6-6-2: See B&A 1300-1303.

B&A CLASS NE-2c 2-6-6-2: See B&A 1304-1307

B&A CLASS NE-2e 2-6-6-2: See B&A 1308-1312.
```

```
NYC CLASS NE-2d 2-6-6-2: 21+&34x32-57-200-363800-63080
        re'36
   1354  1933  Alco-S 56687  2/17  Rt  6/52, SS 10/52
   1355  1934    "    56688   "    Rt  6/52, SS 11/52
   1356          "    56689   "    Rt  9/32, Sc  9/32
   1357  1935    "    56690   "    Rt  5/52, SS 10/52
   1358  1936    "    56691   "    Rt  5/52, SS 10/52
   1359          "    56692   "    Sc  5/34
   1360          "    56693   "    Sc  5/34
   1361  1937    "    56694   "    Rt  5/52, SS 11/52
   1362          "    56695   "    Sc  5/34
   1363          "    56696   "    Rt  4/32, Sc  4/32
   1364          "    56697   "    Rt  4/32, Sc  4/32
   1365          "    56698   "    Sc  5/34
   1366          "    56699   "    Sc  7/34
   1367          "    56700   "    Sc  7/34
   1368          "    56701   "    Sc  7/34
   1369          "    56702   "    Sc  6/34
   1370          "    56703   "    Sc  5/34
   1371          "    56704   "    Rt  4/32, Sc  4/32
   1372          "    56705   "    Rt  4/32, Sc  4/32
   1373  1938    "    56706   "    Rt  7/46, Sc 12/46

NYC CLASS NE-2f 2-6-6-2: 21+&34x32-57-200-363800-63030
   1349        Alco-S 56860 11/17  Rt 10/32, Sc 10/32
   1350          "    56861   "    Rt  3/32, Sc  3/32
   1351          "    56862 12/17  Rt  4/32, Sc  4/32
   1352          "    56863   "    Rt  7/34, Sc  7/34
   1353          "    56864   "    Rt  3/32, Sc  3/32

NYC CLASS NE-2g 2-6-6-2: 21+&34x32-57-200-373000-63030
   1339  1939  Alco-S 62358 12/20  Rt  8/49, Sc  9/49
   1340  1940    "    62359   "    Rt  6/49, Sc  7/49
   1341  1941    "    62360  1/21  Rt  6/52, Sc 11/52
   1342  1942    "    62361   "    Rt  8/49, Sc  9/49
   1343  1943    "    62362   "    Rt  6/52, SS 11/52
   1344  1944    "    62363   "    Rt  6/52, SS 11/52
   1345  1945    "    62364   "    Rt  6/52, SS 10/52
   1346  1946    "    62365   "    Rt  6/52, SS 11/52
   1347  1947    "    62366   "    Rt  6/52, SS 10/52
   1348  1948    "    62367   "    Rt  6/52, SS 11/52
```

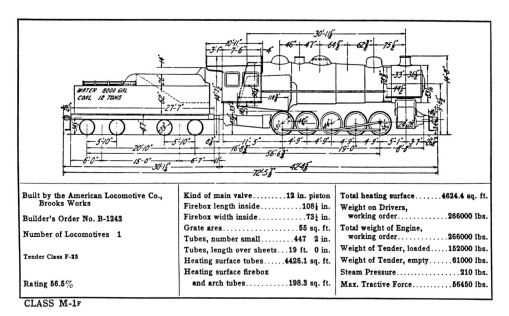

Built by the American Locomotive Co., Brooks Works	Kind of main valve.........12 in. piston	Total heating surface.......4624.4 sq. ft.
	Firebox length inside...........108¼ in.	Weight on Drivers,
Builder's Order No. B-1243	Firebox width inside............73¼ in.	working order............266000 lbs.
	Grate area..................55 sq. ft.	Total weight of Engine,
Number of Locomotives 1	Tubes, number small........447 2 in.	working order.............266000 lbs.
	Tubes, length over sheets...19 ft. 0 in.	Weight of Tender, loaded.....152000 lbs.
Tender Class F-25	Heating surface tubes......4426.1 sq. ft.	Weight of Tender, empty......61000 lbs.
	Heating surface firebox	Steam Pressure.................210 lbs.
Rating 56.5%	and arch tubes...........198.3 sq. ft.	Max. Tractive Force..........56450 lbs.

CLASS M-1F

NYC 1354 class NE-2d, at Rainelle, WV, October 1935. (H.L.Tilton. H.L.Vail collection)

Engine designed for 18°-30' curve.

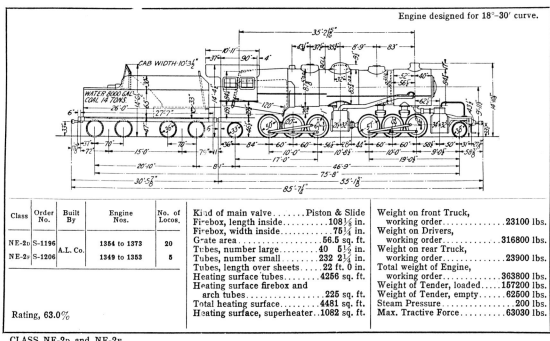

Class	Order No.	Built By	Engine Nos.	No. of Locos.		
					Kind of main valve.......Piston & Slide	Weight on front Truck,
					Firebox, length inside..........108⅛ in.	working order.............23100 lbs.
					Firebox, width inside...........75¼ in.	Weight on Drivers,
NE-2D	S-1196		1354 to 1373	20	Grate area...................56.5 sq. ft.	working order............316800 lbs.
		A.L.Co.			Tubes, number large........40 5½ in.	Weight on rear Truck,
NE-2F	S-1206		1349 to 1353	5	Tubes, number small.......232 2¼ in.	working order.............23900 lbs.
					Tubes, length over sheets....22 ft. 0 in.	Total weight of Engine,
					Heating surface tubes........4256 sq. ft.	working order.............363800 lbs.
					Heating surface firebox and	Weight of Tender, loaded.....157200 lbs.
					arch tubes.................225 sq. ft.	Weight of Tender, empty......62500 lbs.
					Total heating surface........4481 sq. ft.	Steam Pressure.................200 lbs.
Rating, 63.0%					Heating surface, superheater..1082 sq. ft.	Max. Tractive Force..........63030 lbs.

CLASS NE-2D and NE-2F

CLASS NU : 0-8-8-0 HUMP SWITCHER

LS&MS CLASS NU-1a 0-8-8-0 (Orig. P-1a)
5897-5899 re 7097-7099. See LS&MS

P&LE CLASS NU-1b 0-8-8-0: See P&LE 9090-9091.

NYC CLASS NU-1c 0-8-8-0: 26&40x28-52-220-466500-95730
re'36

5900	7100	Alco-B	55908	7/16	Sc	5/47
5901	7101	"	55909	"	Rt	5/47, Sc 6/47
5902	7102	"	55910	"	Sc	4/47
5903	7103	"	55911	"	Rt	5/47, Sc 6/47
5904	7104	"	55912	"	Rt	5/47, Sc 6/47
5905	7105	"	55999	"	Rt	5/47, Sc 6/47

MC CLASS NU-1d 0-8-8-0: See MC 8700-8701 re 7109

NYC CLASS NU-1e 0-8-8-0: 26&40x28-52-220-468500-95730
re'36

5906	7106	Alco-S	62368	1/21	Sc	5/47
5907	7107	"	62369	"	Sc	5/47
5908	7108	"	62370	"	Rt	1/38, Sc 10/38

NYC CLASSES P, Q, R, S, T - See Electric Locomotive Roster.

CLASS S : 4-8-4 NIAGARA

NYC CLASS S-1a 4-8-4: 25x32-79-290-471000-62400 (a)
6000 Alco-S 71454 2/45 Rt 3/56

NYC CLASS S-1b 4-8-4: 25+x32-79-275-471000-61570

6001	Alco-S	73779	10/45	Rt	8/55, SS 9/55			
6002	"	73780	"	"	"	"	"	
6003	"	73781	"	"	"	"	"	
6004	"	73782	"	"	"	"	"	
6005	"	73783	"	"	"	"	"	
6006	"	73784	11/45	"	"	"	"	
6007	"	73785	"	Rt	11/55, SS 12/55			
6008	"	73786	"	Rt	8/55, SS 9/55			
6009	"	73787	"	"	"	"	"	
6010	"	73788	"	"	"	"	"	
6011	"	73789	"	"	"	"	"	
6012	"	73790	"	"	"	Sc	11/55	
6013	"	73791	"	"	"	Sc	10/55	

6014	Alco-S	73792	11/45	Rt	8/55, SS 11/55		
6015	"	73793	"	Rt	8/56		
6016	"	73794	12/45	Rt	8/55, SS 11/55		
6017	"	73795	"	Rt	8/55, SS 9/55		
6018	"	73796	"	Rt	"	"	"
6019	"	73797	"	Rt	3/56		
6020	"	73798	1/46	Rt	3/56		
6021	"	73799	"	Rt	8/55, SS 9/55		
6022	"	73800	"	Rt	8/55, SS 9/55		
6023	"	73801	4/46	Rt	3/56		
6024	"	73802	"	Rt	3/56		
6025	"	73803	"	Rt	8/55, SS 9/55		

NYC CLASS S-2a 4-8-4: 25+x32-79-275-485000-61570 (b)
5500 Alco-S 74365 6/46 Rt 5/51, SS /56

Note a: 6000 had 75" drivers, 275 BP.
Note b: 5500 had Franklin poppet valves.

NYC 5500, Class S-2a.   (J.R.Quinn Coll.)

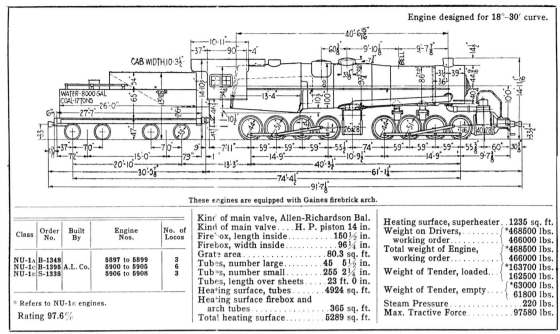

Engine designed for 18°–30′ curve.

CAB WIDTH 10-3½

WATER-8000 GAL
COAL-17 TONS

These engines are equipped with Gaines firebrick arch.

Class	Order No.	Built By	Engine Nos.	No. of Locos
NU-1A	B-1348	A.L. Co.	5897 to 5899	3
NU-1c	B-1395		5900 to 5905	6
NU-1E	S-1338		5906 to 5908	3

* Refers to NU-1E engines.

Rating 97.6%

Kind of main valve, Allen-Richardson Bal.
Kind of main valve.... H. P. piston 14 in.
Firebox, length inside.........150½ in.
Firebox, width inside...........96¼ in.
Grate area...................80.3 sq. ft.
Tubes, number large........45 5½ in.
Tubes, number small........255 2¼ in.
Tubes, length over sheets.....23 ft. 0 in.
Heating surface, tubes........4924 sq. ft.
Heating surface firebox and
arch tubes..................365 sq. ft.
Total heating surface........5289 sq. ft.

Heating surface, superheater..1235 sq. ft.
Weight on Drivers,........{*468500 lbs.
working order..........466000 lbs.
Total weight of Engine,.....{*468500 lbs.
working order..........466000 lbs.
Weight of Tender, loaded..{*163700 lbs.
162500 lbs.
Weight of Tender, empty....{*63000 lbs.
61800 lbs.
Steam Pressure................220 lbs.
Max. Tractive Force.........97580 lbs.

CLASS NU-1A, NU-1c and NU-1E

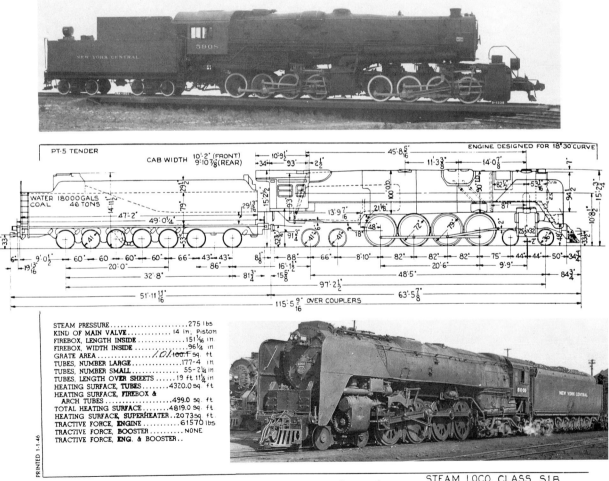

PT-5 TENDER

CAB WIDTH 10'-2" (FRONT) 9'-10⅞" (REAR)

ENGINE DESIGNED FOR 18-30′ CURVE

WATER 18000 GALS
COAL 46 TONS

STEAM PRESSURE.....................275 lbs
KIND OF MAIN VALVE.............14 in; Piston
FIREBOX, LENGTH INSIDE............151 1/16 in
FIREBOX, WIDTH INSIDE..............96¼ in
GRATE AREA.................101.100.5 sq. ft
TUBES, NUMBER LARGE.............177-4 in
TUBES, NUMBER SMALL.............55-2¼ in
TUBES, LENGTH OVER SHEETS......19 ft 11¼ in
HEATING SURFACE, TUBES........4320.0 sq. ft
HEATING SURFACE, FIREBOX &
ARCH TUBES............499.0 sq. ft
TOTAL HEATING SURFACE........4819.0 sq. ft
HEATING SURFACE, SUPERHEATER..2073 sq. ft
TRACTIVE FORCE, ENGINE..........61570 lbs
TRACTIVE FORCE, BOOSTER..........NONE
TRACTIVE FORCE, ENG. & BOOSTER..

PRINTED 1.1.46

STEAM LOCO. CLASS S1B

NYC 6000 class S-1a Collinwood, 2/52 (Prescott)

CLASS U : 0-8-0 SWITCHER

CLASSES U-1a,b,c,d,e 0-8-0: See LS&MS, T&OC, and IHB.

NYC CLASS U-2a 0-8-0:   23+x30-57-185-218000-45710

re'36

750	7450	Alco-B	56058	10/16	Rt	12/51,	SS	2/52
751	7451	"	56059	"	Rt	1/56		
752	7452	"	56060	"	Rt	8/54,	SS	
753	7453	"	56061	"	Rt	7/55,	SS	8/55
754	7454	"	56062	"	Rt	5/52,	SS	9/52
755	7455	"	56063	"	Rt	12/55,	SS	12/55
756	7456	"	56064	"	Rt	1/56		
757	7457	"	56065	"	Rt	12/54,	SS	
758	7458	"	56066	"	Rt	6/52,	SS	8/52
759	7459	"	56067	"	Rt	3/52,	SS	4/52
760	7460	"	56068	"	Rt	3/52,	SS	4/52
761	7461	"	56069	"	Rt	4/53,	Sc	8/53
762	7462	"	56070	"	Rt	5/52,	SS	9/52
763	7463	"	56071	"	Rt	4/55,	SS	6/55
764	7464	"	56072	"	Rt	4/55,	SS	6/55
765	7465	"	56073	"	Rt	7/52,	SS	9/52
766	7466	"	56074	"	Rt	3/52,	SS	7/52
767	7467	"	56075	"	Rt	8/55,	SS	9/55
768	7468	"	56076	"	Rt	3/52,	SS	5/52
769	7469	"	56077	"	Rt	5/52,	SS	9/52
770	7470	"	56078	"	Rt	8/55,	SS	9/55
771	7471	"	56079	"	Rt	12/51,	SS	2/52
772	7472	"	56080	"	Rt	5/52,	SS	10/52
773	7473	"	56081	"	Rt	2/56		
774	7474	"	56082	"	Rt	10/54,	SS	

NYC CLASS U-2b 0-8-0:   23+x30-57-185-218000-45710

710	7410	Lima	5296	1/17	Rt	1/53,	SS	5/53
711	7411	"	5297	"	Rt	1/56		
712	7412	"	5298	"	Rt	1/52,	SS	3/72
713	7413	"	5299	"	Rt	3/52,	SS	3/52
714	7414	"	5300	"	Rt	12/51,	SS	3/52
715	7415	"	5301	"	Rt	10/53,	SS	/54
716	7416	"	5302	"	Rt	2/56		
717	7417	"	5303	"	Rt	5/55,	SS	6/55
718	7418	"	5304	2/17	Rt	9/52,	SS	10/52
719	7419	"	5305	"	Rt	10/53,	SS	/54
720	7420	"	5306	"	Rt	3/52,	SS	4/52
721	7421	"	5307	"	Rt	6/54,	SS	
722	7422	"	5308	"	Rt	2/56		
723	7423	"	5309	"	Rt	12/51,	SS	1/52
724	7424	"	5310	"	Rt	6/53,	SS	7/53
725	7425	"	5356	"	Rt	7/52,	SS	9/52
726	7426	"	5357	"	Rt	12/51,	SS	3/52
727	7427	"	5358	"	Rt	12/51,	SS	1/52
728	7428	"	5359	"	Rt	10/54,	SS	
729	7429	"	5360	"	Rt	2/56		
730	7430	"	5361	"	Rt	12/51,	SS	1/52
731	7431	"	5362	"	Rt	1/56		
732	7432	"	5363	"	Rt	3/52,	SS	4/52
733	7433	"	5364	"	Rt	12/51,	SS	1/52
734	7434	"	5365	"	Rt	4/55,	SS	6/55

NYC CLASS U-2b 0-8-0:   Continued

re'36

735	7435	Lima	5366	2/17	Rt	5/52,	SS	9/52
736	7436	"	5367	"	Rt	12/51,	SS	3/52
737	7437	"	5368	"	Rt	2/56		
738	7438	"	5369	"	Rt	3/52,	SS	4/52
739	7439	"	5370	3/17	Rt	12/51,	SS	3/52
740	7440	"	5371	"	Rt	8/55,	SS	9/55
741	7441	"	5372	"	Rt	1/56		
742	7442	"	5373	"	Rt	6/54,	SS	
743	7443	"	5374	"	Rt	2/56		
744	7444	"	5375	"	Rt	10/53,	SS	/54
745	7445	"	5376	"	Rt	1/53,	SS	4/53
746	7446	"	5377	"	Rt	12/51,	SS	3/52
747	7447	"	5378	"	Rt	7/52,	SS	7/52
748	7448	"	5379	"	Rt	10/52,	SS	12/52
749	7449	"	5380	"	Rt	2/56		
685	7385	Lima	5395	4/17	Rt	7/55,	SS	8/55
686	7386	"	5396	"	Rt	2/59,	SS	2/59
687	7387	"	5397	"	Rt	10/53,	SS	/54
688	7388	"	5398	"	Rt	6/53,	SS	7/53
689	7389	"	5399	"	Rt	10/53,	SS	
690	7390	"	5400	"	Rt	3/52,	SS	4/52
691	7391	"	5401	"	Rt	7/52,	SS	8/52
692	7392	"	5402	"	Rt	6/54,	SS	
693	7393	"	5403	"	Rt	3/52,	SS	4/52
694	7394	"	5404	"	Rt	8/52,	SS	9/52
695	7395	"	5405	"	Rt	2/54		
696	7396	"	5406	"	Rt	10/54		
697	7397	"	5407	5/17	Rt	5/52,	SS	8/52
698	7398	"	5408	"	Rt	7/54		
699	7399	"	5409	"	Rt	6/52,	SS	10/52
700	7400	"	5410	"	Rt	5/55,	SS	6/55
701	7401	"	5411	"	Rt	3/55,	SS	4/55
702	7402	"	5412	"	Rt	10/54,	SS	
703	7403	"	5413	"	Rt	2/59,	SS	4/59
704	7404	"	5414	"	Rt	8/54		
705	7405	"	5415	"	Rt	8/52,	SS	10/52
706	7406	"	5416	"	Rt	2/59,	SS	4/59
707	7407	"	5417	"	Rt	12/51,	SS	1/52
708	7408	"	5418	"	Rt	4/52,	SS	9/52
709	7409	"	5419	"	Rt	6/52,	SS	8/52

MC CLASS U-2c: See MC 8900-8909 re 7550-53,7504-09.

NYC CLASS U-2d 0-8-0:   23+x30-57-185-218000-45710

640	7340	Alco-P	56865	8/17	Rt	7/52,	SS	9/52
641	7341	"	56866	"	Rt	3/52,	SS	4/52
642	7342	"	56867	"	Rt	3/52,	SS	4/52
643	7343	"	56868	"	Rt	3/52,	Sc	5/52
644	7344	"	56869	"	Rt	6/54,	SS	

Builder's photo of NYC 700, class U-2b, built by Lima in 1917.　(H.L.Vail coll.)

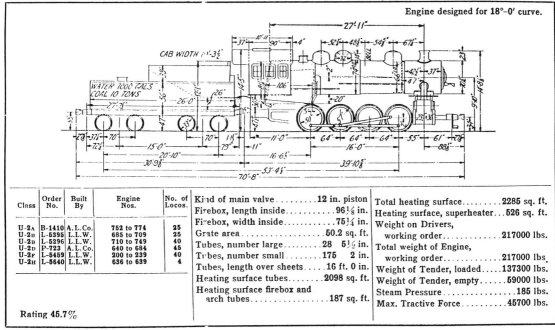

Engine designed for 18°-0' curve.

Class	Order No.	Built By	Engine Nos.	No. of Locos.
U-2A	B-1410	A.L.Co.	752 to 774	25
U-2D	L-5395	L.L.W.	685 to 709	25
U-2D	L-5296	L.L.W.	710 to 749	40
U-2D	P-723	A.L.Co.	640 to 684	45
U-2F	L-5459	L.L.W.	200 to 239	40
U-2H	L-5640	L.L.W.	636 to 639	4

Rating 45.7%

Kind of main valve.........12 in. piston
Firebox, length inside..........96⅛ in.
Firebox, width inside...........75¼ in.
Grate area.................50.2 sq. ft.
Tubes, number large........28 5½ in.
Tubes, number small.......175   2 in.
Tubes, length over sheets.....16 ft. 0 in.
Heating surface tubes.......2098 sq. ft.
Heating surface firebox and
   arch tubes................187 sq. ft.

Total heating surface.........2285 sq. ft.
Heating surface, superheater...526 sq. ft.
Weight on Drivers,
   working order...........217000 lbs.
Total weight of Engine,
   working order...........217000 lbs.
Weight of Tender, loaded.....137300 lbs.
Weight of Tender, empty......59000 lbs.
Steam Pressure...............185 lbs.
Max. Tractive Force.........45700 lbs.

CLASS U-2A, U-2B, U-2D, U-2F and U-2H

NYC 751, class U-2a at Albany, April 1936, just before renumbering to 7451.　(G.Votava)

NYC CLASS U-2d 0-8-0 - Continued
re'36

645	7345	Alco-P	56870	8/17	Rt 12/55,	SS 12/55
646	7346	"	56871	"	Rt 3/52,	SS 5/52
647	7347	"	56872	"	Rt 3/52,	SS 4/52
648	7348	"	56873	"	Rt 3/52,	SS 4/52
649	7349	"	56874	"	Rt 5/55,	SS 6/55
650	7350	"	56875	9/17	Rt 7/52,	SS 10/52
651	7351	"	56876	"	Rt 11/54,	SS
652	7352	"	56877	10/17	Rt 3/52,	SS 3/52
653	7353	"	56878	"	Rt 12/51,	SS 2/52
654	7354	"	56879	"	Rt 1/53,	SS 4/53
655	7355	"	56880	"	Rt 12/51,	SS 2/52
656	7356	"	56881	"	Rt 3/52,	SS 4/52
657	7357	"	56882	"	Rt 3/52,	SS 4/52
658	7358	"	56883	11/17	Rt 5/52,	SS 10/52
659	7359	"	56884	"	Rt 7/52,	SS 9/52
660	7360	"	56885	"	Rt 7/53,	SS 8/53
661	7361	"	56886	"	Rt 2/56,	
662	7362	"	56887	"	Rt 2/56,	
663	7363	"	56888	"	Rt 6/54,	SS
664	7364	"	56889	"	Rt 12/51,	SS 1/52
665	7365	"	56890	"	Rt 10/54,	SS
666	7366	"	56891	"	Rt 4/55,	SS 6/55
667	7367	"	56892	"	Rt 9/54,	SS
668	7368	"	56893	"	Rt 6/54,	SS
669	7369	"	56894	"	Rt 6/54,	SS
670	7370	"	56895	12/17	Rt 6/52,	SS 9/52
671	7371	"	56896	"	Rt 12/54,	SS
672	7372	"	56897	"	Rt 6/53,	SS 8/53
673	7373	"	56898	"	Rt 12/51,	SS 1/52
674	7374	"	56899	"	Rt 6/54,	SS
675	7375	"	56900	"	Rt 7/52,	SS 9/52
676	7376	"	56901	"	Rt 10/55,	SS 11/55
677	7377	"	56902	"	Rt 7/52,	SS 10/52
678	7378	"	56903	1/18	Rt 5/55,	SS 6/55
679	7379	"	56904	"	Rt 3/52,	SS 8/52
680	7380	"	56905	"	Rt 3/52,	SS 4/52
681	7381	"	56906	"	Rt 3/52,	SS 4/52
682	7382	"	56907	"	Rt 7/52,	SS 9/52
683	7383	"	56908	"	Rt 2/59,	SS 2/59
684	7384	"	56909	"	Rt 6/49,	Sc 12/49

MC CLASS U-2e 0-8-0: See MC 8910-8929 re 7510-7529

MC CLASS U-2g 0-8-0: See MC 8930-8939 re 7530-7539

IHB CLASS U-2i 0-8-0: See IHB 167-171.

NYC CLASS U-2f 0-8-0: 23+x30-57-185-218000-45710
re'36

200	7560	Lima	5459	5/18	Rt 7/52,	SS 8/52
201	7561	"	5460	"	Rt 8/54,	SS
202	7562	"	5461	"	Rt 6/52,	SS 9/52
203	7563	"	5462	"	Rt 9/52,	SS 10/52
204	7564	"	5463	"	Rt 3/52,	SS 4/52
205	7565	"	5464	"	Rt 3/55,	SS 4/55
206	7566	"	5465	"	Rt 5/52,	SS 9/52
207	7567	"	5466	"	Rt 3/52,	SS 4/52
208	7568	"	5467	"	Rt 7/53,	SS 7/53
209	7569	"	5468	"	Rt 3/52,	SS 4/52
210	7570	"	5469	"	Rt 6/53,	SS /54
211	7571	"	5470	"	Rt 1/58,	Sc 1/59
212	7572	"	5471	"	Rt 8/54,	SS
213	7573	"	5472	"	Rt 5/52,	SS 11/52
214	7574	"	5473	"	Rt 5/55,	SS 6/55
215	7575	"	5474	"	Rt 6/52,	SS 8/52
216	7576	"	5475	"	Rt 1/53,	SS 5/53
217	7577	"	5476	"	Rt 6/51,	SS 8/51
218	7578	"	5477	"	Rt 6/52,	SS 9/52
219	7579	"	5478	"	Rt 4/53,	SS 7/53
220	7580	"	5479	"	Rt 2/53,	SS 5/53
221	7581	"	5480	"	Rt 5/52,	SS 11/52
222	7582	"	5481	"	Rt 3/52,	SS 4/52
223	7583	"	5482	"	Rt 7/54,	SS
224	7584	"	5483	"	Rt 11/54,	SS
225	7585	"	5484	"	Rt 6/52,	SS 8/52
226	7586	"	5485	"	Rt 3/52,	SS 4/52
227	7587	"	5486	"	Rt 7/54,	SS
228	7588	"	5487	"	Rt 8/54,	SS
229	7589	"	5488	6/18	Rt 3/52,	SS 4/52
230	7590	"	5489	"	Rt 6/52,	SS 8/52
231	7591	"	5490	"	Rt 6/53,	SS 8/53
232	7592	"	5491	"	Rt 7/52,	SS 11/52
233	7593	"	5492	"	Rt 1/53,	SS 2/53
234	7594	"	5493	"	Rt 7/54,	Sc 8/54
235	7595	"	5494	"	Rt 7/54,	SS
236	7596	"	5495	"	Rt 3/52,	SS 4/52
237	7597	"	5496	"	Rt 9/54,	SS
238	7598	"	5497	"	Rt 1/53,	SS 3/53
239	7599	"	5498	"	Rt 2/52,	SS 3/52

NYC CLASS U-2h 0-8-0: 23+x30-57-185-218000-45710

636	7336	Lima	5640	7/18	Rt 6/53,	Sc 8/53
637	7337	"	5641	6/18	Rt 9/54,	SS
638	7338	"	5642	"	Rt 10/52,	SS 1/53
639	7339	"	643	7/18	Rt 2/59,	SS 2/59

B&A CLASSES U-2j,k,l: See B&A 42-47, 54-65.

NYC 7465 and 7450 pushing Second #51 up West Albany hill in 1941.   (G.M.Beischer)

NYC 7362 class U-2d at Collinwood in September 1937.   (Paul Prescott collection)

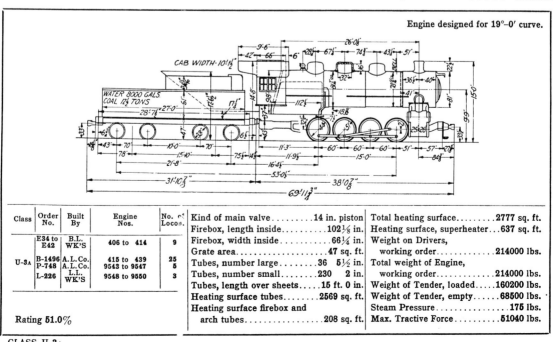

Engine designed for 19°-0' curve.

Class	Order No.	Built By	Engine Nos.	No. of Locos.
U-3ᴀ	E34 to E42	B.L. WK'S	406 to 414	9
	B-1496	A.L.Co.	415 to 439	25
	P-748	A.L.Co.	9543 to 9547	5
	L-226	L.L. WK'S	9548 to 9550	3

Rating 51.0%

Kind of main valve.........14 in. piston
Firebox, length inside.........102⅛ in.
Firebox, width inside.........66¼ in.
Grate area.................47 sq. ft.
Tubes, number large.......36 5½ in.
Tubes, number small.......230   2 in.
Tubes, length over sheets.....15 ft. 0 in.
Heating surface tubes........2569 sq. ft.
Heating surface firebox and
  arch tubes.................208 sq. ft.

Total heating surface.........2777 sq. ft.
Heating surface, superheater...637 sq. ft.
Weight on Drivers,
  working order.............214000 lbs.
Total weight of Engine,
  working order.............214000 lbs.
Weight of Tender, loaded.....160200 lbs.
Weight of Tender, empty......68500 lbs.
Steam Pressure................175 lbs.
Max. Tractive Force..........51040 lbs.

CLASS U-3ᴀ

NYC LINES CLASS U-3 0-8-0 SWITCHER

This class was first ordered by the United States Railroad Administration during World War I for use on numerous railroads throughout the nation. On the NYC it became the standard heavy switcher on all parts of the system. Listed below are the original assignments to component roads:

Class U-3a: 34 NYC, 3 LE&W, 20 IHB, 10 CCC&StL, 10 MC, 5 T&OC, 3 K&M.
U-3b: 50 NYC, 6 B&A, 10 IHB, 10 CCC&StL, 6 MC
U-3c: 50 NYC, 15 CCC&StL, 10 MC
U-3d: 6 CR&I
U-3e: 25 NYC, 5 IHB, 5 CR&I, 20 CCC&StL, 10 MC
U-3f: 25 NYC
U-3g: 5 IHB
U-3h: 2 P&E, 10 MC
U-3j: 25 P&LE
U-3k: 50 P&LE
U-3L: 25 P&LE

NYC CLASS U-3a 0-8-0: 25x28-51-175-219500-51200

	re'36						
415	7815	Alco-B	60085	10/18	Rt	5/52, SS	9/52
416	7816	"	60086	"	Rt	6/56	
417	7817	"	60087	11/18	Rt	5/52, SS	10/52
418	7818	"	60088	"	Rt	2/56	
419	7819	"	60089	"	Rt	4/57	
420	7820	"	60090	"	Rt	1/57	
421	7821	"	60091	"	Rt	5/52, SS	4/52
422	7822	"	60092	"	Rt	2/56	
423	7823	"	60093	"	Rt	5/52, SS	10/52
424	7824	"	60094	"	Rt	3/52, SS	3/52
425	7825	"	60095	"	Rt	3/52, SS	8/52
426	7826	"	60096	"	Rt	9/55, SS	11/55
427	7827	"	60097	"	Rt	3/52, SS	5/52
428	7828	"	60098	"	Rt	11/52, Sc	1/53
429	7829	"	60099	"	Rt	12/52, Sc	1/53
430	7830	"	60100	"	Rt	2/53, SS	4/53
431	7831	"	60101	"	Rt	11/55, SS	12/55
432	7832	"	60102	"	Rt	2/53, SS	4/53
433	7833	"	60103	"	Rt	2/56	
434	7834	"	60104	"	Rt	8/55, SS	9/55
435	7835	"	60105	"	Rt	4/52, SS	10/52
436	7836	"	60106	"	Rt	3/52, SS	4/52
437	7837	"	60107	"	Rt	10/52, Sc	1/53
438	7838	"	60108	"	Rt	5/55, SS	6/55
439	7839	"	60109	"	Rt	3/52, SS	4/52
(a) 406	7806	B.L.W.	51848	6/19	Rt	7/54, SS	
(a) 407	7807	"	51923	"	Rt	10/53, SS	/54
(a) 408	7808	"	51898	"	Rt	2/56	
(a) 409	7809	"	51851	"	Rt	10/53, SS	/54
(a) 410	7810	"	51850	"	Rt	4/53, SS	6/53
(a) 411	7811	"	51897	"	Rt	8/56	
(a) 412	7812	"	51899	"	Rt	3/52, SS	4/52
(a) 413	7813	"	51896	"	Rt	2/53, SS	6/53
(a) 414	7814	"	51849	"	Rt	6/54, SS	

NYC CLASS U-3b 0-8-0: 25x28-51-175-219500-51200

240	7640	Lima	6043	12/20	Rt	7/55, SS	8/55
241	7641	"	6044	"	Rt	1/55, SS	4/55
242	7642	"	6045	"	Rt	4/57	
243	7643	"	6046	"	Rt	6/53, SS	9/53
244	7644	"	6047	"	Rt	10/54, SS	
245	7645	"	6048	"	Rt	5/55, SS	6/55
246	7646	"	6049	"	Rt	5/52, SS	9/52
247	7647	"	6050	"	Rt	5/52, SS	9/52

NYC CLASS U-3b 0-8-0: Continued

	re'36						
248	7648	Lima	6051	12/20	Rt	12/55, SS	12/55
249	7649	"	6052	"	Rt	10/53, SS	12/53
250	7650	"	6053	1/21	Rt	1/56	
251	7651	"	6054	12/20	Rt	7/56	
252	7652	"	6055	"	Rt	2/53, SS	7/53
253	7653	"	6056	"	Rt	12/55, SS	2/56
254	7654	"	6057	"	Rt	5/52, SS	9/52
255	7655	"	6058	1/21	Rt	7/51, SS	7/51
256	7656	"	6059	"	Rt	9/54, SS	
257	7657	"	6060	"	Rt	2/53, SS	5/53
258	7658	"	6061	"	Rt	9/54, SS	
259	7659	"	6062	"	Rt	2/59, SS	2/59
260	7660	"	6063	2/21	Rt	7/52, SS	9/52
261	7661	"	6064	"	Rt	3/52, SS	4/52
262	7662	"	6065	3/21	Rt	2/53, SS	5/53
263	7663	"	6066	2/21	Rt	4/52, SS	10/52
264	7664	"	6067	3/21	Rt	11/54, SS	
265	7665	"	6068	4/21	Rt	3/53, SS	5/53
266	7666	"	6069	"	Rt	12/51, Sc	4/52
267	7667	"	6070	"	Rt	10/53, SS	/54
268	7668	"	6071	"	Rt	3/55, SS	4/55
269	7669	"	6072	"	Rt	2/53, SS	5/53
270	7670	"	6073	"	Rt	9/53, Sc	10/53
271	7671	"	6074	"	Rt	3/52, SS	4/52
272	7672	"	6075	"	Rt	3/52, SS	4/52
273	7673	"	6076	"	Rt	3/55, SS	4/55
274	7674	"	6077	"	Rt	8/55, SS	8/55
275	7675	"	6078	5/21	Rt	3/54, SS	
276	7676	"	6079	4/21	Rt	9/55, SS	11/55
277	7677	"	6080	"	Rt	5/52, SS	10/52
278	7678	"	6081	5/21	Rt	5/52, SS	10/52
279	7679	"	6082	"	Rt	10/54, SS	
280	7680	"	6083	"	Rt	2/56	
281	7681	"	6084	"	Rt	10/53, SS	/54
282	7682	"	6085	"	Rt	10/53, SS	/54
283	7683	"	6086	"	Rt	3/52, SS	4/52
284	7684	"	6087	"	Rt	10/53, Sc	3/54
285	7685	"	6088	"	Rt	7/53, SS	8/53
286	7686	"	6089	"	Rt	4/56	
287	7687	"	6090	"	Rt	2/56	
288	7688	"	6091	"	Rt	2/56	
289	7689	"	6092	6/21	Rt	2/53, SS	6/53

Note a: 406-414 re 3/20 from Mo.Kan. & Tex. 40,
48, 46, 43, 42, 45, 47, 44, and 41.

NYC 7805 class U-3c at East Alton, Ill. in March 1954 .   (John B. Allen)

NYC 7672 class U-3b at Ashtabula in September 1937.   (Paul Prescott collection)

NYC 309 class U-3c at East Youngstown about 1930.   (G.M.Beischer collection)

NYC CLASS U-3c 0-8-0:   25x28-51-175-219500-51200

	re'36					
290	7690	Lima	6256	7/22	Rt 2/59,	SS 2/59
291	7691	"	6257	"	Rt 4/56	
292	7692	"	6258	"	Rt 8/54,	SS
293	7693	"	6259	"	Rt 8/54,	SS
294	7694	"	6260	"	Rt 3/54,	SS
295	7695	"	6261	"	Rt 6/52,	SS 9/52
296	7696	"	6262	"	Rt 6/51,	SS 7/51
297	7697	"	6263	"	Rt 3/55,	SS 4/55
298	7698	"	6264	"	Rt 3/53,	SS 6/53
299	7699	"	6265	"	Rt 10/54	
300	7700	"	6266	8/22	Rt 5/52,	SS 10/52
301	7701	"	6267	"	Rt 10/52,	SS 12/52
302	7702	"	6268	"	Rt 3/52,	SS 4/52
303	7703	"	6269	"	Rt 5/54,	SS
304	7704	"	6270	"	Rt 5/52,	SS 10/52
305	7705	"	6271	"	Rt 3/52,	SS 4/52
306	7706	"	6272	"	Rt 7/52,	SS 1/53
307	7707	"	6273	"	Rt 4/52,	SS 4/52
308	7708	"	6274	"	Rt 3/53,	SS 5/53
309	7709	"	6275	"	Rt 8/54,	SS
310	7710	"	6276	"	Rt 4/55,	SS 6/55
311	7711	"	6277	"	Rt 2/59,	SS 4/59
312	7712	"	6278	"	Rt 5/52,	SS 11/52
313	7713	"	6279	"	Rt 2/55,	SS 4/55
314	7714	"	6280	"	Rt 4/55,	SS 6/55
315	7715	"	6281	"	Rt 3/52,	SS 8/52
316	7716	"	6282	"	Rt 2/56	
317	7717	"	6283	"	Rt 6/52,	SS 11/52
318	7718	"	6284	"	Rt 7/56	
319	7719	"	6285	"	Rt 10/54,	SS
386	7786	Alco-S	63358	8/22	Rt 4/57	
387	7787	"	63359	"	Rt 3/52,	SS 5/52
388	7788	"	63360	"	Rt 10/53,	SS /54
389	7789	"	63361	"	Rt 8/55,	SS 8/55
390	7790	"	63362	"	Rt 2/56	
391	7791	"	63363	"	Rt 9/55,	SS 11/55
392	7792	"	63364	"	Rt 2/59,	SS 4/59
393	7793	"	63365	"	Rt 2/59,	SS 4/59
394	7794	"	63366	"	Rt 2/59,	SS 4/59
395	7795	"	63367	"	Rt 3/52,	SS 4/52
396	7796	"	63368	"	Rt 2/59,	SS 4/59
397	7797	"	63369	"	Rt 3/53,	SS 5/53
398	7798	"	63370	"	Rt 9/53,	SS /54
399	7799	"	63371	"	Rt 9/55,	SS 11/55
400	7800	"	63372	"	Rt 3/52,	SS 7/52
401	7801	"	63373	"	Rt 4/52,	SS 9/52
402	7802	"	63374	"	Rt 4/52,	SS 11/52
403	7803	"	63375	9/22	Rt 2/59,	SS 5/59
404	7804	"	63376	8/22	Rt 4/57	
405	7805	"	63377	"	Rt 4/57	

NYC CLASS U-3e 0-8-0:   25x28-51-175-219500-51200

	re'36					
4300	7900	Alco-S	65498	5/24	Rt 2/53,	SS 6/53
4301	7901	"	65499	"	Rt 5/52,	SS 9/52
4302	7902	"	65500	"	Rt 5/57	
4303	7903	"	65501	"	Rt 7/52,	SS 9/52
4304	7904	"	65502	"	Rt 6/52,	SS 9/52
4305	7905	"	65503	"	Rt 2/59,	SS 5/59
4306	7906	"	65504	"	Rt 12/55,	SS 12/55
4307	7907	"	65505	"	Rt 6/56	
4308	7908	"	65506	"	Rt 12/51,	SS 1/52
4309	7909	"	65507	"	Rt 7/52,	SS 9/52
4310	7910	"	65508	"	Rt 2/52,	SS 3/52
4311	7911	"	65509	"	Rt 3/54	
4312	7912	"	65510	"	Rt 2/59,	SS 5/59
4313	7913	"	65511	"	Rt 2/56	
4314	7914	"	65512	"	Rt 6/54,	SS
4315	7915	"	65513	"	Rt 2/56	
4316	7916	"	65514	"	Rt 2/53,	SS 4/53
4317	7917	"	65515	"	Rt 1/55,	SS 3/55
4318	7918	"	65516	"	Rt 5/52,	SS 11/52
4319	7919	"	65517	"	Rt 10/52,	SS 12/52
4320	7920	"	65518	"	Rt 5/52,	SS 10/52
4321	7921	"	65519	"	Rt 3/52,	SS 4/52
4322	7922	"	65520	"	Rt 10/54,	SS
4323	7923	"	65521	"	Rt 10/54,	SS
4324	7924	"	65522	"	Rt 3/52,	SS 4/52

NYC CLASS U-3f 0-8-0:   25x28-51-175-219500-51200

4325	7925	Alco-S	65946	10/24	Rt 10/56	
4326	7926	"	65947	"	Rt 3/52,	SS 4/52
4327	7927	"	65948	"	Rt 12/51,	SS 1/52
4328	7928	"	65949	"	Rt 3/55,	SS 4/55
4329	7929	"	65950	"	Rt 10/54,	SS
4330	7930	"	65951	"	Rt 6/52,	SS 12/52
4331	7931	"	65952	"	Rt 7/52,	SS 10/52
4332	7932	"	65953	"	Rt 7/52,	SS 8/52
4333	7933	"	65954	"	Rt 10/52,	Sc 12/52
4334	7934	"	65955	"	Rt 3/52,	SS 4/52
4335	7935	"	65956	"	Rt 4/57	
4336	7936	"	65957	"	Rt 3/52,	SS 4/42
4337	7937	"	65958	"	Rt 1/54,	SS
4338	7938	"	65959	"	Rt 10/52,	Sc 12/52
4339	7939	"	65960	"	Rt 10/54,	SS
4340	7940	"	65961	"	Rt 2/56	
4341	7941	"	65962	"	Rt 5/52,	SS 10/52
4342	7942	"	65963	"	Rt 5/52,	SS 10/52
4343	7943	"	65964	"	Rt 10/54,	SS
4344	7944	"	65965	"	Rt 5/52,	SS 9/52
4345	7945	Lima	6878	11/24	Rt 5/52,	SS 9/52
4346	7946	"	6879	"	Rt 9/53,	SS 10/53
4347	7947	"	6880	"	Rt 4/56	
4348	7948	"	6881	"	Rt 2/53,	SS 6/53
4349	7949	"	6882	"	Rt 9/52,	SS 11/52

CLASS X : 4-8-0 12 WHEEL

NYC&HR classes X,X-1,X-3. Formerly classes H,H-1,H-3

Originally Beech Creek #11-20,50-71. See p.84.

NYC 2-TRUCK SHAY: 3-Cylinder 12x12-36-200-139400-27360

		re'36				
1896	7185	Lima	3235	11/23	So 4/48 Lima Works #4
1897	7186	"	3236	"	Rt 12/42, Sc 3/44
1898	7187	"	3237	"	So 4/43 Marcellus & Otisco Lake RR
1899	7188	"	3238	"	Rt 12/42, Sc 5/44
1900	7189	"	3239	"	Rt 12/42, Sc 5/44

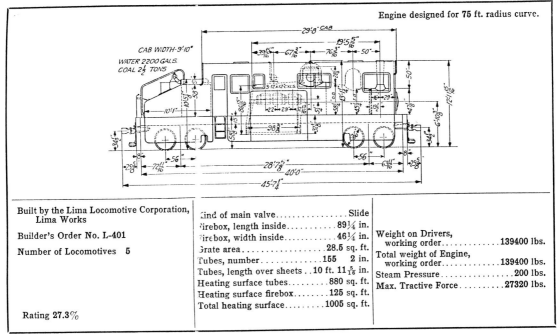

Engine designed for 75 ft. radius curve.

Built by the Lima Locomotive Corporation, Lima Works

Builder's Order No. L-401

Number of Locomotives 5

Rating 27.3%

CLASS—SHAY

Kind of main valve................Slide
Firebox, length inside..........89¼ in.
Firebox, width inside..........46¼ in.
Grate area.................28.5 sq. ft.
Tubes, number............155   2 in.
Tubes, length over sheets ..10 ft. 11 5/16 in.
Heating surface tubes........880 sq. ft.
Heating surface firebox.......125 sq. ft.
Total heating surface........1005 sq. ft.

Weight on Drivers,
    working order............139400 lbs.
Total weight of Engine,
    working order............139400 lbs.
Steam Pressure...............200 lbs.
Max. Tractive Force.........27320 lbs.

Shay 1897 with enclosed carbody for New York West Side Dummy service   (Woodbury)

CUT CLASS P-1a 2-C-C-2 (3000v.dc) 2635 HP-418900 wt.

re'36	Alco	G.E.					(a)
1050	200	67679	10724	11/29	RB 11/55	P-2b	240
1051	201	67680	10725	"	RB 12/55	"	241
1052	202	67681	10726	"	RB 5/55	"	228
1053	203	67682	10727	"	RB 12/55	"	242
1054	204	67683	10728	"	RB 5/55	"	229
1055	205	67684	10729	"	RB 10/55	"	237
1056	206	67685	10730	"	RB 2/55	"	223
1057	207	67686	10731	"	RB 11/55	"	239
1058	208	67687	10732	12/29	RB 10/55	"	238
1059	209	67688	10733	"	RB 6/55	"	230
1060	210	67689	10734	"	RB 6/55	"	231
1061	211	67690	10735	"	RB 9/55	"	235
1062	212	67691	10736	"	RB 4/55	"	226
1063	213	67692	10737	"	RB 7/55	"	233
1064	214	67693	10738	1/30	RB 4/55	"	227
1065	215	67694	10739	"	RB 3/55	"	225
1066	216	67695	10740	"	RB 9/55	"	236
1067	217	67696	10741	"	RB 3/55	"	224
1068	218	67697	10742	"	RB 2/51	P-2a	222
1069	219	67698	10743	"	RB 7/55	P-2b	232
1070	220	68030	10984	3/30	Rt 11/52, Sc		
1071	221	68031	10985	"	RB 8/55	P-2b	234

NYC CLASS P-2a 2-C-C-2: 600v.DC - RB from Class P-1a

former			re'68	
ex-218	222	RB 2/51	PC 4622	SS by'76

NYC CLASS P-2b 2-C-C-2: 600v.DC - RB from Class P-1a

ex-206	223	RB 2/55	PC 4623	dr by'76
ex-217	224	RB 3/55	PC 4624	dr by'76
ex-215	225	RB "	PC 4625	Rt'75-77
ex-212	226	RB 4/55	PC 4626	Rt'75-77
ex-214	227	RB "	PC 4627	Rt'75-77
ex-202	228	RB 5/55	PC 4628	SS by'75
ex-204	229	RB "	PC 4629	SS by'75
ex-209	230	RB 6/55	PC 4630	Rt'75-77
ex-210	231	RB "	PC 4631	dr by'75
ex-219	232	RB 7/55	PC(4632)	Sc by'75
ex-213	233	RB "	PC 4633	dr by'75
ex-221	234	RB 8/55	PC 4634	Rt'75-77
ex-211	235	RB 9/55	PC 4635	dr by'75
ex-216	236	RB "	PC 4636	dr by'75
ex-205	237	RB 10/55	PC 4637	dr by'75
ex-208	238	RB "	PC 4638	dr by'75
ex-207	239	RB 11/55	PC 4639	dr by'75
ex-200	240	RB "	PC 4640	dr by'75
ex-201	241	RB 12/55	PC 4641	dr by'75
ex-203	242	RB "	PC(4642)	Sc by'75

NYC CLASS Q B-B: 600v DC - 1665 HP - 201500 wt.

re'36	Alco	G.E.			
1250	150	66415	9803	3/26	Rt 8/54, Sc 11/55
1251	151	66416	9804	4/26	Rt 8/54, Sc 12/55
1252	152	66417	9805	3/26	Rt 8/54, Sc 11/55
1253	153	66418	9806	4/26	Rt 8/54, Sc 10/55
1254	154	66419	9807	"	Rt 8/54, Sc 12/55
1255	155	66420	9808	"	Rt 8/54, Sc 12/55
1256	156	66421	9809	5/26	Rt 8/54, Sc 12/55

NYC CLASS Ra 2(B-B): 600v DC - 3320HP - 354000 wt.

re'36	Alco	G.E.			
1200	300	66422	9801	9/26	RB 2,4/45 DHT (b)
1201	301	66423	9802	10/26	RB 5,6/45 DHT (b)

MC CLASS R-1 B-B: See MC 7500-7511 re 160-171.

NYC CLASS R-2 C-C: 600v DC - 2500 HP - 266400

1202	302	68230	11153	12/30	Sc 1/56
1203	303	68231	11154	"	So 8/55 CSS&SB 703
1204	304	68232	11155	"	Rt 8/54, Sc 1/56
1205	305	68233	11156	"	Rt 8/54, Sc 11/55
1206	306	68234	11157	"	Rt 8/54, Sc 1/56
1207	307	68235	11158	"	Rt 8/54, Sc 1/55
1208	308	68236	11159	"	So 1/55 CSS&SB 701
1209	309	68237	11160	1/31	Sc 2/43
1210	310	68238	11161	"	Rt 8/54, Sc 1/56
1211	311	68239	11162	"	Rt 8/54, Sc 12/55
1212	312	68240	11163	"	Rt 8/54, Sc 4/55
1213	313	68241	11164	"	RT 8/54, Sc 4/55
1214	314	68242	11165	"	So 1/55 CSS&SB 702
1215	315	68243	11166	2/31	Rt 8/58, Sc 8/58
1216	316	68244	11167	"	Rt 7/62, Sc 4/64
1217	317	68245	11168	"	Rt 7/62, SS 9/63
1218	318	68246	11169	4/31	So 8/55 CSS&SB
1219	319	68247	11170	2/31	Sc 2/43
1220	320	68248	11171	3/31	Rt 8/59, Sc 8/58
1221	321	68249	11172	"	Rt 10/57, Sc 4/58
1222	322	68250	11173	"	Rt 8/56, dr 11/56
1223	323	68251	11174	"	Rt 10/57, Sc 4/58
1224	324	68252	11175	"	Rt 8/58, Sc 9/58
1225	325	68253	11176	"	Rt 9/62, SS 9/63
1226	326	68254	11177	"	Rt 8/58, Sc 10/58
1227	327	68255	11178	"	Rt 12/52, dr 3/53
1228	328	68256	11179	4/31	Rt 7/62, Sc 10/63
1229	329	68257	11180	"	Rt 7/62, SS 10/63
1230	330	68258	11181	"	Rt 12/52, Sc
1231	331	68259	11182	"	Rt 8/54, Sc 11/55
1232	332	68260	11183	"	Rt 8/58, Sc 10/58
1233	333	68261	11184	5/31	Rt 8/58, Sc 9/58
1234	334	68262	11185	"	So 8/55 CSS&SB
1235	335	68263	11186	"	So 8/55 CSS&SB
1236	336	68264	11187	"	Rt 8/54, Sc 11/55
1237	337	68265	11188	"	Rt 7/62, SS 12/63
1238	338	68266	11189	"	Rt 8/54, Sc 12/55
1239	339	68267	11190	6/31	Rt 8/54, Sc 1/56
1240	340	68268	11191	"	So 8/55 CSS&SB 705
1241	341	68269	11192	"	So 8/55 CSS&SB 706
1242	342	68270	11193	"	So 8/55 CSS&SB 707
1243	343	68271	11194	"	So 8/55 CSS&SB 704

Note a: All Class P-1a lettered Cleveland Union
Terminal.   Sold 11/53 to NYC.

Note b: RB to Diesel Hump Trailers 450-453.

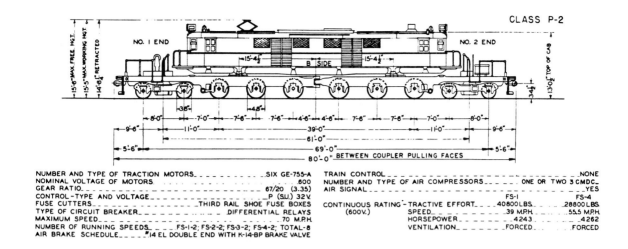

CLASS P-2

NO. 1 END   B SIDE   NO. 2 END

BETWEEN COUPLER PULLING FACES

NUMBER AND TYPE OF TRACTION MOTORS	SIX GE-755-A
NOMINAL VOLTAGE OF MOTORS	600
GEAR RATIO	67/20 (3.35)
CONTROL-TYPE AND VOLTAGE	P (SU.) 32 V.
FUSE CUTTERS	THIRD RAIL SHOE FUSE BOXES
TYPE OF CIRCUIT BREAKER	DIFFERENTIAL RELAYS
MAXIMUM SPEED	70 M.P.H.
NUMBER OF RUNNING SPEEDS	FS-1-2; FS-2-2; FS-3-2; FS-4-2; TOTAL-8
AIR BRAKE SCHEDULE	#14 EL DOUBLE END WITH K-14-BP BRAKE VALVE

TRAIN CONTROL		NONE
NUMBER AND TYPE OF AIR COMPRESSORS		ONE OR TWO 3 CMDC.
AIR SIGNAL		YES
	FS-1	FS-4
CONTINUOUS RATING - TRACTIVE EFFORT	40800 LBS.	28800 LBS.
(600V.) SPEED	39 M.P.H.	55.5 M.P.H.
HORSEPOWER	4243	4262
VENTILATION	FORCED	FORCED

NYC 104 class S-2 electric.   Harmon May 1940. Carried four numbers in 56 years. (G.Votava)

NYC 1237 class R-2.   Normally used in multiple.   Harmon May 1934.   (G.Votava)

NYC&HR CLASS S-1 2-D-2 600v DC-1695 HP-234200 Wt.
(Orig. Class L #6000 1-D-1, wt.200500. Later T-1)

re'05	re'08	re'13	re'36	Alco	G.E.	Built	Retired
3400	3200	1100	100	29935	2100	10/04	1/66 (a)

NYC&HR CLASS S-2 2-D-2 600v DC-1695 HP-229200 Wt.
(Converted from Class T-2 1-D-1 by'09; Wt.200500)

re'05	re'08	re'13	re'36	Alco	G.E.	Built	Retired
3401	3201	1101	101	29936	2101	7/06	Rt 8/50
3402	3202	1102	102	29937	2102*	"	re PC 4702
3403	3203	1103	103	29938	2103	9/06	Rt 11/55
3404	3204	1104	104	29939	2104	"	Rt 2/62
3405	3205	1105	105	29940	2105*	"	re PC 4705
3406	3206	1106	106	29941	2106	"	Rt 11/55
3407	3207	1107	107	29942	2107	"	Rt 2/67
3408	3208	1108	108	29943	2108*	"	re PC 4708
3409	3209	1109	109	29944	2109	"	Rt 1/66
3410	3210	1110	110	29945	2110	"	re PC 4710
3411	3211	1111	111	29946	2111	"	Rt 11/55
3412	3212	1112	112	29947	2112*	"	Rt 1/66
3413	3213	1113	113	29948	2113*	"	Rt '62 (b)
3414	3214	1114	114	29949	2114	"	Rt 11/55
3415	3215	1115	115	29950	2115*	10/06	re PC 4715(c)
3416	3216	1116	116	29951	2116*	"	Rt 5/63
3417	3217	1117	117	29952	2117	9/06	Rt 1/66
3418	3218	1118	118	29953	2118	"	re PC 4718
3419	3219	1119	119	29954	2119	10/06	Rt 2/62
3420	3220	1120	120	29955	2120	9/06	Rt 8/60
3421	3221	1121	121	29956	2121*	10/06	Rt 3/66
3422	3222	1122	122	29957	2122*	"	Rt 8/60
3423	3223	1123	123	29958	2123	"	re PC 4723
3424	3224	1124	124	29959	2124*	"	re PC 4724
3425	3225	1125	125	29960	2125*	11/06	re PC 4725
3426	3226	1126	126	29961	2126*	"	Rt 5/65
3427	3227	1127	127	29962	2127	"	re PC 4727
3428	3228	1128	128	29963	2128	"	Rt 5/63
3429	3229	1129	129	29964	2129*	"	Rt 4/62
3430	3230	1130	130	39735	2455*	"	re PC 4730
3431	3231	1131	131	39736	2456*	"	re PC 4731
3432	3232	1132	132	39737	2457*	"	re PC 4732
3433	3233	1133	133	39738	2458*	"	re PC 4733
3434	3234	1134	134	39739	2459*	"	Rt 11/55

NYC&HR CLASS S-3 2-D-2 600v DC-1695HP-249800 wt.

re'08	re'13	re'36	Alco	G.E.	Built	Retired
3235	1135	135	45290	2874	11/08	Rt 8/54
3236	1136	136	45291	2875	12/08	Rt 8/54
3237	1137	137	45292	2876	1/09	Rt 8/54
3238	1138	138	45293	2877	"	Rt 8/54
3239	1139	139	45294	2878	"	Rt 9/46
3240	1140	140	45295	2879	"	Rt 8/54
3241	1141	141	45296	2880	2/09	Rt 8/54
3242	1142	142	45297	2881	"	Rt 8/54
3243	1143	143	45298	2882	"	Rt 8/54
3244	1144	144	45299	2883	"	Rt 8/54
3245	1145	145	45300	2884	"	Rt 8/54
3246	1146	146	45301	2885	"	Rt 9/46

NYC&HR CLASS T-1a B-B-B-B: 600v DC-2584HP-252200

re'13	re'36		Alco	G.E.	Built	Retired
3247	1147	247	50775	3814	3/13	Rt 8/56

NYC&HR CLASS T-1b B-B-B-B: 600v.DC-2584HP-252200

re'13	re'36		Alco	G.E.	Built	Retired
3248	1148	248	53780	3838	7/13	Rt 8/56
3249	1149	249	53781	3839	"	Rt 5/65
3250	1150	250	53782	3840	"	Rt 8/54
3251	1151	251	53783	3841	8/13	Rt 7/56
3252	1152	252	53784	3842	"	Rt 12/64
3253	1153	253	53785	3843	"	Rt 9/59
3254	1154	254	53786	3844	"	Rt 9/59
3255	1155	255	53787	3845	"	re PC 4655
3256	1156	256	53788	3846	"	Rt 9/59

NYC&HR CLASS T-2a B-B-B-B: 600v.DC-2475HP-279100

re'13	re'36		Alco	G.E.	Built	Retired
3257	1157	257	54205	4657	4/14	Rt 12/64
3258	1158	258	54206	4658	"	Rt 8/56
3259	1159	259	54207	4659	5/14	Rt 11/57
3260	1160	260	54208	4660	"	Rt 9/62
3261	1161	261	54209	4661	6/14	Rt 6/65
3262	1162	262	54210	4662	"	re PC 4662

NYC CLASS T-2b B-B-B-B: 600v.DC-2475HP-247500

re'36		G.E.	Built	Retired
1163	263	5860	5/17	re PC 4663
1164	264	5861	"	Rt 6/65
1165	265	5862	6/17	Rt 9/62
1166	266	5863	"	re PC 4666
1167	267	5864	7/17	re PC 4667
1168	268	5865	10/17	Rt 8/56
1169	269	5866	"	re PC 4669
1170	270	5867	"	Sc 7/46
1171	271	5868	"	re PC 4671
1172	272	5869	11/17	Rt 4/64

NYC CLASS T-3a B-B-B-B: 600v.DC-2488HP-292600

re'36		Alco	G.E.	Built	Retired
1173	273	66705	10062	11/26	re PC 4673
1174	274	66706	10063	"	re PC 4674
1175	275	66707	10064	"	re PC 4675
1176	276	66708	10065	12/26	re PC 4676
1177	277	66709	10066	"	Rt 10/57
1178	278	66710	10067	" (d)	re PC 4678
1179	279	66711	10068	"	re PC 4679
1180	280	66712	10069	"	re PC 4680
1181	281	66713	10070	"	Rt 8/56
1182	282	66714	10071	"	Rt 6/65

* Weight 227700

Note a: 100 donated 3/66 to American Museum of Electricity, Schenectady, N.Y.

Note b: 113 donated 9/62 to Museum of Transport, St.Louis.

Note c: Conrail 4715 donated to Branford Trolley Museum. CT.

Note d: Donated to NRHS Mohawk & Hudson chapter.

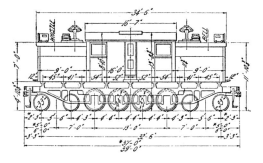

Class S-2.

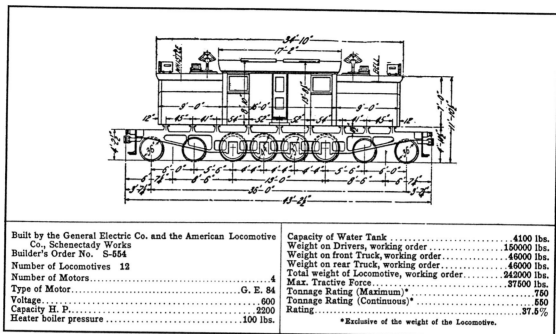

Built by the General Electric Co. and the American Locomotive Co., Schenectady Works
Builder's Order No. S-554
Number of Locomotives 12
Number of Motors..4
Type of Motor..G. E. 84
Voltage..600
Capacity H. P...2200
Heater boiler pressure............................100 lbs.

Capacity of Water Tank ....4100 lbs.
Weight on Drivers, working order.............150000 lbs.
Weight on front Truck, working order..........46000 lbs.
Weight on rear Truck, working order............46000 lbs.
Total weight of Locomotive, working order....242000 lbs.
Max. Tractive Force.....................................37500 lbs.
Tonnage Rating (Maximum)*.................................750
Tonnage Rating (Continuous)*............................550
Rating...37.5%
*Exclusive of the weight of the Locomotive.

CLASS S-3

NYC 273, class T-3a , Harmon   September, 1936.   (G.Votava)

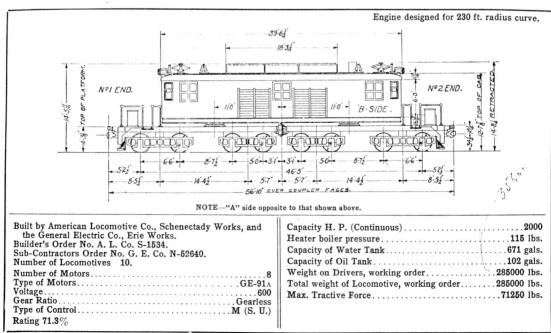

Engine designed for 230 ft. radius curve.

NOTE—"A" side opposite to that shown above.

Built by American Locomotive Co., Schenectady Works, and the General Electric Co., Erie Works.
Builder's Order No. A. L. Co. S-1534.
Sub-Contractors Order No. G. E. Co. N-52640.
Number of Locomotives 10.
Number of Motors...8
Type of Motors...GE-91A
Voltage..600
Gear Ratio...Gearless
Type of Control..................................M (S. U.)
Rating 71.3%

Capacity H. P. (Continuous)..........................2000
Heater boiler pressure.............................115 lbs.
Capacity of Water Tank................................671 gals.
Capacity of Oil Tank.....................................102 gals.
Weight on Drivers, working order.............285000 lbs.
Total weight of Locomotive, working order....285000 lbs.
Max. Tractive Force.....................................71250 lbs.

CLASS T-3A   (Printed Jan. 1, 1929)

ULSTER & DELAWARE. Acquired 2/1932. Formerly RONDOUT & OSWEGO 1866-72, then N.Y.KINGSTON & SYRACUSE 1872-75

```
      Pennsylvania              4-4-0          (Acq. 6/69)                          Wrecked 3/71
 1 Wm.C.More                    2-6-0  Dickson  52 11/69  18x24-49-     - 79000-    So 8/93 N.Y.Const.Co.
 2 Thomas Cornell               4-4-0          (Acq. 6/70)                          Rt'96
 3 John C. Brodhead               "    D.Cooke    12/70  18x24-54                   Exploded 8/86
 4 William Lounsbury              "      "         1/71   "   "                      Rt c'86
 5 Orson N. Allaben               "      "     732 4/71   "   "                      So 8/93 N.Y.Const.Co.
 6 Lewis N. Heermance             "      "     749 7/71   "   "                      Rt'95
 7 re 9 Frank J. Hecker         2-6-0T   "     756 9/71  17x22-48                    Rt'95, Sc'96
 7 (2nd)                        4-4-0  Dickson 360 7/82  18x24-67+                   Rt'06, Sc'07
 8                              2-6-0  Rogers 3060 8/82  17x24-54                    So'88
10                              4-4-0  Dickson 424 5/83  17x24-62                    So c'03
11                                "    Brooks 1014 6/84  18x24-60+                   dr c'03 ?
12                                "      "    1068 6/85   "   "                      dr'96
13              Bx 0-6-0T         "         1063 3/85  17x24-44-105-95260-14070      Sc 10/32
14 (re'99)  1   4-4-0  Dickson 519 5/85  18x24-62-       96500                       Rt'03
15              2-6-0    "     521  "     19x24-56-                                  Sc'08 (or So'07)
 3             4-4-0  Brooks 1234 6/87  18x24-61                                     Rt'04 (Note a)
16 (re'89)  4     "      "    1235  "      "   "                                       "    "
 8 (re'99) 16   2-6-0    "    1538 5/89  14x24-56-     -107900                       Rt'07, Sc'08
16 (re'98)  2 Cx 4-4-0   "    1539 6/89  18x24-61-135- 86300-14630                   Sc 7/32
17 (re'98) 14 Bx 0-6-0   "    1701 7/90  20x24-50-145-118700-23660                   Sc 9/32
 1 (re'98) 17   4-6-0    "    2091 5/92  18x24-56-     107900-                       So 1/07 (Note b)
 5    "  ) 18 Fx  "      2425 4/94  18x24-62-148-118000-15760                        Sc 7/32
11 (re'96)  9   4-4-0  Schen. 4408 4/96  19x24-62-                                   Wrecked 6/11, Sc
           20   (Inspection) Cx "   "  4409 3/96  14x22-62      80900                Sc 9/32
           12   Cx  "    "  4522 3/97  19x24-66-190-129200-21200                     Sc 7/32
            8   Cx  "    "  5153 6/99   "   "   "   "                                Sc 7/32

      re'36 re'48                                       Super..
   19  800        Fx 4-6-0 Schen. 5106 4/99    19x26-60-200-148300-26590            Sc 10/46
   21  801  1216   "   "     "     5107  "      "   "    "   "       "               Rt 1/49, Sc 4/49
   22  802 (1217)  "   "     "     5108  "  '26 20x26-60-200-157000-29470           Rt 7/48, Sc 8/48
   23  803  1218   "   "     "     6070 7/01    19x26-60-200-148300-26590           Rt 4/49, Sc 8/49
   24             "   "   Alco-S 25799 6/02  '20x26-60-200-157000-29470             Sc 5/32
   25  804 (1219)  "   "     "    25800  "      19x26-60-200-148300-26590           Rt 7/48, Sc 9/48
   26  805  1220   "   "     "    25801  "      "   "    "   "       "               Rt 4/49, Sc 8/49
   27  806  1221   "   "     "    29450 4/04    "   "    "   "       "               Rt 1/49, Sc 3/49
   28  807        "   "     "    29451  "      "   "    "   "       "                Sc 4/46
   29             "   "     "    29452  "      "   "    "   "       "                Sc 7/32
   30  808  1222   "   "     "    39952 5/06    20x26-62-200-167000-28520           Rt 1/49, Sc 3/49
   31             "   "     "    39953  "                                           Sc 7/33
   32  809        "   "     "    39954  "  '23 21x26-62-200-176500-31440            Sc 4/45
   33  810  1223   "   "     "    39955  "      20x26-62-200-167000-28520           Rt 1/49, Sc 3/49
   34  811 (1224)  "   "     "    39956  "  '24 21x26-62-200-176500-31440           Rt 7/48, Sc 8/48
   35  812  1225   "   "     "    39957  "      20x26-62-200-167000-28520           Rt 1/49, Sc 3/49
   36  813  1226   "   "     "    43061 6/07    "   "    "   "       "               Rt 4/49, Sc 5/49
   37  814  1227   "   "     "    43062  "  '24 21x26-62-200-176500-31440           Rt 4/49, Sc 5/49
   38  815  1228   "   "     "    43063  "  '23  "   "    "   "                      Rt 1/49, Sc 2/49
   39  816  1229   "   "     "    43064 7/07    20x26-62-200-167000-28520           Rt 1/49, Sc 3/49
   40  817  1230   "   "     "    43065  "  '24 21x26-62-200-176500-31440           Rt 1/49, Sc 2/49
   41  818  1231   "   "     "    43066  "  '24  "   "    "   "                      Rt 4/49, Sc 5/49
```

STONY CLOVE & CATSKILL MOUNTAIN (3'g). Controlled by U&D 1894 to 1900.

```
   1  (Note c)        0-4-4T?(Rhode Is.) acq.5/81                        So'86
   2  Gretchen        2-6-0            acq.'82   15x18-36+-56000         dr'86
   1  Stony Clove  re"2   "   Dickson 358 6/82    "    "    "            So 1/00 Hicks
   2  Hunter       re'1   "      "    530 5/86    "    "    "             "     "
```

KAATERSKILL (3'g). Controlled by U&D 1894 to 1900.

```
   1  Rip Van Winkle re"3 2-6-0 Dickson 423 5/83        15x18-36+-56000 So 8/99 (note d)
   2  D.Van Brummel  re 5   "   Brooks  936 6/83        15x18-37-55000  So 6/99 (note d)
   3  (Note f)       re 4   "      "    801  /82 Acq'93 15x18-37-61000  So 8/99 (note e)
```

Note a: So'06 Salisbury & Albert 5,6.   Note b: Re SI&E 558 re Atl.& StAB 110   Note c: Ex-Worc.& Shrews
Note d: Re Empire Stl.& Iron Co., re 4/05 BR&LCo., re Crystal Riv.Lbr.Co.   Note e: Re Cats.& Tann. 2 and 1.
Note f: Ex-Denver, Leadville & Gunnison 101.

SC&CM narrow gauge #2, 2-6-0 at Phoenicia, N.Y. c.1905.   (Peter Cornwall)

U&D 13 Brooks builder's photo. Lasted until N.Y.C. take-over in 1932.   (G.Votava)

U&D second #1 as built by Brooks in 1892. It was sold in 1907 down South. (NYC 10066-M)

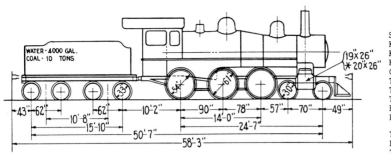

CLASS FX LOCO. N°S 80C-807

STEAM PRESSURE	200 lbs.
KIND OF MAIN VALVE	Slide, *11 in. Piston
FIREBOX, LENGTH INSIDE	96 in.
FIREBOX, WIDTH INSIDE	40½ in.
GRATE AREA	27 sq. ft.
TUBES, NUMBER LARGE	*24 5⅜ in.
TUBES, NUMBER SMALL	320, *166 2 in.
TUBES, LENGTH OVER SHEETS	14 ft. 0 in.
HEATING SURFACE, TUBES	2332, *1689 sq. ft.
HEATING SURFACE, FIREBOX & ARCH TUBES	164 sq. ft.
TOTAL HEATING SURFACE	2496, *1853 sq. ft.
HEATING SURFACE, SUPERHEATER	*379 sq. ft.
TRACTIVE FORCE, ENGINE	26150, *28980 lbs.

* APPLIES TO ENG. N° 802

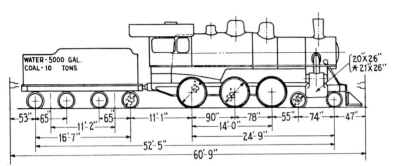

CLASS FX LOCO. N°S 808-818

STEAM PRESSURE	200 lbs.
KIND OF MAIN VALVE	Slide, *11 in. Piston
FIREBOX, LENGTH INSIDE	96 in.
FIREBOX, WIDTH INSIDE	65 in.
GRATE AREA	43.5 sq. ft.
TUBES, NUMBER LARGE	*24 5⅜ in.
TUBES, NUMBER SMALL	304, *169 2 in.
TUBES, LENGTH OVER SHEETS	14 ft. 4 in.
HEATING SURFACE, TUBES	2268, *1742 sq. ft.
HEATING SURFACE, FIREBOX & ARCH TUBES	149 sq. ft.
TOTAL HEATING SURFACE	2417, *1891 sq. ft.
HEATING SURFACE, SUPERHEATER	*387 sq. ft.
TRACTIVE FORCE, ENGINE	28060, *30940 lbs.

* APPLIES TO ENG. N°S 809, 811, 814, 815, 817, 818

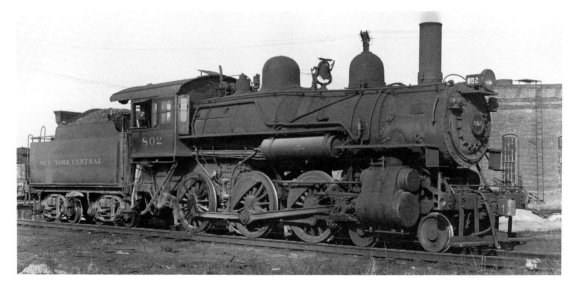

NYC 802, class Fx, formerly U&D 22, one of the lighter 4-6-0's. Superheated in 1926.

NYC 38 before losing old U&D number and adopting 815, later 1228. Class Fx remained.

NYC&HR AND NYCL INDEX BY ROAD NUMBER
(Excluding Former B&A, LS&MS, CCC&StL, MC, OC Locomotives)

1- P.8 9 30 36 40 174
2 - 8 32 36 40 174
3 - 8 32 36 92 174
4 - 8 8 32 37 42 174
5 - 8 20 37 40 174
6 - 8 24 32 42 174
7 - 8 32 36 46 92 174
8 - 8 40 46 174
9 - 8 26 32 40 174
10 - 8 22 32 37 40 174
11 - 8 8 30 32 42 42 174
12 - 8 26 32 38 46 174
13 - 8 26 32 46 174
14 - 8 26 32 42 42 174
15 - 8 20 32 42 50 174
16 - 8 34 50 174
17 - 8 24 32 42 44 174
18 - 8 32 46 174
19 - 8 24 34 44 112 174
20 - 8 34 46 174
21 - 8 24 40 44 174
22 - 8 26 36 46 174
23 - 8 22 34 44 118 174
24 - 8 26 34 42 44 174
25 - 8 36 44 118 174
26 - 8 34 44 174
27 - 8 34 94 118 174
28 - 8 40 94 118 118 174
29 - 8 22 32 46 46 46 118 174
30 - 8 34 40 94 118 174
31 - 8 40 46 174
32 - 8 34 46 112 174
33 - 8 34 37 44 118 174
34 - 8 34 37 94 174
35 - 16 40 94 174
36 - 16 37 94 174
37 - 16 40 94 122 174
38 - 16 34 40 98 112 122 174
39 - 16 34 46 122 174
40 - 16 28 34 46 68 122 174
41 - 9 34 42 46 68 122 174
42 - 10 26 34 46 68 112 122 174
43 - 9 34 46 68 68 112 174
44 - 9 26 36 46 68 122 174
45 - 16 9 34 68 98 174
46 - 16 34 46 68 98 174
47 - 16 34 46 98 122 174
48 - 16 34 46 98 122 174
49 - 16 30 34 98 122 174
50 - 16 34 36 46 94 98 174
51 - 16 34 37 92 98 174
52 - 16 34 42 94 98 112 174
53 - 9 16 22 34 38 46 98 174
54 - 16 28 34 40 98 174
55 - 16 16 34 40 98 174
56 - 16 34 42 98 112 174
57 - 16 34 46 98 174
58 - 16 36 46 98 174
59 - 16 36 40 42 98 174
60 - 16 36 50 98 174
61 - 16 36 50 98 174
62 - 16 22 36 44 98 174
63 - 16 36 46 98 112 174
64 - 16 36 44 98 174
65 - 16 36 46 98 174
66 - 16 36 44 44 98 174
67 - 16 36 46 174
68 - 16 36 44 174
69- P.16 36 44 174
70 - 9 36 44 96 174
71 - 9 9 36 44 96 174

72- p.9 36 94 96 174
73 - 9 9 36 46 96 174
74 - 9 36 94 174
75 - 9 16 20 36 46 84 96 174
76 - 9 9 22 36 46 46 78 84 96 174
77 - 9 22 30 36 44 84 96 174
78 - 10 22 30 36 84 94 96 98 174
79 - 20 24 36 84 94 96 98 174
80 - 10 20 26 36 84 94 96 98 104 174
81 - 10 20 20 36 42 84 94 96 98 174
82 - 10 20 20 36 94 96 98 B&A 174
83 - 10 22 36 92 96 98 B&A 174
84 - 10 22 36 96 98 B&A 174
85 - 10 22 36 96 98 B&A 174
86 - 10 18 20 36 96 B&A 174
87 - 10 20 24 36 96 B&A 174
88 - 10 22 36 96 B&A 174
89 - 10 20 22 36 96 B&A 174
90 - 10 22 36 96 B&A 174
91 - 10 22 36 96 B&A 174
92 - 10 22 36 96 B&A 174
93 - 10 22 24 36 96 B&A 174
94 - 10 22 36 96 B&A 174
95 - 10 22 26 36 96 222 B&A 174
96 - 10 22 26 36 96 222 B&A 174
97 - 10 22 36 96 222 B&A 174
98 - 12 22 36 96 222 B&A 174
99 - 12 22 36 64 96 118 222 B&A 174
100 - 12 16 37 96 102 236 B&A 174
101 - 12 37 50 96 102 B&A 236 174
102 - 12 20 37 50 96 102 236 174
103 - 12 37 50 96 102 236 174
104 - 12 34 37 96 102 236 174
105 - 12 26 32 54 96 102 236 174
106 - 12 22 30 37 96 102 236 174
107 - 9 10 30 37 96 102 236 174
108 - 10 30 34 37 96 102 236 174
109 - 12 34 37 96 102 236 174
110 - 12 34 44 96 102 236 174
111 - 12 34 42 96 102 236 174
112 - 12 28 36 96 102 236 174
113 - 12 22 28 96 102 236 174
114 - 12 30 36 96 102 236 174
115 - 12 20 36 96 102 236 174
116 - 12 28 36 96 102 236 174
117 - 12 20 28 36 96 102 118 236 174
118 - 12 20 36 96 102 236 174
119 - 12 30 36 96 102 236 174
120 - 12 30 36 96 102 236 174
121 - 12 24 36 44 96 102 236 174
122- P.12 20 36 46 96 102 236 174
123 - 12 20 36 112 126 96 102 236
124 - 12 22 36 94 96 102 236
125 - 12 22 32 96 102 236

126- p.12 30 32 82 96 102 236
127 - 12 30 32 96 102 236
128 - 12 28 42 96 102 236
129 - 12 34 42 96 102 236
130 - 12 36 40 96 102 236
131 - 12 20 36 40 96 102 236
132 - 12 36 44 96 102 236
133 - 12 36 42 96 102 236
134 - 14 20 36 46 96 102 236
135 - 14 36 38 96 102 236
136 - 14 36 44 96 102 236
137 - 14 46 50 96 102 236
138 - 13 44 50 96 102 236
139 - 13 20 50 96 102 236
140 - 13 46 50 96 102 236
141 - 13 30 42 96 102 236
142 - 13 24 30 96 102 236
143 - 13 20 24 96 102 236
144 - 13 26 46 102 236
145 - 13 20 20 26 102 236
146 - 13 26 42 98 102 236
147 - 13 26 42 98 102
148 - 13 26 44 98 102
149 - 13 26 46 98 102
150 - 13 26 44 98 102 234
151 - 14 26 40 98 102 234
152 - 14 28 40 98 102 234
153 - 14 28 42 98 102 234
154 - 14 28 30 102 234
155 - 14 28 42 46 102 234
156 - 14 28 44 102 234
157 - 14 28 44 102
158 - 14 24 102
159 - 14 30 44 102
160 - 14 30 44 102
161 - 13 20 44 102
162 - 13 16 24 38 44 102
163 - 14 22 26 98 102
164 - 14 24 40 102
165 - 14 24 38 102
166 - 14 24 24 122 102
167 - 14 24 44 102
168 - 14 24 42 102
169 - 14 24 30 102
170 - 14 24 42 102
171 - 14 24 30 102
172 - 14 24 42 102
173-178 - 14 26 42 102
179 - 14 26 102
180 181 - 10 24 26 102
182 - 10 20 26 42 102
183 - 13 18 26 98 B&A 102
184 - 16 26 38 B&A 102
185 - 16 26 42 B&A 102
186 - 16 26 B&A 102
187 - 16 28 B&A 102
188 - 16 28 94 B&A 102
189 - 16 28 30 B&A 102
190 - 16 28 98 98 B&A 102
191 - 16 28 46 98 102
192 - 16 28 42 98 102
193 - 16 28 44 98 102
194 - 16 28 42 46 98 102
195-196 - 16 28 46 78 92 98
197 - 18 78 92 94 98
198 - 18 28 46 78 92 98
199 - 18 38 46 78 92 B&A
200 - 18 30 78 98 112 126 234 228
201 - 18 28 46 78 84 112 234 228
202 - 18 20 42 46 78 84 234 228

```
203-  p.18 20 46 84 234 228           276-  p.22 28 46 46 96 230 236        440-  p.8 42 44 92
204  - 18 30 46 92 98 98 234 228      277  - 22 28 38 96 230 236            441  - 20 42 92 126
205  - 18 40 46 94 98                 278  - 22 28 40 96 230 236            442  - 24 50 92 126
206  - 18 40 44 98 234 228            279  - 22 28 37 46 96 230 236         443  - 8 38 50 60 92
207  - 18 38 94 98 234 228         280-281 - 22 28 96 230 236             444  - 8 44 92 136
208  - 18 30 98 98 234 228            282  - 22 28 46 96 230 236            445  - 26 44 46 98 102
209  - 18 16 98 98 234 228         283-289 - 22 28 96 230                 446  - 22 44 98 102
210  - 18 18 46 98 234 228         290-292 - 24 28 46 96 232              447  - 30 44 98 102 122
211  - 18 20 44 98 234 228            293  - 24 30 96 232                   448  - 26 44 60 98 102
212  - 18 20 98 234 228               294  - 24 22 96 232                   449  - 26 44 98 98 102
213  - 18 20 20 46 98 234 228      295-299 - 24 30 96 232                 450  - 26 44 98 104
214  - 18 20 98 234 228               300  - 24 22 96 232 234              451  - 20 44 46 98 104
215  - 18 22 98 98 234 228         301-302 - 24 24 96 232 234             452  - 6 30 44 44 104
216  - 18 26 98 112 234 228        303-308 - 24 30 98 232 234             453  - 24 44 104
217  - 18 26 44 98 234 228         309-310 - 26 30 46 98 232 234          454  - 8 38 44 104
218  - 18 26 98 98 234 228         311-318 - 30 98 232 234                455  - 24 44 104
219  - 18 26 98 112 76 234 228        319  - 26 38 98 232 234              456  - 8 40 42 44 104
220  - 20 26 46 98 234 228         320-329 - 26 38 98 176 234             457  - 24 38 44 104
221  - 20 22 26 98 122 234 228        330  - 26 38 46 98 176 234           458  - 26 44 46 104
222  - 20 28 98 112 234 228        331-332 - 26 38 98 176 234             459  - 22 44 104
223  - 20 28 98 98 234 228            333  - 26 38 60 98 176 234           460  - 26 44 46 104
224  - 20 24 28 92 98 234 228      334-339 - 26 38 98 176 234             461  - 8 40 44 104
225  - 20 28 46 92 98 234 228      340-343 - 26 40 98 176 234             462  - 8 38 44 60 104
226  - 20 28 92 98 98 234 228      344-345 - 26 52 98 176              463-464 - 8 44 46 104
227  - 20 28 92 98 234 228            346  - 28 40 98 176                  465  - 8 44 44 104
228  - 20 28 96 234 228               347  - 40 98 176                  466-467 - 8 44 122 104
229  - 20 24 28 96 234 228            348  - 38 98 176                     468  - 8 40 44 104
230-232 - 20 28 96 234 228            349  - 28 40 98 176               469-470 - 8 44 104
233  - 20 30 96 234 228               350  - 28 38 98 176                  471  - 16 42 44 104
234  - 20 8 58 96 122 234 228         351  - 28 38 78 98 98 176            472  - 16 44 136 104
235  - 20 12 16 56 96 122          352-353 - 28 38 78 98 176              473  - 16 44 104
         234 228                   354-358 - 28 38 78 98 98 176           474  - 16 28 44 44 104
236  - 20 20 56 96 234 228         359-364 - 28 38 78 98 176              475  - 16 126 104
237  - 20 20 56 96 98 234 228      365-366 - 28 40 78 98 98 176           476  - 16 22 30 40 104
238  - 20 20 58 96 234 228            367  - 28 40 46 78 98 98 146 176     477  - 9 30 60 146 104
239  - 20 12 46 58 96 112             368  - 28 40 78 98 98 176            478  - 26 46 104
         234 228                      369  - 28 40 78 98 176               479  - 9 30 44 104
240  - 20 44 58 96 230 234            370  - 28 40 78 98                   480  - 9 28 60 126 104
241  - 20 44 60 96 230 234         371-373 - 28 40 84 92                  481  - 16 28 40 60 104
242  - 20 60 96 122 230 234           374  - 28 40 46 84 92                482  - 16 26 30 46 136 104 126
243  - 20 60 96 230                   375  - 28 40 92 98                   483  - 16 30 44 46 104 126
244  - 22 24 60 96 230                376  - 28 40 98 98 98                484  - 16 40 46 104 126
245  - 22 60 96 126 230            377-379 - 28 40 98                     485  - 30 46 104 126
246  - 22 60 96 230                   380  - 28 30 40 98                   486  - 16 44 46 104 126
247  - 22 60 96 98 230 236         381-384 - 28 40 98                     487  - 16 37 40 112 104 126
248  - 22 26 36 60 96 230 236         385  - 28 40 46 98                   488  - 16 37 37 46 104 126
249  - 22 50 96 230 236               386  - 28 30 40 B&A 232              489  - 22 37 46 104 126
250  - 22 34 96 230 236               387  - 28 40 B&A 232                 490  - 28 46 46 104 126
251  - 22 36 96 112 118 118           388  - 28 40 40 B&A 232              491  - 16 37 46 46 104 126
         126 230 236                  389  - 28 36 40 B&A 232              492  - 16 38 46 46 104 126
252  - 22 96 118 230 236              390  - 28 50 B&A 232                 493  - 16 44 46 46 104 126
253  - 22 30 96 112 118 118        391-393 - 30 50 B&A 232                494  - 16 46 46 136 104 126
         126 230 236               394-400 - 30 42 B&A 232                495  - 16 30 46 46 136 104 126
254  - 22 80 118 230 236              401  - 30 34 42 50 B&A 232           496  - 16 30 44 46 46 68 104 126
255  - 22 26 96 98 118 230 236        402  - 30 40 B&A 232                 497  - 16 30 30 38 46 68 104 126
256  - 22 30 34 44 96 118          403-405 - 30 42 B&A 232                498  - 16 30 30 30 68 94 104 126
         230 236                      406  - 30 42 B&A 230                 499  - 16 30 30 44 50 68 104 126
257-259 - 22 36 46 96 230 236         407  - 30 42 36 B&A 230              500  - 16 30 30 30 44 58 62
260  - 22 37 96 146 230 236           408  - 30 42 60 B&A 230                     104 126
261  - 22 37 96 230 236            409-417 - 30 42 B&A 230              501-502 - 16 30 44 146 104
262  - 22 37 96 98 230 236            418  - 30 42 60 B&A 230              503  - 16 38 46 146 104
263  - 22 36 37 46 96 230 236      419 420 - 30 42 B&A 230                504  - 16 38 42 146 104
264  - 22 37 60 96 126 230 236        421  - 30 42 96 B&A 230              505  - 16 38 122 104
265  - 22 37 46 60 96 230 236         422  - 30 42 B&A 230                 506  - 9 38 112 122 104
266  - 22 37 46 60 92 96 98            423  - 30 42 62 B&A 230             507  - 9 38 42 122 104
         230 236                      424  - 30 42 46 230                 508  - 9 38 122 122 104
267  - 22 37 40 42 46 58 60        425-426 - 30 40 92 230                 509  - 9 38 40 122 104
         96 230 236                427 429 - 30 42 92 230                 510  - 9 46 46 122 104
268  - 22 28 58 96 230 236            428  - 30 40 92 230                 511  - 20 38 122 104
269  - 22 28 58 96 126 230 236        430  - 30 42 92 92 230              512  - 9 38 38 122 104
270  - 22 28 30 46 58 96 230 236      431  - 30 40 230                    513  - 30 60 118 122 104
271  - 22 28 60 96 230 236         432-436 - 30 42 230                    514  - 30 38 122 104
272  - 22 28 60 96 122 230 236        437  - 30 42 96 230 B&A          515-517 - 20 38 126 104
273  - 22 28 60 96 146 230 236        438  - 8 42 42 230 B&A               518  - 20 40 126 104
274-275 - 22 28 60 96 230 236         439  - 8 42 44 230 B&A               519  - 10 38 44 126 104
```

NYC&HR PREDECESSOR AND COMPONENT LINES

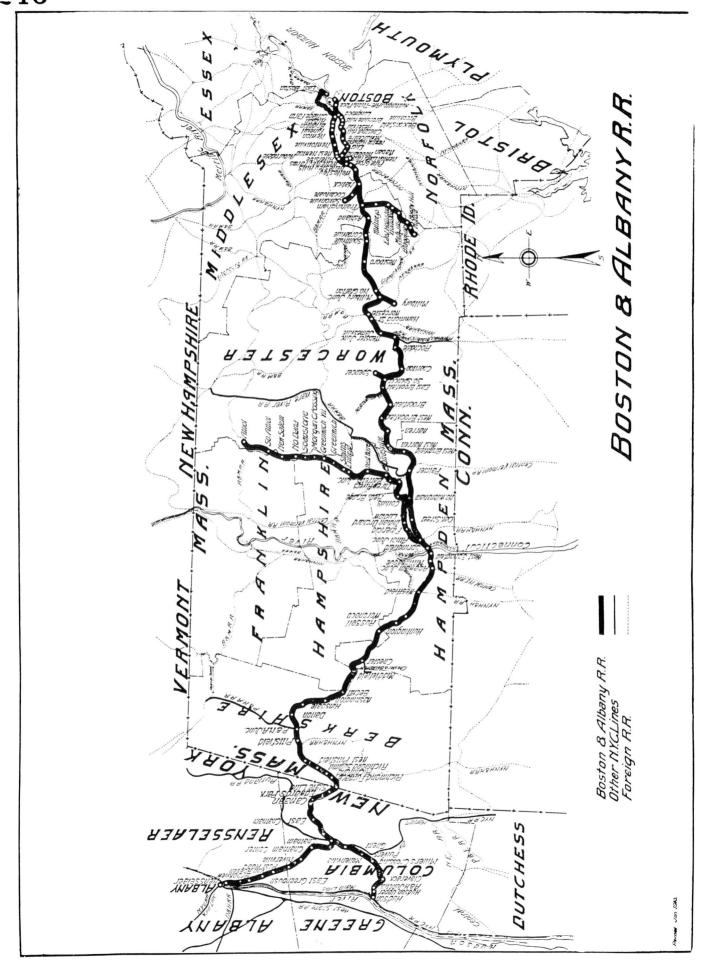

BOSTON & ALBANY R.R.

Boston & Albany R.R.
Other N.Y.C.Lines
Foreign R.R.

STEAM LOCOMOTIVES

OF THE

NEW YORK CENTRAL LINES

PART 2

BOSTON & ALBANY R.R.

248

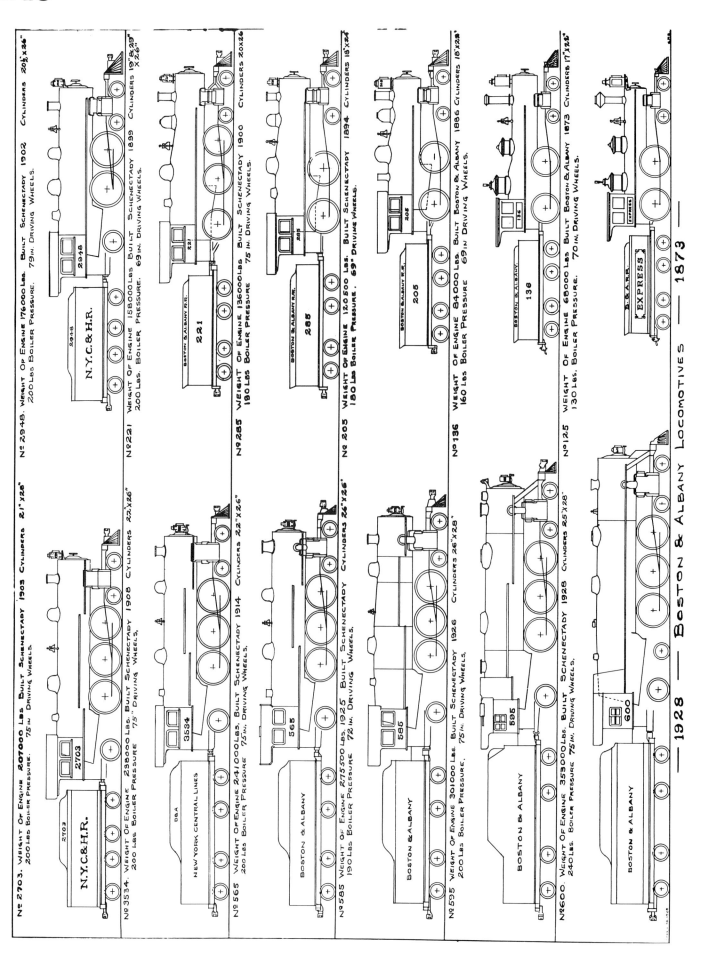

No.2703. Weight Of Engine 207000 Lbs. Built Schenectady 1903 Cylinders 21"x28" 200 Lbs Boiler Pressure. 75in. Driving Wheels.

No. 2948. Weight Of Engine 176000 Lbs. Built Schenectady 1902 Cylinders 20½"x26" 200 Lbs Boiler Pressure. 79in. Driving Wheels.

No.2221 Weight Of Engine 158000 Lbs Built Schenectady 1899 Cylinders 19"&29"X26" 200 Lbs. Boiler Pressure. 69 in. Driving Wheels.

No.285 Weight Of Engine 136000 Lbs. Built Schenectady 1900 Cylinders 20x26 180 Lbs Boiler Pressure 75 in. Driving Wheels.

No. 205 Weight Of Engine 120,500 Lbs. Built Schenectady 1894 Cylinders 18"x24 180 Lbs Boiler Pressure. 69" Driving Wheels.

No.136 Weight Of Engine 84000 Lbs. Built Boston & Albany 1886 Cylinders 18"x28" 160 Lbs Boiler Pressure 69 in. Driving Wheels.

No.125 Weight Of Engine 68000 Lbs. Built Boston & Albany 1873 Cylinders 17"x22" 130 Lbs. Boiler Pressure. 70in. Driving Wheels.

No. 3534. Weight Of Engine 238000 Lbs. Built Schenectady 1908 Cylinders 22"x26" 200 Lbs Boiler Pressure 75" Driving Wheels.

No. 565 Weight Of Engine 241000 Lbs. Built Schenectady 1914 Cylinders 22"x26" 200 Lbs Boiler Pressure 75in. Driving Wheels.

No.585 Weight Of Engine 275500 Lbs. Built Schenectady 1925 Cylinders 26"x26" 190 Lbs Boiler Pressure 72 in. Driving Wheels.

No.595 Weight Of Engine 301000 Lbs. Built Schenectady 1926 Cylinders 26"x28" 200 Lbs Boiler Pressure. 75in. Driving Wheels.

No.600. Weight Of Engine 353000 Lbs. Built Schenectady 1928 Cylinders 25"x28" 240 Lbs. Boiler Pressure 75in. Driving Wheels.

— 1928 — Boston & Albany Locomotives — 1873 —

LOCOMOTIVES OF THE BOSTON & ALBANY

Contents

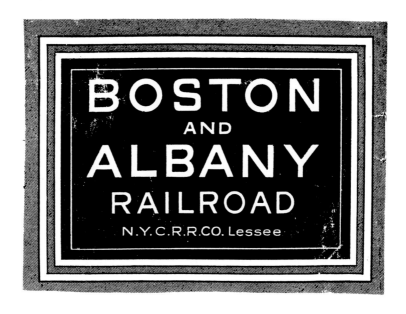

250

BOSTON & WORCESTER (1832-1868)

Note: Names only were used until after 1860, when numbers also were assigned.

B&W Name & No.	Re'67	Type	Builder	c/n	Date	Cyl.	Dr.	Wt.	Disposition
Meteor		2-2-0	R.Steph.	26	1832	10x14	48	-	So'35 Ban.& Pis. (a)
Boston (not used)		"	"	27	"	12x16	60	- (b)	So'34 Alleg. Portage
Meteor (0-4-0?)		"	"	107	4/34	11x16	54	16000	dr'39
Col.Long (for test)		"	Long & Norris		1834				So'34 Bos.& Prov. (c)
Yankee		"	Mill Dam Fdry		7/34				Sc'47
Camel		0-4-0	R.Steph.	143	1/35	10x16	54	20000	So'45 Old Colony (f)
Rocket		"	"	144	5/35	"	"	"	dr'47 (Notes e,f)
Mercury		"	"	120	7/35	"	"	"	Sc'45 (f)
Jupiter		"	"	121	8/35	"	"	"	Sc'45 (f)
Lion		2-2-0	Bury(Eng)	32	1/36	11x16	60	24000	RB'47 4-2-0 "Brookline"
William Penn		4-2-0	Baldwin	25	4/36				So'44 Fitchburg RR
Lowell		2-2-0	Locks & Canals		6/36	11x16	60		So'58 Midland RR "Baring"
Elephant		4-2-0	Baldwin	71	4/37				dr'47
Tartar		"	"	155	7/39				dr'50
Meteor		2-2-0	Locks & Canals		1/40	11x16	60	16000	So'50 Marietta & Cinc.(d)
Mars		4-2-0	R.Norris	108	6/40				dr'51?
Vulcan		"	"	118	7/40				So 11/50 Rut.& Burl.
Buffalo			Locks & Canals		/41				dr c'64
Boston		4-2-0	Baldwin	166	11/41				dr'55
Worcester		"	"	168	12/41				dr'54
Tiger		0-4-0	Hinkley	6	7/42	13x20	48	30000	So'49 R&B "Whiting"
Leopard		"	"	13	3/43	"	"	"	Later 2-2-2? Dr'60-63
Panther		0-8-0	"	16	6/43	13x20	36	44000	So 4/62 U.S.Military RR
Camel		"	"	26	9/44	"	"	"	dr'60
Mercury		4-4-0	"	37	3/45	14x18	66	36000	So'59 Hinkley
Jupiter	40 (149)	"	"	39	4/45	"	"	"	dr'68-69
Comet	37 (146)	"	"	58	3/46	"	"	"	dr'66-67
Ajax	1 110	"	"	60	4/46	15x20	54	46000	dr'68-72
Hercules	2 111	"	"	64	6/46	"	"	"	dr'68-77
Rocket	41 (150)	"	"	94	3/47	15x18	66	44000	dr'68-69 (note e)
Neptune	4 113	"	"	96	"	"	"	"	dr'68-77
William Penn	6 (115)	"	"	107	6/47	"	"	"	dr'68-69
Yankee	5	"	"	108	"	"	"	"	dr'68
Elephant	3 112	"	"	112	7/47	16x20	54	48000	dr'68-74
Brookline (g)	7	4-2-0	RB fr "Lion"		/47	11x16	60	24000	So'67 Port.& Kenn. 18
Vesuvius	11 120	4-4-0	B&W shops		/48	16x20	60	50000	dr'68-70
Hecla	8 117	"	" "		/49	16x20	54	50000	dr'68-78
Aetna		"	Wilmarth		/48	"	"	"	dr'63
Niagara	9 118	"	"		"	"	"	"	dr'68-75
Bee	10 119	"	"		"	"	"	" 44000	dr'62-71
Bison		"	"		"	"	"	" "	dr'60
Falcon	36 (145)	"	"		/49	15x18	66	44000	dr'68-69
Fury	43 (152)	"	"		"	"	"	"	dr'68-70
Carroll of Carrollton		4-2-4	Ross Winans		10/49	17x22	84	50000	returned '56
D.Henshaw	12 121	4-4-0	Wilmarth		/51	16x20	66	48000	dr'68-73
Nathan Hale	13 122	"	"		"	"	"	"	dr'68-74

Note a - Re Bangor & Piscataquis "Pioneer".   Note b - Rebuilt by Mill Dam Foundry.
Note c - Re Boston & Providence "Black Hawk". Note d - Re Mar.& Cinti. "Thomas James"
Note e - Perhaps RB'47, so 8/52 to Aurora Branch RR. Note f - Perhaps 14x16.
Note g - RB to 4-2-2 "Z.E.Coffin".

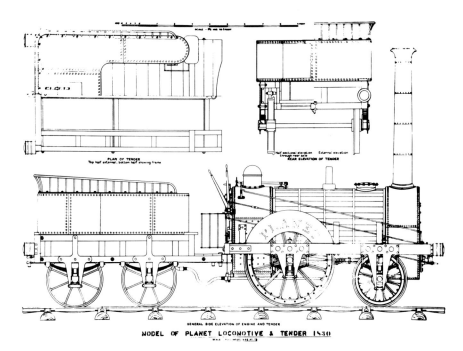

B&W METEOR is believed to have been similar to the English PLANET. (Science Museum London)

B&W VULCAN as built by William Norris about 1843.   (A.F.Stauter collection)

B&W NATHAN HALE was built by a small Boston builder, Seth Wilmarth, in 1851. (Purinton).

BOSTON & WORCESTER: Additions 1854-1868

B&W Name & No.		Re'68	Re'93	Type	Builder	c/n	Date	Cyl. Dr. Weight	Disposition
Worcester	14	123	229	4-4-0	Mason	6	4/54	14x22-72-54000	dr'93-95 (note b)
Tiger	15	124		"	Hinkley	519	5/54	15x24-60-50000	dr'68-76
Boston (d)	17	126		"	"	576	10/55	14x22-54-50000	dr'68-75
Mexico (e)				"	Lowell	144	/56	12x18- 28000	So'60 NY&Bos."Bflo"
Express	16	125		"	B&W Shops		?58?	16x21-72-56000	dr by'76
Despatch (a)	18	127		"	" "		"	" " " "	dr by'77
Camel	19	128		"	Taunton	269	12/59	15x22-60-50000	So'68-81 Nan.Beach 4
Bison	20	129		"	Mason	96	5/60	" " 52000	So by'81 Nan.Beach 5
Meteor (f)	21	130		"	(Port.63 '54)		acq'61	14x22-66-44000	dr'68-69
Leopard	22	131		0-4-0	Hinkley	681	/62	15x20-54-40000	dr by'75
Panther	23	132		4-4-0	"	684	/63	15x24-60-52000	dr by'82
Lion	24	133		"	"	695	"	" " " "	dr by'79
Aetna	25	134		"	"	694	"	" " " "	dr by'83
Mars	26	135		"	Mason	147	12/63	16x22-66-56000	dr by'88
Mercury	27	136		"	"	154	3/64	" " " "	dr by'84
Buffalo	28	137		0-4-0	Hinkley	750	/65	12x22-54-36000	dr by'83 (RB 13x22-48)
Vulcan	29	138	238	4-4-0	Mason	218	11/65	16x22-66-56000	dr'93-95
Union	30	139		"	"	219	12/65	" " " "	Sc 6/90
Atlas	31	140	240	"	"	237	8/66	" 60 "	dr'93-95
Victor (g)	32	141	141	"	"	244	12/66	" " "	dr'93-95
Hero	33	142		"	"	256	4/67	" 66 "	So 5/90
Titan	34	143		0-4-0	"	249	3/67	14x22-48-46000	dr by'87 (RB 16x24)
Pacific	35	144		4-4-0	"	271	9/67	16x22-60-56000	dr by'89
Yankee (2nd)	5	114	114	"	B&A Shops		/68	" " 60000	dr'93-95
Brookline "	7	116		"	" "		/68	" " " "	So by'80 Nan.Beach

WESTERN RR (of Massachusetts) 1839-1868

Note: Names only used until after 1860, when numbers were also assigned. After 1867, when the Boston & Albany was formed, the same numbers were used, without change.

		Type	Builder		Date	Cyl. Dr. Weight	Disposition
Hampden		2-2-0	Locks & Can.		9/39	12x18-54-20000	So'48
Berkshire		"	"	"	"	" " " "	So'48
Hampshire		"	"	"	10/39	" " " "	So 6/47 Cheshire RR
Worcester		"	"	"	11/39	" " " "	dr'59
Suffolk		"	"	"	12/39	" " " "	So'51 Cleve.& Pitts.
Franklin	20	"	"	"	1/40	" " " "	Sc'61
Norfolk		"	"	"	6/41	" " " "	So'51 Akron Branch RR
Middlesex		"	"	"	"	" " " "	dr'61-67
Plymouth		"	"	"	"	" " " "	So'59 Conn.& Pass.R.
Bristol		"	"	"	7/41	" " " "	So'47 Calais RR
Barnstable		"	"	"	3/42	" " " "	So'59
Essex		"	"	"	"	" " " "	So 9/52 Rut.& Wash.
Massachusetts	4 (c)	4-4-0	"	"	11/40	14x18-54-40000	Sc'63
New York	1	"	"	"	1/42	" " " "	Sc'67
Rhode Island	2	"	"	"	2/42	" " " "	Sc'67

Note a - Temporary Name "Prince of Wales". Note b - RB'66 to 15x22-60-56000.
Note c - Renamed "Euxine". Note d - Built for Michigan Central.
Note e - Renamed "Lowell."   Note f - Ex-NY&B. Note g - Renamed "Z.E.Coffin".

WRR MASSACHUSETTS, built by Lowell in 1840. Retouched daguerreotype of 1841. (T.Norrell)

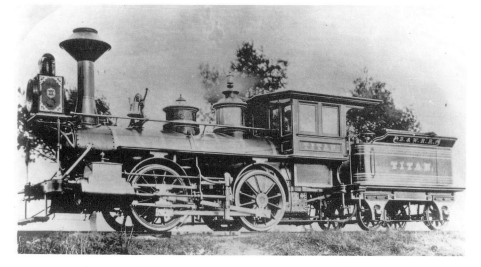

B&W TITAN, a Mason product of 1867. It soon became B&A 143.   (Norton D. Clark)

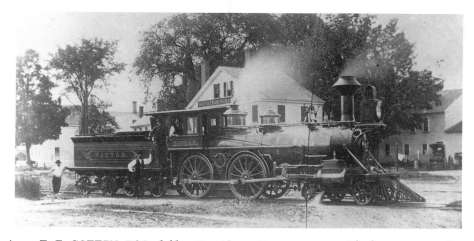

B&W VICTOR, later Z.E.COFFIN B&A 141. Another Mason post-Civil War engine. (Purinton 316)

WESTERN RR - Continued. Additions 1841-1848

WRR Name	No.	Type	Builder	c/n	Date	Cyl.	Driv.	Wt.	to A&WS	Disposition
Chatham (Note d)		?	Ross Winans		9/41			20000		Sc'48
Stockbridge (Note d)		?	" "		"			"		Sc'49
Maryland		0-8-0	" "		"	14+x24		44000		Sc'47
Michigan		"	" "		12/41	"		"		Sc'47
Illinois		"	" "		2/42	"		"		Sc'49
Ohio		"	" "		2/42	"		"		Sc'47
Arkansas		"	Baldwin	175	4/42	"		"		Sc'49
Indiana		"	"	178	5/42	"		"		Sc'49
Missouri		"	"	179	6/42	"		"		Sc'49
Albany re Switcher (e)	60	?	Wm.Norris		1842	12x	-44-	30000		dr'68-71 (c)
Philadelphia	32	?	" "		"	12+x20-	48-	40000	8/52	dr'68-77
Boston (ex 0-4-0)	30	0-4-2	Hinkley	15	4/43	15x20-	48-	32000	12/46	Sc'66
St.Louis	14	4-4-0	"	17	7/43	13+x20-	60-	30000		dr'68-71
Cincinnati		"	"	19	9/43	"	"	"		So'51
Atlantic		0-6-0	Baldwin	205	9/44	16+x18-	46-	40000		Sc'54
Pacific		"	"	206	10/44	"	"	"		Sc'54
United States		"	"	207	"	"	"	"		Sc'58
Springfield		4-4-0	Hinkley	49	8/45	13+x20-	60-	30000		So'51 CC&C
Pittsfield		"	"	72	8/46	"	"	"		So'58
Washington		"	"	74	9/46	"	"	"		So'51 CC&C
Huron		0-6-0	Baldwin	270	10/46	16+x18-	46-	40000	7/51	Sc'58
Superior		"	"	271	"	"	"	"		Sc'58
Vermont re Adriatic	5	4-4-0	Hinkley	69	7/46	16x20-	54-	40000	11/46	dr'68-73
Maine	24	"	"	71	8/46	"	"	"	10/46	dr'68-70
Connecticut	6	"	"	79	10/46	15x20-	"	"	12/46	dr'68-73
Virginia	11	"	"	81	11/46	16x20	"	"	12/46	dr'68-76
Kentucky	8	"	"	84	12/46	"	"	"		dr'68-76
Tennessee	9	"	"	85	"	"	"	"		dr'68-78
Louisiana	22	"	"	99	4/47	"	"			dr'68-74
Iowa	21	"	"	100	5/47	"	"			dr'68-70
Wisconsin	36	"	"	101	"	"	"			dr'68-74
Buffalo	10	"	"	102	"	"	"	"		dr'68-71
Detroit	18	"	"	103	"	"	"	"	6/47	dr'68-69
Delaware	17	"	"	104	"	"	"	"		dr'68-70
Mississippi	25	"	"	128	10/47	"	"	. "		dr'68-69
Pennsylvania	33	"	"	129	"	"	"			dr'68-69
New Jersey re Fulton?	3	(d)"	"	130	11/47	"	"	"	11/47	dr'68-76
South Carolina	35	"	"	140	"	"	"	28000	12/47	dr'68-74
North Carolina (b)	34	"	"	133	12/47	"	"			dr by'67
Ontario re Marmora	39	"	Taunton	8	2/48	"	"	40000		dr'68-76
Champlain		"	"	9	"	"	"	"		So'58
Erie	38	"	"	12	3/48	"	"	"		dr'68-70
St.Clair	42	"	"	13	5/48	"	"	"		dr'68-72
ST.Lawrence	40	"	"	14	"	"	"	"	by'56	dr'68-76
Providence	41	"	"	16	6/48	"	"	"	by'56	dr'68-71
Niagara	43	"	"	19	8/48	"	"	"		dr'68-69
Concord		"	"	20	"	"	"	"		dr by'66
Augusta		"	"	22	9/48	"	"	"	by'56	dr by'60
Nantucket		"	"	23	10/48	"	"	"		dr by'63

Note b - re Richmond. Note c - to H&B 12/54.   Note d - Blt. for Balto. & Port Deposit
Note e - on H&B 10/57.

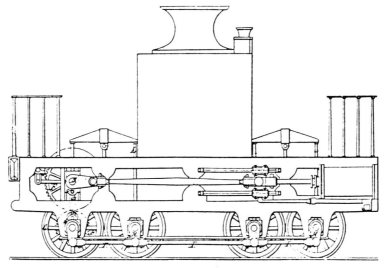

WRR "Mud Digger type, as built by Ross Winans in 1842. Crank and gear drive. (Staufer)

B&W UNION #30, as built by Mason in 1865. Later B&A 139.   (Norton D. Clark)

B&A 137, formerly B&W BUFFALO, from Hinkley in 1865.   (Purinton 57)

WESTERN RR - Continued. Additions 1847-1866:

WRR Name	No.	Type	Builder	c/n	Date	Cyl. Dr. Wt.	to A&WS	Disposition
Greylock re Tobey	44 (b)	4-4-0	Hinkley	98	4/47	14x18-60-40000		dr'68-76
Chicago re Beebe	15	"	"	145	1/48	16x20-60-40000		dr'68-76
Florida	7	"	"	146	2/48	14x18-54-40000	2/48	dr'68-76
Indianapolis	12	"	"	148	"	16x20-60-40000	"	dr'68-71
Nashville	27	"	"	149	"	" " "		dr'68-77
Georgia	19	"	"	150	"	" " "		dr'68-74
New Orleans	31	"	"	152	"	" " "		dr by'67
Louisville	23	"	"	155	3/48	" " "	3/48	dr'68-69
Hampshire re Richmond	20 (c)	"	"	156	"	" " "		dr'68
Columbus	16	"	"	157	"	" " "		dr'68-71
Alabama	37	"	"	159	"	" 54 "		dr'68-71
New Hampshire	29	"	"	166	4/48	" " "	5/48	dr'68-70
New England	28	"	"	171	5/48	" " "		dr'68-70
Montreal re Shaker	26	"	"	201	9/48	" 60 "		dr'68-78
Bristol	13	"	"	209	11/48	15x22-60-40000	yes	dr'68-69
Addison Gilmore	45 (d)	"	WRR Shops		1851	15+x26-72-40000		dr'68-79
Whistler	46	"	" "		1852	16+x22-72-40000		dr'68-81
Wales	47	"	" "		1854	" " "		dr'68-83
Cleveland	57	"	Lowell	119	1853	16x22-66-50000	7/54	So '60
California	54	"	"	120	"	" 54 "		dr'68
Texas	56	"	"	121	"	" " "		dr'68-69
Oregon	55	"	"	122	"	" " "		dr'68-73
San Francisco	61 (f)	"	Taunton	170	7/54	16x20-72-50000	10/54	dr'68-77
Olympus	50	"	Mason	13	1/55	15x22-72-50000		dr'68-80
Apollo	48	"	"	14	"	" " "		dr'68-73
Sonora	53	"	"	15	2/55	" " "		dr'68-83
Nevada	49	"	"	16	1/55	" " "		dr'68-81
Saranak	52	"	"	19	5/55	" " "	5/55	dr'68-81
Panama	51	"	"	20	"	" " "	"	dr'68-83
Albany	62	"	Bemis (Sprfld)		/57	16x26-60-54000		dr'68-73
Pacific re Baltic	64	"	"	"	"	" " "		RB'58,So'90
Atlantic	65	"	"	"	"	" " "		dr c'86
Henry Gray (g)	72	"	"	"	"	" " "		RB'63,dr'68-85
Alger "	59	"	"	"	"	" " "		dr'68-79
Henry Waterman "	58 (e)	"	(Amos.8/53) acq.'56			15x22-66-40000		dr'68-80
Bliss	63	"	WRR Shops		1857	15+x26-72-50000		dr'68-82
Swift	68	"	" "		1858	16+x22-72-40000		dr'68-84
Champlain	66	"	" "		1859	16x26-60-50000		So 5/90
Superior	67	"	" "			" " " "		So 6/90
Dwight	69	"	" "		1860	16+x22-72-50000		dr'68-83
Massachusetts	70	"	" "		1861	16x26-60-54000		Sc 3/90
Huron	71	"	" "		1862	" " "		So 8/90
Chapin	73	"	" "		1864	16+x22-72-54000		dr'68-84
Springfield	74	"	" "		1865	" " "		dr'68-83
Worcester	75	"	" "			" " " "		dr'68-84
Pittsfield	76	"	" "		"	16x26-60-54000		dr c'88
Nantucket	77	"	" "		1868	" " "		dr c'88

Note b - Ordered by Pitts.& N.Adams.   Note c -   #20 re'63 to Franklin.   Note g - On H&B
Note d - Built as 4-2-2 with 81"drivers, 51000 wt.   Note e - Ex Housatonic RR Taghonic
Note f - Renamed Cummings. Built as Southbridge & Blackstone RR Henry M.Holbrook.

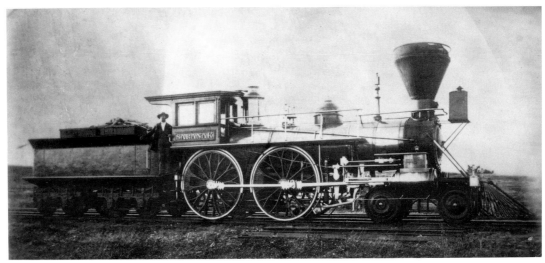

WRR SARANAK, delivered in 1855 by Mason.   Later numbered 52.   (Purinton 117)

WRR SUPERIOR, one of the first "Eddy Clocks", built in company shops 1859. (Purinton 108)

WRR ATLANTIC #65, built at Springfield in 1857.   (Purinton 109)

WESTERN RR - Continued. Additions 1865-1868:

WRR Name	No.	Type	Builder, c/n, Date			Cyl. Dr. Wt.			Disposition
Minnesota	78	4-4-0	WRR Shops		1865	16x26-60-54000			So 5/90
Colorado	79	"	" "		1866	"	"	"	So 5/90
Concord	80	"	" "		"	"	"	"	So 5/90
Montana	81	"	" "		"	"	"	"	dr c.86
Dacotah	82	"	" "		"	"	"	"	dr c.90
Arizona	83	"	" "		"	"	"	"	dr c.80
Greenbush	84	"	Mason	242	10/66	16x24-60-50000			dr c.88
Chatham	85	"	"	243	"	"	"	"	dr c.88
Geo.H.Power	86	"	Taunton	392	"	"	"	"	dr c.82
Hudson	87	"	"	395	11/66	"	"	"	dr c.83
Idaho	88	"	WRR Shops		1866	16x26-60-58000			So 5/90
Nebraska	89	"	" "		"	"	"	"	So 5/90
Michigan	90	"	" "		1867	"	"	"	So 5/90
Maryland	91	"	" "		"	"	"	"	dr c.87
Sampson	92	0-4-0	Hinkley		1867	15x22-48-44000			dr c.88
Goliath	93	"	"	813	"	"	"	"	dr'91
Ohio	94	4-4-0	"	817	"	16x24-60-64000			dr c.86
Illinois	95	"	"	807	"	"	"	"	dr c.85
Missouri	96	"	WRR Shops		"	16x26-60-58000			So 5/90
Indiana	97	"	" "		"	"	"	"	dr'68-78
Arkansas	98	"	" "		"	"	"	"	So 5/90
Alaska	99	"	" "		"	"	"	"	So 5/90
Suffolk	100	"	Grant	494	"	16x24-60-58000			dr c.83
Middlesex	101	"	"	495	"	"	"	"	dr c.84
Hampden	102	"	"	496	"	"	"	"	dr c.84
Berkshire	103	"	"	497	"	"	"	"	dr c.84
New York (2nd)	1	"	WRR Shops		"	16x26-60-58000			dr c.84
New Orleans "	31 (b)	"	" "		"	"	"		dr c.87
Richmond "	34 (b)	"	" "		"	"	"		dr c.87
Rhode Island "	2 (b)	"	" "		1868	"	"	60000	So 6/90
Franklin "	20 (b)	"	" "		"	"	"	"	dr c.93
New Jersey "	30 (b)	"	" "		"	"	"		dr c.85
California "	54 (b)	"	" "		"	"	"		RT'86

HUDSON & BERKSHIRE (1838-1855) and HUDSON & BOSTON (1855-1867)

		Type	Builder, c/n, Date			Cyl. Dr. Wt.			Disposition
Hudson		4-2-0	Norris		1838	10+x18			dr by 9/56
Berkshire		"	"		"	"			dr by 9/56
Pittsfield		"	"		"	"			dr by 9/56
New York		"	"		"	"			dr by 9/56
Chatham		"	"		"	"			dr by 9/56
Adams (Note c)		4-4-0	(Rogers	54	5/44)	11+x22-64			
Albany	(Ex - ?)	"		Acq.12/54		12+	-48		dr'57
James Mellen	(Ex - ?)	"		"	"	13	-54		dr'58-59
Chas.C.Alger	(Ex - ?)	"		"	"	14	-54		dr'57

On H&B 12/57: WRR #3, 58, 59, 60, 72.

Note b - Placed in service by the new B&A RR.
Note c - Acquired by 1849 from N.Y.Providence & Boston RR "Reformer".

LOCOMOTIVES OF THE BOSTON & ALBANY

In September, 1867 the WESTERN RR and the BOSTON & WORCESTER
consolidated to form the BOSTON & ALBANY. During the year that
followed, the locomotive rosters of the two former roads were
combined. WRR engines numbered 1 through 103 became B&A 1 - 103.
Six more engines then on order became B&A 104-109. B&W 1 - 35
became 110 - 144.

During the next 25 years, as older engines were retired their
road numbers were reassigned to new engines, along with higher
numbers which eventually reached 260 by the time of a general
renumbering in 1893. Only seven years later another renumbering
took place, as a result of leasing the B&A to the New York
Central & Hudson River. A final renumbering occurred in 1912,
when the B&A once again adopted its own numbering scheme.

B&A 159, named D.W.LINCOLN when built in 1870. Drawing by H.M.C.Skinner, Fall River, 1874.

B&A 188, formerly MARIPOSA, built 1871 with typical suare sand box.   (Purinton 179)

BOSTON & ALBANY – Additions 1868-1871:

B&A Name and No.		Re'93	Type	Builder	c/n	Date	Cyl. Driv. Wt.	Disposition
Putnam	104		4-4-0	B&A Shops		1868	16x26-60-60000	So 6/90
Washington	105		"	" "		"	" " "	So 6/90
Plymouth	106		"	" "		"	" 66	dr c.85
Norfolk	107		"	" "		"	16+x22-66-60000	dr c.93
Wyoming	108		"	" "		"	16x26-60-60000	Sc 7/90
Brookfield	109	209	"	" "		1869	" " "	dr c.94
Falcon	145		0-4-0	Hinkley	877	"	14x22-48-44000	dr'91
Comet	146		"	"	894	"	" " "	dr'91
Pony	147		"	"	895	"	15x22 " "	Sc c.89
Barnstable	148		4-4-0	B&A Shops		"	16+x22-66-60000	RT c.86
Essex	149		"	" "		"	" " "	dr c.85
Texas	56		"	Rhode Is. 99		4/69	16x24-60-60000	dr c.88
Detroit	18		"	" "	100	"	" " "	dr c.81
G.Twitchell	150		"	" "	118	7/69	17x22-66	RB'81 – See below
Cochituate	151		"	" "	119	7/69	" "	" " "
Hinsdale	152		2-6-0	Hinkley	916	1869	17x24-48-56000	RT c.88
Dalton	153		"	"	917	"	" " "	dr c.87
Westfield	154		4-4-0	B&A Shops		"	16x26-60-60000	Sc c.90
Chester	155		"	" "		"	" "	dr c.86
Russel	156		"	" "		"	" " "	Sc 10/90
Bristol	13		"	" "		"	" " "	So 5/90
Louisville	23		"	" "		"	" "	dr c.85
Mississippi	25		"	" "		"	" "	dr c.86
Pennsylvania	33		"	" "		"	" " 60000	So 5/90
Palmer	43		"	" "		"	" "	dr c.86
W.Penn	115	255	"	" "		"	16x22-66-60000	dr c.96
Meteor	130	278	"	" "		"	" " "	dr c.96
Delaware	17		"	" "		1870	16x26-60-66000	Sc 5/90
Iowa	21	215	"	" "		"	" " "	dr'93-94
Main	24		"	" "		"	" " "	So 5/90
New England	28		"	" "		"	" " "	Sc 7/90
Hampshire	29	207	"	" "		"	" " 64000	dr'93-94
Erie	38		"	" "		"	" " "	dr c'89
Cleveland	57	257	"	" "		"	" " 60000	dr c'96
Vesuvius	120	20	0-4-0	Rhode I. 179		10/70	14x22-48-44000	dr c'94
Jupiter	157		4-4-0	B&A Shops		1869	16x22-60-60000	dr c'89
Rocket	158		0-4-0	Hinkley 939		1870	14x22-48-44000	So 1/91 Ludlow Mfg.Co.
D.W.Lincoln	159	271	4-4-0	B&A Shops		"	17x22-60-68000	Sc 6/07 (Note a)
Huntington	160		"	" "		1869	16x26-60-60000	So 8/90 J.Stewart
Shawmut	161		"	" "		1870	16+x22-66-60000	dr'91-93
James Parker	162		"	" "		"	" " "	dr'93
Fury	163	163	"	" "		"	16x22-60-60000	dr c'99
Wm.Bliss (b)	164	264	"	" "		1871	17x22-66-68000	So 11/06 Coats & Ben.
Charlton	165		"	" "		1870	16x26-60	dr c'90
Adams	166		"	" "		"	" "	Sc 1/90
Becket	167		"	" "		"	" "	dr c'87
Trojan	12		0-4-0	Hinkley		1871	15x22-48-44000	dr'91-93
Agawam	14		"	"		"	" " "	Sc 5/90
Pusher	60		"	"		"	" " "	Sc 7/90

Note a – 271 re'00 to 1216, class C-33a.   Note b – 264 re'00 to 1215, class C-33.

B&A PUTNAM #104, another Eddy Clock built 1868   (Purinton collection)

B&A WILBRAHAM, an Eddy Clock of 1871. Note absence of steam dome.   (Purinton 61)

B&A 16, an Eddy Clock of 1871. The name COLUMBUS is gone, and tender side is blank.(P.113)

BOSTON & ALBANY - Continued. Additions 1871-1872:

B&A Name and No.	Re'93	Re'00	Class	Type	Builder	c/n	Date	Cyl, Dr. Wt.	Disposition.
Vermont	10			4-4-0	B&A Shops		1871	16x26-60-60000	Sc'88-89
Columbus	16			"	" " "		"	" " " "	dr by'93
Middlefield	37			"	" " "		"	" " " "	So 5/90
Providence	41			"	" " "		"	" " " "	dr by'87
Bee	119			"	" " "		"	16x22-60 "	So 7/89 (c)
Wilbraham	168			"	" " "		"	16x26-60 "	dr by'93
Lebanon	169			"	Hinkley		"	16x24-60	dr by'82
Stanwix	170			"	"		"	" "	dr by'86
Delavan	171			"	"		"	" "	dr by'84
Warren	172			"	B&A Shops		"	16x26-60-60000	dr.by'93
Newton	173			"	Mason	402	4/71	" " " "	So 4/90 (b)
Natick	174	131		"	"	403	5/71	16x22 " "	dr'93-95
Alabama	175			"	B&A Shops		1871	16x26-60	dr by'86
Spencer	176			"	" " "		"	" " 60000	dr by'93
Brimfield	177			"	" " "		"	" "	dr by'86
Rochdale	178			"	" " "		"	" " "	So 3/91 Stewart
Allston	179			0-4-0	Hinkley 1024		"	14x22-48-44000	So 11/90 (a)
Brighton	180	101		2-6-0	B&A Shops		"	17x24-60-68000	Sc 11/98
	181								
Tatham	182			2-6-0	Rhode I. 319		"	17x24-54-68000	Sc 9/90
Tekoa	183			"	" 320		"	" " "	dr by'89
Onota	184			"	" 321		"	" " "	Sc 8/90
Globe	185			"	" 322		"	" " "	dr by'87
Luna	186			"	" 323		"	" " "	dr by'88
Juno	187			"	" 324		"	" " "	dr by'88
Mariposa	188			4-4-0	B&A Shops		"	17+x22-66-66000	dr by'93
Utah	189			"	" " "		"	16x26-60-60000	So 6/90
Ajax	110			"	" " "		1872	16x22-60	dr by'88
St.Clair	42			"	" " "		"	18x22-54-66000	So'90 Stewart
Ashland	190	258		"	" " "		"	16x22-50-60000	Sc 7/99
Cunard	191			0-4-0	Hinkley 1084		"	14x22-48-44000	So 2/90
Advance	192			4-4-0	B&A Shops		"	17x26-60-66000	Sc 7/90
Wm.Jackson	193			"	" " "		"	" " "	So'90 Stewart
Westboro	194	276	1225	Cx	" " "		"	16x22-60-60000	Sc 4/07
Framingham	195	272		"	" " "		"	" "	Sc 7/01
DeGrand	196	164		"	" " "		"	17x26-54-66000	dr by'99
Onward	197			"	" " "		"	18x22-54-66000	dr'91-92
Kinderhook	198			"	" " "		"	" " "	dr'93
Schodack	199			"	" " "		"	" " "	dr'91-92
Grantville	200	200	1209	C-32	"	Rhode I. 418	6/72	17x24-60-64000	Sc 4/07
Wellesley	201	201	(1210)	"	"	" 419	"	" " "	Sc 9/00
St.Louis	202			"	B&A Shops		1872	18x22-54-66000	dr'93
St.Lawrence	203			"	" " "		"	18x24-54-66000	Sc 9/90
Stockbridge	204			"	" " "		"	" " "	RT'93
Saxonville	205	205		"	" " "		"	16x22-60-60000	dr'93-94
Arctic	206			"	" " "		"	17x26-54-66000	RT'93
Antarctic	207			"	" " "		"	" " "	So 5/91 Stewart

Note a - to Glen Mfg. Co.   Note b - to Grafton & Upton 2   .Note c - to G&U 1

B¢A 195 was named FRAMINGHAM when built in company shops in 1872.   (Purinton 91)

B&A CUNARD, later #191, one of a handful of switchers built by Hinkley.   (Purinton 55)

Rhode Island built a pair of 8-wheelers like #200, the GRANTVILLE.   (Purinton 92)

BOSTON & ALBANY - Continued. Additions 1872-1874:

B&A Name and No.		Re'93	Re'00	Type	Builder,c/n,Date			Cyl. DD Wt.	Disposition
Active	208	8		0-4-0	Rh.Is.	479	12/72	14x24-48-44000	dr by'94
Alert	209	9		"	"	480	"	" " "	dr by'94
Grafton (a)	210	255		4-4-0	"	477	11/72	16x24-60-64000	Sc 2/01
Millbury (a)	211	257	1220 C-32	"	"	478	"	" " "	So 10/06 (c)
Nonantum	212	212		"	B&A Shops		1873	16x22-60-60000	dr'93-96
Oceanica	213			"	"	"	1872	17x26-54-66000	dr'91-92
Dukes	214	214		"	"	"	"	" " "	dr'93
Adriatic	5			"	"	"	1873	" " 68000	dr'91-92
Connecticut	6			"	"	"	"	" " "	So 3/91 Stewart
Caspian	48			"	"	"	"	" " "	dr'91-92
Oregon	55			"	"	"	"	" " "	dr'91-93
Albany	62	62		"	"	"	"	" " "	dr'91-94
D.Henshaw	121	216		"	"	"	"	16x22-66-60000	dr'93-95
Massasoit	215			"	"	"	"	17x26-54-66000	dr'91-92
Mexico	216			"	"	"	"	" " 68000	So 5/91 Stewart
Tremont	217	217		"	"	"	"	17x26-66-66000	dr'91-95
Olcott	218	218		"	"	"	"	" " "	dr'91-95
Greene	219	119	1842 Ex	2-6-0	Rh.Is.	524	4/73	17x24-54-68000	Sc 11/01
Penfield	220			"	"	525	"	" " "	Sc 4/91
Purves	221	116		"	"	528	5/73	18x26-54-70000	dr'93-94
Babcock	222	122		"	"	529	"	" " "	dr'93-94
Catskill	223			4-4-0	B&A Shops	"	"	" " 68000	So 5/91 Stewart
Adirondack	224			"	"	"	"	" , "	dr'91-93
Malta	225			0-4-0	"	"	"	14x24-48-44000	dr by'93
Wachusett (b)	226	226	1211 C-33	4-4-0	"	"	"	17x22-66-68000	Sc 2/07
Matson	227	127		2-6-0	Rh.Is.	619	8/73	18x26-54-70000	dr'93-95
Allen	228	135		"	"	620	"	" " "	dr'93-95
Morris	229	123		"	"	621	9/73	" " "	dr'93-95
Brown	230	126		"	"	622	"	" " "	dr'93-95
Caribbean	231			4-4-0	B&A Shops	"	"	17x26-54-68000	dr'91-93
Stickney	232			"	"	"	"	18x22-66-68000	dr'91-93
Denny	233			"	"	"	"	" " "	dr'91-93
Java	234	34		0-4-0	"	"	"	14x22-48-44000	So 12/95 (d)
Georgia	19			4-4-0	"	"	1874	18x26-60-68000	dr'91-93
Louisiana	22			"	"	"	"	" " "	dr'93
So.Carolina	35			"	"	"	"	" " "	dr'91
Wisconsin	36			"	"	"	"	" " "	So 3/91 Stewart
Elephant	112	12		0-4-0	"	"	"	14x24-48-44000	So'00 G.H.Keys
N.Hale	122	222		4-4-0	"	"	"	16x22-60-60000	dr'93-95
Parthia	235	6		0-4-0	"	"	"	14x24-48-44000	Sc 4/00
Cuba	236	36		"	"	"	"	" " "	dr'93-94
China	237	7		"	"	"	"	" " "	dr'93-94
Tuscan	238			4-4-0	"	"	"	18x26-60-68000	dr'91-92
Colt	239			"	"	"	"	18x22-66-68000	dr'91-93
Campbell	240			"	"	"	"	" " "	dr'91-93
Sargent	241			"	"	"	"	" " "	dr'91-92
Crocker	242			"	"	"	"	" " "	dr'91-93

Note a - 210, 211 re'96 to 255, 257.   Note b - Renamed "Modoc"
Note c - to Coats & Bennett   Note d - to Glen Mfg. Co.

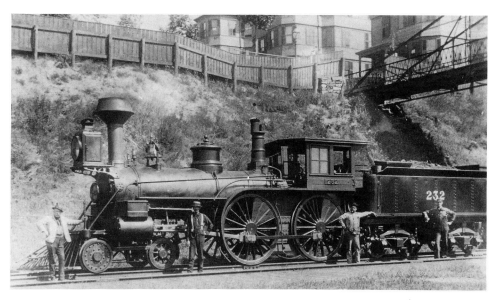

B&A 232, built by the B&A in 1873, at Springfield in 1890.   (Vollrath collection)

B&A 200 as rebuilt with extended smokebox. Later 1209, class C-32.   (Purinton 93)

B&A 214 DUKES, another Eddy Clock of 1873.   (NYC neg. 5644)

266

BOSTON & ALBANY – Continued. Additions 1875-1882

B&A Name	No.	Re'93	Re'00		Type	Builder,			Date	Cyl. DD Wt.	Disposition
Euxine	4				4-4-0	B&A Shops			1875	18x26-60-68000	So 12/90 Stewart
Niagara	118	18			0-4-0	"	"		"	14x24-48-44000	Sc 3/98
Boston	126	261			4-4-0	"	"		"	17x22-66-68000	Sc 2/99
	131	15			0-4-0	"	"		"	14x24-48-44000	dr'93-94
Gillett	243	243			4-4-0	"	"		"	18x22-66-68000	dr'93-95
Kimball	244	244			"	"	"	"	"	" " "	dr'93-95
Fulton	3	3			0-4-0	"	"		1876	14x24-48-44000	dr by'99
Kentucky	8	63			4-4-0	"	"		"	18x26-60-68000	dr'93-95
Virginia	11				"	"	"		"	" " "	dr'91-93
Beebe	15				"	"	"		"	18x22-66-68000	dr'91
Marmora	39				"	"	"		"	18x26-60-68000	RT'91 (a)
Howard	40				"	"	"		"	18x24-72-68000	dr'91-93
Tobey	44				"	"	"		"	18x22-66-68000	dr'91-93
Tiger	124	241	1212	C-33a	"	"	"		"	17x22-60-68000	Sc 7/05
Express	125	253	1214	"	"	"	"		"	18x22-66-68000	Sc 3/00
Nashville	27				"	"	"		1877	18x26-54-70000	dr'91-93
Barnes	32	230			"	"	"		"	18x22-66-68000	dr'93-94
Cummings	61	206			"	"	"		"	18x24-72-68000	dr'93-94
Hercules	111	111			"	"	"		"	18x26-60-70000	Sc 4/00 (b)
Neptune	113	113			"	"	"		"	" " "	So 7/99 McArdle
Despatch	127	227	1177	Cx	"	"	"		"	18x22-66-68000	Sc 2/06
Florida	7				"	"	"		1878	18+x28-54-78000	dr'91-92
Tennessee	9	50			"	"	"		"	" " "	dr'93-95
Shaker	26				"	"	"		"	18x22-72-68000	dr'91-93
Indiana	97				"	"	"		"	18x26-60-68000	dr'91-93
Hecla	117	117			"	"	"		"	" " 70000	So 5/00 G&U 1
	150	250	1213	C-33	"	"	"		RB'81	18x22-66-68000	Sc 6/05
	151	270	1224	Insp.	"	"	"		"	" " "	RB 3/03 Pony 31
Gilmore	45				"	"	"		1879	18x22-72-68000	Sc 7/90
Alger	59	59			"	"	"		"	18x26-60-70000	So 7/99 J.Powers
Lion	133	133			2-6-0	"	"		"	17x26-54-70000	So 6/99 "
C.W.Blakeslee (d)					4-4-0	(Sprfld.'60)					So Conn.Riv.
Olympus	50				"	B&A Shops			1880	18+x28-54-78000	dr'91-93
Chesapeake	58				"	"	"	"	"	" " "	dr'91-93
Arizona	83	83			"	"	"		"	" " 80000	dr'91-94
Brookline	116	221	758	C-30a	"	"	"		"	18x26-60-70000	Sc 6/02 (Note c)
Sacramento	181				"	"	"		"	18x24-66-68000	dr'91-93
Shaker (e)	245	54			"	"	"		"	18+x28-54-78000	dr'91-95
	246	21			0-4-0	"	"		"	14x24-48-44000	So'00 Appleyard
	247	247	1218	C-30a	4-4-0	"	"		1881	18x26-60-70000	So 5/00 McArdle
Columbia	248				"	"	"		1880	18+x28-54-78000	dr'91-93
	249	29			0-4-0	"	"		"	14x24-48-44000	So 2/00 G.W.Keys
(ex-254)?	250				4-4-0	"	"		"	18+x28-54-78000	So 7/90
Whistler	46	232			"	"	"		1881	18x24-72-68000	dr'93-95
	128	213	1217	Cx	"	"	"		"	18x26-60-70000	Sc 10/04
	86	86			"	"	"		1882	" " "	Sc 3/00
	132	30			0-4-0	"	"		"	14x24-48-44000	So'00 Appleyard
	63	263	1223		4-4-0	"	"		"	18x26-60-80000	RT'08

Note a – #39 to Worcester depot as boiler, then donated to Purdue University, then
sent 10/51 to St.Louis Museum of Transport.   Note c – 221 re'99 to 101.
Note d – ex-Springfield & NE RR "Enfield".   Note e – Renamed "Amazon".

B&A 117, as built in 1878. (Purinton 104)

B&A 32, the BARNES, nearly the last Eddy Clock. (Purinton 111)

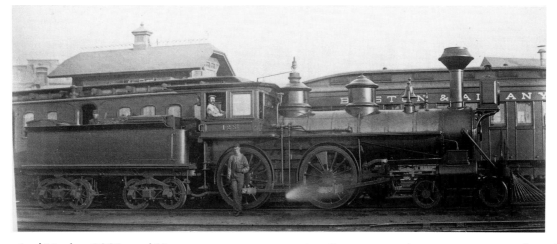

B&A 128, as built in 1881, with no name nor any tender lettering. (Purinton 59)

BOSTON & ALBANY - Continued. Additions 1881 - 1900:

After 1880, B&A motive power was built to relatively few standard designs, and almost all survived into the 1900's after two renumberings. The practice of naming locomotives was discontinued about 1881. Additions to the roster during this period are summarized below:

4-4-0	B&A Shops	1881-1891	18x22-66	Nos. 42,54,56,87,91,94-96,101-103,110,119,129,134-137,142,144,148,152,166,167,169,173,177,184,185. See class C-34 on p.274
4-4-0	B&A Shops	1881-1883	20x26-54	Nos. 18,47,49,51,52,53. See class C-30 on p274.
4-4-0	B&A Shops	1883-1887	20x26-54	Nos. 1,23,25,30,34,41,43,65,68,73-75,81,100,106,149, 153,155,171,175. See class C-31a on p 274.
0-4-0	B&A Shops	1885-1890	16x24-48	Nos. 2,14,31,72,92,143,157,170,191. See A-30 on p270
2-8-0	Baldwin	1886-1891	20x26-48	Nos. 10,66,67,70,71,76-80,82,84,85,88-90,104,105,108 147,154,156,165,183,186,187,251-260. See G-30 p.282
2-8-0	Rhode Is.	1891	20x26-48	Nos. 15,35,39,64. See class G-31 on p.282
0-4-0	Rhode Is.	1891	16x24-48	Nos. 13,17,24,28,33,37,93,98,99. See A-30 on p.270
4-4-0	Rhode Is.	1891-1892	20x26-54	Nos. 48,145,146,158,160,178,179,189,192,193,197,203, 207,213,215,216,220,223,238,241. See C-31 on p.274
4-4-0	B&A Shops	1891-1893	18x22-60	Nos.4-7,36,38,45,60,139,182,199,214. See C-34,a 274
4-4-0	Rhode Is.	1893	19x24-66	Nos. 19,20,26,27. See class C-35 on p.278
0-6-0	Rhode Is.	1893	19x24-50	Nos. 22,44,55,58,97,107. See class B-30 on p.270
4-6-0	Rhode Is.	1893	20x24-70	Nos. 11,12. See class F-30 on p.282

RENUMBERING OF 1893:

A new numbering sceme was adopted in 1893 in which locomotives were grouped by type of service. Nos. 1-49 were switchers, 50-199 were freight, and 200-299 were passenger power.

B&A ADDITIONS 1893-1900: Note that all engines were built by Schenectady Locomotive Works

2-8-0	Schen.	1893	20x26-48	Nos. 161,162,168,172,176,181,198,202,204,206: G-32
0-6-0	Schen.	1894	19x24-52	Nos. 7,8,9,15,20,36. See class B-31 on p270
4-4-0	Schen.	1894	19x24-70	Nos. 205,230. See class C-36a on p.278
4-4-0	Schen.	1894-95	19x24-70	Nos. 206,207,209,215-218,222,229,232,238,240, 243,244. See class C-36 on p278.
2-8-0	Schen.	1894-95	20x26-48	Nos. 50,54,57,62,63,83,96,114,116,120,122,123,126, 127,131,135,141,144. See class G-32 on p.282
4-4-0	Schen.	1896	19x24-69	Nos. 208,210,211,212. See class C-37 on p278
0-6-0	Schen.	1899	19&29x26-52	Nos. 3,18,34 (Compound). See class B-32 on p270.
4-6-0	Schen.	1899	20x26-70	Nos. 220,221. See class F-31 on p.282
4-8-0	Schen.	1899-1900	20x28-54	Nos. 170-180. See class H-30 on p.286
4-4-0	Schen.	1900	20x26-75	Nos. 285-290. See class C-38 on p.278
4-4-0	Schen.	1900	18x24-69	Nos. 201,247,253,258,261. See class C-39 on p.278

RENUMBERING OF 1900 (NYC&HR SERIES):

Shortly after the Boston & Albany was leased by the New York Central & Hudson River in July, 1900, all B&A power was renumbered into a new NYC&HR series as outlined below. Also shown are classes used during 1902-1903 before the NYC Lines classification system began:

84-102	0-4-0	M	A-30	See p.270	1153-1164	4-4-0	C-2	C-36	See p278
386-391	0-6-0	L	B-30	"	1165-1168	"	D	C-35	"
392-394	"	K	B-32	"	1169-1208	"	D-1	C-34,a	See p.274
199,395-399	"	L	B-31	"	1209-1210	"	D-2	C-32	"
715-733	4-4-0	I,I-1	C-31a	See p.274	1211-1216	"	D-2	C-33,a	See p.274
734-753	"	I,I-1	C-31	"	1217-1225	"	D1,D2	Cx	See p.274
754-759	"	I-1	C-30	See p.274	1842	2-6-0		Ex	See p278
760	"	I-1	Cx	"	2030-2031	4-6-0	B-1	F-31	See p282
1139-1144	"	B	C-38	See p.278	2158-2159	"	H	F-30	"
1145-1148	"	C	C-36	"	2506-2569	2-8-0	G	G30,31,32	See p.282
1149-1152	"	C-1	C-37	"	2632-2642	4-8-0	F-1	H-30,a	See p286

RENUMBERING OF 1912 (B&A SERIES)

During the first few years of the NYC&HR lease after 1900, there were no distinguishing marks on B&A motive power. Tenders were simply lettered for the parent road, but about 1905 "New York Central Lines" was substituted, with B&A initials on the coal boards. Apparently this did not satisfy the road's owners, and in 1912 tenders were relettered "Boston & Albany" and an entirely separate numbering scheme was devised for B&A power

1	0-4-0	A-30		See p.270	500-509	4-6-2	K-1	See p294
97-99	0-6-0	B		"	510-554	"	Ka,c,d,e,g,j	"
100-114	"	B-30,32,31		"	600,601	2-6-0	Ed	See p278
115-135	"	B-10e,i,m,o		"	700-703	4-6-0	F-30,31	See p282
200	4-4-0	Insp. Pony	See p.274		704-723	"	F-2c,f	"
201-254	"	C-31,34-39	See p.274,278		800-810	4-8-0	H-30,a	See p286
300-317	2-6-6T	L-1,a	See p.300		900-989	2-8-0	G-30 to 34	See p282
400-405	4-4-2	Ib	See p.290		990-1049	"	G-5,G-6	See p286

After 1912, several additional series and classes were added but the basic scheme remained until early in 1951, when all remaining B&A engines were finally renumbered into the New York Central System series. Very soon thereafter all steam power was gone.

Class A-30.

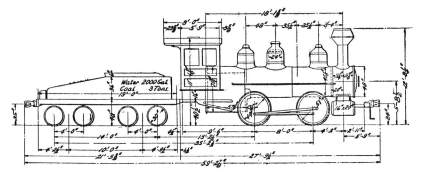

Kind of main valve	Richardson balanced	Heating surface, firebox	74 square feet
Firebox, length inside	51 inches	Heating surface, total	831 square feet
Firebox, width inside	35¾ inches	Weight on drivers, working order	64,400 pounds
Grate area	12.5 square feet	Weight, total of engine, working order	64,400 pounds
Tubes, number	121	Weight of tender, loaded	42,500 pounds
Tubes, length over sheets	11 feet 11⅝ inches	Weight of tender, empty	20,000 pounds
Tubes, diameter outside	2 inches	Steam pressure	130 pounds
Heating surface, tubes	757 square feet	Rating	13.9 per cent.

CLASS A. 0-4-0 SWITCHER

B&A CLASS A-30 0-4-0: 16x24-52-130-64400-13680 (old M)

No.	Re '93	Re '00	Re '05	Builder	c/n	Date	Disposition
69	23	102		B&A Shops		1883	So 8/02 (a)
72	26	92		" "		1885	RT'08
170	38	100	82	" "		1886	RT'08
31	31	95	85	" "		1887	Sc 10/11 (b)
143	10	86		" "		1887	Sc 1/09
92	35	98		" "		1888	Sc 7/07
157	27	93		" "		1889	Sc 8/09
14	14	88		" "		1890	Sc 7/07
191	19	90		" "		1890	RT'08
2	2	84		" "		1891	So 9/08

B&A CLASS A-30 0-4-0 - Continued

No.	Re '93	Re '00	Re '05	Re '12	Builder	c/n	Date	Disposition
13	13	87			Rh.Is.	2550	1/91	Sc 5/11
17	17	89			"	2551	"	Sc 2/07
24	24	91			"	2552	"	RT'08
28	28	94			"	2553	"	RT'08
33	33	97			"	2554	"	Sc 7/09
37	37	99	89	1	"	2555	"	Sc 6/13
93	39	101	83		"	2665	10/91	RT'08
98	32	96			"	2666	"	Sc 5/08
99	5	85			"	2667	"	Sc 11/05

B&A CLASS A-1 2-8-4 : See p.24

CLASS B. 0-6-0 SWITCHER

B&A CLASS B-30 0-6-0: 19x24-51-160-98600-23200 (Old L)

No.	Re '93	Re '00	Re '10	Re '12	Builder	c/n	Date	Disposition
22	22	390		104	Rh.Is.	2860	1/93	Sc 8/26
44	4	387		101	"	2861	2/93	Sc 11/15
55	1	386		100	"	2862	"	Sc 8/15
58	11	388		102	"	2863	"	Sc 8/15
97	25	391		105	"	2864	"	Sc 12/15
107	16	389		103	"	2865	"	Sc 8/27

B&A CLASS B-31 0-6-0: 19x24-52-160-106000-23600 (Old L)

No.	Re '00	Re '10	Re '12	Builder	c/n	Date	Disposition
7	395		109	Schen.	4246	11/94	Sc 12/15
8	396		110	"	4247	"	Sc 9/19
9	397		111	"	4248	12/94	Sc 2/20
15	398		112	"	4249	"	Sc 5/16
20	399		113	"	4250	"	Sc 12/15
36	199	400	114	"	4251	"	Sc 1/19

B&A CLASS B-32 0-6-0: 19&29x26-52-200-112000-27800 (K)
(Converted to B-32a simple)

No.	Re '00	Re '10	Re '12	Builder	c/n	Date	Disposition
3	392		106	Schen.	4929	2/99	Sc 12/23
18	393		107	"	4930	"	Sc 12/23
34	394		108	"	4931	"	Sc 12/23

B&A CLASS B 0-6-0: 18x24-51-145-97000-19600 (Acq.10/07)

No.	Re '00	Re '10	Re '12	Builder	c/n	Date	Disposition
ex GCS 1	421	437	99	(Schen.	3145	7/90)	Sc 1/15
" 2	422	438	98	("	4201	1/94)	Sc 6/16
" 7	423	439	97	("	3972	11/92)	Sc 6/16

B&A CLASS B-10e 0-6-0: 21x28-57-180-162000-33140.
(Built as LS&MS 4518,4519,4520,4540.) (Note d)

No.	Re '12	Builder	c/n	Date	Disposition
401	115	Alco-RI	41774	2/07	RT 3/32
402	116	"	41775	"	RT 5/31
403	117	"	41776	3/07	RT 4/32
404	118	"	41796	"	RT 3/33

B&A CLASS B-10i 0-6-0: 21x28-57-180-162000-33140. (d)

No.	Re '12	Builder	c/n	Date	Disposition
405	119	Alco-RI	43240	8/07	RT 5/31
406	120	"	43241	9/07	RT 4/32
407	121	"	43242	"	RT 3/32
408	122	"	43243	"	RT 7/34
409	123	"	43244	"	RT 9/34

B&A CLASS B-10m 0-6-0: 21x28-57-180-164500-33140.(d)

No.	Re '12	Re 4/51	Builder	c/n	Date	Disposition
410	124		Alco-S	45498	10/08	RT 3/33
411	125		"	45499	"	RT 6/34
412	126		"	45500	"	RT 3/33
413	127		"	45501	11/08	RT 5/34
414	128		"	45502	"	RT 4/35
415	129		"	45503	"	RT 12/34
416	130		"	45504	"	RT 12/34
417	131		"	45505	"	RT 9/35

B&A CLASS B-10o 0-6-0: 21x28-57-180-166000-33140.(d)

No.	Re '12	Re 4/51	Builder	c/n	Date	Disposition
418	132	(Note e)	Alco-S	46996	3/10	Sc 10/35
419	133	"	"	46997	"	Sc 9/40
420	134	"	"	46998	"	Sc 10/39
421	135	"	"	46999	"	Sc 9/47

B&A CLASS B-10s 0-6-0: 21x28-57-180-170000-33140

No.	Re 4/51	Builder	c/n	Date	Disposition
136		Alco-M	52292	11/12	Sc 7/39
137		"	52293	12/12	Sc 6/50
138		"	52294	"	Sc 6/49
139		"	52295	"	Sc 8/39
140		"	52296	"	Sc 6/50
141	6773	"	52297	1/13	SS 6/51
142		"	52298	"	Sc 9/40
143		"	52299	"	Sc 9/40

B&A CLASS B-11L 0-6-0: 21x28-57-180-172000-33140

No.	Re 4/51	Builder	c/n	Date	Disposition
144	6748	Alco-S	54288	12/13	SS 9/52
145	6745(c)	"	54289	"	SS 12/50
146	6746(c)	"	54290	"	SS 6/51
147	6747(c)	"	54291	"	SS 12/50

B&A CLASS B-11o 0-6-0: 21x28-57-180-173000-33140

No.	Re 4/51	Builder	c/n	Date	Disposition
148	6750	Alco-S	55829	5/16	SS 6/51
149	6751	"	55830	"	SS 6/51
150	6752	"	55831	"	SS 6/51
151	6753	"	55832	"	SS 6/51
152	6754	"	55833	"	SS 6/51

Note a:- to J.F.Shaw. Specs: 14x24-48-44000
Note b:- to NYC&HR 8/09. Note c -re 3/46 to 6745-47
Note d:- Super'19. Note e: Built as NYC&HR 538-541

Class B-32.

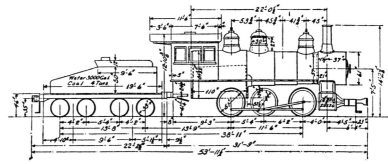

Kind of main valve	American balanced
Firebox, length inside	102¼ inches
Firebox, width inside	33¼ inches
Grate area	23.7 square feet
Tubes, number	212
Tubes, length over sheets	11 feet 6 inches
Tubes, diameter outside	2 inches
Heating surface, tubes	1276 square feet

Heating surface, firebox	144.3 square feet
Heating surface, total	1420.3 square feet
Weight on drivers, working order	118,000 pounds
Weight, total of engine, working order	118,000 pounds
Weight of tender, loaded	64,200 pounds
Weight of tender, empty	31,200 pounds
Steam pressure	200 pounds
Rating	27.8 per cent.

Class B-30.

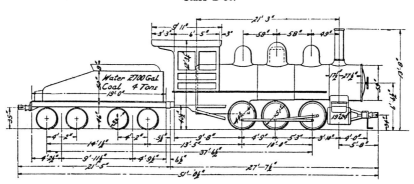

Kind of main valve	Richardson balanced
Firebox, length inside	66 inches
Firebox, width inside	35¼ inches
Grate area	16.2 square feet
Tubes, number	197
Tubes, length over sheets	13 feet, 3 inches
Tubes, diameter outside	2 inches
Heating surface, tubes	1365 square feet

Heating surface, firebox	126 square feet
Heating surface, total	1491 square feet
Weight on drivers, working order	98,600 pounds
Weight, total of engine, working order	98,600 pounds
Weight of tender, loaded	61,940 pounds
Weight of tender, empty	30,000 pounds
Steam pressure	160 pounds
Rating	23.2 per cent.

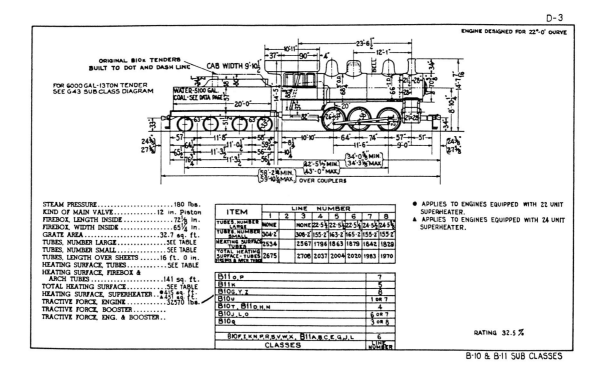

B-10 & B-11 SUB CLASSES

NYC&HR (B&A) 87, class A-30. Built by Rhode Island 1891 as #13, relettered NYC&HR in 1900.

NYC&HR (B&A) 96, another A-30 switcher, built by the B&A in 1891.   (NYC neg. 4779)

B&A 413, one of eight in class B-10m. It became B&A 127 in 1912. (Vollrath collection)

B&A 135, class B-10o, built as NYC&HR 541, but transferred to the B&A. At Boston 7/40.

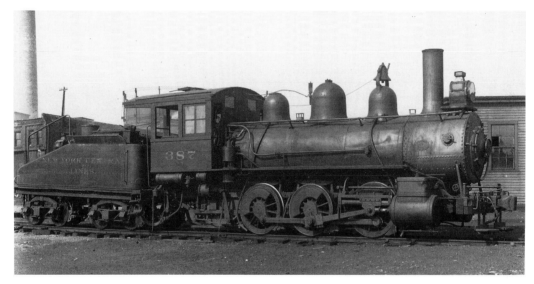

B&A 387, class B-30, one of six built by Rhode Island in 1893. (Purinton 213)

B&A 137, class B-10s, at Allston in May, 1928. Built Alco 1912. (Vollrath collection)

B&A INSPECTION PONY 4-4-0: 16X22-62-145-79000-11200: "BERKSHIRE" #31 (re'12) 200 RB 3/03 from 1224. Sc 6/31.

B&A CLASS C-30 4-4-0: 20x26-54-130-80000- (755 later 18x26. Old class I-1

18	(re'93)	118			B&A Shops	1881	So'00	51	(re'00)	754	B&A Shops 1883	So'06 Coats & Ben.
49	"	94	(re'00)	757	"	"	1882	So'99 ?	52	"	755	"	"	"	Sc 6/05
47	"	140	"	759	"	"	1883	So'99 ?	53	"	756	"	"	"	So'03 Graf.& Up. 3

B&A CLASS C-30a 4-4-0: 18x26-60-130-70000-   (Old D-1): See #758,1217,1218 p.266

B&A CLASS C-30b 4-4-0: 18x26-64-130-80000-   (Old D-1): See #1223 p.266

B&A CLASS Cx 4-4-0: 18x22-66-130-68000- (Old D-1): See #1177 p.266

B&A CLASS Cx 4-4-0: 16x22-60-130-60000- (Old D-2): See #1225 p.266

B&A CLASS C-31 4-4-0: 20x26-54-160-90000-   (Old I) (a)

Re'93	Re'00	Re'12	Builder	c/n	Date	Disp'n.
145	145	744		Rh.Is.	2677	12/91	Sc 5/10
146	146	745	"	2678	"	Sc 1/11 (a)
158	158	748	"	2679	"	Sc 5/09 (j)
179	132	751	"	2680	1/92	RT'08 (a)
160	160	750	(202)	"	2681	"	Sc 6/13 (a)
178	148	746	"	2682	"	So'99
48	109	735	"	2683	"	Sc 2/12 (a)
189	151	747	"	2684	"	Sc 6/12 (a)
192	159	749	"	2685	"	Sc 7/08
193	110	736	"	2686	"	Sc 6/07
197	143	743	"	2692	2/92	Sc 1/11 (a)
203	103	734	"	2693	"	Sc 7/08
207	136	741	201	"	2694	"	Sc 5/13 (a)
213	128	739	"	2695	"	dr by'09
215	129	740	"	2696	"	Sc 7/08 (a)
216	121	737	"	2697	"	Sc 2/09
220	150	752	203	"	2698	"	Sc 9/12 (a)
223	157	753	"	2699	"	RT'08 (a)
238	138	742	"	2700	"	So
241	124	738	"	2701	"	Sc 7/09 (a)

B&A CLASS C-31a 4-4-0: 20x26-54-160-84000- (Old I)(a)

74	74	720	B&A Shops	1883	Sc 3/00 (h)
100	100	726	"	"	"	Sc 6/07 (h)
1	55	715	"	"	1884	Sc 2/06
68	68	717	"	"	"	So 3/02
73	73	719	"	"	"	Sc 6/05
75	75	721	"	"	"	So 6/08 (k)
171	99	725	"	"	"	RT'08 (a)
23	69	718	"	"	1885	RT'08
30	130	728	"	"	"	RT'08
106	106	727	"	"	"	So'99 (c)
149	149	731	"	"	"	Sc 6/06 (a)
25	97	724	"	"	1886	Sc 5/10 (c)
43	166	733	"	"	"	RT'08
65	65	716	"	"	"	So 6/08
81	81	722	"	"	"	RT'09 (k)
155	155	760	"	"	"	Sc 7/09 (d)
34	134	729	"	"	1887	Sc 1/10 (a)
41	92	723	"	"	"	So 7/09 (k)
153	153	732	"	"	"	RT'08
175	139	730	"	"	"	Sc 7/05 (a)

B&A CLASS C-34 4-4-0: 18x22-69-160-94200-14500 Old D-1

Re'93	Re'00	Re'12	Builder	Date	Disp'n.
129	220		B&A Shops	1881	dr'93-99
169	269	1201	"	"	1882	Sc 12/10
87	202	1169	"	"	1883	Sc 5/09
134	234	1181	"	"	"	Sc'08
137	268	1200	"	"	"	Sc 9/05
101	280	1208	"	"	1884	Sc 6/03
102	251	1191	"	"	"	Sc 1/09
103	203	1170	"	"	"	Sc 6/07
136	236	1183	"	"	"	Sc'08
95	259	1194	205,207	"	"	1885	RB'13 RT 8/23 (b)
135	265	1197	206	"	"	RB'10 Sc 9/17 (b)
54	245	1187	208	"	"	1886	RB'10 RT 6/25 (b)
94	249	1190		"	"	Sc 4/06
148	248	1189	207	"	"	Sc 6/14
91	224	1175	209	"	"	1887	RB'10 Sc 9/19 (b)
167	267	1199		"	"	Sc 4/08
177	228	1178	210	"	"	RB'11 Sc 8/23 (b)
185	275	1204	211	"	"	RB'11 Sc 9/23 (b)
56	256	1193		"	"	1888	Sc 9/08
110	262	1196		"	"	Sc 6/09
152	252	1192		"	"	Sc 2/09
38	233	1180	212	"	"	12/89	RB'11 Sc 8/19 (b)
144	208	1206		"	"	Sc by'09 (f)
96	204	1171	213	"	"	10/90	RB'14 Sc 2/20 (b)
142	242	1186	214	"	"	8/90	RB Sc 4/14 (b)
166	266	1198		"	"	3/90	RT'08
173	273	1202		"	"	1890	RT'08
184	274	1203		"	"	11/90	RT'08
42	246	1188		"	"	4/91	Sc 6/07
119	219	1173	215	"	"	1891	RB'11 Sc 1/20 (b)
7	237	1184	222,214	"	"	1892	RB'13 Sc 9/18 (b)

Note a: Old class I-1. As RB: 18x26-57-145-14100.
Note b: Old class H, later D-1. RB to class C-34b
Note c: 724,727 later class C-31c
Note d: 760 class Cx: 18x22-63-150-
Note f: 208 re'96 to 278.
Note h: 74 and 100 built as compounds.
Note i: 7 and 38 built with 60" drivers.
Note j: 748 class Cx re'02 to 1226 class C-31d:
        18x26-66-160-90000 (old class D-1).
Note k: 721,723 class Cx: 18x26-60-145-90000-14100.

B&A CLASS C-32 4-4-0: 17x24-60-130-64000- Old D-2 See #1209,1210,1220 p.262,264

B&A CLASS C-33 4-4-0: 17x22-66-130-68000- Old D-2 See #1211,1213,1215 p.260,264

B&A CLASS C-33a 4-4-0: 17x22-60-130-68000- Old D-2 See #1212,1216 p.260,266

Class C-31.

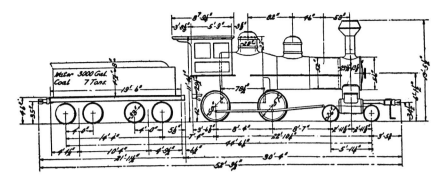

Cylinders	18 x 26 inches
Kind of main valve	Richardson balanced
Firebox, length inside	71¼ inches
Firebox, width inside	35¼ inches
Grate area	17.4 square feet
Tubes, number	221
Tubes, length over sheets	11 feet 2¼ inches
Tubes, diameter outside	2 inches
Heating surface, tubes	1301 square feet

Heating surface, firebox	125 square feet
Heating surface, total	1426 square feet
Weight on drivers, working order	60,000 pounds
Weight on truck, working order	30,000 pounds
Weight, total of engine, working order	90,000 pounds
Weight of tender, loaded	73,800 pounds
Weight of tender, empty	37,000 pounds
Steam pressure	145 pounds
Rating	14.1 per cent.

NOTE.—The cylinders of these engines are being bushed to 16 inches diameter.

Class C-34.

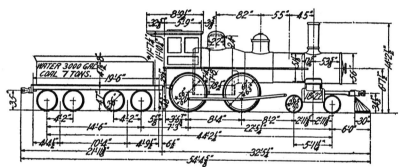

Kind of main valve	Richardson balanced
Firebox, length inside	71¼ inches
Firebox, width inside	35¼ inches
Grate area	17.4 square feet
Tubes, number	221
Tubes, length over sheets	11 feet 0 inches
Tubes, diameter outside	2 inches
Heating surface, tubes	1273 square feet
Heating surface, firebox	130 square feet

Heating surface, total	1403 square feet
Weight on drivers, working order	61,500 pounds
Weight on truck, working order	32,700 pounds
Weight, total of engine, working order	94,200 pounds
Weight of tender, loaded	73,800 pounds
Weight of tender, empty	42,200 pounds
Steam pressure	160 pounds
Rating	14.5 per cent.

NOTE.—Dimensions marked thus * apply to Class C-34A.

Class C-35.

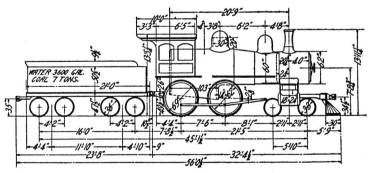

Kind of main valve	Richardson balanced
Firebox, length inside	96¼ inches
Firebox, width inside	33¼ inches
Grate area	22.2 square feet
Tubes, number	248
Tubes, length over sheets	10 feet 7 inches
Tubes, diameter outside	2 inches
Heating surface, tubes	1374 square feet
Heating surface, firebox	142 square feet

Heating surface, total	1516 square feet
Weight on drivers, working order	74,600 pounds
Weight on truck, working order	36,000 pounds
Weight, total of engine, working order	110,600 pounds
Weight of tender, loaded	71,500 pounds
Weight of tender, empty	27,500 pounds
Steam pressure	180 pounds
Rating	17.6 per cent.

B&A 200, inspection Pony BERKSHIRE. At West Springfield. It lasted until 1931.(Vollrath)

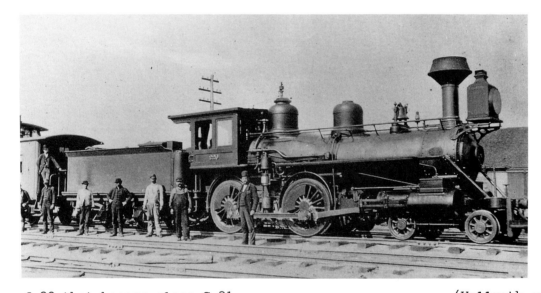

B&A 220, one of 20 that became class C-31.   (Vollrath collection)

B&A 752 class C-31, renumbered 1912 to 203 and scrapped.   (Strum collection)

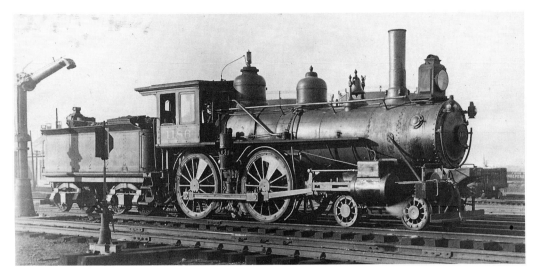

B&A 1186, class C-34, B&A-built in 1890.   Later #214 and scrapped in 1914.   (Strum)

B&A 136 photographed about 1890.   Eventually became #1183, class C-34. (Edson collection)

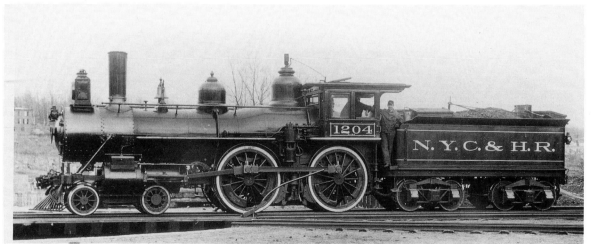

NYC&HR (B&A) 1204, another class C-34.   Later B&A 215.   (Paul Prescott collection)

B&A CLASS C-34a: 18x22-63-160-90000-14700 (Old H,D-1)

Re'93	Re'00	Re'12			Builder	c/n	Date	RB	Disp'n.
36	231	1179	219	(c)	B&A Shops		1891	'10	Sc 9/17
45	225	1176	217	(c)	"	"	"		Sc 3/14
60	260	1195	221	(c)	"	"	"		Sc 1/15
139	239	1185			"	"	"		RT'08
182	223	1174	216	(c)	"	"	1/91		Sc 12/14
4	254	1219		(b)	"	"	1891		Sc 1/12
5	279	1207	218	(a)	"	"	1892	'10	Sc 4/25
6	235	1182	220	(c)	"	"	1891	'13	Sc 11/19
199	277	1205			"	"	1892		Sc 9/11
214	214	1172	223		"	"	1893		Sc 1/15

B&A CLASS C-35 4-4-0: 18x24-69-180-110600-17500
As built: 19x24-69-180-108000 (Old class F, G, D)

				Builder	c/n	Date	RB	Disp'n.
19	281	1165		Rh.Is.	2866	2/93		Sc 3/10
20	282	1166		"	2867			Sc 12/10
26	283	1167	204	"	2868	"		Sc 9/12
27	284	1168		"	2869	3/93		Sc 1/09

B&A CLASS C-36 4-4-0: 18x24-69-180-120500-17700
As built: 20x24-66-180-114000 (Old class E,C)

				Builder	c/n	Date	RB	Disp'n.
206	1145	224		Schen.	4242	11/94		Sc 12/16
207	1146	225	(e)	"	4243	"	'13	Sc 8/26
209	1147	226		"	4244	"		Sc 9/18
215	1148	227		"	4245	"		Sc 12/16

B&A CLASS C-36a 4-4-0: 18x24-69-180-120000-17700
As built: 19x24-66-180000-114000 (Old class G,E,C-2)

				Builder	c/n	Date	RB	Disp'n.
205	1153	228		Schen.	4220	4/94		Sc 5/19
230	1159	229	(f)	"	4219	"	8/13	Sc 4/26

B&A CLASS C-36,b 4-4-0: 18x24-69-180-120000-17700
As built: 19x24-66-180-114000 (Old class C-2)

Re'00	Re'12			Builder	c/n	Date	RB	Disp'n.
216	1154	230	(g)	Schen.	4271	3/95	12/12	Sc 10/26
217	1155	231	(g)	"	4272	"	9/13	Sc 6/26
218	1156	232	(g)	"	4273	"	11/12	Sc 5/29
222	1157	233		"	4274	"		Sc 5/17
229	1158	234		"	4275	"		Sc 11/16
232	1160	235	(g)	"	4276	"	'12	Sc 8/27
238	1161	236	(g)	"	4277	"	'12	Sc 8/28
240	1162	237	(g)	"	4278	"	'12	Sc 8/28
243	1163	238	(g)	"	4279	4/95	'12	Sc 12/25
244	1164	239		"	4280	"		Sc 2/19

B&A CLASS C-37: 19x24-69-180-119000-19210 (Old D,C-1)

			Builder	c/n	Date	RB	Disp'n.
208	1149	240	Schen.	4410	2/96	4/18	Sc 6/34
210	1150	241	"	4411	"	10/17	Sc 8/27
211	1151	242	"	4412	"	6/18	Sc 6/34
212	1152	243	"	4413	"	9/18	Sc 4/31

B&A CLASS C-38: 20x26-75-190-136400-22390 (Old B)

			Builder	c/n	Date	RB	Disp'n.
285	1139	249	Schen.	5387	1/00		Sc 12/26
286	1140	250	"	5388	"	2/19	Sc 7/30
287	1141	251	"	5389	"	12/19	Sc 8/29
288	1142	252	"	5390	"	3/20	Sc 5/31
289	1143	253	"	5391	"	10/19	Sc 5/29
290	1144	254	"	5392	"	7/19	Sc 9/34

B&A CLASS C-39: 18x24-69-190-122400-18400 (Old C-3)

				Builder	c/n	Date	RB	Disp'n.
201	1210	1134	244	Schen.	5639	10/00		Sc 3/24
253	1214	1135	245	"	5641	"		Sc 3/25
247	1218	1136	246	"	5640	"		Sc 11/23
258	1221	1137	247	"	5642	"		Sc 9/25
261	1222	1138	248	"	5643	11/00		Sc 12/25

CLASS D. 4-6-6T DOUBLE ENDER

B&A CLASS D-1a 4-6-6T: 23+x26-63-215-352000-41600

			Builder	c/n	Date		Disp'n.
400	(re 3/51)	1295	Alco-S	67609	9/28		SS 2/52
401	"	1296	"	67610	"		SS 8/51
402	"	1297	"	67611	"		SS 3/52
403	"	1298	"	67612	"		SS 10/51
404	"	1299	"	67613	"		SS 8/51

B&A CLASS D-2a 2-6-6T:
Former Class L-3a. See p.300

B&A CLASS D-2b 2-6-6T:
Former Class L-3b. See p.300

CLASS E. 2-6-0 MOGUL

B&A CLASS Ed 2-6-0: 19x26-63-160-120000-20260. Acqired 12/03 from NYC&HR.

1578	(re'12)	600	(Schen.	3183	8/90)	RB 11/05	RT 9/21
1638	"	601	("	3864	8/92)	RB 12/06	RT 9/21

B&A CLASS Ex 2-6-0: 17x24-54-130-68000- See #1842 p.264

Note a: 1207 re 2nd 1177, later C-34c. Note b: 1219 class Cx: 18x26-69-145- Note c: Later C-34c.
Note e: 1146 old C-2: 19x24-69- RB to C-36b. Note f: 229 RB to C-36c. Note g: RB to C-36b.

Class C-39.

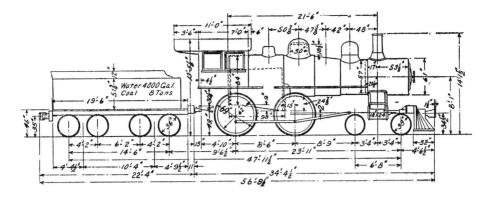

Kind of main valve.....................Allen-Richardson balanced.	Heating surface, total.............................1745 square feet
Firebox, length inside............................90 7/8 inches	Weight on drivers, working order.................78,400 pounds
Firebox, width inside..............................40 1/8 inches	Weight on truck, working order....................44,000 pounds
Grate area.....................................25.3 square feet	Weight, total of engine, working order...........122,400 pounds
Tubes, number..256	Weight of tender, loaded.........................83,800 pounds
Tubes, length over sheets........................12 feet 0 inches	Weight of tender, empty...........................34,500 pounds
Tubes, diameter outside................................2 inches	Steam pressure..190 pounds
Heating surface, tubes...........................1609 square feet	Rating..18.4 per cent.
Heating surface, firebox...........................136 square feet	

B & A

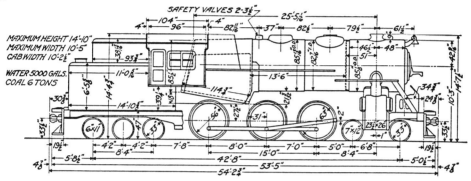

		With Superheater
Number of Locomotives................................5	Small tubes...............................234–2 in.	
Built by the...................American Locomotive Co.	Large tubes...............................48–5 3/8 in.	
Schenectady Works	Length over sheets.........................13 ft.–6 in.	
Builders' Order No............................S–1621	Heating surface, tubes.....................2548 sq. ft.	
Valve gear..Baker	Heating surface, firebox and arch tubes........213 sq. ft.	
Kind of main valve......................14 in. Piston	Total heating surface.......................2761 sq. ft.	
Firebox, length inside........................102 1/8 in.	Heating surface, superheater................788 sq. ft.	
Firebox, width inside..........................85 3/4 in.	Weight in working order on:	
Grate area..................................60.8 sq. ft.	Front truck...........................62000 lbs.	
	Drivers..............................180000 lbs.	
	Total engine.........................242000 lbs.	
	Weight of tender loaded................110000 lbs.	
	Weight of tender empty.................56300 lbs.	

CLASS D–1A

8-1-29

Class C-36.

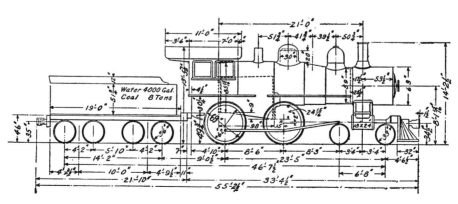

Kind of main valve............................Richardson balanced	Heating surface, total.............................1950 square feet
Firebox, length inside............................90 7/8 inches	Weight on drivers, working order.................76,000 pounds
Firebox, width inside..............................40 1/8 inches	Weight on truck, working order....................44,500 pounds
Grate area.....................................25.2 square feet	Weight, total of engine, working order...........120,500 pounds
Tubes, number..298	Weight of tender, loaded.........................83,800 pounds
Tubes, length over sheets........................11 feet 6 inches	Weight of tender, empty...........................34,500 pounds
Tubes, diameter outside................................2 inches	Steam pressure..180 pounds
Heating surface, tubes...........................1794 square feet	Rating..17.7 per cent.
Heating surface, firebox...........................156 square feet	

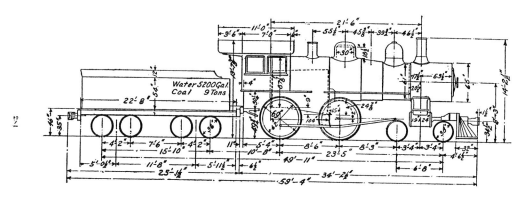

Kind of main valve...........................Richardson balanced	Heating surface, total.........................2080.8 square feet
Firebox, length inside.........................96¼ inches	Weight on drivers, working order.................78,000 pounds
Firebox, width inside.........................40⅛ inches	Weight on truck, working order..................46,000 pounds
Grate area...................................26.9 square feet	Weight, total of engine, working order...........124,000 pounds
Tubes, number................................320	Weight of tender, loaded.........................106,000 pounds
Tubes, length over sheets.....................11 feet 6 inches	Weight of tender, empty..........................44,700 pounds
Tubes, diameter outside.......................2 inches	Steam pressure..................................180 pounds
Heating surface, tubes........................1926 square feet	Rating..18.4 per cent
Heating surface, firebox......................154.8 square feet	

B&A 251, class C-38 at Allston, July 1915.   (Vollrath collection)

NYC&HR (B&A) 1141, class C-38. Note unusual counterweights and small tender. (E.L.May)

B&A 27 as built by Rhode Island in 1893. It became 1168, class c-35.   (Walter Fogg)

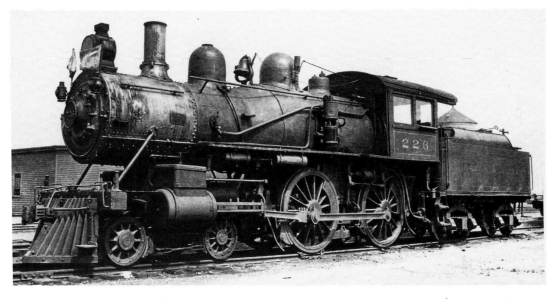

B&A 226, class C-36b, at Allston in July 1915   (Vollrath collection)

B&A 403, class D-la, built 1928 for Boston suburban service. America's biggest tank engine.

(Rail Photo Service)

CLASS F. 4-6-0 TEN WHEEL

B&A CLASS F-30: 20x24-70-180-138000-21600 (Old O,H)

	Re'93	Re'00			Re'12	Bldr.c/n	Date	Disp'n.
11	285	163	2158	2032	700	R.I.2870	3/93	Sc 2/13
12	286	164	2159	2033	701	" 2871	"	Sc 4/13

B&A CLASS F-31: 20x26-70-200-158000-26000 (Old A,B-1)
(As built: 22&34x26-70-190-156000 Compound)

					Bldr.c/n	Date	Disp'n.
220	(re'00)	2030	(re'12)	702	Schen.4927	1/99	Sc 9/15
221	"	2031	"	703	" 4928	"	Sc 1/16

B&A CLASS F-2c: 23x26-69-190-202800-32190 (F-12c SH)

	Re.12	Builder	c/n	Date	Super.	Disp'n.
1900	704	Alco-S	42537	4/07	'19	RT 3/32
1901	705	"	42538	"	'19	RT 3/32
1902	706	"	42539	"	'19	RT 12/29
1903	707	"	42540	"	'20	RT 3/32
1904	708	"	42541	"	'21	RT 3/32
1905	709	"	42542	"	'22	RT 11/33
1906	710	"	42543	"	'22	RT 3/32
1907	711	"	42544	"	'22	RT 4/33
1908	712	"	42545	"	'20	RT 11/30
1909	713	"	42546	"	'20	RT 5/33

B&A CLASS F-2f: 22x26-69-200-211000-31000

	Re'12	Builder	c/n	Date	Super.	Disp'n.
1910	714	Alco-S	44876	12/07	'19	RT 3/29
1911	715	"	44877	"	'19	RT 11/33
1912	716	"	44878	"	'18	RT 10/32
1913	717	"	44879	"	'21	RT 4/32
1914	718	"	44880	"	'19	RT 5/33
1915	719	"	44881	"	'19	RT 3/32
1916	720	"	44882	"	'19	RT 2/32
1917	721	"	44883	"	'21	RT 10/32
1918	722	"	44884	"	'19	RT 6/32
1919	723	"	44885	"	'19	RT 3/32

CLASS G. 2-8-0 CONSOLIDATION

B&A CLASS G-30: 20x26-48-160-132000-27800 (Old M,G)

	Re'93	Re'00	Re'12	Bldr.	c/n	Date	RB	Disp'n.
251	102	2552	924	BLW.	8290	12/86	1/99	Sc 10/18
252	112	2557	929	"	8295	"	4/99	Sc 6/18
253	125	2558	930	"	8728	8/87	12/98	Sc 6/19
254	167	2564(a)	900	"	8729	"	6/00	Sc 9/19
255	142	2559	931	"	8733	"	1/00	Sc 9/18
56	56	2530	902	"	8741	"	3/99	Sc 10/22
257	169	2565(a)	901	"	8798	9/87	2/00	Sc 8/21
258	58	2531	903	"	8800	"	5/99	Sc 9/17
259	95	2550	922	"	8801	"	1/01	Sc 10/16
260	60	2532	904	"	8809	10/87	5/00	Sc 11/22
76	76	2539	911	"	9378	7/88	11/97	Sc 9/16
77	77	2540	912	"	9381	"	11/97	Sc 11/16
84	84	2545	917	"	9383	8/88	11/97	Sc 11/16
85	85	2546	918	"	9384	"	4/00	Sc 3/19
186	72	2538	910	"	9388	"	6/03	Sc 2/19
187	98	2551	923	"	9392	"	6/03	Sc 5/21
10	61	2533	905	"	10579	1/90	12/97	Sc 9/16
82	82	2544	916	"	10582	"	5/01	Sc 3/19
147	147	2560	932	"	10583	"	5/99	Sc 12/22
154	154	2561	933	"	10598	"	12/97	Sc 11/16
165	165	2563	935	"	10586	"	1/98	Sc 10/22
183	107	2555	927	"	10592	"	6/04	Sc 2/19
78	78	2541	913	"	11119	8/90	1/98	Sc 5/19
79	79	2542	914	"	11122	"	5/04	Sc 4/19
80	80	2543	915	"	11127	"	3/01	Sc 9/18
88	88	2547	919	"	11128	"	11/97	Sc 5/19
89	89	2548	920	"	11131	"	11/97	Sc 6/19
90	90	2549	921	"	11126	"	12/98	Sc 4/19
66	66	2534	906	"	12263	10/91	8/02	Sc 10/16
67	67	2535	907	"	12264	"	4/01	Sc 1/19
70	70	2536	908	"	12268	"	1/99	Sc 1/19
71	71	2537	909	"	12271	"	12/97	Sc 9/16
104	104	2553	925	"	12308	10/91	8/04	Sc 6/18
105	105	2554	926	"	12313	"	11/98	Sc 8/17
108	108	2556	928	"	12309	"	3/05	Sc 7/19
156	156	2562	934 (b)	"	12318	"	'01,11	Sc 11/23

B&A CLASS G-31: 20x26-48-160-132000-27800 (Old N,G)

	Re'93	Re'00		Re'12	Bldr.c/n	Date	RB	Disp'n.
15	115	2569	2503	939	R.I.2673	12/91	/08	Sc 10/23
35	87	2567	2501	937	" 2674	"	/09	Sc 10/23
39	93	2568	2502	938	" 2675	"	/11	So 4/22(c)
64	64	2566	2500	936	" 2676	"	/09	Sc 9/23

B&A CLASS G-32: 20x26-48-160-132000-27800 (Old L,G)(d)

	Re'93	Re'00		Re'12	Bldr.c/n	Date	RB	Disp'n.
161	161	2527		963	Sch.4147	7/93		Sc 12/15
162	162	2528	2504	940	" 4148	"	/09	Sc 10/26
168	168	2529	2505	941	" 4149	"	/08	Sc 7/26
172	152	2526		962	" 4150	"		Sc 3/15
176	137	2523		959	" 4151	"	/12	Sc 12/25
181	91	2512		948	" 4152	"	/10	Sc 11/25
198	144	2525		961	" 4153	"	/06	Sc 8/26
202	57	2508		944	" 4154	"	/06	Sc 11/25
204	96	2513		949	" 4155	"	/11	Sc 7/26
206	120	2516		952	" 4156	"	/09	Sc 12/21
	62	2509		945	" 4238	11/94	/10	Sc 4/24
	83	2511		947	" 4239	"	/08	Sc 6/25
	116	2515		951	" 4240	"	/13	Sc 8/26
	122	2517		953	" 4241	"	/07	Sc 6/25
	50	2506		942	" 4282	4/95		So'13(f)
	54	2507		943	" 4283	"	/11	Sc 9/26
	63	2510		946	" 4284	"	/08	Sc 9/25
	114	2514		950	" 4285	5/95		Sc 10/16
	126	2519		955	" 4286	"	/10	Sc 9/25
	127	2520		956	" 4287	"		Sc 11/15
	131	2521		957	" 4288	"		Sc 12/15
	135	2522		958	" 4289	"		Sc 12/15
	123	2518		954	" 4290	"	/11	Sc 8/26
	141	2524		960	" 4291	"	/11	Sc 1/25

B&A CLASS G-33: 20x32-57-195-187000-38400 (Old F)(e)

	Re'00	Re'12	Bldr.	c/n	Date	RB	Disp'n.	#
2500	2564	964	Sch.	5997	9/01	/18	U-33	#30
2501	2565	965	"	5998	"	/18	"	31
2502	2566	966	"	5999	"	/18	"	32
2503	2567	967	"	6000	"	/18	"	33
2504	2568	968	"	6001	"	/17	"	34
2505	2569	969	"	6002	"	/17	"	35
	2570	970	"	25302	11/01	/17	"	36
	2571	971	"	25303	"	"	"	37
	2572	972	"	25304	"	"	"	38
	2573	973	"	25385	2/02	"	"	39
	2574	974	"	25306	"	"	"	40
	2575	975	"	25307	"	"	"	41

Note a: 2564,2565 re 2528,2529
Note b: 934 later class G-30a
Note c: 938 re Hoosac Tun.& Wilm. 39
Note d: Rebuilt engines became class G-32a
Note e: Class G-33 as built: 22&34x32 compound
Note f: 942 sold to Wardwell.

Class F-30.

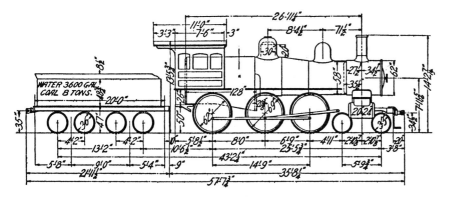

Kind of main valve	Richardson balanced	Heating surface, total	1948.5 square feet
Firebox, length inside	120 inches	Weight on drivers, working order	112,000 pounds
Firebox, width inside	33½ inches	Weight on truck, working order	26,000 pounds
Grate area	27.7 square feet	Weight, total of engine, working order	138,000 pounds
Tubes, number	248	Weight of tender, loaded	73,000 pounds
Tubes, length over sheets	13 feet 8 inches	Weight of tender, empty	27,000 pounds
Tubes, diameter outside	2 inches	Steam pressure	180 pounds
Heating surface, tubes	1774.5 square feet	Rating	21.9 per cent.
Heating surface, firebox	174 square feet		

Class F-2c.

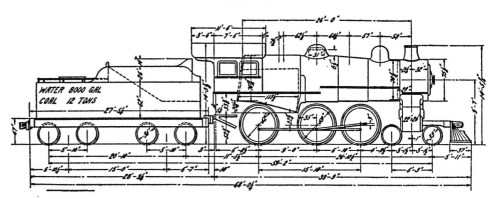

Kind of main valve	12-inch piston	Heating surface, total	3327 square feet
Firebox, length inside	105½ inches	Weight on drivers, working order	152,000 pounds
Firebox, width inside	75½ inches	Weight on truck, working order	46,000 pounds
Grate area	54.93 square feet	Weight, total of engine, working order	198,000 pounds
Tubes, number	400	Weight of tender, loaded	155,000 pounds
Tubes, length over sheets	14 feet 11 inches	Weight of tender, empty	64,200 pounds
Tubes, diameter outside	2 inches	Steam pressure	200 pounds
Heating surface, tubes	3124 square feet	Rating	31.9 per cent.
Heating surface, firebox, including arch tubes	203 square feet		

Class G-30.

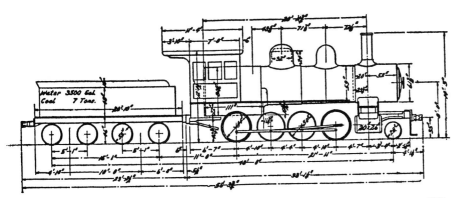

Kind of main valve	Allen-Richardson balanced	Heating surface, total	1726 square feet
Firebox, length inside	103 inches	Weight on drivers, working order	112,000 pounds
Firebox, width inside	41 inches	Weight on truck, working order	16,500 pounds
Grate area	29.3 square feet	Weight, total of engine, working order	128,500 pounds
Tubes, number	228	Weight of tender, loaded	73,300 pounds
Tubes, length over sheets	13 feet 1½ inches	Weight of tender, empty	30,100 pounds
Tubes, diameter outside	2 inches	Steam pressure	160 pounds
Heating surface, tubes	1,566 square feet	Rating	26.4 per cent.
Heating surface, firebox	160 square feet		

B&A 715 class F-2f at Allston in September 1920.   (Purinton 41)

B&A 705 class F-2c. It was reclassified F-12c when superheated in 1919.

Class G-33.

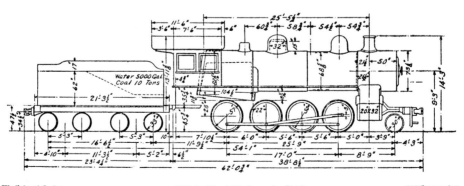

Kind of main valve............................12-inch piston	Heating surface, total............................3150 square feet
Firebox, length inside............................96¼ inches	Weight on drivers, working order............163,000 pounds
Firebox, width inside............................75½ inches	Weight on truck, working order............24,000 pounds
Grate area............................50.2 square feet	Weight, total of engine, working order............187,000 pounds
Tubes, number............................359	Weight of tender, loaded............105,350 pounds
Tubes, length over sheets............16 feet 0 inches	Weight of tender, empty............43,750 pounds
Tubes, diameter outside............2 inches	Steam pressure............195 pounds
Heating surface, tubes............3005 square feet	Rating............38.4 per cent.
Heating surface, firebox............145 square feet	

NYC&HR (B&A) 2500, class C-33. Simpled and rebuilt 1918 to U-33 switcher.   (Vollrath)

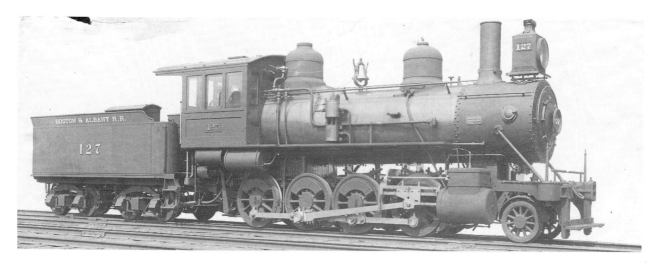

B&A 127 class G-32 Schenectady builder's photo. Later B&A 956.   (Edson collection)

B&A 900, class G-32 Built by Baldwin in 1887, the roads first 2-8-0. Allston,Aug. 1914

(Vollrath)

B&A CLASS G-34 2-8-0: 21x30-63-200-205300-36900

	Re'12		Builder	c/n	Date	Disp'n.
2576	976	(a)	Alco-S	28952	11/03	RT 8/26
2577	977		"	28953	"	RT 5/28
2578	978		"	28954	"	RT 5/25
2579	979		"	28955	"	RT 6/26
2580	980	(a)	"	28956	"	RT 5/28
2581	981		"	28957	"	RT 12/25
2582	982		"	28958	"	RT 7/27
2583	983		"	28959	"	RT 4/26
2584	984	(a)	"	29347	12/03	RT 4/26
2585	985		"	29348	"	RT 12/25
2586	986	(a)	"	29349	"	RT 4/26
2587	987		"	29350	"	RT 5/26
2588	988	(a)	"	29351	"	RT 1/26
2589	989		"	29352	"	RT 7/25

B&A CLASS G-5g 2-8-0: 23x32-63-200-241500-45680.

2590	990	Alco-S	37990	9/05	RB 8/15 (b)
2591	991	"	37991	"	" " "
2592	992	"	37992	"	" " "
2593	993	"	37993	"	" " "
2594	994	"	37994	"	" " "
2595	995	"	37995	"	" " "
2596	996	"	37996	"	" " "
2597	997	"	37997	"	" 10/15 "
2598	998	"	37998	"	" " "
2599	999	"	37999	"	" " "

B&A CLASS G-5w 2-8-0: 23x32-63-200-237000-45680

2600	1000	Alco-S	43003	6/07	RT 12/26
2601	1001	"	43004	"	RT 9/26
2602	1002	"	43005	"	RT 9/26
2603	1003	"	43006	"	RT 5/32
2604	1004	"	43007	"	RT 10/27
2605	1005	"	43008	"	RT 10/32
2606	1006	"	43009	"	RT 5/31
2607	1007	"	43010	"	RT 5/32
2608	1008	"	43011	"	RT 9/34
2609	1009	"	43012	"	RT 5/33
2610	1010	"	43026	"	RT 11/28
2611	1011	"	43027	"	RT 12/29
2612	1012	"	43028	"	RT 5/32
2613	1013	"	43029	"	RT 10/32
2614	1014	"	43030	"	RT 7/34

B&A CLASS G-6e 2-8-0: 23x32-63-200-237000-45680

	Re'12	Builder	c/n	Date	Disp'n
2615	1015	Alco-S	44896	12/07	RT 12/26
2616	1016	"	44897	"	RT 9/26
2617	1017	"	44898	"	RT 5/34
2618	1018	"	44899	"	RT 12/26
2619	1019	"	44900	"	RT 9/26
2620	1020	"	44901	"	RT 7/34
2621	1021	"	44902	"	RT 10/35
2622	1022	"	44903	"	RT 10/27
2623	1023	"	44904	"	Sc 10/27
2624	1024	"	44905	"	Sc 12/34
2625	1025	"	44906	"	RT 12/34
2626	1026	"	44907	"	RT 12/34
2627	1027	"	44908	"	RT 12/34
2628	1028	"	44909	"	RT 10/27
2629	1029	"	44910	"	RT 9/35

B&A CLASS G-6h 2-8-0: 23x32-63-200-242000-45680

2630	1030	Alco-S	45398	10/08	Sc 12/26
2631	1031	"	45399	"	Sc 5/33
2632	1032	"	45400	"	Sc 10/35
2633	1033	"	45401	"	Sc 10/35
2634	1034	"	45402	"	Sc 9/26
2635	1035	"	45403	"	Sc 9/26
2636	1036	"	45404	"	Sc 8/26
2637	1037	"	45405	"	Sc 9/26
2638	1038	"	45406	"	Sc 5/37
2639	1039	"	45407	"	Sc 5/33
2640	1040	"	45408	"	Sc 11/49
2641	1041	"	45409	"	Sc 12/39
2642	1042	"	45410	"	Sc 9/26
2643	1043	"	45411	"	Sc 9/26
2644	1044	"	45412	"	Sc 5/49
2645	1045	"	45413	"	Sc 12/39
2646	1046	"	45414	"	Sc 1/38
2647	1047	"	45415	"	Sc 7/39
2648	1048	"	45416	"	Sc 12/49
2649	1049	"	45417	"	Sc 7/39

B&A CLASS G-6q 2-8-0: 23x32-63-200-242000-45680 (c)

	1050	Alco-S	52279	12/12	Sc 5/49
	1051	"	52280	"	Sc 5/49
	1052	"	52281	"	Sc 1/50
	1053	"	52282	"	Sc 11/49

CLASS H. 4-8-0 TWELVE WHEEL

B&A CLASS H-30 4-8-0: 20x28-54-200-162000-24600.(d)
As built: 22&34x28 compound. 31800 tf. Old F-1

re'00	re'05	re'12	re'12	Builder	c/n	Date	Disp'n
170	2632	3632	2674	800	Schen.	4922	1/99	Sc 10/16
171	2633	3633	2675	801	"	4923	"	Sc 10/16
172	2634	3634	2676	802	"	4924	"	Sc 1/18
173	2635	3635	2677	803	"	4925	"	Sc 10/16
174	2636	3636	2678	804	"	4926	"	Sc 10/16

B&A CLASS H-30a 4-8-0: 20x28-54-200-164000-24600.(e)
As built: 22&34x28 compound. 31800 tf. Old F-1

re'00	re'05	re'12	re'12	Builder	c/n	Date	Disp'n
175	2637	3637	2679	805	Schen.	5393	2/00	Sc 10/16
176	2638	3638	2680	806	"	5394	"	Sc 10/16
177	2639	3639	2681	807	"	5395	"	Sc 11/21
178	2640	3640	2682	808	"	5396	"	Sc 10/16
179	2641	3641	2683	809	"	5397	"	Sc 6/18
180	2642	3642	2684	810	"	5398	"	Sc 11/21

Note a: Converted 1918-1920 tp class G-34a.   Note b: RB 1915 to 2-8-2 class H-5g.   Note c: Later G-16q.
Note d: Reclassified c.1913 to R-30.   Note e: Reclassified c.1913 to R-30a.

Class G-34.

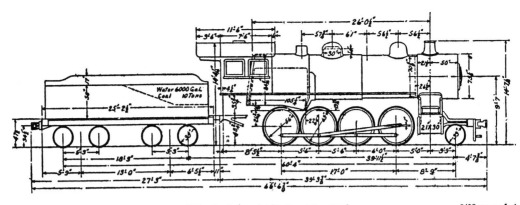

Kind of main valve....................Richardson balanced	Heating surface, total...................3438 square feet
Firebox, length inside..................96¼ inches	Weight on drivers, working order.......167,000 pounds
Firebox, width inside..................75⅜ inches	Weight on truck, working order.........23,000 pounds
Grate area..........................50.32 square feet	Weight, total of engine, working order..190,000 pounds
Tubes, number........................392	Weight of tender, loaded..............116,600 pounds
Tubes, length over sheets............16 feet, 0 inches	Weight of tender, empty...............46,600 pounds
Tubes, diameter outside...............2 inches	Steam pressure.......................200 pounds
Heating surface, tubes...............3284 square feet	Rating..............................36.9 per cent.
Heating surface, firebox.............154 square feet	

Class G-5w.

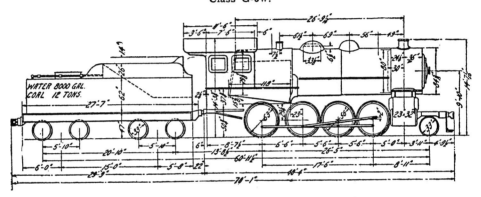

Kind of valve motion..................Walschaert	Heating surface, firebox, including arch tubes....236 square feet
Kind of main valve....................14-inch piston	Heating surface, total................3727 square feet
Firebox, length inside................108¼ inches	Weight on drivers, working order......208,000 pounds
Firebox, width inside.................75¼ inches	Weight on truck, working order........26,000 pounds
Grate area..........................56.5 square feet	Weight, total of engine, working order..234,000 pounds
Tubes, number........................444	Weight of tender, loaded..............155,000 pounds
Tubes, length over sheets............15 feet 0¼ inches	Weight of tender, empty...............64,200 pounds
Tubes, diameter outside...............2 inches	Steam pressure.......................200 pounds
Heating surface, tubes...............3497 square feet	Rating..............................47.2 per cent.

Class H-30.

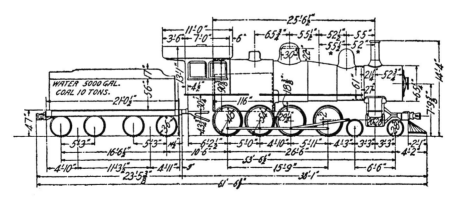

...nd of main valve....................Richardson balanced	Heating surface, total................2516 square feet
...ebox, length inside................108 7/16 inches	Weight on drivers, working order......126,000 pounds
...ebox, width inside.................39⅞ inches	Weight on truck, working order........36,000 pounds
...ate area..........................29.9 square feet	Weight, total of engine, working order..162,000 pounds
...bes, number........................320	Weight of tender, loaded..............110,000 pounds
...bes, length over sheets............14 feet 0 inches	Weight of tender, empty...............45,800 pounds
...bes, diameter outside...............2 inches	Steam pressure.......................200 pounds
...ating surface, tubes...............2346 square feet	Rating..............................29.6 per cent.
...ating surface, firebox.............170 square feet	

NOTE.—Dimensions marked thus * refer to Class H-30A.
NOTE.—For tender capacity of individual engines see serial list.

B&A 1025, class G-6c. Before the A-1's arrived, every freight to the west doubleheaded.
(Vollrath)

NYC&HR (B&A) 2583, class G-34 builder's photo.   (Edson collection)

B&A 2628, class G-6e, at Springfield prior to 1912.   (Chaney collection)

B&A 1008, class G-5w. at Beacon Park, Boston, in August, 1932.   (Pollitt collection)

B&A 1049, class G-6h, at Palmer, Mass. in August, 1938.   (G.Votava)

NYC&HR (B&A) 3639 , class H-30a, later R-30a. Later renumbered B&A 807   (Purinton 293)

CLASS H.   2-8-2 MIKADO

B&A CLASS H-5j 2-8-2: 25x32-63-180-283500-48570 (a)

	Re 4/51	Builder	c/n	Date	Disp'n.
1200		Alco-S	54274	12/13	Sc 7/50
1201	1304	"	54275	"	SS 11/51
1202	1306	"	54276	"	RT 3/55
1203	1307	"	54277	"	Sc 6/51
1204		"	54278	"	Sc 1/50
1205		"	54279	"	Sc 1/50
1206	1322	"	54280	1/14	SS 2/52
1207	1329	"	54281	"	SS 2/52
1208	1340	"	54282	"	SS 10/52
1209	1345	"	54283	"	SS 3/52
1210		"	54284	"	SS 1/50
1211		"	54285	"	SS 5/50
1212		"	54286	"	Sc 9/40
1213	1348	"	54287	"	Sc 1/53

B&A CLASS H-5g 2-6-2: 25x32-63-180-281700-48570 (b)

		Alco-B	c/n	Date	
1214	1350	Alco-B	GO-40134-7	7/15	RT 11/55
1215		"	" 6	"	Sc 12/49
1216	1351	"	" 3	8/15	SS 1/52
1217	1352	"	" 4	"	SS 5/52 (c)
1218		"	" 1	"	Sc 4/50 (c)
1219	1355	"	" 10	10/15	SS 3/52
1220	1356	"	" 2	8/15	SS 3/52 (c)
1221	1358	"	" 5	"	SS 8/52
1222		"	" 8	9/15	So 3/42 (d,c)
1223		"	" 9	"	Sc 3/39

B&A CLASS H-5t 2-8-2: 25x32-63-180-286000-48570 (e)

	Re 4/51	Bldr.	c/n	Date	Acquired		Disp'n.
1224	1425	Lima	5254	10/16	3/39 (ex NYC 1463)		SS 9/52
1225	1426	"	5271	11/16	10/40	" 1480	SS 9/52
1226	1427	"	5244	10/16	2/41	" 1453	RT 11/55
1227	1446	"	5253	"	2/41	" 1462	RT 4/55
1228	1464	"	5255	"	4/41	" 1464	RT 4/55
1229	1449	"	5232	9/16	12/41	" 1441	RT 7/54

B&A CLASS H-10a 2-8-2: 28x30-63-200-342500-63470 (f)

183	(re'36)	2283	Alco-S	63653	2/23	RT 12/53
184	"	2284	"	63695	"	RT 7/52
185	"	2285	"	63696	"	RT 11/51
186	"	2286	"	63690	"	RT 5/52
187	"	2287	"	63691	"	RT 12/51
188	"	2288	"	63692	"	RT 11/51
189	"	2289	"	63693	"	RT 10/52
190	"	2290	"	63694	"	RT 5/52

Note a: Orig. 293400 wt. 57560 tf with booster.
Note b: RB from 2-8-0 class G-5g #990-999. See p.286
Note c: 57560 tf with booster.
Note d: Re Duluth, South Shore & Atlantic 1054.
Note e: #1224= 295300 wt. 57560 tf with booster.
Note f: 74470 tf with booster. All H-10a assigned
　　　　to Line West in 3/26.

CLASS I,   4-4-2 ATLANTIC

B&A CLASS Ib 4-4-2: 20+x26-79-200-188500-22400 (Note g)

	Re'05	Re'12	Builder	c/n	Date	Disp'n.
2948	3948	400	Alco-S	25296	6/02	RT 7/25
2949	3949	401	"	25297	"	RT 6/25
2950	3950	402	"	25298	"	RT 10/24
2951	3051	403	"	25299	"	RT 5/25
2952	3952	404	"	25300	"	RT 1/25
2953	3953	405	"	25301	"	RT 8/24

Note g: Old class A, known as "Trailer type".

　　　　Original specs 21x26-79-200-176000-24000.

CLASS J.   4-6-4 HUDSON

B&A CLASS J-2a 4-6-4: 25x28-75-240-353000-44800 (h)

	Re 4/51	Builder	c/n	Date	Disposition
600	5455	Alco-S	67604	7/28	SS 9/52
601	5456	"	67605	8/28	SS 7/53
602	5457	"	67606	"	SS 8/52
603	5458	"	67607	"	SS 10/52
604	5459	"	67608	"	SS 10/52

B&A CLASS J-2b 4-6-4: 25x28-75-200-356500-44800 (h)

605	5460	Alco-S	68482	8/30	SS 2/53
606	5461	"	68483	"	SS 10/52
607	5462	"	68484	"	SS 3/52
608	5463	"	68485	"	SS 7/53
609	5464	"	68486	"	Sc 9/52

B&A CLASS J-2c 4-6-4: 25x28-75-240-357000-44800 (h)

	Re 4/51	Bldr.	c/n	Date	Disp'n.
610	5465	Lima	7574	4/31	SS 2/52
611	5466	"	7575	"	SS 11/52
612	5467	"	7576	"	SS 7/53
613	5468	"	7577	"	SS 3/52
614	5469	"	7578	"	SS 10/52
615	5470	"	7579	"	SS 3/52
616	5471	"	7580	"	SS 3/52
617	5472	"	7581	"	Sc 9/52
618	5473	"	7582	"	SS 3/52
619	5474	"	7583	"	SS 7/53

Note g: TF 55320 with booster. BP later 225.

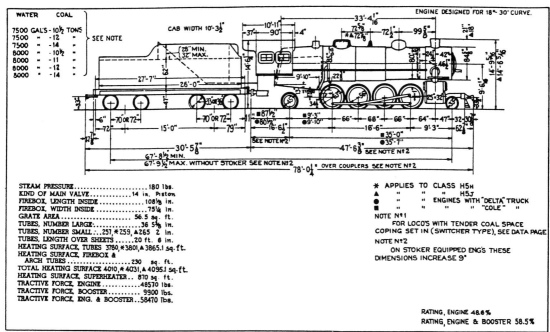

WATER COAL

7500 GAL'S - 10½ TONS
7500 " - 12
7500 " - 14
8000 " - 10½
8000 " - 11
8000 " - 12
8000 " - 14

ENGINE DESIGNED FOR 18° 30' CURVE.

STEAM PRESSURE..................180 lbs.
KIND OF MAIN VALVE..........14 in. Piston
FIREBOX, LENGTH INSIDE...........108½ in.
FIREBOX, WIDTH INSIDE.............75¼ in.
GRATE AREA.....................56.5 sq. ft.
TUBES, NUMBER LARGE...........36 5½ in.
TUBES, NUMBER SMALL....257,*259,▲265 2 in.
TUBES, LENGTH OVER SHEETS......20 ft. 6 in.
HEATING SURFACE, TUBES 3780,*3801,▲3865.1 sq. ft.
HEATING SURFACE, FIREBOX &
    ARCH TUBES..................230 sq. ft.
TOTAL HEATING SURFACE 4010,*4031,▲4095.1 sq. ft.
HEATING SURFACE, SUPERHEATER.....870 sq. ft.
TRACTIVE FORCE, ENGINE...........48570 lbs.
TRACTIVE FORCE, BOOSTER..........9900 lbs.
TRACTIVE FORCE, ENG. & BOOSTER..58470 lbs.

* APPLIES TO CLASS H5H
▲ " " " H5J
● " " ENGINES WITH "DELTA" TRUCK
■ " " " " "COLE" "

NOTE Nº1
    FOR LOCO'S WITH TENDER COAL SPACE
    COPING SET IN (SWITCHER TYPE), SEE DATA PAGE
NOTE Nº2
    ON STOKER EQUIPPED ENG'S THESE
    DIMENSIONS INCREASE 9"

RATING, ENGINE 48.6%
RATING, ENGINE & BOOSTER 58.5%

CLASSES H5H, H5J, H5S & H5T

Class IB.

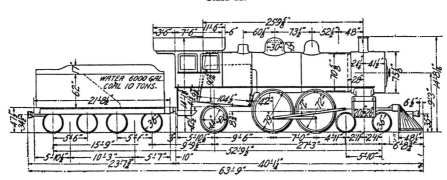

Kind of main valve.........................12-inch piston
Firebox, length inside.....................96¾ inches
Firebox, width inside......................75¾ inches
Grate area.................................50.32 square feet
Tubes, number..............................384
Tubes, length over sheets..................16 feet 0 inches
Tubes, diameter outside....................2 inches
Heating surface, tubes.....................3217 square feet
Heating surface, firebox, including arch tubes.......180 square feet

Heating surface, total.....................3397 square feet
Weight on drivers, working order...........105,000 pounds
Weight on forward truck, working order.....37,000 pounds
Weight on rear truck, working order........34,000 pounds
Weight, total of engine, working order.....176,000 pounds
Weight of tender, loaded...................118,000 pounds
Weight of tender, empty....................48,000 pounds
Steam pressure.............................200 pounds
Rating.....................................24.0 per cent.

B & A

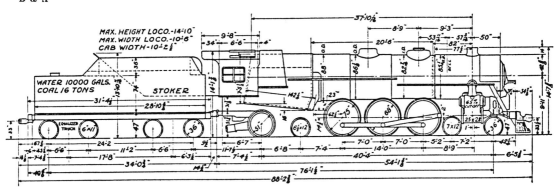

MAX. HEIGHT LOCO.-14'-10"
MAX. WIDTH LOCO.-10'-6"
CAB WIDTH-10'-2¼"

Number of Locomotives.......................5
Built by the........American Locomotive Co.
                    Schenectady Works
Builders' Order No..................S-1620
Valve gear.........................Baker
Kind of main valve.............14 in. Piston
Firebox, length inside.............130 in.
Firebox, width inside..............90¼ in.
Grate area.........................81.5 sq. ft.

WITH SUPERHEATER
Small tubes......................37-2¼ in.
Large tubes......................201-3½ in.
Length over sheets...............20 ft.-6 in.
Heating surface, tubes...........4203 sq. ft.
Heating surface, firebox and arch tubes.......281 sq. ft.
Total heating surface............4484 sq. ft.
Heating surface, superheater.....1951 sq. ft.
WEIGHT IN WORKING ORDER ON:
    Front truck..................65000 lbs.
    Drivers......................187500 lbs.
    Trailer truck................100500 lbs.
    Total engine.................353000 lbs.
Weight of tender loaded..........204600 lbs.
Weight of tender empty...........91100 lbs.

CLASS J-2A

292

B&A 186, class H-10a. Later transferred off the B&A, without change of number.(Purinton)

B&A 1224, class H-5t, ex-NYC 1463. One of six acquired 1939-41.   (Edson collection)

B¢A 400, class Ib. At Allston 5/1922, twenty years after built.   (Vollrath collection)

B&A 601, class J-2a.   Alco Builder's photo. (W.D.Edson coll.)

B&A 605, class J-2b.   Alco Builder's photo. (W.D.Edson coll.)

B&A, class J-2c   LLW builder's photo. (W.D.Edson coll.)

B&A 608, class J-2b, with train #8, the Wolverine, passing Faneuil, Mass. in 1930's.

CLASS K. 4-6-2 PACIFIC

B&A CLASS K-1a 4-6-2: 20 3/4x28-75-200-221200-27300
As built K-1: 21x28-75-200-209000-28800.

Re'05	Re'12		Builder	c/n	Date	Disp'n.
2700	3500	500	Alco-S	28960	12/03	RT 4/28
2701	3501	501	"	28961	"	RT 4/28
2702	3502	502	"	28962	"	RT 8/28
2703	3503	503	"	28963	"	RT 4/28
2704	3504	504	"	29353	"	RT 10/29
2705	3505	505	"	29354	"	RT 4/28
2706	3506	506	"	29355	"	RT 5/28
2707	3507	507	"	29356	"	RT 10/29
2708	3508	508	"	29357	"	RT 3/29
2709	3509	509	"	29358	"	RT 8/28

B&A CLASS K (later Kg): 22x26-75-200-226500-28520(a)

2795	3595	510	Alco-S	27956	12/03	RT 10/28
2796	3596	511	"	27957	"	RT 5/28
2797	3597	512	"	27958	"	RT 6/29
2798	3598	513	"	27959	"	RT 9/29
2799	3599	514	"	27960	"	RT 12/29

B&A CLASS Ka 4-6-2: 22x26-75-200-230000-28520

3510	515	Alco-S	37984	10/05	RT 4/32
3511	516	"	37985	"	RT 4/31
3512	517	"	37986	"	RT 4/32
3513	518	"	37987	"	RT 4/32
3514	519	"	37988	"	RT 4/32
3515	520	"	37989	"	RT 5/30

B&A CLASS Kc 4-6-2: 22x26-75-200-235000-28520

3516	521	Alco-S	43001	6/07	RT 11/33
3517	522	"	43002	"	RT 4/33

B&A CLASS Kd 4-6-2: 22x26-75-200-237000-28520

3518	523	Alco-S	44886	12/07	RT 4/33
3519	524	"	44887	"	RT 4/32
3520	525	"	44888	"	RT 11/34
3521	526	"	44889	"	RT 7/34
3522	527	"	44890	"	RT 5/32
3523	528	"	44891	"	RT 5/33
3524	529	"	44892	"	RT 5/34
3525	530	"	44893	"	RT 6/34
3526	531	"	44894	"	RT 9/34
3527	532	"	44895	"	RT 9/34

B&A CLASS Ke 4-6-2: 22x26-75-200-238000-28520

3528	533	Alco-S	45336	9/08	RT 9/34
3529	534	"	45337	"	RT 6/34
3530	535	"	45338	"	RT 9/35
3531	536	"	45339	"	RT 9/35
3532	537	"	45340	"	RT 9/35
3533	538	"	45341	"	RT 9/35
3534	539	"	45342	"	RT 9/35
3535	540	"	45343	"	RT 9/35
3536	541	"	45344	"	RT 10/35
3537	542	"	45345	"	RT 6/38
3538	543	"	45346	"	RT 12/37
3539	544	"	45347	"	RT 4/39

B&A CLASS Kj 4-6-2: 22x26-75-200-238000-28520

3540	545	Alco-S	49419	2/11	RT 3/38
3541	546	"	49420	"	RT 3/39
3542	547	"	49421	"	RT 11/37
3543	548	"	49422	"	RT 11/37
3544	549	"	49423	"	RT 10/39

B&A CLASS Kj 4-6-2: Continued

Re'12		Builder	c/n	Date	Disp'n.
3545	550	Alco-S	49424	2/11	RT 6/39
3546	551	"	49425	3/11	RT 2/49
3547	552	"	49426	"	RT 3/38
3548	553	"	49427	"	RT 2/49
3549	554	"	49428	"	RT 10/47

B&A CLASS KL 4-6-2: 22x26-75-200-241000-28520

555	Alco-S	52287	12/12	Sc 10/47
556	"	52288	"	Sc 11/48
557	"	52289	"	Sc 10/47
558	"	52290	"	Sc 10/49
559	"	52291	"	Sc 4/49

B&A CLASS Km 4-6-2: 22x26-75-200-241000-28520

560	Alco-S	54268	12/13	Sc 10/47
561	"	54269	"	Sc 5/49
562	"	54270	"	Sc 4/49
563	"	54271	"	Sc 10/48
564	"	54272	1/14	Sc 5/49
565	"	54273	"	Sc 10/47

B&A CLASS K-14g 4-6-2: 26x26-72-190-275500-39420 (b)

Ex-NYC	Re'21	Re'51	Bldr.	c/n	Date	RB	Disp'n.
3171	575	4375	Alco-S	54168	9/13	1/21	SS 8/52
3175	576	4376	"	54172	"	12/20	SS 11/52
3176	577	4377	"	54173	10/13	1/21	SS 2/53
3182	578	4378	"	54179	"	12/20	SS 10/52
3190	579	4379	"	54187	"	8/20	SS 10/52
3192	580	4380	"	54189	"	1/21	SS 2/53
3181	581	4381	"	54178	"	9/21	SS 2/53
3177	582	4382	"	54174	"	11/22	SS 10/52
3172	583	4383	"	54169	9/13	5/23	SS 10/52
3173	584	4384	"	54170	"	6/23	SS 10/52
3179	585	4385	"	54176	10/13	5/23	SS 10/52
3184	586	4386	"	54181	"	6/23	SS 10/52
3185	587	4387	"	54182	"	6/23	SS 10/52
3188	588	4388	"	54185	"	7/23	SS 7/53

B&A CLASS K-14g 4-6-2: 26x26-72-190-269500-39420. (c)

3064	589	4389	BLW.	37360	12/11	9/25	SS 8/52

B&A CLASS K-6a 4-6-2: 26x28-75-200-298000-42900 (d)

590	Alco-B	66088	4/25	Re 5/31	P&LE	9245
591	"	66089	"	Re 6/31	"	9246
592	"	66090	"	Re 6/31	"	9247
593	"	66091	"	Re 6/31	"	9248
594	"	66092	"	Re 5/31	"	9249

B&A CLASS K-6b 4-6-2: 26x28-75-200-301000-42900 (d)

595	Alco-S	67160	12/26	Re 7/31	P&LE	9250
596	"	67161	"	Re 6/31	"	9251
597	"	67162	"	Re 5/31	"	9252
598	"	67163	"	Re 6/31	"	9253
599	"	67164	"	Re 5/31	"	9254

B&A CLASS K-3n 4-6-2: 23+x26-79-200-280200-30900 (e)

ex-NYC			Builder	c/n	Date	Acq	Disp'n.
ex-4737	500		Alco-B	58112	2/18	Acq.10/37	Sc 1/50
4738	501		"	58113	"	"	Sc 4/49
4745	502		"	58120	"	"	Sc 4/49
4747	503		"	58122	"	"	Sc 4/49
4727	504		"	58102	"	3/38	Sc 5/39
4741	505	4741	"	58116	"	"	SS 8/52
4757	506		"	58132	3/18	"	2/39 Sc 4/49

Note a: Class Kg acq. 1910 from NYC&HR. 3595 RB 8/05 W.Albany.   Note d: K-6a,b TF 52620 with booster
Note b: Class K-14g RB from NYC K-11f, later K-14f.   Note c: K-14h RB from NYC class K-11c, later K-14c.
Note e: 506 wt.289100, tf 40310 with booster.

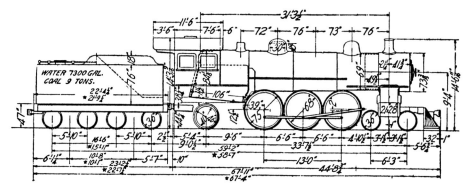

Kind of main valve.........................12-inch piston	Heating surface, total.........................3463 square feet
Firebox, length inside........................96¼ inches	Weight on drivers, working order.............133,000 pounds
Firebox, width inside.........................75¼ inches	Weight on forward truck, working order.........39,000 pounds
Grate area...................................50.2 square feet	Weight on rear truck, working order............37,000 pounds
Tubes, number................................285	Weight, total of engine, working order........209,000 pounds
Tubes, length over sheets.....................19 feet 6 inches	Weight of tender, loaded.....................140,000 pounds
Tubes, diameter outside.......................2¼ inches	Weight of tender, empty.......................61,500 pounds
Heating surface, tubes........................3273 square feet	Steam pressure...............................200 pounds
Heating surface, firebox, including arch tubes.......190 square feet	Rating......................................28.8 per cent.

NOTE.—Dimensions marked thus * apply to engines with 7000 gal. tender.

Class Kᴇ.

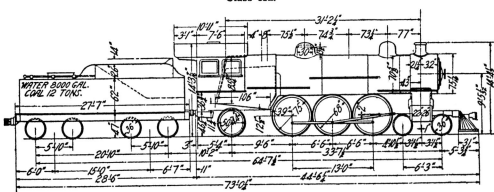

Kind of valve motion.........................Walschaert	Heating surface, total.........................3653 square feet
Kind of main valve...........................12-inch piston	Weight on drivers, working order.............150,500 pounds
Firebox, length inside........................96¼ inches	Weight on forward truck, working order.........42,000 pounds
Firebox, width inside.........................75¼ inches	Weight on rear truck, working order............41,500 pounds
Grate area...................................50.2 square feet	Weight, total of engine, working order........234,000 pounds
Tubes, number................................330	Weight of tender, loaded.....................155,000 pounds
Tubes, length over sheets.....................20 feet 0 inches	Weight of tender, empty.......................64,200 pounds
Tubes, diameter outside.......................2 inches	Steam pressure...............................200 pounds
Heating surface, tubes........................3455 square feet	Rating......................................29.3 per cent.
Heating surface, firebox, including arch tubes.......198 square feet	

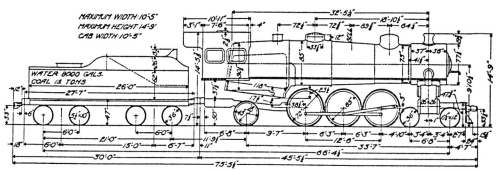

For Wheel Base of Tender With 10,000 Gal. Tanks See Page 96

	WITH SUPERHEATER		
Number of Locomotives..........................14	Small tubes................................248—2 in.		
Built by the...............American Locomotive Co. Schenectady Works	Large tubes...............................34—5⅜ in.		
Builder's Order No............................S-995	Length over sheets........................20 ft.–0 in.		
Valve gear.................................Walschaert	Heating surface, tubes....................3537.1 sq. ft.		
Kind of main valve...........................14 in. Piston	Heating surface, firebox and arch tubes.......232 sq. ft.		
Firebox, length inside........................108⅛ in.	Total heating surface.....................3769.1 sq. ft.		
Firebox, width inside.........................75¼ in.	Heating surface, superheater..............775 sq. ft.		
Grate area...................................56.5 sq. ft.		WITH 10000	WITH 8000
	WEIGHT IN WORKING ORDER ON:	GAL. TANK	GAL. TANK
	Front truck...........49500 lbs...49500 lbs.		
	Drivers...............178000 lbs...178000 lbs.		
	Trailer truck.........48000 lbs...48000 lbs.		
	Total engine.........275500 lbs...275500 lbs.		
	Weight of tender loaded.....201000 lbs...168000 lbs.		
	Weight of tender empty......85700 lbs...63400 lbs.		

NYC&HR (B&A) 2703, class K-1, first Pacifics on the NYC Lines. Later B&A 3503, then 503.

B&A 3530, class Ke, later 535. At South Station, Boston in 1911.   (Chaney collection)

B&A 3517, class Kc. Became B&A 522 in 1912.   (Chaney collection)

B&A 552, class Kj, at Beacon Park, Boston, in September, 1937.   (E.L.May)

B&A 578, class K-14g, converted from NYC K-11f 3182 in 1920. At Beacon Park'37 (E.L.May)

B&A 505 class K-3n, ex-NYC 4741, acquired 1938. At Rensselaer, April 1950.   (E.L.May)

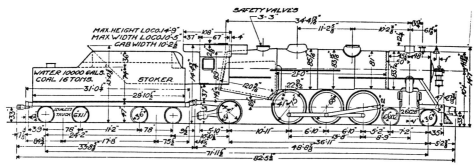

Number of Locomotives	15		With Superheater

Number of Locomotives....................15
Built by the................American Locomotive Co.
Dunkirk Works
Builders' Order No.....................B–1662
Valve Gear............................Walschaert
Kind of Main Valve.................14 in. Piston
Firebox, length inside................108⅛ in.
Firebox, width inside.................90¼ in.
Grate area...........................67.8 sq. ft.

With Superheater
Small tubes............................210–2¼ in.
Large tubes............................45–5½ in.
Length over sheets.....................21 ft.–0 in.
Heating surface, tubes.................3940.0 sq. ft.
Heating surface, firebox and arch tubes....252.0 sq. ft.
Total heating surface..................4192.0 sq. ft.
Heating surface, superheater...........1163.0 sq. ft.
Weight in working order on:
Front truck..........................53500 lbs.
Drivers..............................185500 lbs.
Trailer truck........................59000 lbs.
Total engine.........................298000 lbs.
Weight of tender loaded................204000 lbs.
Weight of tender empty.................88700 lbs.

CLASS K–6A   96

B&A 596, class K-6b, with Boston section of the "Century". Newton, Mass. 1926. (Lorenz)

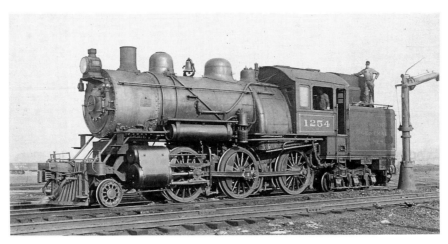

B&A 1254, class L-1, later L-2, then L-3, then D-2a. Beacon Park, c.1911. (Chaney coll.)

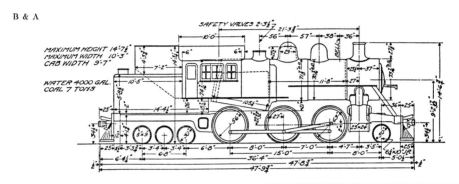

B & A

SAFETY VALVES 2-3½"

MAXIMUM HEIGHT 14'-7¼
MAXIMUM WIDTH 10'-3"
CAB WIDTH 9'-7"

WATER 4000 GAL.
COAL 7 TONS

	WITH SUPERHEATER
Number of Locomotives.......................9+	Small tubes.............................204–2 in.
Built by the.................American Locomotive Co.	Large tubes...........................28–5½ in.
Schenectady Works	Length over sheets.....................11 ft.–8 in.
Builders' Order No.............................S–341	Heating surface, tubes....................1703.0 sq. ft.
Valve gear...................................Baker	Heating surface, firebox and arch tubes........169 sq. ft.
Kind of main valve...................12.10 in. Piston	Total heating surface.....................1872 sq. ft.
Firebox, length inside.................94.3.92⅝ in.	Heating surface, superheater................354.0 sq. ft.
Firebox, width inside......................85¾ in.	WEIGHT IN WORKING ORDER ON:
Grate area...........................55.2 sq. ft.	Front truck.............................27500 lbs.
52.7	Drivers...............................145200 lbs.
	Total engine.........................172700 lbs.
	Weight of tender loaded..................87300 lbs.
	Weight of tender empty...................40000 lbs.

CLASS L–3   118   8-1-29

B&A 304, class L-3, later D-2a. At Riverside, Mass. 1941.   (W.D.Edson)

CLASS L. 2-6-6T DOUBLE ENDER

B&A CLASS L-3: 23x24-63-200-260000-34260 Re'40 D-2a
As built: L-1 20x24-63-200-225000-26800 Re'16 L-2

	Re'12	Builder	c/n	Date	RB	Lima	Disp'n.
1250	300	Alco-S	39654	2/06	11/31	Sc	6/50
1251	301	"	39655	"	11/29	Sc	6/50
1252	302	"	39656	"	12/28	Sc	6/50
1253	303	"	39657	"	3/29	Sc	6/50
1254	304	"	39658	"	10/29	Sc	7/50
1255	305	"	39659	"	12/29	SS	10/52 (a)
1256	306	"	39660	"	8/29	Sc	6/50
1257	307	"	39661	"	2/30	Sc	7/50
1258	308	"	39662	"	5/29	Sc	7/50
1259	309	"	39663	"	7/29	Sc	7/50

B&A CLASS L-3a: 23x24-63-200-263800-34260 Re'40 D-2b
As built L-1a: 20x24-63-200-229000-26800. Re'16 L-2

	Re'12	Builder	c/n	Date	RB	Lima	Disp'n.
1260	310	Alco-S	44868	12/07	10/29	Sc	6/50
1261	311	"	44869	"	4/29	Sc	9/50
1262	312	"	44870	"	12/30	Sc	7/50
1263	313	"	44871	"	2/29	Sc	7/50
1264	314	"	44872	"	1/29	Sc	7/50
1265	315	"	44873	"	4/30	Sc	7/50
1266	316	"	44874	"	3/31	Sc	7/50
1267	317	"	44875	"	8/29	Sc	7/50

Note a: 305 re 6/50 to X305 Selkirk shop engine.

CLASS N. 2-6-6-2 MALLET

B&A CLASS N-1: 20+&33x32-57-210-342000-60770C,80800S
1249   Alco-S 46714 1/10 Re 4/11 NYC&HR 1374

B&A CLASS N-2b: 21+&34x32-57-200-354000-63030C,81000S

1300	Alco-S	52283	12/12	RT	9/32
1301	"	52284	"	RT	4/32
1302	"	52285	"	RT	5/32
1303	"	52286	"	RT	9/32

B&A CLASS NE-2c: 21+&34x32-57-200-354000-63030,81000S

1304	Alco-S	55681	3/16	RT	12/30
1305	"	55682	"	RT	8/32
1306	"	55683	"	RT	12/30
1307	"	55684	"	RT	9/32

B&A CLASS NE-2e: 21+&34x32-57-200-357000-63030C,81000S

1308	Alco-S	56707	3/17	RT	9/32
1309	"	56708	"	RT	5/32
1310	"	56709	"	RT	10/32
1311	"	56710	4/17	RT	10/32
1312	"	56711	"	RT	5/32

Notes: Class N-1 reclassified to NE-1a
       Class N-2b reclassified to NE-2b.

CLASS U. 0-8-0 SWITCHER

B&A CLASS U-33 0-8-0: 23x32-57-180-194500-45490
Rebuilt from 2-8-0 class G-33.

(ex 970)	36	RB	4/17	Sc	5/50
(ex 971)	37	RB	5/17	Sc	5/50
(ex 972)	38	RB	6/17	Sc	5/50
(ex 973)	39	RB	8/17	Sc	6/49
(ex 974)	40	RB	10/17	Sc	6/50
(ex 975)	41	RB	10/17	Sc	7/50
(ex 969)	35	RB	11/17	Sc	4/50
(ex 968)	34	RB	12/17	Sc	1/50
(ex 967)	33	RB	1/18	Sc	6/50
(ex 966)	32	RB	2/18	Sc	5/50
(ex 965)	31	RB	3/18	Sc	5/50
(ex 964)	30	RB	4/18	Sc	1/50

B&A CLASS U-2j 0-8-0: 23+x30-57-185-216500-45710

42 (re 3/51)	7475	Lima	5644	7/18	SS	9/52
43	"	7476	"	5645	"	SS 9/52
44	"	7477	"	5646	"	SS 9/52
45	"	7478	"	5647	"	RT 1/56
46	"	7479	"	5648	"	SS 4/52
47	"	7480	"	5649	"	SS 10/52

B&A CLASS U-3b 0-8-0: 25x28-51-175-219000-51040 USRA

48 (re 3/51)	7720	Lima	6093	12/20	RT	5/52
49	"	7721	"	6094	"	RT 1/55
50	"	7722	"	6095	1/21	RT 4/57
51	"	7723	"	6096	2/21	SS 8/52
52	"	7724	"	6097	3/21	SS 4/52
53	"	7725	"	6098	4/21	RT 1/55

B&A CLASS U-2k 0-8-0: 23+x30-57-185-215000-45710

54 (re 3/51)	7481	Lima	6733	10/23	SS	8/52
55	"	7482	"	6734	"	SS 5/53
56	"	7483	"	6735	"	SS 4/59
57	"	7484	"	6736	"	Sc 8/54
58	"	7485	"	6737	"	SS 8/52
59	"	7486	"	6738	"	RT 8/55
60	"	7487	"	6739	"	RT 8/55
61	"	7488	"	6740	"	RT 12/55

B&A CLASS U-2L 0-8-0: 23+x30-57-185-218000-45710

62 (re 3/51)	7489	Alco-S	65528	6/24	SS	8/53
63	"	7490	"	65529	"	SS 8/52
64	"	7491	"	65530	"	SS 8/52
65	"	7492	"	65531	"	SS 10/52

Alco builder's photo of B&A 1249, class N-1, first NYC Lines mallet. (W.D.Edson coll.)

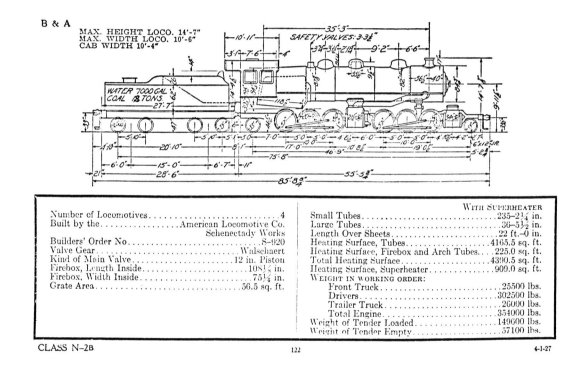

B & A

MAX. HEIGHT LOCO. 14'-7"
MAX. WIDTH LOCO. 10'-6"
CAB WIDTH 10'-4"

WATER 7000 GAL
COAL 13 TONS

	WITH SUPERHEATER
Number of Locomotives............4	Small Tubes.............235-2¼ in.
Built by the........American Locomotive Co.	Large Tubes.............36-5½ in.
Schenectady Works	Length Over Sheets............22 ft.-0 in.
Builders' Order No............S-920	Heating Surface, Tubes............4165.5 sq. ft.
Valve Gear............Walschaert	Heating Surface, Firebox and Arch Tubes...225.0 sq. ft.
Kind of Main Valve............12 in. Piston	Total Heating Surface............4390.5 sq. ft.
Firebox, Length Inside............108½ in.	Heating Surface, Superheater............909.0 sq. ft.
Firebox, Width Inside............75¼ in.	WEIGHT IN WORKING ORDER:
Grate Area............56.5 sq. ft.	Front Truck............25500 lbs.
	Drivers............302500 lbs.
	Trailer Truck............26000 lbs.
	Total Engine............354000 lbs.
	Weight of Tender Loaded............149600 lbs.
	Weight of Tender Empty............57100 lbs.

CLASS N–2B   122   4-1-27

B&A 1312, class NE-2e, at Springfield 12/28. It had only 16 year lifespan. (Vollrath)

B&A 32, class U-33, rebuilt in 1918 from Class G-33 2-8-0. At Beacon Park 9/49.(Vollrath)

B&A 54, class U-2k, builder's photo from Lima.   (Edson collection)

B&A 53, class U-3b, the standard NYC USRA design)   (Pollitt colection)

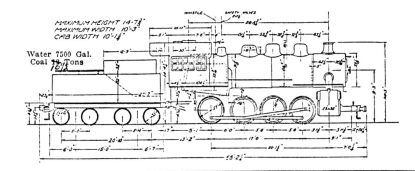

	WITH SUPERHEATER
Number of Locomotives..................12	Small tubes.....................175-2 in.
Built by the............American Locomotive Co., Schenectady Works	Large tubes.....................26-5½ in.
Rebuilt by the...............Boston &·Albany R.R.	Length over sheets..............16 ft.-0 in.
Valve Gear.............................Baker	Heating surface, tubes..........2055.0 sq. ft.
Kind of main valve............12 in. Piston	Heating surface, firebox and arch tubes......145.0 sq. ft.
Firebox, length inside.............96½ in.	Total Heating Surface...........2200 sq. ft.
Firebox, width inside.............75¼ in.	Heating surface, superheater......472.0 sq. ft.
Grate area.........................50.2 sq. ft.	

	WITH 8000 GAL. TANK	WITH 7500 GAL. TANK
WEIGHT IN WORKING ORDER ON:		
Drivers	194500 lbs.	194500 lbs.
Total engine	194500 lbs.	194500 lbs.
Weight of Tender loaded	147500 lbs.	143900 lbs.
Weight of Tender empty	57800 lbs.	57600 lbs.

CLASS U–33   4-1-27

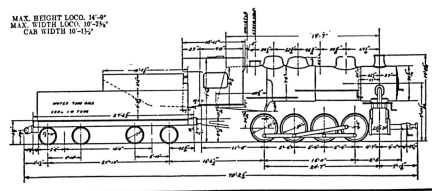

	WITH SUPERHEATER
Number of Locomotives..................8	Small tubes.....................177-2 in.
Built by the............Lima Locomotive Works	Large tubes.....................28-5½ in.
Builders' Order No................L-1056	Length over sheets..............16 ft.-0 in.
Valve gear............................Baker	Heating surface, tubes..........2115 sq. ft.
Kind of main valve............12 in. Piston	Heating surface, firebox and arch tubes........187 sq. ft.
Firebox, length inside.............96⅛ in.	Total heating surface...........2302 sq. ft.
Firebox, width inside.............75¼ in.	Heating surface, superheater......540 sq. ft.
Grate area.........................50.2 sq. ft.	
WEIGHT IN WORKING ORDER ON:	
Drivers	215000 lbs.
Total engine	215000 lbs.
Weight of tender loaded	136500 lbs.
Weight of tender empty	58200 lbs.

CLASS U–2ᴋ

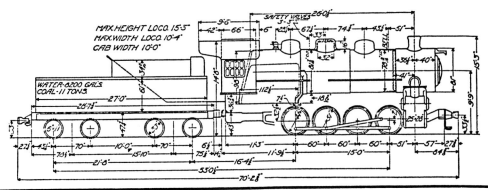

	WITH SUPERHEATER
Number of Locomotives..................6	Small tubes.....................230-2 in.
Built by the............Lima Locomotive Works	Large tubes.....................36-5½ in.
Builder's Order No................L-1013	Length over sheets..............15 ft.-0 in.
Valve Gear............................Baker	Heating surface, tubes..........2560 sq. ft.
Kind of main valve............14 in. Piston	Heating surface, firebox and arch tubes.......208 sq. ft.
Firebox, length inside.............102⅛ in.	Total heating surface...........2777 sq. ft.
Firebox, width inside.............66¼ in.	Heating surface, superheater......637 sq. ft.
Grate Area.........................47 sq. ft.	
WEIGHT IN WORKING ORDER ON:	
Drivers	219000 lbs.
Total engine	219000 lbs.
Weight of Tender loaded	153800 lbs.
Weight of Tender empty	63500 lbs.

CLASS U–3ʙ   4-1-27

CLASS Z. 2-10-2 SANTA FE

B&A CLASS Z-1 2-10-2: 27x32-57-200-352000-69600 USRA. Assigned 3/26 to CCC&StL. Later Canadian National.

1100	Alco-B	60065	1/19	So 8/28	CNR	4200		1105	Alco-B	60070	1/19	So 8/28	CNR	4205
1101	"	60066	"	"	"	4201		1106	"	60071	"	"	"	4206
1102	"	60067	"	"	"	4202		1107	"	60072	"	"	"	4207
1103	"	60068	"	"	"	4203		1108	"	60073	"	"	"	4208
1104	"	60069	"	"	"	4204		1109	"	60074	"	"	"	4209

CLASS A. 2-8-4 BERKSHIRE

B&A CLASS A-1 2-8-4: Lima demonstrator #1 c/n 6883 12/24. Became Illinois Central 7050.

B&A CLASS A-1a 2-8-4: 28x30-63-240-389000-69400 (a)

1400	Lima	6979	2/26	Sc 6/49
1401	"	6980	"	Sc 12/49
1402	"	6981	"	Sc 2/49
1403	"	6982	"	Sc 3/49
1404	"	6983	"	Sc 5/49
1405	"	6984	"	Sc 9/49
1406	"	6985	"	Sc 6/49
1407	"	6986	"	Sc 7/49
1408	"	6987	"	Sc 4/49
1409	"	6988	"	Sc 7/49
1410	"	6989	"	Sc 2/49
1411	"	6990	"	Sc 1/50
1412	"	6991	"	Sc 6/49
1413	"	6992	3/26	Sc 3/49
1414	"	6993	"	Sc 6/49
1415	"	6994	"	Sc 3/49
1416	"	6995	"	Sc 8/49
1417	"	6996	"	Sc 3/49
1418	"	6997	"	Sc 12/49
1419	"	6998	"	Sc 6/49
1420	"	6999	"	Sc 8/49
1421	"	7000	"	Sc 7/50
1422	"	7001	"	Sc 7/49
1423	"	7002	"	So 3/50 (b)
1424	"	7003	"	Sc 7/49

Note a: TF 81400 with booster.
Note b: 1423 re Tenn.Ala.& Ga. RR 601.
Note c: 1434   "   "   "   602.

B&A CLASS A-1b 2-8-4: 28x30-63-240-390500-69400 (a)

1425	Lima	7192	12/26	Sc 12/49
1426	"	7193	"	Sc 6/49
1427	"	7194	"	Sc 8/49
1428	"	7195	"	Sc 8/49
1429	"	7196	"	Sc 8/49
1430	"	7197	"	Sc 6/49
1431	"	7198	1/27	Sc 7/49
1432	"	7199	"	Sc 10/49
1433	"	7200	"	Sc 8/49
1434	"	7201	"	So 3/50 (c)
1435	"	7202	"	Sc 6/49
1436	"	7203	"	Sc 6/49
1437	"	7204	"	Sc 2/49
1438	"	7205	"	Sc 10/49
1439	"	7206	"	Sc 4/49
1440	"	7207	"	Sc 6/49
1441	"	7208	"	Sc 8/49
1442	"	7209	"	Sc 12/49
1443	"	7210	"	Sc 6/49
1444	"	7211	"	Sc 3/49

B&A CLASS A-1c 2-8-4: 28x30-63-240-396100-69400 (a)

1445	Lima	7556	8/30	Sc 12/49
1446	"	7557	"	Sc 11/49
1447	"	7558	"	Sc 12/49
1448	"	7559	"	Sc 3/50
1449	"	7560	"	Sc 12/49
1450	"	7561	"	Sc 12/49
1451	"	7562	"	Sc 12/49
1452	"	7563	"	Sc 12/49
1453	"	7564	"	Sc 12/49
1454	"	7565	"	Sc 12/49

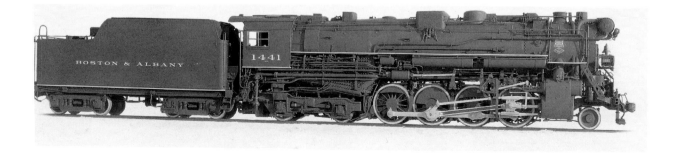

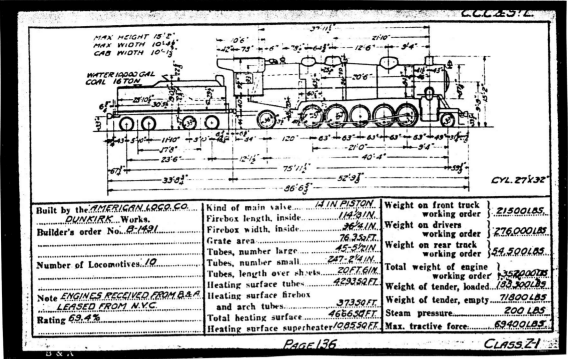

Built by the AMERICAN LOCO. CO. DUNKIRK Works.	Kind of main valve...14 IN PISTON	Weight on front truck working order...21500 LBS
Builder's order No. B-1491	Firebox length, inside...114/8 IN.	Weight on drivers working order...276.000 LBS
	Firebox width, inside...96 1/4 IN.	
	Grate area...76.35 FT.	Weight on rear truck working order...54.500 LBS
	Tubes, number large...45-5 1/2 IN.	
Number of Locomotives...10	Tubes, number small...247-2 1/4 IN.	Total weight of engine working order...352000 LBS
	Tubes, length over sheets...20 FT. 6 IN.	
	Heating surface tubes...4293 SQ FT.	Weight of tender, loaded...183.300 LBS
Note ENGINES RECEIVED FROM B&A LEASED FROM N.Y.C.	Heating surface firebox and arch tubes...373.50 FT.	Weight of tender, empty...71.800 LBS
	Total heating surface...4666.50 FT.	Steam pressure...200 LBS
Rating 69.4 %	Heating surface superheater 1085 SQ FT.	Max. tractive force...69400 LBS.

PAGE 136   CLASS Z-1

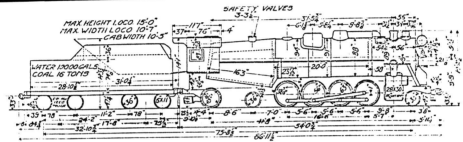

	WITH SUPERHEATER
Number of Locomotives...25	Small tubes...90-2 1/4 in.
Built by the...Lima Locomotive Works	Large tubes...204-3 1/4 in
Builders' Order No...L-1082	Length over sheets...20 ft.-0 in.
Valve gear...Baker	Heating surface, tubes...4773.0 sq. ft.
Kind of main valve...14 in. Piston	Heating surface, firebox and arch tubes...337.0 sq. ft.
Firebox, length inside...150 1/8 in.	Total heating surface...5110.0 sq. ft
Firebox, width inside...96 1/4 in.	Heating surface, superheater...2111.0 sq. ft.
Grate area...100.0 sq. ft.	WEIGHT IN WORKING ORDER ON:
	Front truck...36000 lbs.
	Drivers...249500 lbs.
	Trailer truck...103500 lbs.
	Total engine...389000 lbs.
	Weight of tender loaded...201900 lbs.
	Weight of tender empty...86600 lbs.

CLASS A-1A   22   4 1-27

D-2

ENGINE DESIGNED FOR 18°-30° CURVE

STEAM PRESSURE...220 lbs. ● 240 lbs
KIND OF MAIN VALVE...14 in. Piston
FIREBOX, LENGTH INSIDE...150 1/8 in.
FIREBOX, WIDTH INSIDE...96 1/4 in.
GRATE AREA...100 sq. ft.
TUBES, NUMBER LARGE...204 3 1/2 in.
TUBES, NUMBER SMALL...74 2 1/4 in.
TUBES, LENGTH OVER SHEETS...20 ft. 0 in.
HEATING SURFACE, TUBES...4585.1 sq. ft.
HEATING SURFACE, FIREBOX...284 sq. ft.
HEATING SURFACE, THERMIC SYPHONS 149 sq. ft.
TOTAL HEATING SURFACE...5018.1 sq. ft.
HEATING SURFACE, SUPERHEATER...2111 sq. ft.
TRACTIVE FORCE, ENGINE...69800 lbs. ● 69400 lbs
TRACTIVE FORCE, BOOSTER...11000 lbs. ● 12000 lbs.
TRACTIVE FORCE, ENG. & BOOSTER...80800 lbs. ● 81400 lbs.

● REFERS TO ENGINES WITH LIMITED CUT-OFF
SEE DATA PAGE FOR ENGINE Nº5

●69.4 %
RATING, ENGINE 69.8 %
RATING, ENGINE & BOOSTER 80.8%   ●81.4 %

CLASS A-1c

B&A 1105, class Z-1, one of ten allocated to the B&A by U.S.Railroad Administration.
Alco Builder's photo. (Edson)

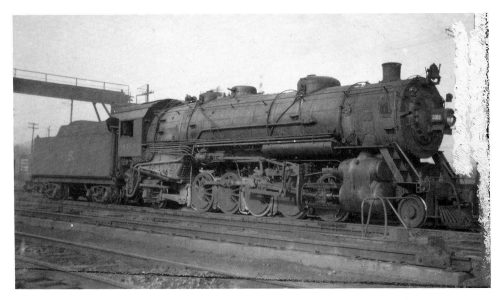

B&A 1109, class Z-1.   These USRA engines were not successful, and were sold to C,N,R.

LLW builder's photo. (W.D.Edson coll.)

B&A 1402, class A-1a, pulling a long freight out of West Sprinfield May, 1941. (R.E. Huke)

B&A 1425, class A-1b at East Chatham, N.Y. in June, 1946. Large tender.   (NYC neg. 7331-1.

B&A 1452, class A-1c "Sports Model" Berkshire at Boston, May 1932   (Pollitt collection)

INDEX BY B&A ROAD NUMBER 1868-1899

B&A 611, class J-2c at Oxford, Mass. with an eastbound Springfield Line train. All New Haven cars. July, 1940 (Collection of W.D.Edson)

Two B&A Berkshires with heavy tonnage leaving Selkirk Yard. (George M. Beischer)